HUMAN BEHAVIOR IN ORGANIZATIONS

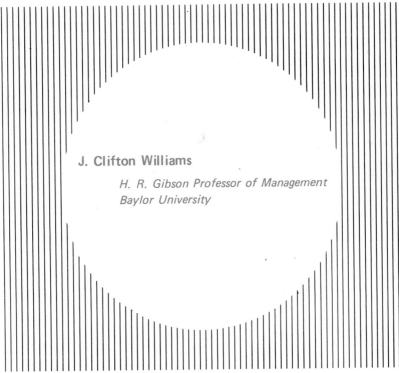

J. Clifton Williams

H. R. Gibson Professor of Management
Baylor University

Published by

G76 **SOUTH-WESTERN PUBLISHING CO.**

CINCINNATI   WEST CHICAGO, ILL.   DALLAS   PELHAM MANOR, N.Y.   PALO ALTO, CALIF.

ISBN: 0–538–07760–3
Library of Congress Catalog Card Number: 76–58799

2 3 4 5 6 7 8 Ki 5 4 3 2 1 0 9 8

Printed in the United States of America

Preface

This book is about people in an organizational setting. Had it been written a decade or two ago, its subject matter would have been called *human relations;* but, since the book avoids the narrow perspective associated with that movement, it is more appropriately designated *organizational behavior* or, as the title indicates, *human behavior in organizations.* This subject is primarily concerned with understanding, predicting, and influencing human behavior in organizations.

Anyone with an interest in relating more effectively to others in a work environment should find this book interesting and valuable. It is, however, written primarily for undergraduate students in colleges and universities. It may also be used by managers and advanced supervisors in development courses or programs of self-study. Although the organizational behavior course in most colleges and universities follows the introductory course and elaborates on the human aspects of management, an introductory course is not a prerequisite for understanding this book.

One of the purposes of a preface is to indicate how a book is unique in relation to others on the same subject. This, of course, is often a matter of opinion. As a professor of organizational behavior, I became convinced that another book was needed because of the difficulty I had in finding a textbook that could adequately deal with the theoretical aspects of the subject without becoming too impractical and difficult to understand. I believe this book is unique to the extent that its contents have practical value even though it does not take a cookbook, how-to approach. Its content can be applied because it is relevant to real-world problems and because it provides the background needed to analyze novel situations and respond intelligently with a sense of goal direction.

In recent years the books used in introductory management courses have increasingly emphasized the behavioral aspects of the subject, often at the expense of important nonbehavioral content. Books in personnel management have tended to do the same, leading to an undesirable overlap with the content of organizational behavior courses. In selecting the content for this book I have deliberately avoided the inclusion of subject matter which is more appropriate for those courses. I have also avoided the inclusion of content which is only of historical interest, regardless of how traditional it has been to include it, and I have attempted to minimize the allocation of space to currently popular but unproved concepts that stand a good chance of rapidly losing their appeal. I hope that this pruning and shaping effort has resulted in a book that is lean and functional.

A great many individuals—scholars, managers, students, and others who cannot be appropriately acknowledged—have contributed to this book. Although many persons have contributed to single chapters, I am uniquely indebted to Dr. Justin Longenecker for his insightful suggestions throughout the manuscript preparation. My wife, Jan, and my children, Eric and Laura, deserve a special word of appreciation for their continuing belief that my writing is worth the price they have to pay for it.

J. Clifton Williams

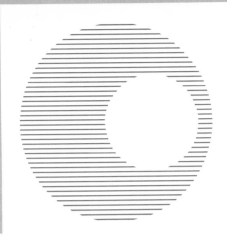

Table of Contents

PART 2 MOTIVATION IN ORGANIZATIONS

PART 3   THE DEVELOPMENT OF LEADERSHIP BEHAVIOR

PART 4 MINIMIZING HUMAN PROBLEMS IN ORGANIZATIONS

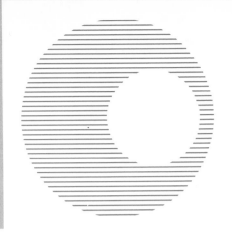

Table of Critical Incidents

PART 4 MINIMIZING HUMAN PROBLEMS IN ORGANIZATIONS

APPENDIX

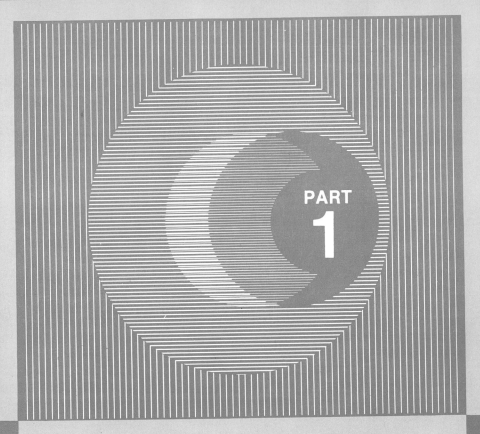

PART
1

The Nature of People and Organizations

Chapter 1

Human Potential in the Work Environment

The scientific, technical, and financial problems encountered by the modern organization are awesome; but none is more challenging than the complex task of understanding people and relating to them in ways that lead to the successful achievement of organizational objectives.

After centuries of relatively stable rural and village life, the industrial revolution dramatically changed the life-style of the average worker, and the rate of change continues to accelerate. As a result, a manager's knowledge of how to deal with the human aspects of organizational life rapidly becomes obsolete and must be continually updated. A major surge of interest in the human aspects of business and industrial organizations began in the 1930s and increased with the growing influence of labor during World War II. This *human relations movement,* as it was called, introduced revolutionary changes in the thinking of scholars and progressive managers. But this was only the beginning of change in the direction of an increasing sensitivity to human needs and a growing sophistication in ways of leading and motivating people in an organizational setting.

HUMANIZING INFLUENCES IN ORGANIZATIONAL LIFE

Thesis: An irreversible emphasis upon the human aspects of organizations which began during World War I and made giant strides during the 1930s gained new impetus during the 1970s. What began as a human relations movement is today most often expressed in terms of the *humanization of work.*[1] It is increasingly a fact of industrial life

---

[1] Robert Kahn defines the humanization of work as "the process of making work more appropriate, more fitting for an adult human being to perform." It should interest the worker and not be degrading, exhausting, or persistently boring. It should utilize the worker's abilities, provide growth opportunities, be supportive of other life roles (husband, wife, citizen), and should provide an acceptable livelihood. Robert L. Kahn, "The Work Module: A Proposal for Humanization of Work," *Work and the Quality of Life,* ed. James O'Toole (Cambridge, Mass.: The M.I.T. Press, 1974), p. 200.

that fair, equitable, and humane treatment of employees is more than just good business or a moral obligation. It has become an enforceable legal requirement.

During the first quarter of the twentieth century, the power of the organization was formidable when compared with that of the individual employee or even with the fledgling unions which were beginning to gain strength. Although specific managers then, as now, demonstrated a degree of concern for the individual, employees in general were regarded as economic units or articles of commerce. The primary concern of the organization was efficiency. Labor was abundant. Employees who were dissatisfied with their treatment were free to leave, but often there was no place to go.

The practical and philosophical basis of management's relationships with people was strongly influenced by two individuals whose writings both captured the spirit of the times and introduced new and exciting concepts to practicing managers. These were Frederick W. Taylor (1856–1915) [2], commonly viewed today as the father of scientific management, and Max Weber (1864–1920),[3] a German sociologist whose influence on organization theory continues to be monumental.

Neither of these men placed primary emphasis on human relations, and, in fact, their ideas sometimes had a dehumanizing influence. Nevertheless, their emphasis on productive efficiency and rationality in organizations was compatible with the humanizing trends which began during World War I and got into full swing in the 1930s. It is, after all, rational to consider all known facts about how people behave in organizations and to adopt management practices that can reduce such employee behaviors as strikes, slowdowns, and absenteeism.

The Human Relations Movement

The beginning of the human relations movement is usually associated with a series of studies conducted by Elton Mayo and his Harvard colleagues at Western Electric Company's Hawthorne plant near Chicago.[4] The Hawthorne studies demonstrated that at that particular time and place productivity could be increased simply by altering the social relationships in the workplace. The experimenters were attempting to establish a relationship between variables in the physical environment (the level of lighting, for example) and productivity. They were surprised, however, to find that the employees' response to being studied, to being considered important, and to new patterns of supervision had

[2] Frederick W. Taylor, *Principles of Scientific Management* (New York: Harper & Row, Publishers, 1947). Originally copyrighted by Taylor in 1911.

[3] Max Weber, *The Theory of Social and Economic Organization,* Trans. A. M. Henderson and Talcott Parsons (New York: Oxford University Press, Inc., 1947).

[4] Elton Mayo, *The Human Problems of an Industrial Civilization* (Cambridge, Mass.: Harvard University Press, 1933); and F. J. Roethlisberger and W. J. Dickson, *Management and the Worker* (Cambridge, Mass.: Harvard University Press, 1939).

more bearing on productivity than the experimental variables which were being manipulated. For example, production increased when the amount of lighting was decreased as well as when it was increased.

The human relations movement was motivated by a number of factors. Guilt over the treatment of employees and genuine concern for their welfare were important, but perhaps no more so than a desire to stem the rising tide of unionism and to deal with problems of rising labor costs and shortages. As employees became better educated and enjoyed a higher standard of living, they began to expect more. At the same time management was learning new ways to lead, to motivate, to deal with employee grievances, and to meet the developing needs and expectations of employees. The times were right for radical change.

During the prosperous decade following World War II, the human relations movement achieved a bandwagon effect. Human relations training for supervisors became a fad; and much of what was written, taught, and practiced during this time had a recognizable aura of unrealistic idealism about it. Many practicing managers gave lip service to the need for improved relations with subordinates but made few actual changes in behavior. Still, the human relations movement began an irreversible trend.

Adaptation to Radical Change

The decade from 1965 to 1975 again produced dramatic social changes that required a significant accommodation on the part of managers. The riots of the 1960s, the challenges to authority spawned by two generations of permissive child rearing and accentuated by the Vietnamese War, and the rising demands of a variety of minority groups which collectively constitute a majority of Americans combined to challenge a way of life and a style of management. Traditional concepts of morality have changed, the stabilizing influence of the family has diminished, and the motivating influence of the Protestant work ethic has increasingly been called into question.[5]

There are growing expectations today that one's work should be interesting and fulfilling in addition to providing security and affluence. There are also expectations, backed by force of law, that all discrimination on the basis of race, ethnic background, religion, sex, and age should be immediately ended; that the workplace should be free from all conditions that might conceivably be dangerous; and that an organization's products should be safe, of high quality, and sufficiently inexpensive to be noninflationary. All this is to be accomplished without polluting or defacing the environment. The organization is expected to abdicate its selfish ways, to abhor obscene profits, and in all ways to become

---

[5] According to Max Weber's 1904 treatment of the subject, the Protestant ethic provided the psychological conditions which made possible the rise of capitalism. An interpretation of Calvinistic theology, the Protestant ethic made the accumulation of wealth not just acceptable, but an obligation. Work is a calling, not a curse; productivity and frugality are virtues. For persons influenced by this ethic, to be lazy and unproductive is to waste one's God-given talents. Max Weber, *The Protestant Ethic and the Spirit of Capitalism,* trans. Talcott Parsons (London: George Allen and Unwin Ltd., 1930).

publicly responsible. It is not with tongue in cheek that these demands are being made by a great many powerful groups and individuals.

The Challenge to Management

Needless to say, the challenge to management is impressive. Only progressive and efficient organizations can survive, and only sophisticated and knowledgeable managers can succeed. Managers must have more than technical knowledge and an intuitive grasp of what is required to organize and lead effectively. They must become aware of the subtleties of formal organizations, informal group processes, authority, power, and communication within an organizational setting. They can no longer be content with effete, uncreative, intuitive decision making at a time when their competitors are using more sophisticated methods. Managers must gain a deep understanding of human behavior as it is expressed in an organizational setting. In the final analysis, organizations are made up of individuals who are increasingly demanding to be viewed as individuals rather than as economic units in a heartless, impersonal bureaucracy. It is to these management challenges that this book is addressed.

VIEW OF THE INDIVIDUAL

Thesis: Consciously or unconsciously, all managers make certain assumptions about human nature. Upon these assumptions, leadership styles are developed, policies are formulated, and actions are taken. It is essential to effective management that these assumptions be valid. This ordinarily requires that assumptions be explicit and that their implications be explored.

The manager who relies primarily on wage incentives, formal authority, and external controls to motivate subordinates is influenced by assumptions about human nature that differ from those of the manager who attempts to maximize the subordinates' sense of self-worth and desire to assume responsibility. Some managers behave as though their subordinates are just so many isolated individuals or a disorganized rabble who relate to the organization but not to one another. In contrast, other managers expect a work group to develop complex social relationships which influence group members in ways that may either contribute to or interfere with the achievement of formal organizational goals.

The effectiveness with which managers relate to individuals and groups in organizations is a function of their assumptions about human nature. For this reason it is important that these assumptions be spelled out and that evaluations be made concerning their consistency with what is known about human nature from collective experience, expert judgments, and scientific experimentation. We look now at a few of the assumptions which are most likely to be useful in understanding people in a work environment.

Individual Differences in Ability

If there is any one characteristic of people which is universally valid and important, it is that they differ. To say that all persons are created equal is a statement of human rights under the law. It communicates nothing at all about human nature. As a matter of fact, people differ greatly in intelligence, aptitudes, physical strength, manual dexterity, knowledge, skill, interests, personality traits, motivation, and many other attributes which potentially influence behavior and productivity.

Figure 1–1 shows the distribution of mental ability (general intelligence expressed in terms of IQ) throughout the population. Notice that mental ability essentially follows a normal probability or bell-shaped curve. There are few persons with an extremely low or extremely high IQ, and the number of persons with a given IQ increases toward the center of the distribution (that is, toward the average IQ of 100).[6] Simple as the observation may seem, it is significant that most people are just average and, therefore, cannot be expected to perform well on many jobs that demand the complex mental processes required, for example, in most scientific and professional positions.

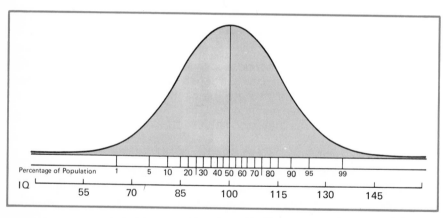

Figure 1–1   The Distribution of Mental Ability Throughout the Population

Individual differences in mental ability have broad implications for organizational behavior. For example, we should expect the assembly line worker with an IQ of 128 to be bored and dissatisfied. In fact, we might hypothesize that all efforts to make assembly line work meaningful and interesting will be wasted on this particular individual. The situation would be totally different for a worker with an IQ of 90 or 100. For people with borderline or subnormal intelligence, the boring assembly-line job is often extremely challenging. Sometimes it is even

[6] In statistical terms the IQ scores shown in Figure 1–1 are standard scores with a mean of 100 and a standard deviation of 15. Although other approaches to the computation of IQs have been employed, this is the most generally accepted one today for the measurement of adult intelligence.

too complex to be performed without provoking unacceptable stress in the employee. Obviously, people are suited for greatly differing types of work—a fortunate circumstance since job demands vary widely.

Most abilities are distributed throughout the population in a pattern similar to that of mental ability, and many of them influence performance on the job.[7] There is, of course, no one-to-one relationship between ability and productivity. Differences in motivation, experience, and work habits may result in many persons with high native potential performing below the level of others whose aptitudes are marginal for the task in question.

Rationality and Emotionality

During the early part of this century managerial behavior was strongly influenced by the prolific writings of Max Weber. His "bureaucratic" organization is built around the concepts of rationality and impersonality. The duties of every manager are clearly defined, career paths are specified, selection and promotion decisions are objectively made on the basis of job requirements, and the relationships among organizational members are determined by rules and policies. Predictability is possible and organizational goals are achieved because incentives are provided to ensure that organization members will voluntarily submit to the legitimate authority of the organization.

About the same time that Weber was extolling the virtues of a rationally contrived organization, Sigmund Freud was emphasizing the importance of unconscious motivation and human irrationality. Freud, the founder of the psychoanalytic school of psychology, stressed the complexity of human motivation and pointed out that the outward manifestations of an individual's psyche are like the tip of the submerged iceberg (Figure 1–2, page 8).

Although Weber's contributions to organizational theory were invaluable, his assumptions about the rational nature of people were misleading. Today we know that employees do not always behave rationally, at least in an economic sense. They sometimes strike, for example, in order to demonstrate their power and independence, even when they know full well they cannot recover their economic losses. They restrict production, sacrificing pay for peer approval, and give up high-paying jobs in order to do work they find satisfying.

We are rational—but only to a point. We plan, set goals, think, reason, and live by creeds and values. But we also become frustrated and behave in ways that can be perceived as rational only by someone who understands all our deeply embedded, sometimes conflicting needs, aspirations, and perceptions. In many situations our motivation is unconscious so that not even we understand our own actions.

---

[7] Historically psychologists have attempted to isolate a variety of special aptitudes which relate to success in different types of work, but most of these aptitudes have been shown to have a strong general intelligence component. People do differ greatly in verbal and quantitative abilities. Other important abilities relate to performance on mechanical, clerical, and manual jobs.

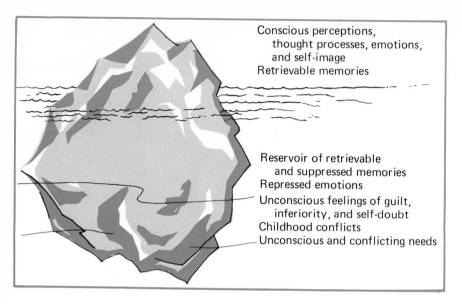

Conscious perceptions,
    thought processes, emotions,
    and self-image
Retrievable memories

Reservoir of retrievable
    and suppressed memories
Repressed emotions
Unconscious feelings of guilt,
    inferiority, and self-doubt
Childhood conflicts
Unconscious and conflicting needs

**Figure 1–2   The Iceberg Model of Personality—
The Largest Portion Is Hidden**

Constraints of Attitude and Perception

The fact that one's environment strongly influences behavior is indisputable. The person whose early background consistently provides rewards for hard work and responsible behavior will probably perform more acceptably on the job than one whose history is characterized by rewards for antisocial behavior and opposition to the established order. There is no doubt that human behavior, like that of lower animals, is to a significant extent conditioned by its consequences (reward and punishment). This does not, however, necessarily lead to the conclusion that humans have no freedom or autonomy.

Freedom of Choice. A number of prominent psychologists have assumed that human freedom is an illusion—that the choices an individual appears to make are totally determined by the impact of past events upon and within the individual. Like the billiard ball that comes to rest at a specific spot on the table, because of the velocity and angles of the other balls with which it comes in contact, human choices are thought to be totally determined. This, of course, is an assumption. It is only an assumption, and one that many of us do not accept.

Many people do not subjectively perceive themselves in this way. It is significant that behavior and expectations are strongly influenced by what a person believes to be true. Individuals feel responsible for their actions. In fact, they sometimes feel so strongly that on a deep, unconscious level they develop intense feelings of guilt when they fail to live up to their self-expectations. Also, people consciously believe that their choices are real, regardless of any awareness of philosophical arguments to the contrary. The fact that they hold others responsible for their actions, too, is further evidence that, for practical purposes, people are committed to that very lofty view of humanity which states that individuals have a capacity for choosing between alternatives and for assuming responsibility for their behavior. Organizations cannot function optimally without these pragmatic assumptions.

Levels of Freedom.   Practically speaking, some people have more freedom than others. For example, two sales representatives with equal ability have an opportunity to make a sale. One, who believes the sale is possible, is free to attempt it. The other believes that the probability of making the sale is zero and is consequently bound by that belief. Subjectively, to attempt the sale would be pure folly. This dimension of freedom, or lack of it, may also be seen in the simple task of cutting a pie. There are many conceivable ways of cutting it, but the person who assumes that pie slices must be wedge shaped is limited by that assumption.

To varying degrees everyone loses freedom through limitations posed by past experience, ignorance, prejudices, beliefs, assumptions, attitudes, opportunities, and the like. Some employees feel boxed in, while others in the same environment experience the exhilarating freedom that comes from an awareness that many courses of action are available. Objective observers can clearly see that in many cases the constraints lie within an individual's self-perception and perception of the external environment rather than in a real lack of ability or opportunity.

Perceptual Filters.   No one sees all the world as it really is. Everyone has a point of view that serves as a filter through which the external world is viewed. A coal miner with a long history of working for low wages under dangerous conditions has learned to view managers as ruthless exploiters. As a result, any statement made by a manager is viewed with skepticism, regardless of how true it may be. Managers who believe that people are inherently lazy and selfish will naturally interpret the behavior of others through that filter and consequently will have no difficulty finding reinforcing evidence for that viewpoint.

One of the most important filters through which the world is interpreted is one's own self-image. The manager whose self-perception is, "I am an intelligent, tough-minded, experienced problem solver," may see a given organizational problem as a welcomed opportunity. To the manager who is plagued by self-doubt that same problem may be perceived as a danger area to be avoided at any cost.

Many of the filters through which one perceives the real world can be recognized as attitudes. An *attitude* is a predisposition to evaluate an object in a favorable or unfavorable manner. The attitude object may be, for example, a person, group, religion, process, or form of government. Attitudes involve both feelings and beliefs. Thus, a business owner who has negative attitudes toward unions may believe that they are bad for business, for the nation, for management, and for the union members. These beliefs are accompanied by strong feelings, and the interaction of the two provides a component of personality that is highly resistant to change. Once the attitude is formed, this manager may be blinded to any conceivable good in unions because everything unions do is interpreted through that attitude.

The drawings shown in Figure 1–3 illustrate that *seeing is believing* cannot always be taken too literally and that what is depends to some extent upon the complex process of human perception. To understand people in organizations (or anywhere else) managers cannot be naive realists, acting as though what they perceive is always what really is. Individuals begin to understand others only as they are able to switch perceptual sets and view the world from the perspective of others. To some extent, each of us has a distorted view of the real world, but it is to this uniquely private reality that we individually react and within which each of us lives.

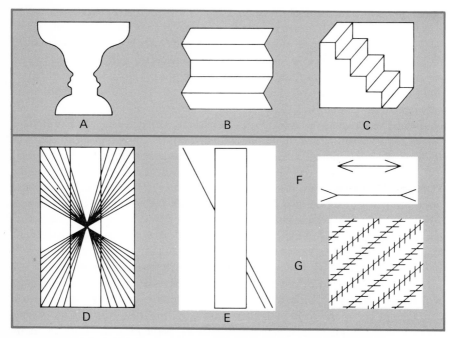

In the upper series of illusions what is seen depends upon what is perceived as foreground and background. (A) This may be seen as a vase or two faces. (B) The center section may be seen as close up or in the distance. (C) This view of a stairway may be from above or below (slowly rotate the page to get a reversal). (D) The vertical lines are straight. (E) The bottom line is the extended one. (F) The lines are of equal length. (G) The long lines are parallel.

Figure 1–3   Subjective Reality Is a Matter of Perception

Sociability and Interdependence

The early rational and economic views of individuals gave no recognition to the fact that people are inherently social beings. We now recognize that employees attempt to satisfy a variety of social needs in the work situation and that for most people employment which does not provide for this satisfaction is unacceptable.

Social needs take a variety of forms: the need for companionship, for support in doing one's work, and for someone with whom to communicate in order to relieve personal frustration and work-stimulated boredom. But social needs have an even deeper meaning. Personality itself develops in interaction with others. One's self-concept emerges as feedback is received from others concerning one's abilities, appearance, personality characteristics, and general acceptability. At a very early time in life, dependencies upon others are formed, and some forms of dependence persist throughout life. People need approval and affection from one another in order to maintain self-respect and security. In the work situation, individuals spontaneously interact to develop informal but highly organized behavior which is important to the satisfaction of these needs. Effective managers must understand and relate to these informal groups as well as to individual employees.

Differing Needs

Employees cannot be treated as though their needs are all alike. Everyone has certain primary needs (the needs for food, rest, self-respect, and the approval of others, for example), but even these needs vary greatly in intensity. As a person goes about satisfying these, new needs emerge, such as the need for power, achievement, recognition, and the need to engage in certain interesting activities. These are learned, secondary needs. As such, they may be strong in one person and virtually nonexistent in another.

Chapters 5 and 6 describe in some detail the nature and function of human needs and their relationship to motivation. For now, the important point is that human needs vary greatly from person to person, making generalizations difficult.

A Sense of History

When an organization attempts to motivate employees to be more productive or cooperative, the response may be unexpected because of influences within individuals or groups which result from past experience. The point is sometimes made that, because the basic physiological needs (food, shelter, and the like) of most workers are satisfied today, these needs no longer serve as motivators. In one sense, this is a valid statement, but it fails to take into consideration the importance of memory and the anticipation of future events.

There are still large numbers of people in the work force, many of whom are in high-level positions, whose childhood memories of the Depression of the 1930s are vivid. These memories influence both present perceptions and future expectations. Employees are influenced by abuses suffered under previous employers and even by events which were related to them by their parents and grandparents. Personality may be visualized objectively as a stream of consciousness flowing in the present; but subjectively we experience ourselves as liberated from the bonds of time—free to relive the past and project ourselves into the future.

Theories X and Y

There are, of course, innumerable statements which one might make about human nature, but they would not all have a direct bearing on how people should be dealt with in the work environment. The late Douglas McGregor [8] did an excellent job of conceptualizing some of the assumptions about human nature which are relevant to organizational behavior. He labeled these, *Theory X,* the classical or traditional view, and *Theory Y,* a progressive view upon which he believed an enlightened model for human relations in organizations could be developed.

Theory X.   This theory holds that the average person inherently dislikes work, is innately lazy, irresponsible, self-centered, and security oriented, and consequently is indifferent to the needs of the organization. Because of these characteristics, the average person must be threatened, coerced, and controlled. In fact, most people prefer to be directed and controlled. They seek security above all, prefer to avoid responsibility, and both want and need external control in the work situation. Because people are basically gullible and immature, management should experience little difficulty in using a highly directive and manipulative style of supervision.

Theory Y.   Experience has shown that Theory X assumptions result in a great deal of difficulty for management although they remain popular with some managers. McGregor's Theory Y makes the opposite assumptions. People do not inherently dislike work and are not inherently lazy. Rather they have learned to dislike work, to be lazy, and to be irresponsible because of the nature of their work and supervision. They have a high capacity for developing an intrinsic interest in their work, for committing themselves to organizational objectives, and for working productively with a minimum of external controls.

Critique.   Theory Y represents a far more realistic set of assumptions about human nature. It provides the optimism about people which managers must possess if they are to win the cooperation and enthusiastic support of employees in achieving organizational goals. Increasingly managers who make Theory X assumptions are met with extreme resistance and cannot function effectively.

Two points should be made with reference to these theories. First, the Theory X characteristics are said to be inherent or innate. To be such, they would necessarily apply to everyone, which is obviously absurd. On the other hand, under Theory Y, people are said to have the potential or capacity for the responsible behavior and attitudes described. If anyone possesses these qualities, and a

---

[8] Douglas McGregor, *The Human Side of Enterprise* (New York: McGraw-Hill, Inc., 1960).

great many people do, then everyone has the potential for them. However, potential must be developed or actualized, and it is questionable that a favorable work environment can by itself always accomplish this feat, at least at a cost an organization can afford.

Second, McGregor speaks of assumptions about the average person, and one must ask, "Average on what dimensions?" Are we talking about intelligence? education? experience? Average is a statistical concept. The average person is a nonexistent, hypothetical construct. When we make assumptions about the average person, at best we are referring to most people, and in doing so must recognize that there are exceptions.

The notion that people are innately or inherently lazy and irresponsible is in no sense defensible, but it is an indisputable fact that some people have developed these qualities and strongly resist change. The assumptions we make about the nature of most people tend to exert a controlling influence on the management styles we adopt, and Theory Y provides a worthy foundation for a manager's general leadership pattern. One cannot, however, afford to ignore individual differences. For practical purposes some employees do fit the Theory X model, and the supervisor who attempts to lead them with Theory Y assumptions will probably fail.

ORGANIZATIONAL NEEDS AND DEMANDS

Thesis: An organization can survive and achieve its objectives only through the application of efficient processes and methods. Historically a primary means of achieving efficiency has been a division of labor which has deprived large numbers of employees of the opportunity to engage in work that is intrinsically satisfying. To provide employees with meaningful work is perhaps the greatest challenge currently being presented to management. It has yet to be demonstrated, however, that the feat is possible or that a significant investment in making all jobs intrinsically satisfying is worthwhile.

An organization is formed when the specific and limited objectives of its founders can be achieved only through the cooperative efforts of a group of individuals. Organizations make possible the achievement of certain goals and efficiencies which would not be possible through individual effort, and, consequently, organizations make possible a higher level of compensation for their members than each could achieve working alone.

As organizations grow, their efficiency may be increased by the use of highly specialized machines, by simplified work methods, and by the employment of specialized personnel. As a result, it often happens that one employee does nothing but routinely punch insurance claims data into computer cards, another performs the simple operations that combine two components of a carburetor, while still another checks for errors in the recording of telephone directory information. The resulting problems of boredom and disinterest constitute one of the major problems of industrial life.

Closely related to this problem is the fact that organizational life requires that its members conform to a broad spectrum of behavioral expectations. The rules, regulations, work standards, and social norms which collectively define acceptable performance are often experienced by employees as being unacceptably restrictive and by observers of organizational behavior as promoting immaturity and irresponsibility. We look now at a few of the many demands organizations make upon their members and upon member reactions to these demands.

The Nature of Work

The scientist, artist, manager, or engineer whose fascinating work has become an obsession may indefinitely postpone vacations and voluntarily work long hours with little concern for external rewards. In contrast, the bright, but bored, accounts payable clerk watches the clock in eager anticipation of the moment the workday yields to the leisure time activity of working in the garden or engaging in some other energy-consuming and fatiguing activity. We commonly speak of mothers who work as though those who spend their day rearing a family do not work. Obviously the term *work* is an ambiguous one.

The concept of work lends itself to a variety of interpretations. To the ancient Greeks, it was a curse. To the early Hebrews, it was a form of punishment resulting from the sinful nature of humanity. To Marxists, work is an opportunity for the oppressed worker to escape the tyranny of capitalistic oppression and joyously participate in building an improved material environment. To many peoples, work is an opportunity to serve God and humanity, to utilize their natural talents, and to fulfill their vocation or calling to service.

In practice, the meaning of work is uniquely personal, depending upon one's philosophy, opportunities, specific work situation, and a variety of other factors which influence perceptual processes. One definition that includes several aspects of work and avoids the popular notions that work is paid employment or activity engaged in from necessity rather than for pleasure is simply the statement that work is "an activity that produces something of value for other people." [9] Although organizational behavior deals primarily with work for which one is paid, the compensation received is by no means restricted to monetary pay and the notion that work is somehow intrinsically distasteful may itself be the main curse of work in organizations.

Instrumental and Intrinsic Aspects of Work

Most employees do not work primarily for pleasure. Their work is an instrument for the achievement of certain valued objectives. It is, for example, a means

---

[9] Homo Faber, *Work in America—Report of a Special Task Force to the Secretary of Health, Education, and Welfare,* James O'Toole, Chairman (Cambridge, Mass: The M.I.T. Press, 1973), p. 2.

of earning money and providing for security and leisure time. However, this does not mean that work is only a means to an end. In fact, research studies indicate most employees would continue to work even if they should inherit enough money to make work unnecessary. The intrinsic, or noninstrumental, reasons for continuing work vary greatly with groups and individuals. Blue-collar workers, many of whom are instrumentally oriented, would continue to work primarily to keep occupied, while middle-class employees are more likely to be motivated by interest and accomplishment.[10]

For many employees work provides a sense of identity. The employee who says with pride "I work for IBM" is saying, "If you want to know who I am, just think of the well-established qualities of my employer and note the kinds of people IBM employs." Another employee, who identifies more with a prestigious vocational field than with an organization, responds to questions about employment with, "I am a tool and die maker," or "I'm an engineer." In contrast, to be both unemployed and to have no trade or profession, especially if one has no income, is subjectively to be a nobody. This can be an ego-crushing experience, as many welfare recipients report.

People whose services are in demand subjectively perceive themselves to be worth something. The belief that one is worthwhile is somehow validated in work. People who can look with pride upon something they have produced (a painting, a house, a manufactured product, or an idea) are rewarded by the identification. One of the major problems encountered in assembly-line manufacturing is that employees perform such a minor operation on the product that they are unable to identify with or even to visualize, in some instances, the finished product. Such work can only be instrumental and is consequently less rewarding than some other types of work.

The Division of Labor

There was much to be said for the approach to manufacturing before the industrial revolution. Artisans who made a pair of shoes from beginning to end had a personal investment in the product and could justifiably feel an intense pride in the fruits of their labor. On the other hand, a shoemaker could produce very few shoes and was consequently destined to be poor, at least when compared to the modern factory worker. Employees today enjoy luxuries which could be afforded only by the very rich in earlier times.

A primary contributor to the efficiency of the factory system was the division of work into small, simple jobs (a process sometimes referred to as *job dilution*). In 1832, Charles Babbage extolled the virtues of the division of labor, outlining its advantages:

---

[10] A summary of current research on this topic may be found in George Strauss, "Job Satisfaction, Motivation, and Job Redesign," *Organizational Behavior: Research and Issues,* edited by George Strauss, Raymond E. Miles, Charles C. Snow, and Arnold S. Tannenbaum (Madison, Wis.: Industrial Relations Research Association, 1974), p. 28.

1. The reduction of learning time (In contrast to the years an apprentice must serve, an assembly-line worker can reach peak performance within a few hours.)

2. A reduction in wasted materials during learning

3. The small amount of time lost when employees are moved from one job to another or when they change occupations

4. The specialized and often simple tools which may be employed

5. The high level of skill acquired by the frequent repetition of the same process by an individual

6. The stimulation an employee receives to think of new tools and processes to perform the specialized function assigned.[11]

These and other benefits which were believed to be inherent in the division of labor were expressed in the work of Frederick W. Taylor. Taylor advocated the scientific study of all jobs in order to maximize labor efficiency. Through time and motion studies, jobs were reduced to the fewest and simplest movements, and, where possible, Taylor's piece-rate system of payment was installed as a means of encouraging workers to produce at their peak. Although organizations continue to utilize many of the efficiency methods advocated by Taylor, they are aware that these methods often lead to negative attitudes and counterproductive behavior. For example, creative ideas about how to improve production (Point 6) are often intentionally hidden from management, and even employees who are paid incentive wages sometimes restrict production.

Employee Alienation

In recent years much has been written about employee *alienation.* This term refers to an estrangement from the organization and indifference, if not outright disdain, toward work. Presumably this alienation results from the dull, fragmented jobs which are a product of the division of labor and from the impersonality of large bureaucratic organizations. Studies consistently show that the problem is worse among young, well-educated employees who are less tolerant than their elders of these dehumanizing conditions. The typical proposed solution to the problem is some form of job enrichment which will make the work intrinsically satisfying.

Job Enrichment Projects.[12]   Several companies have attempted to make routine jobs more challenging—both in the factory and in the office. The companies

---

[11] Charles Babbage, *On the Economy of Machinery and Manufactures* (London: Charles Knight, 1832), pp. 169–176.

[12] The terms *job enrichment, job enlargement,* and *job redesign* are currently used interchangeably in organizational behavior literature. Some authors, however, have used job enlargement to refer to the addition of routine functions to a job, making it more complex, in contrast to enrichment through the addition of responsibility and autonomy.

include the American Telephone and Telegraph Company; Xerox; Donnelly Mirrors Corporation; Texas Instruments; Motorola; Corning Glass; Maytag; Prudential Insurance; General Foods; and Merrill Lynch, Pierce, Fenner and Smith. In many cases, they have performed enrichment experiments in a single location and on a very limited basis. In Europe, experimentation has taken place in such well-known companies as Saab, Volvo, and Fiat.[13]

The enrichment projects themselves have varied greatly. Some involved little more than placing two or more simple, routine tasks in a series. (For example, a telephone directory assembler both enters items and proofreads for errors). Others have added responsibility, sometimes to the point that one may question the competence of the worker to handle it. Janitors personally order needed janitorial supplies. Machine service employees are given additional authority to decide upon expenses, to make work schedules, and to order their own supplies. Teams of workers are allowed to set production goals and solve production problems. Employees are allowed to rotate from assembly line to bench work, and the fractionated tasks of processing a stock certificate are combined into a single job.

Generally speaking, only successful cases have been reported in published literature. In many cases quality and quantity of work and also morale improved while absenteeism, turnover, and wasted materials were significantly reduced. However, the results are still inconclusive. There is little doubt that attention and concern on the part of management are capable of producing temporary favorable results (called the Hawthorne Effect). In many cases, however, costs as well as productivity increased. At times the employees and their unions resist the changes, preferring instead to suffer the boredom and opt for shorter hours. In some specific instances, profitable and lasting improvements have been made, but the results are not so conclusive as to convince skeptics of the general applicability of job enrichment.

The Extent of the Problem.   There is no agreement concerning the extent of the alienation problem. A tendency exists for behavioral scientists, as well as other observers, to interpret data through the preconceived prisms of their viewpoint. To some extent, what one sees is a function of the particular industry, organization, and work group studied. For example, automobile assembly-line workers might be expected to experience more alienation than comparable employees in new industries such as electronics. In the latter, a high degree of sensitivity to the needs of employees has been often expressed in the formulation of organizational policy. Generally speaking, assembly-line and machine-tending jobs are viewed as more boring than most others, although some white-collar jobs (key-punch operations and routine clerical functions, for example) may run a close second.

---

[13] Summaries of job enrichment experiments and references to earlier publications may be found in the following articles: Strauss, op.cit., p. 38; and Sar A. Levitan and William B. Johnson, "Job Redesign, Reform, Enrichment—Exploring the Limitations," *Monthly Labor Review,* Vol. 96 (July, 1973), pp. 35–36.

Based upon Bureau of Labor Statistics data concerning jobs with assembly-line or operative features, Faber and his associates have concluded that the problem is less widespread than popularly believed:

> It is clear that classically alienating jobs (such as on the assembly line) that allow the worker no control over the conditions of work and that seriously affect his mental and physical functioning off the job probably comprise less than 2 percent of the jobs in America. But a growing number of white-collar jobs have much in common with the jobs of auto workers and steelworkers. Indeed, discontent with the intrinsic factors of work has spread even to those with managerial status.[14]

One of the difficulties in determining the extent of dissatisfaction is that the techniques used to survey workers are sometimes inadequate. For example, a Gallup poll asks only, "Is your work satisfying?" Nevertheless, there has been considerable research on the subject, leading George Strauss to this position:

> Very briefly, my thesis is as follows: most workers report satisfaction with their work, and there is no evidence of rising dissatisfaction. Although the typical worker reacts positively to having more challenging work, he has learned to cope with a lack of challenge (sometimes at a considerable psychic cost); blue-collar workers at least tend to focus their lives away from their jobs and to give higher priority to economic benefits and adequate working conditions than to intrinsic job challenge. As a consequence, they are motivated to produce only a "fair day's work" (whatever this may be in local context). Job design schemes, such as job enrichment, offer hope of increasing satisfaction and productivity in some cases, although perhaps their main advantage lies in providing a more flexible work force, in improving communication among workers, and in increasing the supply of "amenities" on the job.[15]

In many situations the challenge of providing interesting and intrinsically rewarding work is a worthy one, but the extent of the problem is apparently not as widespread as some observers seem to think.

Routine versus Boring Work.   Many jobs require employees to perform the same routines hour after hour. Assembly-line and machine-tending jobs are obvious examples, but even managers have such routine functions as reading and preparing reports. Routine, however, is not in itself necessarily boring and dissatisfying. It may be dull in the sense that it allows for little or no variety or autonomy, but not all employees are concerned with these qualities. Boredom is a psychological condition that results in part from one's environment and in part from the attitudes and perception of the individual.

Consider what occurs in the classroom! The lectures of one professor are highly interesting, and even motivational and exhilarating, to one student, while

---

[14] Faber, op.cit., p. 9.
[15] George Strauss, op.cit., p. 20.

to another they are boring and uninteresting. What is boring, subjectively speaking, is a matter of perception, and the qualities that induce boredom are as often brought to the classroom by the student as by the lecturer. In this regard, it is equally important that people with a high need for self-expression, autonomy, and creativity not be placed on routine jobs and that routine-loving people not be placed in jobs that require a deep sense of responsibility and ability to solve problems. It is significant that most organizations appear to have as much difficulty finding employees who are willing to tackle challenging jobs as they have in solving the problem of too much routine.

Adaptation to Routine. Employees have an amazing capacity to adapt to routine jobs. Of course, some adapt more easily than others, and some never adapt. It would, indeed, be surprising if an uneducated employee whose intelligence and aspirations are low had as much trouble adapting as the mentally alert, ambitious individual who was forced to drop out of college because of financial problems. Naturally adaptation is easier for persons who are properly placed. It is, in fact, preferable to transfer a misplaced individual to a more suitable position, rather than demand the psychological change required for adaptation.

For many employees and managers, work is a central value. It is a means of self-expression and an opportunity for personal development and ego-satisfaction. In contrast, employees on routine jobs often accept their employment solely as a means to an end. Work is something one does to provide a livelihood, security, and retirement benefits. Meaning is found not in the work itself but in the fact that one is responsibly working, providing for the needs of one's family, and making a valuable contribution to society. The factory worker may not enjoy working as such, but this becomes a serious problem only to the person who has been led to believe that work should be intrinsically satisfying.

Varieties of techniques are used on the job to avoid the pain of excessive boredom. The most common is probably daydreaming about the "really important" activities that take place away from work: family time, recreation, vacations, and the like. Another boredom-reducing device is to contrive various games involving creative ways of performing tasks, getting ahead and then resting, or unofficially trading off tasks with a co-worker. There are other less desirable forms of adaptation, too, such as loafing, engaging in intensive union activity, chronic complaining, absenteeism, and frequently changing employers. The more poorly matched an employee is to the job, the higher the probability that adjustment techniques will be undesirable.

The Trouble with Adaptation. Organizations can survive and attain their objectives only because their members are willing to adapt to some extent to organizational demands. The managerial task of efficiently turning out a product or service requires that a certain degree of individuality be sacrificed in order to achieve organizational objectives. There are major differences in perceptions of what this aspect of organizational life does to or for its members.

From one perspective, organizations require their members to behave in ways that promote or perpetuate immaturity. Chris Argyris has for a number of years called attention to those aspects of organizations that tend to reward dependence, submissiveness, the development of few rather than many abilities, and the development of a short time perspective. As employees accept inducements to behave *rationally,* that is, rationally in terms of organizational goals and rules, they develop submissiveness before the power of the organization. As this continues over time, they begin to suppress or deny their self-actualizing tendencies and to define responsibility and maturity in terms of their ability to conform to organizational demands. Healthy-minded individuals who cannot make the adaptation to the norms of this immature subculture become extremely frustrated and cannot function harmoniously within the system.[16]

A Focus upon Individual Differences.   There is no doubt that the conditions Argyris described do exist in some organizations. It is probable that most researchers and practitioners would regard his position as an overgeneralization, but it does make a point. Specifically, it focuses attention upon the need to provide meaningful work whenever possible and to so organize and manage that the employees' uniqueness, maturity, and sense of responsibility are respected, preserved, and developed.

On the other hand, a number of facts about organizations and the individual seem to run counter to the lofty view of people and the pessimistic view of organizations that Argyris presents.

1. Even among traditional organizations there are vast individual differences in the nature of the work and the leadership patterns employed. Thus, the tendency to stereotype organizations is hazardous.

2. Most organizations actively promote the personal worth and development of their members. The constantly changing social and economic environment increasingly demands of an organization's members a capacity for adaptability and the acquisition of new skills and knowledge.

3. Contrary to the view that organizations promote or perpetuate irresponsibility and conformity, studies of successful managers suggest that even with all the organizational support provided (such as organizational structure, formal authority, and policy and procedure), managers have about all the responsibility they can handle and neither reward submissive and irresponsible subordinates nor perceive themselves to be rewarded by such behavior. In a very real sense the nurturing and protective structure provided by organization is what enables a manager to withstand the tremendous pressure of work without collapsing from a psychic overload.

4. The justification for a movement to make work at all levels more intrinsically rewarding does not require that most workers be dissatisfied. The facts rather consistently show that most workers adapt remarkably well to their work—so much so that one of the major problems with job

---

[16] Chris Argyris, "Personality vs. Organization," *Organizational Dynamics,* Vol. 3, No. 2 (Fall, 1974), p. 217.

enrichment programs is overcoming employee resistance to changing from the routine to which they have become accustomed. Managers should be able to enrich certain jobs without seriously undermining efficiency while at the same time being thankful for the many employees who do not seriously object to routine.

Many researchers consistently focus attention upon the virtues of autonomy, creativity, freedom, and responsibility in the work place. However, the rewards of job security, routine duties, and protection from excessive demands are highly valued by a significant number of employees. Consideration of individual differences among people suggests that if all routine jobs were made significantly more challenging (where this is taken to mean more complex and thus requiring more ability) a great many more people would be condemned to the welfare rolls. The following conclusion, drawn by Reif and Luthans, is noteworthy:

> The introduction of a job enrichment program may have a negative impact on some workers and result in feelings of inadequacy, fear of failure, and a concern for dependency. For these employees, low level competency, security, and relative independence are more important than the opportunity for greater responsibility and personal growth in enriched jobs.[17]

STUDY AND DISCUSSION QUESTIONS

1. Contrast Robert Kahn's 1974 definition of the humanization of work with the prevailing attitudes toward employees prior to the human relations movement.
2. In what sense was the time right for greater attention to the human aspects of organizations at the time of the Hawthorne Studies?
3. What is the meaning and significance of the Protestant work ethic?
4. What is the probable source of a manager's assumptions about people if they are not based upon scholarly research and the collective experience of successful managers?
5. What are some of the implications for management of the fact that most human abilities are normally distributed throughout the population?
6. What problems would a naive realist be likely to have in a management position?
7. Why, in general terms, do organizations break complex jobs down into simple ones and require that their employees conform to a broad spectrum of standards and norms?
8. Evaluate this statement: Employees have a right to work that is interesting and fulfilling.

---

[17] William E. Reif and Fred Luthans, "Does Job Enrichment Really Pay Off?" *California Management Review,* Vol. XV, No. 1 (1972), pp. 30–37.

9. Evaluate these statements: The average blue-collar worker has learned to live with routine work. Those who cannot adapt should change jobs. Those who can adapt are in many ways compensated for that adaptation.

10. Assume that the studies quoted in this chapter are valid and that a relatively small percentage of the work force is involved in the extreme forms of routine, fatiguing, and monotonous work, and that they resist job redesign efforts. Is this an argument against job enrichment? What meaning should be given to such facts?

CRITICAL INCIDENT

The Enlightenment

The Centurion Equipment Company, one of the most successful companies of its kind, is a manufacturer of garden tractors, which, with slight style variations, are sold under four different brand names. One line is sold through a network of distributors, and the remaining three are sold through nationwide chain stores. The assembly-line methods employed, similar to those used in the auto industry, have proved to be workable. All jobs have been engineered for maximum efficiency.

For several months prior to the incident described here, the director of personnel, Jean Murdock, had attempted to interest the president, Harold Woznick, and the manufacturing superintendent, William Grobe, in job enrichment projects for the factory. She was finally successful in getting a meeting called to discuss the subject. The following is a sample of the sometimes heated discussion:

Grobe:

Jean, I've had it with your job enrichment propaganda. It has taken me years to set up an assembly line that works smoothly and efficiently. Productivity is high, quality is on standard, and nobody's complaining. So why rock the boat?

Murdock:

But that's not the whole story. It is true that things seem to be going well, but we do have a 3 percent turnover a month and more absenteeism than we should have. There's certainly room for improvement. Anyway, why subject our employees to boredom and drudgery if we don't have to. I've been reading about a number of cases in which . . . .

Grobe:

Hold it, Jean. How can you be sure the workers won't get bored with your so-called enriched job after they have been on it a week? So, instead of just mounting engines, they mount the wheels, too. Big deal.

You cut down on their efficiency, foul up their daydreams, and make it harder for me to train new people when our present employees become part of your 3 percent turnover statistics. I'm not sure I think the enrichment idea applies here. Someone suggested that a better answer might be to keep the routine and shorten the workweek when we are forced to make a change. I just don't want to change anything when we don't have to.

Woznick:

Perhaps there are some jobs that we could and should redesign. Do we have to go all or nothing with this idea?

Murdock:

Of course, we don't! But we have some jobs that are so monotonous they're inhuman. It appears to me that . . . .

Grobe:

And they're just the ones I wouldn't want to touch. By the way, Jean, those jobs may not be as monotonous for the people who are on them as they would be for you. Any job on the line would bore you. And what do you mean by inhumane? Whoever said work was supposed to be fun? Work is work. It's OK not to like it. If work were fun, our employees would be paying us to let them work here.

Questions

1. What are the strengths and weaknesses in Grobe's position?
2. How could Murdock have made her position more convincing?
3. What position would you take. Why?
4. What additional information is needed in order to answer Question 3 intelligently?

Chapter

2

Evolving Concepts of Organizations

Organizations develop because individuals cannot meet their needs and fulfill their aspirations without cooperative effort. From the simple task of lifting a log in the construction of a cabin to the complex task of building a space shuttle, some degree of organized behavior is necessary. In the former case, the advantage of organized behavior may lie only in the fact that two people have more lifting capacity than one. In the latter, organization involves a large number of specialists interacting to produce a whole that is infinitely greater than the sum of its parts. Whether the objective of an organization is to make a profit, to provide services, or to provide pleasure for its members, the underlying assumption is that the value of the outputs (such as products, services, and salaries) will somehow exceed that of the inputs (e.g., money, raw materials, human effort). The universal compulsion of people to organize attests to the validity of this assumption.

This chapter presents an overview of organization theory as it has evolved during the twentieth century. It provides a skeleton or a superstructure which will serve as a reference point for future chapters.

By definition, organization theory deals with concepts rather than with practical application. Thus, it is somewhat heavy and abstract in nature. It is not the kind of material that business students, who are usually very practical, prefer. It is, however, necessary. It provides a foundation and a springboard for the more applied content of some future chapters. It will probably be advisable to reread this chapter. It will make much more sense the second time around.

INTRODUCTION TO ORGANIZATIONAL THEORY

Thesis: There is nothing more practical than a good theory. Because of the many variables involved in organizational life, it is especially important that practicing managers possess theoretical frames of reference within which specific events may be given meaning and predictions made. All managers operate from a theoretical base. It is important that this theory be made explicit and that it meet the standards of logical thinking and empirical testing.

The enormous variation in the size, purpose, and complexity of organizations makes generalization difficult. Statements made about an organization such as General Motors may not apply to a small nonunion research and consulting firm, and vice versa. Yet generalizations must be made if our understanding of organizations is to progress. A suitable place to begin is with a statement about the nature of formal organizations.

Formal Organizations

A *formal organization* is a rationally structured system of interrelated activities, processes, and technologies within which human efforts are coordinated to achieve specific objectives.[1]

First of all, *formal* organizations, such as we are accustomed to observing in businesses, educational institutions, hospitals, and government, are differentiated from *informal* organizations which spontaneously develop whenever people interact closely for a period of time. Informal organization exists in such forms as cliques, gangs, and cooperative work groups. As we shall see in Chapter 4, these informal groups often develop a high degree of structure, including leadership patterns and enforceable standards of acceptable behavior. Because of the overlapping memberships of formal and informal organizations, the latter play a significant role in the life of the formal organization. Unless otherwise specified, however, the term *organization* should be understood to mean formal organization.

Organizations are *rationally structured* in that such elements as the allocation of work, lines of authority, and policies and procedures are designed to fulfill the organization's ultimate purpose and achieve its short-term goals. The organization is a system in that all its parts—its structure, activities, processes, and technologies—are interdependent. A change in one area potentially affects all other areas. Finally, organizations do not exist without people. It is the coordinated *human efforts* which result in the achievement of the *specific objectives* which have been set by the organization's founders and/or members.

Organization Theory

Generally speaking, a *theory* is a systematic statement of the interrelated principles and concepts that explain a specified set of observations. For example, motivation theory would explain such behaviors as an employee's accident prone-

---

[1] For a compilation of definitions given by such organization theorists as Chester I. Barnard, Ralph Davis, Victor Thompson, and Ralph Stogdill, read Henry L. Tosi (ed.), *Theories of Organization* (Chicago: St. Clair Press, 1975), p. 2.

ness, low productivity, aggressiveness, or general insecurity. Theory is intended to give meaning to or to show the relationship between otherwise unexplainable facts. It subsequently provides a basis for prediction and control.

Organization theory attempts to explain how organizations function and to predict the result that a given change will have on organizational effectiveness. One might ask, for example, what effect the involvement of employees in managerial decision making might have upon productivity and profit. Under ideal conditions organization theory would enable a manager to predict that in a given situation one organizational structure would produce good results while another would not.

Unfortunately many aspects of organizational theory are not yet developed to the point that a high level of prediction is possible. Theorists are not in total agreement concerning the content of organization theory. One problem in defining its limits lies in the fact that the most significant organizational unit is the individual. At what point does organizational theory become personality, leadership, learning, or motivational theory? There is no categorical answer to this question. It depends upon one's point of view. Certain organizational theories have little to say about these subjects while others are preoccupied with them.

It will soon become apparent that theorists are highly selective in the subject matter they discuss. Actually there is no single organizational theory that deals effectively with all aspects of organizational life, nor is such a theory expected. Organizational theory is fragmented. A given theorist focuses upon an area viewed as most important, most interesting, or most in need of investigation. Nevertheless, the twentieth century has produced a rich and exciting body of organizational theory, much of which has far-reaching implications for the practicing manager as well as for the researcher whose primary concern is understanding.

CLASSICAL ORGANIZATION THEORY

Thesis: Most organizations are strongly influenced by classical theory. Some of its assumptions are questionable, many of its principles are deficient, its assertions are too sweeping, and its application has often led to undesirable results. It is, nevertheless, a brilliant expression of organization theory and a standard of reference which cannot be ignored or considered insignificant by theorist or practicing manager.

Classical organization theory represents a relatively well-defined body of concepts and principles which were formulated during the first half of the twentieth century and were predominant in the thought and practice of managers during most of that period. Three streams of thought converged to produce classical theory: (1) bureaucratic theory, (2) scientific management, and (3) administrative theory (or principles of management).

A constantly recurring theme in classical theory is the search for *universals*
—guidelines and principles which are applicable to all organizations. Because of
this emphasis, classical theory tends to be somewhat mechanical, inflexible, and
conservative. In its purest form, it tends to appeal to people with a need for
clear-cut and rigid categories. It is relatively uncluttered by a great mass of
important data which deals with such subjects as the behavior of informal groups
and human values, attitudes, and needs. Nevertheless, classical theory provided
the foundation and point of departure for later theories.

Bureaucratic Theory

The basic structure of classical theory was provided by Max Weber and is
referred to as bureaucratic theory.[2] In popular usage, the term *bureaucracy* is
associated with large, inefficient organizations whose members spend more time
muddling through an endless maze of red tape than achieving organizational
objectives. A *bureaucrat,* an official of such an organization, is perceived as a
nameless, robot-like individual whose primary concerns are job security, clock-
watching, retirement, and a slavish obedience to unnecessary rules.

There is much evidence to justify the popular use of these terms, but they
are not what Weber had in mind; and the Weberian definitions continue to be
meaningful in the literature of organization theory. A *bureaucrat* is one of the
managers or administrators above the work level but below the decision-making
level. Accordingly, the *bureaucracy* refers to a group of in-between functionaries
(middle and lower-level managers) who carry out policy rather than make it
(Figure 2–1), and a *bureaucratic organization* is one that is structured along
hierarchical lines with employees at the bottom, bureaucrats in the middle, and
executive leadership at the top.

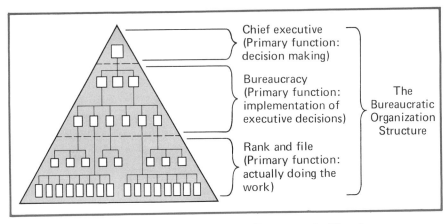

Figure 2–1   Weber's Concept of Bureaucratic Structure

---

[2] Max Weber, *The Theory of Social and Economic Organization,* Trans. A. M. Henderson and
Talcott Parsons (New York: Oxford University Press, 1947).

The presence of a bureaucratic hierarchy is just one of many characteristics of the classical organization. These will be discussed after a brief look at the two remaining contributors to classical theory: scientific management and administrative theory (or principles of management).

Scientific Management

Weber was concerned primarily with organizational structure, especially as it relates to the management hierarchy. In contrast, Frederick W. Taylor, usually referred to as the father of scientific management, was preoccupied with the everyday operational efficiency of an organization, primarily at the employee level. He was particularly impressed with the fact that many employees performed far below their potential, either because of low motivation or because methods and tools were inefficient.

Taylor is best known for his work in time and motion study.[3] His methods, to which present industrial engineering practices may be directly traced, demonstrated that productivity could be dramatically increased by eliminating unnecessary movements and sequencing the remaining ones for maximum efficiency. He was able to show, for example, that by providing bricklayers with helpers (who, naturally, received lower wages), efficiently positioning the brick and mortar, and using a minimum number of movements, a bricklayer could achieve a level of productivity previously considered impossible. Such efficiency methods were especially well suited for assembly-line manufacturing processess and were almost universally accepted.

Taylor emphasized standard practices (all employees doing a job the same way—the most efficient way); standards of performance (a specified level of productivity per hour or day); breaking complex jobs down into simple, routine ones (job simplification or job dilution); and the development of specialized tools to increase the efficiency of operators.

Although his emphasis was primarily on the needs of the organization for productive efficiency, Taylor was not, as he has sometimes been pictured, an advocate of a heartless exploitation of the individual. Quite to the contrary, he viewed increased efficiency as beneficial to the employee by providing increased income through greater productivity. In spite of inequities and problems along the way, this is exactly what has occurred. No better example can be cited than automobile assemblers whose earnings now exceed those of many managers in small and inefficient organizations.

Administrative Theory

A number of theorists attempted to abstract certain universal principles by which organizations should be structured and operated. Although their approach

---

[3] Frederick W. Taylor, *Scientific Management* (New York: Harper & Row, Publishers, 1947). Originally copyrighted by Taylor in 1911.

was similar to Weber's, the two streams of thought developed somewhat independently, especially during the first quarter of the twentieth century.[4] One of the early expressions of organizational principles was made by James Mooney and Allan Reiley.[5] Later a publication by Luther Gulick and Lyndall Urwick [6] and the translation of a book by French industrialist Henri Fayol [7] continued the trend toward specifying universal principles of the ideal organization.

As one should expect, the advocates of universal principles were not in complete agreement. The principles most often emphasized were the division of work (each employee performing a specialized function), unity of command (each employee reporting to only one superior), coordination (the harmonious integration of the different aspects of an organization), span of supervision (the number of subordinates reporting to one manager or supervisor), the hierarchical arrangement of functions and authority, and the subordination of the individual to institutional authority. Urwick [8] proposed twenty-nine principles, a considerably larger number than his fellow classicists advocated. Although this was far fewer than the number of variables considered by later theorists, it was a recognition that many different variables contribute to an organization's effectiveness.

NEOCLASSICAL ORGANIZATION THEORY

Thesis: Neoclassical theory evolved as a reaction to the deficiencies in classical theory. Building upon the classical foundation, neoclassical theory incorporated the findings of behavioral scientists, particularly those identified with the human relations movement. Accordingly, neoclassical theory was a step in the direction of humanizing organizations and correcting some deficiencies in classical theory.

The contributions made by classical theory were enormous. One cannot help being awed by the genius of Max Weber, in particular. Much of what he and the other classicists wrote continues to occupy a central position in organization theory. But classical theory had shortcomings which became painfully obvious with experience and with the enlightenment which resulted from behavioral science research.

---

[4] In emphasizing the independent development of these streams of thought, Hicks and Gullett point out that the theory of bureaucracy was developed by a scholarly group of sociologists, while administrative theorists were a more practical group, including many operating managers. Herbert G. Hicks and C. Ray Gullett, *Organizations: Theory and Behavior* (New York: McGraw-Hill, Inc., 1975), p. 159.

[5] James D. Mooney and Allan C. Reiley, *Onward Industry* (New York: Harper & Row, Publishers, 1931).

[6] Luther Gulick and Lyndall Urwick (eds.), *Papers on the Science of Administration* (New York: Institute of Public Administration, 1937).

[7] Henri Fayol, *General and Industrial Management,* trans. Constance Storrs (London: Sir Isaac Pitman & Sons, Ltd., 1949). This was first published in France in 1916.

[8] Lyndall Urwick, *The Elements of Administration* (New York: Harper & Row, Publishers, 1943), p. 119.

The most serious flaw in classical theory arose from its assumptions about human nature, especially the simplistic notion that the motivation to work can be understood primarily in economic terms. Running a close second was the indefensible position that organization principles can be regarded as universal —i.e., applicable to all organizations. The latter assumption gave classical theory a rigid, mechanical dimension that blinded its proponents to a great many facets of organizational behavior.

The Human Relations Movement

To the extent that neoclassical theory can be identified with the human relations movement, it may be seen as a reaction to the so-called pathologies of classical theory. Although reformers sought to build upon rather than to destroy classical theory, they were of a different persuasion from the classicists. If classicists were at times undesirably tough-minded, authoritarian, and task-oriented, human relationists, at the opposite extreme, were unrealistically people-oriented. They have often been accused of being concerned only with making employees happy, as if this would inevitably result in high productivity or as if productivity were unimportant. To the extent that this is true, the movement was naive, blinded in part by its praiseworthy humanitarian values and its sometimes over-zealous desire to save the individual from the organization.

Although the origin of the human relations movement is generally associated with the Hawthorne experiments,[9] it was the hundreds of research studies and articles which followed during the 1940s and 1950s that constitute the most significant content of the movement.[10] Although much of the research employed relatively unsophisticated designs and dealt with minute fragments of organization life, the overall effect was to produce a body of information which contributed significantly to the development of organization theory.

The human relations researchers included psychologists, sociologists, anthropologists, political scientists, professors of management, and practicing managers. Their subject matter was broad, but a few areas stand out. Heavy emphasis was placed on the study of informal groups, employee satisfaction, group decision making, and leadership styles. Although the findings of psychologists on the nature of perception and motivation were introduced into management literature, the focus of the human relations movement was upon the group

---

[9] Two landmark publications dealt with this research which was conducted at the Western Electric Company, Hawthorne Works, Chicago. They were Elton Mayo, *The Human Problems of an Industrial Civilization* (New York: Macmillan, Inc., 1933) and F. J. Roethlisberger and William J. Dickson, *Management and the Worker* (Cambridge, Mass.: Harvard University Press, 1939).

[10] A typical human relations textbook of this period was Burleigh B. Gardner and David G. Moore, *Human Relations in Industry* (Homewood, Ill.: Richard D. Irwin, Inc. 1955). A general view of the human relations position may be found in Rensis Likert, *The Human Organization* (New York: McGraw-Hill, Inc., 1967). The contributions of such writers as Chris Argyris, Frederick Herzberg, Douglas McGregor, Robert Blake, and Jane Mouton are presented in D. S. Hickson and C. R. Hinings, *Writers on Organization* (Baltimore, Md.: Penguin Books, Inc., 1971).

rather than the individual and upon democratic rather than autocratic leadership. Relatively little attention was given to organizational structure.

The Neoclassicist

Classical theorists are easy to identify. One is, however, on less stable ground in labeling a writer or researcher as human relationist or neoclassicist, the latter being the broader category. Many who were identified with the human relations movement have become more sophisticated and no longer accept the thinking associated with the human relations movement of the 1950s.

Although neoclassical theory is sometimes equated with human relations theory, this practice is not altogether justified. Contributions to neoclassical theory were made by a diverse collection of individuals. Many researchers were behavioral scientists and managers searching for truth (and often for a publication) while having little concern for or identification with the value-oriented, humanistic applications which characterized the human relations movement. The industrial sociologists often fell into this category.

The human relations movement has gradually given way during the last two decades to a more sophisticated discipline known as *organizational behavior*. The latter deals with the same subject matter as human relations, essentially the content of this book, but is more concerned with research, understanding, and theory development. Today, the term *human relations* is avoided by many writers who do not wish to be labeled as do-gooders with good intentions and a reputation for manipulating people but with little depth of understanding. Although a minority influence gave the term this negative connotation, it is, nevertheless, being replaced by the term *organizational behavior*. The best of the human relations theory is now classified as neoclassical.

Problems to Which Neoclassical Theory Is Addressed

The deficiencies of classical theory are the primary subject matter of neoclassical theory, although they are often dealt with indirectly and in piecemeal fashion. These deficiencies are sometimes called the pathologies (illnesses) of bureaucracy, or *bureaupathologies*. Seven of the more commonly observed pathologies of bureaucratic organizations are briefly described in the sections that follow.

Overconformity. An organization's survival depends upon the willingness of its members to sacrifice a degree of individuality and to conform to certain behavioral norms. But conformity can be taken too far, limiting creativity and individual growth and at times rewarding immature behavior.[11] Where willing-

---

[11] Probably the most influential spokesman for the position that organizations tend to reward and promote immature behavior is Harvard Professor Chris Argyris. A statement of his thinking may be found in Chris Argyris, "Personality vs. Organization," *Organizational Dynamics,* Vol. 3, No. 2 (Fall, 1974), p. 217.

ness to conform becomes a standard by which behavior is evaluated, managers throughout the hierarchy sometimes become carbon copies of top management in attitudes, beliefs, and behavior.[12]

Obscured Goals.   Following an organization's rules, policies, and procedures to the letter may become so important to its members that they lose sight of the organization's reason for existence. This may often be observed in government agencies where employees sometimes appear to be more intent on complying with rules than with meeting the needs of the public, although the problem is much in evidence in business as well.

Uncontrolled Growth.   Organizational units have a tendency to proliferate beyond what can be justified on the basis of increased productivity. Ambitious managers sometimes strive for bigger budgets, more employees, and expanded operations with little appreciation for their effect on overall productivity and profit.

Rigidity.   The many stabilizing elements within organizations—lines of authority, position descriptions, policies, work rules, traditions, vested interests—make adaptation to environmental change difficult. Thus, in the middle 1970s a large restaurant still refused to accept credit cards, and internal resistance to change prevented a department store chain from adopting discount marketing methods which could have enabled it to avoid bankruptcy.

Specialization Problems.   Specialists pose some unique problems in that the development of expertise in one area leads to a neglect of others and often to a conflict-producing tunnel vision. The brilliant accountant who perceives all the company's problems from an accounting perspective may thereby be hindered in understanding the problems of marketing or manufacturing. To maximize the benefits of specialization is often to increase problems of communication and coordination.

The problems arising from task specialization (making simple, routine jobs out of complex jobs) were discussed in Chapter 1. The efficiencies gained are accompanied by problems of boredom and minimal utilization of human ability.

Loss of Motivation.   The more an organization is routinized through rules and standards, the fewer are the opportunities for exercising initiative and exerting maximum effort. Seniority provisions and other measures which are taken to make jobs secure are often accompanied by a loss of motivation for personal growth and increased productivity. Especially in stable, noncompetitive organizations whose personnel feel secure, motivation for high productivity may be re-

---

[12] William H. Whyte, Jr., overstated his case but gained national recognition for his attacks upon organizations as demanding an unhealthy conformity of their members. His book, *The Organization Man* (New York: Simon & Schuster, Inc., 1956), is still worthwhile and interesting reading for the student of management.

placed by a Parkinson's law mentality in which the "work expands to fill the time available for its completion." [13]

Subordination of Human Needs. The standardization and impersonal treatment in large bureaucracies often give members the feeling that they are expendable components of a big, heartless machine. In many profit-making organizations, productivity and profit goals are predominant. Managers are sometimes encouraged to put career goals above all others (such as family and health), and employees are treated only as economic units. Because of the limited purpose of the organizations, people are perceived only in terms of their contribution to organizational objectives. Little concern may be shown for their intrinsic value.

CLASSICAL POSITION AND NEOCLASSICAL RESPONSE

Thesis: Classical theory is concerned with organization structure and with the way in which the services of people can best be utilized. While recognizing the value and necessity of structure, neoclassical theory introduces a real concern for the individual and a conviction that the value of people must not be sacrificed on the altar of organizational principles and objectives.

Seven important classical principles, or pillars of organization, are briefly discussed in this section with the neoclassical response to each. Generally speaking, the classical position may be stated more categorically and precisely than the response. The neoclassical response represents a great many voices, but they are generally characterized by a desire to improve the welfare of employees, to humanize the workplace, and to incorporate the research findings of the behavioral sciences into organization theory.

Division of Labor

From one point of view the division of labor refers to task specialization: the practice of making small, simple jobs out of large, complex ones. Thus, instead of a tailor making an entire suit, each of many semiskilled workers performs a specialized function. One lays out patterns, another cuts the material, while still another sews collars or stitches buttonholes. Professional and technical specialization also is a form of division of labor. Specialists—accountants, engineers, or machinists—perform within a relatively narrow but valuable area of expertise. Professional specialization contrasts with task specialization in which

---

[13] C. Northcote Parkinson. *Parkinson's Law and Other Studies in Administration* (Boston: Houghton Mifflin Company, 1957). Parkinson showed how the number of employees increases out of proportion to the work to be done. For example, the power of the British navy declined drastically from 1914 to 1967 while the number of officials increased from 4,366 to over 33,000.

workers are valued for high productivity on work that requires a minimum of knowledge.

Classical Position.   To the classicist, task specialization is a means of gaining maximum productive efficiency and reducing costs at the work level. But Taylor was an advocate of task specialization at the managerial level as well (called *functional management*).Under such a scheme, one person would handle time-keeping, another machine repair, another product quality, and so forth. As we shall see later, the increased use of professional and technical specialists has to a great extent diluted management jobs, particularly at the foreman level.

Neoclassical Response.   The division of labor is accepted by neoclassicists, but its dehumanizing effects are emphasized. Employees in excessively specialized jobs often exhibit boredom, indifference, negative attitudes, low motivation, and immature behavior. This means that, apart from any value judgments about the dehumanizing impact of unchallenging jobs, the efficiencies gained by job dilution are partially offset by negative side effects.

At the professional level, specialization creates poor communication and coordination. The language of the specialist is often difficult for others to understand, and specialization brings about a perceptual distortion and a tendency to protect one's area of interest. For example, the sales department in one company was in constant conflict with the accounting department over the fact that sales were lost because high standards of customer credit were maintained. Neither seemed able to understand and respond to the needs of the other.

Hierarchical Structure

The positions and jobs of bureaucratic organizations are arranged in a *hierarchical structure,* meaning that they are scaled from highest to lowest on the basis of authority, status, and breadth of responsibility.

Classical Position.   From the classical viewpoint the building blocks of organizations are jobs or positions. (Weber called the bureaucratic positions *offices,* a term which is still used extensively, especially in government.) The duties of each position are clearly defined, and the authority relationships among positions are specified. Thus, all members of the hierarchy are aware of their own positions in relation to superiors, peers, and subordinates.

Because the attributes of a position (responsibilities, authority, and the like) are relatively stable, regardless of who occupies the position, the organization has stability and resists pressures to be changed by the whims and personal goals of its members. Because authority relationships are clearly defined, the ability to command and get compliance is theoretically assured.

Neoclassical Response.   The principle is sound to a point, but it is too simply stated. Neoclassicists attack the notion of authoritarian leadership, preferring democratic or participative leadership in which the role of formal authority is minimized. They also believe that the structure of the hierarchy should not be rigid. A position should, to some degree, reflect the characteristics of the person filling it; and the effects of the authority hierarchy should be softened by committee action and participative management programs. Finally, organizations are composed of people, not just positions. To minimize this fact is to subordinate people unnecessarily to the often unsympathetic demands of the organization.

Limited Span of Supervision

The optimum *span of supervison* (called *span of control* by classical theorists) refers to the number of subordinates a manager can supervise effectively. The appropriate size of the span was a hotly debated issue among classicists, but neoclassicists have refused to take it seriously. Classicists are perceived as asking the wrong questions and making invalid assumptions.

Classical Position.   Classicists believed there was an ideal number of subordinates, but there was no general agreement on what the exact number should be. They believed, however, that the smaller the span of supervision, management, or control, the better the control would be. Good control was perceived as tight control. Some believed that a supervisor's effectiveness would decline when the span exceeded five or six subordinates and that under certain circumstances a span of three might be ideal.

Neoclassical Response.   Control took on new meaning for the neoclassicist. The ideal control was believed to be self-control rather than external control through authority. This being the case, the classical notion that a manager should supervise only a limited, specific number of subordinates required alteration. A number of variables affect the proper span of supervision. Among the more important are:

1. The qualifications of the manager (e.g., experience and leadership skills)

2. The nature of the technology (e.g., routine assembly-line versus a job shop operation in which the manufacturing methods change constantly)

3. The qualifications of subordinates (e.g., skill level, self-discipline, and motivation to be productive)

4. The number of personal contacts the supervisor makes with subordinates and others (One manager may have fewer personal contacts while supervising fifty relatively autonomous store managers or routine factory workers than another manager, say a company president, has with four or five vice-presidents.)

5. The degree of staff support (e.g., assistants, quality control inspectors, engineers, secretaries, and personnel specialists)

6. The number of nonsupervisory functions a manager performs (such as serving on committees, making reports, relating to customers, and handling correspondence)

Figure 2–2 illustrates how the optimum span of supervision depends upon other variables in the work environment. It should be obvious that there can be no simple formula for deciding upon the ideal span of supervision. The classical notion that there is one best span for all situations is totally without support.

Type of Work Performed	Competence of Supervisor	Competence of Subordinates	Motivation of Subordinates	Possible Span of Control
Routine assembly	Superior	Superior	High	50*
Routine assembly	Marginal	Low	Low	20
Office — clerical	High	Moderate	Moderate	12
Systems analysis	High	Moderate	High	6

*These figures are presented only as examples of how span of supervision may vary depending upon the situation. They should in no sense be regarded as norms.

Figure 2–2 Span of Supervision as Dependent upon a
Number of Other Interacting Variables

In one situation, say a routine assembly operation, an acceptable span might be fifty. In another, where several employees require their supervisor's personal attention (a computer programming department, for example), a span of six or eight might be excessive. In all cases, the neoclassicist prefers the broadest possible span of supervision. This is consistent with a Theory Y view of people and a conviction that self-discipline under general supervision is preferable to the external control of authoritarian leadership.[14]

It is noteworthy that span of supervision has a direct bearing on the shape of the organization pyramid (Figure 2–3). The narrow span of the classicist results in a tall structure while the broad span of the neoclassicist results in a somewhat flatter structure. Neoclassicists prefer the flat, decentralized organizations because decision making occurs at the lowest possible level; each member is given the greatest possible amount of autonomy; and the inner control which results from individual goal setting and personal commitment is maximized. This is consistent with a neoclassical preference for participative leadership and general rather than close supervision.

---

[14] For an explanation of how control is maintained in complex, modern organizations refer to Peter B. Evans, "Multiple Hierarchies and Organizational Control," *Administrative Science Quarterly*, Vol. 20 (June, 1975), pp. 250–259.

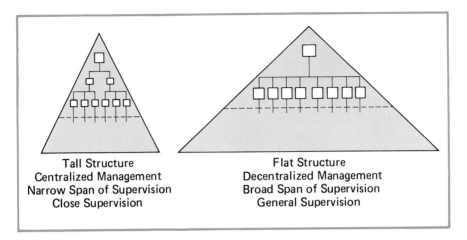

Figure 2-3   Relationship Between Span of Supervision
and Organization Structure and Function

Unity of Command

Unity of command means that a given individual takes orders from only one superior.

Classical Position.   Unity of command is universally applicable because the person who receives directions from more than one person is apt to get conflicting signals. This would disrupt the chain of command, reduce predictability, and place the subordinate in an untenable position.

Neoclassical Response.   The principle is valid to a point, but it does not always apply in the rigid, mechanical fashion envisioned by the classicists. Some adaptation is necessary because of the influence of staff and the concept that authority should be related to competence. In practice, the difference between accepting the advice of a staff expert and obeying the command of a line manager may be difficult to discern, and failure to take the expert's advice may be as disastrous as failure to accept the command. The more complex organizations become, the lower the probability that the unity of command principle can be applied in every situation.

Equal Responsibility and Authority

This principle states that the individual who is assigned a job should be delegated the authority needed to insure its completion. An unstated assumption is that the use of authority is the primary means of achieving organizational objectives.

Classical Position.   The logic of the classicist was simple: it would be irrational and unfair to expect managers without the appropriate authority to get results in terms of the job assigned. A manager assigned the job of manufacturing a product could hardly be expected to succeed without the authority to spend money; to hire personnel and direct their activities; to utilize space, materials, and equipment—to take whatever action is necessary to achieve the assigned objective.

Neoclassical Response.   Although neoclassicists accept the equal responsibility and authority principle, they understand that more is involved in achieving an objective than the exercise of formal authority. The classicist's statement of the principle seems to imply that degree of authority and ability to achieve the assigned objective are perfectly correlated. To the contrary, the exercise of authority may at times interfere with employee motivation and result in resistance and hostility. Leaders whose formal authority is minimal are sometimes better off for the lack of it because they are more inclined to use persuasion, suggestion, and other nonoffensive types of influence while taking steps to win the enthusiastic support of subordinates. The point is also made that a manager may officially possess formal authority but be lacking in the ability to exercise it. There are many kinds of authority and power, a factor not considered by the classicists.

This position does not deny the value of authority. Managers known to possess formal authority are less likely to have to use it than are managers who are perceived as weak. Formal authority is good, but it should be used sparingly. It should be held in reserve and, except as a last resort, should be subordinated to leadership behavior, expertise, and cooperative goal seeking.

Line and Staff

Organizations are composed of two types of managers. *Line managers* are those who are in the central chain of command. Marketing and production are always considered as line departments because they contribute directly to the organization's primary objective. Line managers receive authority from above and delegate to lower echelons of the hierarchy. *Staff managers* include the specialists who advise and otherwise serve line managers but have no formal authority over the primary operations. Personnel, advertising, and purchasing are considered staff departments, and their leaders are classified as staff managers. (Actually in large organizations there is a chain of command within staff departments—a line within staff—but this is not what we mean by line organization).

Classical Position.   In classical theory, line and staff are easily distinguishable. Line operations pertain to the vertical structure of the organization (delegating, assuming responsibility, maintaining unity of command, and the like) and are called the *scalar process* (from the scale of authority and responsibility). In contrast, staff positions are related to the *functional process* and are a part of the horizontal growth of the organization.

Although staff personnel usually perform specialized functions such as accounting, engineering, and industrial relations, in some cases they are junior administrators who function in positions as assistants to line managers. Since staff personnel support the line organization in a service or advisory capacity, staff is subordinate to line and is generally perceived as weak and inferior.

Neoclassical Response. Concepts of line and staff were greatly altered by neoclassical thought. As business became more technical and complex, staff specialists came to play an increasingly important role in decision making. Even in the early part of this century, when Taylor's impact was first felt, industrial engineers and other staff personnel were calling the shots on production methods, rates, and related production matters. Yet classical theorists could find no place for staff in the decision structure because it conflicted with the unity of command principle.

Glenn Stahl, Robert Golembiewski, and others have pointed out that the classical concept of staff as advisors of and inferior to line is not only a questionable concept but actually was never totally accepted in practice.[15] There are numerous examples in the military where staff officers operate more as colleagues than as inferior aids or advisors. It was obvious to most observers that when Henry Kissinger was serving as a foreign affairs advisor to President Nixon he was actually more powerful than the Secretary of State and often (even before Kissinger became Secretary of State) was in a position to make foreign policy because of his expertise and proximity to the President.

This same phenomenon occurs in industry where personnel move freely between line and staff positions and where influential staff specialists unofficially speak with the authority of their line superiors. For example, an individual was a staff advisor for scientific affairs to the president of IBM one day and the next he was managing a factory (a line position). A top level Conoco executive was assigned as an assistant to a division production vice-president because he was available and had the ability to solve problems. Within a short time, this staff assistant was promoted to the position of production vice-president in another division of the company. Such persons are never lacking in power merely because they occupy staff positions.

Obviously whether a staff manager is weak or powerful and influences or does not influence decisions cannot be totally predicated on the basis of line-staff identification. Thus, the unity of command problem must be solved in order to avoid excessive line-staff conflict. The neoclassical concept of authority helps to deal with this problem in two ways. First of all, the point is made that formal authority is not the only kind of authority or source of power. Power is also associated with expertise and personal qualities such as charisma and social dominance. Secondly, the dispersion of the decision-making function throughout the organization diminishes the problem somewhat. Staff, like line personnel, can make certain decisions and be held accountable for them. In fact, the neoclassicists are strong advocates of group problem solving in which expertise and formal authority become inextricably intertwined, and awareness of line-staff distinctions

[15] This and other research on staff are summarized in Philip J. Browne and Robert T. Golembiewski, "The Line-Staff Concept Revisited: An Empirical Study of Organizational Images," *Academy of Management Journal,* Vol. 17, No. 3 (September, 1974), p. 407.

is minimized. Needless to say, staff managers have for many years increased their power relative to line. Only in doing so was it possible for the organization to take advantage of the benefits of specialization (a principle which lies at the heart of classical theory), but the price paid in line-staff conflict has often been high.

Rationality

The principle of rationality has many dimensions, but essentially it means that the structure and function of organizations are goal directed and, for the most part, free of contamination by emotion and human sentiments.

Classical Position.   Rationality finds many expressions in the bureaucratic organization. The positions and authority are logically planned according to the bureaucratic principles already discussed. Rules (policies, procedures, regulations, and standards) provide the guidelines for individual behavior. Jobs are simplified as required to maximize efficiency, and personnel decisions (such as selection, promotions, compensation, and disciplinary matters) are made on the basis of performance rather than personal bias. The rationality principle in personnel decisions is called *impersonalization* and occupies a central position in bureaucratic theory.

Neoclassical Response.   In principle the rationality concept is admirable and should not be abandoned. It does, however, produce some negative side effects that require attention. The classical approach tends to subordinate the individual to the organization in an unhealthy manner, requiring excessive conformity and destroying the individuality needed to stimulate change and high motivation. It is good that impersonalization helps eliminate prejudice in personnel decisions, but it may also result in treating employees as though they were numbers or machines.

Classical rationality is at points irrational in that it fails to consider the importance of individual differences and to recognize the fact that all people are emotional as well as rational. Rationally, from the classicist's viewpoint, people should exert more effort in order to earn more money, but often this does not happen. This and many other expressions of the classicist's rationality principle sound rational but omit too many important facts about human nature to be workable. The classicist's illusion of rationality is often maintained only by thinking in rigid, oversimplified terms. The greater rationality of the neoclassicist is expressed in an attempt to take all the data into consideration when making generalizations, especially the great mass of empirical data concerning the nature of individuals and groups.

MODERN ORGANIZATION THEORY

Thesis: The term *modern organization theory* does not imply that neoclassical theory is out of date. In fact, the two coexist, interact, and in places are indistinguishable. Modern theory, however, is more daring, less encumbered by entanglements with classical theory, and more committed to an as yet unrealized integration of its components into a unified system.

Although the lines between neoclassical and modern theory are by no means tightly drawn, modern theory does have some distinctive characteristics. Like neoclassical, modern theory draws heavily upon empirical research but differs in its attempt to be integrative. Also, modern theory breaks more thoroughly with the rigid, mechanistic aspects of classical structure and is inclined to view organizations as living organisms which are constantly in the process of moving, changing, and adapting.

Modern organization theory is not all modern from a time perspective. Although modern theory generally dates back to the 1950s, Chester I. Barnard's 1938 definition of organizations had a distinctly modern ring about it, and Barnard is often viewed as a modern theorist. Setting the pace for modern theory, he defined organizations in terms of a system of consciously coordinated and interrelated personal activities and forces.[16] Yet Barnard had a significant influence upon neoclassical theory, too. Because a number of writers are associated with both neoclassical and modern theory, it is impossible to pigeonhole individuals according to the two classifications. Even the concepts involved often defy classification.

A Systems Approach

Modern theory views an organization as a total system rather than concentrating on a single aspect without regard for its relationship to the whole. The point is emphasized that all parts of an organization are interrelated and that a change in one area affects all others. Thus, a change in executive personnel, promotion policy, methods of accounting, or quality control standards could have implications for apparently unrelated parts of the organization. For example, promotion of an executive who is an advocate of automation may trigger labor unrest which ultimately leads to a strike. A minor change in accounting procedures may force a change in record keeping that disrupts the sales force, and the transfer of an employee may upset the equilibrium of an informal work group of which management is not even aware.

As shown in Figure 2–4, there are many kinds of organizational *inputs* or resources of which the organization is composed. The unplanned inputs contribute to organizational irrationality and to undesirable outputs (e.g., personal frustrations and losses rather than profits).

Of growing importance in organizational theory is the impact of the external environment: Congress passes an Occupational Safety and Health Act, Arab

---

[16] Chester I. Barnard, *The Functions of the Executive* (Cambridge, Mass.: Harvard University Press, 1938), p. 73.

Inputs	Transformation Variables in the Organization	Environmental Variables Affecting Output	Output
Money	Technology	Economic	Product Sales
Materials	Product mix	conditions	
Raw materials	Objectives	Market	Service
Subassemblies	Decisions	conditions	
Energy	Policies	Competition	Profit or Loss
Technology	Management	Cultural values	
Processes	Motivational	and attitudes	Dividends
Scientific	systems	Government	
discoveries	History and	requirements	Satisfactions
Personnel	traditions	World affairs	
Intelligence	Informal	War and peace	Frustrations
Aptitudes	group action	Trade barriers	
Expertise	Communication	Product demand	Personal growth
Attitudes	systems	Union relations	
Motives	Cooperation	Community relations	Wages and
Experience	and conflict	Labor supply	salaries

Figure 2–4   Organization as an Interactional System

nations place an embargo on oil, and the economy heats up with simultaneous inflation and recession. Modern theorists point out the importance of maintaining a dynamic equilibrium with the external environment and of regarding organization as an "open system" in continual interaction with a changing environment.[17] *Dynamic equilibrium* refers to a balance which the organization is able to maintain only by continually adapting and adjusting.

Figure 2–4 shows some interrleated variables which influence organizational behavior. The systems approach to studying organizations focuses attention on the fact that, because these variables are always influencing one another, we can understand any given part (e.g., decision making) only by understanding how it influences and is influenced by all the other continually changing parts (e.g., the organization's objectives, policies, communication systems, as well as environmental variables such as market conditions and government regulations).

Unfortunately the means of quantifying these interacting variables are not available and are not likely to be available any time soon. A literature review reveals that we know so little about how an organization's subsystems interact (e.g., the communication and motivational systems) that it is difficult to develop a workable organizational theory based on a total systems approach.[18] Therefore, at the present time, systems theory is more an ideal toward which to strive than a practical foundation for developing functional organization theory.

[17] Fremont E. Kast and James E. Rosenzweig, *Organization and Management* (New York: McGraw-Hill, Inc., 1970), p. 119.

[18] Fremont E. Kast and James E. Rosenzweig, "General Systems Theory: Applications for Organization and Management," *Academy of Management Journal,* Vol. 15, No. 4 (December, 1972), p. 451.

Integrating Processes

Modern organizational theory has given considerable attention to the linking processes by which the parts of an organization are integrated into a dynamic, functioning unit. Three of these are communication networks, organizational objectives, and decision making.

Elaborating upon early studies of communication by neoclassicists, modern theorists study the communication networks by which decision centers are linked and information is received, transmitted, and stored. Cybernetic models [19] are sometimes used to describe certain aspects of communication systems. Like the heat-seeking missile that receives information from its moving target and adapts accordingly, the organization is constantly in the process of adapting on the basis of information input. The cybernetic frame of reference has permitted theorists to be more precise in describing an organization's communication centers and networks.

The objectives, or goals, of an organization serve to integrate its activities by establishing a rational basis for purposeful behavior and decisions. Goal-setting theory has been applied in many diverse settings as numerous organizations have established systems to "manage by objectives." This is a process by which coordinated individual goals are set by key personnel at all organizational levels.

A critical aspect of the integrating process is decision making, and the theory developed in this area has been both prolific and practical. Early studies by Herbert Simon and others on how to program a computer to simulate human problem solving led to extensive studies on decision-making and problem-solving processes. A timely new discipline of *decision theory* has for several years been emerging. It is especially needed now because the complexity of large-scale organizations has reduced the usefulness of decisions based on unanalyzed intuition and enforced by formal authority.[20]

Matrix Organization

A variety of organization structures that differ from the bureaucratic model and violate classical principles of organization are included in modern theory. *Matrix organization,* also called project management and program management, is one such structure that has proved effective in recent years. It has most often been used when a new product must be developed, say a new military aircraft, while maintaining production of existing models.

---

[19] The term *cybernetics* was introduced by Norbert Wiener, an MIT mathematician, to refer to the science of receiving information and developing reaction and control systems. It deals primarily with the concepts of communication, information processing, and feedback and response in machines and living organisms. See Norbert Wiener, *Cybernetics, or Control and Communication in the Animal and the Machine* (New York: John Wiley & Sons, Inc. 1948).

[20] Herbert A. Simon, *Administrative Behavior* (3d ed.; New York: The Free Press, 1976). A comprehensive view of modern decision theory is found in E. Frank Harrison, *The Managerial Decision-Making Process* (Boston: Houghton Mifflin Company, 1975).

Matrix organization is ordinarily conceived as a temporary appendage to a traditional structure, although on major projects *temporary* could mean several years. The main advantage of a matrix organization is that an objective can be achieved without the expense and time required to develop a totally new organization. In many instances, personnel can be drawn from throughout the parent organization without seriously impairing its efficiency. This is especially true of scientific and technical personnel whose work is creative and who lack the routine duties associated with line management. When the special project is completed, the personnel assigned to it usually return to their regular jobs or are reassigned to other projects.

Depending upon the task, the project manager may develop a large personal staff or may operate virtually alone except for the support received by members of the permanent organization. The matrix organization may consist of temporarily assigned staff members working at the project site or working in their usual job location—laboratory, shop, office, etc. Since one of the advantages of matrix organization is that it maximizes use of existing facilities, as well as personnel, some efficiency may be lost when employees are brought together in a central location. This is, however, necessary on some projects.

Many of the employees who actually perform the project work are never assigned to the project manager. They continue to work under their usual supervisor while performing the tasks needed to complete the special project. They may, in fact, apply their expertise to two or more projects simultaneously. Since project managers work through the existing organization, over which they exert no formal authority, one would expect innumerable conflicts to arise, as indeed they sometimes do. On the other hand, the matrix organization can be made to work effectively. There are a number of elements in the dynamics that make it work.

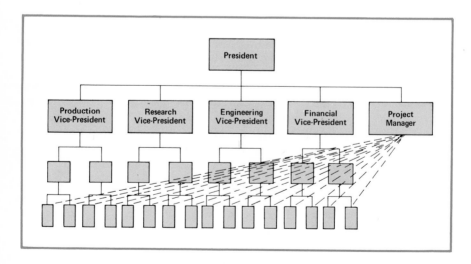

Figure 2–5   Matrix Organization Structure

1. The project manager, a respected member of the executive team, is known to have a high level of competence and the support of the president.

2. Each line manager has a responsibility to perform certain functions which are necessary to achieve the project objectives, and each has access to the resources (money, people, materials, space, etc.) needed to do the job.

3. A complex network of schedules and communication techniques is maintained to coordinate the work, reduce friction, and ensure the completion of the project.

4. Although formal authority exists within the traditional line organization, its impact is softened because the organization places a high value on cooperation, expert judgment, committee action, and scientifically analyzed decisions.

Matrix organization can best be understood within the modern paradigm of a living organism which is constantly changing and adapting.[21] Within such an organization, authority to make decisions flows to expertise rather than to formal position in a rigid hierarchy. Since authority of competence is equated with authority of position, matrix and other new organization designs are not new patches sewed on old garments. They are genuine departures from classical structure. Bureaucratic designs are satisfactory for stable organizations (those with regularized production processes, stable product lines, low employee turnover, fixed sales outlets, etc.), but they are often unable to cope with the complex problems which many organizations face today.

STUDY AND DISCUSSION QUESTIONS

1. Why do practicing managers need to know organizational theory?
2. What is the major difference between a formal and an informal organization?
3. What are the major differences between classical and neoclassical theory?
4. Classical theory includes the work of both Weber and Taylor. What do they have in common that justifies their grouping in this way?
5. What problems are involved in the concept of universal principles of organization?
6. What is the difference between human relations and organizational behavior?

---

[21] An understanding of organizations on a continuum from mechanistic to organic types is presented in easy to understand form in M. B. McCaskey, "Introduction to Organizational Design," *California Management Review,* Vol. 17 (Winter, 1974), pp. 13–20. Also see Don Helbriegel and John W. Slocom, Jr., "Organizational Design: A Contingency Approach," *Business Horizons,* Vol. 16 (April, 1973), pp. 59–68.

7. What are the two different ways in which the division of labor principle is expressed?
8. In what ways does the bureaucratic hierarchy contribute to the stability of an organization?
9. How have neoclassicists reacted to the span of supervision principle?
10. Evaluate the classical notion that staff is generally weak and inferior when compared with line management.
11. In what sense might the classical principle of impersonalization be thought of as contributing a humanizing element in organizations?
12. To what extent has modern organization theory been successful in developing a systems theory of the total organization?

CRITICAL INCIDENT

The High Command

In 1947 the Schwartz and Mason Company was founded to produce and market a small line of drugs which originated with the discovery by Dr. Stephen Schwartz, a practicing physician, of a uniquely effective formula to treat nasal congestion. Medical endorsement of this product led to rapid expansion of the company, the gross sales of which were over $40 million a year by 1976 when this event occurred.

As indicated on the chart below, Schwartz was officially chairman of the board and Frank Mason was president, although from the beginning the two had functioned harmoniously as equal partners in the management of the business. Ownership was split 60–40 with Schwartz the majority shareholder. Schwartz

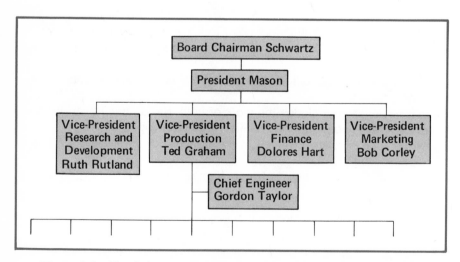

Figure 2–6   The Schwartz and Mason Company Organization Chart

gradually reduced his medical practice, spending an increasing amount of time in the business and in travel. Mason, a highly competent executive with a financial background, was in the business full time from the beginning.

Although Schwartz and Mason had no aspiration to become a major drug company, they were growth-oriented and had discovered that the manufacture of private label cosmetics provided a compatible and profitable diversification. They produced two such product lines and were in the process of adding a third.

As shown on the organization chart, there are few top managers in the company. Eleven first-line production supervisors report to Graham; so the organization is relatively flat, and the span of supervision is broad. All line managers are competent, well paid, and highly motivated "members of a problem-solving team" (a descriptive phrase often used by Mason). One uniquely competent staff manager is Gordon Taylor, the chief engineer. He spent two years in medical school before dropping out, and he later earned an industrial engineering degree in night school. A mature and highly respected member of management, Taylor is involved in most of the important management decisions, especially those which relate to production. In production matters his judgment is unusually sound and is recognized as such.

For several months the company had been moving toward the development of the production unit to manufacture the third line of cosmetics. Most of the new equipment had been received. Since the new product was to be produced and packaged to the specifications of the customer, there were few major decisions yet to be made about the venture. The only issue over which there had been some debate was the physical placement of the new line within the plant.

The day before Dr. Schwartz was to leave for an extended world cruise, he consulted with Taylor about the location of the new unit:

Schwartz:
Now that you've given it some thought, what do you think?

Taylor:
I think we should combine the production facilities of all three cosmetic units in order to take maximum advantage of our equipment. That way when we're caught up on one line we can use its blending and possibly its labeling and packaging equipment for another line. Of course, this will mean that all three units will have to be located in the new warehouse area. Moving the two existing lines will cause some problems, but it can be done, and in the long run it will pay off.

Schwartz:
That's the answer, and we need to get on with it. You make sure it gets done. When I get back I would like to see the new unit in full production alongside the other two.

This was the last conversation Schwartz had with anyone within the company before he left to prepare for his vacation. Taylor wished that Graham and Mason had been present since he knew that both of them had reservations about the action he had recommended.

Questions

1. What classical principles of organization were violated in this situation?
2. How serious is the problem caused by the fact that the so-called universal principles have been breached?
3. How should Taylor handle the situation?
4. What additional information is needed in order to understand this situation?

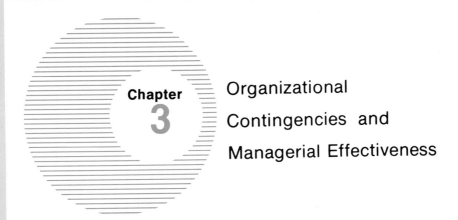

Chapter 3

Organizational Contingencies and Managerial Effectiveness

When managers are unusually successful or when they fail, the popular notion is that their success or failure is due solely or primarily to their personal performance. Those who are unfamiliar with the intimate details of the latter tend to ask, "What did the discharged manager do wrong? Was it a matter of poor decision making? inadequate leadership behavior? inability to compete in corporate politics? a lack of sophistication in business matters?" These questions are often based on the assumption that the organization has little, if any, responsibility for a manager's success or failure. Such an assumption is usually invalid.

In this chapter we examine a few of the many organizational characteristics that influence managerial effectiveness and success. Such an emphasis does not imply, however, that managers are victims of organization, unable to influence its performance. Because of vast individual differences, an impenetrable barrier to one manager is a challenge to another. One may convert the apparent barrier into an asset in reaching organizational goals and achieving personal success, while others passively assume that their fate is determined by an all-powerful organization. Nevertheless, managerial effectiveness is determined by the organization as well as the individual.

SITUATIONAL AND CONTINGENCY MANAGEMENT

Thesis: The search for universal principles of management often leads to sweeping generalizations which cannot be defended because what works in one situation may not work in another. Contingency management, the most recent trend in understanding organizational behavior, takes a diagnostic approach in an attempt to isolate certain characteristics of the organizational environment and make "if-then" statements: if a given characteristic is present, then a certain management practice will apply.

For the past two decades, it has been popular to talk in terms of *situational leadership* (or management). In its common usage, the term conveys the idea that a leadership approach which works well in one situation (e.g., the presidency of a college fraternity) may be a total failure in another (e.g., the supervisor of a construction crew). When generalized, this concept carries the notion that the success of any given management practice in one situation is no assurance that it will succeed in another where conditions are different. Thus, organizational goal setting (management by objectives) has been highly successful in some companies and a miserable failure in many others. Situational management has made no serious attempts to describe the specific conditions under which a given management practice will succeed.

The terms *situational management* and *contingency management* are often used interchangeably. However, Luthans has made a meaningful distinction between the two.[1] *Situational management* proposes that the organizational environment must be analyzed before choosing an appropriate course of action. *Contingency management* takes the same basic point of view but attempts to go a step further by specifying the relationship between managerial action (say deciding on the most effective span of supervision) and other relevant variables (for example, a manager's leadership skills, the nature of the work, and the abilities of subordinates). As research provides new insights into such relationships, contingency management offers considerably more promise than the situational approach.[2]

According to Kast and Rosenzweig, contingency management is "a middle ground between the view that there are universal principles of organization and management and the view that each organization is unique and that each situation must be analyzed separately."[3] Contingency management does not involve a search for universal principles, but it does seek to draw generalizations within limited contexts. For example, Fiedler's research led him to conclude that task-oriented leaders perform best in situations that are very favorable or unfavorable, while people-oriented leaders perform best in situations of intermediate favorableness (as he defined these terms). This is a contingency if-then approach (if certain conditions exist, then a certain leadership style is best).[4] The situational approach merely states that the most appropriate style depends upon the situation. It does not attempt to specify the if-then conditions.

A number of theorists in different areas (personnel management, planning, leadership, organization design, and behavior modification) are using the contingency framework, and a few have become enthusiastic supporters of it. On the

---

[1] Fred Luthans, *Introduction to Management: A Contingency Approach* (New York: McGraw-Hill, Inc., 1976), p. 31.

[2] The situational approach is presented in the following publications: Howard M. Carlisle, *Situational Management* (New York: AMACOM, 1973); and Robert J. Mockler, *Management Decision Making and Action in Behavioral Situations* (Austin, Texas: Austin Press, 1973).

[3] Fremont E. Kast and James E. Rosenzweig, *Contingency Views of Organization and Management* (Chicago: Science Research Associates, 1973) p. ix.

[4] Fred E. Fiedler, "Predicting the Effects of Leadership Training and Experience from the Contingency Model: A Clarification," *Journal of Applied Psychology,* Vol. 57, No. 2 (1973), p. 110.

other hand, while praising the contingency approach for courageously seeking to establish functional relationships between management practices and environmental conditions, Moberg and Koch are correct in warning against going too far too fast. They point out the dangers of overgeneralizing from the crude beginnings of situational research and note that, in spite of the warnings which offer a word of caution or an apology for the tentativeness of the contingency models, they "both overstate the convergence among existing findings and underestimate the problems of applying them."[5]

While recognizing the dangers of overgeneralizing, an attempt is made in this chapter to describe some of the environmental variables which influence managerial effectiveness. In later chapters, some specific applications of contingency theory, as such, will be discussed in greater detail.

IDENTIFIABLE EXPECTATIONS

Thesis: Managerial effectiveness is contingent upon a balance between two environmental extremes: (a) so little position structure that a manager is unable to identify critical job requirements and (b) so much structure that the position cannot be adapted to the unique qualifications of the manager who occupies it.

As the classicists so ably pointed out, position stability is a critical factor in making an organization predictable and thus making possible coordinated effort in achieving goals. Because positions remain stable as individuals flow through them, predictable behavior may continue in the face of high personnel turnover, rapid expansion, and other conditions which would otherwise result in chaos.

The Need to Know What Is Expected

Few management positions are so simple that the incumbents can know exactly what is expected of them. A position description helps define expectations, but it is never complete. It represents only the general superstructure of the position. And just as the steel frame of a building shows little of its style, warmth, and uses, the position description only outlines what is expected of a manager. Like a highway map which cannot show stoplights, rough roads, and washed out bridges, the position description serves a general purpose but leaves much to the discretion of the user.

The structure provided by a position description is supplemented by supervisory directives, policies, and procedures (many of which are not expressed in writing), and by organizational goals and controls. All these contribute to managerial effectiveness. To the extent that managers know what is expected,

---

[5] Dennis J. Moberg and James L. Koch, "A Critical Appraisal of Integrated Treatments of Contingency Findings," *Academy of Management Journal*, Vol. 18, No. 1 (March, 1975), p. 122.

they can behave rationally. They can also have reasonable expectations concerning the standards by which their performance will be assessed. In the absence of these conditions, even managers with outstanding potential may find it difficult to perform effectively.

The Managerial Role

As the term is used here, *role* refers to a set of behaviors which is generally regarded as appropriate for a given individual in a specific situation. Like the actor who adapts from one drama to another, we all play many roles, each requiring behavior which may be inappropriate elsewhere. Thus, a manager plays one role as a subordinate and quite another as a peer or superior. The role of parent must be played in one situation; and the role of manager, lover, or United Fund drive chairperson in another. The confusion of these roles can be disastrous.

There is, of course, no simple book of rules which describes the many facets of the managerial role. Successful managers are sensitive to their environments, constantly observing and reading the subtle cues, hints, and innuendos by which the unwritten role expectations are communicated. This brief excerpt from a conversation between a new foreman and his superior illustrates the point that not all expectations are expressed in position descriptions and policy manuals.

Foreman:
Are you telling me I have to give up Tuesday night poker with the men I've worked with for eight years?

Superintendent:
I am not saying that. I have no right to say who your friends should be or what you should do outside your work.

Foreman:
But you're suggesting that I should make a break with my friends. You think it's best.

Superintendent:
Let's put it this way. Your subordinates are accusing you of favoritism toward your close friends, and it's hurting your effectiveness. In addition, the other foremen are not cooperating with you because they think you're a union steward in disguise, and you can't survive for long without their support. They clam up when you enter the room because they're afraid you will talk out of school. You apparently want to force me into the uncomfortable position of telling you how to handle your personal affairs. I will just say this: I shouldn't have to tell you! To succeed in this job you're going to have to see and respond to some cues that you've elected to ignore. Your Tuesday night poker game is just a symptom.

In this illustration, the superintendent is finding it difficult to maintain the fiction that managers do not get involved in the private lives of their subordinates;

and the foreman is having an understandable problem adapting to the managerial role. This is the characteristic effect of a broad spectrum of unwritten and often unstated expectations to which an effective and successful manager must respond. A manager may be expected to work long and irregular hours and to be supportive of certain attitudes held by higher-level managers. Only managers who are aware of and responsive to such expectations will be likely to receive the support necessary to be effective and to be personally successful.

Autonomy and Flexibility

Although formal structure and role expectations may strongly support a manager's efforts to be effective, they can also be a hindrance. Two conditions must be present before they are likely to be supportive. First, they must be flexible enough to permit expression of the individuality involved in adapting position requirements to one's unique abilities and needs. The second, a closely related condition, is that organizational standards and values must be relatively consistent with those held by the manager in question.

Most management positions yield to considerable modification over a period of time. Subordinates are selected who can perform well in areas in which the superior is weak or disinterested, new and challenging problems are sought out, and tasks are shifted, within limits, from one manager to another. Much of a position's potential for adaptation depends upon the initiative and motivation of its occupant.

On the basis of extensive research in a variety of companies, Henry Mintzberg has shown that what managers say they do varies greatly from what they actually do.[6] Following the classical view, they often say that they plan, organize, coordinate, and control. In reality, however, their work involves a variety of unrelenting, short-term (typically from a few seconds to thirty minutes), fragmented, and unplanned activities designed to meet the needs of the moment. Given this lack of rigid structure in most management positions, managers who are proficient in planning, organizing, and delegating have almost unlimited possibilities for shaping their jobs for an optimal match with their personal abilities and needs.

SUPPORTIVE ORGANIZATIONAL SYSTEMS

Thesis: Organizations vary greatly in the extent to which they provide managerial support. Depending upon the favorability of the environment, a manager's job may be easy or difficult, possible or impossible. In a highly favorable environment, a marginally qualified manager may perform well; in an unfavorable environment, a superbly qualified manager may fail miserably.

---

[6] Henry Mintzberg, "The Manager's Job: Folklore and Fact," *Harvard Business Review,* Vol. 53, No. 4 (July–August, 1975), pp. 49–61. This is a condensation of a book by Mintzberg, *The Nature of Managerial Work,* published by Harper & Row, Publishers, in 1973.

An endless number of organizational conditions interact to determine the favorability of the manager's environment. In this section we look briefly at five conditions which prove to be important in most organizations. These are concerned with (1) motivational systems, (2) communication systems, (3) personnel practices, (4) growth opportunities, and (5) advancement opportunities.

Motivational Systems

An organization's motivational systems consist of all the means by which the work-related behavior of its members is influenced. The most obvious of these have to do with financial compensation—programs and policies by which wages and salaries are used to reward desirable behavior. Other motivational forces are expressed in the extent to which promotions and recognition follow desirable behavior and the degree to which loyalty and interest in the work itself result in positive behavior. The various forms of punishment, designed to discourage undesirable behavior, are also part of the overall motivational system.

How do an organization's motivational systems relate to managerial effectiveness? Where motivation is generally high, even a manager with mediocre leadership ability may get acceptable results. The system itself gets results whether or not the manager is performing acceptably. However, where motivation is generally low because of organizational conditions over which the manager has no control, personal efforts to motivate subordinates may be unsuccessful.

The following comment from an attitude survey is a good example of a motivational stance that is difficult to overcome. This view was typical of those expressed by most employees in this newspaper composing room.

> I have worked for this company for over twenty years, and I know almost all there is to know about it. Management doesn't really care whether we live or die except that some of us might be hard to replace. Whether you do good work or bad work doesn't matter—you are paid the same either way. Whether you get promoted depends more on your willingness to play politics than on your ability to do the work. I'm not blaming my foreman for this. He's a victim of the system, too. He has good intentions, but they don't matter. I'm convinced that nothing will ever be any different until we unionize and run the show ourselves.

Effectiveness is also related to a manager's own motivation to perform. A certain degree of technical and human relations ability is required, but differences in managerial effectiveness are as often attributable to motivation as to ability. Simply stated, some organizations make it rewarding for a manager to perform at a high level while others are structured to reward mediocrity. Accordingly, some organizations find it exceedingly difficult to attract and hold managers with high potential.

Communication Systems

Chapter 15 discusses the process of communication in organizations. At this point, our objective is only to show the relationship between an organization's communication systems and managerial effectiveness. Three closely interrelated aspects of the communication process demonstrate this relationship. They are (1) access to information, (2) feedback systems, and (3) written policies and procedures.

Access to Information.   The most critical aspect of managerial effectiveness is the ability to make good decisions. This, in turn, is contingent upon the availability of information and the ability to communicate freely with other organizational members who can contribute useful facts or ideas.

Feedback Systems.   Organizations have a variety of devices for obtaining feedback. Management reports concerning profits, productivity, quality, sales, employee turnover, and other aspects of organizational life provide valuable information on the extent to which managerial actions are effective. In addition, performance evaluations and attitude surveys may provide feedback on the basis of which a manager may adapt rather than continue an undesirable course of action. These opportunities for feedback are normally built into the fabric of the organization, and their potential for influencing managerial performance varies greatly from one organization to another.

Feedback devices necessarily involve many informal channels of communication which can make an environment either favorable or unfavorable to managerial effectiveness. In commenting on the poor performance of a departmental superintendent, a management consultant made the following observation:

> Mrs. Grossman is not altogether to blame for her plight. She made one big mistake, and it continues to haunt her. Because she resented the condescending treatment of her male peers, she became too aggressive and let them know she didn't need their help. But she does need it, and she is not getting it. She lacks the benefit of the exchanges that take place at coffee breaks and lunchtime where much of the really meaningful, work-related communication is taking place. In a real sense she is isolated from the organization. She does not know what is going on most of the time, and she is not getting the benefit of the special consideration the other supervisors are showing for one another's needs. There is no question about her competence, but she is out of the system and cannot perform well under such conditions.

Written Policies and Procedures.   Many of the problems a manager faces have been faced before, perhaps with minor variations. It is customary for recurring problems to be dealt with by means of written policies and procedures. This leads to consistency of action and eliminates the frustration and time pressures which result from handling each problem as if it were an isolated event. It would, for example, be foolish to make every credit decision without reference to policies and procedures which capture past experiences and set forth guidelines for dealing with the request of a specific customer or prospect.

The development of policies and procedures is a decision-making process which establishes the limits within which future decisions are made. The manager who has the benefit of current, wisely developed policies and procedures uses these as criteria or standards for decision making. They define what a good decision consists of and thus make good decisions possible. In some organizations, small ones especially, most of the guidelines are locked in the brain of a chief executive. Since subordinate managers must guess at what these guidelines are, they are often forced to be either dependent decision avoiders or high-risk decision makers whose careers are in constant jeopardy.

Personnel Practices

Over a period of time, an organization's personnel policies strongly influence its character and personality. Consider the impact of personnel selection. One organization exercises great care in selection in the conviction that each new employee is a valued individual with a unique contribution to make. Special attention is given to how each new employee will relate to existing personnel and to whether the individual's values, standards of behavior, and leadership style are compatible with those held by the organization.

Another organization pays little attention to selection in the expectation that turnover will be high under any circumstance. Employees who are productive and compatible will remain with the organization; those who are not will leave or be fired. These two approaches usually produce organizations with quite different temperaments. Some organizations consistently build upon personnel with outstanding potential in terms of the jobs and challenges available, while others are staffed primarily by personnel whose qualifications are marginal.

The implications for managerial effectiveness are obvious. Some managers have such outstanding talent with which to work that they could hardly fail. Others are expected to get results with problem subordinates, and attempts to replace ineffective subordinates are met with extreme resistance from other employees and managers. Effective management may be further thwarted by practices of nepotism, bias in giving promotions and raises, and a variety of other behaviors which sooner or later encourage the manager with high potential to change organizations rather than fight the system.

Theodore Levitt points out that the process by which a manager is selected is a critical element in managerial success. It is as though meticulous care in selection is required in order to give higher-ranking managers the confidence and motivation they need to provide a new manager with the backing required for success. Commenting on the elaborate screening through which successful managers usually pass before employment, Levitt makes a subtle, but important, point: [7]

> The purpose was to determine whether his particular talents, competences, attitudes, styles, and personality were appropriate for the tasks and problems of the new situation he would enter. He turned

[7] Theodore Levitt, "The Managerial Merry-Go-Round," *Harvard Business Review,* Vol. 52, No. 4 (July–August, 1974), p. 121.

out to be successful not alone for what he brought to the situation but for what his selectors saw in him as suitable for the situation. Those two things are not the same, though they may seem so at first.

Personnel policy influences managerial effectiveness in at least one other way—namely, the degree of staff support to which a manager has access. The quality of professional services in such areas as engineering, accounting, and personnel can sometimes make the difference between success and failure. They are specialized functions upon which a manager may have a high degree of dependence but little control. They are often the critical determinants of managerial effectiveness.

Growth Opportunities

Organizations which provide little opportunity for management growth are unable to make optimal use of managerial talent. Managers are most effective when challenged to use their full potential. Although personal characteristics are important determinants of whether a manager's abilities will be developed and used, environmental constraints are also a factor.

The motivation for personal growth is closely linked to advancement opportunities, but other factors are also involved. The two interrelated questions concerning growth opportunity are (1) whether top management actively encourages management development and (2) whether managers who continually learn and develop new skills are subsequently rewarded for doing so. Affirmative answers to most of the checklist questions presented in Figure 3–1 (page 58) indicate that an environment is favorable for growth.

Advancement Opportunities

Where advancement opportunities are perceived as few or nonexistent, managers typically (1) lose their motivation to grow, with a resulting loss of effectiveness or (2) are motivated to grow only in order to move on to greener pastures in another firm. In either case, the organization suffers.

The availability of advancement opportunities and the expectation of advancement are not the same thing, and the latter is in many respects more important. Recently a senior engineer who was slated by his superiors to succeed the retiring production vice-president resigned, completely unaware that he was being considered for the post. In fact, he was afraid of being laid off because of the company's recent loss of contracts. The position he took actually paid less than the one he had left, but it offered more stability and prospects for continual promotions.

Expectations for advancement are shaped by a number of factors in the work environment. The actual frequency with which openings occur is important, but for a given individual it may not be the most important factor in determining promotions. Professor Eugene Jennings, whose book, *The Mobile Manager,* pro-

MANAGEMENT DEVELOPMENT PRACTICES	Yes	No
1. Definite expectations exist that managers shall continue to learn and develop new skills. _____	☐	☐
2. The organization requires annual goal setting for personal growth and follows up on progress made. _____	☐	☐
3. Released time is provided for special seminars and other forms of education and self-improvement. _____	☐	☐
4. Tuition and other expenses for work-related development activities are paid by the organization. _____	☐	☐
5. Development is encouraged by in-house seminars, lectures, behavior-modification projects, and related activities. _____	☐	☐
6. Managers are rewarded for developing subordinates. _____	☐	☐
7. Evidence of serious individual efforts to learn, mature, and develop skills is rewarded. _____	☐	☐
8. Managers are encouraged to coach subordinates for development purposes. _____	☐	☐
9. Programs of job rotation, designed to broaden managerial experience, are sponsored. _____	☐	☐
10. The organization makes every effort to utilize the highest level of talent developed by each manager. _____	☐	☐
11. To the extent that internally developed talent is available, promotions are made from within. _____	☐	☐
12. Managers are provided with all possible information concerning position openings, expected opportunities, and position requirements as an aid to long-range career planning and personal growth. _____	☐	☐

Figure 3–1   Checklist of Management Development Practices

vides some brilliant insights into the conditions which are correlated with upward mobility, notes that a manager must have both visibility and exposure in order to advance.[8]

Visibility is the opportunity to see one's superiors in action, to learn how they think and operate, and to become aware of what they value. *Exposure* is the ability to be seen by one's superiors and to demonstrate one's competence (or incompetence). To some extent these conditions are a function of the leadership style of high-level managers. Managers can influence their own visibility and exposure (Jennings calls these *visiposure*), but they do not have complete control over these conditions.

---

[8] Eugene Emerson Jennings, *The Mobile Manager* (New York: McGraw-Hill, Inc., 1967), pp. 30–34.

ORGANIZATIONAL CONTROLS

Thesis: An organization can best achieve its objectives when its members require a minimum of supervision because they are competent and goal-oriented. Nevertheless, even under optimal conditions of individual commitment and self-control, organizations need formal controls.

The control function of organizations consists of the following:

1. *Establishing standards by which all aspects of organizational life are evaluated.* Most organizations have formal standards relating to spending, production, sales, product quality, safety, inventory, personnel selection, acceptable employee behavior, and so forth.

2. *Establishing feedback systems by which actual performance is compared with predetermined standards.* These are best exemplified by management reports which show, often on a daily basis, expected and actual performance. A manager whose budget report shows the amount allocated for a particular item, the amount spent to date, the amount committed but not spent, and the amount remaining, is provided with a practical basis for the control of expenditures.

3. *Taking appropriate action to ensure that substandard performance is improved and that standards will be met in the future.*

It is common practice to refer to the standards and feedback systems as *controls* although it should be obvious that they serve a control function only if managerial action is involved. They are not a substitute for supervision, but they minimize requirements for personal supervision. A correlate of this is the fact that self-control or self-management is possible only when the standards and expectations spelled out in formal controls are available as guidelines for behavior.[9]

Controls and Managerial Effectiveness

The availability of effective control systems has a direct bearing both on managerial effectiveness and the success of the total enterprise. This can be seen in the case of a rapidly expanding manufacturing firm whose financial controls were inadequate. Its chief financial officer, an ultraconservative, major shareholder, was slow to change to the sophisticated types of financial controls required in this fast-paced and volatile organization. As a result, sales often outpaced production; a higher level of inventory was maintained for costly,

---

[9] Two articles which provide insights into the nature of controls are Robert J. Mockler, "The Corporate Control Job: Breaking the Mold," *Business Horizons,* December, 1970, pp. 73–77; and William H. Sihler, "Toward Better Management Control Systems," *California Management Review,* Vol. 10, No. 3 (1971), pp. 33–39.

slow-moving items than for others that were fast moving and subject to wide fluctuations in demand; and the company experienced almost daily cash-flow problems. Because of system inadequacies, a succession of office managers and accountants resigned or were discharged because of presumed incompetence, and for several years the company wavered on the brink of disaster.

Poor controls make unnecessary demands upon managers. They require that a manager spend an inordinate amount of time in direct supervisory relationships, and the excessively close supervision is resented. Subordinates do not always have favorable attitudes toward controls (toward demanding production and quality standards, for example), but at least the controls introduce an element of predictability into the environment. In reducing the amount of superior-subordinate contact, controls also reduce the subordinates' feelings of being controlled and personally dominated by a superior.

Problems Caused by Controls

Because rewards and penalties are associated with meeting the standards established in control systems, the standards often become ends in themselves. Knowing that their effectiveness will be evaluated against a set of standards, managers meet the standards, or appear to do so, at the organization's expense. Two brief examples illustrate this point.

> In one organization, sales quotas were often met by forcefully selling merchandise customers did not need, selling merchandise to be shipped in a subsequent month, and selling merchandise with the understanding that it would be returned. This managerial behavior was designed to postpone the day of judgment on the assumption that by some means that day could be postponed indefinitely.

> In assembly-line manufacturing, where each of a large number of employees performs a minor operation on a product, the end of a work period normally leaves many production units on the line at various stages of completion. In one plant, for example, at the end of the day, approximately sixty incomplete inflatable life rafts are left in the plant —some almost completed and others just begun. At the end of the week, when a production report is due, the superintendent sometimes "bleeds the line." Instead of continuing to start new units until the end of the work period, employees at the beginning of the line are assigned to help those nearer the end so that when the time of accounting comes a maximum number of units will have been produced. Contrary to the expectations of superiors, however, there are few, if any, partially completed units on the floor, and the crash effort to meet a production quota has drastically reduced efficiency.

Some common abuses of controls can be avoided by minor changes in the system. Sihler points out that the way controls are established is often a reflection of management attitudes and philosophy.[10] Controls which reflect a basic distrust

---

[10] Ibid., p. 34.

of and lack of consideration for people tend to invite abuses; and when top management evaluates performance only on the basis of results, with no consideration for how they are achieved, subordinate managers often behave irrationally to achieve the desired results.

THE DELEGATION PROCESS

Thesis: Delegation at higher levels of an organization is a primary determinant of a manager's opportunities to perform well. While a manager's success and effectiveness are not totally dependent upon the superior's willingness to delegate, they may be severely limited by it.

Delegation is the organizational process by which (1) a manager assigns specific duties to a subordinate, (2) the subordinate is provided with a grant of authority commensurate with the duties to be performed, (3) the subordinate assumes responsibility for satisfactorily performing the duties, and (4) the subordinate is held accountable for results.

Like most definitions, this is an oversimplification. For example, it seems to imply that only authority is necessary for satisfactory performance of the assigned duties. As we shall see, delegation is a highly complex and dynamic process involving a number of interacting variables. We say, for example, that managers should always be given authority to match the responsibility that they are expected to assume, but in practice there is no simple way to accomplish this. The amount of authority needed depends upon such factors as leadership style, attitudes of subordinates, the extent to which managers perceive themselves to have authority, and the extent to which managers possess the authority that comes from expertise and personality characteristics.

Extent of Delegation

Delegation occurs any time a subordinate performs work for which that person's superior is ultimately responsible. It occurs, for instance, every time a secretary types a letter for a superior, even when little or no discretion exists for the secretary to influence the ultimate product.

The extent to which a subordinate is permitted to determine the means of task performance may vary from none to all. Some managers specify detailed means and supervise closely to see that results are accomplished by those means. Others specify the results to be achieved and leave the means to the discretion of the subordinate. Both qualify as delegation, but in the latter case the manager delegates more completely.

Clarifying the Levels of Delegation. A manager often begins by delegating only the most elementary aspects of a job, supervising closely to ensure effective completion. Then, as it becomes obvious that the subordinate is capable of assuming more responsibility, an increasing amount of work is delegated. Finally, the superior may feel confident in specifying only the results desired.

Some managers, for reasons to be discussed shortly, have extreme difficulty in allowing subordinates to make decisions and work on their own long after they are capable of doing so. Such managers do delegate, but they delegate much less than they could. This means that both they and their subordinates assume less responsibility than they are capable of assuming. Managers who refuse to delegate tasks for which great amounts of authority are required involve themselves in unnecessary detail and thereby limit both their contributions to the organization and their promotion potential. To achieve a high degree of success, a top-level manager must develop and supervise subordinate managers who possess a high level of authority and who will assume responsibility for important managerial functions.

A technique used by one management consultant, a specialist in management development, illustrates the problems of minimal delegation. He makes use of a program, always with the full support of the chief executive, in which a study is performed to determine how the organization's managers actually spend their time. The duties performed are then classified according to predetermined standards as managerial, staff specialist, clerical, secretarial, and so forth. Given the percentage of time spent in each type of activity, the manager's total job is evaluated on the basis of the average earnings of employees in each category. It is a shocking experience for $50,000 a year executives to discover that much of their time is occupied with tasks which should be performed by $18,000 a year assistants or $9,000 a year secretaries. It is a strong incentive to delegate more completely and to use as much time as possible for performing managerial functions.

Since the aggregate amount of responsibility assumed in an organization is directly related to the extent of effective delegation, good management generally favors maximum delegation. This amount, however, may vary greatly over time. Since new personnel are continually entering an organization and experienced personnel theoretically are able to assume increasing responsibility, the amount of work a manager delegates is constantly in flux. This poses no serious problem as long as duties and authority are reasonably well defined at any given point in time.

Although duties and authority can never be perfectly defined, managers need to be aware of (1) when to take action solely on their own, (2) when to take action and inform their superiors of that action, (3) when to plan an action and inform their superiors of what will be done unless the superiors intervene, (4) when to ask their superiors for a decision, and (5) when to take no initiative unless specifically told to do so.

Awareness of when to act at each of these levels comes only from experience in a particular environment and is influenced greatly by the perception, sensitivity, management philosophy, self-confidence, and risk-taking tendency of the manager. One effective manager, an executive vice-president, has increased his authority and responsibility by following this philosophy:

> When I'm not sure whether I have the authority to take a certain course of action—when it is really a gray area—I assume I have it and take whatever action seems appropriate. If I later discover that I have overstepped my authority, I apologize. This has worked for me for twenty years. Someone has to interpret the gray area, and it may as well be me.

Another manager takes an entirely different approach:

> I'm careful not to make decisions in areas where I'm uncertain about my authority. I don't want the embarrassment of having to apologize or back down. When I'm not sure of where I stand, I ask for a clarification.

Everything else being equal, managers of the former type will grow in power and responsibility more rapidly than the latter. They stand a greater chance of losing their jobs, or having clashes with superiors, but their aggressiveness will ordinarily lead to a rapid expansion of authority and responsibility. These cases demonstrate the fact that the subordinate as well as the superior defines the limits within which delegation will occur. Managers who complain that they lack the authority to perform effectively sometimes lack it because they have not reached out to grasp it.

Upward Delegation.   Managers who have difficulty in delegating often find themselves victims of upward delegation. This refers to the process by which subordinates bring problems to their superior for a decision instead of personally assuming responsibility and taking the risk involved in decision making. The superior may be critical of subordinates for not being able to make decisions while unconsciously encouraging the practice because it is ego-enhancing.

A new manager who replaces one who delegated poorly can usually reverse the upward delegation process by turning the questions back on subordinates and gradually refusing to make the decisions which the subordinates should be making. Only if this is done can subordinates be held accountable for results.[11]

Nondelegable Duties.   Theoretically managers can delegate all the duties for which they are responsible, but in practice this is not possible. Most managers perform a variety of functions which are much like the work of their subordinates. They read and edit reports, for example. They answer correspondence, some of which may require minimal ability but cannot ordinarily be delegated (e.g., answering a letter from a very important customer). At times, even a chief executive, such as the President of the United States, must become involved in speech writing, entertaining, studying, and other activities which are not delegable.

It is important to note that responsibility can never be delegated. Managers remain accountable to higher levels of management for all the tasks which they

---

[11] For some practical ideas on this subject see Lewis A. Allen, "How to Stop Upward Delegation," *Nation's Business,* Vol. 61 (1973), pp. 67–69.

delegate to subordinates. The manager whose subordinates fail to produce cannot be absolved of responsibility by blaming the incompetence or low motivation of subordinates. This principle applies at all organizational levels. Accountability is always to one's immediate superior.

Favorable Conditions for Delegation

Ineffective delegation occurs for a variety of reasons. Attempts to remedy the situation are usually unsuccessful unless the causes have been diagnosed and corrected. Figure 3–2 presents a checklist in which many of the causes of poor delegation are/listed. Use of this instrument as a diagnostic tool will help ferret out possible causes that might otherwise go undiscovered.

CAUSES OF POOR DELEGATION	Yes	No
1. Subordinates lack the aptitude needed to do the work.	☐	☐
2. Subordinates are inadequately trained.	☐	☐
3. Managers have no confidence in subordinates.	☐	☐
4. Managers have misconceptions about delegation.	☐	☐
5. Managers are too cautious — afraid to take risks.	☐	☐
6. Higher-ranking managers constantly interfere.	☐	☐
7. Managers feel more secure doing than delegating.	☐	☐
8. Managers enjoy doing and dislike supervising.	☐	☐
9. Managers are too intolerant of subordinates' mistakes.	☐	☐
10. Superior-subordinate working conditions are too close.	☐	☐
11. The organization has unclear goals and/or work standards.	☐	☐
12. The general organizational climate is one of distrust.	☐	☐
13. Managers do not know their subordinates' capabilities.	☐	☐
14. Systems for monitoring performance are inadequate.	☐	☐
15. Managers are too detail minded — have limited perspective.	☐	☐
16. Too little value is placed on developing subordinates.	☐	☐
17. Managers are afraid of losing power through delegation.	☐	☐
18. Organizational working conditions are unstable and chaotic.	☐	☐
19. Decision making is too concentrated at the top.	☐	☐
20. Managers want all the credit for themselves.	☐	☐
21. Planning for the purpose of delegating is poor.	☐	☐
22. Subordinates avoid responsibility by delegating upward.	☐	☐
23. It is organizational philosophy to supervise closely.	☐	☐
24. The organizational systems of motivation are inadequate.	☐	☐
25. Managers desire to keep subordinates dependent.	☐	☐
26. Subordinates lack the information needed to perform well.	☐	☐
27. Superiors fail to provide adequate back-up authority.	☐	☐

Figure 3–2   Checklist of Causes of Poor Delegation

THE ORGANIZATIONAL STATUS SYSTEM

Thesis: Whenever people associate closely with one another over a period of time it is inevitable that status differences will be recognized. Most organizations take deliberate steps to establish and maintain a status system. Personnel on all levels tend to support it.

Status refers to the ranking or relative position of an individual within a group.[12] Status is highly correlated with prestige and is based upon the predominant values held by members of the reference group. Although society in general has certain values by which status is assigned, an individual may have high status in one group and low status in another. An irresponsible, noncontributing member of a work group may have extremely low status on the job but high status with a group of friends because of physical prowess and expertise with a switchblade.

The aggregate values, techniques, and symbols by which these relative rankings are established and maintained within an organization are called a *status system.* As we shall see, the status system plays a major role in making an organization orderly and in structuring relationships between people which make effective management possible.

Status Categories

Status can best be understood in terms of four general categories: objective, subjective, scalor, and functional.

Objective status refers to the ranking of people on the basis of generally accepted standards of evaluation. For example, in our society there is general agreement that physicians have higher status than nurses, that managers have higher status than workers, that skilled craftsmen have higher status than machine tenders, and so forth.

Subjective status refers to the perception of one's own status. An understandable bias often enters the picture when we rank ourselves. It is interesting to note that even the lowest employees on the objective scale can find some basis for viewing others as having lower status than themselves. The janitors of one building perceive themselves as above those of another because of the physical quality of the building they work in or because of its occupants or because of cultural biases relating to such personal attributes as race, national origin, religion, age, or sex. For example, members of recently arrived immigrant groups are typically accorded a low status. Noncommissioned military officers often perform an interesting twist of logic by which they look with some disdain upon their commis-

---

12 Although the subject of status is one about which there is little serious disagreement, authors differ greatly in the content they select for presentation. For a treatment of status as a motivator see Luthans op. cit., pp. 272–273. The most thorough treatment of the subject was one of the first truly comprehensive writings: Chester I. Barnard, "Functions of Status Systems in Formal Organizations," in William F. Whyte (ed.), *Industry and Society* (New York: McGraw-Hill, Inc., 1946), pp. 46–70.

sioned superiors; and veteran construction workers sometimes elevate themselves by pointing up the inexperience and impractical "book-learning" of the young, college-educated engineers and architects with whom they work.

Scalar status is based upon the formal organizational hierarchy. Thus, the president has higher status than the vice-president who in turn has higher status than managers at lower levels. Scalar status is perfectly correlated with formal authority.

Functional status is based upon the type of work one performs, without reference to formal authority within the organizational hierarchy. For instance, a research physicist has higher status than a bookkeeper. This is because of personal and work characteristics, not because the physicist has any organizational authority over the bookkeeper.

It is notable that one's status on the job, whether scalar or functional, tends to generalize to one's relationships with others outside work. The corporation president, CPA, attorney, or physician is accorded higher status than the foreman, bookkeeper, secretary, or nurse, wherever they are. This generalization is a major reason why most personnel are highly motivated to seek and retain status in organizations.

Establishing and Maintaining the System

The most obvious means of establishing employee status is the use of titles. One's status may be elevated by this means even when duties and responsibilities remain the same. It is not uncommon, for instance, for the term *maintenance personnel* to be used instead of *janitors*. The former title communicates higher status, especially to people outside the organization.

Unlike the military, the clergy, and educational institutions, business organizations have few ceremonies (such as parades, inaugurations, ordinations, and graduations) by which status is formally conveyed; but promoted employees are given recognition in company publications and the public news media, and a wide variety of status symbols separate the status levels. Among these are

1. Clothing: tie and suit versus sport shirt versus coveralls

2. Office location: a large corner office with windows or, in some companies, a particular floor or proximity to a top executive

3. Office furnishings: notable differences in quality of furniture, wall decorations, and carpeting

4. Parking space: private, close, preferably with the name indicated

5. Support in doing work: private secretaries, staff assistants, access to consultants

6. Other privileges: use of company automobiles and aircraft, liberal expense accounts, freedom to set one's own work hours (or, at a lower level, freedom from having to punch a time clock), inclusion in certain social groups, access to inside information, permission to use first names, and

related privileges which are not officially spelled out but which are highly visible to those within the company

At the employee level, the status system flourishes, even in informal work groups. Insiders recognize status differences based upon seniority, the type of machine one operates, whether one's work is clean or dirty, whether one is willing to stand up to the boss, and a large number of other criteria, many of which are difficult for outsiders to detect. Generally speaking, at all organizational levels status differences are related to requirements of ability, education, training, and experience.

The system of status differences is vigorously defended because of its link with self-esteem, sense of identity, and personal security. A few companies have attempted to eliminate status differences because of the barriers they sometimes pose to free communication and good human relations; but what usually occurs is that obvious status symbols are simply replaced by more subtle ones. Communist nations provide the best examples of the futility of trying to eliminate status differences. The observation that everyone is equal, but some are more equal than others, is still true.

Functions of the Status System

A status system serves both the individual and the organization. For the organization, its greatest contribution is probably the manner in which it helps to define levels of authority and competence. Everyone needs to know where formal authority lies and who has the competence to serve as an authority on a particular type of problem. Status differences indicate who has a right to issue commands or to give an opinion worthy of being held in high esteem. The status system also serves the organization because of its role as a motivator. "Status pay" is sometimes valued even more highly than financial compensation.

Both high status and low status serve a purpose for the individual. The person with high status is given recognition for ability, education, productivity, or another valued quality. Thus, it is advantageous to seek higher status at any organizational level. At times, however, it is also psychologically rewarding to claim low status. Thus, the laborer is protected from excessive demands by a right to say, "You will have to ask my supervisor," or "I'm not paid to make decisions. I just do what I'm told." Likewise, the chief financial executive is protected by the disclaimer, "The question is really out of my field. I suggest that we call in a tax specialist for an opinion."

Employees have a need to attribute high status to those from whom commands are received. Recently promoted supervisors often have difficulty because their subordinates question the justification of someone so much like themselves telling them what to do. On the other hand, when we are able to view our superiors as outstanding and identify with them, we draw upon their status and thereby grow in self-esteem. A related phenomenon occurs when combat soldiers exaggerate and embellish tales of bravery about their superiors as a means of reducing fear and bolstering their own self-confidence.

Generally speaking, subordinates prefer to view their supervisors as superior and are usually willing to rationalize in order to maintain the illusion. For this reason, when they are forced to face the fact that a supervisor is incompetent, their reaction is often a pendulum swing to aggressiveness and hostility. Early studies referred to the status hierarchy as a "pecking order," a term drawn from the observation that chickens (and other animals, for that matter) establish definite superior-subordinate rankings. It is also notable that when one fowl develops a defect, an injury, or even a feather out of place, the pecking does not cease until the defective fowl is eliminated.

STUDY AND DISCUSSION QUESTIONS

1. Luthans, Kast, Rosenzweig, and many others believe that contingency management is superior to situational management as a framework for understanding organizational behavior. By what logic can this point of view be supported?

2. Think of an individual, perhaps someone you know well, who possesses all the personal qualifications you think would lead to success in management. What conditions within the organizational environment may cause such an individual to perform poorly?

3. Why are the specific features of a managerial role not written out in an organization handbook or position description?

4. What conditions of organizational life support a manager's efforts to modify his or her position for a more favorable match between position demands and the individual's abilities?

5. In what sense does an organization's long-term approach to personnel selection influence the effectiveness of a given manager?

6. What did Levitt mean by his statement that a manager "turned out to be successful not alone for what he brought to the situation but for what his selectors saw in him as suitable for the situation?"

7. Where opportunities for advancement are perceived as nonexistent, what motivation do managers have for personal growth?

8. Why is it true that, within the work environment, self-control or self-management is possible only when the standards and expectations spelled out in formal controls are made known?

9. Under what circumstances would it be wise for a manager to delegate only the most elementary aspects of a job, supervising closely to ensure completion according to expectation?

10. Imagine an organization in which no status symbols are visible. What negative consequences might be expected?

CRITICAL INCIDENT

The Performance Review

At the end of Tom Ryan's first year as production superintendent, he and his immediate superior, Daniel Butler, met to discuss Ryan's performance. It was after work hours, both men were prepared to be open and honest and, everything considered, the climate was favorable for such an interview.

Ryan and Butler had frequent occasions to discuss work-related problems. As a result, Ryan expected the session to contain no big surprises. For the most part he had received excellent performance ratings. Nevertheless, as the conversation continued, Ryan realized that he and Butler did not see eye-to-eye on everything. A few exerpts from the interview will accent some of these differences.

Butler:
When I look back over the year I see some definite progress. Production is up, and unit costs are down. Grievances are down, too. There is no way I can complain about your results. In fact, I have to give you the credit for these improvements, just as the president does. In the interest of offering constructive criticism, I would say, however, that at times we seem to have been pulling in different directions.

Ryan:
For instance?

Butler:
I'm thinking about two or three things. One has to do with the long hours you have spent with your foremen—your training sessions. I've wondered whether you might be overdoing it a bit. I have had some question, too, about the money you've spent attending seminars and trade association meetings. I have never wanted to make an issue of it; but I have wondered about some of your expense items—traveling first class, for example.

At this point, Ryan realized that Butler was, as Ryan expressed it, getting some things off his chest; so he encouraged Butler to bring up any other points about which there might be some disagreement or dissatisfaction.

Butler:
I'll be honest with you. Knowing that this meeting was scheduled, I jotted down a few things. I will briefly tell you what they are, and then we can take them up one at a time if you like.

First of all, I have wondered why you hired Browden and Smith without going through the Personnel Department. They're turning out to be first-class foremen, but you really stirred up a hornet's nest by not going through the traditional channels. There is no rule that says you have to go through Personnel, but we always have.

You brought up the idea of the new cost accounting system in the production meeting without talking to me about it first. Quite frankly I think it's a waste of money, but once Engineering picked up on the idea it was sold and I couldn't influence the final decision.

This sounds small when I talk about it, but I think you went overboard redecorating your office. I used that office for six years without carpeting on the floor and now . . .

Ryan:

I want to hear the remainder of your list, Dan, but I just have to respond to that one. You personally approved the budget to remodel my office, and I stayed within it. My wife spent endless hours shopping for bargains, and the pictures are some we stored away when we moved here because they didn't fit the decor of our home. Not only that, but . . .

Butler:

I know, Tom, I know; but the fact remains that when anyone walks into your office they get the impression it should belong to the president. . . .

The session turned out to be a long and stressful one. Both men made their views known, and there were indeed some points of disagreement. Ryan was understandably disturbed to find that, in spite of his accomplishments, he was not personally as successful as he had perceived himself to be.

Questions

1. What personal behavior and environmental variables have led to Ryan's present situation?
2. What facts do you need to know in order to answer Question 1 with confidence?
3. In what way should Ryan modify his behavior?

Chapter 4

Informal Organizations

An organization can be described in terms of such characteristics as authority structure, purpose, technology, and policies. Classical organization theorists, indeed, were inclined to behave as if these formal attributes of an organization were all of it. This viewpoint was dramatically changed, however, by the Hawthorne studies [1] of the 1930s and the behavioral science research which followed.

Neoclassicists discovered a vast array of small, informally organized groups, or subcultures, within formal organizations. Such groups do not appear on the organization chart but nonetheless have their own leadership, goals, standards of acceptable behavior, and means of membership control. The impact of such groups becomes especially noteworthy when their own limited objectives take precedence over goals of the formal organization. It should not be concluded, however, that informal groups are necessarily opposed to the formal organization. Informal groups have both a positive and a negative influence in most organizations.

A variety of names has been given to these informally organized groups, notably primary groups, informal groups, informal organizations, and shadow organizations. They are most commonly referred to as *informal groups*. A collection of individuals becomes a group when members develop interdependencies, influence one another's behavior, and contribute to mutual need satisfaction. Informal relationships are those associations between individuals which are not explicitly prescribed by the formal organization. As we shall see, informal relationships constitute a highly significant aspect of organizational life. Many mistakes of classical theorists could have been avoided had they been aware of the nature and importance of informal relationships.

---

[1] These studies were conducted by Elton Mayo and his Harvard colleagues at the Western Electric Company's Hawthorne plant near Chicago. Publication references were presented in Footnote 4 of Chapter 1.

NATURE OF INFORMAL GROUPS

Thesis: Informal groups develop in order to meet a variety of individual needs which are not met by the formal organization. Their presence is not, however, an indication that the formal organization is inadequate or deficient since informal groups exist in all organizations.

Most of us belong to several groups. This is equally true of the employed and unemployed. Outside our work, families constitute a major type of informal group. Some family groups are small and loosely held together; while others are large and clannish, sometimes including distant relatives who are, nevertheless, quite close psychologically. Sharing a common name, ancestry, and values provides a bond that is far stronger than the lines of formal organization. Mafia families, for instance, are particularly noted for their closeness and goal directedness. More common are the many family groups held together by bonds of love, religion, and mutual dependency.

Other informal groups are based upon common interests, such as bridge, golf, drama, music, karate, aviation, gardening, or intellectual pursuits. Friendship groups have sometimes developed among neighbors who would have had little in common had not the location of their homes or apartments brought them together. As we shall see, family groups, social groups, and friendship groups have much in common with informal groups found in work situations.

Autonomy within Structure

A formal organization structures the behavior of its members. They enter the organization with a wide diversity of interests, goals, attitudes, and other personal attributes which would lead to utter chaos if no behavioral guidelines were provided. Accordingly, an organization provides position descriptions, goals, policies, procedures, and the like to structure member activity. These reduce individual autonomy and promote purposeful, cooperative behavior.

In spite of the structure provided by formal organizations, much discretion is left to the individual. As Fred Katz points out, even a detailed job description leaves undefined much of an employee's life within the organization.[2] New employees are immediately presented with subtle clues and direct communication about differences between the picture presented by management and the way organizational life really is. The informal communication process itself is one of the major undefined areas of organizational behavior, and yet without it many organizations could not function. It provides a source of coordination which is vital to the smooth functioning of an organization.

Katz views informal groups among blue-collar personnel as relatively autonomous subcultures which are often alien to the decorum expected of the

---

[2] Fred E. Katz, "Explaining Informal Work Groups in Complex Organizations: The Case for Autonomy in Structure," *Administrative Science Quarterly,* Vol. 10, No. 2 (September, 1965), pp. 204–223.

white-collar employees. He notes particularly the constant sexual allusions of male workers, the hazing of lower status employees, and the practical jokes and prankish physical contact which are characteristic of the blue-collar culture but are taboo in the white-collar culture. In contrast, the formal role expectations of white-collar employees are relatively compatible with the roles they play in other areas of life such as school, church, and community affairs.

The freedom of action which permits the development of subcultures may have both positive and negative consequences for an organization. On the positive side, it allows employees to express their individuality, to be known and accepted by others for the unique persons they are, and to find a degree of freedom from the routine which characterizes much work at the lower levels. However, when the organization is perceived as the enemy, the autonomy becomes destructive, and the sometimes awesome power of informal groups is used to undermine achievement of formal goals.

Informal Groups and Mobility Patterns

The nature of informal groups, at either the employee or the management level, is influenced by the upward mobility patterns within an organization.[3] Different types of groups are likely to develop under conditions of (1) promotion on the basis of merit, (2) promotion on the basis of seniority, and (3) no possibilities for promotion.

The most significant factor in each of these three conditions is the "reference groups" whose standards are used to evaluate one's own attitudes, abilities, and performance. Employees who perceive themselves as having a good chance of being promoted into the supervisory ranks, like managers who anticipate a series of promotions, are more sensitive to the attitudes and opinions of their immediate superiors than are employees who see little possibility for mobility. The former are more likely to be in competition with their peers than in collusion with them.

Where promotion opportunities are nonexistent or promotions are based primarily upon seniority, competition between peers is minimized and identification with peers is high. Close friendships can develop under these circumstances. And, since promotions are not related to performance, the need to make a favorable impression on one's superiors is minimal.

Where no mobility is possible, employees are motivated to form self-protectionist groups that often conflict with the needs and goals of the organization. Since there is no motivation for mobility, the group's responsiveness to superiors is low. Group pressures may be strong to "make progress" by such devices as restricting production, increasing power, and resisting upward movement of lower status groups.

Groups with no promotion opportunities often focus their attention upon social rewards as though the work were merely a necessary evil, unworthy of

---

[3] For a critical analysis of the literature on this subject see Noel Tichy, "An Analysis of Clique Formation and Structure in Organizations," *Administrative Science Quarterly,* Vol. 18 (June, 1973), pp. 194–208.

serious emotional involvement. This defensive reaction makes the routine and relative meaninglessness of a job more acceptable psychologically. Group attention is focused on important personal interests such as sports, hobbies, family, and other concerns unrelated to work.

Need Satisfaction in Informal Groups

Because individual needs vary greatly and are satisfied in unique ways, it is not possible to list all the human needs which are satisfied, to some degree, at least, in informal groups. However, more than forty years of research have demonstrated a few areas in which informal groups meet the needs of their members.

Companionship. Group affiliation provides an opportunity for close association with others, which, in itself, is a source of satisfaction. Stated negatively, it enables an individual to avoid the pain of loneliness and the ego-crushing experience of rejection. Stated positively, group affiliation gives one a sense of belonging—of being a person rather than a number or an article of commerce.

Reassurance and Support. There is power in numbers. Just knowing that one other person is supportive may give an individual the courage to express a conviction or take a stand on an important issue. The support of a unified group often serves to greatly reduce fear, anxiety, and apprehensiveness. The group provides the self-confidence an employee or manager needs to face the work situation with a degree of equanimity. Without support, the organizational environment could be unbearably frustrating and threatening.

Reduction of Tension. This is, of course, closely related to reassurance and support, but it is not identical. Informal groups often contribute to a reduction of internal tension through humor and horseplay that prevent members from taking themselves and their work too seriously. Tension is also reduced through *catharsis,* the process by which merely talking about a problem or source of irritation makes one feel better. Catharsis takes place, for example, when an employee who is hostile toward a superior finds emotional release by talking to a peer. The verbalization of feelings tends to decrease them. When repressed, they accumulate and may result in irrational behavior and feelings over which one has little control.

Sense of Identity. Groups give one a sense of personal identity—a sense of being somebody. The size and impersonality of formal organization often give rise to the feeling that personal identity is lost. If, however, one feels a strong identity with an informal group, personal identity is maintained even within the context of a large organization. It is especially ego-enhancing to be identified with a high prestige group—for example, a group recognized for high productivity, possession of unusual skills, or power to deal effectively with management.

Improved Communication. Informal groups are sometimes developed around a person who has access to information which contributes to group security. Secretive managers keep subordinates ignorant concerning actions which affect their welfare and thereby invite formation of informal groups to fill the void.

Reduction of Boredom. The point was made in an earlier chapter that routine work is not necessarily boring work. Interest or boredom depends upon the individual and the work situation. In many work groups, boredom is minimized by group interaction. Most of us have had experiences in which doing nothing —waiting for a plane, for instance—was far from boring because of the opportunity it provided to talk with or just be with someone with whom we have an emotional bond or common interest. When an assembly of individuals becomes a group, just being together, especially where conversation is possible, becomes an end in itself. As long as the work does not seriously interfere with group interaction the likelihood that it will be perceived as boring is minimal.

INFORMAL GROUP LEADERSHIP

Thesis: Informal group leaders emerge in response to the needs of the group, and their leadership is accepted because of the contribution they make to the achievement of group goals.

Informal group leaders are not appointed or elected as they are in formal organizations. In fact, group members may not even be fully aware that leader-follower relationships exist. An informal leader emerges spontaneously, depending upon the needs of the moment, and when the specific needs are satisfied, the leader may again become indistinguishable from other group members. Because leadership needs change, the most appropriate leader in one situation may be unqualified to lead in another.

Some of the major roles played by informal group leaders are noted below. Although one person may play all the different roles, it is probable that leadership will be rotated among the membership.

The Representative to Management

The individual who serves as a representative to management is ordinarily talented in two important areas: courage and communication skills. The role may be played by the diplomat who enjoys good relations with management or by an aggressive, power-oriented type who simply is unconcerned about being liked by management. The former is often viewed by management as potential for a supervisory position. The latter may become a union steward, or, in the absence of union protection, may find it necessary to change employment frequently.

The Technical Expert

Individuals with expertise (an unusually high level of knowledge or skill) are particularly influential in groups whose work is somewhat technical and involves problem solving. Mechanics, electricians, and plumbers, as well as engineers, research scientists, and accountants, are often in need of expert leadership. An individual with little ability as a representative to management or as a supervisor may play this role. It requires a minimum of courage, leadership ability, or human relations skills.

One major corporation which has an unusually flat organizational structure and a highly participative form of management has formalized the position of technical expert.[4] Individuals in this position are given special training and are designated *technical consultants,* but they have no supervisory or administrative duties. Their leadership flows from an officially sanctioned authority of competence.

The Information Source

Certain individuals are looked to for leadership because they are well informed about company politics and matters relating to the well-being of the group. They may have access to inside information because of white-collar friends or relatives within the company; or they may be avid readers of publications which provide insights into trends within the industry and/or a specific organization (such as closing down of plants, anticipated expansion, acquisitions, or development of new product lines).

The Enforcer

At times, members refuse to conform to group norms and must be disciplined. Depending upon the nature of the group, this may require gentle persuasion of a verbal nature or the use of muscle. At any rate, certain group members are better prepared to play this role than others and thus emerge at their own initiative or at the urging of the group to assume the leadership role needed on such an occasion. Some of the techniques used are discussed in the next major section of this chapter. Although this role may not always be a pleasant one—for certain people it would be extremely unpleasant—it can be rewarding. The leader in this situation is recognized as having certain talents and is thereby accorded a position of prestige within the group.

The Tension Reducer

Sometimes this person is a comic whose puns lighten the conversation or whose jokes are always new to the group. At other times, the tension reducer is a philosopher or human relations expert who helps the group interpret situations in such a way that tension is minimized. The role sometimes calls for a

---

[4] Although this is a well-known organization with multibillion dollar sales, it is closely held; and top management requests that individuals associated with the company in a managerial or consulting capacity not use its name in publications.

compromiser who can take opposing points of view held by group members and make them compatible. This can be an important leadership function, especially if friction between members threatens to destroy the group or reduce its effectiveness. In a large apparel company, one manager's career was greatly enhanced by her skill in reducing conflict among her fellow managers. On one occasion, she received a promotion solely because no one else could relate without conflict to a majority of the managers who reported to her in the new position.

The Crisis Manager

Groups are sometimes threatened from without—for example, by plans to increase production standards or to change methods which require relearning or mass layoffs. In such cases, the leader who emerges may or may not be the type of individual who assumes leadership under normal circumstances. Perhaps the role calls for a bright tactical strategist, an individual with insight into the thinking of management, or an individual who is able to persuade the group to accept the inevitable without taking action which would cause irreparable damage to the group.

As implied earlier, it is possible for an informal group to have a single leader, but this would be unusual. Because of dominant personality characteristics or unusual charisma, group members may perceive a specific individual to be *the* leader of the group, but even under such circumstances other members may lead on specific occasions.

Implications for Management

Much of what is known about informal group leadership can serve as a model for managers who aspire to become outstanding leaders. Without attempting to eliminate informal groups, it makes sense for supervisors to behave in such a way that strong informal leadership is unnecessary.

First-line supervisors should realize that on occasions they must represent subordinates who feel oppressed by the actions or policies of higher managers. Depending upon the human relations skills of a supervisor, playing the role of an advocate for subordinates may involve a high level of risk. If subordinates have a legitimate complaint, however, such action is called for. It should be noted that risk is also involved in abdicating this role and leaving it to an informal leader.

First-line supervisors are in a strategic position to provide subordinates with information. Yet many supervisors, following the lead of their superiors, keep employees ignorant concerning what is going on in the organization. Management sometimes provides so little information about how the job should be performed that a new employee must depend upon peers to survive during the first few days of employment. It is difficult to overemphasize the critical nature of the first week on the job.

Management should invest heavily in orienting the new employee to the physical and psychological environment and to the work itself. Many organizations have elaborate induction training programs which relieve the first-line supervisor of much of the burden of getting new employees oriented favorably toward the organization. In fact, some induction programs provide a psychological and biographical profile of supervisors to give new employees the feeling that they know their supervisors personally. Such programs reflect an awareness of the needs of employees and demonstrate management's concern for satisfying them. It is only by satisfying these needs that managers can lead, in the best sense of the word, and reduce the individual employee's excessive dependency upon peer groups.

CONTROLS IN INFORMAL GROUPS

Thesis: Three important, interrelated characteristics of informal groups are their inclination to establish standards of acceptable member behavior, their ability to detect deviations from such standards, and their power to demand conformity to them. So effective is the control of a group over its membership that it often renders the power of management ineffective.

All cultures have norms or standards with which members are expected to comply and against which the behavior of members is evaluated. These behavioral expectations are expressed in a variety of forms, such as mores, religious values, ethical standards, rules of etiquette and decorum, laws, policies, and procedures. They necessarily relate to only a small segment of the range of possible behaviors, but within a given subculture such standards define the rules for belonging. They specify the behaviors which are relevant to group survival and enhancement, leaving all other possible ways of behaving to the discretion of the individual or of some other group of which that individual is a member.

Group Norms

In informal groups, these behavior expectations are called *norms*. More than any other aspect of group life they serve to define the nature of the group. They express the collective values of its membership and provide guidelines which ensure the successful achievement of its goals as shown in the following examples.

1. Group A consists of fifteen no-mobility employees who work in a chemical plant. They rotate over three shifts and are primarily involved in loading ships with pelletized fertilizer. The following norms are of central importance to this group:

    (a) One employee shall not exert so much effort that other employees appear to be unproductive by comparison.
    (b) When employees are unable to perform well, because of a hangover or fatigue, others will cover for them; however, abuse of the off-day privilege will not be tolerated.
    (c) Employees will not discuss with management anything derogatory about another group member.

(d) Employees will not express favorable attitudes toward management and the company in general.

The norms of Group A stand in stark contrast to those of the following group:

2. Group B consists of eleven young women in a secretarial pool of the same organization. Each looks forward to promotion into a position as executive secretary. The promotion decision is usually made on the combined basis of seniority, competence, and ability to relate to a given executive. Group B reflects a need for nondestructive internal competition. Among the norms which are most obvious are the following:

(a) Dress and hair must always be smart and fashionable in order to maintain the image that "the pool" is the place for an executive to select an attractive, efficient secretary (rather than hire an outsider through the Personnel Department).
(b) Taking the initiative with executives in order to be selected is taboo —especially if such initiative involves flirting.
(c) It is never permissible to make remarks or stimulate rumors that may interfere with a peer's promotion, even though the remarks or rumors are true.
(d) Poor productivity and poor quality work from anyone capable of high performance is unacceptable, since it reflects negatively on the group.
(e) An employee does not recommend friends or acquaintances to fill vacancies unless they fit the model required to maintain the favorable image the group enjoys.

The norms of informal groups are not formally agreed upon. They tend to evolve as the collection of individuals becomes a group. They are not always rational or functional since they may be perpetuated by habit and tradition long after their usefulness has passed. As a result of past labor strife, for example, group members sometimes maintain norms against communicating freely with management even though such communication could allay fears, remove distrust, and provide a cooperative spirit of mutual benefit.

How Norms Are Communicated

The communication systems which operate within informal groups are most impressive. Employees with previous work experience have some insight into norms typically held by groups in their type of work and geographical area. Nevertheless, norms vary somewhat from one situation to another, and new employees are therefore sensitive to pick up cues concerning acceptable and unacceptable behavior. The normal insecurity experienced by new employees provides high motivation for painstakingly *mapping* the environment; that is, for making rapid and sensitive observations which will serve as a sound basis for behavior.

New employees are typically given help in detecting group norms. Conversations are staged—half consciously in many cases—to educate the new employee, and fellow employees volunteer advice about appropriate behavior. If the new employee refuses to conform, a more persuasive tactic is used. For example, a group member passes along the word that "the last 'rate buster' we had in this department had a transportation problem. He found it very difficult to drive home from work with flat tires." If information and threats fail to get conformity, direct action is always possible.

Modifying Deviant Behavior

Not all norms are equally important to a group. For example, inappropriate dress may not elicit the same response as passing along inside information to management or exceeding a work quota. Groups tend to have *crucial norms,* those which, when violated, threaten the survival or well-being of the group, and *peripheral norms* which are viewed as less important. In other words there are felony and misdemeanor violations. The penalty to be paid usually corresponds to the seriousness of the offense.

A number of possible actions can be taken by a group to control individual behavior:

1. *Unfriendliness or the cold shoulder treatment.* This is strong enough action to get results with sensitive individuals who have a strong need for acceptance. Others, however, will not even be aware of it.

2. *Verbal expressions of hostility and criticism.* This approach leaves no doubt about the feelings of the group. It may or may not get the results desired.

3. *Ridicule.* This may involve assigning the offender an undesirable nickname and/or continually making the offender the butt of jokes and pranks.

4. *Spreading unflattering gossip about the offender.* This can be a very damaging type of aggression—strong enough to cause the offender to be discharged or to resign.

5. *Harassment.* This may take many forms: the offender's time card is punched early and then placed behind another card where it cannot be easily found; or the individual's lunch box is hidden. On one occasion, a pair of expensive calipers was placed in an employee's lunch box, and the plant guards were tipped off about it.

6. *Disruption of work.* Even where an employee works in relative independence of others, it is possible for peers to interfere with the offender's productivity. Defective raw materials or tools are selectively issued to the offender; misleading information is supplied; reports are lost or held up; or the individual's schedule is disrupted by forced waiting periods or the deliberate mistakes of others. The latter often have been observed at the management level. One tactic, where inspectors collude with production workers, is the practice of switching product identification so that substandard production is attributed to the offender. It is difficult for a worker to succeed against these odds.

7. *Overt intimidation and threats.* The offender becomes the object of painful physical hazing with the stated or implied threat that it could become even

more serious. This may be half veiled as humor or harmless horseplay, but the message is clearly communicated. At times the message is more strongly emphasized through destruction of the offender's property such as a slashed tire or seat cover, a dented fender, or a scratch on a new paint job. In some circumstances the offender's children are intimidated by the children of the other employees. This adds a vicious dimension to the pressure of the group.

8. *Physical violence.* Finally, the history of the labor movements abounds with examples of beatings and even killings. Such events are often associated with attempts to unionize a plant or with strikebreaking by management, but the motivation for such actions is usually fomented in informal groups rather than formal union organizations. Again, the theme is the same: individuals are punished for refusal to conform to critical group norms. Antiquated and immoral as such tactics may appear, they are, nevertheless, still in vogue. For example, within the 1970s strikebreakers have been ambushed and killed, labor leaders have been murdered, and nonstriking truck drivers have had heavy concrete blocks dropped through their windshields as they passed under freeway overpasses.

The emphasis here has been upon punishment as a means of enforcing group norms. Positive reinforcement is, of course, also used. Individuals who comply are rewarded by being accepted, protected, and provided with a high degree of support in meeting the demands of the formal organization. The combined positive and negative reinforcements are sufficient to gain the conformity of most employees in a work group.

Group Influence upon Attitudes, Beliefs, and Perceptions

Where group pressures for conformity are strong, group members are highly motivated to remove the dissonance between what they feel and believe and the way they are required to behave. For example, employees with high potential for rapid promotion but who are compelled to support a seniority promotion policy are placed in a psychologically untenable position. On the one hand, they know that their best interests are served by freedom to compete and earn promotions. On the other hand, they know that group structure makes this course of action impossible. A common way of dealing with the conflict is through rationalization and unconsciously distorted perception.

The rationalization process gets abundant support from the group. Since much of the employee's information is filtered through the attitudes and biases of the group, and since expression of contrary attitudes brings immediate condemnation, the potentially mobile employee easily learns to think this way:

I might move a little faster if I could be promoted on merit. But, in view of the arbitrariness of management, there is no assurance of it. It is better to bet on a sure thing rather than be dependent upon the whims of management.

Once an employee begins to accept group values, it becomes difficult to distinguish fact from fiction. We all perceive reality from our own point of view. When that perception is influenced strongly by the emotional impact of group pressure, we find it difficult to switch perceptual sets and see an opposite viewpoint. Behavioristic psychology has in recent years made the point that behavioral changes lead to attitude changes in order to bring about a consistency between the two.[5] Informal groups are masterful at changing both, and their members develop perceptual filters which admit into consciousness only selected "facts" which reinforce existing attitudes and beliefs.

GROUP COHESIVENESS

Thesis: Informal groups differ greatly in their ability to agree upon goals, maintain control over members, and achieve long-term objectives. The single, most important contribution to group effectiveness is group cohesiveness.

Cohesiveness is defined as unity of purpose and action. It is an expression of the degree to which group members are committed to common goals, to a set of norms for the guidance of behavior, and to one another as individuals. As a group's cohesiveness increases, its members assume increased responsibility for results. Individuals who are low in motivation become more highly motivated when placed in situations fostering group motivation for success.[6] Whether this motivation will benefit the organization depends, of course, upon the group's orientation toward the formal organization. Group success may be defined in terms of high productivity or effectiveness in restricting productivity, depending upon the predominant attitudes, beliefs, and perceptions of the group.

Determinants of Cohesiveness

Cohesiveness is determined by a number of interacting factors. Because they interact with one another and with many aspects of the formal organization, their isolation for analysis creates a somewhat artificial situation. Nevertheless, it is practical to abstract a few causes of group cohesiveness. Nine of these are especially important.

1. Homogeneity

2. Group size

3. Opportunities to communicate

---

[5] For a survey of the literature and an extensive bibliography on the implications of operant conditioning and behavior modification techniques see Craig E. Schneier, "Behavior Modification in Management: A Review and a Critique," *Academy of Management Journal,* Vol 17, No. 3 (September, 1974), pp. 528–548.

[6] Alvin F. Zander, "Productivity and Group Success: Team Spirit vs. the Individual Achiever," *Psychology Today,* Vol. 8, No. 6 (November, 1974), pp. 64–68.

4. Group isolation

5. External threat

6. Group success

7. Individual mobility

8. Membership in other groups

9. Availability of effective leadership

Homogeneity. The homogeneity of a group depends upon the similarity of member characteristics and interests. For example, a group of individuals with the same racial or ethnic background and the same socioeconomic status is likely to be more cohesive than a group whose members differ widely in these characteristics.

Cohesiveness is increased most when the common attributes of its members are particularly relevant to group purposes and goals. Thus, in a work group whose primary goal is improving the economic status of its members, a common need for more money may contribute more to group unity than would similarity in sex, race, religion, or type of work.

Several studies support the general hypothesis that homogeneous groups have a higher degree of both job satisfaction and cohesiveness. On the other hand, homogeneous groups are less effective in problem solving than are those with greater diversity of membership.[7] Thus, group homogeneity is a mixed blessing for the group and for the formal organization of which it is a part.[8]

Group Size. Everything else being equal, small groups are more likely to be cohesive than are large ones. The larger a group becomes, the more heterogeneous are its members, and the fewer common interests they hold. As in the case of formal organizations, large groups become impersonal. When it is difficult for members to know one another well, large groups tend to break up and produce small, homogeneous groups. Group members are attracted to others with similar interests, attitudes, values, and abilities;[9] and this interpersonal attraction is strongest among a very few individuals who know one another well.

Opportunities to Communicate. Groups in which members can communicate freely are apt to be more cohesive than groups in situations where face-to-face communication is difficult. For example, the combined noise level and requirement for intense concentration of sewing maching operators minimize conversation except during break periods. In many factories, noise levels are so high they

---

[7] Nicholas Dimarco, "Life Style, Work Group Structure, Compatibility, and Job Satisfaction," *Academy of Management Journal,* Vol. 18, No. 2 (June, 1975), p. 321.

[8] Additional insights into the implications of group problem solving are found in Irving L. Janis, *Victims of Groupthink* (Boston: Houghton Mifflin Company, 1972). This book presents a psychological study of foreign-policy decisions and fiascos, including the Bay of Pigs failure, and some poor decisions made prior to Pearl Harbor, during the Korean War, and during the Cuban missile crisis.

[9] Gerald H. Graham, "Interpersonal Attraction as a Basis of Informal Organization," *Academy of Management Journal,* Vol. 16 (December, 1971), pp. 483–495.

cause hearing damage. Contrast these situations with offices in which employees are physically close to one another in a quiet environment performing work which requires personal interaction. When employees are required to converse in order to do their work, they are ordinarily free to discuss the personal concerns that increase cohesiveness.

Group Isolation. The conditions just discussed show how environmental conditions may decrease cohesiveness by isolating group members from one another. In contrast, isolation of one group from other groups increases internal cohesiveness. This effect is demonstrated by a situation in which a company moved into a new building designed for closer personal relationships. In the old building, most white-collar employees worked in one large room. Because there were no partitions to delineate the different departments, departmental identification was weak, and loosely structured informal groups cut across departmental lines. As soon as the departments were separated, cohesive cliques began to form along departmental lines. This proved to be a mixed blessing. Morale and intradepartmental teamwork improved, but conflict among departments increased.

External Threat. Members of a threatened group typically band together for survival. A classic example of this on an international level occurred in the 1950s and 1960s when the leaders of Communist China unified a country that for centuries had been ruled by provincial war lords. Their primary tactic was to convince the citizens that the country was in imminent danger of attack by the United States. More recently, the same strategy has been used with Russia cast in the role of the enemy.

Within business organizations, management is the most likely source of threat. In industries, specific companies, or geographical localities with a history of labor-management conflict, a pervasive spirit of distrust and group paranoia make it easy to interpret a wide range of management behaviors as threatening. The filtering process through which group leaders interpret and screen management communications is often designed to maintain the perceived external threat and consequently to maintain a high degree of group cohesiveness.

Group Success. Since everyone likes to be identified with a winner, group success contributes to cohesiveness. When group members perceive a group to be unusually successful, they take pride in it, draw personal strength from its power and status, and go to great lengths to maintain the group's prestige. When the prestige results from management's recognition of high productivity, outstanding product quality, a low accident rate, or other behavior valued by the organization, this success-based cohesion serves to increase productivity motivation. Unfortunately, group success may also be defined in terms of behavior which is detrimental to the organization, such as restricting production, reducing the effective authority of a supervisor, or breaking rules without facing the consequences.

Individual Mobility. Where employee turnover is high because of resignations, discharges, transfers, or promotions, group cohesiveness is difficult to maintain.

Leadership and membership roles are difficult to establish, and the impact of new members prevents the crystallization of group norms. Without a relatively stable membership and identifiable norms, what might normally be a close group is little more than a collection of psychologically isolated individuals.

Membership in Other Groups.   Membership in several groups reduces the influence or control any single group is able to exert upon an individual. The most cohesive and effective work groups are composed of members for whom the group occupies a central life position.[10] They value the group's goals and have a narrow, sometimes fanatic commitment to their achievement. The following individuals illustrate this point.

> Following in his father's footsteps, Mason Clark has worked on a General Motors' assembly line all his adult life and cannot imagine doing anything else. He has few social contacts outside work and spends most of his leisure time gardening, working in his shop, and watching television. He is married, and his one child, age 21, is no longer living at home. He is a member of no organizations other than the United Auto Workers Union, and his greatest ambition is to save enough money to take an early retirement. Although his work is routine and not especially challenging, it is his one major contact with people, and he identifies strongly with the union and a small group of workers with whom he has been associated for several years.
>
> In contrast, Judy Holden is an engineer who has been employed by Texas Instruments for five years. Although she identifies with TI and her local work group, she thinks of herself first of all as an engineer and only secondarily as an engineer working for TI. She has deep commitments to her large family, with whom she spends a great deal of time. She is active in her local Catholic Church; she coaches a Little League baseball team and is on the Boy's Club board of directors. She has broad interests and takes pride in the fact that she has taken a number of correspondence and evening courses in electronics, mathematics, and other subjects related to her field. She perceives herself to be a professional and enjoys associating with fellow engineers in local, state, and national associations. She is enthusiastic about the many groups with which she is associated, but is not controlled by any one of them.

College-educated, white-collar employees often have a broader perspective and more group contacts than do blue-collar employees. For this reason they are less likely than blue-collar employees to develop deep commitments to informal groups in the work situation. White-collar employees also tend to be more competitive with one another and to identify more readily with the goals and norms of the formal organization.

Availability of Effective Leadership.   On many occasions a group is unified primarily by the impact of a dominant, charismatic personality. Although groups

---

10 The term *effective* as used here refers to the ability of the group to achieve its objectives. As indicated earlier, its objectives may or may not be in the best interests of the organization.

are typically led by different members at different times, one member may be so outstanding that practically all members identify with that individual. To a significant degree, the cement that provides group solidarity in such a situation is the one person rather than a network of interdependencies. In other situations potential leaders influence members in different directions and none is capable of unifying the factions.

Dealing with Hostile Groups

Factors affecting group cohesiveness have practical applications when dealing with groups which are hostile to managment. On some occasions, management must reduce the solidarity of a group which opposes its policy. The first step should be to determine why the group opposes rather than supports management. It may be that management should deal directly with some underlying problems rather than treat symptoms by attempting to reduce the power of an informal group.

Even after management has done everything possible to eliminate group hostility, the remaining negative attitudes may still justify steps to reduce the group's effectiveness. Such action should be carried out as unobtrusively as possible to prevent further group solidification in response to the external threat. How can this be done? The answers may be found by reviewing the factors which make for cohesiveness. One or several of the following actions may be appropriate, although such actions may be costly both in terms of money and morale:

1. Increase the rate of turnover within the group through transfers, layoffs, or whatever means are feasible.

2. Remove undesirable leaders and transfer in employees known to be capable of influencing the group in a positive way. (One large organization has found that individuals who are misplaced in a work group because of overqualification are a nuisance at the employee level but perform admirably in supervisory, inspection, and other white-collar positions.)

3. Modify the physical environment to reduce the level of interaction among group members and/or to dilute group solidarity by increasing member interaction with other groups.

4. Train first-line supervisors in leadership techniques, increase communication from management, improve the organization's motivational systems, handle employee grievances as early as possible, and take other constructive steps to reduce threats to the group and to encourage individual employees to identify with the formal organization.

Hostile groups do not develop without cause; unless the cause is discovered and rationally treated, management's efforts to cope with them will probably fail. Unfortunately managers are sometimes so hostile and defensive themselves that they are blinded to possible causes arising from their own actions. In diagnosing, it helps to determine whether such feelings are widespread or are restricted to a local plant, department, work shift, or to the subordinates of one manager. Consideration should also be given to what changes occurred prior to the development of the hostility and to whether it is a result of industry-wide problems, such as low wages or a long history of labor-management strife.

The presence of hostile work groups is not unusual, and the situation cannot always be corrected. Success is most likely, however—whether the groups are within the employee or managerial ranks—when management takes a diagnostic approach (using an attitude survey, for example) and then systematically proceeds to solve the underlying problem.

FORMAL-INFORMAL GROUP RELATIONS

Thesis: Informal groups are not always supportive of the formal organizations, but their development is inevitable, and, all things considered, they are a positive force in organizational life.

Managers who have experienced frustration with hostile employee groups sometimes conclude that the ideal would be total elimination of informal groups. Aside from the fact that destruction of informal groups would be impossible, it certainly would be unprofitable. Informal groups sometimes pose serious problems for the organization; they typically prevent it from being as rational as it would be without them. But it is precisely at this point that they make their greatest contribution, introducing warmth, humanity, and opportunity for individual expression.

Informal groups provide an element of emotionality and concern which at times stands in stark contrast to the tough-minded personnel decisions which managers are required to make. Given the problems of employee motivation and morale which have resulted from job dilution, many jobs would be intolerable without the psychological input provided by informal groups.

Figure 4–1 (page 88) shows some of the advantages and disadvantages of informal groups. In some instances similar behaviors are listed on both sides. Some informal groups resist management policies and goals, while others actively support them. In fact, a group may resist the leadership of management at one time and actively support it at another. The apparent contradictions are resolved, in part, by the fact that the positive or negative impact of a group's behavior is contingent upon a large number of variables—management actions, labor-management history, etc.—which are inherent in the nature of informal groups.

To maintain their identity and solidarity, groups enforce their norms and thus reduce individual freedom. On the other hand, they provide opportunities for individual expression. Both of these conditions may occur in a given group, whether its sentiments and behavior favor or oppose the organization. Both the members of a group and the organization pay a price for the benefits which result from group action. The point of Figure 4–1 is simply that, on the balance, formal organizations benefit from their informal groups.

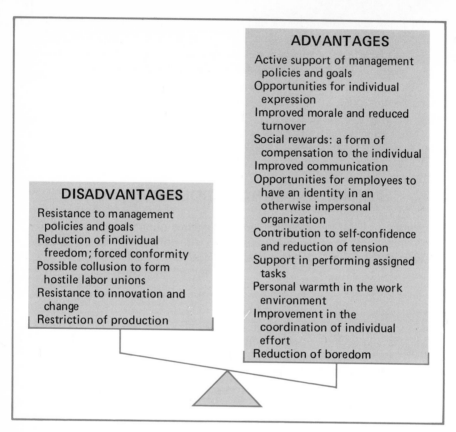

Figure 4–1   The Advantages of Informal Groups Outweigh the Disadvantages

Formalizing Informal Groups

Hostile employee groups often form the nucleus of formal labor organizations. When a group which opposes management policies and practices develops strong leadership, effectively enforces norms, and demonstrates a high degree of cohesiveness, the logical next step is to organize officially and to form alliances with like-minded groups in other organizations. This step is facilitated by the aggressive organizing tactics of a number of international unions.

Since most managers would prefer to deal directly with their employees rather than experience the loss of control which results from dealing with a union intermediary, they sometimes employ highly aggressive and irrational tactics to suppress informal groups. Although union-management relations are more appropriately the subject of Chapter 13, one word of caution is in order at this point: poorly planned, aggressive attempts to destroy informal groups often serve to increase their hostility and cohesiveness. The best way to deal with such groups is to (1) diagnose and treat the cause of the group's alienation and hostility and (2) unobtrusively employ some of the techniques described earlier for weakening group cohesion. The objective should not be to destroy the group but to make it work for rather than against the organization.

Types of Informal Work Groups in Unionized Organizations

One of the most thorough studies of the nature of informal groups in the work environment was conducted by Leonard Sayles during the middle 1950s. He examined 300 work groups in 30 industrial plants and from his observations developed a classification system based primarily on their relationship to the formal organization. The four classifications observed by Sayles are:

1. Apathetic groups

2. Erratic groups

3. Strategic groups

4. Conservative groups[11]

Apathetic Groups. Of all the groups studied, the ones Sayles classified as apathetic are the least likely to express grievances or engage in collective action to influence management or the union. These groups usually consist of relatively low-paid individuals whose work requires a minimum of teamwork. Group cohesion is low, and internal jealousies and bickering are commonplace. Leadership is widely dispersed over several members. Although there is little unity of action, there is much suppressed discontent.

Erratic Groups. The dominant characteristic of this type group is inconsistency. Although serious problems may be neglected for long periods of time, a minor grievance will trigger a wildcat strike or major protest. Because of their explosiveness and irrationality, they are generally regarded by management as dangerous to the organization. In spite of their centralized leadership, their pressure tactics tend to be poorly controlled. The jobs of employees in these groups usually require a high degree of interaction. The employees typically do essentially the same kinds of work (assembly work, for example). Relationships with managements may change rapidly from excellent to extremely poor and back again.

Strategic Groups. These groups consist of employees at a higher level than those in the two previous groups. Members tend to be union regulars. Their pressure tactics are consistent, highly organized, goal directed, and oriented toward crucial rather than trivial issues. The groups are highly cohesive, and their activities are strictly in the self-interests of the membership. Their productivity is ordinarily acceptable to management.

---

[11] Leonard R. Sayles, *Behavior of Industrial Work Groups: Prediction and Control* (New York: John Wiley & Sons, Inc., 1958), pp. 7–39.

Conservative Groups. These groups consist of the most skilled and independent plant employees—machine maintenance crews, for example. Their abilities are in short supply, they are well paid, and their productivity is usually acceptable to management. They seldom act without warning, typically are not union activists, and evidence little internal conflict. They occupy the enviable position of being able to work elsewhere if management does not comply with their demands. As a result, they are usually treated very well. Because of their independence, they have few grievances. As often as not, it is management that has a grievance to express. Most highly skilled groups value their freedom and autonomy to the point that they sometimes attempt to write their own rules rather than respond graciously to the desires of their superiors.

STUDY AND DISCUSSION QUESTIONS

1. The statement is made in this chapter that (1) informal groups develop in order to meet a variety of individual needs which are not met by the formal organization and (2) their presence does not indicate that the formal organization is inadequate or deficient. How can both of these statements be true?

2. Why are groups which are composed of employees with no opportunities for promotions more likely to oppose the formal organization than are high-mobility employees?

3. In what ways do informal groups contribute to the reduction of tension within individual group members?

4. What problems of communication are involved in labeling certain types of work as boring? How do these relate to informal groups?

5. Why will a group accept the leadership of an individual who has no organizational authority or other formal right to play the leader role?

6. In view of the thoroughness with which a group is able to detect and punish deviations from norms, how can one build a case for the idea than informal groups provide an opportunity for individual expression which is not allowed by formal groups?

7. The point is made that homogeneous groups are less effective in problem solving than are those with greater diversity of membership. What logical explanation would you give for this research finding?

8. When a group is threatened from without, cohesion is often increased as a defensive measure. How should this affect managerial action to decrease the cohesiveness of an antimanagement group?

9. Under what circumstances would it be advisable for management to structure the work environment so that the formation of informal groups is encouraged?

10. Why is it inevitable that informal groups will develop in formal organizations?

CRITICAL INCIDENT

The Neophyte

That first day on the job was an eye-opener for Karla Blake. It was not at all what she expected it to be. The selection process had been a pleasant experience. The personnel offices were quiet and modern. The interviewer had been warm and friendly. The interviewer had, in her opinion, gone overboard to explain company policy to the small group of women who were being hired and had given her a booklet which described the insurance programs and answered such questions as what an employee should do when late, absent, or sick.

Karla reported to the personnel department at 8 a.m. as directed. After a brief wait, she and five other new sewing machine operators were escorted to the second floor where they were introduced to Karla's supervisor. Since the day shift had already begun their work, the noise was deafening, and Karla did not understand the supervisor's name. Karla had been a seamstress all her adult life and regarded herself as an expert. At least, she had made most of her own clothes and those of her daughters who were now away at college. But she was awed by the speed with which the women were working and could hardly believe there could be so much difference between the power of her own sewing machine and the heavy duty commercial models. She was also impressed by the vastness of the sewing room. She estimated that there must be between 200 and 300 operators working in the one large room.

The forelady briefly explained to Karla that all she had to do was the simple operation of sewing together two sides of a pre-cut piece of cloth to form part of a shirt sleeve. She was warned that her machine was dangerous and that she should take care not to get her fingers caught in it. Her supervisor then left, and Karla was on her own. The supervisor did stop by three or four times during the day, however, to offer constructuve criticisms. Karla could not tell for sure whether the forelady was tough and angry or just spoke loudly to be heard over the noise of the machines.

On two or three occasions during the morning, a fellow operator offered a suggestion that made Karla's work a little easier. At 9:45, about fifteen operators in Karla's work area all stopped their machines and took a short rest break. Jane Schmidt, whose machine was nearest to Karla's, invited her to join them, explaining that break periods were taken in shifts. During the break and lunch periods, Jane and three other women were particularly helpful in making Karla more confident that she could handle the job. Jane explained that, although the production pace looked terribly fast, it really was no problem after the first few days of the training period. "Any experienced operator," Jane explained, "can easily increase her production by 20 percent, but no one has any intention of doing so."

The women also recommended that Karla join the union immediately as protection against arbitrary action by management. They also pointed out the dangers of being too friendly with the supervisors. "If you are, everybody will think you're a stoolie," one woman volunteered. Karla's husband was a manager in another company, and she generally had an unfavorable attitude toward unions; but after the first day her attitude began to change. She was particularly impressed after hearing a conversation about a woman whom the others called Lynda and referred to as a "free rider," an employee who receives the benefits of union action without being a union member. They pointed out that when Lynda's machine needed adjusting she sometimes had to wait for hours to get help because the mechanics all belonged to the union. Since everyone except trainees was paid by the piece, this resulted in a considerable loss of income.

Questions

1. What group norms are present in this incident?
2. What positive and negative inducements does the group employ to ensure conformity to the norms?
3. What can management do to prevent employee groups from alienating new employees from the organization?

Motivation in Organizations

Chapter

5

Understanding

Human Needs

If an organization is to function effectively it must somehow find ways of involving people in its objectives. It must solicit a type of individual commitment that will ensure maximum effort with a minimum of external supervision and control. Managers need a conceptual framework by means of which they can understand the behavior of others in the work environment, predict the consequences of alternative courses of action, and inspire cooperative effort toward organizational goals. The subject of motivation is addressed to these challenges.

Because there are so many different ways to view human motivation, different theorists and researchers often sound as though they are dealing with entirely unrelated subjects and exhibit a tendency to treat a single aspect of motivation as though it were the whole, or as though it were the only part that really matters. An attempt is made in this chapter to avoid taking a narrow, extreme position on the assumption that a number of different theories can all be valid since they lead to practical outcomes.

INTRODUCTION TO MOTIVATION

Thesis: The ability to understand why people behave as they do and the ability to motivate them to behave in a specific manner are two interrelated qualities which are important to managerial effectiveness. Fortunately they are qualities which a manager can acquire.

Motivation in organizations is a complex subject and should not be treated as if it were otherwise. At the same time a manager need not understand the intricate details of each motivation theory in order to make use of its practical contributions. A certain amount of theory is necessary to integrate and systematize what we know about the subject. A knowledge of motivation theory provides a framework for drawing generalizations and for analyzing novel motivation problems. However, the manager who becomes too involved in theorizing may lose the ability to make practical application of the theory.

In practice, a manager applies an understanding of motivation theory primarily in two ways. The first is highly intuitive—a half-conscious awareness of why someone, reacts in a particular manner or how the individual will react to being treated in a specific way. People differ greatly in their sensitivity to the needs and motives of others, and these differences are a product of learning experiences which date back to infancy. Fortunately the fact that we have all been students of motivation throughout our lives simplifies the task of learning objective concepts and facts in this area. On the other hand, objectifying and pressing into conceptual form the "feel" we have for why people behave as they do tends to educate the intuition and to sharpen and sensitize the intuitive processes which are so critically important in everyday relationships with people.

The second application of motivational theory is cognitive and objective. We are confronted with the task of understanding the motives behind specific behaviors. For example, why is no one in the department willing to accept a promotion to foreman? Why do first-line supervisors refuse to enforce the work rules? Why does the productivity in two comparable plants differ significantly? Since these types of problems do not require instant action, a manager has time to employ an objective, rational analysis through the use of a motivational model which provides a systematic framework for thinking critically and avoiding too limited a perspective. Chapter 6 includes such a model. Its use will serve to further educate the intuition, to increase a manager's ability to understand why others behave as they do, and to motivate in situations where instant action is required.

NEED SATISFACTION

Thesis: Human motivation can best be understood in terms of the needs we have in common and the different means by which these needs are satisfied. When a *need* (a physical or psychological deprivation) is aroused, an individual develops a *drive* toward a *goal* or *incentive* (that which is perceived as capable of satisfying the need or removing the deprivation).[1] This process by which behavior is energized is called *motivation.*

Everyone has needs which must be satisfied if life itself is to be sustained. For purposes of discussion these needs may be grouped into two general categories—physiological and psychological—although few psychologists would attempt to draw hard and fast lines between the two. Because a person functions as a whole, integrated unit, our classifications for purposes of understanding are somewhat artificial. Nevertheless, we have no acceptable alternative to an analytical approach which focuses on one dimension at a time as if it were not an integral part of the whole.

---

[1] We commonly define the term *need* in a circular fashion. When we say that we have a need for water, for example, what we really mean is that when the water in our bodies falls below a certain level we experience a need, a deficit, which goads us into action (motivates us) to find water. Technically speaking, the deficit, not the water, is the need, but it is convenient to ignore this technicality.

Physiological Needs

The physiological needs for air, water, food, rest, and the like are concerned with the preservation of life. Because the physiological needs are part of a life support system, we have no difficulty in understanding their purpose and the implications of failure to satisfy them. Our motivation to satisfy them can at times become acutely intense and prolonged.

Although we recognize the ultimate end served by our physiological needs, the immediate motivation for their satisfaction does not require this awareness. The immediate motive is typically a desire to remove or avoid pain or to participate in a pleasurable experience. Although pain is subjectively experienced as undesirable, no rational person would want to eliminate the potential for experiencing pain, for it is the automatic alarm system by which we learn that a physiological need is not being satisfied and one of the compelling forces that goads us into action.

Psychological Needs

The definition of psychological needs is complex, and experts are by no means consistent in their approach to the task. Freudians insist upon linking psychological needs to primitive biological urges of a sexual nature. Behaviorists refuse to discuss needs at all, preferring instead to focus on how the environment reinforces behavior. A third general point of view is represented by a loosely structured group of behavioral scientists including Otto Rank, Kurt Goldstein, Eric Fromm, Carl Rogers, Gordon W. Allport, and Abraham Maslow. The contributions of these men differ markedly, but they all have in common what is usually called an *organismic-holistic* point of view.[2]

Organismic-holistic psychology stresses the idea that an individual functions as a whole and is simultaneously influenced by a number of factors, including physiological needs, need for maintaining and enhancing one's self-image, and one's perception of a given situation. From this point of view we are all motivated for self-preservation and enhancement; but for this statement to make sense, it must be kept in mind that in the organismic-holistic view the *self* includes all that one is. Beginning with the physical body and self-image, the self is extended, in a sense, to include everything and everybody with which a person identifies, such as family, friends, school, profession, religion, and possessions. You can experience in a personal way just how much a part of you these outside identifications are when someone puts the first dent in the fender of your new car, attacks your school, or makes derogatory remarks about your family.

Three observations may be made with reference to the relationship between the physical-social-psychological self depicted in Figure 5-1.

1. Everyone has a need for self-preservation and enhancement. When it appears that this is not so, it is only because we have failed to analyze

---

[2] For further information on this point of view read Desmond S. Cartwright, *Introduction to Personality* (Chicago: Rand McNally & Company, 1974), pp. 13–70.

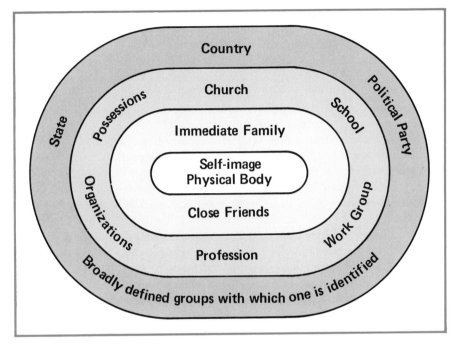

Figure 5–1   Possible Dimensions of the Self

carefully enough the true motives behind overtly self-destructive behavior. For example, a highly successful computer salesman made a series of blunders during the final stages of negotiating the biggest sale of his career. The sale failed to materialize, and his career was seriously jeopardized. He later realized that he had unconsciously caused his own failure because he felt guilty about this and other occasions on which he had sold computer hardware to customers who really did not need it. Through the overtly self-destructive behavior, the salesman was attempting to maintain self-respect.

2. Psychological needs are highly social in nature. Our self-images are strongly influenced by the feedback we get from others, and our inner standards are largely learned from others for whom we have respect and/or upon whom we depend. As a result, our need for self-esteem is closely intertwined with a need for belonging or being accepted by others.

3. We are continually involved (consciously and unconsciously) in a process of matching our inner standards with our behavior, as we perceive it, of course. When we fail to live up to our expectations (an inner standard is not met), our attention is drawn to this fact by an *alarm reaction,* expressed in the form of irritation, tension, apprehensiveness, anxiety, fear, or guilt feelings. These varieties of pains, like physical pain, warn us of real or imagined danger. We are then motivated to perform in a manner which will remove the pain and restore an inner sense of security, self-acceptance, and equilibrium.

Primary and Secondary Needs

We all have certain physiological and psychological needs, and everyone strives for self-preservation and enhancement in the broad sense in which the self has been defined. An awareness of these basic needs enables us to understand similarities in the motivation and subsequent behavior of people. We begin to understand motivation at this point, but it is only a small beginning. Analyzing the differences among people is much more difficult.

In order to understand how motivation differs from person to person it is practical to make a distinction between primary and secondary needs. The *primary needs* include the physiological needs and the basic psychological needs for self-esteem, self-respect, and self-acceptance (or whatever related terms one prefers to use to describe the need to preserve and enhance the social-psychological self). The *secondary needs* are derived from the primary needs and contribute to their satisfaction. They are learned standards a person has internalized and a set of self-expectations that have become highly important. In one sense they are wants and goals that have become central to one's values because their acquisition is critical to maintaining an adequate self-image.

Although there are theoretically as many secondary needs as there are means by which the primary needs are satisfied, only three are described here: power, achievement, and affiliation. All these are found in large numbers of Americans. They are to some extent culturally determined in that they are rewarded in most subcultures of American life.

The Need for Power.[3]   Persons with a high need for power have learned that the acquisition of power is an effective means of self-preservation and enhancement. The manager with a high need for power is willing to take risks involved in competing with others in order to gain power and make optimal use of it. Such a person is motivated to strive for promotions, often with great intensity. Eyeball-to-eyeball confrontations, showdowns, and involvement in organizational politics are often a part of the power-seeker's life-style; and, although the role is a dangerous one, the payoff from playing the power game and winning is worth the risk.

The Need for Achievement.[4]   Persons with a high need for achievement play solitaire rather than poker. They have learned to satisfy their primary needs by means of a game in which the product itself symbolizes their contribution. Although achievement involves an element of competition, it avoids the head-on clashes involved in power-seeking. Sometimes extreme introverts, who carefully avoid the power game, are able to gain considerable power through the low-risk game that allows them to gain the status of recognized authority in a special field.

---

[3] For a discerning article on the need for power by a recognized authority on the subject read David C. McClelland, "The Two Faces of Power," *Journal of International Affairs,* Vol. XXIV, No. 1 (1970), pp. 29–47.

[4] A comprehensive treatment of achievement motivation is found in J. S. Atkinson and T. N. Feather (eds.), *A Theory of Achievement Motivation* (New York: John Wiley & Sons, Inc., 1966).

Individuals with a high need for achievement and a low need for power often choose staff positions such as accounting or engineering, while those with a high need for power prefer a position in sales or line management. Thus, the type of secondary needs one develops is logically related to vocational choice as well as to behavior on the job.

The Need for Affiliation.   Many people find greater need satisfaction in being loved than in being powerful or in achieving. They prefer to avoid power because people with power must often make decisions that alienate others. Those with a high need for affiliation care very much what others think about them, and acceptance by others is the primary clue that is used to demonstrate their own acceptability. Their first priority is to belong, to be accepted, and they are motivated to behave accordingly.

Extremely high needs for power and affiliation in a given individual are somewhat incompatible. On the other hand, people with a high affiliation need may achieve in many situations and in the process actually increase rather than decrease their feelings of belonging. Achievement and power are also compatible needs, although the presence of one does not necessarily indicate the presence of the other.

NEEDS AS STANDARDS

Thesis: Employees enter the workplace with greatly varying self-expectations. Some have extremely high standards, demanding of themselves outstanding performance regardless of external controls and incentives. Others, whose performance standards are low, feel comfortable doing as little work as possible. Thus, a manager's potential for motivating subordinates is to some extent limited by the selection process.

Implied and stated throughout this chapter is the idea that needs constitute a set of standards against which an individual constantly makes a self-evaluation. When we are relatively successful in meeting our needs, we feel safe, satisfied with ourselves, and contented. When we perceive that a need is not being met, we are motivated to behave in ways we believe will lead to need satisfaction. Figure 5–2 graphically expresses this relationship between needs, expressed as internalized standards, and motivation. At a given point in time (A), we are engaged in a sequence of activities which is intended to satisfy a variety of needs (that is, to meet the standards we have accepted for ourselves). At point (B) we become aware (through insight, fear, apprehensiveness, guilt, shame, etc.) that a standard or aspiration is not being met, that we are not moving steadily and directly toward (C). In effect, we become aware that a need is not being satisfied, that our actual or anticipated performance (D) is falling short of our self-expectations (C). The unpleasantness of this experience and the desire to restore the pleasurable equilibrium that exists when we are on target is the triggering mechanism (stimulation or motivation) to do whatever is required to get back on target (to move from

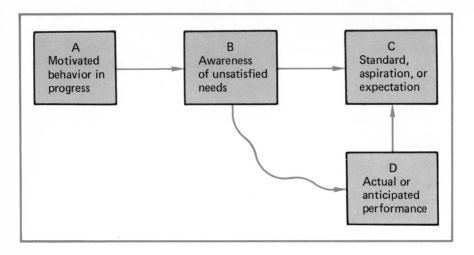

Figure 5–2   Standards as Motivators

D to C). As long as a discrepancy exists between C and D, a motivational basis for improved performance exists. An example will clarify this concept.

Bill Taylor, a senior business major, began interviewing, along with his classmates, in the late fall of the year before he was to graduate in June. Because he had been a good student, he expected to be able to choose among several attractive job offers. His need level (C) was established. By February it was becoming painfully obvious that his friends were receiving job offers and he was not; that is, he became aware (B) that his actual performance (D) was below his standard or expectation (C). As his awareness of the situation grew, his anxiety mounted and the intensity of his need was expressed in two ways: (1) a preoccupation with the difference between his expected and actual behavior (C > D) and (2) a tendency to have doubts about his own potential (a direct threat to his self-image, which occurred as he compared himself with his successful peers—another C > D discrepancy). As a result, he was motivated to act in order to remove the discrepancy and threat. Not knowing what to do, he sought the advice of a friendly management professor, who suggested that he trim his hair and beard and replace his sandals and cut-off jeans with more conventional attire. Although he had long since given up such traditional behavior, his need for employment proved to be stronger than his need to be like a small group of friends with whom he had begun to identify. As a result, the interviewers were able to see him for the outstanding prospect he really was (C = D), his anxiety disappeared, and his faltering self-confidence was restored.

One strategy by which people maintain a favorable self-concept (or, at least, avoid intense feelings of guilt, shame, anxiety, etc.) is to refuse to commit themselves firmly to any demanding standards. Being late for work, turning in low-quality work, and being reprimanded for breaking rules do no damage to the self-image of persons who see nothing wrong with such behavior. Others bring to the job high and firm self-expectations and are receptive to the challenges of their supervisors to perform at levels consistent with their highest potential.

The internalized standards by which we judge ourselves are expressed in many different forms. For example:

Self-perception of abilities (I have superior intelligence.)
Work standards (I do only what is required to get by.)
Moral or ethical standards (I don't lie or steal.)
Aspirations (I intend to become a company executive.)
Interests (I work only to support my fishing habit.)
Status (I am not required to punch the time clock.)
Goals (I plan to get an outstanding performance rating this year.)

Theoretically anyone can be motivated to perform acceptably, but it should be obvious that in some cases the costs to the organization would be prohibitive. Persons with demanding and deeply internalized work standards are more productive, require less supervision, and are more likely to have attitudes that contribute to a positive work environment than persons whose standards are average or low.

THE CONCEPT OF NEED HIERARCHY

Thesis: Human needs are insatiable. As one need is reasonably well satisfied, an individual's aspirations and expectations are raised and a new level of need arises. For several years it was generally assumed that the hierarchy formed by the emergence of new and higher level needs was common to all people, but such a viewpoint has now been discredited.

One point of view which has stimulated considerable thought and research on human needs was proposed by the prominent psychologist, Abraham Maslow.[5] The major aspects of his contribution are as follows:

1. Within a given individual there are great differences in the motivational force of different needs. What motivates at one point in time may have no motivational potential at another. This is true for two reasons: (1) certain needs develop only after others are satisfied and (2) a satisfied need is not a motivator.

2. Human needs may be classified along a definite scale of priority which constitutes a *need hierarchy.* Lower level needs are satisfied first, and higher order needs develop only as lower level needs are reasonably well satisfied. As lower level needs are satisfied, the emerging, higher level

---

[5] For a broad sampling of Maslow's thinking see Abraham E. Maslow, *Motivation and Personality* (2d ed.; New York: Harper & Row, Publishers, 1970).

needs take precedence as motivators. This does not mean that needs on the different levels cannot motivate at the same time, but there is at any given time a level of needs within the hierarchy that is uniquely active.

Maslow's Need Hierarchy

The need hierarchy shown in Figure 5–3 and outlined below was viewed by Maslow as applying to people in general. Moving from the lowest level to the highest, it is described as follows:

1. *Physiological needs.* These are the needs mentioned earlier in this chapter—food, water, rest, etc.

2. *Safety needs.* These are concerned with protection from danger and threats. The drive to achieve economic and job security would logically be included in this category (for example, seniority provisions and pension plans). Maslow also suggested that the desire for savings accounts and various forms of insurance would also be calculated to satisfy needs at this level.

2. *Belonging or social needs.* Included here are the need for acceptance by others and the need for love, affection, and friendship (the affiliation needs mentioned earlier).

4. *Esteem needs.* This level moves beyond merely being accepted and refers to a need to be held in high esteem by others and by oneself. Maslow speaks of the need for a "firmly based self-esteem" in that one's esteem is based on real capacity, achievement, and the respect of others. At times he appears to equate the esteem needs with self-respect.

5. *Self-actualization.* Once the lower level needs have been reasonably well satisfied a new discontent develops. This is expressed as a need to do what one is best suited for, to achieve at the level of one's highest potential,

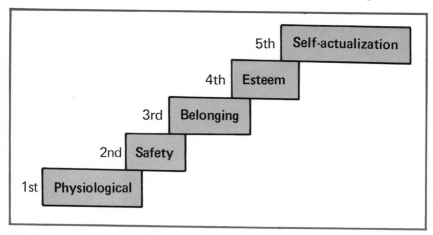

Figure 5–3   Maslow's Need Hierarchy

to become everything one is capable of becoming. So complex and open-ended is this need that it is safe to say that human needs are insatiable.

Critique of Maslow's Theory

For years after Maslow's theory was published it was accepted more or less uncritically by large numbers of persons, probably because it focuses our attention upon some important truths about human needs. It does, however, contain some serious flaws, not the least of which is the fact that it has not withstood experimental testing. We look now at the pros and cons of the theory.

Positive Contributions. Directly or indirectly Maslow's theory calls to our attention three important points about human needs.

1. Satisfied needs do not motivate. To effectively motivate we must focus on currently active needs. For example, for the mass of Americans the need for job security is currently weak, at least when compared with the 1920s and 1930s. In a highly mobile society, opportunities to find work elsewhere, seniority provisions, programs of unemployment compensation, and policies which make arbitrary dismissal unlikely combine to reduce employees' dependence upon an employer and the intensity of their need for safety.

2. We should expect a shift in employees' needs, depending upon general economic conditions. The need for money, for example, can logically be expected to be lowered when the masses of workers are experiencing financial prosperity. However, when depression or inflation bring general economic hardship, the motivational value of money should increase.

3. An increasingly large number of persons, especially, but not exclusively, at the management level, are developing expectations and needs at the self-fulfillment level. Some of these expectations are in all probability currently unrealistic (for example, some expectations relating to job enrichment at the rank and file level), but they must nevertheless be dealt with in one way or another. It does not follow that an expectation ceases to function as an active need merely because it is objectively unrealistic.

Questionable Concepts. Maslow developed his theory on the basis of clinical observation rather than rigorous experimentation, and in spite of the great amount of attention it has received, there has been no convincing experimentation to support it. For the theory to be valid, an increase in need satisfaction on a given level (safety, for example) must cause the strength of that need to decrease and result in an increase in the importance of the next higher level need (belonging). This process continues up the hierarchy in lock-step fashion. Presumably at the top level (self-actualization), a reversal occurs, and need satisfaction results in increased rather than decreased motivation.[6] Although this may occur in the lives of some people, it is not characteristic of everyone.

---

[6] Maslow added this idea in later writings. See A. H. Maslow, *Toward a Psychology of Being* (2d ed.; New York: Van Nostrand Reinhold Company, 1968), p. 30. Also A. H. Maslow, op. cit., 1970.

On the basis of the research conducted over the past twenty-five years, Maslow's theory may be questioned on the following basis:

1. Although it may be generally true that satisfied needs do not motivate, the meaning of satisfaction is unclear. At the physiological level it is evident that one is not motivated to eat, for example, immediately after a big meal. But humans have memory and the ability to anticipate the future when hunger will again occur. How then can it be said that even these needs are ever satisfied completely?

   At the higher levels the problem is even more complex; and, although specific needs emerge as uniquely active at certain times, it has yet to be demonstrated that the lower level, so-called satisfied, needs cease to motivate. The executive, for instance, whose self-actualization needs are strong, may still be motivated to act out of a need for esteem, belonging, and safety.

2. When the physiological needs are reasonably well satisfied (in a sense that one has no real fear of being unable to meet them in the foreseeable future), there appears to be no way to predict which of the higher level needs will increase in importance for a particular person. Because of the learned or acquired nature of needs, there are large differences between people in terms of the sequence in which needs emerge.

3. There is no acceptable way to predict the time lag which exists between the satisfaction of one need and the increased importance of the next higher one. In fact, in Maslow's latest revision of his theory, he suggests that the hierarchy may unfold throughout a lifetime.[7] The levels would, in effect, correspond more or less to the developmental stages of childhood, adolescence, and various levels of adulthood. There is evidence that the emergence of needs may relate more to age and career level than to the satisfaction of lower level needs.

   Some people whose needs appear to be reasonably well met live a lifetime without becoming self-actualizers in Maslow's sense. The theory does not take into account such a possibility.

The research studies concerning Maslow's theory are thoroughly summarized in articles by Hall and Nougaim [8] and Lawler and Suttle.[9] These articles also report original studies which employ more acceptable experimental designs than any of the other research reported to date. Neither study found support for Maslow's multilevel theory.

A two-step theory has received some support in the literature. Following this line of thinking, the person who is unemployed or new on the job is likely to be preoccupied with physiological and safety needs; but, as these are reasonably

---

[7] Maslow, op. cit., 1970, p. 20.

[8] D. T. Hall and K. E. Nougaim, "An Examination of Maslow's Need Hierarchy in an Organizational Setting," *Organizational Behavior and Human Performance,* Vol. 3, No. 1 (February, 1968), p. 12.

[9] Edward E. Lawler, III, and J. Lloyd Suttle, "A Causal Correlation Test of the Need Hierarchy Concept," *Organization Behavior and Human Performance,* Vol. 7, No. 2 (April, 1972), p. 265.

well satisfied, other needs begin to emerge. On the basis of his own and other research, Lawler concluded that "at the present time it is probably prudent to accept the two-step view." [10] The two-step view wisely avoids any attempt to predict which of the higher level needs will predominate once the lower level needs have been satisfied.

HERZBERG'S TWO-FACTOR THEORY

Thesis: Herzberg's two-factor theory has been valuable in stimulating research and concern for making the work itself more rewarding. However, its usefulness as a workable motivational theory is quite limited.

In recent years massive numbers of research studies and publications have been stimulated by the *two-factor theory* proposed by Frederick Herzberg. This theory should not be confused with the two-step hierarchy previously discussed. Herzberg based his original theory on two sets of data—a review of published literature on job attitudes [11] and a series of interviews with 200 engineers and accountants in the Pittsburgh area.[12] In the interview each employee was asked to think of a time when he had felt particularly good and one when he had felt particularly bad about his job. He was then asked to describe the conditions leading up to these feelings. The result was that employees tended to name different conditions as leading to their good and bad feelings. For example, interesting work was associated with good feelings, but lack of it was not ordinarily associated with bad feelings; and low status was associated with bad feelings, but high status was not associated with good feelings.

Herzberg concluded that many of the factors which managers have traditionally believed to be motivators, such as pay and the nature of supervision, do not really motivate at all. The two-factor idea is that the job factors which are generally regarded as motivators should actually be divided into two groups: one consisting of *motivational factors,* or what he called *satisfiers,* and the other consisting of *maintenance factors,* or *dissatisfiers.*

The motivating factors are *intrinsic* or *job content* factors. They occur at the time the work is performed and make it rewarding in and of itself. *Job maintenance* factors, on the other hand, are extrinsic or *job context* factors. They are part of the work environment but not of the work itself. As Herzberg continued to elaborate on his two-factor theory, he referred to intrinsic and extrinsic factors as *motivators* and *hygiene factors* respectively and to the theory as the *motivation-*

---

10 Edward E. Lawler, III, *Pay and Organizational Effectiveness: A Psychological View* (New York: McGraw-Hill, Inc., 1971), p. 28.

11 F. Herzberg et al., *Job Attitudes: A Review of Research and Opinion* (Pittsburgh: Psychological Services of Pittsburgh, 1957).

12 F. Herzberg, B. Mausner, and B. Snyderman, *The Motivation to Work* (2d ed.; New York: John Wiley & Sons, Inc., 1959).

hygiene theory.[13] Figure 5–4 is intended to clarify Herzberg's sometimes confusing terminology. It also presents a list of satisfiers and dissatisfiers as classified by his research.

TWO-FACTOR THEORY (Motivation-Hygiene Theory)	
FACTORS Motivation Factors Job Content (Intrinsic) Factors Satisfiers	**FACTORS** Maintenance (Hygiene) Factors Job Content (Extrinsic) Factors Dissatisfiers
EXAMPLES Achievement Recognition Advancement Responsibility The work itself Growth possibilities	**EXAMPLES** Company policy and administration Supervision Peer relations Relations with subordinates Status Pay Job security Working conditions

Figure 5–4   Herzberg's Terms and Factor Classifications

One of the most controversial aspects of the two-factor theory is the proposition that job satisfaction and dissatisfaction are not two ends of a continuum but rather are two separate and distinct variables; that is, the presence of job content factors is satisfying and motivational, but the absence of such factors is not the cause of dissatisfaction. The presence of job context factors is not motivational, but their absence causes dissatisfaction. Since motivation and maintenance factors are viewed by Herzberg as qualitatively different variables, and since pay is a maintenance factor, we would have to conclude that pay is not a motivator. Aside from the fact that this contradicts a mountain of evidence, such a conclusion is unsatisfactory in that it is a perfect example of all-or-nothing, either-or thinking about human motivation. The hundreds of research studies and systematic observations about motivation simply do not support this type of thinking, and there is a question about whether Herzberg's own research supports the idea that a given factor should always be placed in one classification or the other.

Few theories have received more attention than the two-factor theory, and there is still not complete agreement concerning its value. However, the research evidence against it appears to have the edge, particularly since it was generated through the use of a wide variety of methodologies. Evidence for the theory, collected primarily by Herzberg's original method, has been widely criticized as being an artifact of the method itself. After a thorough critique of the published literature, Campbell and his associates had this to say:

---

[13] F. Herzberg, *Work and the Nature of Man* (Cleveland: World Publishing Company, 1966).

The most meaningful conclusion that we can draw is that the two-factor theory has now served its purpose and should be altered or respectfully laid aside. Theories are never true or false, but exhibit only varying degrees of usefulness. The Herzberg theory has stimulated a great deal of argument and considerable research activity. On these grounds it has been useful. However, on the basis of the data that it has generated, it also seems to be an oversimplification. Repeated factor analytic studies of job attitudes have failed to demonstrate the existence of two independent factors corresponding to motivators and hygienes.[14]

Herzberg's two-factor theory has been useful in focusing our attention upon the importance of job content factors, particularly in view of their relevance to job enrichment and job satisfaction. However, it has long been recognized that a high level of job satisfaction does not necessarily result in a high motivation to produce. Research to date would seem to indicate that whether or not a job context or job content factor will motivate, rather than merely make employees happier, depends upon a number of different environmental and psychological conditions which are discussed in Chapter 6.

INTERESTS AS MOTIVATORS

Thesis: High intrinsic interest in one's work will, under certain conditions, result in an increased motivation to produce. It may also motivate an individual to accept employment or to remain on a job, to think creatively, and to identify with the goals and objectives of the organization.

When a student says, "I am interested in management," the meaning is quite unclear. It may simply mean "I want to become a manager," or "I want to study management." It could mean "I am motivated (by what, I don't know) to enter the field of management." Perhaps this interest in management stems from parental pressure, or from a knowledge that top managers earn high salaries, or because the student identifies strongly with a particular professor of management.

On the other hand, "I am interested in management" may imply an intrinsic satisfaction in doing what managers do—that is, an interest in the work itself. Most of us have had work experience that did not seem like work at all because of the intensity of our interest in it. Time passed quickly, concentration was strong, and, despite all the effort exerted, it was pleasurable. Interests, in this sense, are an important form of motivation. They are, in fact, an ideal form of motivation for both the organization and the employee. An organization reaps the benefits of high productivity, creativity, initiative, and few personnel problems; the employee is compensated with a pleasurable work experience in addition to regular forms of reimbursement.

---

[14] John P. Campbell et al., *Managerial Behavior, Performance, and Effectiveness* (New York: McGraw-Hill, Inc., 1970), p. 381.

The Nature and Intensity of Interests

Since interests are learned, interest in a particular subject or type of work varies greatly from person to person, depending upon the nature and degree of one's past exposure to it. Some people have relatively shallow interests. They tend to be uninterested in everything; while others are virtually consumed by interest in their hobbies, studies, work, and other activities. To some extent the quality of being interesting is a function of the activity or object in question (a job, a hobby, etc.); but it is probably more often a function of a person's attitudes, curiosity, and intellectual ambitiousness. Those with generally low interest levels probably will not respond as favorably to what management may regard as interesting work as will others with high interest levels. However, interests are to some degree motivators for everyone; and management should carefully consider individual differences in interests when making selection, placement, and promotion decisions. Certainly it is not, as was once thought, an advantage only to the employees for their work to be interesting. The managerial goals of high motivation and job satisfaction are both supported when employees are intrinsically interested in their work.

One way to understand interests is in terms of needs. For example, think for a moment of an individual you know who has developed a deep and lasting interest in music. He or she is constantly drawn to it; and not to be able to hear, compose, or play music is to suffer a void that cannot be filled by any other activity. Once a person learns through continued experience to associate a deep satisfaction with a particular activity, a need is created for that activity, and one who can satisfy such a need through work is doubly rewarded.

When Interests Motivate

Interests are not always motivational, if by motivation we are referring to effort that will increase productivity. Some people are highly motivated to be optimally productive because of characteristics within themselves which have little to do with the type of work they are doing or the environmental factors surrounding the job. They have set high expectations for themselves, and have internalized high work standards; and, since they typically do their best because of other needs, interests have little effect on their productivity. On the other hand, people with low work standards often do well only in areas where interest is high. This is exemplified by the fact that some high-ability students consistently make A's in courses they enjoy, while their grades in other courses range from A to F.

It should not be concluded that attempts to match interests with work and to make work more interesting are of value only for those employees with poor work habits. Motives for accepting a job, for being productive, and for leaving that job may be quite different. Aside from what interesting work does to enable an employee to satisfy needs for self-fulfillment or self-actualization, an organization needs the creativity, emotional involvement, and loyalty that are typically found in employees who are interested in their work. For the person who is already exerting maximum effort to produce, interesting work may provide motivation for other behaviors which are valued by the organization. Productivity is important in all jobs, but it is certainly not the only activity toward which motivated behavior in organizations must be directed.

UNCONSCIOUS MOTIVATION

Thesis: Most of us desire at one time or another to understand our own motives. On the other hand, we also desire to maintain a favorable self-image. This means that often we will be totally biased, both in drawing conclusions about our own motives and in reporting to others why we behave as we do.

Since the early 1930s, a popular method of research on the importance of various motivational factors has been self-report.[15] This typically involves asking workers to rank the importance of various factors as work motivators. As mentioned earlier, Herzberg's original research was based on data obtained from the interview, one form of self-report technique. This has been a valuable, and, at times, a valid approach to understanding motivation, but a note of caution should always be involved in its use. The truth is that much motivation is unconscious, and, to the extent that this is the case, it is impossible for people to describe their own motives. Some motives are hidden from consciousness by a desire to look good to ourselves and others, and our motivations are often so complex that we are unable to sort them out.

High-ability workers who restrict production because they fear rejection by peers may not be sufficiently objective to admit their dependence upon peer approval. In fact, they may not even be consciously aware that they are performing below their potential. Employees who are frequently absent from work because of minor illnesses may have little if any insight into the fact that their excessive absences may be due to a sympathy-getting syndrome developed during childhood. Even rational and objective employees may be hard pressed to communicate accurately whether they are more motivated by, say money, security, or interesting work, when all three are motivational; and their answers to questions about motivation may change with general economic conditions and other job-related variables. We too often ask people for information about their own motivation which cannot possibly be given.

The fact that we are unaware of many of our own motives is not all bad. The many defense reactions by which we psychologically protect ourselves from reality are, to a point, quite valuable. It is also true that preoccupation with our own mental processes may result in diminished attention to the needs of others and to those aspects of our work that require intense concentration. At any rate, it follows that at times we are much more capable of understanding the motives of others than we are our own.

---

[15] Edward E. Lawler, III, op. cit., and Herzberg, F., et al., op. cit., pp. 40–42.

INTERNALIZED MOTIVATION

Thesis: Employees who believe in and identify with the organization—its purpose, its people, its policies, and its goals—serve both themselves and the organization better than employees who are motivated principally by incentives to produce and a fear of doing otherwise.

It has long been recognized that reward and punishment leave something to be desired as motivators. Employees do work for extrinsic rewards, such as money, and at specific times and under certain circumstances their efforts are motivated by a fear of being punished, but these alone are relatively poor motivators. If other motivators are not operative alongside these, employees may slow down or stop working altogether when external controls are absent; and, unless rewards are strategically planned, employees may never produce beyond minimum requirements.

Harry Levinson refers to the assumption that people can be successfully motivated by reward and punishment as the "great jackass fallacy." [16] The image that comes to mind when one thinks of the reward-punishment approach is that of the jackass being lured forward by a carrot or driven from behind by fear of a stick. If carrot-and-stick motivation dominates a manager's thinking, subordinates will not be treated with the dignity and respect they deserve and often demand.

It is generally accepted by those who understand human motivation that some degree of *internalization* of organizational standards and goals by members of the group is necessary for that organization to function effectively. If employees do not accept the idea that a rule or regulation is meaningful and just, no amount of external control will be adequate to produce the desired behavior. The analogy of law enforcement is applicable here. The police officer serves an important function in apprehending lawbreakers and making citizens fear punishment should they decide to become offenders. But the critical determiner of whether laws will be obeyed is the citizen's belief in and commitment to the law. This has been clearly demonstrated in situations where a law has not had general public support. National prohibition of the sale of alcoholic beverages failed miserably, as have attempts to enforce speed laws when the people involved have not really believed in them. The best controls are internal. On the other hand, the existence of strong internal controls does not preclude the use of reward and punishment as motivators.

Indoctrination

The process of internalization is sometimes referred to as *indoctrination.* Through this process, people who are expected to behave in a certain way are

---

[16] Harry Levinson, "Asinine Attitudes Toward Motivation," *Harvard Business Review* (January-February, 1973), pp. 70–76.

somehow led to believe that they should behave in that way. When we internalize an organization's standards and values, we accept them as our own. Then when we fail to live up to them by being late for work or by making a costly mistake, for example, we are our own worst critic.

Internalized work standards become a part of one's own value system. Failure to live up to these standards becomes an occasion for remorse or regret, and outstanding performance with reference to them is a cause of pride and satisfaction. It is only when an organization's goals and standards have to some extent been internalized that employees have a basis for feeling that their work has meaning—that it makes a worthwhile contribution. Thus, indoctrination serves the employee as well as the organization.

The Internalization Process

On the first day of employment, workers are provided information concerning rules, regulations, policies, procedures, and performance expectations; and, if their attitudes toward work are reasonably mature, they willingly accept a broad spectrum of such standards. In effect, they agree to sacrifice certain personal freedoms and to conform to specified organizational norms in return for pay and other forms of compensation. In time employees become aware of more subtle and covert expectations and must choose whether to internalize them, to conform because of possible rewards and punishments, or to refuse to conform and live with the consequences.

To some extent internalization is a form of "social role taking." An employee with a work history has developed a general image of the role or behavior expectations of an accountant, supervisor, chief executive, or whatever. Most employees accept the fact that organizations cannot survive without the predictability and control that result from the sacrifice of a certain degree of individuality which accompanies the internalization of job expectations. On the other hand, effective managers are sensitive to the need of employees on all levels to remain unique, self-respecting individuals who have not sold their souls along with their skills, effort, and, perhaps, their loyalty.

DEFENSIVE AND ABNORMAL BEHAVIOR

Thesis: Defensive and abnormal reactions clearly are motivated behaviors and are understandable within the context of our need for self-preservation and enhancement. The manager who is naive with reference to these behaviors will be unable to understand and rationally react to a significant dimension of organizational life.

During the past twenty years major changes have been made in the treatment of persons with serious personality problems. With the discovery of tranquilizing drugs it became possible to remove large numbers of seriously ill people from mental institutions and return them to their home environments and to useful, productive work. The 1960s and 1970s have not reduced the occurrence of psychological problems, but the number of people requiring prolonged hospitalization has greatly decreased. People who in years past would have required hospitalization now receive outpatient treatment and continue to work, often without awareness on the part of their superiors of the nature and seriousness of their problems. The symptoms of the disorders are commonly seen as excessive tardiness or absenteeism, inability to relate effectively to other people, withdrawal, alcoholism, or drug addiction.

Several large companies now cope with problems of alcoholism and drug use as though they are routine medical problems; and, where specialists are available in this area, managers should take full advantage of the opportunity to make referrals. However, most problems resulting from defensive and abnormal behavior on the job must be dealt with by line managers as they occur. This means that managers must have greater than average insight into their nature. Fortunately these problems can be understood within the general frame of reference already established.

Barriers to Need Satisfaction

We begin by taking a look at what happens when individuals are chronically unable to view themselves as acceptable and worthwhile. As shown in Figure 5–5, at a given point in time we may conceptualize an individual engaging in a variety of activities designed to satisfy needs. To get a feel for what chronic inability to meet one's needs involves, consider the case of George, a young man who flunked out of college and began working as a machinist's helper.

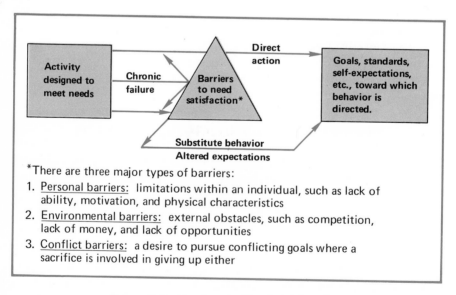

*There are three major types of barriers:
1. Personal barriers: limitations within an individual, such as lack of ability, motivation, and physical characteristics
2. Environmental barriers: external obstacles, such as competition, lack of money, and lack of opportunities
3. Conflict barriers: a desire to pursue conflicting goals where a sacrifice is involved in giving up either

Figure 5–5   Barriers to Need Satisfaction

Because of early parental influence George developed an aspiration to become a lawyer, and during his teen years this aspiration was a continual source of satisfaction and recognition. He developed a strong need to become a lawyer.

Unfortunately some barriers stood between George and a successful legal career. To begin with, he had a *personal barrier* to need satisfaction: he lacked the mental ability to pass his law courses. Because of this deficiency he faced a major *environmental barrier:* a group of bright, highly motivated young law students with whom he had to compete for grades. George could see no way out. He was trapped. He could not meet his need, but neither could he get it out of his system. His aspiration to become a lawyer had become a significant part of his self-identity, and to give it up would require the ego-crushing admission that he and others had long overrated his potential.

George's problem was compounded by the fact that his parents could not accept the truth either. They had too often gained status with their friends by boasting about their son's brilliant future. George was acutely aware of their disappointment and was constantly reminded of their insistence that his leaving school would be temporary . . . that he would return and complete his education after a brief period of adjustment. Unfortunately he was unable to face his problem head-on and solve it in a healthy, direct, realistic manner. Instead he found it necessary to make some internal adjustments that involved self-deception and reality distortion. Some of the many alternatives open to him are discussed in the following section.

Defensive Behavior

When relatively direct attempts to overcome barriers and meet needs are unsuccessful and the need itself cannot be modified, a psychological adjustment must be made. The most common adjustment is to employ one or more *defense reactions.* These are ways of thinking which are calculated to cushion the blow to the self and thereby enable a person to continue to maintain a favorable self-image. A few of the most common defense reactions are:

1. *Rationalization:* a form of self-deception in which a socially acceptable justification is developed to avoid having to face a nonacceptable view of oneself. For example, an executive fails because of poor business decisions, but insists that the cause of failure was an unfavorable economy.

2. *Flight into fantasy:* inappropriate daydreaming. A management trainee who is frustrated by low status and unchallenging work daydreams about a future in the executive suite rather than creatively working to make such a future a reality.

3. *Projection:* unconsciously rejecting an unacceptable thought, desire, impulse, etc., by blaming it on someone else. The executive who has ceased to be promoted because of nonperformance projects failure onto superiors by believing that they block opportunities and favor other candidates.

4. *Aggression:* destructively attacking the real or imaginary source of frustration. This may be expressed verbally in slander and gossip or physically in such behaviors as sabotage or fighting.

5. *Scapegoating:* behaving aggressively toward someone who cannot fight back as a substitute for aggression toward the source of one's frustration. A foreman who is angry at his superior takes it out on subordinates or family.

6. *Overcompensation:* as a means of handling inadequacy in one area, exaggerated and inappropriate behavior is expressed in another. For example, an individual who feels ill at ease with people may talk too much and too loudly in a vain attempt to gain social acceptance. On a less extreme level, called *compensation,* students who flunk out of school make up for feelings of shame by intensively applying themselves in a substitute career. Various forms of *substitution* can be wholesome forms of defense, except when they involve giving up too soon on a worthwhile initial objective or lowering one's self-expectations when the going gets rough.

7. *Repression:* blotting out of consciousness certain ideas, memories, etc., that cause conflict and tend to lower self-esteem. This is exemplified by supervisors who selectively forget their own errors and blunders, refuse to accept constructive criticisms of superiors, and thus are unable to make the behavioral changes required for effective performance.

8. *Reaction formation:* a pendulum swing in the opposite direction from one's true desires or impulses as a means of maintaining self-control or self-respect. A highly ambitious manager whose career is stymied accepts defeat and becomes an extreme advocate of the stupidity of working hard and playing the upward mobility game.

9. *Withdrawal:* physically and/or psychologically pulling away from people and conflict. This is exemplified by the shy individual whose protection is to be excessively quiet or by the manager whose reaction to departmental conflict is to avoid becoming involved—to act as though the conflict were nonexistent.

Defense reactions such as these clearly are motivated, goal-directed behavior, and the goal is still self-preservation and enhancement. We all use defense reactions at times, and, when not used excessively or for too long a time, they are helpful and effective in achieving short-term need satisfaction.

Neurotic and Psychotic Behavior

Sometimes a person who is unable to maintain a favorable self-image, even with the use of defense reactions, resorts to chronic dependency upon them. They are used like alcohol or drugs to provide escape from reality. The means of escape often increases the problem and contributes to a spiral of decreasing effectiveness which is typically viewed as abnormal behavior.

Abnormal behavior can best be understood as an exaggeration or extension of so-called normal behavior. The mentally ill person has a chronic inability to adjust: either to find need satisfaction directly or to accept altered or modified standards of self-judgment. As a result, such a person may exhibit one or many behaviors which others recognize as being unhealthy (overuse of the defense reactions just described, suspicion, illogical thinking, etc.).

When people become mentally ill (neurotic or psychotic) it is not because a foreign substance, such as bacteria, has entered their psyches. Rather, in their desperate attempts to find self-acceptance they have had to resort to extreme, costly, and inefficient devices (defenses) for coping with their personal problems. Lay people are often unable and/or unwilling to diagnose a person as abnormal, but professional psychologists and psychiatrists can detect certain clusters or syndromes of unhealthy behaviors which they classify as a type of neurosis or psychosis.

A *neurosis* is, relatively speaking, a mild personality disorder in which there is a lack of gross personality disorganization. Even before the discovery of tranquilizers, neurotics seldom had to be hospitalized and were often found in the work environment. They include, for example, people with phobias, high anxiety, and preoccupation with imaginary illnesses as well as those who are excessively perfectionist or given to constant worrying and mild depression. A *psychosis* is a severe personality disorder in which the defenses employed are so extreme that an individual loses touch with reality (through hallucinations, delusions, and extreme withdrawal, for example).

Since today only chronically ill psychotics and occasionally neurotics are hospitalized, managers must relate to large numbers of people who would be totally incapacitated except for their continued medication. They are people with problems and are thus a problem for their supervisors. They are often the people with whom the supervisor has the most direct contact: the chronic absentee, the troublemaker, the low producer, and the individual who has difficulty relating to others. At this point we are concerned primarily with understanding their motivation. Chapter 19 will provide insights into how to supervise them.

STUDY AND DISCUSSION QUESTIONS

1. Why is it valuable for managers, who are of necessity concerned with practical problems, to study motivation rather than rely on their intuitive ability?

2. Why is it unnecessary for an individual to understand the underlying purpose of a need in order to be motivated to satisfy it?

3. What is meant by the *self* in the organismic-holistic view? What is misleading about saying that our most basic need is for self-preservation as that term is popularly used?

4. In what sense do the needs of people differ? How did these differences occur?

5. Three of the many needs in which people differ are power, achievement, and affiliation. Assign a rating of 1 (low), 2 (average), or 3 (high) to the

degree of each of these needs you would expect to find in the individuals described below:

(a) A sensitive, submissive career file clerk

(b) An unsociable professor who has authored five books

(c) An insensitive and overbearing line supervisor

6. In what sense is a need an inner standard against which self-evaluation takes place? What are the signals by which we may become aware that a standard has not been met?

7. A manager can motivate some employees more easily than others to be productive. Which type of person is easiest to motivate?

8. Describe and evaluate Maslow's concept of need hierarchy.

9. Describe and evaluate Herzberg's motivation-hygiene theory.

10. Under what circumstances do interests motivate employees to be more productive?

11. Why should we be suspicious of a study in which employees are asked to rank the following in order of their importance as motivators: money, security, good supervision, a comfortable work environment, and friendly co-workers?

12. Describe the meaning and importance of *internalized motivation* as the term is used in this chapter.

13. What is abnormal behavior? Why does a manager need to understand the motivation behind it?

CRITICAL INCIDENT

The Sales Plateau

Although Mark Cooper was nearing retirement as sales manager, he was deeply concerned about his inability to increase sales as his competitors were doing. He knew from the experiences of other Chevrolet dealers that the problem had nothing to do with the product; and he had no reason to believe that a problem existed in the areas of service, advertising, or the public image of the company.

His top salesman, Jeff Borman, typically earned unusually high commissions, almost twice what the lowest paid salesman, Keith Brock, was earning, although Borman seemed more interested in becoming sales manager than in earning money as such. It was generally known that his income from inherited investments was substantial.

Most of the other sales staff earned relatively high commissions when compared with the commissions paid by competitors, and on an annual basis there was very little difference in earnings from one salesperson to another. The commission structure had been established when automobile sales were relatively low, and, even though the continued expansion of a large nearby Army base had resulted in unusually high sales companywide, the commission rate remained the same. The owner believed that this was an important factor in building a high-quality, stable sales force.

When members of the sales staff, which consisted of eight people besides Borman, were interviewed concerning their preference for a sales manager they all expressed a vague disapproval of Borman for the position although no one gave any concrete reason for the opinion or seriously recommended anyone else. Brock was the only one who actually expressed a direct criticism of Borman; and his comment was, "I just don't think Borman has what it takes to be a manager." Brock's feelings were obviously strong.

In attempting to understand why sales had leveled off, Cooper observed that the salespeople did not seem to compete with one another for the sales prospects and often failed to follow up on leads even though, from Borman's performance, it was obvious that such a practice produced sales. Knowing what to do did not seem to be the issue. The problem was, in Cooper's opinion, purely a matter of motivation.

Questions

1. Analyze the possible motives of Cooper, Borman, and Brock.
2. What plausible explanations may be given for Cooper's inability to increase sales?
3. What changes could increase the overall motivation of the sales staff? What negative side effects could result from such a change?
4. How seriously should Cooper consider the attitudes of the other salespeople toward Borman's possible promotion?
5. What additional information do you need in order to analyze this incident?

Chapter 6

Motivating Subordinates and Followers

Managers differ greatly in their approaches to motivating the individuals who report to them. Because the personalities and learning experiences of managers are different, it is understandable that their motivational styles differ, too. Since there are also vast differences in the needs of subordinates and in the environments where motivation occurs, managers are called upon to be adaptable and to possess a repertoire of motivational techniques rather than to rely upon a stereotyped best method.

There is, of course, no one best way to motivate. This chapter presents a variety of conceptual models within which a manager may formulate an effective motivational strategy for a specific situation.

MOTIVATION, EQUITY, AND EXCHANGE

Thesis: A useful way of conceptualizing certain facets of motivation and couching them within a framework which deals directly with employee-organization relationships is to interpret motivation as a system of exchange.[1] This is not a comprehensive motivation theory. It is a simplified, practical way of viewing limited but important aspects of a complex relationship.

Two assumptions are made when an employment agreement is reached: first, that both the employee and the organization have something to offer that will meet certain needs of the other; second, that the two parties can maintain a relationship in which an equitable exchange is possible. The organization and the employee may not always share a common view of what constitutes an equitable exchange. Intensive individual or collective bargaining may be required before

---

[1] In a general sense, this concept may be traced to George C. Homans, "Social Behavior Exchange," *American Journal of Sociology*, Vol. 63, No. 6 (May, 1958), pp. 597–606. A review of the literature on this point of view may be found under the topic of "Equity Theory" in Richard M. Steers and Lyman W. Porter, *Motivation and Work Behavior* (New York: McGraw-Hill, Inc., 1975), pp. 135–179.

employee and organization (ordinarily represented by a manager who is also an employee) can agree upon an acceptable balance.

In some situations the agreement is determined solely by which side is more powerful, and the needs of neither are fully met. Under such circumstances motivation on both sides is low, and each produces at the minimum level required to maintain the employment relationship. At another time or in another situation, open communication and mutual concern result in an optimal exchange in which motivation is high because the needs of each are satisfied to the greatest extent possible.

The Minimum Exchange

The simplest exchange relationship is expressed as a fair day's work for a fair day's pay. This sounds like a good working principle, and in one sense it is; but perceptions of fairness are inevitably biased, and, when applied in its crudest form, the principle leads to conflict and low motivation. As long as the organization and employee consider only their own needs and attempt to get as much as possible while giving as little as possible, both are forced into an adversary position in which one or the other typically perceives the exchange as inequitable. On the other hand, when either party to the exchange is able to break the deadlock and become committed to meeting the other's needs as well as its own, the way is paved for optimal need satisfaction and motivation.

Optimizing the Exchange

Moving beyond the principle of a fair day's work for a fair day's pay, we look now at other possible exchanges. First of all, what can the organization offer besides money? Potentially it can offer the partial satisfaction of a wide range of needs that employees are often expected to satisfy through the paycheck and off-the-job activities. Some organizations, for example, provide security, supportive social relationships, satisfying and enjoyable work, and opportunities for creative self-expression. Through effective supervisory relationships and opportunities for achieving and assuming responsibility, an organization can provide partial fulfillment of an employee's basic psychological needs, totally apart from the need fulfillment which is achieved through financial compensation.

An employee, regardless of position and status, has much more to offer the organization than a fair day's work. Of course, some employees do offer only their labor. They are hired hands in the truest sense of the word, while others in the same job offer creative thought and problem-solving behavior. An employee may offer loyalty, cooperation, and attitudes and behavior that reflect a genuine identification with organizational goals and purposes.

As a practical matter, an effective exchange system is partially covert or hidden. With reference to certain contributions, parties to the exchange should deliberately avoid open power bargaining which makes behavior on each side contingent upon what the other side does. In one sense, contingency motivation

Some Organizational Contributions to the Exchange	Some Employee Contributions to the Exchange
Financial compensation	Loyalty
Security	Cooperation
Social relationships	Problem-solving behavior
Fair treatment	Support of goals
Responsibility	Dependability
Growth opportunities	Initiative
Status and power	Creativity
Safe working conditions	Productivity

Figure 6–1   Some Factors in the Organization-Employee Exchange

is the most nearly perfect expression of an exchange system (for example, when compensation is clearly dependent on productivity), but in some situations this is inappropriate.

Certain actions must be unilateral to be effective. For example, management should consistently relate to subordinates in a way that contributes to their sense of self-respect and dignity. Management should exert maximum effort to treat employees fairly and provide for their safety on the job without expecting anything in return. Only if these behaviors emerge from an inner character and a genuine concern for others will they be likely to elicit a favorable exchange response. Generous, nonmanipulative actions from either side communicate that a sincere effort is being made to meet the other's needs. This creates trust and a quality of relationship that prevent the exchange system from degenerating into a mechanical, impersonal, and overtly selfish form of power bargaining.

Perceptual Aspects of Equity

What constitutes a fair and equitable exchange is a matter of perception. For example, employees on a given job may believe that they are being well paid until they discover that similar jobs in other companies pay more. Then their perception of the exchange is modified, and they see themselves as being treated unfairly. Incidentally, in the absence of documented facts, employees tend to overestimate what others are being paid, which suggests that secrecy concerning what employees are being paid presents motivational problems similar to those involved in making pay information public.

Systematic differences in the perception of employees and managers may contribute to inequity problems. For example, perceptual differences are sometimes seen when an employee is offered a promotion to supervisor. Because of overtime pay at the employee level, the supervisory position may offer little if any pay increase. Because managers place a high value on opportunity, achievement, managerial status, and a salaried position, they may be unable to understand why the promotion to supervisor would not be welcomed in spite of the pay. The employee, in contrast, may be placing maximum value on the security enjoyed as a union member and the friendship and support of fellow workers.

Exchanging this status for the unfamiliar, high-risk supervisory position may be perceived as unacceptable unless a substantial pay raise is involved.

COERCIVE MOTIVATION

Thesis: The use of coercion as a motivational style is generally unproductive. It debases and demotivates the employee and creates unnecessary problems for management. On the other hand, some degree of fear motivation is always present in healthy individuals as a defense against the temptation to behave inappropriately when other potential motivators are ineffective. Thus, fear motivation is not all bad.

Classical organization theory resulted in a style of management that relied heavily on coercion or the fear of sanctions for motivating employees; this approach is still very much alive although it is increasingly ineffective. It has serious shortcomings, the most obvious of which is the fact that no one likes to be on the receiving end of the relationship. To the extent that a manager is able to get compliance with an order by threatening a subordinate, coercive motivation has been successful, but in a deeper sense it may have failed.

Problems with Fear Motivation

The subordinate who complies because of fear resents the tactic. Especially if coercion is the supervisor's typical motivational style, the subordinate is likely to build up hostility and express it in hidden ways which are seriously damaging to the organization and the supervisor. Resentment may be expressed in the form of marginal productivity or behavior designed to arouse the resentment and hostility of other employees. Unhealthy as these actions are, they may not be as serious as the resulting absence of positive attitudes and behavior. Where coercive motivation is extensively applied, initiative, loyalty, and creative problem solving are greatly diminished. The organizational environment may be rich in other potential motivators, but fear and its resulting hostility reduce their effectiveness.

When Fear Is Healthy

The point has been made elsewhere that a given behavior, especially a complex behavior such as sustaining a high level of productivity, is seldom the result of a single motive. Fear probably operates as one of these motives for most employees in most organizations. To suggest that there may be some positive value in fear motivation is not inconsistent with the proposition that using coercion as a motivational style is undesirable.

Confident, self-actualizing individuals are not devoid of all fear. In fact, strange as it may seem, even highly successful managers are often characterized by a fear of failure. They are not basically fearful people; they are not dominated or debilitated by fear. Rather, they tend to have a fear of failure because they constantly accept challenges that tax their abilities to the utmost degree. Successful managers recognize the risks involved in the kind of behavior required of them and know that there is always a possibility of failure. The fear is a warning signal and a defense against carelessness in a dangerous environment. In general, such fear is healthy, similar to fear of crossing a busy intersection before the light changes. It often reflects an awareness of real danger and provides a healthy motivation for avoiding unnecessary risk taking.

Realists know that in the best managed, most positively motivated organizations there are some danger areas. These should not be so numerous that one fears to enter confidently and take the bold action sometimes necessary to perform effectively. Still, there are some pitfalls into which a prudent person should not step. So long as there are activities in which an employee may engage that lead to failure or for which disciplinary action may be taken, there is a realistic basis for fear motivation. Granted that the ideal motivation for an employee to refrain from stealing company property is conscience or an identification with and respect for the organization, if it must be a fear of punishment that controls the employee's behavior, then fear has served a useful purpose for both the organization and the potential offender.

Fear as a motivational force may produce either positive or negative results. It is never absent as a potential motivator, but ideally it comes into play only as a last resort when positive forms of motivation have failed.

MONEY AS A MOTIVATOR[2]

Thesis: Money is a symbol that represents different things to different people. Because of this and other factors, some people will be more highly motivated than others to work for money, but for practically every employee, making money is one motive for working. Usually it is an important one.

Some researchers have failed to make the important distinction between motivation to work for money and motivation to work harder in order to earn more money. Others have arrived at the indefensible conclusion that money either is not a motivator or is not an important motivator, and still others have proceeded with little apparent recognition of the fact that money is often just one of many motives that interact in a complex way to produce a given behavior. If money had the same meaning to everyone, it would be easy to draw generalizations about it; but, because of its different symbolic meanings and its almost unlimited potential as a medium of exchange, the conditions under which it motivates vary greatly.

---

[2] The most comprehensive treatment of money as a motivator may be found in Edward E. Lawler, III, *Pay and Organizational Effectiveness: A Psychological View* (New York: McGraw-Hill, Inc., 1971).

The Meaning of Money

For the very poor, money symbolizes immediate satisfaction of the basic needs for food, health care, clothing, and shelter; but most employed Americans do not function at this level, and for them the symbolism becomes more complex. At higher economic levels money may symbolize security, status, power, or prestige; or it may serve to point up the fact that a person is a winner in a tricky and complicated game of business. For some it is a criterion of value or worth. More than we may wish to admit, the statement that a person is worth a million dollars may reflect the depth to which materialism is a part of our basic value system. In fact, money may psychologically be a god, one's supreme value and highest good. Its reward strength necessarily relates to its unique meanings for a given individual.

Changes in the Need for Money

Those who belittle the potential of money to motivate sometimes point to the fact that most employed persons in this country have their basic needs met reasonably well and thus the motivational value of money is reduced or nonexistent. Although there is a grain of truth to be found in this idea, it overlooks the fact that the reason these needs are satisfied is precisely because people are motivated to work and earn money which can in turn be used as a medium of exchange.

Although the motivational value of money may change after a person's basic needs have been reasonably well satisfied, human beings have a way of continually redefining their needs. At one point in time, satisfying the need for food is viewed as having the staples needed to avoid hunger. At another time, it means being able to buy a balanced diet of precooked foods and high-protein beef. Still later it may mean the ability to afford frequent dining out in expensive restaurants. The necessities of dental care change imperceptibly from the ability to get an aching tooth filled to being able to afford an orthodontist. Even after the necessities of life are satisfied, money will continue to motivate an individual in whose thinking money is linked with the acquisition of such qualities as power, recognition, prestige, belonging, and love. Such linkages are easily formed in our culture.

Whether money will motivate is to some degree a matter of the amount of money involved and the amount an individual is already earning. Generally speaking, the more people earn, the more they must receive to be motivated to work harder or longer. For example, the clerk who earns $7,000 a year may be motivated by the prospect of earning an 8 percent raise, a total of $560. To an executive who is earning $70,000 such a prospect would be considered an insult. A comparable percentage increase would be more acceptable, although many top executives require a pay increase of 25 to 30 percent as an inducement to change companies.

Money often ceases to motivate because an individual has reached a *comfort level.* Admittedly, inflation, media advertising, and built-in product obsolescence make this an unlikely prospect for most people who work for a living, but such people do exist. Reaching a comfort level is typically the choice to live within one's income by controlling wants and spending in order to gain a degree of independence and freedom. This may be the response of a mature and productive employee. It need not be associated with an individual whose living and work standards are low.

Needs in Conflict

One of the important determinants of whether money will motivate is the price one must pay to earn it. This is not simply a matter of the fatigue and effort involved. An even more serious consideration is the prospect of a conflict between modes of need satisfaction. The employee who is paid on a piecework basis must weigh carefully whether the needs satisfied with increased earnings will offset being rejected by peers as a rate-buster. Even if the financial payoff is sufficient to make the sacrifice of peer support worthwhile, an internal conflict that partially neutralizes the motivational impact of money is created within the worker.

At times value conflicts reduce the attractiveness of money. For example, a salesperson may refuse to misrepresent a product, or a certified public accountant may sacrifice a client rather than compromise principles. In another case, making more money conflicts with health needs. Some employees refuse to take certain accident risks or to continue working under intense pressures when ulcers are obviously developing. The behavior required to earn more may also conflict with a need for love and self-respect when, for example, continual travel disrupts family life. In other situations, increased effort simply interferes with leisure-time activities, and the employee's response is to reject overtime work or a promotion into management.

A Symbol of Success

For top executives the motivational value of money often lies primarily in its ability to symbolize success. For executives who have acquired personal wealth through stock options and private investments, for example, even a substantial raise may have little practical effect except to increase income taxes. Yet, under these circumstances, a raise does communicate appreciation for continuing peak performance. Failure to receive a raise, especially if executives in a comparable position get one, may subjectively be viewed as a pay cut. Under such conditions, money may very well fit Herzberg's description of a dissatisfier in which a raise does not motivate increased effort, but failure to get it causes dissatisfaction. On the other hand, if raises contribute to sustained optimal effort, it can hardly be said that money has no motivational impact.

The Probability of a Payoff

Money will motivate increased effort only if employees believe that working harder or producing more will result in more money. Unfortunately many compensation systems reward performance and nonperformance equally. The typical end-of-year bonus, in particular, is notably unrelated to behavior in the minds of those who receive it.

Money motivates best when it is received immediately after the behavior it purports to reward. For example, one manager of direct sales representatives in Colombia, South America, pays the representatives at the close of every day just to make sure they see clearly the relationship between behavior and reward. The practice would not be feasible today, but there was a time when, as a means of keeping motivation high for work that was both difficult and boring, sewing machine operators were paid in coin when each bundle of garments was turned in. General Radio, one of the oldest electronics companies in the United States, is unique in that it varies the monthly compensation and short-term bonuses of many of its salaried personnel in an attempt to increase the motivational value of money.[3]

COMPETITION

Thesis: Because the performance of others provides employees with a meaningful barometer of success where more objective measurements are lacking, spontaneous competition between employees is one of the important motivational forces within organizations. Competition which is deliberately promoted by management may be effective under certain circumstances, but it should be used with caution and combined with other forms of motivation which are less likely to be viewed as manipulative and cause destructive conflict.

In a capitalistic, private enterprise system, competition is by definition national policy. In the United States, antitrust laws have been passed to preserve competition on the assumption that competition among companies is in the public interest. Under competition, managers are highly motivated to produce better products and services at the lowest possible cost to the consumer. Anyone who has experienced or studied the abuses of power under monopoly has little difficulty in accepting the idea that competition is good. Yet it is easy to see that competition leaves behind it a continuous line of casualities. When marginal and inefficient companies fail, their owners and employees are hurt, sometimes seriously. Another problem of competition among organizations is that it leads to monopoly unless it is carefully regulated. Competition within organizations has comparable advantages and disadvantages.

The Nature of Competition

The urge to compete is by no means universal although it is highly promoted in our culture. It is a secondary need, a learned means of satisfying more basic needs. Since all kinds of games reward the winner, most children learn to enjoy

---

[3] David A. Weeks, "A Fluctuating Paycheck for Managers," *The Conference Board Record* (April, 1968).

competition, and this enjoyment continues into adulthood. Obviously some people who are fierce competitors in athletics or street-fighting avoid academic competition and vice versa. We learn to compete in areas where we are most likely to succeed and it is, therefore, not surprising that some people learn not to compete at all.[4]

Competition always exists as a motivator within organizations. Where one potential job opening exists and there are several contenders, it is inevitable that a certain degree of competition will develop. Motivation to compete, like money motivation, has many facets and offers many forms of potential need satisfaction. In competing for a promotion, an obvious dimension of the competitive urge is the lure of money, power, and prestige. Competition gives many people a sense of goal directedness that both increases achievement and provides a satisfying sense of purpose. There is also a game aspect to competition within and among organizations. Playing the game is fun, and the prospect of winning reduces boredom and makes fatigue more acceptable. This effect is easily observed in the willingness of athletes to exert extreme effort and often to endure pain in order to win.

Successfully competing with worthy opponents is ego-enhancing. It contributes to a sense of self-worth, and most of us learn early in life not to be seriously hurt if we invest heavily in winning and then lose. In many situations it is all but impossible to find acceptable measurements for performance other than comparison with other people; and for persons who perceive themselves to be outstanding performers being rated high within a respected peer group may provide a better norm than would an absolute standard.

For the great mass of average performers in any area, who perceive themselves to be as good as the next fellow, the desire to avoid being classified at the bottom rung of the ladder may also provide a degree of competitive motivation. Competition does not always involve a drive to be number one. The level to which one aspires depends upon past experience and upon what one has learned to perceive as realistic in relation to other people.

Competition within Work Groups

A distinction should be made between the more or less spontaneous, natural competition that develops in a work environment and competition promoted by management. Attempts to stimulate competition as a means of increasing productivity are usually unsuccessful among blue-collar workers and white-collar workers who are on relatively routine jobs (such as office clerks, key punch operators, and members of a stenographic pool). Employees who too obviously demonstrate their superiority and desire to win the favor of superiors are rejected by their peers and pressured to behave in ways that will not make their fellow employees appear mediocre by comparison.

---

[4] A few subcultures do as much to discourage competition as we do to promote it. Among the Zuni, Hopi, and Arapesh Indians, a strong anticompetition, procooperation sentiment prevents the development of a strong desire to compete in any area.

Attempts to stimulate competition among employees (as contrasted to line or staff management) are challenged by two limitations within the work environment. The first, described in Chapter 1, involves the fact that abilities are typically distributed throughout the work group in such a way that most employees are just average. This means that the few whose outstanding abilities enable them to stand head-and-shoulders above the others under competitive conditions can be successfully discouraged from competing by the other group members.

The second limitation on competition is inherent in the fact that in many situations employees are rewarded for seniority rather than merit. Under such circumstances competition serves a useful purpose only for management. Employees will not ordinarily compete just to please management, especially when doing so has negative consequences in terms of peer rejection and punishment.

Competition among Salespeople

Sales managers have learned to be relatively successful with competition motivation, mainly for two reasons. First of all, they tend to recruit people who are likely to have competitive natures—people who have learned to satisfy their needs through competition. Secondly—and this is why it is appropriate to recruit competitive people—the sales situation can usually be structured to provide an opportunity for individuals to be directly rewarded for their effort and ingenuity. Most sales contests are set up so that everybody can win. The salesperson who loses a contest but earns increased commissions is not left with the feeling of having been manipulated into working only for the good of the company.

However, competition among salespeople often has negative side effects. Salespeople sometimes promote low-profit but easy-to-sell items, lie to and exert undue pressure on customers to buy unneeded merchandise, and otherwise engage in behavior that may hurt long-term sales. In the heat of a sales contest they may also engage in behavior that undermines the success of a competing salesperson (stealing leads, for example) or increases sales at the expense of the organization (for example, by excessive price cutting or orally committing the company to perform unusual warranty services).

Although people outside the sales field are often critical of techniques used to increase competition (such as offering a $500 gift certificate to a salesman's wife if he meets his quota) some rather unusual methods are accepted, and even welcomed, by commissioned salespeople. They know from experience how difficult it is to stay motivated when prospective customers are saying no. Contests generate enthusiasm and excitement because they are associated with high sales. When properly conducted, they increase commissions, decrease boredom, and, for the winners, add a material bonus along with status and prestige.

Competition among Managers

Highly competitive managers, like salespeople, are not beyond putting their own interests above the organizations they purport to represent. They sometimes withhold information in order to make a competing manager look bad, even when the competitor is an immediate superior. They may start unflattering rumors or otherwise behave in ways designed to destroy competitors rather than defeat them in fair competition.

An organization cannot function efficiently when its resources are wasted on internal conflict, and the inevitable competition among managers often results in undesirable conflict along with the very valuable motivational contribution it makes. One of the important functions of a manager is to serve as a mediator between competing subordinate managers. Managers must prevent competition among subordinates from becoming destructive, and they must also guard against the possibility that destructive competition will be rewarded within the organization. The objective is not to eliminate competition among managers, but to keep it within reasonable limits and to make sure it does not prevent competitors from cooperating to achieve organizational goals.

Competition Between Groups

Some of the destructiveness of competition among people is diminished when competition is switched from individuals to groups. It is commonly observed that when one work group accepts the challenge of beating another, group cohesiveness and cooperation, as well as motivation, increase. Often the advantages of intragroup cooperation offset any disadvantages that might result from intergroup competition.

Between-group competition is most effective when it arises, or appears to arise, spontaneously. A manager may create conditions that will lead to competition, by posting group production records, for example, but caution must be exercised in overtly encouraging competition. If a manager's behavior is viewed as an attempt to get something for nothing, it may backfire and significantly decrease motivation.

EXPECTANCY MODELS OF MOTIVATION

Thesis: At the present time, there is no motivation model which effectively combines our existing knowledge into a comprehensive motivation theory. Expectancy models are no exception, but they do provide the most promising framework yet developed for evolving such a theory.

Expectancy theory[5] is typically associated with the work of Vroom[6] and Porter and Lawler,[7] although the basic theory was developed in the 1930s,

---

[5] *Expectancy theory* is also called cognitive expectancy theory, instrumentality theory, and valence-instrumentality-expectancy theory (VIE). Expectancy theory is a general term and the one least likely to represent the thoughts of a particular researcher.

[6] V. H. Vroom, *Work and Motivation* (New York: John Wiley & Sons, Inc., 1964).

[7] L. W. Porter and E. E. Lawler, III, *Managerial Attitudes and Performance* (Homewood, Ill.: Dorsey-Irwin, 1968).

primarily by psychologists E. C. Tolman and Kurt Lewin. More recently, an integrative hybrid theory was proposed by Campbell and his associates.[8] Although the latter was not intended as a formal theory, it represents a much needed elaboration of earlier expectancy theory.

Valence

In expectancy theory, *valence* refers to the value a person places on a particular *outcome* (consequence of an action). For example, an employee may visualize a promotion as the likely outcome of outstanding performance on the job. Valence for the promotion would be high for a person with a strong desire for the promotion, neutral for a person who is indifferent about it, and negative for a person who is repelled by it.

Depending upon the strength and direction of one's preference for an outcome, valence varies from -1.00 to $+1.00$ as shown in Figure 6–2. Common sense suggests that the higher the valence of an outcome the stronger a person will be motivated to obtain it. Theoretically a minus valence of a certain size is as motivational as a comparable positive valence. For example, a desire to avoid getting fired expressed by a valence of $-.90$ would supposedly have the same motivational force as a desire for a raise with a positive valence of the same size ($V = +.90$). There are, however, some long-range side effects of outcomes which have a negative valence (the use of threats and intimidation, for example) that make their motivational impact different from that of positive outcomes. A strong threat of getting fired may motivate a manager to work more diligently, but resentment because of the threat may later have an unpredictable motivational impact. Inability to account for such variables may be a weakness in expectancy theory.

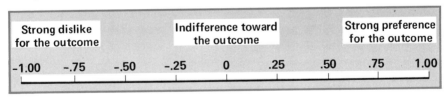

Strong dislike for the outcome			Indifference toward the outcome			Strong preference for the outcome		
-1.00	-.75	-.50	-.25	0	.25	.50	.75	1.00

Figure 6–2 The Range within Which Valence May Vary

Expectancy

Expectancy refers to a person's judgment of the likelihood that a specific outcome will follow a specific course of action. For example, an expectancy could express an employee's judgment that a pay raise will be the outcome of increased productivity. Expectancy is a subjective probability estimate which may vary from highly realistic to totally unrealistic. Regardless of whether it is objectively

[8] John P. Campbell et al., *Managerial Behavior, Performance, and Effectiveness* (New York: McGraw-Hill, Inc., 1970).

valid, expectancy is a major determinant of whether an incentive, such as the prospect of a raise or promotion, will motivate a given individual.

Since expectancy is a probability estimate, it ranges from zero, total disbelief that a specific outcome will result from a course of action, to 1.00, absolute belief that the specific outcome will result from the action. Let us say that in private conversation, company president, Gary Jones, tells accountant, Carolyn Watson, "If you will go back to night school and get your MBA, your chances of becoming financial vice-president are excellent." Consider the probable motivational impact of this statement under the following conditions:

1. Watson thinks: Jones has never kept his promise yet. Why should he do so this time? Here expectancy is somewhere near zero.

2. Watson is intrigued with the prospect: He hasn't guaranteed that I will get the job, but I believe I have a fair chance of getting it. Expectancy is equal to about .50.

3. As Watson interprets Jones's statement, if she earns the degree, the promotion is assured: Jones would never make such a statement just to motivate me to finish my MBA. If I get the degree, the job is mine. (E = .99)

Motivational Force

High valence or high expectancy alone will not motivate. In the example just presented, Watson would not be motivated by the lure of the promotion, even under the third set of conditions (E = .99), if it were not attractive to her. On the other hand, regardless of how much she wanted the promotion (even if V = 1.00), her motivation to finish the degree in order to get it would be nil if she perceived that she had no chance of getting it (E = 0).

Because both high expectancy and high valence are necessary for motivation, the expectancy model may be expressed as follows:

$$\text{Motivational Force (MF)} = \text{Expectancy (E)} \times \text{Valence (V)}$$

Thus, when either expectancy or valence has a zero value, the motivational force of the outcome is also zero. If both E and V = 1.00, MF also would be +1.00. The range of values from 0 to 1.00 (or 0 to −1.00 where the motivation is to avoid the outcome) represents intermediate degrees of motivation. In solving a motivational problem or deciding upon a motivational strategy, we obviously do not have specific Expectancy and Valence figures to work with, but the model provides a valuable framework within which to conceptualize the variables involved.

A Hybrid Expectancy Model

John P. Campbell and his associates made a significant contribution to expectancy theory by expanding the model.[9] They pointed out that a series of

[9] Ibid., p. 381.

expectancies, or subjective probability estimates, determine the motivational force of an outcome. In developing the probability estimate of an outcome following an action (for example, increased pay following the solution of a complex problem), perceptions of the task and one's own abilities are critical.

On the basis of these perceptions, a person makes a probability estimate about whether the task can be completed. This is followed by other expectancies concerning (1) the likelihood that the reward will be forthcoming if the task is completed and (2) the likelihood that, if received, the reward will satisfy personal needs (for example, that more money will make one more secure, will bring increased pleasure, or result in another form of psychological payoff). Such variables complicate expectancy theory, but it is a realistic complication.

The hybrid expectancy model makes a meaningful distinction between a *first-level outcome,* an external reward such as money, promotion, or recognition, and a *second-level outcome* which is the satisfaction of inner needs, or lack of it, toward which the first-level outcomes are purportedly directed. An employee may have a strong expectancy $(E = .90)$ that a certain high level of performance will result in a promotion (first-level outcome). If, however, the promotion is perceived primarily as leading to loss of friends and a high level of personal frustration rather than to self-esteem and a sense of achievement, it will not be a strong motivator. This will especially be true if the valence of achievement is

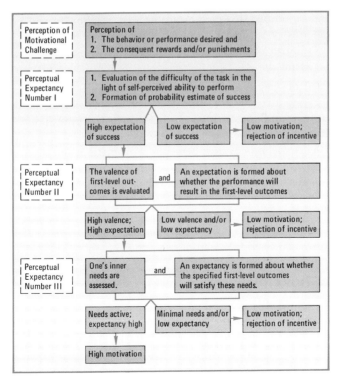

Figure 6–3   An Expectancy Model of Motivation

low (the employee places a low value on it) and the valence of friendships is high (friendships are highly valued). This distinction between internal and external goals and rewards helps to objectify many of the motivational conflicts within the individual.

Figure 6–3 presents a schematic of an expectancy model which includes the major contributions of Campbell and his associates. The term *needs* normally is not used in expectancy theory but is used here to show the relationship between expectancy and need theory.

MOTIVATION AS REINFORCEMENT

Thesis: The reinforcement approach to motivation follows the behavioristic model of ignoring what takes place within the psyche while concentrating on the process of reinforcing desirable behaviors. Often viewed by nonbehaviorists as simplistic, reinforcement theory has much to offer that is practical and theoretically sound.

Reinforcement theory (also called *contingency theory*) is an approach to understanding and modifying human behavior which is based upon reinforcement principles of learning. In its most elementary form, reinforcement refers to the positive or negative consequences (reward or punishment) which follow a behavior and determine, to some extent at least, whether it will be repeated. Reinforcement theory is closely identified with behaviorist B. F. Skinner, although a large number of other persons have been responsible for developing its principles and applications.

Reinforcement theory has much in common with the expectancy models just described. They are alike in that both stress the importance of the relationship between a behavior and its consequences (the reward or punishment which follows it). A major difference between the two lies in the fact that expectancy theory deals with such internal processes as perception, evaluation, and subjective probability, while contingency theory attempts to avoid reference to internal psychological processes and deal only with behavior. In fact, behaviorists prefer not to use the word motivation. They think instead in terms of modifying behavior. The founder of the behaviorist school of psychology, John B. Watson (1878–1958) and his modern-day followers believe that only the behavior, as contrasted to the subjective experience of people, can be scientifically studied.

Behavioral Principles

Reinforcement theory is based on a few simple principles of learning which are treated in a straightforward, noncontroversial manner in practically any introductory textbook in psychology. They have no necessary connection with philosophical behaviorism. As Perry London [10] suggests, we would do well to

---

[10] Perry London, "The End of Ideology in Behavior Modification," *American Psychologist,* Vol. 27 (1972), pp. 913–920.

separate the technology involved in working with human behavior from behaviorism as such.

The following behavioral principles form the basis for the reinforcement model of motivation.[11]

1. Reinforced behavior tends to be repeated. A reinforcer is any consequence that increases the likelihood that a specific behavior will occur in the future. (For example, when praise is the outcome, it increases the likelihood that the performance will be repeated.)

2. Reward (positive reinforcement) is more effective than punishment in motivating a person to perform in a particular way.[12] Punishment is to be avoided whenever possible.

3. An important form of reinforcement is feedback on performance. Even the simple feedback that comes from knowing a supervisor is aware of a behavior may positively reinforce it. On the other hand, when behaviors deemed to be positive are ignored, they may cease to occur.

4. For best results a reward should follow as soon as possible after the occurrence of the behavior one seeks to reinforce.

5. A clear distinction should be made between a need for training and a need for motivation (reinforcement). These two problems are often confused so that attempts to motivate fail because an employee needs training or training is unsuccessful because of weak motivation.

6. Desired performance should be clearly defined and stated. It is only when the behavioral objectives are made explicit and concrete that they can be measured and rewarded.[13]

7. Reward should be given for movement toward the desired target behavior. Rewarding so-called successive approximations provides assurance that an individual will continue to move in the right direction. Behavior modification technology often provides for graduated "schedules of reinforcement" by which people move from wherever they are (their *baseline behavior*) to target behavior.

Evaluation

It is inevitable that a behavior will be followed by consequences which will, to some extent, determine whether it will be repeated. Individuals who criticize

---

[11] For an excellent summary of the literature in this area read Craig E. Schneier, "Behavior Modification in Management: A Review and Critique," *Academy of Management Journal,* Vol. 17, No. 3 (1974), pp. 528–548.

[12] This material is intentionally presented in familiar terms. A behaviorist would not use the word *motivation* as it is used here. A thorough description of the learning principles involved in contingency theory may be found in W. Clay Hammer, "Reinforcement Theory and Contingency Management in Organizational Settings," in H. L. Tosi and W. C. Hammer, eds., *Organizational Behavior and Management: A Contingency Approach* (Chicago: St. Clair Press, 1974).

[13] For an example of behavior modification read Harry Wiard, "Why Manage Behavior: A Case for Positive Reinforcement," *Human Resources Management,* Vol. 2, No. 2 (1972) pp. 15–20. Also, "Where Skinner's Theories Work," *Business Week* (Dec. 2, 1972), pp. 64–65.

behavior modification as unjustifiable manipulation are invited to keep this in mind. Behavior theory proposes that it is better to analyze and control the consequences of a behavior than to leave them to chance. Making the consequences known is not manipulative. To the contrary, it provides the employee with an optimal opportunity to make deliberate choices between explicitly defined alternatives.

Managers often behave like a mother who encourages her son to have tantrums by showing him an excessive amount of attention when such behavior occurs (conceivably the most rewarding gift she could offer) and by occasionally or frequently giving in to his demands. The everyday, unplanned patterns of reinforcement, which are as common in organizations as in parent-child relationships, are expressed in the example of managers who were unable to motivate their subordinates to turn in their reports on time. The managers needed the reports on the 15th of the month in order to have their own reports prepared by the 20th. When bribes, scolding, reasoning, and threatening failed to work, the consequences of turning in reports (1) late and (2) on time were analyzed. They found that they had been punishing subordinates who were on time by sending reports back for corrections and additions. Subordinates who turned their reports in on time were never rewarded because they were perceived as doing only what they were paid for and expected to do.

The reinforcement model of motivation takes many forms and has much to offer a manager who is concerned with understanding and, to some degree, controlling behavior. People with a bias against philosophical behaviorism would do well to lay aside any feelings which might prevent their taking advantage of the potential contributions of reinforcement motivation theory. The point cannot be made too strongly that we do in fact continually reinforce behavior. What could be more intelligent than understanding and rationally controlling the reinforcement processes within an organization?

HOW TO ANALYZE A MOTIVATION PROBLEM

Thesis: One of the major problems in analyzing a motivational problem is understanding the many variables within the individuals involved. A practical alternative is to deal with the problem as behaviorally as possible, emphasizing primarily the consequences of behaviors and how they can be altered in order to positively reinforce desired behaviors.

A *motivation problem* exists within an organization when there is a discrepancy between expected and achieved results and when the discrepancy is due to lack of effort rather than to lack of ability or opportunity. For example, the motivational problem may be expressed in terms of the failure of employees to obey a specific safety rule (smoking in a restricted area only), failure to perform certain supervisory practices (handling disciplinary problems in private), or failure to follow a procedure (checking a customer's credit balance before every shipment). A *performance problem* exists any time an employee's behavior falls short of expectations, but such a problem may not be caused by low motivation. The determination of whether nonperformance results from low motivation is a matter of rejecting at least four other possible causes of the substandard behavior.

1. *A problem of communication.* In this case failure to perform is caused by the employee's misperception of what is expected.

2. *A problem of ability.* The person in question lacks the physical or mental ability to perform according to expectations and is therefore untrainable.

3. *A problem of training.* In this case performance would be inadequate regardless of motivational level until training occurs.

4. *A problem of opportunity.* The employee knows what to do and how to do it but is held back by environmental conditions (for example, inadequate tools, obsolete methods, being paced by the performance of others or by market conditions).

Once it has been established that the problem is due to low motivation, further analysis is called for. We begin with the simple proposition that the substandard behavior persists because it is more rewarding than any alternative behavior currently available to the individual in question. From management's point of view, it may seem totally irrational for the employee to persist in a behavior which is in direct opposition to the preferences of management. It should be noted, however, that understanding motives requires that we get into the other person's shoes and see a situation from that unique vantage point. What is rational to a manager may not appear rational to a subordinate because the two are viewing the facts through entirely different prisms.

Guidelines for Analysis

A convenient way to analyze the motivation for a particular behavior is to examine its consequences, insofar as possible, from the viewpoint of the person whose behavior we are studying. A format for visualizing the problem is presented in Figure 6–4, but first let us take a look at some of the basic principles or guidelines to be used in our motivation analysis. Since each of these has been considered in some detail elsewhere, little additional detail is presented here.

1. One principle involved in analyzing a motivation problem is that rewarded behaviors tend to be repeated and behaviors that are not rewarded (or that are punished) are not repeated.

2. For a factor (such as the work itself, pay, praise, or a promotion) to serve as a motivator, the individual we hope to motivate must *believe* it will satisfy an active need. The higher the subjective probability of each of the following, the greater the likelihood that a factor will be a motivator: (a) That the expected performance standard can be reached

(b) That the hoped-for reward will be forthcoming
(c) That the reward will satisfy an active need

RELATIVELY LOW MOTIVA-TIONAL VALUE	BALANCE OF CONSEQUENCES TABLE*		RELATIVELY HIGH MOTIVA-TIONAL VALUE
	Effect of the Consequences		
O	Organizational	Personal	P
	Timing of the Consequences		
D	Delayed	Immediate	I
	Probability of the Consequences		
G	Gamble	Certain	C
	Perceived Importance of the Consequences		
1	1 (low) through 5 (high)		5
	A. Foremen Enforce the Rules		
	Possible Positive Consequences		
D-G	Recognition by management		P 3
D-G	Receiving a promotion or raise		P 3
O-D-G-2	Increased productivity		
O-D-G	Improvement in accident rate		4
	Possible Negative Consequences		
	Conflict with subordinates		P-I-C-5
	An increase in work load		P-I-C-5
O	Increased trouble with the union		P-I-C-5
O- G-2	Decreased productivity		I
O- G-2	Reduction in quality of product		I
	Increase in peer pressure		P-I-C-5
	B. Foremen Do Not Enforce the Rules		
	Possible Positive Consequences		
	Good relations with workers		P-I-C-5
	Comfortable work load		P-I-C-5
	No difficulty with peers		P-I-C-5
	Possible Negative Consequences		
-2	Pressure from higher management		P-I-C
O-D-G-1	High dollar cost to the company		
O-D-G	Less than optimal accident rate		4

*Sources: The basic idea for this table came from the lecture and discussion content of a University of Michigan seminar in "The Management of Behavior Change," James V. McConnell, senior seminar leader. The perceived importance of the consequences factor is an expression of one dimension of cognitive expectancy theory.

Figure 6–4   Balance of Consequences Table

3. Generally speaking, rewarding desirable behavior is a more effective motivator of high performance than punishing undesirable behavior.

4. A given behavior (whether it is good or bad) is more strongly reinforced when the reward or punishment follows *immediately* than when it is *delayed.*

5. The motivational value of a promised—or anticipated—reward or punishment is higher when it is *certain* to occur than when its occurrence is subjectively viewed as a *gamble.*

6. The motivational value of a reward or punishment is higher when it affects the individual *personally* than when it has an effect only on the *organization* of which the individual is a part. For example, a quality control inspector who must personally assume responsibility for a returned product will be more highly motivated to avoid the shipment of defective merchandise than will the inspector who knows the defective merchandise will merely be traced back to the quality control department.

7. Motivation to perform in a specified manner will be higher when the standard in question has been internalized than when the individual is only being extrinsically rewarded.

A Motivation Problem

Let us look now at a typical problem in management behavior and formally analyze it from a motivational viewpoint. Consider the case of a general superintendent of an automobile parts remanufacturer who had a problem getting his foremen to enforce the work rules. For example, workers were allowed to use the grinder without wearing their goggles; one worker punched the time clock for another who left work early; and, contrary to company policy, frequent personal calls were made on company telephones during working hours. The foremen knew the rules and had the authority and interpersonal skills needed to enforce them. They knew what they should do, but they were not motivated to do it.

After proceeding through the steps to determine that the problem was one of motivation rather than communication, ability, training, or opportunity, the analysis began by seeking the answers to seven strategic questions.

1. Have the expected performance standards been internalized? If not, why not? The apparent answer to this question was no. In this particular case the reason seemed to lie in the fact that the organization had a history of (1) always making rules and never modifying or discarding them when they became obsolete and (2) not enforcing the rules once they were made. This tended to communicate the idea that rules were relatively unimportant. The president and other top officials set the pace for this lax behavior.

2. What are the positive and negative consequences of enforcing the rules? (In what ways is the desired behavior rewarded and punished?) The

answers to this and the following four questions are expressed in the Balance of Consequences Table presented in Figure 6–4.

3. What are the positive and negative consequences of not enforcing the rules? (In what ways is the undesirable behavior rewarded and punished?)

4. Is each of the positive and negative consequences perceived as having *personal* application or as merely having beneficial or harmful effects on the *organization* (P or O)?

5. Is each of the positive and negative consequences of enforcing and not enforcing the rules perceived (by the foremen whose behavior we want to change) as being *immediate* or *delayed* (I or D)?

6. How important is each of the positive or negative consequences as a need satisfier to this specific group of foremen? This is expressed on the Balance of Consequences Table on a scale of *one* (of little importance) to *five* (of great importance insofar as the analyst is able to determine).

7. Is each of the positive and negative consequences perceived as being *certain* to occur or, to some degree, a *gamble* (C or G)?

The judgments expressed in the Balance of Consequences Table are valid and useful only to the extent that they represent the point of view and subjective probability estimates of the foremen whose motives are being analyzed. Assuming the investigation has been objective, so that the judgments do in fact represent the foremen's viewpoint, let us take a look at what the data mean.

The foremen perceive their present behavior to be more rewarding than the behavior their superiors prefer. Notice, in particular, that the perceived negative consequences of enforcing the rules are highly motivational (four of the six consequences are rated P-I-C-5, personal-immediate-certain-highly important), while the perceived negative consequences are not (all consequences are perceived as being delayed and a gamble). On the other hand, note that the positive consequences of not enforcing the rules, compared with the positive consequences of enforcement, strongly indicate that nonenforcement is more rewarding. (All three consequences of not enforcing the rules are rated P-I-C-5, which indicates the highest possible motivation.)

The foremen do place a high value on promotions and raises (shown by the rating of P, personal, and 5 in importance in the right-hand column beside these factors), but the motivational value of the factor is minimal because a promotion or raise would not be received immediately and might not be received at all (as indicated by the D-G, delayed-gamble, in the left-hand column). In other words one foreman is saying,

> I would very much like to have a raise or promotion, but the probability that the enforcement of the work rules will lead to either is quite low. And even if I should get either a raise or a promotion in exchange for my cooperation, it would be so long in coming that I really can't get excited about it.

This illustrates a point made in the discussion of expectancy theory; namely that when either element in the equation (Motivation = Expectancy $\times$ Valence) is low, motivation will be low. The prospect of winning a million dollars in a lottery would be extremely motivational to some people, but not to the person who thinks that the probability of winning it is nil.

When we look at the negative consequences of nonenforcement, it becomes obvious that the foremen know they will receive pressure from their superiors (the P-I-C in the right-hand column), but they are not greatly disturbed about it (the 2 rating on importance in the left-hand column). The foremen obviously do not think that they will be seriously hurt by any punitive action management might take. On the other hand, they would be deeply concerned by what they believe to be the certain and negative consequences of enforcing the rules (indicated by the four P-I-C-5 ratings given to such factors as conflict with subordinates and an increase in work load).

Once an accurate analysis has been made, motivating the desired behavior is essentially a matter of altering the consequences. In the case just presented, several steps may be taken. First of all, a committee of foremen might be established to work with personnel specialists in revising the rules to make sure all are relevant and accepted as such by the foremen. The foremen would then be informed of the importance of enforcement and the changed policy of top management in this regard. Since all foremen and workers are made aware of what is taking place and the seriousness with which the move is being taken by management, group pressures can be made to work for, rather than against, enforcement; and to the extent that hostility results from the enforcement, top management, rather than the foremen, can be the major recipient. "Rules enforcement" may be added to the semiannual foreman performance appraisal scale as a means of stressing the fact that enforcement is more rewarding than nonenforcement. As a last resort, one or more foremen who refuse to cooperate can be suspended or discharged. These actions will tip the balance of consequences in the direction of compliance.

This type of analysis has many applications in spite of its lack of quantitative preciseness. The alternative to such a model is typically a fuzzy type of thinking that fails to take into consideration many important variables. Although some important dimensions of motivation are omitted or incompletely dealt with here, it is, at least, a start in the direction of scientifically analyzing a motivation problem. It capitalizes on an important principle used in decision theory; namely, that complex decisions are often improved by breaking them down into a large number of bite-sized pieces and then combining those pieces in the process of arriving at a final conclusion.

MOTIVATIONAL CONSTRAINTS

Thesis: Motivating subordinates to produce at acceptably high levels, one of a supervisor's major concerns, is often blocked by organizational constraints that require lock-step behavior. Procedures, controls, and technology which are intended to optimize productivity often destroy a supervisor's potential for motivating subordinates to perform above the lowest acceptable level.

One of the most obvious motivational constraints results from the necessity for making personnel decisions on the basis of seniority. If workers with the capacity for outstanding productivity know that seniority rather than merit will be the sole criterion of promotions, their motivation for peak production may be undermined. The same can be said for situations in which raises are based on negotiated contracts or length of service, rather than performance. Treating unequal people as though they were equal tends to motivate everyone to perform at as nearly the same level as possible, and often this is the lowest acceptable level.

In many work environments productivity is determined more by the technology involved than by the employees who apply it. An operator whose main duty is to monitor instruments for deviations from standards in the production of petroleum products may have little to do with the rate of productivity and may work at or near capacity only when a breakdown occurs. Assembly-line workers are often paced by a conveyor belt and the productivity of others on the line. An office worker who performs at a level that permits completion of specific tasks within a specified time may have nothing to do once the tasks are finished. In situations such as these, conditions outside the individual worker are the controlling elements in productivity. In such cases, attempts to increase productivity are more apt to be made by engineers and job analysts than by managers, and a manager's role as a motivator may only be to keep workers on the job, cooperative, and willing to apply the minimal effort required of them.

In some large business and government organizations, motivation for excellence is squelched by the effect of an inordinate number of guidelines, policies, rules, and regulations that define both what is to be done and how. The concept of outstanding performance implies that individuals have some degree of autonomy and freedom to choose between alternatives. In the absence of such freedom, employee motivation consists mostly of willingness to conform.

In situations where technology and organizational controls are the primary determinants of productivity, an acceptable level of performance is often maintained even when motivation to perform is low and attitudes toward the organization are negative. In a sense, the structured environment provides an alternative to employee motivation. Experience has shown that large numbers of persons are capable of functioning throughout a lifetime in such an environment. However, the highly structured environment has the potential both for degrading personality and exercising a stultifying effect on the organization.

STUDY AND DISCUSSION QUESTIONS

1. In what way does the practice of power bargaining detract from the motivational benefits to be received from the exchange system?
2. What are the positive and negative implications of fear motivation?

3. Why is reward generally a better motivator than punishment? Under what circumstances might punishment be better?
4. Defend this statement: It is unrealistic to believe that all fear motivation can or should be eliminated from an organization.
5. In recent years many knowledgeable persons have questioned the motivating power of money. Why do you think this is so? What do you think of such a position?
6. Under what conditions do you think money would motivate a highly paid executive to work harder?
7. Why do most people in our culture enjoy competition?
8. Under what circumstances does competition motivate best?
9. What is the major theme of expectancy models of motivation?
10. Contrast and evaluate the reinforcement and expectancy models of motivation.
11. Name some motivational constraints found in organizations.

CRITICAL INCIDENT

The Sinking Boat

When production supervisor, Davina Slivka, left the meeting with her superiors, she was dejected, frustrated, and furious. She related these events to her assistant, Helen Conrad:

> I have never had so much poor advice from three such insensitive men in all my life. Each has his own reason why production is low on the evening shift, and nobody understands our problems. Bates suggested that we should let a few heads roll. He really thinks that all we do at night is drink coffee! I wish I were back in the union. I would have told him where to go.

Mrs. Slivka was the supervisor of 45 women engaged in the production of inflatable lifeboats under a series of contracts with the Air Force and the Navy. Like most of the women on her shift, she had little work experience other than her four years with the tire manufacturer by whom she was employed. After serving as an assistant supervisor for six months, she was promoted to supervisor of the evening shift at the time it was started. That was three months before this incident occurred.

Although the manufacturing methods used on the evening shift were similar to those Mrs. Slivka was accustomed to, a different model boat was being produced, a totally new time study had been made, and 30 of the 45 employees had been hired specifically to work on the new contract. Harvey Bates, the production superintendent, insisted that unusual care be exercised in studying the piece rates in order to avoid setting them too low, which was what he thought had been done on the day shift.

Although no one on the evening shift had been able to reach the production standard and thus begin drawing a piece-rate pay, morale was high. Mrs. Slivka had been able to develop a good working relationship among the women, the base rate paid during the training period (of unspecified duration) was generally considered high relative to the going rate in that geographical area, and the employee benefits were outstanding. Perhaps, because most of the women were married and perceived themselves as providing a second income, they were not too upset at being unable to earn the unit bonus available to higher producing employees. The high production quotas were a frequent topic among the women, including Mrs. Slivka, and she felt exceedingly fortunate just to be able to keep the employees from giving up and leaving the company.

In the hope of increasing production on the evening shift one of the devices Mr. Bates employed was to post the average daily production of both shifts, using a graphic method that made the differences quite obvious. On several occasions he talked with Mrs. Slivka about her inability to increase production significantly and recommended that she get tough if necessary to get the job done. As she saw it, most of the women were conscientious, hard-working, loyal, and doing their best to get production up. Bates had one rejoinder: "The production figures indicate otherwise."

Questions

1. What motivational problems are likely to be involved in this situation?
2. What do you think is the best way to handle the situation?
3. What additional information is needed before a course of action can be recommended with confidence?

Chapter 7

Goal Setting in Organizations

An organization is created to achieve certain objectives of its founders. It exists for a purpose, and the behavior of its members must make a contribution to the fulfillment of that purpose in order to have value and meaning within the organizational context.

The individual members of an organization have their own private objectives and, understandably, view employment as a means of achieving them. As a result, the possibility always exists that the objectives of the organization will be subordinated to the diverse private interests of its members. On occasion, jobs are created, expenditures are made, and projects are undertaken which serve no major organizational purpose and have meaning only in terms of the private goals of parasitic members who feed upon the organization but do not significantly contribute to it. Because this is an ever-present danger, an organization must constantly make its objectives explicit and exert a special effort to involve its members in those objectives.[1]

This chapter purposely begins with a discussion of the benefits to be gained from goal setting since the failure of a goals program in an organization can most often be traced to the fact that its managers do not appreciate its value. From this, the chapter proceeds to deal with the practical aspects of establishing a goals program.

THE BENEFITS OF GOAL SETTING

Thesis: Goal setting may bring about significant changes in a manager's typical modes of thinking, perceiving, and behaving. The occurrence of these changes, or lack of it, accounts, in part, for the success or failure of individual managers and of an organization's goals program.

---

[1] Although the terms *objectives* and *goals* are popularly used as synonyms, writers in this field often make a distinction between the two. *Objectives* are desired outcomes, such as obtaining or retaining a dominant share of a product market. *Goals* are concrete and specific formulations of these objectives and include a completion schedule. For example, a goal may be set to increase market share by 10 percent each year for a specified time.

Managers who have for the first time begun to set goals in a systematic way differ greatly in the value they place on goal setting and in their concept of what it involves. Because they think differently, they behave differently, and, as shown in Figure 7–1, these changes are positively expressed in results. Although the organization benefits directly when its objectives are reached, it is not the only beneficiary. Each goal-directed manager also experiences personally the many tangible and intangible rewards of high achievement.

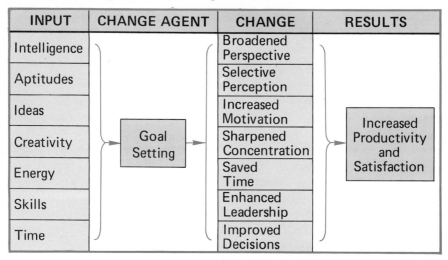

INPUT	CHANGE AGENT	CHANGE	RESULTS
Intelligence		Broadened Perspective	
Aptitudes		Selective Perception	
Ideas		Increased Motivation	Increased Productivity and Satisfaction
Creativity	Goal Setting	Sharpened Concentration	
Energy		Saved Time	
Skills		Enhanced Leadership	
Time		Improved Decisions	

Figure 7–1   The Benefits of Goal Setting

A Broadened Perspective

Managers often need help to avoid becoming so preoccupied with one aspect of the business that other important areas are neglected. This was the case in a struggling plastics company whose young president, an aggressive promoter-salesman, pushed sales to the limit while giving so little attention to finances that he sold the company into receivership. He seemed to believe that success was inevitable as long as sales continued to be strong at a price which would permit a reasonable profit. Because of inexperience in the financial area, however, the president failed to consider the enormous costs of manufacturing and shipping the company's products and the lag time between these expenditures and payment by the customers. In order to finance sales, he finally mortgaged the last of the company's assets, the accounts receivable (the presumably collectible debts of customers). A short time later the bank took over the company when one of its large, slow-paying customers went out of business.

The most serious problem in the example just stated is that the president had tunnel vision—he lacked the broad perspective needed to visualize all the important aspects of the business at one time. Goal setting encourages balanced achievement in all areas which are vital to an organization's success. It forces management to pull back from the pressures of day-to-day operations and systematically look at the different facets of current operations in terms of organizational purpose and long-term objectives.

Selective Perception

Persons with clearly defined goals are provided with a special set of filters which accents that part of the environment which contributes to goal achievement and suppresses as irrelevant much that would otherwise clutter one's consciousness. Intensely goal-oriented managers selectively perceive their environments in terms of their goal-oriented needs. For example, managers who are deeply committed to achieving a specific level of production become preoccupied with that need and continually view their environment in terms of resources for achieving their objectives. Millions of stimuli constantly compete for their attention, but only a relatively few are admitted to consciousness. These are selectively filtered through the needs and desires with which the goal-oriented managers are most preoccupied.

The manner in which selective perception enables a manager to become aware of opportunities and resources which would otherwise be hidden is seen in this statement by a first-line supervisor at General Tire and Rubber Co.:

> I had 45 operators on my shift, but not one that I was willing to promote into the inspector position until the personnel director helped me spell out exactly what kind of person I needed. Then I discovered that the one to be promoted was right under my nose. I couldn't see her good qualities because I didn't know what I was looking for, and I didn't particularly like her. She was too strong, too efficient, and too willing to sound off when everything didn't go just right. She was exactly what the inspector job called for.

Increased Motivation

The process of goal setting emphasizes the importance of investing mental and physical resources in areas that have the highest potential for a payoff. To experience the attracting force of a goal is, in effect, to anticipate the rewards inherent in reaching it. The more clearly a goal and its rewards are visualized, the greater is its motivational pull.

Sharpened Concentration

When the normally diffused attention of managers is focused on a really important goal, they tend to develop an intense concentration of thought and energy. Such concentration increases the availability of mental resources needed to think clearly and solve problems. Absentminded daydreaming is characteristic of clock-watchers; it is never characteristic of individuals who are concerned with results.

Saved Time

Goal setters waste little time in the pursuit of intriguing ideas or courses of action that lead nowhere in particular. Goal setting itself is a time-consuming process, but the time invested is rapidly recovered through the efficiency which results from focusing on ends instead of means. The constant awareness that a specific result must be achieved by a specified time and that one's contribution will be measured in terms of that result inevitably motivates an individual to view time as a uniquely valuable resource.

Enhanced Leadership

Nobody wants to follow a leader who has no sense of direction. By contrast, people feel secure in following a purposeful, goal-directed leader. Commitment to goals suggests to others that a manager is knowledgeable, competent, and likely to succeed. Achievement-oriented people find it easy to identify with an achieving, purposeful supervisor. Furthermore, an increase in goal-directedness contributes to a high degree of self-confidence, a personal attribute found in most successful managers.

Improved Decisions

Goals serve as criteria against which decisions are made and evaluated. This is illustrated in the experience of a university sophomore whose first year of studies was almost a waste of time because of her lack of direction. When, during her second year, she set a goal to earn a BBA degree as a first step toward becoming an attorney her decision processes changed abruptly. Realizing that high grades would be required to enter law school, her daily decisions for time allocation were made in the light of her ultimate career objective. The goal also influenced her decision not to pledge a time-consuming sorority and to back away from a courtship that could have led to marriage early in her educational career. Thus, her entire life-style became goal-oriented.

Goal setting, like policy formation, is itself a decision-making process. Once a decision has been made to reach a particular corporate or individual goal, many other decisions can be made by reference to it. The role of goals in decision making is seen in this statement to a superior by a thoroughly frustrated and hostile production manager:

> How can you hold me accountable for anything! I don't know from one day to the next whether I'm supposed to be expanding production capacity or closing down operations. One day I read a memo that convinces me I should lay off workers, and the next day I get the feeling that the president is going to be all over me because inventories are so low we can't fill our orders. Since I'm not sure what our objectives are, any decision I make around here is a shot in the dark.

PERSONALITY AND GOAL SETTING

Thesis: Because individual differences in goal-seeking behavior are deeply entrenched in personality, resistance to organizational goal setting can be expected in most organizations. Resistance may even be encountered in some individuals whose lives are generally goal directed but who choose to avoid the discipline and paperwork required by a formal goals program.

The role of goal setting in the development and functioning of personality first received serious attention by the renowned psychologist, Kurt Lewin, in the 1930s, and a steady stream of fruitful research and theory has continued since that time.[2]

Goal seeking begins in infancy and by adulthood has matured into a highly complex mental activity. Children who are rewarded for high achievement tend to become goal-directed adults. On the other hand, children who encounter unrealistic expectations and low anticipation of reward are early discouraged from goal setting and may develop a lifestyle almost void of conscious goal-setting activity. The personal influence of parents, teachers, and peers often combines with the impact of laws, rules, cultural expectations, and fixed schedules (school, sports, and music lessons) to externally guide an individual through school and into a career while requiring a minimum of purposive, intentional behavior. This externally directed person learns to value the lack of conflict involved in drifting with the stream and waiting to see what happens rather than risk the possibility of failure involved in setting a goal to make something happen. In many organizations, even in some managerial positions, this externally directed behavior is rewarded. In practically all organizations, people who are not goal directed thrive in positions where opportunities for initiative and autonomy are limited.

As one might expect from the vast differences which exist among people, many individuals are resistant to the goal setting involved in formal programs. Psychologist Fred Massarik notes that among persons for whom goal setting in any formal sense is anathema, or simply irrelevant, two major polarities of personality appear—the *spontaneous* and the *anomic:*

> The spontaneous, though lacking clear daily goals, face the unfolding of the day's events with immediate and intentional response, drawing, in the process, on a well-integrated repertoire of personal resources. While they make no effort to spell out what they will do *today,* they are guided by long-term, or even by lifelong, goal patterns. These provide a stabilizing general framework, leaving room for considerable

---

[2] For a varied exposure to the literature on personality and goal setting consult C. Buhler and Fred Massarik (eds.), *The Course of Human Life, a Study of Goals in the Humanistic Perspective* (New York: Springer Publishing Co., Inc., 1968); Charles L. Hughes, *Goal Setting—Key to Individual and Organizational Effectiveness* (New York: American Management Association, 1965); and David A. Kolb and Richard E. Boyatzis, "Goal-Setting and Self-Directed Behavior Change," (only) in David A. Kolb, Irwin M. Rubin, and James M. McIntyre, *Organizational Psychology—A Book of Readings* (2d ed.; Englewood Cliffs: Prentice-Hall, Inc., 1974), pp. 349–369.

freedom and improvisation in dealing with the current exigencies of living.

The anomic are, like the spontaneous, devoid of daily goals, and perhaps make no intentional responses other than those concerned with direct need satisfactions. Their repertoire of personal resources is relatively impoverished, and to them no long-term or lifelong configuration of goals is available to establish a broad context within which purposeful daily activity may plausibly occur. At the extreme, this personality structure includes the alienated and the drifter, for whom neither the day ahead nor the sweep of a lifetime has substantial meaning.[3]

Although the ranks of management are not free of goal-resistant personalities, effective managers do tend to be goal seekers. The goal-oriented manager is rewarded by opportunities for autonomy and self-direction. Among such persons success is perceived as a matter of deliberate, intentional action rather than luck. Events are perceived as occurring because of choice, not chance. The future is viewed as relatively predictable because of one's ability to learn from the past, anticipate future events, intelligently adapt to unforeseen circumstances, and overcome obstacles by force of will and rational action.

In view of the broad individual differences in goal-directedness and everyone's natural resistance to change, it is unrealistic to expect goals programs to be equally effective at all organizational levels. Although, in unusual circumstances, goals programs are effective with blue-collar employees, they have most often been successful within the ranks of management. The opportunity managers have to progress on the basis of merit and their consequent need to be responsive to the desires of their superiors are often incentives to become goal directed, even when it runs counter to deeply ingrained personality patterns. Resistance to goal setting is, however, sometimes strong and persistent among managers as well as lower level employees.

MANAGEMENT BY OBJECTIVES

Thesis: Management by objectives (MBO) is a managerial philosophy and technique which has the potential for creating self-directed behavior change and for increasing productivity. The failure of MBO in specific settings does not detract from this potential.

The work day of a typical employee is defined in terms of hours on the job rather than results achieved. From the worker's point of view, acceptable performance often means being on time for work, keeping busy, and conforming to work rules. This is a normal response to supervision which attempts to achieve productivity exclusively by means of job design, lock-step procedures, close

---

[3] Fred Massarik, "Today as an Integrating Factor," in C. Buhler and Fred Massarik, op cit., p. 396.

supervision, and other devices which divert the attention of employees from the objectives of the organization.

Definition

Management by objectives or *management by results* deemphasizes external controls and, to the greatest extent possible, focuses attention on ends rather than on means. Although the current theory and practice of management by objectives has evolved from the research, experience, and critical thought of many writers and practitioners, the contributions of three men, Peter Drucker,[4] George Odiorne,[5] and John W. Humble [6] are especially notable. Odiorne defines the MBO process in these terms:

> In brief, the system of management by objectives can be described as a process whereby superior and subordinate managers of an organization jointly identify its common goals, define each individual's major area of responsibility in terms of results expected of him, and use these measures as guides for operating the unit and assessing the contribution of each of its members.[7]

Evaluation

Since MBO programs differ greatly, there is a sense in which MBO must be understood and evaluated in terms of its application to each situation. For this reason, it is difficult to make generalizations about either its nature or effectiveness. Nevertheless, from a strictly logical point of view, the system is highly defensible. Since it allows the individual maximum discretion in determining the means by which goals will be reached, it contributes to a supervisory style that respects the subordinate and provides an opportunity for meaningful work. Performance evaluation under MBO tends to be centered on results and behavior rather than personality and is consequently less likely to involve bias and irrelevant judgments. Furthermore, on the basis of theoretical considerations alone, one would predict that under MBO results would be better than under alternative management systems.

Research to date supports the hypothesis that goal-directedness such as that expressed in MBO does, in fact, increase productivity. Kolb and Boyatzis cite several studies which support the proposition that conscious goal setting leads to increased achievement, and they conclude from their own research that goal setting for personal development also yields favorable results:

---

[4] Peter F. Drucker, *The Practice of Management* (New York: Harper and Row, Publishers, 1954).

[5] George S. Odiorne, *Management by Objectives* (New York: Pitman Publishing Corporation, 1965).

[6] John W. Humble, *Management by Objectives in Action* (U.K.: McGraw-Hill Publishing Co., Ltd., 1970).

[7] Odiorne, op. cit., pp. 55–56.

The experiment presents convincing evidence that conscious goal setting plays an important role in the process of self-directed behavior change. Individuals tend to change more in those areas of their self-concept which are related to their consciously set goals. These changes are independent of the difficulty of the change goal and thus do not appear to be a result of an initial choice of easy-to-achieve goals.[8]

Locke summarizes and integrates the research published prior to 1968 on the relationship between conscious goals and task performance citing studies which demonstrate that (1) difficult goals result in a higher level of output than easy goals, (2) specific difficult goals produce a higher level of output than a goal of "do your best," and (3) behavioral intentions regulate choice behavior.[9]

Application

The research of Latham and Baldes [10] provides an illustration of the kinds of results that have been obtained from successful MBO programs. The research was done in a single company within the logging industry, but it was a controlled follow-up on previous research with 292 Southern pulpwood producers.

The problem dealt with increasing the weight of a load of logs being transported from the woods to the mill. Because the logs vary in length and diameter, it is a matter of judgment as to how many and what type the trucker hauls in order to approximate the maximum legal limit. Data were collected on the net weight of 36 trucks over a 12-month period.

Latham and Baldes concluded that the results of this and previous research strongly support the external validity, for the logging industry, at least, of goal-setting theory. Performance improved immediately upon the assignment of a specific hard goal. (The assigned goal was 94 percent of the legal limit, as opposed to "do your best to approximate the legal limit.") The following statement attests to the practical significance of the goal-setting program:

Corporate policy prevents a detailed public discussion of the impact of this particular study on the company. However, it can be said that without the increase in efficiency due to goal setting it would have cost the company a quarter of a million dollars for the purchase of additional trucks in order to deliver the same quantity of logs to the mills. This figure does not include the cost for the additional diesel fuel that would have been consumed or the expenses for recruiting and hiring additional truck drivers.[11]

---

[8] Kolb and Boyatzis, op. cit., p. 363.

[9] Edwin A. Locke, "Toward a Theory of Task Motivation and Incentives," *Organizational Behavior and Human Performance,* Vol. 3, No. 2 (1968), pp. 157–189.

[10] Gary P. Latham, and James J. Baldes, "The Practical Significance of Locke's Theory of Goal Setting," *Journal of Applied Psychology,* Vol. 60, No. 1 (February, 1975), pp. 122–124.

[11] Ibid., p. 124.

THE NATURE OF GOALS IN ORGANIZATIONS

Thesis: Goal setting, the heart of an MBO program, has always been an important aspect of effective management, but the goal setting of MBO is more than a restatement of common practices. Goal setting is gradually becoming less an intuitive art and more a scientific methodology.

Since the very existence of an organization is an expression of purposive behavior, it follows that organizational goal setting has historically been a part of the management process. Management by objectives does, however, possess two unique characteristics which may potentially alter managerial behavior:

1. A strong emphasis on the importance of consciously formulating goals and

2. A body of information upon which a workable goals system can be developed and integrated into the organization

Managers differ greatly in goal-setting effectiveness, as do the methodologies they employ. In one sense, the evolution of MBO as a management system has been a process of capturing the diverse experiences of those managers who have been most effective in setting and reaching goals and systematizing the results for use by others. There is currently no standardized MBO terminology or methodology in spite of the fact that much literature has been published on the subject and increasing agreement is emerging on what constitutes effective MBO practice. Perhaps the most serious problem which exists for persons who attempt to integrate and systematize the available information on MBO is that the process necessarily differs with size and nature of the organization and the unique views of MBO held by the persons involved. Although each writer selects for presentation what appears to represent the most advanced state of the art, it should be understood that the content presented is always a sample of a very heterogeneous body of information.[12]

Strategic Objectives and Goals

In recent years managers have become increasingly aware of the importance of long-range corporate planning.[13] The complexities of modern business are such

[12] In addition to the references previously cited, persons interested in pursuing the subject in greater depth should find the following books helpful: Charles L. Hughes, *Goal Setting* (New York: American Management Association, 1965); Paul Mali, *Managing by Objectives* (New York: Wiley-Interscience, 1972); George S. Odiorne, *Management Decision by Objectives* (Englewood Cliffs: Prentice-Hall, Inc., 1969); Edward C. Schleh, *Management by Results* (New York: McGraw-Hill, Inc., 1969).

[13] Much has been written on corporate planning, and persons who are interested in gaining a depth understanding of MBO should become familiar with this literature. A bibliography and a concept of planning which has been applied in a large number of companies of all sizes is presented in a concise 158-page book, Russell L. Ackoff, *A Concept of Corporate Planning* (New York: Wiley-Interscience, 1970).

that effectiveness in making current operating decisions requires the broad perspective that long-range objectives and goals provide. In their most general form, long-range strategic objectives are broad statements of organizational purpose or reason for existence. In business organizations purpose is expressed primarily, but not exclusively, in terms of making a profit. Some organizations have also found it meaningful to make explicit other purposes such as fulfilling specified responsibilities to customers, to the public, and to their own employees.

As shown in Figure 7–2, there are differences in the nature of the goals set by top management, middle management, supervisory management, and non-supervisory employees. For purposes of communication, goals at different levels are assigned different names, beginning with strategic goals at the top, moving downward through tactical goals, and ending with projects or tasks. This should not be interpreted to mean that managers have no project-level goals. It does show, however, where each type of goal tends to originate.

Where MBO is practiced, organizational purpose is expressed by top management in the form of *strategic objectives* (formulations of desired outcomes). They provide an overall umbrella for goal setting at all management levels and may relate to any aspect of the organization such as profits, market standing, labor relations, technology, and management development. *Strategic goals* are concrete and specific statements of these objectives. In addition to their specificity, they differ from strategic objectives in that they are to be achieved within a designated period of time. Strategic goals may be long range (extending several years into the future) or short range (one year or less). They are strategic in that their achievement is crucial to the organization's success and they serve to communicate the meaning of success to the lower levels of the organization.

Especially in medium and small organizations, there is a point at which top management may become excessively involved in the means of reaching strategic goals although that point is difficult to define.[14] Consider, for example, the following goals statements:

> *Goal A.* During the 1980 fiscal year company profits will be increased from $500,000 to $650,000. (This is clearly a strategic goal and is, therefore, to be set by top management.)
> *Goal B.* During the 1980 fiscal year employee turnover will be reduced from 4 percent per month to 3 percent.

Note that Goal B is a subgoal of A—one of the means by which Goal A is to be achieved. Still lower level goals may be set which will be a means to achieve the turnover goal, but such subgoals should not be classified as strategic goals. As shown in Figure 7–2 top management normally should be primarily concerned with strategic goals, or the ends toward which the organization is striving. To the extent that they become involved in setting subgoals (tactical

---

[14] In this regard, March and Simon discuss a "means-end analysis" in which general goals are broken down into successively smaller and detailed subgoals. See J. March and H. Simon, *Organizations* (New York: John Wiley & Sons, Inc., 1958), p. 191.

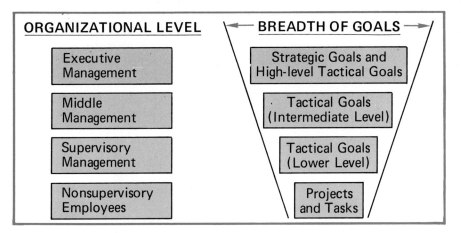

Figure 7–2   Relationship Between Level of Management
and Breadth and Type of Goals

goals) they run a risk of minimizing the active participation of lower managers in goal setting.

Tactical Goals

Tactical goals are the subgoals which undergird and make possible the achievement of strategic goals. They are set throughout the organization, even at the employee level in unusual cases (as in the case of the logging industry example presented earlier). Ideally MBO should extend to the lowest organization level, but such involvement is difficult to achieve.

Since goals must often be broken down into a series of successively smaller subgoals, there is a point at which the difficulty level of a given subgoal does not warrant the analytical treatment applied to strategic goals or relatively complex tactical goals. For example, tactical subgoals beneath the goal to reduce employee turnover by one percent a month within a year might include:

1. Modification of the reward system in order to motivate supervisors to work at the task of reducing turnover and to motivate operators to become long-term employees

2. Development of the human relations skills of first-line supervisors to the point that they understand how to work on the turnover problem on a daily basis

3. Determination of the causes of turnover by means of an attitude survey, interviews of present operators, and exit interviews

4. Analysis of employment data in order to isolate variables that will predict turnover prior to employment

5. Improvement of the physical environment by appropriate painting and by upgrading the heating and air-conditioning systems

The first goal could turn out to be rather complex. The fifth goal, by contrast, may require little attention other than a written order and assignment of a target completion date. It is important that simple goals not be treated as though they are complex. Some companies become so enamored of their complicated systems and procedures that results are subordinated to goal-setting techniques.

Tactical goals are at times minor goals in the sense of being uncomplicated and easy to achieve, but they are critical to making a goals system function successfully. Unless they are established as goals in their own right, they may well be neglected and lead to a collapse of the entire goals system. They are a crucial link between strategic goals and daily behavior.

Official versus Operative Goals

Many studies of organizational behavior have been guided by an overrationalistic point of view in which goals are taken for granted or in which the assumption is made that the static, official goals of the organization are the real goals that control everyday decisions and behavior.

Official goals are found in corporate charters, annual reports, and similar publications designed primarily for public consumption. Such statements as "to make a profit," "to earn the maximum return on investment," or "to provide a specific service" are purposely vague. The *operative goals* are more concerned with the actual operation of the organization and, consequently, are more practical and specific. Perrow explains the differences in the two in this way.

> Where operative goals provide the specific content of official goals they reflect choices among competing values. They may be justified on the basis of an official goal, even though they may subvert another official goal. In one sense they are a means to official goals, but since the latter are vague or of high abstraction, the "means" become ends in themselves when the organization is the object of analysis. For example, where profit-making is the announced goal, operative goals will specify whether quality or quantity is to be emphasized, whether profits are to be short run and risky or long run and stable, and will indicate the relative priority of diverse and somewhat conflicting ends of customer service, employee morale, competitive pricing, diversification, or liquidity.[15]

Over a period of time, operating goals may become so deeply embedded in tradition and major operating policy that official statements become virtually meaningless. The important point is that official statements of corporate goals are no substitute for current, carefully formulated, and realistic strategic goals. In the absence of such strategic goals, tactical goals may become ends in themselves.

---

[15] Charles Perrow, "The Analysis of Goals in Complex Organizations," *American Sociological Review,* Vol. 26, No. 6 (December, 1961), pp. 854–865.

Performance versus Development Goals

Performance goals are related to achievement in an individual's official position and may relate to sales volume, production, services, profits, and the like. *Development goals,* on the other hand, refer to the growth of individuals in the organization.[16] The contrast is seen in the following examples:

A performance goal of a manufacturing foreman: "Within the next six months the number of returns for reworking in my department will be reduced by 25 percent. Improvements will be evident the first month and will continue steadily until the 25 percent goal is reached."

A development goal of a sales manager with aspirations to move into general management: "During the next twelve months I will improve my understanding of accounting and finance to the level of a university student with two years of study in these subjects."

Development goals are often neglected, in part because of pressures to reach performance goals and in part because development is often intangible and difficult to measure. It is important to make the performance-development distinction, if for no other reason than to call attention to the vague, nonspecific manner in which most organizations treat development needs. Personal development serves a two-fold purpose: to prepare the individual to perform at a higher level and to provide compensation for contributions to the organization. Its importance is sufficient to warrant consideration at the strategic goal level and at tactical levels throughout the organization.

PREREQUISITES FOR A SUCCESSFUL MBO PROGRAM

Thesis: Whether an MBO program will succeed depends upon the nature of the program and the environment in which it is applied. Some organizations should move gradually toward MBO rather than take a chance that the organizational body will reject MBO as a "foreign element."

Although there is no guarantee that the most perfectly contrived MBO program will succeed in a given organization, there are certain precautions management may take to increase the likelihood of success. Any one of the prerequisites listed below may, under certain conditions, be absent to a degree without causing failure of an overall MBO program, but each is important and contributes to a program's success.

Participation by Top Management

Top management cannot limit its involvement in MBO to endorsement of the program. In addition to insisting that middle managers and first-line supervi-

---

[16] For an elaboration on performance and development goals read Henry L. Tosi, John R. Rizzo, and Stephen J. Carroll, "Setting Goals in Management by Objectives," *California Management Review,* Vol. 12, No. 4 (1970), pp. 70–78.

sors take the program seriously, the president and other members of top management should become actively involved in formulating corporate objectives and high-level goals.

Grass Roots Participation

When top corporate executives set goals without the participation of lower ranks of management and then authoritatively delegate the goals downward, they miss the major point of MBO. The motivational and humanizing aspects of an MBO program are based on the assumption that any given manager in the hierarchy has taken part in the goal-setting process and has made a commitment to reach specified goals. In a strictly top-down approach, neither of these elements is likely to be present.

Availability of Information

Effective goal setting requires extensive and accurate information. The manager who is kept in the dark about the goals of top-level managers is in no position to set realistic individual goals. In addition, a manager must have access to a broad spectrum of information pertaining to costs, availability of resources, willingness of peers and others to cooperate, market conditions, and the effect of one's actions upon other units within the organization.

Control over Means

The concept of MBO assumes that a manager has a degree of control over the means (processes, people, materials, and money) by which goals will be reached. If this is not the case, it is unrealistic to expect goal setting to alter managerial behavior and thereby affect results. A foreman in a Texas cement plant, which is closely controlled by its New York home office, expressed well the predicament of a manager whose position is too narrow to permit a significant influence on results:

I sometimes wonder why I'm even here. Productivity in this company has little to do with human effort. It's a matter of plant capability. As for my other management functions, Personnel does the hiring, and it takes an act of Congress to get anybody fired. Raises are determined by collective bargaining between people I've never seen. A clock and a clerk do the timekeeping, Payroll mails out the checks, Maintenance does the housekeeping, Mechanical keeps the equipment going, Q.C. oversees the product quality; and I'm supposed to supervise a department, but I can't say good morning without consulting the union contract. I'm not sure what I am, but don't call me a manager. Every union member in the plant has more freedom of action than I do!

Motivation to Take Risks

A manager who has always been evaluated on the basis of activities performed, rather than results achieved, is understandably threatened when required to set goals. A commitment to achieve specific objectives and an agreement on the standards by which performance will be evaluated inevitably involve a manager in risk-taking behavior. There is always the possibility of failure when an individual participates in MBO.

When an MBO program is installed, a manager's only motivation to participate may be a fear of the consequences of doing otherwise. The reluctant participant may give lip service to goal setting while subtly resisting and undermining the system. The goal-setting behavior of managers and nonmanagers alike may have much in common with that of machine operators who deliberately withhold valuable information about production methods and produce below their potential. Employees on any level who believe that a commitment to high productivity may entail a penalty, such as the threat of failure or harder work without more pay, will somehow subvert the system. From their point of view, it is the rational thing to do.

A Belief in People

Generally speaking, MBO requires a Theory Y view of people (discussed in Chapter 1) and an experience-based trust in the individuals who are expected to set goals and assume responsibility for results. MBO assumes that it is the nature of people to be challenged by a goal and to respond favorably to responsibility, autonomy, and the opportunities for growth which are inherent in such a system.

Many MBO programs fail probably because historically the top corporate management has been oriented toward a Theory X viewpoint and simply cannot make the change MBO requires. It follows, too, that employees who have been selected and retained on the basis of their suitability for working in a Theory X environment may be unable to adapt rapidly enough to satisfy the demands of MBO.

Organizations change, but like the individuals of whom they are composed, they change slowly and grudgingly. Management should be cautious about trying to change the environment too rapidly in order to make it suitable for MBO. The successful installation of a fully developed crash program should be expected only if the environment is unusually favorable.

ESTABLISHING AN MBO PROGRAM

Thesis: Goal setting in organizations is a long, technical process of serious planning and decision making. As such, it possesses the potential for influencing every major aspect of an organization's life and should not be undertaken unless management is prepared to invest heavily in time and emotional involvement.

Because organizations differ greatly in the many aspects that affect the success of an MBO program, there can be no one best process for integrating it into the organization. Those responsible for its installation should always evaluate the total environment before deciding upon a course of action. The adoption of a "canned" and supposedly universally applicable program is seldom advisable.

While granting the need for tailoring MBO to each unique environment, the following is suggested as a very general model for establishing an MBO program.

Phase I: Preparation

All members of management and others who are expected to participate in MBO are systematically informed about the nature and benefits of MBO. To the maximum extent possible, participants are made aware of the personal advantages of functioning within an MBO system. Participants should, if possible, have all their fears concerning it allayed.

Phase II: Formulation of Strategic Objectives and Goals

It is top management's function to provide the purpose and criteria by which subsequent goal setting will be guided. In this regard three suggestions are in order:

1. Organizational purpose should be broad enough to allow flexibility as environmental changes occur. Some nineteenth century manufacturers would still be in business had they perceived their purpose in terms of providing transportation instead of making horse-drawn carriages.

2. Organizational purpose should be expressed in terms of as many strategic objectives as are needed to provide a meaningful statement of what the organization would like to become or achieve. For example,

    (a) To maximize profits within the limits posed by ethical and legal behavior and other stated objectives
    (b) To contribute to the well-being of the organization's members by providing unusual opportunities for productivity, compensation, and challenge
    (c) To take affirmative action to include a reasonable portion of the area's disadvantaged and minority citizens in the company's employment and growth and advancement opportunities

3. The strategic goals for achieving the major corporate objectives should be established prior to the setting of tactical goals organization-wide. A knowledge of the former will give a quality of realism to the tactical goals which are subsequently set. The strategic goals should be stated concretely, specifically, and measurably; but they should be relatively free of statements of means that might unnecessarily restrict freedom of action at lower levels of management. For example, the statement, "expansion of production capacity by 50 percent within the next 18 months," is preferable to "expansion of the production capacity of present plants by 50 percent during the next 18 months."

Phase III: Tentative Goal Setting at All Levels

Working within the parameters of broadly based corporate goals, middle and first-line managers formulate a set of tactical goals (the means for achieving strategic goals) for presentation to higher levels of management. Top management also formulates a set of high-level tactical goals it believes will best serve the purposes of the organization. Tactical goals, even those of top management, are at this point in time *tentative* (experimental and subject to change), because they have yet to be integrated and made consistent throughout the hierarchy.

At each management level this phase may be broken down into three steps:

Step 1. *Goal Definition*
Is the goal specific, measurable, and apparently achievable?

Step 2. *Goal Analysis*
  A. Barriers to Achievement
  What barriers will interfere with goal achievement?

  (a) Personal barriers (for example, attitudes, motivation, experience, education, and skills)
  (b) Environmental barriers (actions of a competitor, inadequate technology, limited funds, or high interest rates)
  (c) Conflict barriers (conflict with other goals for resources; mutually exclusive goals such as acquisition by a major corporation versus maintaining autonomy and independence)

  B. Tactics and Resources
  How will each barrier to achieving the goal be overcome?
  C. Cost of Achievement
  How much time, money, emotional involvement, and diversion from other worthy goals will be necessary?
  D. Expected Payoff
  Will the profits, growth, and opportunities be worth the necessary cost of achievement?
  E. Risk Evaluation
  Will possible losses warrant the risk involved in achieving the goal?

Step 3. *Decision Making*
Is the net return sufficient to warrant the investment required to reach this goal? If the answer is yes, proceed to Phase IV.

Phase IV: Proposal, Interaction, and Revision

In a series of meetings throughout the different levels of the organizational hierarchy, proposed goals are discussed and evaluated. Compromises and trade-offs result in a final set of goals with which everyone can live. Although conflicts must at times be settled by means of formal authority, by the time Phase IV is concluded, all managers have a set of objectives which are in some sense personalized and to which each is willing to make a commitment.

Effective goal setting is necessarily an iterative process, often involving several cycles or repetitions of the working sessions within which goals are discussed, modified, and restated. This, of course, is time-consuming. It is, however, a necessary process if goals are to be meaningful to the individuals involved and are to integrate the activities of the organization.

Phase V: Agreement on Goals and Standards of Evaluation

As an integral part of defining the goals upon which agreement has been reached, the superior and subordinate jointly decide upon the standards by which the latter's performance will be evaluated. To avoid future misunderstandings and to provide a means of crystallizing the subordinate's goal commitment, the agreement concerning frequency of evaluations and the standards for measuring results should be committed to writing with copies transmitted to the next higher level of management.

Phase VI: Daily Implementation

Far too many MBO programs make no systematic provision for translating goals into day-to-day planning and. decision making. As a result, statements of goals gather dust and only in a general way influence organizational behavior.

One systematic way of bridging the gap between goals and everyday activity is to encourage all managers to begin each day with a brief but relatively formal planning session. Managers ask themselves: What specifically can I do today that will contribute to the achievement of my goals? The answers to these questions may be organized around seven themes:

1. *Initiation.* What projects should be started today?

2. *Continuation.* On what projects should progress be made today?

3. *Completion.* What projects should be completed today?

4. *Priorities.* In what sequence should today's tasks be done in order to make efficient use of resources and meet fixed deadlines or target dates?

5. *Follow-up.* What projects should be reviewed today to insure successful completion within the allotted time?

6. *Time allocation.* In addition to the above mentioned activities, how can today's time best be spent? Which activities that are typically handled personally can be delegated? How can interruptions be controlled? How can necessary tasks be completed in less time? What specific time-wasting activities can be eliminated?

Phase VII: Follow-up and Performance Evaluation

As shown in Figure 7–3, the MBO process is incomplete without evaluation. General rather than close supervision is the style of the MBO manager, but this

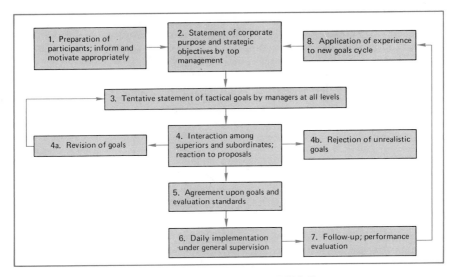

Figure 7–3   A Prototype of an MBO Program

does not mean that the superior retires from the arena of action. As one manager put it, "I still inspect what I expect."

Assuming that a manager has a feedback system which provides adequate information about the subordinate's progress, *management by exception* may be practiced.[17] Direct supervision becomes necessary primarily when there is reason to believe subordinates are falling behind schedule or utilizing unacceptable means to achieve their objectives. Of course, in addition to these interventions, the superior and subordinate will freely exchange information on an informal basis. However, as a means of stressing the seriousness of a goals commitment, midcourse corrections in goals are preferably made only during regularly scheduled performance evaluation sessions. Since individual goals within an organization are interdependent, appropriate communications should be made when a major goal is changed.

PERFORMANCE EVALUATION UNDER MBO

Thesis: When an individual's own efforts and ingenuity are largely responsible for the results obtained, performance evaluation based on results can be effective, but some dangers are involved in using only results as a criterion. Two managers with equal results may have dif-

---

[17] The term *management by exception* is commonly used to refer to the supervisory practice of making order giving and involvement in the means by which subordinates achieve their goals the exception rather than the rule. For practical purposes *general supervision* and *management by exception* are synonymous, but the latter term does call attention to an important aspect of supervisory style.

fered greatly in opportunity to achieve, degree of improvement, performance on variables which were not evaluated, and in the means by which their results were obtained.

Performance appraisal, ordinarily a distasteful task for managers, is usually less objectionable under MBO. Tosi and Carroll note that the implementation of MBO alters the expectations of organizational members about performance appraisal and evaluation.[18] To the extent that subordinate and superior have established standards of measurement and evaluation during the goal-setting process, assessment should present the subordinate with no surprises and the superior with no compelling reason to feel uncomfortable as an evaluator.

Performance appraisal interviews are ordinarily conducted for the purpose of justifying a personnel decision (a salary action, for example) and/or motivating improved performance. These objectives are often in conflict. When the appraisal interview attempts to handle both functions in a single discussion, it typically has little influence on future performance. On the other hand, when the performance appraisal deals only with evaluation against specific goals upon which manager and subordinate have previously agreed, appreciable improvement in job performance is realized.

Performance appraisal under MBO has some advantages over traditional ratings, but evaluating solely on results has two serious limitations. First, the means by which results are achieved, critically important to the organization in the long run, may be obscured by the attention given to results. The superior must ask, "What price did the subordinate pay to achieve the objectives agreed upon?" "Did the methods employed by a salesperson, for example, contribute to long-term customer goodwill or to alienation?" If the emphasis on results causes managers to decrease their concern for people, MBO may signal a return to an archaic leadership philosophy in which people are seen only as means to an end.

The second problem with evaluating only on results is that managers sometimes press hard to present favorable results on assessed variables while neglecting those on which no evaluations are made. For example, short-term profits may be made at the expense of long-term profits where only the former are the subject of quarterly performance reviews.

To the extent that these limitations of evaluation by results are manifested, it becomes necessary to revert to evaluations of both means and ends, which is the method typically used where MBO is not practiced. The MBO emphasis on results is a worthy one, but it does not diminish the fact that the means by which results are achieved are also important.

SYSTEM IMPLICATIONS OF MBO

Thesis: MBO is much more than a method for increasing productivity through goal setting. For goal setting to get maximum results, MBO

---

[18] Henry L. Tosi and Stephen Carroll, "Management by Objectives," *Personnel Administration* (July–August, 1970), p. 45.

must be integrated into the organization in such a way that it influences and is influenced by all major subsystems and processes.

MBO is not in itself an all-inclusive approach to managing, but its implications are broad for a number of subsystems within an organization. For example, where promotions have been strongly influenced by personality characteristics and political considerations, some reexamination of policy is called for. Where management compensation has been controlled by job classification and length of service, it may be necessary to make changes which will permit a closer relationship between productivity and pay.

Management development practices will ordinarily be influenced by MBO. The behavior patterns of high and low achieving managers should be contrasted to determine whether management development efforts are being directed toward change that will improve results. Contrary to the assumption made in most development programs, it may be that the manager who has a strong desire to manage and is strongly committed to the achievement of clearly defined objectives will, with a minimum of help from formal programs, find the means.[19] Under MBO managers will be justifiably critical of programs that are expensive and time-consuming but bear no demonstrable relationship to results.

While MBO is not intended to replace traditional managerial controls, it should to some extent move an organization in the direction of substituting internal for external controls. The more completely MBO becomes a reality, the greater the likelihood that external controls will dampen the creativity, initiative, and a sense of responsibility MBO tends to stimulate. This is consistent with the fact that MBO favors a high level of delegation, general rather than close supervision, and decentralization rather than centralized organizational structure.

Depending upon the degree of delegation and goal setting practiced before its installation, MBO may drastically change the organization's patterns of communication. Since goal setting demands a high degree of information exchange and interaction between the different levels of management, MBO tends to change the quality of communication. Superior and subordinate typically move in the direction of a greater sense of shared responsibility, and status barriers give way to an increased awareness of mutual interdependence and common interests.

Finally, MBO virtually replaces organizational planning as it is practiced in most organizations, or, depending upon one's perspective, adds a significant dimension to traditional planning. The critical difference is that MBO involves the entire organization in certain aspects of the planning process and provides a much needed framework for translating plans into day-to-day behavior.

THE FUTURE OF MBO

Thesis: The brief history of MBO leaves much to be desired. Enough showcase examples exist in organizations of all sizes to dem-

---

[19] For an elaboration of this general concept read J. Sterling Livingston, "Myth of the Well-Educated Manager," *Harvard Business Review* (January–February, 1971), p. 85.

onstrate its value, but the many more examples of failure have seriously damaged its reputation. Any fair and objective evaluation of MBO must deal with the fact that there are many MBO methods applied in a variety of organizations by persons with greatly differing levels of commitment and expertise.

For the most part the MBO programs which have failed have been characterized by one or more of the following:

1. *Authoritarian leadership.* MBO requires a high level of participation by a large number of individuals. It is not a quick route to increased productivity. There is a price to pay.

2. *Hasty implementation without organizational preparation.* Outside MBO "specialists" skillfully sell and hastily install canned programs without reference to whether the organizational climate is favorable (the attitudes, motivation, leadership styles, and the like).

3. *Excessive paperwork.* MBO is equated in the minds of participants with the completion of large numbers of elaborate forms. Managers go through the motions of goal setting but only to satisfy the demands of their superiors.

Although MBO has to some extent become a fad, it is not likely to pass from the scene as most fads do. It will mature rather than die, since it is firmly undergirded by accepted managerial practices of strategic planning, goal setting, and participative management. Some companies will continue to reject MBO, but its name and specific techniques are unimportant when compared with the philosophy and fundamental practices which are its essence. Companies that reject MBO would do well to make a distinction between its essential features and the techniques and paperwork of one particular program which they find objectionable.

STUDY AND DISCUSSION QUESTIONS

1. Prior to the human relations movement, management philosophy and practice tended to emphasize productivity at the expense of people. What is to prevent MBO from doing the same thing?
2. In what ways does the goal setting of MBO typically differ from goal setting in an organization that has no MBO program? Is the difference of any importance?
3. What are the major differences between the following types of goals: (a) strategic and tactical and (b) official and operative?
4. Why are developmental goals more often neglected than performance goals? Just how important are developmental goals?
5. In what significant ways does goal setting affect a manager's thought processes?

6. Why do managers sometimes resist goal setting? What do you think superiors should do about such resistance by a subordinate manager when a corporate decision has been made to institute management by objectives?
7. Describe an organization in which MBO will probably fail.
8. Describe what you think a company president should do in an ideal MBO program. Would you recommend that the president's role differ depending upon the size of the organization?
9. Evaluate this statement by a manager in terms of what you know about MBO: MBO is a waste of time. We need more people with their heads in *today's* ball game instead of spending so much time thinking about what's going to happen in the future.
10. Why do you think goal setting tends to work best at the management level?
11. MBO and management by exception are often found in the same organization. Why is this true?
12. Planning has long been accepted as an important part of a manager's work. How does it relate to MBO?
13. Why is it generally assumed that performance appraisal under MBO offers fewer problems than under alternative managerial systems?
14. What problems are likely to occur where a manager's performance is evaluated only by results achieved?

CRITICAL INCIDENT

The Master Plan

Dr. William Stern and his wife, Charlotte, both of whom are electrical engineers, founded Stern Electronics five years prior to this incident. The company produces a line of sophisticated electronic surveillance equipment which the Sterns invented and obtained government contracts to manufacture. William Stern, the company president, naturally has turned to Mrs. Stern, his business partner and the company's director of research, for consultation on virtually all matters relating to the company. Before officially starting the business, they designed a master plan for the company and continued to revise it as the company grew. Since Stern Electronics was privately held, they thought it inappropriate to discuss the details of their long-range objectives with their employees.

Since the product was unique and in great demand, sales were no problem. Even though the company was making acceptable profits, there were some rather serious problems in production. When Dr. Stern had his usual Monday morning meeting with his production vice-president, Martin Cantos, it became painfully obvious that the production situation was not improving. In Stern's opinion productivity was low, and costs were too high. Cantos's record was exemplary before joining the company, but Stern believed that in Stern Electronics his decisions had been poor and his results unimpressive. He left no doubt in Cantos's mind that he would have to produce or, in Stern's words, "give someone else a crack at solving the problem."

Cantos felt confident that he could solve the production problems, but he seemed to be making little headway. He was simultaneously attempting to cope with rising costs, worker motivation, and some complicated technical problems. He believed that most of the technical problems could be solved by the acquisition of a piece of expensive specialized equipment. Cantos had discussed the purchase with Stern on several occasions but had yet received no indication as to whether funds were available. Neither did Stern make clear that he believed such an investment would be advisable in terms of the company's profit and growth objectives.

Recognizing the need for planning, Cantos set up monthly planning meetings for the eight managers in the manufacturing department. These were conducted on Saturdays in the conference facilities of a local hotel. They usually began with a breakfast and lasted all morning. At first everyone was enthusiastic about the meetings; but after four or five months, it became obvious that their major function was to provide an opportunity to vent grievances and argue about how the department's problems should be solved. Most of the managers felt that their time could be better spent at the factory or with their families.

During one of the monthly planning meetings, Clara Moore, the manufacturing superintendent, expressed her feelings this way.

> We're wasting our time in these sessions. Nothing ever happens when we reach a conclusion, even when we are reasonably certain that we know what we're doing. Most of the time what we do is get together and share our ignorance.

Cantos usually reacted defensively to this kind of talk and issued directions which he was convinced would get positive results and dispel the impression that the meetings were all talk and no action. On one occasion he invited Dr. Stern to a meeting in the hope that his prestige and input might make them more effective, but Stern declined with the comment, "I would rather you handle the meetings yourself. I think they're a good thing, but meetings are just not my management style."

Questions

1. What obvious problems exist in this situation?
2. What changes would have to occur before an effective MBO program would be possible?
3. Assume the role of a management consultant employed by Dr. Stern to evaluate the situation. On the basis of the information you have, what sort of recommendation can you make concerning the advisability of establishing an MBO program at this time?
4. What additional information would help you make a recommendation?

Chapter 8

Authority and Power

A manager must have authority and power in order to function effectively. Since the individual members of organizations act out of private interests, perceive the world in different ways, and behave emotionally as well as rationally, power is needed to buttress a manager's leadership skills and ensure the achievement of the organization's objectives. A significant reason for managerial success lies in the manager's ability to understand organizational power relationships, to develop a viable power base from which to manage, and to use power discreetly.

Authority and power are interlocking concepts which lend themselves to a variety of interpretations. As used here, *power* refers to the ability of one individual to influence the behavior of another (without reference to how this is accomplished). *Authority* is the right of an individual to employ power (or an individual's right to influence the behavior of another). The implications of these definitions will be explored in some detail.

FORMAL AUTHORITY

Thesis: A manager's position within an organization conveys certain rights to use power. This authority may be viewed as a contingent grant, received initially as part of a formal position but standing in need of reinforcement from other power sources.

Formal authority is the institutionalized right to employ power. It is a delegated right which accompanies a manager's formal position. If it could be isolated from other forms of authority (and it cannot be), it would be independent of any particular individual and available equally to anyone who might occupy a given position. Formal authority is a *contingent* (conditional) *grant* in that the absolute amount of functional authority a manager possesses depends upon a number of variables, most of which are related to managerial behavior.

In real life the authority associated with a position is never totally defined, and perhaps should not be, since different occupants have different needs for power and are capable of handling different degrees of responsibility. Clues about a position's formal authority may be picked up from position descriptions, observations of the behavior of previous occupants, observation of persons in comparable positions, statements made by one's superior, size and nature of budgets managed, the difficulty of assigned tasks, and other such factors. These clues are sometimes vague and subject to much interpretation on the part of all members of the organization, including the powerholder in question. Thus, much of the initial authority grant may be subject to question at the outset.

Position Power

Position power, as used here, may be defined as that ability to influence the behavior of others which is derived primarily from a manager's position within the organization—that is, from a manager's formal authority. This is not a static and constant quantity. Rather, it continually fluctuates, typically following a general tendency either to increase or decrease systematically from the initial, ill-defined authority grant. In a sense it is a potential for influence that may or may not become actualized in the experience of a particular manager.

Many a bright, ambitious manager has clashed head-on with the position power of an immediate superior. The superior may, relatively speaking, be ineffective and still possess a considerable amount of position power. Here are seven of the major sources of such power:

1. *Reward power.*[1] Managers have a certain ability to reward performance: through raises, promotions, praise, for example, and through withholding punishment which normally would be justified.

2. *Coercive power.* The manager may apply sanctions of various sorts: suspension, layoff, discharge, demotion, and the like.

3. *Control of strategic information.* Power with reference to subordinates, peers, and even superiors may result from a manager's ability to control access to information needed by others in order to perform well or deal with the political aspects of their jobs.

4. *Control over resources.* Control over money, materials, or personnel may give tremendous power. A financial executive often exerts a high degree of control over peers as well as subordinates. Even the personnel manager, who is normally thought of as being in a relatively weak position, may wield power through the ability to influence the personnel resources available to line managers.

---

[1] For a discussion of five important sources of power (reward, coercive, legitimate, referent, and expert) read John R. P. French, Jr., and Bertram Raven, "The Bases of Social Power," *Studies in Social Power,* by D. Cartwright (Ann Arbor: Research Center for Group Dynamics, University of Michigan, 1959) pp. 150–168.

5. *Status and prestige.* The position itself may open doors that would otherwise be closed. For example, a given officeholder has access to high-level executives on an informal, social basis which would not be available to a lower level manager.

6. *Delegatory power.* Position power conveys the right to make subordinates more powerful or less powerful through delegation. Delegatory power also enables a manager to delegate tasks in a manner that may offset a personal weakness or accent the weaknesses of another person.

7. *Control over policy and rules.* At a given organizational level a manager is able to set policy, make rules, and otherwise take action that will both serve the organization and be personally enhancing. For example, one newly appointed operating manager very effectively increased her own power by systematically restructuring the vaguely defined positions of her subordinates. By taking the initiative to clarify the duties and authority of others, she underscored her own authority and power to act.

Limitations of Position Power

Professional observers of organizational behavior are not altogether in agreement concerning the effectiveness of position power. Sometimes, in order to make a point, an author takes an extreme position and in the process presents a distorted picture of the facts. One such position is a reaction against the classical emphasis on formal authority. It is expressed in this well-known statement by Herbert Simon:

> Theoreticians of history have often questioned the extent to which "leaders" really lead. How broad is the area of indifference within which a group will continue to follow its leadership? In a very real sense, the leader, or the superior, is merely a bus driver whose passengers will leave him unless he takes them in the direction they wish to go. They leave him only minor discretion as to the road to be followed.[2]

This is obviously a strong statement of the fact that a manager's authority must be accepted to be effective, but it is important that we avoid carrying the analogy too far. It would appear to present a limited view of the facts in that it fails to take into consideration the impact of the position power which is often available to a manager. It is true that when a manager gives an order subordinates are free to disobey, but they are not free to disobey without having to face the consequences. One could, depending upon the situation, just as easily take the position that the awesome power of the organization, as expressed through formal authority, leaves followers with little choice but to follow. Either position is extreme and untenable.

The notion that a leader's task is to take followers where they want to go was characteristic of the human relations literature of the late 1940s and early

---

[2] Herbert A. Simon, *Administrative Behavior* (New York: Macmillan, Inc., 1947), p. 134.

1950s. Most of these studies stressed the very real power of informal groups but tended to ignore altogether the organizational power structure. It is not too surprising that such a movement would spawn the anarchistic viewpoint that followers rather than the leader have the last word about their goals and objectives.

Managers would do well to recognize the considerable power of their subordinates without being excessively awed by it. In the real world, managers who are too impressed with the power of subordinates sacrifice their initial grant of position power only to find that subordinates have neither the authority to provide them with a monthly paycheck nor the inclination to assume the responsibility which should be associated with such authority. It cannot be said that managers who believe they have the power to take a given action always do, but it is generally true that managers who believe they do not have power are limited by that belief.

THE AUTHORITY OF COMPETENCE

Thesis: Managers who are endowed with relevant knowledge, analytical skills, and other abilities which are in high demand thereby increase their power. This type of power is often more effective than position power in getting results without negative repercussions from subordinates.

We generally refer to individuals with outstanding knowledge or expertise in a field as *authorities*. Even when such persons have no formal authority within an organization they have great power to influence organizational behavior. For example, line managers often take the advice of consultants on major policy and operating decisions. By their very nature consultants rely heavily upon their *authority of competence*—the right of a person to influence others by virtue of recognized ability and expertise.

In the absence of evidence to the contrary it is normally assumed that a manager possesses the technical and/or managerial expertise required to perform assigned duties satisfactorily. Superiors, peers, and subordinates cautiously confer upon the new office holder a contingent grant of authority of competence which carries with it certain rights and behavioral expectations. For example, other organizational members tend to accept without serious question certain authoritative opinions and judgments within the area of the manager's expertise. The grant is contingent in that it will be withdrawn if the manager's subsequent behavior proves that it was unjustified.

From a practical point of view this means that a manager must ultimately earn the initial authority grant. At times others greet a new officeholder with exceptionally high competence expectations, but in the final analysis all assumptions must be tested on the firing line. Thus, the power of managers to influence behavior depends upon performance as well as position. So it is that an experienced top sergeant may have more influence on the decisions of a field commander than a crowd of young officers of superior rank, and a manager at a given organizational level may be more powerful than one or more managers higher up the line.

Success-oriented managers typically place a high value on the opportunity an organizatioin provides for personal growth. They continually expand their authority by increasing their expertise rather than by being content with the official power expansion provided by promotions. Since expertise has no value unless it is expressed, they volunteer to assume additional responsibility—taking on the undesirable jobs and complex problems passed over by less ambitious managers—until their expertise is recognized and their power is felt within the organization.

Once a manager's *expert power* is recognized and accepted by others, no distinction is made between it and position power. However, for purposes of understanding, it is helpful to note the bases upon which expert power is attributed to an individual. The following are among the most often observed contributors to expert power.

1. Formal education (degrees, specialized courses, and academic honors)

2. Depth of relevant knowledge (without reference to formal education)

3. Successful on-the-job experience

4. A history of successful problem solving and decision making

5. A willingness to tackle difficult problems which others have avoided or failed to observe

6. Formal status as an expert (for example, appointment to a position normally held by an expert or designation by one's superior as the person to consult on certain problems)

Managers acquire expert power in different ways and to different degrees. Possession of expertise alone does not ensure that a manager will gain expert power. To be expressed as expert power, the expertise must be recognized and valued.

AUTHORITY OF THE PERSON

Thesis: Without reference to their competence or formal authority, managers differ greatly in their ability to influence others. Each possesses attitudes, personality characteristics, and behavior patterns which interact to produce a uniquely personal form of influence. This constitutes an accepted and important source of power.

Classical organizational theory made little allowance for the impact of personal influences on organizational life. One such influence that throws askew the most rationally contrived theories of formal authority is *authority of the person* (the recognized right of a manager to influence others—a right based on previously established personal relations, personal leadership skills, and charisma).

For purposes of discussion this topic is subdivided into personality factors and motivational factors.

Personality Factors

There are undoubtedly a great many factors related to personality which directly affect an individual's personal power. The three discussed here—social ascendancy, domination, and referent power—are closely intertwined: social ascendancy contributes to domination which, in turn, is expressed in referent power.

Social Ascendancy.   *Power,* as we have used the term, is a social concept; that is, it refers to relationships between people. The term *social ascendancy* is a personal concept. It refers to certain characteristics of an individual which are, in turn, expressed as social power. Socially ascendant individuals tend to assert themselves in the presence of other people. They feel free to say what they think and are relatively unconcerned about the approval of others. Everything else being equal, the socially ascendant manager is more powerful—has a greater influence on the behavior of others—than the manager who is restrained and unassertive.

Domination.   Although all forms of personal power are present in formal organizations and interact with other forms of power, *domination* can best be understood by reference to informal relations. It occurs any time one individual gives a command or makes a request and another complies because of the personal qualities (other than expertise) of the one making the request. Thus, within an informal group of friends, one or more individuals may tend to make the decisions; influence the behavior, attitudes, and life-styles of the group; and, in general, behave as though formal superior-subordinate relationships prevail.

It is the nature of some individuals to cower before another person who is self-confident and assertive. Sometimes the nonassertive person becomes submissive to a specific manager even though the latter is not particularly forceful and has no motivation to dominate. Because people differ in the dominance-submissive personality characteristic, it is inevitable that when they are continually thrown together in any form of social interaction a "pecking order" (superior-subordinate relationship) will develop. It should be noted that this status and power hierarchy often serves to meet the needs of followers as well as leaders. The nonassertive role is preferred by many persons since it typically involves a minimum of responsibility and risk-taking.

Referent Power.   French and Raven use the term *referent power* to describe the power superiors sometimes enjoy because their subordinates identify with them.[3] *Identification* in this sense typically involves the three elements described here:

---

[3] French and Raven, op. cit., p. 266.

1. The superior-subordinate relationship provides the subordinate with certain important need satisfactions (for example, security, status, and a sense of belonging).

2. The subordinate strives to be acceptable to the superior (sometimes expressed in attempts to be like the superior). The subordinate often admires and has affection for the superior.

3. The subordinate typically accepts the superior's goals and salient values.

Referent power is a singularly valuable type of power for a manager to possess. It usually grows out of a manager's deep and consistent concern for people and exists in significant amounts only when a manager is unusually successful in applying human relations skills.

Identification is facilitated when the superior is gifted with charisma or personal charm and attractiveness. It is, for example, easier for subordinates to identify with a beautiful woman or handsome man than with one who is physically repulsive. Any behavior which is generally accepted as favorable (friendliness, intellectual brilliance, sense of humor, or an interest in others) may contribute to the leader's charisma.

The qualities that make a leader charismatic and facilitate identification need not be consciously identifiable by the follower to be effective. The recognition of charisma in an individual is to some extent a matter of personal opinion, residing in the eye of the beholder. This being true, the factors which contribute to identification are more likely to be emotional than rational. Nevertheless, charisma is an undeniable source of personal power and is a significant aspect of the stuff of which relationships among people are formed.

Motivational Factors

David McClelland, a psychologist who has spent much of his life studying the motivation of managers, had assumed that the heads of achieving organizations would be persons with a high need to achieve until he was confronted with the fact that the president of one of the most achievement-oriented firms in his studies scored exactly zero on his need for achievement scale.[4] From this and other observations McClelland concluded that managers are primarily concerned with influencing others to achieve and that they are more likely to have a high need for power than a need for achievement.

Most of us are somewhat suspicious of others who seek power. We cannot help but question the power-seeker's motives and wonder whether the power will be used wisely. Even managers who themselves seek additional power tend to question their own motives. Actually, power, in and of itself, is morally neutral, but it may be employed to achieve either good or evil ends by means which do or do not respect the rights of others. Likewise, persons who have a high need for power are not in themselves more or less honorable than those who have a

---

[4] David C. McClelland, "The Two Faces of Power," *Journal of International Affairs,* Vol. XXIV, No. 1 (1970), pp. 29–47.

high need for, say, achievement, or affiliation (the need to belong and be accepted by others).

Although different managers seek power for different reasons there are four primary reasons why successful managers seek power.

1. Management positions tend to attract individuals with a high need for power. They derive satisfaction from directing the activities of others, making decisions, and having others defer to them. Such persons may react favorably to interpersonal conflict and to the risks associated with assuming responsibility.

2. Managers need power in order to accomplish their organizational objectives. They cannot succeed without power because they must constantly deal with powerful persons and groups.

3. Managers need power as a means of reducing the insecurity and frustration which are a result of having to get work done through other people.

4. Power contributes to a manager's self-esteem and sense of personal worth. Power is valued in its own right, apart from its utility. Semantic studies indicate that being powerful is identified with goodness, health, and beauty; while its polar opposite, weakness, is identified with evil, sickness, and ugliness. Persons who do not seek power are no less interested in ego enhancement; they have simply learned to satisfy their needs in other ways.

DETERMINANTS OF LEGITIMACY

Thesis: The use of power is legitimate when it is right and proper in a moral sense. Unfortunately, individuals and groups within organizations often perceive rights and morals differently. As a result, the question of who has the right to make certain decisions and to take certain actions is debatable.

Authority was defined early in this chapter as the *right* of one individual to influence another, in contrast to power which is the *ability* to influence. Obviously, there are times when an individual has the power to influence another without having the right. For example, the mugger influences behavior by offering two unacceptable choices: your money or your life. The right of one person to manipulate another is also questionable. The manipulator influences through deception: the person being influenced is ignorant of the manipulator's motives and intent. These behaviors are not considered legitimate because the power-holder violates the rights of the persons influenced. We look now at some of the variables which determine whether a power act is perceived as legitimate.

Weber's View of Legitimacy

The most widely publicized view of legitimacy follows a line of thinking developed by Max Weber. For him a power act is legitimate only when acknowledged as such by the subordinated individual. Subordinates voluntarily accept authority because they believe that the superior has a right to command and they have an obligation to obey. In situations where the superior gains compliance without this type of willing cooperation (for example, when disciplinary action is threatened), the employee has submitted to coercion, not authority, in the same sense that a slave chooses to obey rather than be beaten or killed. Coercion is a form of social control, but it should not be associated with legitimate power according to Weber. He visualized three forms of legitimate power: [5]

1. *Legal* (Rational). Legitimacy is based on the individual's commitment to the organization, its purposes, policies, and rules. The superior is perceived to have been objectively selected on the basis of leadership ability; and the best interest of everyone is served by working within the rational, impersonal organizational framework.

2. *Traditional.* Legitimacy is based on the subordinate's belief that the powerholder has a right to command because of a preordained right (without reference to the powerholder's personal qualities). For example, a king, priest, or member of an elite caste holds legitimate power over persons who believe in the particular political, religious, or social system within which the leader is endowed with authority.

3. *Charismatic.* Legitimacy is based on a belief in and commitment to the powerholder as an individual. Charismatic power is legitimate because followers freely choose to obey and are in a personal way compensated by their association with the leader. The charismatic leader wields power through the ability to inspire and to solicit the fanatic loyalty of devoted followers.

The Question of Rights

Although Weber's concept of legitimacy is widely accepted, it is not altogether satisfactory to the individual who is interested in understanding the power relationships which exist in real, live organizations. The following statement by Peter Blau pinpoints the major problem with Weber's viewpoint:

> The power to sanction formally invested in the bureaucratic official has paradoxical implications for authority. In terms of the concept advanced, the direct use of sanctions by a manager to compel subordinates to carry out his orders does not constitute the exercise of authority. Quite the contrary, it shows that his directives do not command their unconditional compliance. It is this official power of sanction, on the other hand, that makes subordinates dependent on the bureaucratic superior, and this dependence, in turn, is the ultimate source of his authority over them.[6]

---

[5] A. M. Henderson and Talcott Parsons, eds. and trans., Max Weber: *The Theory of Social and Economic Organization* (New York: Oxford University Press, 1947), pp. 56–77; and H. P. Secher, trans. and introd., Max Weber; *Basic Concepts in Sociology* (New York: The Citadel press, 1962), pp. 71–84.

[6] Peter M. Blau, "Critical Remarks on Weber's Theory of Authority," *The American Political Science Review,* Vol. LVII, No. 2 (June, 1963), pp. 313.

Expressed another way, when a manager must coerce because subordinates refuse to obey otherwise, by definition (Weber's definition) that manager's power act is not legitimate. Weber's concept of legitimacy makes interesting theory, but it should be unacceptable to management.

Most managers would seriously question the value judgment in the notion that an action has legitimacy only when subordinates comply in a spirit of unconditional, willing obedience. The failure of subordinates to comply or to comply willingly obviously indicates something about the effectiveness of a power act, but it does not necessarily indicate anything about its moral or ethical rightness.

If we are to think of legitimacy in terms of an individual's right to influence the behavior of others, we must deal realistically with the fact that the question of rights always involves value judgments. Management and labor (or superior and subordinate at any level) often perceive a situation differently, and the most morally qualified panel of jurists would often have difficulty deciding who has the right to take authoritative action. For example, does management have the right to require longshoremen to load wheat into foreign ships bound for Russia? In 1975 a significant number of longshoremen thought that management had no such right and therefore engaged in a wildcat strike. Even though the labor contract provided what appeared to be clearly an affirmative answer, the question of rights was still debatable in the opinion of the parties involved. Considering the possibilities for perceptual bias, it would be simplistic to define our terms in such a way that management's command automatically lacks legitimacy merely because subordinates refuse to obey.

Although there is no one best way to interpret legitimacy, we may, within the framework established to this point, draw three practical conclusions:

1. The refusal of subordinates to obey, even when severe sanctions are threatened or applied, does not negate management's right to command or the subordinates' obligation to obey.

2. Management may have the authority, that is, the right to influence the behavior of subordinates, without having the ability to do so.

3. We should not expect authority in organizations always to be rationally discernible and incontestable. By their very nature, rights are subject to question and the object of contest. The perception of rights will necessarily remain in a state of flux, and the question of who has the authority to command will often be decided on the basis of who has the power to influence behavior rather than who has the right to influence it.

The Rights of Ownership

Most managers, past and present, would probably be willing to accept the following as a statement of the source of their authority:

Under our democratic form of government the right upon which managerial authority is based has its source in the Constitution of the

United States through the guarantee of private property. Since the Constitution is a creature of the people, subject to amendment and modification by the will of the people, it follows that society, through government, is the source from which authority flows to ownership and thence to management.[7]

Although this represents an early view of the rights of management, it is still a strong and valid statement as far as it goes. Its primary limitations as a statement of managerial authority are that (1) it pertains only to formal authority, omitting any reference to the earned authority of competence and authority of the person, and (2) it fails to take into consideration nonmanagerial sources of authority within the organization which are also grounded in the Constitution and will of the people. It is, nevertheless, a valuable statement of one major source of managerial authority.

Bottom-Up Authority

Traditionally the subject of authority within organizations has been dealt with as if its flow were only downward from the top. Although this condition is the one most managers would prefer, it is a distorted view of the authority and power relationships which actually exist. There are in fact sources of authority other than ownership. These are often in conflict with the power of management and dilute it to some extent.

The Authority of Organized Labor. The National Labor Relations Act of 1935 (the Wagner Act) for the first time clearly legitimized at the national level the authority of organized labor. Workers were given the right to organize with some degree of immunity from the power of management, to bargain collectively, and to use their collective power (through the strike, for example) to challenge the authority of employers. In a deliberate move to reduce the imbalance of power between an organization and an individual worker, the federal government created an environment in which industrial warfare—the power of management pitted against the power of organized labor—became national policy.

The labor-management competition, endorsed by law, presents some interesting implications in the area of rights. Granted that each party has an initial right to employ power to protect its own interests, many of the so-called rights of each are thereafter determined by which of the two is more powerful. Who has the right to decide on wages, hours, and general personnel policies? The answer: whoever has the most power. Although, in practice, elements of personal morality, reason, and human relations are involved in the bargaining process, it remains the rule that might makes right. Incongruous as it may be, the legitimacy, the ethical sanctification, of authority is often decided on the basis of trial by combat.

The labor-management power struggle is a never-ending process in unionized companies, sometimes involving extreme bitterness and hostility. This, of

---

[7] Elmore Peterson and E. G. Plowman, *Business Organization and Management* (Chicago: Richard D. Irwin, Inc., 1949), p. 62.

course, is not always the case. The mood is often that of two powerful football teams that fight with all possible force, aggressiveness, and cunning on the field and then socialize at a friendly aftergame party or that of opposing trial lawyers who do their best to win in the courtroom but remain friends afterward.

The Authority of Individual Rights. Each employee, from the floor sweeper to the president, lays claim to certain rights and powers by virtue of being a human being in a free society. Each maintains an area of privacy and self-rule which remains inviolate and beyond the legitimate reach of the organization's power. The manager who fails to respect this private domain is usually confronted with a noteworthy contest of power.

The basis for what is here called the authority of individual rights lies partially in broadly accepted moral and ethical values, some of which are expressed as constitutional and legal rights. For example, regardless of our commitment to an organization or an individual leader, most of us would feel a sense of moral indignation if a supervisor were to attempt to use his power to influence our religious beliefs or require us to act contrary to those beliefs. Such behavior is perceived as a violation of our rights—an encroachment into that area over which we reserve the right to rule.

Each of us has a slightly different way of defining just what this area of privacy is, depending upon our values, self-concepts, and learned expectations. Most employees would probably agree that supervisors have no right to physically abuse them (push and shove, for example) or even to touch them (say through an act of intimacy or affection). Some would say that a supervisor has no right to verbally abuse a subordinate, by "bawling out," for example. One research engineer put it this way to his superior who had just reprimanded him for the way he handled a project:

> Let's get something straight. You have the authority to do a lot of different things to me when I foul up. Perhaps you can even fire me. But one thing you have no right to do is talk to me as if I were a dog, or a naughty child, or somebody who is inferior to you as a human being. I'm as much a man as you are; so don't talk down to me!

Because people have different expectations, managers must know their subordinates as individuals in order to be maximally effective. Supervisors who are insensitive and/or disrespectful of the rights of subordinates are perceived as using their power in illegitimate ways. The resulting conflict tends to erode the supervisor's future ability to influence behavior, even in legitimate areas.

It should be noted that management, in its official role, is confronted with the individual authority of its own members as well as that of nonmanagerial personnel. Thus, the power of management is never totally consolidated, and the roles which managers must play are often in conflict. At one point in time a manager is a defender of the organization; at another, that same manager is motivated strictly by self-interest, often at the expense of the organization. It is obvious from a study of the summary of managerial and worker authority presented in Figure 8–1 that much of a manager's power is individual rather than organizational and can therefore be used in dealing with superiors as well as with subordinates.

CLASSIFICATION	SOURCE OF RIGHTS	EXAMPLES OF POWER
Formal authority	Ownership-delegation	Rewarding subordinates Control over budgets
Authority of competence	Demonstrated expertise	Solving complex problems Services in demand
Authority of person	Personal qualities	Persuasiveness Ability to win loyalties
Authority of individual rights[1]	Accepted morality	Refusal to be owned Requiring fair treatment
EMPLOYEE AUTHORITY		
CLASSIFICATION	SOURCE OF RIGHTS	EXAMPLES OF POWER
Formal authority	Ownership-delegation	Control over a machine Control over information
Authority of competence	Demonstrated expertise	Problem solving Withholding productivity
Authority of the person	Personal qualities	Persuasiveness Trouble-making
Authority of individual rights	Accepted morality	Refusal to be owned Demanding constitutional rights
Authority of organized labor [2]	Legislation	The strike Picketing and boycotting

[1] In one sense a manager's authority of individual rights relates more to his or her role as an employee than as a manager. However, since this power contributes to the manager's dignity and self-respect, it is also a positive image builder and is therefore a contributor to managerial power.

[2] Although there is no form of managerial authority which is directly parallel to the employees' authority of organized labor, managers do, of course, unite to meet specific power confrontations from below, and by virtue of their formal authority relationships they continually function more or less collectively.

Figure 8–1   Managerial and Employee Authority

EXTERNAL SOURCES OF AUTHORITY

Thesis: As society becomes more complex, management power diminishes. Although the wealth controlled by management has increased, its power has been greatly reduced by the involvement of federal, state, and local governments in all areas of business life.

To some extent the challenge to the power of management which organized labor presents is from within the organization. When bargaining takes place at the local level, at least, the organization is dealing with its own employees. There are, however, outside challenges to management's authority which may be even more demanding than those from within the organization, the most important of which is the influence of government.

There was a time when a business owner's greatest complaint about government interference was the requirement of detailed records for tax purposes. Today even a relatively small business owner must spend endless hours studying government regulations, complying with them, making reports, and defending whatever action is taken. As society becomes more complex, federal government, in particular, continues to reduce the authority of management and to substitute its own.

The areas in which the power of government limits organizational power are too numerous to mention; but examples include the right to make decisions concerning employment, promotion, wages, prices, employee safety, product safety, product design, advertising, transportation, borrowing and lending, competitive practices, and a host of other areas which were once generally believed to lie solely within the legitimate domain of managerial authority. The point should be clear that the so-called rights of management are constantly in a state of flux and are gradually diminishing.

There are, of course, other institutions in the organization's external environment which limit the effective power of management. Public opinion, for example, is important to most organizations because of the public's power to regulate (as in the case of transportation and public utilities) and because the general public consists of customers. At times management's freedom of movement is almost totally limited by the actions of competitors, lending institutions, or major customers or suppliers. Although the power of management remains substantial, only those managers who are skilled in its acquisition and use are able to manage effectively.

GENERALIZED DEFERENCE TO AUTHORITY

Thesis: The acceptance of managerial authority is in part dependent upon beliefs, perceptions, and attitudes which are deeply imbedded in our society. Generally speaking, Americans are suspicious of authority and repelled by the notion of blind obedience. These qualities tend to limit the power of management.

The United States was in part founded by individuals who sought to escape the tyranny of unbridled power. The freedoms spelled out in our Constitution and checks and balances designed to prevent one branch of government from becoming too powerful reflect their consciousness of the dangers of power and their determination not to be excessively controlled by it. The concept of democratic government (or democratic leadership) represents an antiauthority philosophy, which is deeply ingrained in the people of most freedom-loving countries of the world; and our general commitment to it is in itself sufficient to create some problems with authority of any sort.

Although individuals view power in greatly differing ways, widespread behaviors can often be observed which indicate strong sentiment against potentially uncontrolled power. During the Watergate investigation the news media sometimes sounded as though the office of the President, quite independent of its incumbent, had degenerated into a dictatorship. Secret agreements of any sort came under attack, and a few powerful individuals appeared willing virtually to destroy the CIA rather than risk the danger of power that is not subject to the direct scrutiny of the press and the will of the voters.

Other evidences of antiauthority sentiment are seen in a rejection of authoritarian styles of child-rearing, a hesitancy to punish lawbreakers, and the failure of authority in educational institutions at all levels. The street riots of the 1960s, the refusal of significant numbers of men to participate in the Vietnamese war, and the extensive use of illegal drugs are all evidences of generalized negative attitudes toward authority.

The lack of respect which many Americans have for authority greatly diminishes the power of managers. This point should not, however, obscure the fact that a vast majority of our population does respect the law and honors our institutions. For example, the campus riots of the 1960s may have somewhat reduced the level of autocracy on college campuses, but administrators are still in charge and faculty members are still basically in control of the classroom. Because a democracy permits citizen involvement in the legal process and because most of our institutions are perceived as legitimate, there is little likelihood that anarchistic movements can be sustained for long periods of time.

In spite of all the obvious antiauthority sentiment, the managers of most organizations still have the authority to manage as long as they use discretion and avoid overreliance on formal authority. Since most people still show a degree of deference to authority, managers who are sophisticated in the acquisition and use of power need not suffer from lack of it.

DELEGATION AND POWER

Thesis: Delegation is one of the most effective ways for a manager to acquire power. The manager who attempts to hoard power loses it, while the one who develops powerful subordinates through delegation generates the maximum amount of power available for the achievement of organizational objectives.

It is common for managers to refuse to delegate for fear they will lose power in the process. This is especially characteristic of weak or insecure managers who sense that delegation may further weaken their positions. The presence of powerful subordinates may pose a threat in two interrelated ways: first, through a fear that the subordinate will take the superior's job, and second, through a fear that the superior's ineffectiveness will be accented in contrast with a powerful and effective subordinate.

In some situations it may be realistic for a manager to fear the presence of powerful subordinates. However, assuming that a manager is reasonably competent, the development of powerful subordinates through delegation usually has the effect of strengthening the superior. The manager of a unit composed of individually powerful subordinates is able to coordinate and control their collective power in the interest of achieving organizational objectives. The poor delegator has no such power available.

It is noteworthy that delegation does not reduce a manager's initial grant of power. Theoretically the delegator's power and responsibility remain constant even when the power of subordinates is dramatically increased. Thus, the effective delegator optimizes both the absolute amount of power controlled and the total responsibility assumed by members of the organization. The delegator's powerful subordinate managers have less need to use power directly than do weak managers in comparable positions. Consequently, the former have more potential for using such forms of influence as persuasion and suggestion. These less obvious power acts, in turn, increase the managers' personal power and decrease the likelihood that countervailing power will develop (such as the personal power of hostile subordinates or the power of a union).

A mature attitude toward the power of subordinates was expressed to a foreman by his immediate superior in the General Tire and Rubber Company:

> In the past 30 years I've helped train more foremen who became plant managers than any other man in this company. Considering my education, I've probably gone as far as I can go; but I'm proud to say I've never held anyone back. I can call any one of 50 men in the home office who know me by my first name. I've never thrown my weight around, even when I could have. If I ever need help, I'm sure they will go to bat for me.

Managers who try to maintain power at the expense of subordinates undermine their own positions.

AN EFFECTIVE NONUSE OF FORMAL AUTHORITY

Thesis: The most effective use of authority is usually the least obvious one. Although formal authority must at times be expressed directly and bluntly, it serves best to increase a manager's potential for using unobtrusive forms of power such as persuasion and suggestion.

Managers who rely heavily on their formal authority place themselves in an untenable position with reference to their subordinates. When compared with other managers, who depend more upon their expertise, persuasiveness, or personal relationships with subordinates, the authority-oriented manager appears to be weak. Nothing symbolizes the possession of power better than a powerholder's ability to avoid its use in situations where it could be legitimately applied. When a manager who is perceived as weak refrains from the direct use of power, the act is perceived by subordinates to be motivated by fear; but when a powerful manager does the same thing, the act is perceived to be a result of choice behavior and is therefore seen as magnanimous.

The most perfect power act is often the least obvious one. This is best exemplified when subordinates perform an act, or refrain from performing it, because they anticipate the reaction of a superior. For example, commission sales representatives for a certain printing company do not accept single orders under

$100 (even though company policy allows them to do so) because they know their superior thinks such orders are unprofitable. In this particular case, the sales representatives do not agree fully with their supervisor's judgment, but authority controls their behavior. In such cases subordinates are not likely to make a conscious distinction between formal authority, authority of competence, and personal authority. Ideally all three function simultaneously; but when competence and personal authority fail, formal authority provides an effective backup.

Persuasion

In certain work environments subordinates have learned to expect and respond favorably to direct, unequivocal commands. Combat soldiers must obey commands or endanger their own lives and the lives of others. Construction bosses often use direct commands, especially where noise levels are high and immediate obedience is sometimes necessary to coordinate the activities of a work group and to avoid accidents. There is a time and place for direct commands in the experience of any supervisor, and subordinates typically recognize and accept this fact.

On the other hand, effective managers can often more easily solicit the active cooperation of subordinates by convincing them that a particular task needs to be performed or that it should be performed in a certain way. The manager who *persuades*—who influences subordinates by providing them with convincing reasons for behaving in a specific way—communicates a degree of respect for their mentality which leads to a strengthening of the superior-subordinate bond. The use of persuasion also contributes to the growth and understanding of the subordinate, thus reducing the need in the future for order-giving and external controls.

Although persuasion tends to substitute reason for a formal power act, it would be erroneous to assume that persuasion is independent of formal organizational power. As a matter of fact, the subordinate may be incapable of drawing a distinction between the power and the reasoning of a superior.

Powerholders have a unique ability to gain and hold the attention of subordinates and are often given the benefit of the doubt because of their access to privileged information and their presumed competence. When relating to a superior, subordinates often withhold critical judgment and avoid decisions without being aware that they are doing so. Of course, managers who gain a reputation for faulty reasoning and illogical conclusions may undermine their potential for using persuasion and thereafter have to resort excessively to formal authority.

Two very practical warnings are in order with reference to the attempted use of persuasion with subordinates. They are exemplified by the behavior of these two managers:

> Jane Morris, a production superintendent in an automotive parts remanufacturing plant, had spent most of her career as a staff engineer and had a strong aversion to issuing any sort of a direct order. Actually she felt quite uncomfortable as a formal powerholder. Because she was obsessed with the virtues of persuasion over formal power, she wasted

endless hours arguing with subordinates who had only a fraction of her expertise. She finally learned, with the help of a management counselor, simply to tell a subordinate, "I'm sorry you don't agree, but that's the way we're going to do it." Unknowingly she had taught her subordinates to be inappropriately argumentative.

The second manager was entirely different from Morris, but he, too, had a problem with the use of persuasion.

Jim Cullen, a highly successful entrepreneur, did not dislike having to use power; in fact, he was sometimes too authoritarian. His problem was that he could not simply issue an order, have it obeyed, and then let the matter drop. He wanted his subordinates to agree with his thinking, when, from their viewpoint, he was often incorrect and illogical. His need for their approval caused his subordinates to view him as domineering and overbearing. As one of his two vice-presidents expressed it, "I'm perfectly willing to follow his orders, but I will not pretend to agree with him. I respect his right to influence my actions, but I resent his attempts to control my thoughts."

These two cases suggest two practical conclusions for the practicing manager:

1. Since attempts to persuade are not always successful, managers who rely heavily upon persuasion to gain the compliance of subordinates may undermine their own ability to be persuasive. When persuasion fails, a manager must often fall back on the right to the last word, and this should not be done apologetically.

2. The person who is forced to agree—overtly, at least—has not been persuaded. It is typically less objectionable to comply with orders with which one disagrees when one is not also called upon to endorse them.

Suggestion

Effective supervisors are sensitive to the fact that the issuance of commands draws heavily upon one's formal authority and may in time undermine it. The use of persuasion provides an alternative form of influence, but even this may at times be unnecessarily directive. An even less offensive alternative is the use of suggestion. The supervisor who uses *suggestion* sets an example, proposes a course of action, hints that a course of action may be appropriate, or calls to the subordinate's attention a possibility for action which might otherwise be overlooked. For example, instead of saying, "I would like you to follow last year's format when you write your report," a manager suggests, "Before you finalize the format of your report you might want to see if last year's report has something to offer."

The substitution of suggestions for direct commands permits subordinates to experience a greater sense of self-esteem and dignity than is ordinarily possible when continuous submission to a superior's direct orders is required. Even when the suggestion is synonymous with a command, they can appreciate their supervisor's preference for using suggestion and respond accordingly.

The use of suggestion by a powerholder must be considered a power act, but it is an indirect power act and more acceptable to subordinates than is a direct order. It somehow communicates to the subordinate: You are not the sort of person who has to be commanded. Because you are a sensitive and responsible person, you are capable of deciding for yourself the best course of action. Even when the suggestion is obviously a veiled command, the subordinate is given an opportunity to rationalize and interpret the communication in a way that is self-enhancing.

HOW MANAGERS ACQUIRE POWER

Thesis: Managers differ greatly in the means by which they acquire and use power. Each possesses a unique power style based on a combination of position power, personal characteristics, competencies, and power tactics.

In our discussion of the nature and legitimacy of power the point has been made that managers need power to function effectively. Since they are called upon to achieve objectives through other people in an environment which is controlled by power centers, they must at times depend upon one form or other of power in order to be successful. Figure 8–2 (page 186) presents a summary of some of the interacting conditions and behaviors which ordinarily contribute to the acquisition of managerial power.

It should be obvious that no two managers acquire or use power in exactly the same manner. One relies heavily on formal authority and somehow maintains a high level of effectiveness, another depends more upon personal persuasiveness, while still another maintains power primarily because of unusual ability to solve complex problems. The many contributors to the development of power constantly interact within the individual and the external environment to produce a unique managerial *power style* (defined as the manner in which a manager acquires and uses power).[8]

The uniqueness of a manager's power style is demonstrated in the life of a regional vice-president of a major oil company. He is unusually quiet and unassertive in social situations, is apparently not a seeker of power, and is in no sense charismatic, but his power within the company is unmistakable. He explained his success and his rather awesome influence in this way:

I started to work for this company during the depression. Although I had a degree in petroleum engineering, I worked as a laborer in the oil fields for three years and did practically every dirty job in the production division. Early in my career, I earned a reputation for making good

---

[8] Anyone with an interest in pursuing this subject will find the following book practical and easy to read: Michael Korda, *Power! How to Get It, How to Use It* (New York: Random House, Inc., 1975).

A FAVORABLE ENVIRONMENT FOR THE ACQUISITION OF POWER

1. A profitable organization; availability of vast resources
2. Minimal external controls (from government, banks, etc.)
3. Minimal countervailing powers (unions, hostile employees, etc.)
4. An organization characterized by growth and change
5. Decentralization and delegation as organizational policy
6. General rather than close supervision; maximum autonomy

EXPANSION OF AN INITIAL GRANT OF POSITION POWER

1. Directly seeking additional power grants when appropriate
2. Obtaining control of critical resources (money, materials, etc.)
3. Discreetly using rewards and punishment
4. Making optimal use of policies, regulations, and controls
5. Upgrading the technology and processes controlled
6. Selecting strong subordinates; delegating maximally

A POWER-ORIENTED PERSONALITY

1. A high motivation to obtain power
2. Expression of socially ascendant behavior
3. Demonstration of self-confidence in social relations
4. Skillful use of the power of persuasion
5. Taking calculated risks versus inhibited, cautious behavior
6. Charismatic behavior; development of loyal followers
7. Mastery of a body of valuable and scarce information

THE ACHIEVEMENT OF A HIGH LEVEL OF PERFORMANCE

1. The achievement of impressive results; overfilling one's position
2. Working hard and long; making personal sacrifices
3. Seeking out rather than avoiding problems
4. Skillfully solving difficult problems
5. Making decisions that are right most of the time
6. Initiating action rather than accepting the status quo

THE USE OF TACTICAL BEHAVIORS WHICH INCREASE POWER

1. Making friends; forming alliances
2. Avoiding antagonisms and the development of opposition power
3. When in doubt, exceeding authority rather than underrating it
4. Directly using formal authority only when necessary
5. Avoiding power acts that are likely not to succeed
6. Occasionally (and discreetly) demonstrating power
7. Constantly doing favors; creating obligations; earning credits
8. Using skill in compromising and making trade-offs
9. Being willing to lose small battles in order to win big ones
10. Seeking wise counsel; developing trust; behaving with integrity

Figure 8–2   Some Factors Which Contribute to the Acquisition of Power

decisions. It became a challenge to me to do my homework better than anybody else—regardless of the cost to me—and to be right most of the time. Of course, it was easier to be an expert when my education and experience were far beyond what my job required, but I've tried to keep from losing that early reputation. I'm a very nonpolitical, nonsocial manager, but it's my way—the only one I feel comfortable with.

STUDY AND DISCUSSION QUESTIONS

1. Should a manager with outstanding leadership skills really need position power in order to be effective? Explain.

2. Why can a manager's authority not be clearly and absolutely defined? How does a newly appointed manager know how much authority he or she has?

3. In what sense is a manager's position power a contingent grant?

4. In what way does a manager's perception of the amount of power possessed by subordinates affect the manager's power?

5. In what way might the actions of a superior contribute to a manager's expert power?

6. Think of an individual you know who is unusually endowed with the ability to influence others over whom that person has no formal authority. Describe the personal qualities which appear to lie behind this power.

7. Some people have a strong need for power. They seek it and enjoy it. Is the power of these people more likely to be misused than is the power of people who have no such need? Explain.

8. What problems are involved in defining the legitimacy of a manager's power act strictly in terms of whether it is accepted by the persons supervised?

9. From what different sources does one individual derive the right to influence another?

10. After an extended strike the XYZ Company granted its employees, along with other concessions, the right individually to decide whether to work overtime when asked to do so. Relate this method of establishing rights to the concept of legitimacy as moral rightness.

11. Why do Americans as a group respond less favorably to authority than do people in some other countries?

12. How is delegation related to power?

13. What justification can there be for treating persuasion and suggestion as forms of power?

14. Evaluate the following statement: Power tends to corrupt, and absolute power corrupts absolutely.

CRITICAL INCIDENT

The Olmstead Company

The headquarters of the Olmstead Company, a manufacturer of men's work clothes and casual slacks, is located in a North Carolina city of 40,000 population where Joseph Olmstead founded the organization in 1947. The company consists of seventeen plants, all located within a 200-mile radius of the home office. Company sales run about $65,000,000 a year. All the company's products are sold to six large retailing chains which have national outlets and which also buy similar products from other manufacturers.

Seven years ago, when the company was unionized, Olmstead resigned from the presidency and has since been primarily involved in other businesses while still serving as Board Chairman of the Olmstead Company. With 25 percent ownership of the stock, Olmstead is the largest single stockholder. He and four close associates, whose companies were acquired through stock trades, control about 60 percent of the stock. The remainder is widely dispersed. Primarily because of foreign competition and high union wages, company profits and stock prices have declined steadily; and the principal stockholders now feel that some action should be taken. They are considering several alternatives, including closing down the least profitable plants, accepting an acquisition offer by another company (basically a stock trade), and selling the company to its union employees. Although the latter possibility is looked upon with disfavor by most of the company's executives, it remains a serious possibility in the thinking of the major stockholders. Accordingly, they have established a committee to study the union's proposal and make a recommendation. The committee consists of the following persons:

William Craft, age 58, president since Olmstead resigned. He owns little stock and recently has been under considerable stockholder pressure because of the profit situation. His relations with the union are good—too good, according to Olmstead. He also maintains close personal ties with key executives in the customer organizations. His managerial and technical skills are generally respected throughout the company.

Terry Boyce, age 28, production superintendent of the home office plant, a nephew of Joseph Olmstead. He is described as a dependable plodder—the stable kind of individual who effectively keeps the routine operations running. Boyce evidences no ambition to become a corporate executive.

Sarah Shils, age 50, controller, an eight-year employee. She is one of the highest paid executives in the company and is respected by everyone who knows her for her genius in the financial area. She is an attractive, likable woman, and the wife of a prominent banker and community leader. Before entering the business world, Mrs. Shils was deeply involved in community affairs and was president of several charitable and social organizations.

Lewis Woodfin, age 35, a union steward who played a major role in the company's unionization. Woodfin is poorly educated but highly intelligent, verbally fluent, and possesses qualities that make others listen and identify with him even when they disagree with his point of view. On several occasions he has turned down opportunities for promotion to foreman and for a full-time position with the union. Because of his position as a senior mechanic, he has broad contact with plant employees, and he values highly his close personal relations with them.

Leo Ballentine, age 38, a middle manager with direct responsibility for sales and customer relations. He is also responsible for the general supervision of personnel, warehousing, and shipping. Although no one seems to know just how it happened, Ballentine has continued to acquire responsibility. His relations with Woodfin and the labor force in general have always been excellent, and he does not attempt to hide the fact that he would some day like to be the company president. He is independently wealthy, but this does not seem to affect his ambition or productivity.

Olmstead's primary goal in establishing the study committee was to get a feel for the political implications of selling the company to the union. He wonders whether the sale itself will destroy the company, and he does not want that to happen. It appears to him that the action of this committee may help determine the likelihood of the company's success under union ownership.

Questions

1. What are the sources of the power each individual possesses? What, if any, behaviors or conditions might serve to reduce the power of each?
2. What external conditions affect the power structure of the company?
3. What tactical behaviors for influencing others are likely to be used by the individuals involved in this incident?
4. What motives of the committee members are likely to influence the position each takes on the issue under consideration?
5. Is the committee recommendation more likely to be influenced by logic or power? Why?
6. What additional information is needed to understand this incident adequately?

Chapter

9

Effective Discipline

The ideal organization would consist of mature, rational, self-disciplined members who produce optimally and comply with its rules because they believe that such standards are meaningful and good. In such an organization, the goal directedness and other internal controls of its members would make punishment and fear of punishment unnecessary.

Unfortunately this organization does not exist. People are emotional as well as rational. They are motivated to achieve conflicting goals and have learned to satisfy their needs in ways that are sometimes injurious to the organization and to other employees. And because some employees view certain of their employer's expectations as unreasonable, unnecessary, and unfair, they decide to flout the rules even while maintaining a basic commitment and loyalty to the organization.

Another group of employees is basically lacking in the self-discipline which is needed to function effectively and harmoniously in any organizational setting. This group includes those with marginal mental abilities as well as the alcoholic, drug addict, neurotic, psychotic, the openly rebellious, and the morally bankrupt. Also included is a vast array of persons whose attitudes and values predispose them to use other people and to attempt to get more than they are willing to give.

Most employees understand, accept, and abide by the organization's rules, regulations, and performance expectations. However, there is always a minority whose behavior must be punished, not as an application of a divine right of the organization to make its members pay for their sins, but as a necessary means of modifying the behavior of the individual offender and communicating to everyone else that certain behaviors will not be tolerated. In this sense, disciplinary action is just one of the many facets of an organization's motivational system.

CAUSES OF EFFECTIVE DISCIPLINE

Thesis: The application of sanctions following unacceptable behavior is only a minor part of the broad task of maintaining organizational discipline. The foundation for effective discipline lies in the commitment of employees to be productive and to support the rules of the organization.

In its broadest sense *discipline* in organizations may be defined as a state of orderliness or control in terms of the standards by which acceptable behavior and performance are measured. Thus, an organization with substandard productivity and/or poor conformity to its rules would be poorly disciplined when contrasted with one whose employees are highly productive and supportive of its behavior standards.

When, for any reason, organizational discipline begins to break down, management takes whatever actions are deemed most appropriate to restore it. This commonly includes reeducation of employees concerning management's expectations and attempts to provide incentives which will motivate employees to perform according to expectations. It may also include *disciplinary action:* an application of punishment calculated to prevent future occurrences of the offense in question. Disciplinary actions seldom go unnoticed, and this is good since they are intended to impress both the offender and other employees who are potential offenders.

To rule-conscious offenders it may appear that disciplinary action is the major determinant of overall organizational discipline. This, of course, is far from true. Disciplinary action is only the tip of the iceberg. Underneath are four primary determinants of the effectiveness of disciplinary action: careful selection of employees, an effective motivational system, meaningful rules and regulations, and an awareness that rules will be enforced.

Careful Selection of Employees

Since organizations are made up of people, selection practices are significant in determining how a given organization will function. Some select their personnel carefully, giving consideration to emotional maturity, sense of responsibility, and personal integrity. They obviously have a distinct advantage over organizations which treat the selection function as if it were unimportant or select only on the basis of technical competence.

Organizations tend to develop personalities in the sense that they reflect the salient characteristics of their leaders in the kinds of people they select and retain. Three brief examples of companies of comparable size (about 300 employees) illustrate this point:

1. Company A, a strategic subcontractor on an important national defense project, operated on a cost-plus basis and so had no incentive to be efficient. Its president was a "swinger" and gathered around him a group of individuals with whom he felt comfortable. For most of the managerial personnel and a significant number of secretaries and office clerks, the lunch break involved heavy drinking. After the midafternoon cocktail break, practically no productive work occurred.

2. Company B, a manufacturing company, started in the owner's garage in a low-income section of Dallas. Since the labor market was tight and the company's wages were low, it tended to attract large numbers of employees whose poor work habits and undisciplined personal lives made it difficult for them to hold down a job in most companies. As Company B grew, friends of the present employees were hired. Employees were often fired for drinking on the job, fighting, absenteeism, and even for theft, only to be rehired when vacancies could not be filled. The company could hardly have been less disciplined.

3. Company C is a custom fabricator of steel superstructures for industrial buildings. It was founded in 1927 by three men whose high personal standards and professional competence in management and engineering led them to an almost fanatical compulsion to employ only the type person with whom they would personally like to be associated. These were persons with high moral character, dedication to productivity, and a pride in workmanship. After fifty years this small but highly profitable company operates internationally but still maintains the same internal discipline that characterized its founders.

It is obvious that each of these companies has a unique personality, closely related to the type of persons it has recruited, selected, and indoctrinated in its ways of behaving. It should also be apparent that the internal discipline within each organization is dependent upon the characteristics of its individual members and that some types of disciplinary action may be appropriate in one organization and inappropriate in another.

An Effective Motivational System

In well-disciplined organizations, employees are provided with positive incentives to be productive and to live by the rules. Self-disciplined employees, who are highly productive, punctual, observant of work rules, and respectful of the rights of others, are rewarded for their behavior. In poorly disciplined organizations, where such internal controls are weak, management must often resort to disciplinary action in order to maintain its standards of conduct and productivity.

As indicated in previous chapters, positive forms of motivation do not succeed with all employees. If they are successful for most employees, however, the need for disciplinary action is minimal. Goal-directed employees who find satisfaction in their work and are motivated to seek such rewards as recognition, status, increased pay, and promotion are not likely to present management with disciplinary problems.

Necessary Rules and Regulations

Some organizations are noted for their excess of red tape, rules, and regulations. All forms have two carbons whether they are needed or not. Rules that are made to deal with a specific problem are kept in force long after the problem is solved. In one company, for example, sales representatives were required to file detailed reports on the use of company automobiles for out-of-town trips as a means of controlling their use for personal travel. The company changed its policy to allow company automobiles to be used as the employee saw fit, but the rule on out-of-town travel reports was retained and was, of course, a prime source of irritation. No one was sure why the reports were required, but no one wanted to plead ignorance and question top management about the matter.

The point is simply this: when rules do not make sense to the employees to whom they apply, they are resented and frequently broken. Rules, especially those that might lead to disciplinary action, should be periodically reviewed and discarded or modified as needed. The review committee should have broad representation of employees at different organizational levels, both for the purpose of providing input into the review process and for communicating to employees at various levels the reasons for a given rule.

When too many expectations are formally spelled out as rules and regulations, it suggests to employees that they lack the intelligence and maturity for self-discipline. When employees become too rule conscious, frustration and resistance to the rules increase. One company which had just moved into a new building made a big mistake after someone wrote on a wall. Instead of cleaning the wall and treating the action as an isolated incident, the company posted a *Do not write on the wall* sign and made an announcement over the public address system about the importance of preserving the attractiveness of the new building. By publicizing an isolated incident, the company invited problems. Thereafter, large numbers of employees could not resist the temptation to decorate the walls with graffiti.

Awareness That Rules Will Be Enforced

Even employees who fully endorse an organization's rules do not always live by them. Most of us endorse the painfully slow speed requirements in school zones, but the awareness that such areas are carefully patrolled strengthens our commitment to do what we believe is right and good. Likewise, employees are more likely to conform to an organization's standards if they are confident that they will be punished for failing to do so. More than fear motivation is involved in such conformity. Management's willingness to enforce its rules strengthens the employees' belief that such rules have value.

Members of an organization need the security and predictability of knowing that work standards will be maintained. The failure of a single employee to obey a safety rule may endanger the lives of many, and the failure of one individual to produce a quality product may prevent others from doing their work satisfactorily. Thus, all members of an organization—not just management—are rewarded when necessary rules are enforced.

PERSONAL BARRIERS TO OBJECTIVITY

Thesis: Learning how to administer disciplinary action poses no great problem. However, a serious problem does arise in the actual administration of disciplinary action because managers must cope with their own emotions evoked by such actions.

For most managers, taking disciplinary action is an unpleasant task. For some it is an excruciatingly painful experience, especially when the punishment must be severe. The following case illustrates the kinds of emotional problems and reactions which can be involved.

> Carl Warren knew that he should fire his assistant, Jeff Blair. First of all, Carl had to admit that he had made a mistake in selection. Jeff was hired over the protest of Carl's superiors who did not like the idea of Carl bringing in an old friend. From Jeff's first day of work his relations with Carl's superiors were bad. They thought he was arrogant and did not like to work with him. In discharging Jeff, Carl also had the problem of having to face Jeff's wrath and accusations, part of which were justified. Jeff really was not given the opportunity he was promised, but it was top management that failed to come through. And there was Betty, Jeff's wife, to think about, too. She would be hurt deeply through no fault of her own. Other questions: How would it affect Jeff's career? Would irreparable harm be done? Does Jeff really have to be fired? Under the circumstances, how would top management react if he were not fired? Who really was at fault in this situation? Perhaps a great many people were.

As shown in Figure 9–1, a decision to discharge an employee, or take other disciplinary action for that matter, may be the occasion for a wide range of

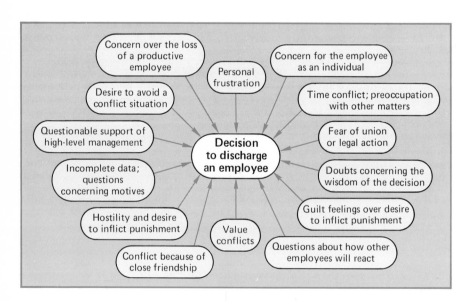

Figure 9–1 Conflicts Surrounding a Discharge Decision

concerns, conflicts, and self-doubts. Just how these will be handled depends upon the unique psychological makeup of the individual manager. One tender-hearted company president must work himself into a frenzy and convince himself that the subordinate is a villain before he can face a disciplinary situation. A middle manager in the same company simply reacts by procrastinating; his subordinates call him a "gutless wonder." Another manager waits so long to get his facts assembled and his case planned that the disciplined employee thinks that any punishment at all is unjustified. Still another feels so guilty over taking disciplinary action, regardless of the cause, that she is the one who always suffers most. Her admirable qualities of sympathy and compassion diminish her objectivity. Her boss gave her a wall plaque which aptly states that "A Thick Skin Is a Gift of God." Incidentally her reaction pattern is as often found in men as in women.

A few managers relish conflict, but their approach to disciplinary action may be as distorted by inappropriate emotion as if they were conflict avoiders. Managers who handle the emotional aspects of disciplinary action best are often characterized by statements such as these:

1. The person receiving punishment is being hurt, but pain is not all bad. There is a learning opportunity in this action that may prevent an even more damaging experience later on. Somebody should have taken action long ago.

2. I have an obligation to the subordinate being disciplined, but I have other obligations, too. I am being paid to do a job, and this is part of it. If I allow theft to go unpunished and lazy, unproductive employees to remain on the payroll, I am part of the problem and I am being less than honest.

3. If a disciplinary problem is handled properly, the person being punished cannot blame others. The employee who knows what is expected, knows the penalties for not behaving accordingly, and knows that sanctions will certainly be applied takes the matter out of my hands. I am left with no choice and should perform my duty without reservation or apology.

Such statements as these are indicative that a manager is placing the disciplinary action in perspective. There are, of course, other mature ways to perceive the situation, but there is no generally acceptable substitute for a philosophy or viewpoint that will enable a manager to step away from the specific disciplinary event and see it within the larger context of the organization and a system of values that respects the rights of all parties to the conflict.

ANALYZING A DISCIPLINARY PROBLEM

Thesis: Effectiveness in the administration of disciplinary action is often dependent upon a manager's understanding of the reasons for disciplinary problems. Knowing that an employee has performed in an unacceptable manner without understanding why often leads to the treatment of symptoms while underlying problems remain unsolved.

Behaviors which lead to disciplinary action seldom occur as isolated actions. Except in rare cases involving serious offenses, it is unusual for disciplinary action to be taken the first time an offense is committed. When it is customary for an employee to be on time or to call in when ill, a supervisor expects a justifiable excuse when an exception occurs. When, however, a pattern of offenses begins to emerge, the natural tendency is to assume that one is dealing with a recalcitrant employee and to begin taking action which will demonstrate that the consequences of such behavior are unpleasant.

The notion that desirable behavior should be rewarded and undesirable behavior punished is logical and is consistent with good learning and motivation theory. On the other hand, to react to undesirable behavior with a kind of automatic, unthinking tendency to punish leaves much to be desired. Such a reaction is characteristic of the bull-of-the-woods, autocratic supervisor of the 1920s and is not likely to be effective in modern organizations—not in the long run, at least.

The Need for Analysis

Since all behavior has a cause, it is reasonable to expect that between the time that an individual's behavior is acceptable and the time that substandard performance occurs, something has happened to bring about the change (see Figure 9–2). That something (the intervening influence or precipitating cause) may lie within the individual, in the form of an accumulation of hostility or an inner conflict which develops from a family problem. Or it may be primarily environmental: the employee's usual method of getting to work is no longer available, forcing dependence upon a highly unreliable means of transportation; or the employee becomes friends with others whose influence is negative as far as work is concerned.

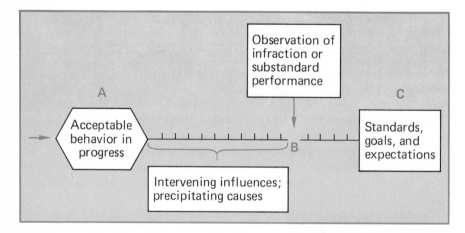

Figure 9–2   The Causal Nature of Behavior and Performance Changes

If the manager's impulsive reaction is to punish, the cause of the problem may be overlooked. And because the manager deals only with the symptoms (the undesirable behaviors) rather than the disease, the symptoms may persist. This is seen in the case of a factory superintendent whose persistent reprimands and threats were singularly unsuccessful in reducing absenteeism. The simplistic explanation given to a management consultant who was asked to review the situation was, "We're just getting a poor quality of employee these days. People just don't want to work." As a matter of fact, most of the employees had been with the company for many years. They were absent because they were fatigued from too much overtime for too many months. Disciplinary action could never have solved this problem.

There are, of course, situations in which understanding causes is not particularly helpful. There is a reason why an employee is habitually inclined to be irresponsible, to drink on the job, to steal company property, and consistently to behave in other unacceptable ways. It is important that a supervisor be sufficiently informed and sensitive to know when the problem is one that is solvable with a prudent combination of advice, counseling, and firm pressure to perform, and when the problem is chronic and too complex and deep-seated to handle successfully. Managers should not attempt to play the role of social worker or psychiatrist.

There are times when a manager's understanding of the antecedents of a given behavior leads to an unjustifiably tender-minded approach to discipline. For example, the president of a small manufacturing company made a habit of hiring boys in their late teens who were school drop-outs and problems for their families. His efforts at rehabilitation were admirable, but the boys were often unproductive rule-breakers who were resented and imitated by other employees. The president's awareness of the personality-based causes of the boys' behavior led to an unrealistic permissiveness which undermined organizational discipline and apparently was not helpful to the boys.

Some Causes of Disciplinary Problems

The process of determining why undesirable behavior occurs will vary with the individual manager and the situation. Certainly it requires open channels of communication between supervisor and subordinate, and the supervisor must be motivated to look for causes rather than deal with problems only at a shallow behavioral level. The supervisor must be a good listener and be able to ask probing questions without being offensive or arousing defensive behavior.

A distinction should be made between unacceptable behavior which results from willful decision making (stealing company property, loafing, or falsifying reports) and behavior which is beyond the control of the individual because of lack of ability or training, inadequate materials, or lack of opportunity. For example, the declining sales of two individuals may be due to entirely different factors. Although the efforts of one salesperson are increased, sales are reduced because of competition and a depressed local economy. The other, who has become lazy and irresponsible, sells in a territory which offers unlimited opportunity. The sales of the two are comparable, but they obviously should not be dealt with in the same way.

Although there is no simple way to determine the causes of unacceptable behavior, it helps to work with guidelines for the analysis process. Figure 9–3 provides a checklist of possible causes of disciplinary problems. When the cause is not readily apparent, a manager may use an instrument of this kind to suggest causes that might not otherwise come to mind.

POSSIBLE CAUSES OF PROBLEMS	Fits Poorly		Intermediate Degrees of Fit				Fits Well	
	1	2	3	4	5	6	7	8
APTITUDES AND ABILITIES								
Inadequate mental ability	☐	☐	☐	☐	☐	☐	☐	☐
Poor common sense judgment	☐	☐	☐	☐	☐	☐	☐	☐
Inadequate verbal abilities	☐	☐	☐	☐	☐	☐	☐	☐
Inadequate quantitative abilities	☐	☐	☐	☐	☐	☐	☐	☐
Inadequate special aptitudes	☐	☐	☐	☐	☐	☐	☐	☐
Physical limitations	☐	☐	☐	☐	☐	☐	☐	☐
KNOWLEDGE AND SKILLS								
Inadequate knowledge of requirements	☐	☐	☐	☐	☐	☐	☐	☐
Inadequate general education	☐	☐	☐	☐	☐	☐	☐	☐
Inadequate specialized education	☐	☐	☐	☐	☐	☐	☐	☐
Inadequate job-related skills	☐	☐	☐	☐	☐	☐	☐	☐
PERSONALITY AND MOTIVATION								
Low motivation	☐	☐	☐	☐	☐	☐	☐	☐
Inadequate self-discipline	☐	☐	☐	☐	☐	☐	☐	☐
Low self-expectations	☐	☐	☐	☐	☐	☐	☐	☐
Poorly developed work habits	☐	☐	☐	☐	☐	☐	☐	☐
Poorly developed value system	☐	☐	☐	☐	☐	☐	☐	☐
Emotional problems	☐	☐	☐	☐	☐	☐	☐	☐
Preoccupation with family problems	☐	☐	☐	☐	☐	☐	☐	☐
Excessive use of alcohol	☐	☐	☐	☐	☐	☐	☐	☐
Inappropriate use of drugs	☐	☐	☐	☐	☐	☐	☐	☐
Problems in relating to authority	☐	☐	☐	☐	☐	☐	☐	☐
ENVIRONMENTAL FACTORS								
Vague productivity requirements	☐	☐	☐	☐	☐	☐	☐	☐
Vague rules and regulations	☐	☐	☐	☐	☐	☐	☐	☐
Limits on opportunity to produce	☐	☐	☐	☐	☐	☐	☐	☐
Negative influence of peers	☐	☐	☐	☐	☐	☐	☐	☐
Poor materials, tools, or procedures	☐	☐	☐	☐	☐	☐	☐	☐
Improper supervision	☐	☐	☐	☐	☐	☐	☐	☐
Poor motivational systems	☐	☐	☐	☐	☐	☐	☐	☐
Poor employee placement	☐	☐	☐	☐	☐	☐	☐	☐

Figure 9–3 Causes of Disciplinary Problems

TAKING DISCIPLINARY ACTION

Thesis: Much of the unpleasantness and damage to the organization and the employee can be removed from disciplinary action by the use of appropriate methodology. Failure to take certain precautions, on the other hand, can lead to poor human relations, decreased productivity, serious legal action, and irreparable personal loss to the individuals involved.

Historically the management of disciplinary problems has been taken lightly. Discipline was one of many subjects included in training programs for first-line supervisors, but it was hardly seen as worthy of serious consideration by higher levels of management. If a supervisor made a mistake or handled a disciplinary problem indiscreetly, the employee might be hurt, but the organization was not likely to suffer greatly.

Today things have changed. Perceptive managers recognize that the manner in which disciplinary cases are resolved may have a significant influence on job-related employee attitudes and behavior. But beyond this, the many possibilities for claims of discrimination under federal and state law make it mandatory that disciplinary action be taken properly. It is also significant that disciplinary problems are the single category of grievances most often referred to an arbitrator for a solution.

Who Takes Disciplinary Action?

An employee's immediate superior is usually the person most directly involved in taking disciplinary action. This manager may, of course, occupy a position anywhere along the hierarchy from first-line supervisor to president. Managers who fail to assume this responsibility, even when superiors are willing to relieve them of it, sacrifice a major source of power and influence. Even when the decision to take disciplinary action has actually been handed down by a superior, the supervisor who fails to take responsibility for it will often be seen by subordinates as weak.

This emphasis on the crucial role of the immediate supervisor should not be taken to mean other persons are not involved. Especially when the action is to discharge an employee, it is usually advisable for supervisors to discuss the matter with a superior and/or a technical advisor in the industrial relations or legal department. The decision to discharge a manager is virtually always the subject of discussion among that individual's superiors, underscoring the importance given to such decisions in most organizations.

There are, of course, other persons who may enter into the disciplinary process. In unionized companies, the union steward is usually brought into the discussion, either because the union contract requires it or as a matter of courtesy and a means of avoiding later trouble with the union. About one-fourth of all nonsupervisory employees are covered by union contracts. These, along with most government employees, work under formally defined conditions with respect to discharge and other conditions of employment.

In many disputes over disciplinary action, impartial arbitrators, mutually agreed upon by the company and union, play a significant role in determining whether the action taken by management shall be allowed to stand. Under the Labor Management Relations Act of 1947 (Taft-Hartley Act), Congress expressed a preference for private rather than public settlement of disputes. In 1957, the Supreme Court held in the *Lincoln Mills* case that federal courts could enforce agreements between unions and management, including agreements to arbitrate disputes.[1]

Guidelines for Disciplinary Action

The occasions for disciplinary action run the gamut from infrequent tardiness to smoking in the explosives storeroom, and the environments range from small, family operated companies to international organizations dominated by militant unions. On one occasion the offender is a minimum-wage laborer; on another occasion the offender is a $100,000-a-year executive. This variety makes generalizations about the disciplinary process difficult. Nevertheless, some generalizations are possible as long as intelligent adaptation is made for each unique situation.

Preparation.   Impulsive disciplinary action is seldom advisable. Managers who are inclined to "bawl out" a subordinate at the point of an infraction may find satisfaction in expressing their own feelings and establishing their dominance over the subordinate, but their actions usually fall far short of achieving long-term behavior modification. Preparation for disciplinary action has a twofold purpose. It is needed to minimize the possibility of impulsive, ill-advised action—to make sure the action taken is fair and that it achieves its purpose. Preparation is also important because managers are called upon to defend their actions.

Although it is wise to avoid even the appearance of secretly and maliciously gathering evidence to use against an employee, it is often necessary for a manager to collect solid evidence over a period of time, meticulously keeping records of offences, disciplinary actions, and warnings. Since cases are sometimes brought before the quasi-legal bodies involved in formal grievance or arbitration proceedings, a manager must be in the right and be able to prove it. In some situations, where witnesses are likely to change their stories, it may even be necessary to obtain written statements or affidavits.

It is often advisable to avoid a highly legalistic approach to handling a disciplinary problem, but it is never advisable to be slovenly in record keeping. Even in companies where there is no union, there are always federal and state laws to be dealt with, and the resulting prospect that one's action will have to be defended in the courts.

---

[1] Robert W. Fisher, "When Workers Are Discharged: an Overview," *Monthly Labor Review,* Vol. 96 (June, 1973), p. 6.

One major benefit of thorough preparation for disciplinary action is that it may be found to be inappropriate. As shown in Figure 9–4, what at first appears to be a need for some form of punishment may turn out to be a need for training, motivation, or the removal of obstacles that prevent performance from matching the expectations of management. Even when the problem is an infraction of the rules, rather than substandard performance, it can often be solved through positive action rather than punishment. Preparation for disciplinary action, by reviewing employee records and asking appropriate questions, for example, may suggest the need for a sequence of actions designed to produce the desired employee behavior. It is particularly important that prior to taking disciplinary action a manager make sure the subordinate understood what was expected, was able to do it, and then elected not to do it.

Immediacy. Although preparation is important and impulsiveness is an invitation to disaster, punishment should follow as soon after the infraction as possible. Quick justice is more acceptable to the offender and is thus more effective. Immediately after the infraction, subordinates expect punishment and are less

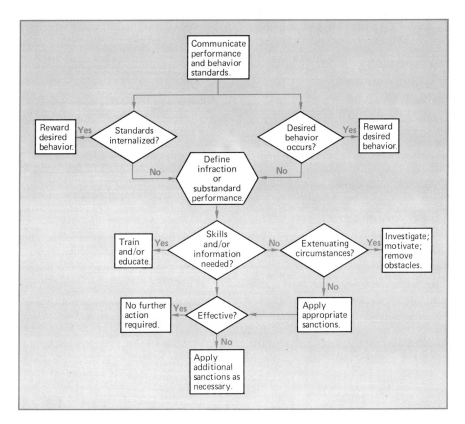

Figure 9–4 The Analysis-Action Sequence in Handling Disciplinary Problems

likely to view it as unjust than if they are led to believe they have escaped it. When the association between the infraction and punishment is strong, the probability of punishment makes repetition of the offense less likely.

In cases of serious infraction, possibly deserving termination, some companies prefer to lay the employee off for a short time (sometimes with pay in order to avoid union complictions) until the needed information is gathered and a decision is made (the remainder of a day, for example). Such a practice underscores the gravity of the situation. It permits swift action, gives the employee a brief time to reconsider the merits of abiding by the rules, and gives management enough time to make a deliberate decision.[2]

No Surprises.   Punishment is typically viewed as unjust by the offender, by arbitrators, and by the courts when it represents a major change in policy without warning. The following case illustrates the point that even the relatively serious offense of stealing company property may be rationalized and justified when it is viewed as de facto company policy:

> Sure, I had a crescent wrench in my lunch box, but I'm no thief. Everybody does it. I could give you dozens of examples, but I won't. One thing I will say is that taking company property is not restricted to hourly employees. Look at the way management uses company cars and gasoline for personal trips. And in the shops we're always fixing something for management—using company labor, tools, and parts. I'm always hearing stories from the front office about how managers combine vacations and company paid business trips or use their expense accounts for personal entertainment. I'm willing to live by the same rules everybody else does, but I won't sit still for being singled out. Let's face it: the way most employees think is that as long as you don't overdo it, taking company property is a form of employee benefit—like vacations and insurance.

Sometimes a new manager makes the mistake of reversing the lax policy of a predecessor without notifying subordinates of the change. A simple memo communicating the fact that certain enforcement changes are beng made would avoid unnecessary problems and begin to establish a basis for trust. Strictly from a legalistic viewpoint an employee has a good argument for claiming arbitrary and discriminatory action when it can be proved that the case in point is an isolated enforcement of a rule.

Certainty.   Generally speaking, the certainty of punishment is more important than the severity. In a few cases severe punishment, even on the first offense, is

---

[2] John Huberman presents a case involving a unionized plywood mill of about 550 employees in which, after an unacceptable accumulation of minor infractions and prior to being discharged, the employee is directed to "go home for the rest of the day and consider whether he does or does not wish to abide by company standards." The employee is given full pay as a last expression of the company's hope that he or she will wish to stay and abide by the rules. See John Huberman, "Discipline Without Punishment," *Harvard Business Review,* Vol. 42 (July–August, 1964), p. 66.

called for, but these are the exceptions. A large, unionized oil company, for example, has a firm policy of firing anyone caught smoking in an area of a refinery not specifically set aside for that purpose. The constant danger of explosions seems to justify this in the minds of employees as well as management.

Certainty of punishment means that there is a high probability that an offender will be caught and appropriately punished. To be more specific, it means that employees perceive that the probability of being caught and punished is high (that is, the subjective probability is high).

Consistency.   The consistency of managerial action requires the enforcement of a given rule equally for all employees, but it also implies equal punishment for a given offense. The latter is a much more complex problem.

Just when is punishment consistent? Does it require that identical punishment always be given for a certain offense? Probably not. Consider the case of two individuals who are insubordinate: on different occasions each of two linemen refuses to do a certain potentially dangerous job. However, one has had extensive training in how to avoid all possibility of bodily harm while the other has not. Appropriate punishment for the trained lineman might be a transfer to less desirable work (depending upon company policy and common practice). The lineman who has not received safety training should not be punished. Certainly it would be inconsistent to treat the two employees identically.

In a second case two employess are repeatedly late for work, but one is indifferent and surly while the other is penitent and makes an honest effort to improve. The employee who is making an effort to be on time may need counseling to provide insight that will help solve the problem; a strongly worded, written reprimand and warning would be more suitable for the other.

Consistency of punishment must also be related to an individual's unique needs and consequent reaction to punishment. Consider, for example, two employees who receive a one-week suspension without pay, both starting on the first day of deer-hunting season. One has no financial problems and has been known to take vacation time to go deer hunting, while the other has a pressing need for money and has no interest in hunting. Again, the inequity is obvious. Punishment should always be fair and should fit the offense, but to be so it must be tailored to the needs of the individual.

Objectivity.   Difficult as it may be, close friends and well-liked subordinates should be dealt with as if no affectional bonds exist. Employees are generally aware of a manager's personal feelings for subordinates, either positive or negative, and are highly sensitive to expressions of bias in either direction.

Because of the possibility for bias or the appearance of it, first-line supervisors, in particular, are well advised to avoid emotional entanglements with subordinates. Subordinates can accept orders, criticism, and punishment more graciously when a degree of social distance exists between themselves and their superior than when the superior is perceived as a peer. Of course, where a manager is supervising persons in the work group from which he or she was promoted, attempts to break off close personal relationships and establish a social distance may be seriously damaging, at least in the short run. There are no easy answers to problems arising out of such relationships, but the fact remains that effective disciplinary practices demand objectivity and impersonality.

Confident Action.   Disciplinary action should not be taken unless it is justified and procedurally correct (after preparation, with warning, immediate, consistent, and objective). However, when these conditions have been met, a manager has every reason to proceed with firmness and confidence. It is obviously inappropriate for a manager to exhibit arrogance or delight in taking disciplinary action; but an apologetic, self-doubting attitude is equally inappropriate. Firm, confident action reinforces the notion that what the manager is doing should be done. Apologetic action raises doubts about its propriety and consequently weakens its effectiveness.

The Disciplinary Interview

The disciplinary interview (or interviews) will necessarily reflect a manager's personality and leadership style as they interact with the nature of the offense, the characteristics of the offender, and the nature and history of the organization. Nevertheless, the following interview guidelines are generally applicable:

1. Enter the interview with as many facts as possible. Check the employee's personnel records for previous offenses or evidence of exemplary behavior and performance. It may be appropriate to contact the offender's previous supervisors.

2. Conduct the interview in a quiet, private place. This reduces defensiveness and emotionality and at the same time reduces the likelihood that other employees will identify with and become supportive of the offender. The tendency to identify with the underdog, especially if that individual is a friend, is sometimes irresistible, regardless of the facts.

3. Avoid aggressive accusations. State the facts in a simple and straightforward way: "Bill, I received a call from Personnel this morning. They reported that you were again involved in a fight during work hours. I would like to hear your side of the story."

4. Make sure the employee understands the rule and the reason for its existence.

5. Allow the employee to make a full defense. Be a good listener. Ask probing questions, but do not attempt to use trickery or intimidation. Be straightforward and open. In some cases it is advisable to have a third person present to witness the employee's responses and the fairness of the questioning. Statements made during a first interview are sometimes denied in later quasi-legal hearings (grievance and arbitration proceedings).

6. Stay cool and calm. Do not scold or behave as though the superior-subordinate relationship were that of parent and child. Never use foul language or touch the employee. Such behaviors are subject to gross

misinterpretation, and the memory of them may be quite different from reality.

7. Admit it if you made a mistake. One of the practical advantages of avoiding accusations is that the manager is not placed on the defensive when it turns out that the situation is not what it appeared to be.

8. Allow for honest mistakes on the part of the employee. Consider extenuating circumstances and the unique perceptions of the offender. It is important that a balance be maintained between the extremes of being too soft and willing to rationalize for the offender and too hard and unwilling to view the situation from the other side.

9. Even when punishment is required, try to express confidence in the employee's worth as a person and ability to perform acceptably in the future: "Harry, you've really fouled up, and obviously you will not be getting the promotion which was practically in your hands. But I believe you're the type person who will profit from your mistake and be more successful in the long run because of it. I want you to know that if I see you're really trying to do a good job, I will go out of my way to help you."

10. Avoid the temptation to continue to punish. Prescribe the punishment and carry it out, but do not inject the additional punishment of being hostile or cool toward the offender. Keep in mind that the objective of disciplinary action is behavior change (rather than punishment as such) and that it can never take the place of positive motivation.

Types of Disciplinary Action

In practice most managers tend to apply a limited number of disciplinary actions for which there is precedent within the organization. The many delicate issues relating to the preservation of human rights and personal dignity, not to mention the impact of the law and union power, make experimentation in this area somewhat hazardous. Although managers are not limited to the commonly applied sanctions, it is valuable for a manager to be aware of these alternatives to the discharge (sometimes called *industrial capital punishment*). Fairness requires that the punishment match the offense.

Oral Reprimand.   The most common and least severe form of punishment is an oral reprimand. It should not be a scolding or bawling out. Its intent should be to communicate to the employee in a mature, matter-of-fact, and believable manner that the behavior in question is unacceptable and should not be repeated. A notation of the action is placed in the employee's personnel file.

Written Reprimand.   When an oral reprimand is unsuccessful, a manager may strengthen it by putting it in writing. One copy is given to the offender and another filed for future reference. The written reprimand may carry a warning that future infractions will be followed by a specified and undesirable consequence. This approach follows a pattern of *progressive discipline,* meaning that increasingly severe penalties are assessed until, if necessary, the employee is discharged. Most companies have a policy of removing the written reprimand from the employee's personnel folder after a period of good behavior (typically six months to a year).

For many thick-skinned, insensitive individuals, oral reprimands are not actually experienced as punishment, but documented reprimands communicate clearly that punishment will be forthcoming unless a change is made. Thus, reprimands are often motivational. Both oral and written reprimands may be repeated and cumulative in their severity, but they should not be used indefinitely as a substitute for firm action.

Job Transfer.   Employees are sometimes transferred to less desirable work or to a less desirable shift as punishment for misconduct. Having to give up, say, freedom of movement or daylight hours may be viewed as a serious penalty, depending upon the individual offender.

Demotion.   Of all the possible forms of punishment, this is among the least desirable although it is used occasionally. Demoted employees lose face and often become disgruntled troublemakers whose attitudes and behavior harm the company. Many companies find socially acceptable ways of reducing the responsibility of personnel who have been promoted beyond their capabilities or who experience declining abilities because of age or illness. But this is not the same as demoting because of a rule infraction, a practice which should be used with caution.

Reduced Compensation.   It is generally inadvisable to *dock* an individual's pay (deduct a portion of wages), although military and professional sports organizations have done so through the use of fines; and docking is sometimes appropriate to pay for specific damages. For strictly legal reasons, if no other, earned wages should be paid. On the other hand, in many industrial situations employees are passed over for raises, promotions, and end-of-year bonuses as a consequence of undesirable behavior or poor performance.

Suspension without pay is a common penalty, but its success is doubtful. Employees often return with tales about their pleasurable vacations, and, assuming that the employee's services are in demand, the organization may be punished more than the offender. On occasion it is advisable to reduce an employee's rate of pay—when a raise is followed by substandard productivity, for example. This does not involve the loss of face present in a demotion because it can be handled as a confidential transaction. Actually, in times of rapid inflation, being passed over for a raise has the effect of a pay cut.

Dehiring.   The term *dehiring* has been used to describe the common practice of encouraging an employee to resign.[3] As a popular substitute for firing an employee, dehiring offers the advantage of being less damaging to the offender's

---

[3] Lawrence Steinmetz, *Managing the Marginal and Unsatisfactory Performer* (Reading, Mass.: Addison-Wesley Publishing Co., Inc., 1969).

career and causing less disruption within the organization. In many cases the employee picks up dehiring clues such as lack of raises, undesirable assignments, and cool treatment from superiors. In other situations the message is communicated directly: "We do not want to terminate you, but we do want your resignation." Depending upon the circumstances, the employee may be given an opportunity to find employment elsewhere before resigning.

Discharging.   When employees are dismissed, especially employees with several years of service, both the individual and the organization are hurt. The employee may have difficulty finding comparable employment, and the organization loses its investment in training and may have to accept a less productive replacement. Especially at the managerial level, this can be quite costly.

It is significant that few employees are discharged because of incompetence. The cause of discharge is usually related to work habits, such as the use of alcohol and drugs or similar personality-related factors. Reviews of published literature on cases of reinstatement under the Labor Management Relations Act and private arbitration reveal that, although high seniority employees with good work records tend to make it after reinstatement, junior employees tend to get fired again.[4]

There is evidence that most companies are reluctant to discharge employees, perhaps too much so, and that persons who are dismissed could avoid it if they were motivated to do so. Those discharged are most often young, unstable employees with no family relationships and a tendency to change jobs frequently. In many cases an employee discharge is more like suicide than capital punishment. Managers typically discharge subordinates only because they are forced by the subordinates to do so.

EMPLOYEE GRIEVANCES

Thesis: When employees have grievances, regardless of the cause or validity, the organization is better served by bringing the grievances into the open and dealing with them directly than by suppressing them. This fact argues forcefully for the value of formal grievance procedures in nonunionized as well as unionized companies.

Most union contracts provide that employees can be discharged only *for cause.* In fact, practically all cases in which a dispute arises over disciplinary action involve the issue of what constitutes reasonable cause for management action. Just how such disputes are settled varies greatly from the small nonunion company to the large unionized organization.

Union members and the nonunion employees of government are guided by detailed rules and regulations in drawing conclusions about whether they have a legitimate grievance against their employer. Their rights are also expressed in numerous laws, executive orders, and rulings of courts and quasi-judicial bodies

---

[4] Fisher, op. cit., p. 9.

such as the National Labor Relations Board and Civil Rights Commission. Employees of private, nonunionized organizations typically have fewer guidelines against which to base a grievance against their employers. Such employees are, however, becoming increasingly assertive as a result of government actions which define and protect their rights. Only the most uninformed employees need feel that they are at the mercy of an unscrupulous employer.

Grievances in Nonunion Companies

Nonunion workers in small companies have a measure of protection because of their right to seek redress through such agencies as the Equal Employment Opportunity Commission and the courts. However, such employees usually prefer to abide by the disciplinary action of management rather than take the costly and uncertain route that the courts provide. Because of this, small nonunion companies can and often do discharge employees without just cause.

Many large nonunion companies provide a formal procedure for use by employees who believe they have been treated unjustly by management. Perceptive managers know that such grievances need to be brought into the open and dealt with fairly. Supervisors sometimes act out of spite or ignorance in making personal decisions relating to pay, transfers, promotions, and the like, as well as when taking disciplinary action. Employees need protection against such treatment. In the absence of this protection the organization is hurt through the effects of low motivation and morale, employee hostility, and other factors which reduce the self-discipline and productivity of the work force.

The grievance procedure of nonunion companies often permits an employee to file a formal grievance with a "grievance committee." The committee usually consists of representatives from different organizational levels, including rank and file employees. This committee is responsible for gathering the facts, providing the parties involved with an opportunity for an impartial hearing, and handing down a decision. Appeals to a high-level review committee or to higher levels of management may be provided for. A key advantage of a formal grievance process, in addition to giving employees protection from arbitrary action, is that supervisors are strongly motivated to prevent grievances from arising and to settle quickly grievances that do occur.

Grievances in Unionized Companies

The union contract ordinarily contains clearly defined, formal guidelines for the handling of grievances. Employees who cannot find relief through their supervisors enlist the support of a union steward who in turn contacts the supervisor and attempts to resolve the problem. Most grievances are settled in this relatively informal manner.

When the grievance cannot be settled at the first level, the employee and the steward carefully express the grievance in writing and appeal to a higher level. Depending upon the size of the organization, the second level may be composed of the union business agent and members of an industrial relations staff, or a shop committee and, say, the general manager. The larger the company, the more numerous are the levels of appeal. If union and company representatives are unable to agree, the last resort is to refer the case to an impartial arbitrator. This formal, legalistic procedure is, of course, frustrating, time-consuming, and expensive. Managers who have worked within such a system and move to nonunion companies often oppose the establishment of any type of formal grievance procedure. However, all things considered, the advantages of formal procedures in nonunion plants probably outweigh the disadvantages. The suppression of grievances leads to serious problems, one of which may be unionization.

One of the complex and interesting problems in unionized systems concerns the role of union stewards.[5] They are faced with the problem of acting simultaneously as a subordinate employee with specific duties and as a representative of an aggrieved employee who must relate to management as an equal and often as an antagonist. The success of the grievance system is influenced significantly by the attitudes and skills of union stewards. They can greatly reduce the number of grievances by effectively influencing the behavior of uninformed or troublemaking employees, and their good judgment can lead to quick settlements. On the other hand, their militancy and overzealousness may give the grievance process the aura of a fiercely fought criminal court battle and result in serious damage to labor-management relations.

THE INDULGENCY PATTERN

Thesis: One way to deal with disciplinary problems is to relax standards, look the other way, and gain a degree of approval, if not respect, from subordinates by a policy of leniency and permissiveness. But the approval of subordinates is not the ultimate goal of management, and the result of this pattern is a capitulation to nondiscipline.

During the 1950s the term *indulgency pattern* was used by Alvin Gouldner to describe a common approach to discipline which he observed in his extensive research in the gypsum industry.[6] He defined the indulgency pattern as "a connected set of concrete judgments and underlying sentiments that predispose workers to react favorably to the plant and to trust their supervisors." Workers placed a high value on leniency, interpreted as meaning that supervisors avoided constant checking to see if employees were working. Employees were allowed to use their spare time as they saw fit, and rules were not strictly enforced as long as there were no gross abuses. Employees were allowed to do personal work in the company shops (repair jobs, for example), and tools and raw materials, including quantities of the company's gypsum board, were available without charge.

---

[5] For a discussion of the conflicting role of the union steward, read William H. Leahy, "Landmark Cases Involving Union Representatives," *Personnel Journal,* Vol. 51 (April, 1972), pp. 241–245.

[6] Alvin W. Gouldner, *Patterns of Industrial Bureaucracy* (New York: The Free Press, 1954), pp. 45–56; and Alvin W. Gouldner, *Wildcat Strike* (New York: Harper Torchbooks, 1954), pp. 18–22.

Variations of the Pattern

The indulgency pattern takes a variety of forms in different companies. Often the looseness of discipline is expressed in the form of covert trade-offs between first-line supervisors and subordinates without the approval of high-level management. A supervisor is well liked and supported by subordinates who receive special privileges: one employee is allowed to punch the time clock for another who leaves early, infractions of rules are overlooked, and errors or mistakes are covered up. Supervisors who play the indulgency game are rewarded with extra effort when an important job must be completed, and work group pressures are applied to bring a troublemaking employee into line.

Evaluation

At its best the indulgency pattern is an undesirable accommodation made at the point of interface between labor and management. An alternative to strict legalism and blind commitment to rules, it is one means by which a first-line supervisor is able to cope with the complex and conflicting pressures from above and below. At its worst the indulgency pattern degenerates into a form of mutual blackmail in which employees are allowed to be relatively unproductive and ignore the organization's work rules; in return they help to conceal from higher level management the costly compromises of the first-line supervisor. This pattern is especially prevalent in the large organizations of industries in which profits are not heavily dependent upon concentrations of efficiently producing employees.[7]

The organization, of course, is the loser where an excessive indulgency pattern exists. The problems involved in taking disciplinary action are solved by lowering expectations to the point that no problems exist. It is a pathological condition into which organizations degenerate and from which they find great difficulty extricating themselves. Although there are no painless solutions to the problem, it seems reasonable to assert that rules which are not enforceable should be eliminated and that any rule worthy of retaining should be enforced.

Although degrees of the indulgency pattern exist in the informal relations of most organizations, its extreme forms are both undesirable and unnecessary. The indulgency pattern is the logical result of managerial failure to assume full responsibility for the unpleasant task of taking disciplinary action and the complex task of developing motivational systems that lead to self-discipline within the individuals of whom the organization is composed.

STUDY AND DISCUSSION QUESTIONS

1. What is the difference between organizational discipline and disciplinary action?

---

[7] Certain industries, such as oil and chemicals, are less dependent upon the productive efficiency of their nonprofessional employees than are labor-intensive industries, such as apparel and automobile manufacturing.

2. In what sense is the level of discipline within an organization a function of personnel selection?

3. What are the principal relationships between an organization's rules and the level of organizational discipline?

4. How can managers best handle the personal barriers that typically interfere with effective discipline?

5. A strictly behavioristic approach to dealing with disciplinary problems would primarily emphasize the importance of rewarding desirable behavior and punishing undesirable behavior. Is this an adequate approach to solving disciplinary problems? Why or why not?

6. Why are disciplinary problems more likely to be regarded as important today than, say, during the 1920s?

7. Following the precedent set by criminal court judges, arbitrators sometimes decide in favor of an accused and obviously guilty employee because of a technicality. For example, a guilty employee is allowed to go without punishment because the supervisor allowed another employee who did the same thing to get off with an oral reprimand. What are the pros and cons of such a practice?

8. The point is made that close personal relationships between supervisor and subordinates often lead to bias in the handling of disciplinary problems. How should this problem be dealt with where a supervisor is in charge of a work group from which he or she has recently been promoted?

9. Students and supervisors alike have been known to make statements similar to the following when dealing with disciplinary cases: "Since the employee is a loyal member of a strong union, we can't fire him." Evaluate this statement.

10. Evaluate the use of demotion as a form of punishment.

CRITICAL INCIDENT

The Dummy

Morris Sands had worked in the warehouse for six months as a laborer and for 18 months as a forklift operator. He was promoted to warehouse clerk about two months prior to this incident. When his predecessor decided to retire after serving eight years as a warehouse clerk, Sands was asked to replace him because of Sands' outstanding performance during his two years with the company.

The job of warehouse clerk represented a considerable increase in pay and responsibility for Sands. His primary duty was to determine whether incoming shipments were consistent with purchase orders and bills of lading. He was required to make a notation when orders were supposedly shipped but were not received, when unavailable items were placed on back order, and when merchandise was damaged. The items received consisted mostly of office and laboratory

supplies, cutting tools, and various metals from which custom parts were manufactured in the company's machine shops.

Sands worked with his predecessor for three weeks before assuming his new
responsibilities. During this training period he was conscientious, and no difficulty was noted. However, soon after he took full responsibility for the job a
number of complaints were received concerning damaged merchandise and incorrect or short shipments. In each case Sands' supervisor, Martha Clark, talked
with him, patiently explaining how such an error could have occurred and
encouraging him to exercise more care in his work. Sands expressed appreciation
for her help and assured her that it would not happen again.

On three or four occasions, Clark noticed Sands standing around talking
with other warehouse employees and suggested that he spend more time at his
work in order to avoid errors. Each time this happened Sands called Clark's
attention to the fact that (1) there really was not enough work to require all his
time, (2) he was caught up on his work, and (3) he had been taking Clark's
suggestions about being careful in checking incoming shipments. Clark became
increasingly frustrated over Sands' performance and wondered if Sands was really
trying. One of the clerks in the front office increased her suspicions by spreading
the word around that Sands was a dummy who made mistakes that no one in
his right mind would make.

After a few days of relative quiet Clark felt that everything might be working
out. Then she received a call from her superior, Milton Scott. The conversation
went something like this:

Scott:
  "I just got another complaint about Sands. Have you talked with him?"

Clark:
  "Certainly. Almost every day. I just can't seem to get through to him."

Scott:
  "Then fire the dummy. I've heard the last complaint I want to hear."

That afternoon Clark called Sands into her office to carry out Scott's orders.
Sands could hardly believe what he was hearing. He kept repeating the same
statement, "I've done everything you asked me to do. Why didn't you tell me
I was in trouble? My old job was open last week. I would gladly have gone back
to it. I was a real pro on the forklift."

Questions

1. What is wrong with the way this situation was handled?
2. What should Clark do now?
3. What additional information is needed for an analysis of this situation?

PART
3

The Development of Leadership Behavior

Chapter 10

Leadership Theory and Practice

The success of an organization is dependent upon many factors, but none is more important than the impact of its leaders. They make the decisions which determine both organizational purpose and the means by which that purpose is fulfilled. Their actions determine whether the potential of the organization's members will be actualized or lie dormant and whether the emotional tone of the organization will be characterized by warmth and enthusiasm or coldness and apathy.

Leadership in organizations is behavior whereby one person motivates others to work toward the achievement of specific objectives. Managers differ greatly in their leadership styles, and effective leaders vary their leadership behavior according to the needs of the situation. Although our knowledge of leadership behavior leaves much to be desired, an impressive and expanding body of information on leadership is available. This chapter presents some of the major theories of leadership and their practical implications.

LEADERSHIP IN ORGANIZATIONS

Thesis: All managers are leaders, because they influence, to varying degrees, the behavior of other persons within the organization. Some are poor leaders; they have little influence except that which their formal authority permits them to exercise. Others combine personal leadership qualities with position power and prestige to produce a powerful influence on subordinates, peers, and superiors alike.

Popular definitions of leadership are by no means consistent. It can be argued, for example, that managers [1] may motivate their subordinates through the use of organizational power (through various forms of reward and punish-

---

[1] Leading is only one of several managerial functions. Managers also control budgets, solve technical problems, and perform other functions which are not directly involved in leadership. Thus, managers are organizational leaders, but *leadership* and *management* are not synonymous.

214

ment) while exhibiting a minimum of leadership behavior. Following this line of thinking, managers have subordinates by virtue of their formal positions, but they may not have followers. They may lack the quality of relationships with subordinates that would motivate the latter to support with enthusiasm their superior's efforts to achieve organizational objectives. From this perspective, merely possessing the means of controlling subordinates' behavior does not in itself qualify as leadership. Leadership would involve an ability to influence that goes beyond organizational authority and taps the resources inherent in the personal relationships that exist between leader and follower.[2]

The notion that leadership involves an ability to influence that transcends authority underscores an important aspect of leadership— namely, that the quality of leadership must, in part, be judged in terms of leader-follower relationships. On the other hand, it would be a mistake to define leadership so narrowly that any manager would be excluded. Positions are structured in such a way that a new manager can lead subordinates—can influence them to behave in ways that contribute to the achievement of organizational objectives—prior to any opportunity to establish personal relationships with them. A formal organizational position also enables a manager to get a job done even after negative relationships have been formed (for example, after subordinates have become hostile because of an unpopular management decision). Because these possibilities exist, it would appear that leadership in organizations is not altogether the fragile and friendly relationship it is often pictured to be. Nevertheless, managers who rely too heavily upon formal authority are in danger of losing some or all of their ability to lead.

We commonly refer to an individual as a leader as though leadership were only an attribute of the person. We say, "Mary is an outstanding leader," as though she would be outstanding in any setting and under all circumstances. This is a very nontechnical and imprecise use of the term. Actually it makes sense to think of leadership more as a form of behavior than as a personal quality. In her sorority Mary may be a leader, but at work she may primarily be a follower. Or she may, within her sorority, exercise leadership behavior in one setting and be a follower in another. From a behavioral viewpoint a person is a leader only when leading. Otherwise that individual may be said to have varying degrees of leadership potential, depending upon the situation.

STUDIES OF LEADERSHIP CHARACTERISTICS

Thesis: In recent years leadership studies have placed primary emphasis upon the importance of environmental influences on leadership success and in the process have inappropriately de-emphasized personal characteristics. Yet, on the basis of published research, it must be concluded that certain characteristics do favor success in the leadership role, regardless of the situation in which leadership occurs.

---

[2] For an elaboration of this concept see Daniel Katz and Robert L. Kahn, *Social Psychology of Organizations* (New York: John Wiley & Sons, Inc., 1966), p. 334.

One attempt to isolate factors which contribute to leadership effectiveness centers around studies of traits or personality characteristics. This approach, which enjoyed its greatest popularity from about 1920 to 1950, assumed that personal attributes, such as intelligence, social dominance, initiative, persistence, and the like, were the primary cause of leadership success and failure.

Because the early trait studies employed poor experimental design and relied heavily on notoriously unreliable and invalid "personality inventories," the results were ambiguous and conflicting. In most of the studies no consideration was given to the possibility that different situations might require different characteristics or that a specific situation might either require so little of the leader or be so unfavorable that personal qualities would have little if any bearing on success. A variety of other deficiencies was present in many of the research studies: the criteria of leadership success were inadequately defined, the studies were unable to specify how much of a given trait was needed or to demonstrate an unequivocal cause and effect relationship between the presence of a trait and leadership success.

One analysis of 20 studies conducted prior to 1940 resulted in a total of 79 traits, 65 percent of which were listed in only one study. In addition to listing a ridiculously large number of poorly defined and overlapping traits, these studies provided management little assurance that it could either select leaders with such traits or develop those traits in existing managers.

Because of the gross deficiencies in early trait studies and a growing awareness of the importance of the organizational environment to a leader's success, the view developed that leadership is entirely situational in origin—that for practical purposes no personal characteristics are predictive of leadership success. As Ralph Stogdill, an authority on leadership, has pointed out, this view overemphasized the situational and underemphasized the personal nature of leadership.[3]

After comparing a 1948 survey of leadership characteristics with 163 studies conducted between 1948 and 1970, Stogdill concluded that a selected group of characteristics do, in fact, differentiate (1) leaders from followers, (2) effective from ineffective leaders, and (3) high-echelon from low-echelon leaders.

> The leader is characterized by a strong drive for responsibility and task completion, vigor and persistence in pursuit of goals, venturesomeness and originality, drive to exercise initiative in social situations, self-confidence and a sense of personal identity, willingness to accept consequences of decision and action, readiness to absorb interpersonal stress, willingness to tolerate frustration and delay, ability to influence behavior, and capacity to structure social interaction systems to the purpose at hand.[4]

---

[3] Ralph M. Stogdill, *Handbook of Leadership* (New York: The Free Press, 1974), p. 72.
[4] Ibid., p. 81.

STYLES OF LEADERSHIP

Thesis: Leadership style refers to the pattern or constellation of leadership behaviors that characterize a given leader. Because each leader feels most comfortable with a particular style and tends to be relatively consistent in its use, the effectiveness of a specific leader will vary from one situation to another.

Some leaders tend to be *authoritarian,* relying heavily on the power of their formal positions, while others are more *participative* (inclined to involve subordinates in organizational planning and decision making). Highly authoritarian leaders usually place a high value on completing assigned tasks while neglecting the needs of subordinates. Leaders who are inclined toward participative management show more concern for the needs of their subordinates often at the expense of achieving organizational objectives. A leader may, of course, exhibit a strong concern for both task and people. The two emphases are not incompatible.

Sometimes style is expressed in terms of *closeness of supervision.* Managers often have the option, on the one hand, of keeping themselves informed concerning the details of their subordinates' work and exercising close personal control at all times, or, on the other hand, of delegating freely and concentrating attention more upon results than upon the means by which the results are achieved. While close supervision tends to be associated with authoritarian leadership and centralized organizations, *general supervision* is more likely to be associated with some form of participative leadership and decentralized organizations.

One extreme form of general supervision is *laissez-faire,* or *free-reign,* leadership. A leader using this style almost abdicates the leadership role, allowing subordinates more or less to lead themselves. Although such a style could lead to total disaster, there are a few situations in which it appears to be reasonably effective (for example, the supervision of certain highly responsible research scientists or college professors). Figure 10–1 shows the interaction patterns of three major leadership styles.

Since these and other elements of leadership style can be applied in varying degrees and combinations and must be integrated with the unique personality

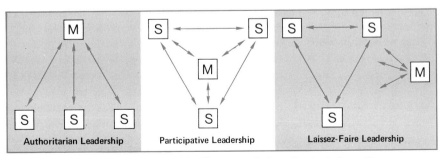

Figure 10–1   **The Primary Manager-Subordinate Interaction Patterns of Three Leadership Styles**

makeup of a given manager as it interacts with a specific environment, no two leadership styles are exactly alike. Among the many other elements of leadership style we might consider are such variables as (1) the leader's approach to motivating subordinates (the use of coercion, incentives, etc.), (2) the leader's unique approach to making decisions, (3) the extent to which the leader's personal charisma and authority of personality influence relationships with subordinates, and (4) the leader's ability to vary his or her leadership behavior to meet the unique demands of different situations.

AUTHORITARIAN LEADERSHIP

Thesis: Authority is a valuable and necessary aspect of organizational life, but a strictly authoritarian leadership style is inappropriate in today's organizations.

Persons with organizational power lead with varying degrees of authoritarian control. Although many understand the need for the support and cooperation of subordinates, the temptation for a powerholder to rely upon position power, rather than upon an alternative form of influence, is sometimes overwhelming. The Caesars of Rome moved progressively from a relatively democratic form of government to a totally autocratic one. Ultimately they proclaimed themselves gods and demanded to be treated as such.

The temptation to place excessive reliance upon formal authority is no less real for a manager than for a totalitarian ruler. When opportunities arise for choosing between persuasion and command, or personal influence and authority, the power-based alternatives are often preferred for their simplicity, efficiency, and immediate effectiveness. Machiavelli's words express the sentiments of a true autocrat:

> Is it better to be loved than feared, or the reverse? The answer is that it is desirable to be both; but, because it is difficult to join them together, it is much safer for a prince to be feared than loved, if he is to fail in one of the two. . . . Men have less hesitation in injuring one who makes himself loved than one who makes himself feared, for love is held by a chain of duty which, since men are bad, they break at every chance for their own profit; but fear is held by a dread of punishment that never fails you.[5]

Leadership in Classical Theory

Authoritarian leadership has its theoretical basis in classical organizational theory [6] and in capitalistic doctrines concerning the rights inherent in private

---

[5] This is taken from *The Prince,* written by Niccolo Machiavelli in the early part of the sixteenth century. See Allan Gilbert, trans., *Machiavelli* (Durham, North Carolina: Duke University Press, 1965), p. 62.

[6] For a brief review of classical organizational theory refer to Chapter 2.

ownership of property. Historically managers, especially owner-managers, have understandably believed that management has a right to make organizational decisions and to issue commands and expect them to be obeyed. From the classical viewpoint, leadership, as personal influence, is considered unnecessary since the primary basis for influence is organizational authority.

The authoritarian approach to leadership is logical and rational, given the assumptions of classical organizational theory. The problem lies in the fact that people are not as simple and rational as the model implies. Human behavior is controlled as much by emotions as by logic, and perceptions of rights change as the values of society change. Although classical theory provides an invaluable point of departure for understanding organizations, it is in many ways naive and unrealistic. It simply does not take all the facts into consideration.

The Authoritarian Personality

Sometimes a leader develops an authoritarian style by imitating other managers. Another tries a variety of leadership behaviors and finds that in a specific setting the authoritarian approach works best. If an authoritarian style is based on one of these simple forms of learning, a manager can learn to use other methods when appropriate.

There exists, however, an individual whose authoritarian leadership style is based on deeply ingrained personality characteristics. This person we describe as an *authoritarian personality*. The parents of this leader were highly authoritarian, and their leadership approach was successful; that is, the child submitted to the authority rather than rebel and refuse to accept it. As a result, the adult behavior of this individual follows the parents' authoritarian style. Because leaders with authoritarian personalities learned in early life to believe in the rights of superiors to dominate their subordinates, they are submissive toward superiors, while dominating their subordinates.

It might at first appear that authoritarian personalities would have difficulty relating to superiors, and in one sense they do. If they feel hostility or resentment toward superiors, they repress or bottle it up lest it be expressed and jeopardize the relationship; but they usually vent these feelings through relationships with subordinates, causing the subordinates to develop hostile feelings in return.

The superior and subordinates of an authoritarian personality see two entirely different persons. The subordinate sees one who is strong, powerful, and dominant; and the superior sees one who is weak and submissive. Actually the apparently paradoxical behavior of authoritarian personalities is quite consistent. If their background and personality development are considered, they could hardly be expected to behave otherwise.

It should be noted that the submissiveness before superiors is almost as undesirable as domination of subordinates. Mature leaders, even those who are relatively authoritarian, are not submissive. They are not passively dependent individuals who grovel before the controlling power of a superior. Rather, they identify with and assume a comfortable working relationship with their superiors.

The Antiauthoritarian Personality

A close relative of the authoritarian personality is exemplified by an individual we will call George:

> George had authoritarian parents, too, but he reacted by rebelling instead of submitting. Just the thought of someone telling him what to do makes him bristle. Although he occupies a formal position in management, his real identification is with the underdog subordinate whom he perceives as being pushed around by management. Although he resents authority, he, too, is often attracted to an authoritarian management style—doing to others as others did to him. George may look to subordinates like an authoritarian personality, but he differs in one important aspect: he is not submissive to his superiors. He may, in fact, be openly aggressive; and this usually ensures his demise in the management hierarchy.

It is interesting to note that where an authoritarian style is an outgrowth of deeply ingrained personality characteristics there may be considerable inconsistency between what the leader believes and does. The professor with a total intellectual commitment to participative techniques may be a model of authoritarian leadership in the classroom. The corporate manager whose formal education has provided an arsenal of prepackaged, ready-to-use participative techniques may intellectually proclaim their virtues but emotionally reject them as just so much theoretical garbage. Behavior is more often influenced by long-standing habits and gut-level feelings than by what one rationally holds to be true and good.

THE CHARISMATIC LEADER

Thesis: Although charismatic leaders are rare, they are not yet an extinct species in business organizations, and elements of the charismatic style are found in many managers. The greatest weakness in this style is that the superior-subordinate relationship is presumed to be between a superior leader and an inferior subordinate.

One variation of the authoritarian style is what Max Weber called *charismatic leadership* (based on charisma, the "gift of grace"). Such leaders differ from the typical autocrat primarily in the extent to which leadership style is calculated to focus attention upon their own "superhuman" qualities and the extent to which their authority is personality-based as well as position-based. Like kings or feudal lords, charismatic leaders think of themselves as having certain attributes that make them superior to and better than their subordinates. Subordinates are expected not merely to obey, but also to show reverence and personal loyalty.

Employees who do not respond to the lord-vassal treatment typically leave the organization, by choice or otherwise, and those who remain are ideally suited for reinforcing the leader's self-deceptive, ego-enhancing behavior. Charismatic leaders are most likely to be found among entrepreneurs who have somehow succeeded beyond all expectations and lack the insight to know that their success is not solely the result of their own genius. Managers who are talented and powerful, but unduly egotistical, may have an especially difficult time avoiding the undesirable elements of charismatic leadership in their relations with subordinates. When these qualities are combined with an unwillingness or inability to delegate, the stage is perfectly set for a charismatic style.

Managers who fail to delegate decision making to subordinates automatically increase their subordinates' dependence and place themselves in an unrealistically exalted position. Subordinates who must constantly seek advice, even with regard to trivia, are by definition placed in humble, demeaning, and inferior positions. In a real sense, this leadership style creates a self-fulfilling prophecy. The prophecy of the leader's superiority relative to others is reinforced by the fact that the decisions made are often the right ones only because he or she is the judge and standard of rightness. The actual quality of the leader's decisions might well be inferior to the decisions many subordinates would make if they had the authority, but such a possibility is never put to the test.

Although a charismatic leader may be highly endowed with charisma (personal charm or magnetism that attracts others and establishes bonds of identification), it would be incorrect to assume that persons with charisma will necessarily adopt a charismatic style, as the term is used here. Adolph Hitler, whose generals were treated as if they were personal servants, and India's Mahatma Gandhi, whose political followers sought his personal blessing, were both charismatic leaders and both possessed unusual personal charisma. To a limited extent, the same may be said for Franklin D. Roosevelt or John F. Kennedy, whose followers often spoke of them in hushed, messianic terms. On the other hand, large numbers of leaders who possess a relatively high level of personal charisma never make it the focal point for their leadership behavior. Although charisma is obviously a desirable quality, especially for someone in a leadership position, it is not in itself a sufficient basis upon which to develop a leadership pattern.

PATERNALISM

Thesis: Paternalism was one of management's great mistakes. From it management learned that employees will not willingly tolerate a relationship in which they are made to feel dependent and in which they are expected to work out of feelings of gratitude.

Of the many expressions of authoritarian leadership, paternalism ranks among the least successful. Although some company presidents still try to maintain the fiction that their employees constitute a family, attempts to recognize the company, its founder, or its president as a father who assumes responsibility for the welfare of his children, have in their extreme forms been discontinued in America. It is noteworthy, however, that in some foreign countries, particularly in Japan, paternalism is still very much alive.

From its late nineteenth century beginning with company welfare programs, paternalism reached its heyday in the 1920s, mostly as management's attempt to stave off the rising tide of unionism. This fathering approach to leadership expressed itself primarily in two ways. First of all, management made a concerted effort to be good to its employees. In practice this meant the establishment of fringe benefits, cafeterias, company purchasing plans, recreational programs, and a host of other programs intended to make employees happy and, hopefully, more productive.

The second expression of paternalism was somewhat more ominous. In many companies, among the more notable of which was the Ford Motor Company, organizational influence was not confined to the work situation. Company social workers were sent into the homes of employees to help them be more effective in handling their personal affairs. Employees were encouraged to practice financial budgeting, physical hygiene, and "high morality." (Divorce and drinking alcoholic beverages often topped the list of unacceptable moral behaviors.) Some organizations exercised additional controls over their employees through company-owned towns (company stores, housing, and recreational facilities). Owing one's soul to the company store was almost a reality for many employees in the 1920s and 1930s.

Whatever honorable motivation may have been involved in paternalism, the ultimate result was to reduce employees to the role of dependents. Since the fringe benefits and welfare programs were presented by management as though they were gifts, rather than compensation, it became obvious that they could be withdrawn anytime employees failed to comply with company demands. The unacceptability of this crude use of power was increased by management's attempts to package it as goodness and concern for people, a tactic which was certain to provoke resentment and hostility. The long-range effect of paternalism apparently was to increase rather than decrease unionism.

PARTICIPATIVE LEADERSHIP

Thesis: When compared with authoritarian leadership, participative leadership expresses greater confidence in the subordinates' willingness and ability to assume responsibility, involves subordinates in decision making to a greater extent, and accepts more fully the notion that management has a responsibility to subordinates as well as to superiors. No manager can perform effectively over an extended period of time without some degree of employee participation.

Although the terms *participative* and *democratic* leadership are used interchangeably, the latter is a less desirable term in that it tends to communicate the notion that managerial decision making is a matter of vote taking. Because of our popular use of the word *democracy,* we necessarily read meaning into it that ordinarily cannot be accepted by management. To be specific, the participation of subordinates in management decision making can never be taken so far that it undermines a manager's right to the last word. A purely democratic process would make accountability impossible. Since line managers remain accountable for results, regardless of their leadership style, they cannot afford to abdicate the decision-making responsibility. The term *consultative* leadership is sometimes used in preference to participative leadership because it clearly avoids the connotation of pure democracy.

Participative Techniques

Managers have many opportunities for involving subordinates in organizational planning and decision making. Some companies, for example, have experimented with "junior boards of directors," composed of middle managers, and others have formalized elaborate programs of employee representation on major planning and decision-making bodies of the organization. We look now at the four participative methods which managers are most likely to employ.

Delegation.   Delegation is not ordinarily classified as a participative technique. Yet if the objective of participation is to involve subordinates in decision making, delegation should be high on the list. Since the determination of which decisions should be delegated is often difficult, a manager's leadership philosophy and degree of commitment to participative management certainly come into play. The manager who is committed to maximum participation will insist that decisions be made at the lowest possible level in the organization, while a more autocratic manager will prefer to centralize decision making.

Question Asking.   Managers who respect the knowledge, opinions, and judgment of their subordinates may achieve a relatively high level of participation by simply asking questions. While authoritarian leaders are busy playing the role of oracle and telling others what to do, participative leaders are asking for information and insights that will improve the quality of their decisions and at the same time underscore the responsibility of their subordinates to think and solve problems. One manager formalized this practice and the philosophy by posting a small sign on the wall behind his desk. It read *DBMQ,* which he interpreted as *Don't bring me questions.* Implied was the alternative: *Bring me recommendations.*

Experienced managers learn not to be afraid subordinates will think the manager's question asking is a reflection of ignorance, a form of buck-passing, or an attempt to avoid responsibility. It is actually a form of tough-minded management, not recommended for leaders who are unable to accept criticism, relate effectively to strong subordinates, or live with the challenge of new ideas and creative change.

Committee Action.   Committees are a vital means of continually gaining input from a large number of organizational members. Most companies have certain *standing committees* to deal with continuing or recurring problems (for example, near the top of the management hierarchy an executive committee handles a variety of problems relating to corporate policy, goals, and operations). Depending upon the organizational structure, *special committees* may be established to deal with budgets, employment policies, grievances, disciplinary problems, and a variety of other organizational problems and activities.

The nature and function of committees vary according to the demands of the specific situation. Some are *permanent committees* with rotating membership, or membership determined by position within the organization, while others are *ad hoc,* special purpose committees, which are dissolved when their mission is completed. A decision may be delegated to a committee, or the committee may be asked to make a recommendation to a higher level governing body or to a specific manager. Ordinarily the latter course of action is followed, since it is difficult to fix responsibility for a committee decision, and a committee decision actually may be made by one or two of its dominant members.

Ad hoc committees of rank and file workers are sometimes used as a means of bypassing one or more levels of management in order to provide a manager with information concerning special problems or attitudes toward pay, working conditions, supervision, and other work-related matters. Such committees provide management with insights into employee sentiments and attitudes which are essential for effective decision making.

Since committee membership can be rationally selected, committees are ideally suited for handling situations in which coordination and interaction among members is important. Representatives from, say, sales, marketing, credit, and manufacturing may dynamically interact concerning a common problem to produce insights which could be gained only from such interaction. Committee action contributes significantly to the coordinative as well as the problem-solving function of an organization.

Shared Goals.   Authoritarian leaders are not prone to become involved in management by objectives and similar goal-oriented programs. Although MBO programs do exist in which all the planning is centralized and the objectives are authoritatively delegated, such programs miss the point of what management by objectives is all about. Ideally an MBO program is highly participative, at least in the sense that each manager is able to exercise a degree of initiative and discretion in determining individual goals and the means for reaching them.

Authoritarian leaders often resist the loss of personal power that they fear will result from clear statements of goals. As organizational goals are clearly defined and the criteria against which decisions are to be made and evaluated are thereby clarified, differences between the roles of managers and their subordinates begin to diminish. Since effective goals programs involve a diffusion of responsibility throughout the organization, they require a concomitant increase in the authority of persons whose responsibilities have been increased. Authoritarian leaders often feel threatened by their subordinates' power, while the participative leader is more likely to view a high level of subordinate power and responsibility as an ideal toward which to strive.

Advantages of Participative Leadership

Many advantages have been claimed for participative over authoritarian leadership. While recognizing that they do not apply in every situation, a manager should be aware of some of the major benefits to be derived from participation.

Improved Decisions. Participation improves a manager's ability to make decisions. This point is especially convincing when we consider that the resources available through participation are above and beyond those available to the purely authoritarian decision maker. Since participation does not require managers to give up the ultimate right to choose between the available alternatives, they lose few of the benefits of authoritarian decision making when participative methods are employed.

Facilitation of Change. When employees, on any level, have had a voice in the formulation of a policy or course of action, they are less likely to resist its implementation. Because of their participation, they can understand the reasons behind the change and anticipate its positive as well as its possible negative consequences.

Identification with Leadership. Since participation affirms the value of subordinates by expressing the belief that they can make worthwhile contributions, it reduces defensiveness and increases the likelihood that a positive relationship will develop between superior and subordinate. Subordinates can more easily form a positive, personal identification with a participative leader than with an authoritarian one.

A High Level of Achievement. To the extent that participation leads subordinates to accept organizational goals and to internalize the organization's standards and values, it should lead to increased productivity, fewer grievances, reduced turnover, and to the achievement of other objectives by which managerial success is typically measured.

Conditions Necessary for Participation

Managers are by no means universally successful in their attempts to use participative methods. In fact, for managers who are authoritarian because of deep-seated personality characteristics and, therefore, likely to be inept in their use of participative methods, a rapid shift to a high level of participation could be disastrous. Certain conditions must be present for participative management to be optimally effective.

1. *Adequate Time.* Since participation ordinarily requires more time than authoritarian decision making, participative methods work best in situations where a manager is able to anticipate problems and plan ahead.

2. *Psychological Preparation of Subordinates.* Optimal participation requires that subordinates be psychologically prepared to contribute intelligently. They must have access to information which may typically be

withheld from them; they must believe that there is some personal benefit to be derived from participation and must not be too threatened by possible negative repercussions from it (for example, pressure from peers).

3. *Psychological Preparation of Management.* Managers must be convinced that participative leadership will pay off in terms of their own success. They must be psychologically prepared to deal with feelings, attitudes, and ideas from which an authoritarian leader may be relatively insulated. Only if they are highly motivated to change to participative methods will managers be willing to tolerate the frustrations involved in participative leadership.

4. *Belief in Participative Methods.* Managers who aspire to be successful using participative methods must have an in-depth belief that their subordinates have a contribution to make. Insincere or token attempts at participative leadership on the part of persons who see participation only as a gimmick or manipulative technique will ordinarily be seen for what they are and consequently be resented and resisted by subordinates. Since participative management is based on an optimistic view of human nature, the manager who believes that people are inherently lazy and prefer to avoid responsibility is not likely to succeed with a participative style.

5. *Dual Accountability.* Managers who employ participative methods must be willing to accept the idea that they have a responsibility and a form of accountability to subordinates as well as superiors. Participative leadership implies the existence of a partnership of sorts and a mutual respect that cannot be taken lightly when a conflict arises between the organization and a manager's subordinates. Managers must at times be their subordinates' advocate and representative to higher level management as well as the transmitter of commands from above.

TWO-DIMENSIONAL MODELS

Thesis: The two dimensions of leadership effectiveness which have received the most attention from researchers are (1) behaviors that are primarily concerned with achieving organizational objectives and (2) behaviors that are intended to meet the needs of followers or subordinates. Successful managers tend to place high emphasis on both.

Historically one school of thought stressed the achievement of organizational objectives while another focused attention on human needs. Traditional organizational theory, based primarily upon Max Weber's bureaucratic theory and Frederick W. Taylor's scientific management, showed little concern for the individual. Achieving results was everything; the individual was often viewed as merely a means to an end. On the other hand, the human relations movement, which began in the 1930s with a series of studies at Western Electric's Hawthorne plant, took the opposite approach. As the movement developed, the needs of the organization were de-emphasized, and the long-neglected needs and rights of the individual reigned supreme in the human relations literature.

In their reaction against the authority-oriented leadership of traditional theory, the leaders of the human relations movement interpreted the results of their experiments as though organizational authority were nonexistent or inherently evil. Placing all its hope on democratic leadership, narrowly conceived, the human relations movement lacked the realism and tough-mindedness to survive in its early form. It did, however, produce a major stream of thought that, over a period of time, was integrated with traditional concepts to produce a realistic and workable body of leadership theory.

Initiating Structure and Consideration

During the 1950s the two major dimensions of leadership behavior were first expressed as *initiating structure* and *consideration,* terms which became commonplace in leadership literature.[7] Initiating structure is intended to communicate the idea that task-oriented leaders rely heavily upon providing structure within which the behavior of subordinates is deemed acceptable. For example, they set goals, establish policies and procedures, issue directives, and otherwise limit the freedom of their subordinates. At the other extreme is consideration for people or concern for the needs of subordinates as individuals.

The two-dimensional view of leadership emphasizes the inadequacy of either initiating structure or consideration without the other. It suggests that a leader must be a mediator between the demands of the organization and the needs of the individuals upon whom the organization must depend for the achievement of its objectives.

The Managerial Grid®

A variation of the two-dimensional approach was developed by Robert Blake and Jane Mouton. Beginning with a rather simple two-dimensional model called the Managerial Grid, they developed an elaborate system for evaluating and developing managers. As shown in Figure 10–2 (page 228), leadership style is expressed in terms of concern for people and concern for production, corresponding roughly to consideration and initiating structure.

According to Blake and Mouton the 9,9 leadership style is always preferred. They object to the notion that a leader's style should be changed to meet the demands of each unique situation since such an approach undermines trust and respect. Situational leadership is seen as void of positive values which reflect a concern for helping others, for contributing to the development of subordinates, and for changing the negative aspects of the leadership environment.

In spite of their commitment to the 9,9 leadership style, Blake and Mouton do not advocate indifference to the situation or leadership environment. But

---

[7] E. Fleishman, E. F. Harris, and R. D. Burtt, *Leadership and Supervision in Industry* (Columbus: Ohio State University Press, 1955).

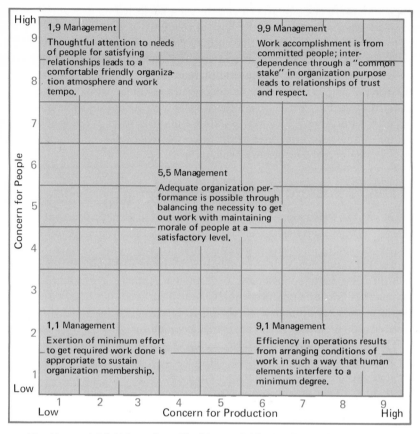

Figure 10–2   The Managerial Grid

rather than accept the *flexibility* of shifting from one leadership style to another, they advocate a *versatility* in which commitment to certain principles remains constant while searches are made for solutions to problems arising in each situation. For example, if the transfer of a manager to another geographical area is called for, that individual is not ordered to go, nor is subtle leverage applied to produce the desired behavior. Rather, the subordinate is helped to see the costs and benefits in terms of career, family, friends, etc., of accepting the transfer. Thus, the decision is based on free choice.[8]

The 9,9 leadership style, as conceptualized by Blake and Mouton, is based on certain principles which are not to be sacrificed in the interest of short-term

---

[8] Robert R. Blake and Jane Srygley Mouton, "Does It All Depend on the Situation? . . . Or Is There One Best Way to Lead?—Flexibility or Versatility," unpublished paper copyrighted by Scientific Methods, Inc., 1977, p. 14.

expediency. For example, a 9,9 style prefers freedom of choice to enforced compliance, active participation in problem solving and decision making over unilateral action, and self-direction guided by goal setting over external control. By consistently applying such principles the leader is perceived as developing relationships of trust and avoiding the image of being shifty or untrustworthy that could result from applying first one style and then another.

Tannenbaum and Schmidt [9] attempt to deal with the conflict managers experience in selecting a leadership pattern with which they can be comfortable and effective. Figure 10–3 shows Tannenbaum and Schmidt's concept of a two-dimensional approach to leadership. Again, the extremes of boss-centered and subordinate-centered leadership can be recognized as comparable to the models discussed earlier. Tannenbaum and Schmidt stress the notion that the "appropriate style of leadership for a particular manager depends not only upon his or her own needs and preferences but also upon the total organizational environment, including the nature of subordinates." Carefully avoiding the idea that there is

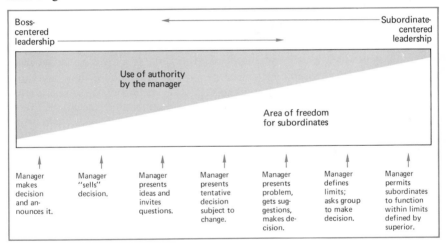

Figure 10–3 Continuum of Leadership Behavior

any one best leadership pattern for all situations, they point out four "internal forces" that will face the manager in the process of choosing a leadership pattern or style:

1. The manager's value system: personal convictions or beliefs about how much responsibility should be given to subordinates for making decisions and participating in decision making

2. The manager's confidence in subordinates: perception of their knowledge, competence, and beliefs about how much they are able to contribute to the decision-making function

---

[9] Robert Tannenbaum and Warren H. Schmidt, "How to Choose a Leadership Pattern," *Harvard Business Review,* Vol. 36, No. 2 (March–April, 1958), pp. 95–101.

3. The manager's own leadership inclinations: whether he or she feels more comfortable taking a directive or a team role

4. The manager's feelings of security in an uncertain situation: personal need for structure and predictability versus level of tolerance for ambiguity and uncertainty

A CONTINGENCY MODEL

Thesis: In Fred E. Fiedler's "contingency model" leadership effectiveness depends primarily upon leadership style and the favorableness of the situation (leadership environment). The quality of leadership is more likely to be improved by modifying the environment than by attempting to change the leader's behavior.

In contingency theory, leadership style is defined as the extent to which a manager is "task-oriented" versus "relationship-oriented" (again, corresponding roughly to initiating structure and consideration). Style is measured by means of a least preferred co-worker (LPC scale).[10] The measuring instrument itself is a simple, bipolar adjective scale (for example, good-bad and strong-weak) which is commonly used in attitude measurement. According to Fiedler's studies, leaders who describe in favorable terms the co-workers with whom they have been least able to work are "relationship-oriented," while leaders whose least preferred co-workers are described critically are "task-oriented."

Situational favorableness is defined by Fiedler as the degree to which the situation itself provides the leader with power and influence over the behavior of subordinates. To be more specific, situational favorableness depends upon (1) leader-member relations, (2) the extent to which the task is structured or clearly defined, and (3) the amount of formal organizational power the leader possesses (the power to hire, fire, give raises, etc.).

On the basis of a number of studies, conducted in many different field and laboratory settings, Fiedler draws several conclusions about leadership and its development. Notable among these are the following:

1. Task-oriented leaders perform best in situations that are very favorable or unfavorable; while people-oriented leaders perform best in situations of intermediate favorableness.

2. Neither formal leadership training nor leadership experience contributes greatly to effectiveness in the leadership role. Because of the difficulty in changing the leader's behavior, leadership effectiveness can best be improved by changing the favorableness of the situation (e.g., altering a leader's position power, selecting subordinates who fit the leader's style, restructuring the leader's job, or transferring the leader to a position that matches his or her style).

---

[10] Fred E. Fiedler, "Validation and Extension of the Contingency Model of Leadership Effectiveness: A Review of Empirical Findings," *Psychological Bulletin,* Vol. 76, No. 2 (1971), pp. 129–148. Also see Fred E. Fiedler, "How Do You Make Leaders More Effective? New Answers to an Old Puzzle," *Organizational Dynamics* (Autumn, 1972), pp. 3–18.

Fiedler's contingency theory makes a significant contribution to the understanding of leadership effectiveness, but it probably goes too far in its de-emphasis of management development and adaptability. Modifying the position to fit the manager, to the degree prescribed by Fiedler, would be highly disruptive to an organization, considering the frequency with which managers change positions. Managers who aspire to be optimally effective would be ill-advised to believe that they can reach their goal without being willing and able constantly to grow, change, adapt, and modify their behavior to meet the demands of different situations and different types of subordinates.

PATH-GOAL THEORY OF LEADERSHIP

Thesis: Path-goal theory of leadership, a form of contingency theory with great potential for explaining leadership behavior, is currently attracting the attention of serious researchers. Research findings to date, however, are conflicting. They do effectively demonstrate that a great number of variables, including individual leader characteristics, are required to explain the difference between effective and ineffective leadership.

Path-goal leadership theory is based on expectancy motivation theory and the concepts of consideration and initiating structure.[11] According to this theory, leaders are effective in terms of their ability to motivate subordinates to reach organizational goals and to find satisfaction in their work. Although path-goal theory is rapidly evolving, at the present time, it may be generally expressed as follows:

1. The leader may improve the motivation of subordinates by making the rewards for productivity more attractive to them (i.e., by increasing the valence of goal achievement). For example, a manager has the potential for rewarding high productivity with raises, promotions, recognition, and praise, thereby increasing its attractiveness as a goal.

2. When the work of subordinates is poorly defined, a manager may increase motivation by providing structure (clarifying goals, giving supportive and helpful supervision, training subordinates, etc.) which will reduce the job's vagueness and ambiguity and thereby increase the expectation of successful goal achievement. Since, in expectancy theory, motivational force = valence X expectancy, this should increase employee motivation and consequently increase leader effectiveness.

3. When the work of subordinates is already highly structured (e.g., repetitive assembly-line or machine-tending work), this theory assumes that goal-path relationships are clear and that initiating structure will be viewed by subordinates as unnecessary and too directive. Thus, it would

---

[11] Robert J. House, "A Path Goal Theory of Leader Effectiveness," *Administrative Science Quarterly* (September, 1971), pp. 321–338; and Robert J. House and Terrence R. Mitchell, "Path-Goal Theory of Leadership," *Journal of Contemporary Business* (Autumn, 1974), pp. 81–97.

lead to subordinate dissatisfaction. This highly structured situation calls for increased consideration for the personal needs of the individual (e.g., understanding, praise, and related forms of support).

Path-goal theory appears to be quite logical, and there is some experimental evidence to support it.[12] There is, however, good research to show that in its original form the theory is too simple—that is, it does not take enough variables into consideration.[13] It applies to some people but not to others. In some unstructured situations, for example, when leaders take the initiative by clarifying goals and otherwise reducing ambiguity in the work environment, subordinates react unfavorably. Some employees either do not want their goal-path structured or believe in their own ability to provide whatever structure is needed without help from their superior. There is evidence that the reaction of subordinates to structure by a superior is related to a number of personal characteristics, including education, need for achievement, perceived ability, willingness to accept responsibility, and need for independence. A leader should not, therefore, assume that subordinate motivation will always be increased by giving structure to the path that leads to a goal, even when that path is very vague. There is, however, fairly strong evidence that increasing consideration for subordinates whose work is already highly structured does increase their job satisfaction.

The value of path-goal theory lies not so much in its proved ability to predict and interpret leadership effectiveness as in its ability to stimulate good research. The foundations upon which it is based are sufficiently broad that an endless number of variables can be related to leadership effectiveness within the context of path-goal theory.

LEAVING A MARK

Thesis: Environmental favorableness is an important determinant of a leader's success, but managers are a part of that environment and capable of changing it. While one manager is submissive to an unfavorable organizational environment and conforms to all its demands, another manager acts to change it. Strong leaders leave their mark on the organization.

The leadership literature from Max Weber to Fred Fiedler is interesting and challenging but it can hardly be described as inspiring. Its emphasis is on theories

---

[12] Robert J. House and G. Dressler, "The Path-Goal Theory of Leadership: Some Post Hoc and A Priori Tests," in J. G. Hunt and L. L. Larson, eds., *Contingency Approaches to Leadership* (Carbondale, Ill.: Southern Illinois University Press, 1974), pp. 29–55; and H. P. Sims, Jr. and A. D. Szilagyi, "Leader Structure and Subordinate Satisfaction for Two Hospital Administrative Levels: A Path Analysis Approach," *Journal of Applied Psychology,* Vol. 60, No. 2 (April, 1975), pp. 194–197.

[13] John E. Stinson and Thomas W. Johnson, "The Path-Goal Theory of Leadership: A Partial Test and Suggested Refinement," *Academy of Management Journal,* Vol. 18, No. 2 (June, 1975), pp. 242–252; A. D. Szilagyi and H. P. Sims, Jr., "An Exploration of the Path-Goal Theory of Leadership in a Health Care Environment," *Academy of Management Journal,* Vol. 17, No. 4 (December, 1974), pp. 622–634; and H. K. Downey, J. E. Sheridan, and J. W. Slocum, "Analysis of Relationships among Leader Behavior, Subordinate Job Performance and Satisfaction: A Path-Goal Approach," *Academy of Management Journal,* Vol. 18, No. 2 (June, 1975), pp. 253–262.

and principles rather than the personal qualities of the leaders to which they relate. In contrast, the writings of Eugene E. Jennings focus attention on the leader. He argues forcefully for the idea that we have lost the will to lead and have even developed a silent, but active, hostility toward leadership.[14]

Not to be confused with the "great man" of the trait approach or with Weber's charismatic leader, Jennings' leader does, in fact, have qualities of greatness. Leadership at its best is a high-risk venture requiring personal initiative and the courage to deviate from the standards of mediocrity promulgated by our society. Unlike the low-confidence chairperson, coordinator, facilitator and therapist-type bureaucratic executive, Jennings' leader leaves a mark on the organization. The leader is no public relations expert who senses group sentiments and merely takes the group where it wants to go. Although Jennings recognizes that a situation must be ripe for greatness to be expressed, he also points out that the leader must be prepared to be a value-creator and a tradition-breaker. Unwilling to be bound by situational unfavorableness, the optimally effective leader takes the position that aggressive action can often overcome a bad situation.

The notion that leaders should or often do leave their mark on an organization and the people with whom they interact is not a new idea. It is, in fact, a very old one, but one that needs to be occasionally restated. In the real world, leadership consists of very dynamic relationships between leaders and followers. Because it is centered in personal relationships, leadership must often be understood in terms of human emotions and nonrational needs as well as rationally formulated and empirically tested theories. It should not, therefore, be surprising that the personal qualities of both leaders and followers are important variables in the leadership equation.

STUDY AND DISCUSSION QUESTIONS

1. In what technical sense is a manager always a leader?
2. Why did early research studies cause some scholars to conclude that personal characteristics are not related to leadership success? From your own observations, how would you evaluate such a conclusion?
3. In the absence of special training in participative leadership, why do managers tend to gravitate toward an authoritarian style?
4. Differentiate the leadership style of the authoritarian personality from that of the great mass of authoritarian leaders who have learned the style through imitation or trial and error.
5. What distinctions would you make between a charismatic leader and a leader who has charisma? Should a leader with charisma necessarily be classified as a charismatic leader, as the term is used here?
6. What are the primary shortcomings of paternalistic leadership?

[14] E. E. Jennings, *An Anatomy of Leadership: Princes, Heroes, and Supermen* (New York: McGraw-Hill, Inc., 1960).

7. In what sense is participative leadership not democratic?
8. In what ways are participative methods superior to authoritarian leadership as a general managerial style?
9. From one point of view, authoritarian leadership is the approach taken by the strong, tough-minded, and courageous manager. From another perspective such a manager is more likely to use a participative style. Be prepared to support either point of view in classroom discussion.
10. Evaluate Fiedler's emphasis on improving leadership effectiveness by modifying the environment rather than the individual.
11. Evaluate the statement that a leader must be prepared to be a value creator and a tradition breaker.

CRITICAL INCIDENT

The Too Mobile Manager

Charles Batson gathered his personal belongings, turned in his keys, and prepared to leave for the day. It was his last day. He had been fired from the second highest paying position in the company after fourteen months of outstanding achievement. It was not a new experience for Batson, who had averaged changing jobs every three years during his 20-year career in production management, but he was disappointed and did not want to go through another job change.

At one point during the termination interview, Lester Howard, President of Executive Mobile Homes, Inc., had made a statement that kept returning to Batson as he drove back to his apartment. Batson remembered it this way:

> Charles, I'm truly sorry it had to come to this. In slightly over a year you've changed this company from a mom-and-pop operation into a sound business. I give you credit for our success, but either you leave or a half dozen other key managers do. You're a great hatchet man, but the deadwood is gone now. Let's face it, you're a short-term operator.

In trying to ferret out the implications of Howard's statement, Batson thought back over the last fourteen months. He had, indeed, started with something less than a business. In whipping the organization into shape he had conducted time and motion studies, set up a cost accounting system, instituted a quality control program, and totally revised the manufacturing process. The production department was unquestionably efficient, and Batson was enormously proud of it.

He was not so proud of some of the steps he was forced to take to reach his goal. A number of skilled workers had to be discharged when their jobs were diluted to enable unskilled labor to perform them. Some supervisors were discharged, too. Batson worked closely with each of the six general supervisors until he knew every detail of their jobs. Three of the six were just too rigid to change their methods and were given an opportunity to resign. This statement by one of the three who left was characteristic of their inability to adapt to the new system:

> Batson, what do you care how we do the job as long as it gets done? I've been building mobile homes ever since the industry began, and I know what I'm doing. If you will just get off my back, I'll see to it that we make homes that meet all your standards, including costs.

Batson thought back over the insurance programs and retirement plan that he had installed, and marvelled that no one seemed to appreciate them. He also took note of the fact that everybody, including the stockholders and the president, was now making much more money than before he revolutionized the company; but this fact had not resulted in any warm feelings toward him.

Batson mused that he really would not have a great deal of difficulty getting another job. He had always been able to sell himself. In college he was everybody's candidate for the man most likely to succeed. During his senior year he was captain of the football team, leading man in a successful drama, and president of the student body. Today was a bad day; but he knew that his persuasiveness, superior ability, and willingness to work hard were still going for him; and he was determined not to make the same mistakes again.

Questions

1. How would you describe Batson's leadership style?
2. What should Batson have done differently?
3. What additional information would be helpful in answering Question 2?

Chapter

11

Personal Dimensions of Leadership Effectiveness

Organizational behavior cannot be understood by viewing people as though they were all alike. One is, however, tempted to do so because of the many uncontrolled variables introduced when the influence of individual differences is taken seriously. Classical theorists such as Weber, Fayol, and Taylor confined their contributions primarily to a study of organizational structure, principles of management, and techniques of productive efficiency. Neoclassical thinkers broke with the relatively neat, impersonal categories of the classicists by studying the nature of informal groups. Ultimately such person-centered subjects as leadership, perception, learning, motivation, and the nature of conflict became a significant part of the literature of organizational behavior. Tempting as it has been to avoid the individual in studying organizational behavior, it has not been possible.

It is for several reasons important that the individual be included in a study of managerial effectiveness. If some managers with certain personal characteristics (such as specific personality traits, aptitudes, acquired needs, attitudes, and interests) are more effective than others, it is important that these qualities be recognized and that their impact in different environments be studied. To the extent that the personal characteristics of effective and ineffective leaders are different, they should be taken into consideration when selecting and promoting managers; and the implications of such differences for management development should be understood. Finally, if personal characteristics are related to managerial effectiveness—and research clearly shows that some characteristics are—these factors should be considered in developing leadership theory and drawing conclusions about its practical applications.

A REVIVED INTEREST IN THE INDIVIDUAL

Thesis: Managerial effectiveness is contingent upon many variables; some are environmental, and some are personal. Although cautious interpretation is in order, research provides excellent insights into variables in both categories.

Chapter 3 dealt with environmental variables which affect managerial performance. In this chapter, we look closely at personal characteristics which also influence a manager's ability to perform effectively. They are not independent of organizational variables. Rather, the two interact in highly complex ways to produce unique behavior patterns and, at times, to produce improbable successes and failures.

Identifying common personal characteristics of effective managers is less ambitious than attempting to isolate universal characteristics of leaders without reference to the setting in which they lead.[1] Although leadership and management are closely related, they are not identical. Managers are leaders, but not all leaders are managers. There are leaders, for example, on the football field, in the parent-teachers association, and in the university student body, but they need not be managers. This chapter focuses specifically on managerial effectiveness with leadership skills included as one of several personal qualities involved.

A revival of interest in the contribution of personal characteristics to managerial effectiveness is strongly evidenced by the research of the past decade. After reviewing a number of published studies, John P. Campbell and his associates conclude that:

> Taken together, these studies provide good evidence that a fairly sizable portion (30 to 50 percent) of the variance in general managerial effectiveness can be expressed in terms of personal qualities measured by self-response tests and inventories and by predetermined rules or statistical equations.[2]

A surprising degree of support for the notion that individual characteristics are an important ingredient of managerial effectiveness comes from Fred Fiedler, a strong advocate of the importance of the environment:

> On the basis of evidence which we have presented so far, it would certainly not seem very fruitful to predict leadership status or leadership effectiveness from personality traits. At the same time,

---

[1] From the time psychological testing became popular, during World War I, to about 1945, the focus of leadership studies was on the isolation of personality traits (such as extroversion, social ascendancy, or aggressiveness) which characterized effective leaders. Paralleling the classical organizational theorists, who were searching for universal principles applicable to all organizations, leadership theorists sought to isolate a set of traits which were universally descriptive of effective leaders. Because this approach stressed only personal qualities of the leader and omitted any reference to the nature of followers, the favorability of the environment, and other situational variables, the trait-listing approach was sometimes called "the great man" theory of leadership. In this early research, which was often very crude, business managers were just one of many types of leaders who were studied as a single group.

[2] John P. Campbell et al., *Managerial Behavior, Performance and Effectiveness* (New York: McGraw-Hill, Inc., 1970), p. 195.

a number of studies indicate fairly conclusively that we can predict, to some extent, the effectiveness of *managers* from personality tests and inventories.[3]

Ralph M. Stogdill, who for many years has been a recognized authority on leadership behavior, based the following statement on a thorough survey of published research studies in a variety of settings:

> It can be concluded that the clusters of characteristics listed above differentiate (1) leaders from followers (2) effective from ineffective leaders, and (3) high-echelon from lower echelon leaders.[4]

Stogdill obviously goes beyond Fiedler by concluding that, leadership, one of several complex behaviors of effective managers, can be partially accounted for by personal characteristics (e.g., a strong drive for responsibility and task completion, self-confidence, willingness to tolerate frustration and delay, etc.). Stogdill's conclusions are based on practically all the research literature published prior to 1974.

Marvin Dunnette adds further credence to the notion that managerial behavior cannot be understood apart from the influence of individual characteristics.

> In choosing to include these four chapters about the methodology and instrumentation available for measuring human attributes, the editor obviously accepts the major thrust of traditional trait concepts and rejects the basic arguments put forward over the last several years by those who claim that human behavior is a function almost exclusively of the situation in which it occurs.[5]

Dunnette and many other behavioral scientists take an interactionist position in which it is recognized that individuals interpret and shape situations rather than passively submit to their influence.

PERSONAL CHARACTERISTICS: PROBLEMS AND CONTINGENCIES

Thesis: Personal characteristics influence managerial effectiveness in complex ways. They interact with one another and the situation to produce outcomes which lead to varying degrees of managerial effectiveness. It is only through an awareness of certain

---

[3] Fred E. Fiedler and Martin M. Chemers, *Leadership and Effective Management* (Glenview, Ill.: Scott, Foresman and Company, 1974), p. 31.

[4] Ralph M. Stogdill, *Handbook of Leadership: A Survey of Theory and Research* (New York: The Free Press, 1974), p. 81. (The specific characteristics to which Stogdill refers are listed in Chapter 10 of this textbook; see Footnote 4, Chapter 10.)

[5] Marvin D. Dunnette (ed.), *Handbook of Industrial and Organizational Psychology* (Chicago: Rand McNally & Company, 1976), p. 469. (This 1,740-page handbook consists of original contributions by many of the country's most outstanding behavioral scientists.)

contingencies, certain "if-then" conditions, that the effect of personal characteristics can be understood.

It is well to simplify burdensome and overly complicated theories and to avoid complex explanations when simple ones are effective. But oversimplification can be a problem, too. It leads to shallow answers and to reliance upon rigidly held half-truths. Classical theorists erred in their quest for universally applicable principles of organization. Similarly, those who seek to define the personal characteristics of effective managers may generalize too far on the basis of too little knowledge. This section provides the background needed to avert such a possibility.

A Probability Frame of Reference

Although it would be convenient to specify the amount of a given characteristic (say an IQ of 125) required for effectiveness in a particular managerial position, this is not possible. At best, we can define the position and make a statement concerning the probability that a given characteristic will contribute to a manager's effectiveness in it.

In the best studies of managerial effectiveness, a statistical relationship is established between a measurement of a characteristic (say intelligence) and one or more criteria of success (performance evaluations or promotions, for example); that is, statistics are used to show what effect intelligence has on performance evaluations or promotions. Only in extreme cases, however, can a specific amount of a certain characteristic be regarded as necessary for effective performance. The more cautious and realistic approach is to conclude that individuals with a given characteristic have a higher probability of success than those who lack it.

The relationship between measurements of personal characteristics and measurements of success may be graphically expressed in the form of an expectancy chart (Figure 11–1). The ratings referred to in this illustration were obtained in assessment centers which were designed to evaluate managerial potential.[6] On the basis of their combined ratings on a number of personal characteristics, the managers in this study were divided into four categories (left column of Figure 11–1). Note the tendency for managers with high ratings to rank high on the success criterion (managers receiving two or more promotions). Statistical tests indicate that the differences shown in Figure 11–1 would occur by chance less often than one time in 1,000. Individuals rated more than acceptable in terms of their personal characteristics are twice as likely to receive two or more promotions as those rated acceptable, and are almost ten times more likely to meet the

---

[6] An *assessment center* is both a place and a method. The place is somewhere other than the workplace in order to provide freedom from work pressures and interruptions. The method involves *situational tests* in which assessees (usually six managers at a time) work together to solve a problem or achieve an objective. Trained observers rate their performance on several carefully defined characteristics (e.g., initiative, communication skills, decisiveness, motivation, and persistence) which are thought to relate to success in the position for which assessment is being made. AT&T and other large companies have done extensive research with the method. Results have been impressive.

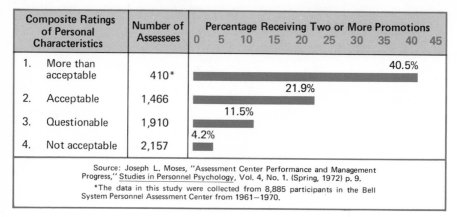

Composite Ratings of Personal Characteristics	Number of Assessees	Percentage Receiving Two or More Promotions
1. More than acceptable	410*	40.5%
2. Acceptable	1,466	21.9%
3. Questionable	1,910	11.5%
4. Not acceptable	2,157	4.2%

Source: Joseph L. Moses, "Assessment Center Performance and Management Progress," Studies in Personnel Psychology, Vol. 4, No. 1. (Spring, 1972) p. 9.

*The data in this study were collected from 8,885 participants in the Bell System Personnel Assessment Center from 1961–1970.

Figure 11-1   The Expectancy Chart Method of Relating Personal Characteristics to Managerial Success

promotion criterion than those rated not acceptable. In the Bell System (AT&T), personal characteristics are clearly related to success.

One of the most extensive studies of the relationship between personal characteristics and managerial effectiveness was conducted by the Standard Oil Company of New Jersey.[7] The 443 managers who participated in the study held a variety of line and staff positions. Psychological test scores and background information were used as indicators of personal characteristics. These were correlated with three measures of managerial effectiveness: position level, salary history, and effectiveness rankings. When the composite personal characteristics scores were related to an overall success index, approximately half (49 percent) of the variation in managerial effectiveness was related to personal characteristics as measured in the study.[8] Although the Standard Oil Company of New Jersey study is one of the better research studies on this subject, it is only one of many that shows a substantial correlation between individual characteristics and managerial effectiveness.

The Ambiguous Managerial Position

One way to increase the precision with which characteristics of effective managers are isolated is to single out a particular kind of manager for study. The president of General Motors is a manager, but so is the president-owner of Dameron's Delicatessen. It is unlikely that the ideal profile for the two managers

---

[7] H. Laurent, "EIMP Applied to the International Petroleum Co.," *Standard Oil of New Jersey Technical Report, 1966.*

[8] The term *related to* is preferred to *caused by* in correlation studies to emphasize the fact that causation is inferred rather than proved. The fallacy of automatically equating correlation and causation is seen in the fact that in children there is a high correlation between mental ability and foot size. Yet it would be foolish to conclude that one causes the other. To the contrary, both are influenced by a third variable, age (or growth and maturation).

is the same. The manufacturing supervisor, quality control superintendent, director of personnel, office supervisor, and chief engineer are all managers; and individuals who succeed in these positions may have certain characteristics in common. On the other hand, certain qualities are unique to each category. For example, successful office supervisors ordinarily need more detailed technical knowledge about processes and methods than do higher level line managers. The higher managers progress, the greater is their need for the ability to plan, organize, and make complex decisions.

Managers are often tritely defined as people who achieve objectives through the efforts of others. While this definition is appropriate in most cases, it does not allow for the fact that both line and staff managers spend much time performing nonmanagerial work. Because there are many different kinds of managers performing a variety of duties, one must be cautious in generalizing about managerial characteristics. The generalizations in this chapter will refer primarily to line managers above the supervisory level—to individuals who have responsibility for achieving organizational objectives through other people as well as for performing a variety of other tasks.

Problems in the Measurement of Managerial Effectiveness

One of the problems in isolating characteristics of effective managers is that research studies must somehow define and measure managerial effectiveness. Many measures of effectiveness have been used, such as performance evaluations, number of promotions during a specific period, level achieved in the management hierarchy, and salary. Virtually any criterion used is subject to one or another form of bias, although in recent years most researchers have made serious attempts to use meaningful and reliable criteria.

In discussing criteria, the terms *success* and *effectiveness* are used interchangeably. However, managers often succeed (that is, receive raises and promotions), because of political skills that have little to do with their other abilities needed to perform effectively. Another factor which calls for caution in using promotion and salary as indicators of effectiveness is the element of luck. Successful managers create part of their so-called luck, but some of it is due to the chance factor of being in the right place at the right time.

One study shows that managers considered promotable are significantly more aware of their superiors' views than are nonpromotable managers.[9] This could be the result of a manager's unusual empathy and perceptiveness, or it could result from a unique opportunity to observe one's superiors. Managers who are fortunate enough to begin their careers under superiors who are highly promotable, excellent models, and who are committed to the development of subordinate managers may succeed while other managers with comparable personal qualities fail or achieve only marginal success.

---

[9] George H. Labovitz, "More on Subjective Executive Appraisal, an Empirical Study," *Academy of Management Journal,* Vol. 15, No. 3 (September, 1972), pp. 289–302.

The Effect of Compensating Characteristics

Isolating the differentiating characteristics of effective managers is complicated by the fact that an individual always functions as a whole. Characteristics do not exist in isolation. Rather, they constantly interact with each other. Even though a manager lacks one desirable characteristic, strength in another area compensates for the deficiency and results in effective overall performance.

The effect of compensation is clearly operating in the following example taken from the author's assessment files. The name is, of course, fictitious.

Charles Clark functions effectively as the production manager of a manufacturing firm of about three hundred employees despite the fact that his IQ, as measured by the Wechsler Adult Intelligence Scale (WAIS), is in a range where one would normally predict failure. His IQ of 114 is about average for the first-line foremen in that company and considerably below the average IQ (127) of the other managers at Clark's level.

Although Clark is not known for his brilliance, he is respected, and he performs satisfactorily because of other outstanding qualities. He works extremely long hours, and through much effort he keeps abreast of advancements in his field. His common sense judgment is high, his human relations skills are outstanding, and he is methodical and organized. He is secure enough to hire technical advisers who are much better problem solvers than he is, and he delegates effectively. His predecessor, a brilliant engineering student while in school and a highly creative and analytical technical expert, failed miserably, in spite of his superior mental ability, because he related poorly to people. His predecessor's intellectual abilities failed to compensate for the lack of human relations skills.

Even though some compensation occurs, certain characteristics typically contribute to success. A success-related characteristic does not ensure success, nor does its absence always lead to failure. Its presence or absence does, however, affect the probability of success.

SELECTED CORRELATES OF MANAGERIAL EFFECTIVENESS

Thesis:　Since situational demands differ, it is not possible to describe personal characteristics which are critically important in all managerial positions. It is, however, possible to describe personal characteristics which significantly contribute to success in most managerial positions.

How many personal characteristics are related to managerial effectiveness? Too many factors are involved for this question to be answered definitively. For example, research studies show varying degrees of correlation between characteristics and effectiveness, and no one can say exactly how large a correlation must be to be considered important or practically significant. Another problem arises from the fact that researchers may use different terms to refer to essentially the same characteristic. Still another consideration is the fact that many of the personal characteristics which correlate with managerial effectiveness also correlate with one another. Decisiveness and self-confidence, for example, are overlapping concepts because self-confident managers are more likely to be decisive than are managers whose self-confidence is low. It is likely that studies which list more than, say, ten to twelve personal characteristics, do so only because statistical analyses have not been performed to eliminate the inevitable overlapping of personal characteristics.

No attempt is made in this chapter to present an exhaustive discussion of personal characteristics of effective managers, nor is any claim made that those presented are independent of one another. They are, however, representative of the characteristics most often found to relate to managerial effectiveness.

Superior Mental Ability

Although mental ability (intelligence) does not always differentiate the various levels of effectiveness within management, research shows that effective managers are usually characterized by superior intelligence.[10] It is difficult to specify exactly what constitutes superior intelligence. One problem is inherent in the type of test used to measure this quality. For example, the exhaustive AT&T studies used the SCAT (School and College Ability Test),[11] and an elaborate University of Minnesota study of 452 managers in 13 firms used the 12-minute Wonderlic Personnel Test.[12] The use of diverse tests with different norms makes comparisons difficult.

It is virtually impossible today for a manager to succeed in most organizations without a college education. In fact, the AT&T studies showed that high achieving students from highly rated universities who participated actively in campus activities were more likely to achieve high salaries (one measure of

---

[10] For a critical presentation of outstanding studies on this and other characteristics, refer to Campbell, et al., op. cit., Chapters 8 and 9. Also note the conclusions of Ghiselli and Grimsley and Jarrett that differences in intellectual competence are related to the degree of success achieved at high levels of management: Edwin E. Ghiselli, "Managerial Talent," *American Psychologist,* Vol. 8 (1963), pp. 631–664; and Glen Grimsley and Hilton F. Jarrett, "The Relation of Past Managerial Achievement to Test Measures Obtained in the Employment Situation: Methodology and Results," *Personnel Psychology,* Vol. 26 (1973), pp. 31–48.

[11] For a comprehensive view of these studies see D. W. Bray and D. L. Grant, *The Assessment Center in the Measurement of Potential for Business Management,* Psychological Monographs, Vol. 80 (1966), Whole. No. 625. Also Joseph L. Moses, "Assessment Center Performance and Managerial Progress," *Studies in Personnel Psychology,* Vol. 4, No. 1 (Spring, 1972), p. 7–12; and Douglas W. Bray, Richard J. Campbell, and Donald L. Grant, *Formative Years in Business: A Long-Term AT&T Study of Managerial Lives* (New York: John Wiley & Sons, Inc., 1974).

[12] T. A. Mahoney et al., "Identification and Prediction of Managerial Effectiveness," *Personnel Administration,* Vol. 26 (1963), pp. 12–22.

managerial effectiveness) than were individuals who lacked these qualities.[13] Since earning a degree typically screens out people who are average and below in intelligence, it is understandable that superior intelligence is required to compete within the ranks of management.[14]

Some studies have shown little correlation between managerial performance and the intelligence of present managers. The reason for this is usually obvious. If high intelligence is one criterion for selecting managers, all managers within an organization will be so much alike in this characteristic that differences are masked by differences in motivation, work habits, leadership behavior, and other success-related characteristics. If management were represented by the full spectrum of intellectual abilities, the correlation between intelligence and success would be extremely high. Those with below average intelligence would most certainly fail, those near the mean would very likely fail, and most of the successes would be considerably above the average category.

Psychological assessments conducted by the author over a 15-year period strongly suggest that IQs from about 120 to 135 are in the ideal range for managerial success.[15] This ranges from the 91st to the 99th centiles of the general population on the best adult intelligence test (the Wechsler Adult Intelligence Scale). Individuals with IQs from 115–119 are acceptable in some managerial positions but seldom in top companies with strong competition for promotion. Managers with IQs below 115 are at a distinct disadvantage when competing with other managers, except at the first-line supervisory level. Those with unusually high IQs (say, over 135) sometimes become undesirably theoretical and/or become bored with the routine which exists in many line positions.

Managers who are far above the people they supervise, say managers with IQs in the 140s and above, are sometimes intolerant of the relative slowness of subordinates. This may result in human relations problems which reduce overall management effectiveness although it would be incorrect to assume that extremely high intelligence will necessarily have this effect. On the average, staff managers are more highly educated and more intelligent than line managers. In staff positions involving complex problem solving very superior intelligence is

---

[13] Research results differ on the importance of university achievement (usually measured by grades) and managerial success. For support of the notion that there is very little relationship between the level of academic and managerial success see J. Sterling Livingston, "Myth of the Well-Educated Manager," *Harvard Business Review* (May-June, 1971), pp. 79–89.

[14] Psychologists have arbitrarily broken down the total IQ range into several categories. For simplicity in communication these are avoided with one exception. The average category includes the middle 50 percent of the population and ranges from 90–110. Those above 110 are here referred to as superior in a very nontechnical sense, and those below 90 are simply categorized as below average.

[15] Though highly consistent with published studies, these conclusions concerning intelligence, are based partly on unpublished clinical observation by the author. The data consist of approximately 600 management assessments made in 22 different companies ranging in size from small, family-owned businesses to multinational organizations. In most of these, the Wechsler Adult Intelligence Test (Verbal) was administered along with a battery of other tests, a background study, and an interview. In many instances, the author worked with these managers in development programs and/or had other opportunities to observe their behavior through various consulting relationships.

usually an asset. Should this intellectual superiority interfere with personal relations, the problem is usually less serious than for line managers.

Although space does not permit a detailed discussion of the nature of intelligence, it is noteworthy that it consists of a number of interrelated aptitudes such as ability to learn, practical judgment, and verbal, quantitative, and abstract reasoning. Because an overall IQ consists of different components, two IQs of, say, 120 points are not necessarily equivalent, and different strengths are important in different managerial positions (e.g., high quantitative reasoning is especially desirable for financial executives but is less important for personnel and sales executives). Because of the practical nature of business organizations, a high degree of practical judgment or common sense reasoning is desirable in all managerial positions.

Emotional Maturity

Effective managers often have a fear of failure because they continue to accept challenges that require peak performance. However, since the fear is a natural and realistic function of the risk involved in such a life-style, they should not be considered fearful people. Effective managers are basically self-confident and free from fears, anxiety, and guilt feelings which are capable of interfering with performance.

Emotional maturity is expressed in many characteristics of effective managers. They tend to perceive themselves in a favorable light (to have positive self-images), and their perceptions of reality have a minimum of distortions because of emotional needs and ego-defensiveness. Although their aspirations and self-expectations continue to increase as goals are reached, effective managers generally have realistic expectations for themselves and others.

Characteristic of mature individuals, effective managers have a sense of purpose and meaning in life. They have sometimes been described as possessing a *strong self-structure*. This means that they know who they are, where they are going, and how they are going to get there. This appears to be more a function of decision making about oneself than a result of philosophizing, reasoning, and extensive self-analysis. It is associated with decisiveness, self-confidence, practicality, and with a desire to avoid excessive speculation and get on with the task of achievement.

Contrary to popular opinion, successful managers do not tend to be ulcer prone. This condition is more characteristic of the harried, frustrated manager whose career has been blocked by personal characteristics or external circumstances. Top managers tend to be highly resistant to the stresses of business life in spite of long hours of work and continual problem-solving activity. They are not prone to engage in escape activity, such as excessive drinking, drug use, problem avoidance, rationalization, and poorly planned job changing. The incidence of divorce and other family problems is no higher for successful managers than for the general population.

Leadership Skills

The point has already been made that many different approaches to leadership are effective because leadership environments differ greatly. The research and literature surveys of Ralph Stogdill are particularly enlightening concerning the personal characteristics which contribute to the leadership skills of managers. On the basis of the positive findings of 163 research studies, Stogdill isolated the following task-related characteristics of effective leaders:

1. Need for achievement, desire to excel

2. Drive for responsibility

3. Enterprise, initiative

4. Responsible in pursuit of objectives

5. Task orientation

In addition he isolated nine social characteristics of the the leader:

1. Ability to enlist cooperation

2. Administrative ability

3. Attractiveness

4. Cooperativeness

5. Nurturance

6. Popularity, prestige

7. Sociability, interpersonal skills

8. Social participation

9. Tact, diplomacy[16]

These characteristics are obviously intercorrelated; and they also overlap some of the other characteristics discussed in this chapter, particularly motivation. In view of the global nature of leadership, however, this should be expected. Some writers prefer to use the term *supervisory qualities* rather than leadership characteristics (or traits), presumably to avoid having to deal with the fact that leadership behavior is expressed in an unusually wide variety of situations, managerial and otherwise, and is therefore a difficult term to define.[17]

One personal quality which contributes to leadership skills is *empathy*. It relates to one's ability to understand the needs and motives of others—to place oneself in another's shoes and become aware of how he or she thinks, perceives, and feels. This is a quality on which people differ greatly, depending upon early

---

[16] Ralph Stogdill, op. cit., pp. 80–82.

[17] See Thomas W. Harrell and Margaret S. Harrell, "The Personality of MBA's Who Reach General Management Early," *Personnel Psychology,* Vol. 26, No. 1 (Spring, 1973), pp. 127–134.

life experiences. Consider the case of the following supervisor whose unusually high level of empathy caused her some serious on-the-job problems.

> Jane's early years were spent in approximately ten different homes. Her divorced parents did not want her, and several relatives tolerated her for short periods of time to keep her off the streets. Very early in life, she learned to be sensitive to their every gesture, voice tone, or other behavior that might provide a cue which would be useful in her struggle to survive in this particular jungle. As an adult, her ability to understand the needs and motives of others was uncanny, but in many cases she would have been better off to have been less aware. She tended to become too involved in the personal lives of her subordinates and to lose objectivity in personnel decisions. She was too people-oriented and too little task-oriented.

At the opposite extreme is the manager who is relatively insensitive, as Jane may well have been had she been inclined to suppress her sensitivity in order to avoid the hurt of knowing how others felt about her. This example illustrates the important point that the ideal amount of certain characteristics is not always the maximum amount.

Stogdill's attractiveness factor is an interesting one. A number of assessment centers have used the word *impact* as an apparent synonym, and both of these are related to charisma. Appearance, self-image, friendliness, the projection of a favorable self-image, and motivation to be attractive to others are all related to this characteristic. Too often an assumption is made that such qualities are inborn or that they are otherwise beyond the control of the individual manager. Neither assumption is altogether valid, and both are counterproductive for the manager who would like to be more effective.

Problem-Solving Skills

Effective managers are problem solvers rather than problem avoiders. They accept problems as a challenge and as an opportunity to prove their superiority and worthiness for advancement. This ability is, first of all, related to motivation. Effective problem solvers have learned, often early in life, that solving problems is rewarding. Without this motivation, effectiveness is likely to be minimal because of the risk involved. Problem solving requires more than application of analytical skills, although this is important. For line managers, it also involves the high-risk behavior of making decisions and taking action (which may or may not be successful).

Problem solving may also involve the unpopular action of defining and attacking a problem at a time when other managers prefer to close their eyes to its existence or when they disagree concerning its nature and solution. This means that problem solvers are often irritants and boat rockers, and this requires self-confidence, and, at times, an exceedingly thick skin.

Problem solving is related to a number of other individual characteristics, among which are the possession of relevant knowledge, goal-directedness, creativity, decisiveness, intelligence, emotional maturity, and optimism regarding the likelihood that one's efforts will be successful. Relevant knowledge is not synonymous with formal education. At times it relates to information—about people, processes, products, and the like—which can be acquired only through practical experience over a long period of time. The higher managers progress, the broader their knowledge must be in order to obtain a grasp of overall organizational problems and to make decisions which will not have adverse, unforeseen implications for seemingly unrelated parts of the organization.

Decisiveness, an important aspect of problem-solving skills, has at least two major components: (1) the self-confidence to take reasonable and calculated risks and (2) a strong self-structure. The former is important to the problem solver because decisions sometimes result in failure, and a manager must be able to live with that ever-present possibility. The manager who experiences failure as defeat and humiliation will ordinarily value safety more highly than achievement and may therefore be controlled by excessive cautiousness in decision making. In contrast, the manager who views failure as an opportunity to learn from experience can afford to be decisive.

The role of a strong self-structure in decisiveness is associated with the fact that people who have made decisions about themselves possess internalized standards against which decisions may be made effortlessly. Consider, for example, two controllers who have an opportunity to embezzle a large sum of money. The one who has already made the firm decision that he is not a thief can be decisive. The decision is made in an instant but without impulsiveness. In contrast, the controller with a poor commitment to standards of personal morality may struggle with the decision for months and, after making it, have serious questions about whether it was the right decision.

Personal Organization

People differ greatly in the extent to which they feel comfortable in a chaotic, disorderly environment. Some of these differences are deeply embedded in personality and are difficult to change; others are related more to habit or training and can be modified with relative ease. Managers with a deep need to impose order and system upon chaotic situations are more likely than others to learn effective organization techniques, to feel comfortable with the structure of complex organizations, and to systematize their work in ways which enable them to handle a wide variety of duties. Managers who prefer an unstructured life-style often feel boxed in and overcontrolled by the employing organization and require special assistance in handling their organizing functions.

Personal organization involves more than the formalities of such activities as defining jobs, establishing procedures, and delegating authority. It affects one's ability to use time efficiently, to set priorities, to establish controls, and to manage by objectives. The issue of managerial effectiveness hinges upon the question of whether a manager will organize with the aid of a sensitive, intuitive feel for the activity or whether dependency must be placed primarily upon a textbookish, intellectual understanding of when and how to organize. The so-called natural-born manager is a myth, but the nearest thing to such a manager is the individual whose early training and personality development provide an intuitive grasp of the managerial functions of organizing, deciding, and motivating subordinates to reach organizational goals.

Communication Skills

The ability to communicate orally and in writing is highly correlated with managerial success. Line managers spend most of their time in one or other kind of communication: directing, informing, report writing, listening, and attempting to persuade.

The practical nature of business students often detracts from the task of learning some of the basic skills of communication. Many think that such academic pursuits as learning to spell, to write grammatically correct sentences, or to perform as a fluent public speaker will contribute little to their success. This is far from realistic. Aside from the need to make one's ideas known and to be sensitive to what others are trying to say, communication skills are one of the primary means by which others decide whether a manager is educated or uneducated, knowledgeable or ignorant, brilliant or dull. To some extent these judgments may be unfair and unrealistic; but they are made, and they affect both the promotability and the effectiveness of the manager.

Students of management often play down the importance of spelling and grammar on the assumption (or rationalization) that as managers they will have secretaries to worry about such trivia. But in the real world it does not necessarily work out that way. There is always the question of who will catch the secretary's errors. In addition, the aspiring manager whose vocabulary is limited and whose grammar is poor cannot avoid displaying this limitation in conversations and meetings with superiors.

The ability to communicate is, of course, more complex than the mastery of speaking and writing skills. Empathy is an important dimension of communication in that it contributes a sensitivity to the needs and motives of the persons with whom one proposes to communicate. Empathy provides cues concerning the appropriate times to speak and to listen, and it enables one to sense the meaning of nonverbal cues expressed in voice inflections, gestures, eye contact, and body movements. The empathic manager has an awareness of the importance of timing. Often it is when and how one speaks rather than what one says that determines the effectiveness of communication.

Finally, the ability to communicate involves trust. Whether a given communication is viewed with skepticism, doubt, interest, or acceptance may be more a result of who makes a statement than what is said or how it is said. This accounts in part for the fact that some managers whose language skills are minimal achieve a relatively high level of success. Because they are trusted and have a reputation for dependability, they succeed in spite of their inadequacy. There is always the possibility, however, that their success would be even greater were it not for the language deficiency.

Personal Integrity

In recent years many managers have been severely criticized for taking and giving bribes, making illegal political contributions, fixing prices, and a host of other behaviors which suggest a generalized character flaw. In many instances such behavior has led to sweeping attacks upon the integrity of managers as a group, as though the role itself demands moral compromise, lack of concern for others, and a selfish, manipulative life-style.

Although there are obviously large numbers of business managers (as well as leaders in government, schools, churches, and other institutions) who lack personal integrity, such behavior is not typical of effective managers. In most organizations managers who tell the truth, operate within the law, and have a genuine sense of concern for the well-being of others are more likely to be effective and successful than are those whose word must be questioned, who are prone to behave unethically, and who are concerned only with self-gain.

To function effectively, organizations require a high degree of predictability. Managers must be able to trust one another and relate to employees in ways that create trust and respect. These qualities are equally important as managers relate to customers, suppliers, bankers, government, and the general public. If there were no more compelling reason than expediency, effectiveness in management would favor persons with character and integrity.

As a matter of fact, business managers often prove to be among the most responsible leaders in civic, religious, and charitable organizations, and evidence does not support the notion that such activities are motivated primarily by business interests. Participation in such organizations is quite common among managers who are already successful, as well as among those who have humanitarian or religious values and seek a deeper level of expression than their work permits. It is also significant that, when managers themselves describe the characteristics of effective managers, fairness and high integrity are among the descriptive adjectives most often mentioned.[18]

Motivational Patterns

Effective managers are highly motivated and have a high activity level.[19] Early research seemed to show that effective managers were most motivated by

---

[18] Lawrence I. Sank, "Effective and Ineffective Managerial Traits Obtained as Naturalistic Descriptions from Executive Members of a Super-Corporation," *Personnel Psychology,* Vol. 27 (1974), pp. 423–434.

[19] Persons with a high activity level are always on the move. They are energetic, inclined to get involved in many different kinds of tasks, and they enjoy keeping busy.

achievement (i.e., by an intrinsic satisfaction in overcoming obstacles, achieving objectives, and seeing the fruits of their efforts). More recently, however, research indicates that effective managers are more motivated by a need for power.[20]

The need for power may be fulfilled by the satisfaction a manager receives from controlling great amounts of wealth, making important and difficult decisions, and directing the activities of other people. It is also expressed in a seemingly insatiable desire for upward mobility and increased personal income. The latter are typically related to the manager's contribution to organizational growth and profits. It is not surprising that managers who contribute significantly to these goals are appropriately rewarded for it.

These motivations stand in sharp contrast to the motives of many who are less effective in the managerial role. Prominent among the latter are managers with a high affiliation need. This strong need for approval, nurturance, support, and friendship clashes with the necessity for making objective personnel decisions and for taking a courageous, but unpopular, stand on issues which are perceived as vital to organizational success. Effective managers need to have a genuine concern for people, but they cannot afford to be too dependent upon the approval of others. Power gives independence and enables a manager to be effective in doing what must be done without being crushed by the pressures with which a decision maker must cope on a daily basis.

A high level of motivation and a high energy level are vital to the manager with high aspirations because the work is often difficult, the hours are long, the pressures are intense, and the risks are high. Managers who cease to receive promotions before their full potential is reached often do so because they consciously or unconsciously prefer the relative comfort of a secure position to the conflict involved in the continuing struggle upward. In short, their success is less than it could be because of lack of motivation. This is often a good choice for the individual and may benefit the organization since there is a limited number of positions at the top of the pyramid. Managers may function effectively long after their success, as measured by promotions, has leveled off.

Administrative Skills

Administrative skills is a catch-all term. Like leadership, it is correlated with other characteristics discussed in this chapter. As used here, it involves activities such as the following:

1. Developing techniques for paper flow, such as correspondence and interoffice memoranda, and for performing other routine office functions which cannot be delegated

2. Developing organizational policies, procedures, and controls without introducing unnecessary red tape

---

[20] David C. McClelland and David H. Burnham, "Power Is the Great Motivator," *Harvard Business Review,* Vol. 54, No. 2 (March-April, 1976), p. 100–110.

3. Organizing, planning, and clarifying organizational objectives

4. Coordinating a variety of seemingly unrelated functions to enable the organization to function as a whole, integrated unit rather than as a conglomeration of disconnected parts

5. Conducting meetings that efficiently achieve their objectives

These skills can be learned, and, therefore, are often related to the length and quality of a manager's experience. Yet there are great differences in the speed and thoroughness with which they are learned, and there is no guarantee that a manager will profit from experience. Some managers, for example, with long years of experience still cannot handle their correspondence. They shuffle papers back and forth from one side of their desks to the other, procrastinating, questioning, waiting, and hoping that problems—especially the morass of trivial problems—will somehow go away.

The manner in which one unusually effective executive handles his correspondence illustrates how managers develop guidelines to ensure their own efficiency. After months of frustration over a mounting volume of incoming mail, he established a rule: read a piece of correspondence only one time. Some exceptions must be made, but for him the rule is effective. Instead of placing a letter in a stack to be reread and answered later, he dictates a response, sends it to a subordinate for information or for answering, decides it is unworthy of an answer, or disposes of it in some other way. He uses a "hold file" for items he chooses to ignore unless a further communication requires that action be taken. Periodically the bottom half of the file is destroyed. He also leaves instructions that he is not to be disturbed while his correspondence is being answered except for genuine emergencies. These techniques may be unworkable for another manager, but they are a good example of the way an effective manager establishes mastery over one worrisome administrative problem. Simple as this problem appears to be, some managers never learn to handle it effectively.

THE DEVELOPMENT OF MANAGERIAL ABILITY

Thesis: Personal characteristics which contribute to managerial effectiveness are, for the most part, subject to modification. One important attribute of effective managers is a motivation to develop themselves in ways that will contribute to increased personal effectiveness.

Scientists have long debated and researched the question of the relative contributions of heredity, environment, and individual initiative to the formation of personal characteristics. Actually all three are important.

Heredity establishes limits within which mental ability, for example, may develop. Some people lack the genetic background to learn and reason at a level necessary for managerial work or for the education it requires. Still, it is evident that a favorable environment influences the degree to which one's hereditary potential is actualized. Regardless of background, any normal person has the potential to become a more effective learner—for example, by learning how to concentrate more intensely, by developing better study habits, and by improving reading skills. People can learn how to think more analytically by using appropriate mathematical and qualitative decision models. Hereditary potential which has remained dormant during childhood and adolescence because of lack of opportunity and/or motivation can often be actualized in adulthood as an individual experiences a strong need for abilities and skills in order to achieve career objectives and otherwise meet personal needs. The notion that mental abilities are unalterably fixed by heredity has long been rejected by competent researchers. This fact has far-reaching implications for the development of managerial abilities during adulthood, particularly abilities which relate to decision making.

Both mental abilities and personality characteristics are resistant to change. They are especially resistant when one person aspires to effect a change in another—when, for example, a manager wants to change a hypersensitive subordinate into one who can make tough decisions about people without worrying excessively about losing their approval. When, on the other hand, the subordinate with such a problem is intensely motivated to make the change, he or she can often find the means for doing so. The change may occur only after many painful experiences and a gradual process of desensitization through insight, perceptual modification, and growth in self-confidence. Nevertheless, changes in managers' personality and ability do occur, enabling them to assume increasing levels of responsibility as their careers unfold.

Since vocational decisions often are little more than chance happenings, many lower level managerial positions are filled by individuals whose personality characteristics are poorly suited for their work. This is especially true of managers with (1) an unusually strong need for the approval of others, (2) low tolerance for withstanding work pressures, (3) poor insight into the needs and motives of others, (4) a tendency to make poor decisions (for whatever reason), and (5) low motivation and/or ability to influence the behavior of others. Such individuals are handicapped and often find that the changes necessary for managerial effectiveness are too unnatural and painful to be worthwhile. In such cases, a switch to another career field is usually advisable.

For those managers who choose to remain in the field, a variety of techniques exist for defining and satisfying developmental needs.[21] It is generally conceded, however, that one of the best means of developing managerial skills is to work under the supervision of an effective manager within an organization in which superior managerial skills are recognized and rewarded. Just as parents and other influential persons serve as models for the early development of leadership potential, an immediate superior with exemplary talent serves as a live model with whom subordinates may identify and thereby develop the personal qualities needed to play the managerial role. Although many development techniques have significant contributions to make, few are comparable to this type of superior-subordinate relationship. The use of a combination of techniques is, of course, ideal.

---

[21] An excellent presentation of modern techniques for developing managers along with extensive bibliographic references may be found in Andrew J. DuBrin, *The Practice of Managerial Psychology* (Elmsford, New York: Pergamon Press, Inc., 1972).

STUDY AND DISCUSSION QUESTIONS

1. Why is it less difficult to isolate characteristics of successful managers than characteristics of leaders?
2. Why is it important that a probability frame of reference be assumed in order to understand the relationship between personal characteristics and managerial effectiveness?
3. In the Standard Oil of New Jersey study, 49 percent of the variance in managerial effectiveness was accounted for by personal characteristics. What is most likely to account for the remaining 51 percent of the differences in effectiveness?
4. In what sense do managerial effectiveness and managerial success differ?
5. What is the meaning and significance of *compensation* as the term is used in this chapter?
6. Two managers are highly motivated to succeed, have excellent formal educations, are high in leadership abilities, and have equally favorable environments within which to manage. Their levels of effectiveness, however, differ greatly. What might account for these differences?
7. If there were no research studies which show a positive relationship between intelligence and managerial effectiveness, what common sense reasons could be given in support of the proposition that the relationship exists?
8. What are the probable reasons that successful managers are less ulcer prone than those whose careers have been blocked by personal characteristics or external circumstances?
9. Problem solving is typically viewed as an intellectual activity which draws heavily on formal education and technical knowledge. In what sense is it also related to such personality characteristics as motivation and self-confidence?
10. A high level of motivation to succeed is an important determinant of whether a manager will be successful. Why would this be especially true of managerial versus nonmanagerial employees?
11. Given the fact that large numbers of people with above average intelligence and college degrees are capable of developing the characteristics normally associated with managerial success, why is it inadvisable for many of them to do so?

CRITICAL INCIDENT

The Improbable Success

The time had come for the final decision as to whether Winston Hauser would be promoted to regional vice-president. His experience within the major oil company by which he was employed was broad, and the VP position would be a logical next step for him. Hauser's superior, senior production vice-president Roger Helm, strongly recommended him, but the executive committee could not agree. Company president, Ralph Stewart, argued against him:

> I've been aware of Hauser's good record for several years, but for some reason I had not met him until our recent interview. And, quite frankly, I was disappointed. I had to carry the conversation. I think the man is shy and unsociable.

Helm was not inclined to give in easily. Knowing that in the final analysis Stewart would have to approve the promotion, Helm addressed him directly:

> Ralph, I agree that Hauser won't win any medals for being a conversationalist, but he has some outstanding qualities. His decisions are unbelievably sound. He makes fewer mistakes than any man I've ever supervised. He is bright, well organized, persistent, and totally honest. His people trust him. When he expresses an opinion, they listen, and they take his advice. They think he hung the moon.

The committee meeting rapidly became a two-way conversation. Stewart obviously did not like Hauser, and let it be known that, as he expressed it, "their chemistry was different."

Stewart:
After work yesterday I took Hauser by the club for a drink. He ordered a coke. He didn't make a big deal out of it, but it made me feel that he was very different from me—different from us. We will be spending a lot of time together if he's promoted. Do you think he can fit into the executive group?

Helm:
He is different, but perhaps that is not all bad. I know what you are saying, and I respect the point you're making, but Hauser grows on you. He is a warm, sensitive human being. You're right. He is shy in a way, if by that you mean that he is uncomfortable in some social situations. He obviously felt uncomfortable with you. But he is a tough-minded manager and can be hard as nails when he has to be. Nobody pushes him around. They don't even try. He gets excellent cooperation from his subordinates. They respect his judgment, expertise, and integrity. He's not flashy, but he is a winner, and his subordinates know that.

Stewart:
He has some admirable qualities, but he still may not be vice-presidential material.

Helm:
I'll stake my job on him. I'll assume full responsibility for the decision. I want someone heading that division who will get the job done, and Hauser will. He always has.

Stewart:

Roger, I value your judgment. You know Hauser better than anyone else and should have a major voice in determining who will fill the position. But I would like to get an outside consultant's opinion about him. Then we'll get back together and make a decision.

Questions

1. Analyze the incident in terms of the content of this chapter.
2. What is occurring here which suggests that managerial success and managerial effectiveness are not always synonymous?
3. Assume that you are the consultant who is asked to make a recommendation concerning Hauser's promotion. What questions would you want to have answered before making your decision?

Chapter

12   The First-Line Supervisor

One of the most important members of management is the first-line supervisor—the lowest ranking member of the management hierarchy and the manager with direct responsibility for supervising nonmanagerial employees. Because the first-line supervisor performs a difficult "linking-pin" function between management and employees, the supervisory position possesses problems which are not found in other management positions. This chapter defines some of the major problems of supervisors and provides insights into current approaches to solving them.

A CONFLICT OF ROLES

Thesis: The important problems of first-line supervisors center around the question of identity. Before supervisors can function effectively, they must answer the question, Who am I? in a manner that is satisfactory to themselves and to their superiors, subordinates, and peers.

The identity problem of first-line supervisors arises from circumstances which are not present at higher management levels. Because supervisors are usually promoted from the employee ranks, they often possess attitudes, ways of perceiving, and personal bonds which hamper their identification with management. The supervisor, furthermore, must look continually in two directions and be a buffer between the conflicting interests of labor and management. Success demands that the supervisor meet the needs of both parties while maintaining personal integrity and credibility.

The Supervisor: A Manager by Law

Both the foreman of a labor gang and the corporate president are supervisory in that they are directly responsible for achieving results through subordinates. The term *supervisor,* however, normally refers to the person who manages hourly paid, nonmanagerial employees rather than other managers. In manufacturing, supervisors are usually referred to as foremen or foreladies. Depending upon the situation, the first-line manager may also be called a supervisor, head nurse, office manager, unit director, overseer, gang boss, or crew chief.

The line of demarcation between employees and supervisors was clarified somewhat by the Taft-Hartley Act (the National Labor-Management Relations Act). This 1947 statute clarified the intent of the Wagner Act (the National Labor Relations Act) of 1935 under which large numbers of supervisors had claimed immunity from management retaliation for their union activity. The Taft-Hartley Act made it clear that first-line supervisors are a part of management and are therefore denied special protection for union activities. The Act defined a supervisor as

> . . . any individual having authority, in the interest of the employer, to hire, transfer, suspend, lay off, recall, promote, discharge, assign, reward, or discipline other employees, or responsibility to direct them, or to adjust their grievances, or effectively to recommend such action, if, in connection with the foregoing, the exercise of such authority is not of a merely routine or clerical nature, but requires the use of independent judgment.[1]

Although supervisors are permitted to form supervisor unions, they can, since 1947, be discharged for doing so.

Perceptions of the Supervisor's Role

The supervisory role lends itself to a variety of interpretations. From a legal viewpoint, at least, the supervisor is more than just another worker, although many supervisors feel a stronger identification with subordinates than with management. Who, in reality, are supervisors? What is their true identity? The answer varies between and within organizations, but one or more of the following role perceptions usually applies:

1. A special class of *in-the-middle* managers

2. Strategically placed management representatives

3. Human relations specialists

A Special Class of In-the-Middle Managers.   In many organizations, supervisors may be realistically described as caught in the middle—as lacking an adequate identity. They are no longer employees (technicians, clerks, laborers, workers, or whatever they may have been called), but neither are they fully managers either. New supervisors, at least, often find that their role falls short of their expectations.

---

[1] National Labor-Management Relations Act, 1947 (as amended), Section 101, Subsection 2(11).

The identity problem arises, in part, from the fact that neither subordinates nor higher managers are sure they can trust the new supervisor. In this statement, a production supervisor reflects upon her feelings soon after her promotion:

> I had been with the company for twelve years and knew all too well the derogatory kinds of things workers have to say about management—regardless of how good a job management is doing. It became painfully obvious that I was no longer one of them when they quit making such statements in my presence. They even cleaned up their language when they talked with me. They put on an act for me because I was now a supervisor.
>
> Unfortunately the other supervisors didn't really trust me either. I was too close to the employees, and they weren't sure whether I would keep my mouth shut. Perhaps they were right in neutralizing their conversation when I came around. I found it hard to resist passing along choice bits of inside information in order to regain some of the status I had lost with my old work group. I knew I had to have their cooperation to be a success.
>
> I had to lean heavily upon the other supervisors for advice just to survive, and they really came through. I soon felt a close kinship with them, especially after several occasions when we covered for one another to avoid getting in trouble with the production manager. We're a closely knit, self-help organization. We don't have a union; but don't kid yourself, we're organized.

Barriers to Upward Identification.   The unique problem of keeping the goodwill of subordinates while relating to higher management tends to increase the cohesiveness of supervisory groups. Managers who supervise only other managers have little appreciation for the difficulties of relating to employees on a continuing basis—especially when those employees are hostile, resentful, and poorly motivated. Supervisors often believe that only peers who face similar pressures can know what they are experiencing. This, in turn, establishes a psychological barrier to identifying with their superiors.

The organizational environment poses still other barriers to upward identification. Since most supervisors are promoted from the ranks, their attitudes, values, interests, motivational patterns, education, and other important characteristics are different from those of college-educated managers. On a superficial level, these differences are seen in language, dress, and the subject matter of casual conversation. At a deeper level, a psychological barrier arises from the fact that college graduates identify with superiors in anticipation of future promotions. In contrast, first-line supervisors normally expect no more than one promotion, and they typically regard supervisory positions as dead-end jobs. It is no wonder that upward identification is often weak or nonexistent.

Making Peace with Subordinates.   Supervisors must get results in order to succeed. To do this they must somehow come to terms with subordinates.

While continuing to represent management, supervisors must understand the needs and motives of subordinates and solicit their cooperation. Supervisors interpret and administer management policy and must know when to compromise and when to stand firm.

Establishing sound relationships with subordinates requires supervisors to listen to their grievances and to alleviate them even when this requires taking an unpopular position with higher management. At this point, management is most likely to question the supervisor's loyalty—to suspect that the supervisor has not learned to think like a manager. Yet this in-between manager must take such risks in order to be effective.

A Janus Face.   The point has often been made that, like Janus, the Roman god of gates and doors, supervisors tend to become two-faced, one of which is acceptable only to higher management and the other acceptable only to subordinates. In his now classical article, written during the period when supervisors were unionizing under the protection of the Wagner Act, Fritz Roethlisberger referred to the supervisor as the "master and victim of double talk." [2] Double talk, in Roethlisberger's terms, means "translating what is into a semblance of the way it ought to be." In saying that supervisors become Janus-faced, we need not imply that they must become deceitful in order to play the role. A more generous and partially valid way to visualize the role is to see it as a peace-making buffer between superiors and subordinates.

Because of cultural and communication barriers, the gap between upper level management and the worker would be at times insurmountable—without the supervisor's mediating skills. Unfortunately this role permits supervisors who are either inept or manipulative to do great damage to the organization. Like double agents in international espionage, such individuals may serve only themselves while convincing both superiors and subordinates of their loyalty. There is little evidence, however, that many supervisors choose this method of coping with their dilemma. The role can be, and often is, played with integrity and openness.

Strategically Placed Management Representatives.   From one point of view, first-line supervisors are perceived as important members of the management team. They should, therefore, be given the authority and prestige befitting such a position. They should be consulted on all technical or personnel decisions which affect their work or about which they have valuable information.

Because of the importance of supervisors to the overall management of the organization, extreme care should be exercised in their selection and development. Special attention may be given to their potential for further education and for management development. Under no circumstances should managerial promotion policies discriminate against supervisors. Every effort should be made to break down barriers between supervisors and higher management, thus avoiding the popular notion that supervisors are a special, in-the-middle, class of employee.

---

[2] Fritz J. Roethlisberger, "The Foreman: Master and Victim of Double Talk," *Harvard Business Review,* Vol. 23 (Spring, 1945), pp. 283–298.

Human Relations Specialists. Since many functions previously performed by supervisors are now performed by others, such as engineers and personnel specialists, the one remaining specialty of the supervisor is human relations. From this perspective, human relations involves personal interaction with subordinates for the purpose of maintaining high motivation, morale, and job satisfaction. The supervisor counsels employees about job-related problems, adjusts grievances, takes disciplinary action, and assists subordinates in planning for personal development.

Both supervisors and their superiors are aware of the importance of good human relations to the achievement of organizational goals, including productivity. Management does acknowledge, however, that other specialists share in the responsibility for production. In some situations, the actions of others may have a greater impact upon production than do the actions of supervisors. Among such persons are industrial engineers, machine design engineers, production planners and schedulers, and a host of others whose technical recommendations and decisions directly affect productivity.

To view the first-line supervisor as a human relations specialist is more appropriate in some supervisory positions than in others. The same is true of the two previously discussed roles. Perhaps the most realistic view of supervisors is that to varying degrees they are a special class of in-the-middle managers; they are strategically placed management representatives, even though higher management may be unaware of it; and, more than other managers, they are human relations specialists.

SUPERVISORY RESPONSIBILITY AND AUTHORITY

Thesis: During the past fifty years, the authority of and range of duties performed by first-line supervisors have steadily declined. Even so, their duties today require a higher degree of education and expertise than in the past.

It seems paradoxical that modern supervisors must have greater ability than their predecessors even though their authority has declined and their duties have narrowed. The paradox is, however, more illusory than real. Since a number of specialists now perform duties which were once performed by supervisors, the range of supervisory duties has been reduced considerably. On the other hand, the organizational environment has become more complex—so much so that modern supervisors could not possibly perform all the functions performed by their predecessors.

The decline in supervisory authority is indeed real, but it is not altogether due to changes in the supervisor's role and status. The decline follows a trend toward less authoritarian leadership throughout organizations generally and a loss of managerial power to government and to organized labor. Superior ability is required, therefore, because supervisors must be effective with less authority than their predecessors had.

The Supervisor of the Past

First-line supervisors of the early 1900s contrast sharply with those of today. The supervisor of the past was exemplified by the factory foreman. Although a few women held supervisory positions in industries such as apparel manufacturing, most supervisors were men.

The factory foreman of the past has often been described as the "bull-of-the-woods." Because of his ability to hire and fire, to promote, and to give pay raises, his power over his subordinates was virtually unlimited. This was particularly true where the labor supply was abundant and union power was weak or nonexistent.

The trademark of the bull-of-the-woods foreman was power, not expertise. Because he was typically promoted from the ranks, he possessed a technical knowledge of the jobs he supervised. This was often the limit of his expertise, however. Although he selected personnel, he had no special training to enable him to do it well. His knowledge of motivation, settlement of grievances, disciplinary methods, and related supervisory functions was primarily based on common sense. In practice the common sense approach was shaped by an authoritarian philosophy. The foreman's stance was uncomplicated:

> I'm the boss, and you had better not forget it. When you accepted this job, you knew the pay was low, the work was hard, and the hours were long. If you don't want to work under these conditions, you're free to leave. If you stay, you are expected to do what you are told. It's that simple!

The power of the supervisor has continually declined, and in some situations it has declined so far that supervisory effectiveness has declined. On the other hand, the supervisor of the early 1900s was too powerful—a virtual dictator—and abuses of power were commonplace. The abuses were only one of the many factors, however, which interacted to bring about changes in the supervisory role.

Factors Affecting Supervisory Role Changes

A number of environmental changes, which accelerated during the second quarter of the century, dramatically affected the supervisor's role and function. The most important of these were an increase in the size and complexity of organizations, an increase in the level of specialization, the growing influence of unions and government, and an increasingly affluent society.

Increased Size and Complexity of Organizations. At the turn of the century, most businesses were small, and organizational structures were simple. Although professional, hired managers were gaining prominence, owner-managers operated most businesses. Since only a relatively small body of common business practice had developed (relating, for example, to management, finance, accounting, manufacturing, quality control, personnel, and legal affairs), each organization strongly reflected the personality of its leaders. Decision making and styles of leadership were more individualistic than they are today.

With increases in organizational size and the advent of professional management came complex organizational structures and a drive for uniformity in methods of relating to employees. These changes, in turn, called for a reduction of the supervisor's individuality, a trend which was accelerated by the human relations movement. The common sense approach and intuitive supervision became obsolete.

Finally, the increased size and complexity of organizations resulted in a morass of policies and procedures—a body of canned decisions applicable to everyone. They covered such functions as hiring, compensation, timekeeping, promotions, disciplinary action, production methods and schedules, product quality, safety—virtually every aspect of the work environment in which individual discretion might cause inconsistency and nonpredictability. The free-wheeling bull-of-the-woods supervisor had no place in such an environment.

Increased Specialization. As organizations grew in size and complexity, a knowledge explosion occurred. Beginning in the 1930s, and receiving impetus from the World War II industrial growth, the burgeoning discipline of management drastically changed the expectations for management education at all levels. Technical advancements and the emergence of new industries made old production methods obsolete. Scientific discoveries, growing out of the time-compressed research of defense programs, accelerated the rate of automation, displacing large numbers of employees and requiring retraining for workers and supervisors alike.

These changes increased the value and importance of specialists—individuals whose concentrated knowledge and skill in narrow areas permitted them to perform expertly. Thus, personnel specialists in selection and placement performed a service that supervisors had neither the time nor expertise to perform well. Over the span of a half century, tasks previously performed by supervisors were absorbed by a variety of specialists, including accounting clerks, engineers, timekeepers, personnel counselors, quality control inspectors, production schedulers, and many others.

Under the old system, the life of factory supervisors was relatively simple. They performed many functions which today seem inappropriate for supervisors. They were able to do so, however, only because the performance expectations were lower then, and supervisors were not burdened by requirements for detailed records and reports. Modern specialists deal with information of which supervisors of the past were either unaware or which they considered unimportant. An example is the mass of data collected and evaluated in employee selection. The complex environment in which a modern supervisor works is shown in Figure 12–1 (page 264).

Specialization and Coordination. A coordination problem is caused by specialization. Where the efforts of many individuals are required to achieve an objective, bottlenecks, priority conflicts, and personality clashes are commonplace.

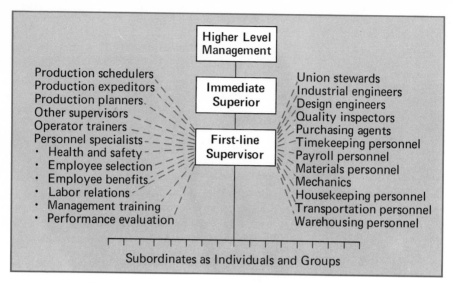

Figure 12–1   **Personnel with Whom a Modern
Production Supervisor May Interact**

One approach to coordinating specialized work is the use of coordinating specialists such as production schedulers and expediters. Even so, responsibility for coordination falls heavily upon supervisors. When machine breakdowns occur, supervisors must contact the maintenance department to request repairs. Supervisors bring together employees, union stewards, and labor relations specialists to deal with complex grievances. They also serve as intermediaries between employees and other specialists to solve problems relating to product quality, safety, timekeeping, training, and raw materials. But this role is sometimes difficult to play. It is complicated by problems of authority and accountability.

Specialization and Accountability.   Who is responsible when production falls behind schedule because of machine failure? The production supervisor reports a breakdown to the machine maintenance department but has no authority to establish repair priorities. A first-come-first-served rule may depersonalize the decision and treat all breakdowns as though they are equally important. If the maintenance supervisor sets priorities on a day-to-day basis, opportunities abound for bias and inappropriate use of power.

An example of the accountability problem comes from an attitude survey conducted with the supervisors of a large apparel manufacturer. One of the supervisors expressed the problem this way:

> I can't get the work out when the machines are down, and when they're down I have to wait forever to get them repaired. Whenever there's work to be done and I see a mechanic loafing, my blood boils, but there's nothing I can do about it. I know I'll catch it from the machine operator and from my boss, but my hands are tied. Our mechanics are

prima donnas. Because they're in high demand, they work less and get paid more than any employees in the plant. Let's face it: the supervisors in this plant are held accountable for production, but we don't have the authority to be productive.

Supervisors commonly experience frustrations of this kind. Subjectively the experience is one of being excessively dependent upon others. For example, supervisors depend upon others for

1. Personnel who are able and willing to work

2. Realistic production standards

3. Efficient production methods

4. Machine design and maintenance

5. Motivational systems (such as financial incentives)

6. Quality raw materials or subassemblies

7. Realistic production scheduling

A breakdown in any one of these areas may seriously affect productivity. In some situations, productivity is so controlled by machine design, assembly-line processes, and organization-wide motivational systems that the supervisors' actions have little effect upon it. In such situations, the supervisor logically has responsibility for little besides employee satisfaction, and even that is influenced by factors beyond the supervisor's control (such as the routineness of jobs and company-wide morale factors).

The Influence of Unions. Union power has significantly altered both the power and functions of supervisors. In unionized companies, union stewards stand between supervisors and their subordinates in solving disciplinary and grievance problems. Stewards and other union representatives often become involved in minor disputes which would not even occur in nonunionized organizations. The following incident, which occurred in a unionized chemical plant, illustrates this point.

While a carpenter waited, two plumbers were called in to reroute a water line which interfered with the construction of a storage bin. Although they arrived about 9:00 A.M., the warehouse foreman noticed that at 9:30 they had not begun to work. The plumbers explained that the lighting was poor and suggested that the foreman call the electrical department about it. When the foreman called and discovered that the electricians were busy, he personally set up two floodlights and wired them with extension cords which had been stored in the warehouse area. As he finished, the foreman noticed that the plumbers were gone. They soon reappeared, however, with a union steward who protested that the union contract forbade foremen from performing manual work.

The warehouse foreman called the maintenance superintendent who agreed with him that his act was not a contract violation. The

superintendent then ordered the plumbers to begin work. They refused
and walked off the job. By late afternoon the issue was settled, but only
after the local union president and company labor relations specialists
entered the dispute.

The anticipation of incidents such as this makes supervisors in unionized
companies extremely cautious about what they say and do. In some companies,
supervisors simply assume that their authority is inadequate and automatically
invoke the formal grievance machinery when a grievance occurs. This has the
effect of further weakening their positions. It strengthens the position of the union
steward, who often continues to plead the employee's cause after the supervisor
has turned the case over to the labor relations specialist.

Unions have further limited the power of supervisors by reducing or eliminating supervisory authority to give promotions and wage increases based on
merit. Instead promotions are based on seniority, and across-the-board pay raises
are decided through collective bargaining. Reduction of the supervisor's power
has the positive effect of reducing the incidence of unfair and arbitrary supervisory actions. On the other hand, it has often made supervisory positions so
unattractive that they are difficult to fill. It is also difficult to clearly define
objective standards for evaluating the performance of supervisors in such positions.

The Influence of Government.   The controlling influence of government, like
that of unions, limits the supervisor's autonomy and decision-making power.
Since government controls affect most aspects of the supervisor's relations with
subordinates, they increase the supervisor's dependence upon staff specialists.

Since the passage of the Fair Labor Standards Act in 1938, the federal
government has become increasingly involved in employee compensation. This
law and its subsequent amendments specify minimum wages, for example, and
outline conditions for the payment of overtime pay after forty hours of work a
week. Other laws prohibit discrimination in hiring and in subsequent personnel
decisions of all types (e.g., pay, layoffs, promotions, and discharges) on the basis
of race, color, religion, sex, national origin, or age (the Civil Rights Act of 1964
and the Age Discrimination in Employment Act of 1967).

State and federal antidiscrimination laws are designed to eliminate bias in
personnel decisions—to ensure that only performance-related criteria are used
in such decisions. Totally apart from morality and legality, the objectives of these
laws are worthy organizational objectives. On the negative side, however, such
laws do reduce supervisory effectiveness in at least one important way. They cause
supervisors to be overly cautious in making personnel decisions. Lazy, ineffective,
and dishonest employees are employed or allowed to remain on the payroll to
avoid claims of discrimination. As other employees observe such abuses and
realize that they will be tolerated, the abuses tend to increase.

Almost everyone can claim discrimination or *reverse discrimination* under
one or more legal categories. The legality of the latter is now being tested in the
courts. Reverse discrimination occurs when a member of a legally protected

special group (say a woman, a 50-year-old white male, or a member of a racial minority) is given preferential treatment over a better qualified, better performing individual who is not protected (a 20-year-old white male, for example). The infinite number of possibilities for charges of discrimination result in extensive record keeping, frequent consultations with legal experts regarding personnel decisions, and a cautious, defensive posture in dealing with subordinates.

Other laws, especially the Wagner Act (National Labor Relations Act of 1935), specify in great detail what supervisors can and cannot do when employees attempt to unionize or after they are unionized. Numerous amendments and decisions of the National Labor Relations Board and federal courts have greatly increased the number of laws affecting organized labor. Still other federal, state, and municipal laws involve the supervisor in action designed to protect the health and safety of employees. The Occupational Safety and Health Act (OSHA) of 1970 goes further than most laws in giving government administrators the power to demand action and to impose heavy penalties for management's failure to respond immediately. Here, as elsewhere, government has become an ever-present, authoritarian superior of the first-line supervisor and the entire management group.

An Affluent and Educated Society.   If there were no other factors to influence the supervisor's role, economic and educational changes would alone require its modification. The changed market place has increasingly demanded that supervisors be less authoritarian and more considerate.

As the level of general education increased, employees learned to expect better treatment from their supervisors. This change occurred while the nation was becoming more affluent and mobile. All these elements increased the independence of employees. Labor legislation of the 1930s and economic and cultural changes begun during World War II spawned a new, nonagrarian society, characterized by an accelerating rate of change in all aspects of life. It was inevitable that the supervisory role would also change dramatically.

The Work of the Supervisor

Because supervisory positions differ greatly from one organization to another, it is difficult to generalize concerning job requirements. In one study, 549 supervisors, representing a diversity of organizations, ranked fifteen supervisory functions in order of perceived importance.[3] With a relatively high degree of consistency from one industry to another, the following rankings were given:

1. Setting goals

2. Improving present work methods

3. Delegating work

---

[3] Blake D. Lewis, Jr., "The Supervisor in 1975," *Personnel Journal,* Vol. 52 (September, 1973), pp. 815–818.

4. Allocating manpower

5. Meeting deadlines

6. Controlling expenditures

7. Following progress of work

8. Evaluating employee performance

9. Forecasting manpower requirements

10. Safety

11. On-the-job instruction

12. Discussing performance with employees

13. Handling employee complaints

14. Enforcing rules

15. Conducting meetings

The supervisors in this study agreed that goal setting is the most important because of its role in providing purpose, direction, and criteria for performance evaluations. This and other rankings, however, would have differed had the study focused on the amount of time spent in each activity. Goal setting, for example, requires relatively little time compared with a number of other activities.

Supervisors spend most of their time reacting to various stimuli in the work place: employee questions or complaints, production problems, and requests from superiors for information or action. Although most of the supervisor's time is spent in contact with subordinates, supervisors complain that they are unable to get the work out because of too much paper work and too many meetings (with superiors, other supervisors, and specialists). Paper work has in recent years been reduced somewhat by the actions of staff personnel and the use of computers for routine reporting; but legal problems now require supervisors to prepare thorough reports on promotions, grievances, disciplinary matters, and accidents.

The following are among the supervisory functions on which the greatest differences in time usage exist.

1. *Personnel selection.* In some organizations, selection is performed exclusively by the personnel department while in others the supervisor makes the employment decisions. In the latter case, the supervisor may interview the applicants, in addition to studying data prepared by the personnel department on one or more applicants.
2. *Grievance handling.* In unionized organizations and others with formal grievance machinery, more time is required than in organizations where the supervisor has the authority to dispose of grievances as they occur.
3. *Controlling expenditures.* Some supervisors have their own budgets and are able to make decisions which directly affect expenses (e.g., purchasing and work methods). Others work within rigid structures in which these functions are performed by staff personnel.

4. *Job training.* The training of subordinates is a major supervisory responsibility in some organizations. In others, the function is performed exclusively by staff specialists.

THE IDENTIFICATION OF SUPERVISORY POTENTIAL

Thesis: Most first-line supervisors are promoted from the worker ranks, often upon the basis of performance which bears little relationship to success in supervision. The knowledge and techniques are available, however, for selecting supervisors with a high probability of success.

For supervisors, higher level managers often select friendly, outgoing individuals who are top performers on nonsupervisory jobs. Although these qualities are admirable, they are relatively poor predictors of supervisory success.

Success-Related Characteristics

Because demands of supervisory positions differ widely, progressive organizations continually gather and analyze data concerning the characteristics of successful and unsuccessful supervisors in specific positions. These data are then used to improve the effectiveness of subsequent selection decisions.

Much of the information presented in Chapters 10 and 11 applies to the selection of first-line supervisors. Emphasis should, for example, be placed upon an applicant's leadership skills, motivation to become a supervisor, and ability to work under constant pressure. The applicant's mental ability, adaptability, and motivation to learn are also important characteristics since the new supervisor must often learn an entirely new set of skills. Although the supervisor's intelligence need not be as high as that of upper level management unless promotion into upper level management is likely, it should be above average and should contain a liberal amount of practical judgment.

Most supervisory positions require a relatively high level of empathy and skill in interpersonal relations. Although certain human relations skills can be learned, such as how to counsel employees or conduct disciplinary interviews, most managers endeavor to promote only individuals whose background has already given them an intuitive understanding of people.

The Recruitment of Supervisors

Except in times of rapid expansion, most companies promote supervisors from within the organization. A few hire only college graduates as supervisors, reasoning that the position is the bottom rung of the management ladder and should be filled by someone who is promotable. This approach avoids certain problems which occur when supervisors who were promoted from below identify more strongly with labor than with management and when employees resent supervision by someone who has recently been a peer.

There are, however, good reasons for maintaining a continuing flow of promotions into supervisory positions from employee ranks. Such a practice weakens the tendency for labor and management to form into rigid, mutually exclusive, and antagonistic groups. It provides employees with possibilities for promotion and reduces feelings of being hopelessly boxed in. It provides management with current, first-hand information about how employees think and feel. Employees can identify more easily with a management group which includes individuals who have come from their ranks, speak their language, and presumably understand their problems.[4]

The value of promoting individuals from the employee ranks outweighs the value of appointing college graduates to most supervisory positions. Any organizational policy which reinforces the demarcation line between management and employees has the potential for causing serious problems.

Techniques for Selecting Supervisors

It is a common practice for personnel specialists to evaluate potential supervisors who are recommended for promotion. The specialist, in turn, recommends who, if any, of the applicants should be promoted. In addition to describing the candidate's strengths and weaknesses, the personnel report may also include recommendations for training and managing the new supervisor.

The methods used to evaluate supervisory applicants vary from a casual interview to an intensive psychological evaluation. Large companies with sophisticated personnel research departments are more likely than others to recognize the seriousness of the decision and to invest accordingly. Since assessments at this level often cost from $500 to $1,000, with many individuals being appraised but not selected, the investment is sizable, indeed.

A thorough supervisor assessment may require from one to three days, depending upon the methods used. A one-day assessment may include a background study and evaluation and the administration of standardized psychological tests for mental ability, supervisory knowledge and attitudes, leadership style, personality characteristics, interests, and values. The assessment may also include one or more depth interviews to obtain general information and to probe for answers to specific questions which relate to the applicant's success potential. Other evaluation instruments may be administered which are clinically rather than statistically evaluated. The applicant may, for example, write a self-description essay, compose stories in response to picture stimuli, and respond to a wide variety of items in a simulated supervisor's in-basket (i.e., handle the items typically found in a supervisor's incoming mail).

---

[4] There is actually little support for the notion that a supervisor promoted from the ranks can understand employees' problems better than the college-educated supervisor. If employees perceive this to be true however, it is a factor to be considered. Actually thousands of potential managers who graduate from college annually have had several years of experience in a variety of nonmanagerial jobs.

The longer evaluation process normally compares six applicants at one time by rating applicant behavior on *situational tests*—standardized situations or problems similar to those which the prospective supervisor will face on the job—to which the applicants respond as individuals and groups. This *assessment center* method has been extensively validated and used by the American Telephone and Telegraph Company and others.[5]

The Motivation for Accepting a Supervisory Position

Many employees who are offered supervisory positions understandably reject them. They are asked to move from the top of one career pyramid to the bottom of another—from secure, often comfortable jobs which command the respect of peers to the insecurity and stress of the lowest rung on the management ladder. Other employees believe that a supervisory position will meet a variety of important needs and, thus, actively seek it.

One sample of 2,054 first-line production supervisors indicated that the five factors listed below are the most important motives for accepting a supervisory position. The number beside each is the percentage of the supervisors selecting that factor as one of three (from a list of 15) which was most instrumental in attracting them to supervision.

1. More money (63 percent)

2. Greater responsibility (45 percent)

3. Challenge of a more difficult job (44 percent)

4. More security (41 percent)

5. A first step toward management (38 percent) [6]

Below factor No. 5, the percentages dropped sharply, indicating that these five motives were dominant in this company.

In some companies, there is little, if any, financial incentive for becoming a supervisor. A meager 10 percent to 20 percent pay increase is immediately offset by a loss of overtime pay and by the addition of hours worked. Supervisors have some financial advantage in being on salary, however, especially where frequent work stoppages result in a loss of wages for hourly employees. In spite of these advantages, supervisors who are paid only slightly more than the union wage scale often identify with the union and sympathize with its objectives. When supervisors know that their own pay raises are linked to the raises union members receive, it is understandable that they sympathize with union demands.

Security is often a higher motive for declining than for accepting an offer for advancement into supervision. This is particularly true for employees who

---

[5] Joseph L. Moses, "The Development of an Assessment Center for the Early Identification of Supervisory Potential," *Personnel Psychology,* Vol. 26, No. 4 (Winter, 1973), pp. 569–578.

[6] Robert H. Schappe, "The Production Foreman Today—His Needs and His Difficulties," *Personnel Journal,* Vol. 51 (July, 1972), p. 491.

rely more upon seniority than upon their own competence and ability. There are, however, employees who value the opportunities provided by a supervisory position more than the security of seniority and union protection. Such persons usually have other characteristics, such as self-confidence and desire for autonomy which are useful in supervision. Although motivation to become a supervisor does not in itself qualify one for that role, the lack of such motivation may usually be considered a disqualifier.

RESHAPING THE SUPERVISOR'S ROLE

Thesis: As presently constituted in many organizations, the supervisor's position is destined to cause unnecessary frustration and marginal effectiveness. Proven remedies for these conditions are available, however, to organizations which are willing to make the necessary investment.

The extensive unionization of supervisors between 1935 and 1947 stimulated a flurry of activity intended to bring supervisors back into the management fold. Although many such activities (human relations seminars, for example) failed to strike at the root of the problem, a variety of effective solutions has evolved. The appropriateness of each is dependent upon current conditions in a particular organization. The management actions described below, among others, have proved effective in reducing the frustration of supervisors and increasing their ability to perform effectively.

Selection for Growth Potential

Extreme care is needed in the recruitment and selection of supervisors. This may even involve hiring employees with a view to having supervisory talent available several years hence. Supervisory selections should be made from those employees with intellectual superiority, leadership potential, high motivation to lead, and potential for progressing into higher levels of management.[7]

Motivation for Growth and Advancement

Where the opportunities are available first-line supervisors should be encouraged to move into higher management rather than to view themselves as an in-between special class. This begins with selecting supervisors who have the ability and motivation to continue their formal education. It also involves providing incentives for continued education and making promotions without prejudice against managers who have risen from the ranks.

---

[7] In Schappe's study of 2,054 supervisors, 37 percent had earned some college credit. (Robert H. Schappe, op.cit., p. 491.) Selection of the best-educated and brightest of those employees who are otherwise qualified facilitates their movement into higher levels of management. Since such persons are usually overqualified for their nonsupervisory jobs, it is also beneficial in removing potentially dissatisfied employees from the employee ranks.

Upgrading the Position

In many organizations major changes in job design are needed to increase the authority, responsibility, and prestige of supervisors. A possible way to accomplish this with production supervisors is to flatten the organization—to eliminate some of the management levels between the first-line supervisor and the production manager, as shown in Figure 12–2.[8]

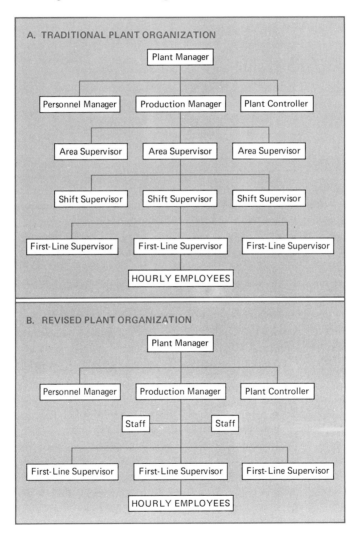

Figure 12–2 **Traditional and Flat Organization of Plant Production Management**

[8] Laurence M. Smiley and Paul R. Westbrook, "The First-Line Supervisory Problem Redefined," *Personnel Journal,* Vol. 54 (December, 1975), pp. 621–622.

This form of organization is possible only if the production manager and first-line supervisors have ample staff support. The production manager is thus freed to interact directly with a large number of supervisors. The supervisors have an opportunity to participate in policy decisions, the authority to make operational decisions on their own, and the information needed to supervise effectively.

Changes from the traditional to the revised flat organization structure should be made slowly to avoid loss of control. It is noteworthy, however, that the flat structure is more than a theoretical model. Such structures are now in operation and functioning successfully.

Facilitating the Transition to Supervisor

Professional guidance is typically needed to facilitate the transition from employee to supervisor. This involves more than supervisory training. Formal programs, both group and individual, enable the new supervisor to anticipate problems and to develop a repertoire of possible solutions. Some common problems are relating to former coworkers, dealing with the effects of the job change upon one's family, learning to play a leadership role, adapting to the supervisory peer group, organizing and controlling time, coping with the pressures of the supervisory position, and managing feelings of insecurity and inadequacy in the new role.

Providing Career Guidance

It is important that the new supervisor understand that the first-line supervisor's job is not the end of the line. To avoid this and provide motivation for personal growth and outstanding performance, the supervisor needs professional assistance in career planning. This should be made available on a continuing basis and is linked to planning for training in skills and general education.

STUDY AND DISCUSSION QUESTIONS

1. What is the nature of the identity problem faced by first-line supervisors?
2. Why is it important that first-line supervisors have a strong identification with management?
3. In a situation where labor and management relations are in continual conflict, is it possible for a first-line supervisor to relate to both sides without being two-faced in a hypocritical, deceitful sense? Explain.
4. Explain this statement: Modern first-line supervisors perform a much narrower range of duties than did their predecessors. On the other hand, greater ability and skill are required of modern supervisors.
5. In what ways did the emergence of large organizations require supervisors to sacrifice much of their decision-making function?

6. What major problem does a supervisor face in coordinating the activities of others to achieve productivity goals?
7. Make a list of activities a modern supervisor might perform in response to government regulations and controls.
8. Assume the position of a production superintendent searching for a new first-line supervisor from a group of production workers. What behavior would provide helpful clues in making the identification?
9. What problems would likely result from consistently filling first-line supervisory positions with recent college graduates who are expected to progress into higher management?
10. What problems are commonly observed in the financial compensation of first-line supervisors?

CRITICAL INCIDENT

Promotion Problems

Charles Gresham began his career at Mosley Electronics on the assembly line, but, because of his two years of college and his Army experience in electronics, he was soon given a technician's job. As a technician, he was one of many who located problems in computer subsystems after they failed to pass quality control tests. Between 1966 and 1977, he received five promotions and gained a reputation for being a mature, highly analytical problem solver.

In June of 1977, Gresham received his first management assignment. He was promoted to supervisor over the twelve senior technicians with whom he had worked for several years, including two men, Ralph Corley and Mel Janek, who were his closest friends. In fact, the three families had developed close bonds of friendship because of a mutual interest in camping. They had taken numerous trips together and in some ways felt a family kinship.

Gresham's promotion brought forth hearty congratulations from his two friends. After all, the position paid well and managers at Mosley Electronics were held in high esteem by the company's 3,000 nonunion employees. Soon after Gresham's promotion, however, problems began to arise. The first occurred when Gresham recommended another subordinate over Corley for a temporary duty assignment in Europe. Corley did not complain directly about the action, but his wife told Gresham's wife that Corley should have received the assignment. "We would be on our way to Amsterdam," she asserted, "if Charles weren't afraid he would be accused of favoritism."

Because Gresham's new job required long hours, there was less time for camping trips; and, when they did occur, the warm, relaxed, uninhibited relationships of the past were no longer present. On occasion, Gresham was forced to hedge when asked questions about company plans and to take an unpopular stand on controversial management issues, which, in turn, reinforced the fact that the friendships could no longer survive in their early form. Gradually the camping trips were dropped, and the old group seldom got together without other friends or department members present.

Gresham regretted the loss of his close friends; but, being deeply committed to his new career, he was also concerned that negative feelings on the part of Corley and Janek might cause difficulty on the job. The transition was softened somewhat by the fact that the wives of the three men continued to visit frequently. This was, however, a mixed blessing.

On one occasion, confidential information that Charles Gresham had shared with Mrs. Gresham was inadvertently passed on. Although the event caused no serious problems at work, Gresham unconsciously began talking less often with his wife about business problems. Her reaction was, "We're losing our friends. That's frustrating, but I can live with it. But perhaps you're leaving me behind, too. I miss knowing what you're doing and what's important to you. I'm happy for your success, but it is your success—not our success. You work too much, and you are too involved in it. You're moving into another world that I don't understand and don't like."

Questions

1. What is the underlying cause of Gresham's problems?
2. How should Gresham solve his problems?
3. What additional information is needed in order to answer Questions 1 and 2?

Chapter 13

Union Influences on Organizational Behavior

Approximately 25 percent of the nonagricultural labor force in the United States is unionized. Union influence on organizational behavior is, however, greater than this figure would suggest; and, in many organizations, management must seriously consider union power in all major decisions. In some organizations, the union is virtually a partner—usually an unwelcomed partner—in managing the enterprise.

Many organizations, both large and small, have no unions. Even in such organizations, however, the impact of unions is felt. The managers of nonunion companies are aware that their policies and procedures are constantly being compared with those of unionized companies. They may use high wages, liberal fringe benefits, and even participation in decision making to avoid the loss of control associated with unionism.

UNION PHILOSOPHY AND DEVELOPMENT

Thesis: The growth of labor unions in America has, for the most part, been motivated by the desire of employees to influence decisions which affect their welfare. The labor movement essentially has been oriented toward the use of power to achieve economic advantages rather than promote a political philosophy.

An individual is at a distinct disadvantage when dealing with a large corporation. This was especially true prior to the human relations movement when authoritarian management was commonplace and employees were typically regarded as expendable articles of commerce rather than as persons. The resulting imbalance in bargaining power and the abuses suffered by workers at the hands of unenlightened, arbitrary managers led to formation of unions as early as the Colonial Period.

Unions in an Affluent Society

The intense commitment of many union members is not altogether explainable in terms of present working conditions. Large numbers of union members make more than $15,000 a year, plus extensive economic supplements (fringe benefits), live in the surburbs, own at least two automobiles, send their children to college, and enjoy more leisure time than the managers for whom they work. Top union leaders are well-paid executives, supported by a professional staff of attorneys, accountants, and economists who bear no resemblance to the traditional image of a proletariat or downtrodden working class.

In view of the current well-being of American workers, why does unionism continue to thrive? There are at least three good reasons. First, unionism is seen as the goose that laid the golden egg. The union is perceived as being the cause of worker strength and prosperity and is thus worthy of preservation and expansion. Second, human needs and wants are insatiable. There is always a desire for higher income, better working conditions, more interesting work, and greater autonomy and security. Finally, the employment experiences of parents and grandparents are not altogether forgotten, especially those which were bitter and traumatic. These memories are passed from one generation to another and interact with present dissatisfactions to cause distrust of management and loyalty to the union.

Early Growth of Unions

Small *craft unions* of the Colonial Period were primarily fraternal societies of skilled tradesmen such as stonemasons, shoemakers, and carpenters. They existed as self-help organizations concerned with training apprentices and with the general enhancement of their membership. But they possessed little potential for influencing powerful employers. Labor historians often cite the Philadelphia cordwainers (shoemakers), formed in 1792, as the earliest union in the United States. It was not until 1850 that such local associations began to form national unions. In that year, a national union of photographers was formed, followed by the stonecutters union in 1853 and the hat-finishers union in 1854. Within two decades, over thirty such national unions had been formed.

Amalgamation of Unions

Once national unions were formed, the next logical step was to combine them into still larger units. The first effective amalgamation was the Knights of Labor in 1869. This organization, spearheaded by the garment workers, welcomed existing craft unions as well as other skilled and unskilled labor. By 1886, a peak membership of 703,000 was achieved. The diversity of membership, the impact of several unsuccessful strikes, and unfavorable public opinion, however, led to its rapid demise.

The decline of the Knights of Labor was accompanied by the formation of the American Federation of Labor (AFL) in 1886. This loosely knit group of craft unions (25 at the beginning) avoided affiliation with *industrial unions,* that is, unions made up primarily of unskilled and semiskilled employees. Under the strong leadership of Samuel Gompers, the AFL grew rapidly as an association of the labor elite.

The Congress of Industrial Organizations (CIO) was organized in 1936 to meet the needs of the rapidly expanding unions in the mass-production industries. The organization was headed by John L. Lewis, the powerful president of the United Mine Workers, and was supported by other labor leaders who disagreed with the exclusivist policies of the AFL. The CIO became aggressive in unionizing the mass-production industries. Unlike the AFL, the CIO welcomed all employees, including minorities, and became active in local, state, and national politics. In 1955 the two groups merged to form the AFL-CIO. By 1974, Bureau of Labor Statistics data indicated that AFL-CIO membership totaled about 16.5 million.[1] A few large unions, such as the Teamsters and United Auto Workers, have withdrawn from the AFL-CIO. Such unions are classified as independents. The Teamsters, with about 2.2 million members, is the nation's largest independent union.

Figure 13–1 (page 280) shows the structure of the AFL-CIO. Ultimate authority rests with the elected delegates at the biennial convention. The number of delegates from each union is based on paid-up memberships. The executive branch of the organization consists of the elected president, secretary-treasurer, and thirty-three vice-presidents. Supporting these executives are large staffs (concerned with such activities as accounting, civil rights, education, legislation, and public relations) and standing committees (such as civil rights, ethical practices, political affairs, education, and safety).

Trends in Union Membership

As shown in Figure 13–2 (page 281), union growth has been uneven. In fact, since the end of World War II, the number of union members has declined relative to the size of the total labor force. This has occurred for a number of reasons, not the least of which is the expansion of jobs for white-collar employees not traditionally associated with the labor movement. The programmers, systems analysts, keypunch operators, computer operators, and technicians of the computer industry are examples of such personnel. Although many employees in these positions become union members, others identify closely with management and shy away from union membership.

The dramatic spurt in union growth between 1935 and 1945 can be accounted for by three factors. The first was the 1935 passage of the National Labor Relations Act (Wagner Act) which guaranteed the right of collective bargaining. This was strategically followed by the formation of the CIO, with its aggressive tactics for organizing the masses of semiskilled and unskilled workers. Finally,

---

[1] U. S. Department of Labor, Bureau of Labor Statistics, *Directory of National Unions and Employee Associations* (Washington, D. C.: U. S. Government Printing Office, 1974), p. 66.

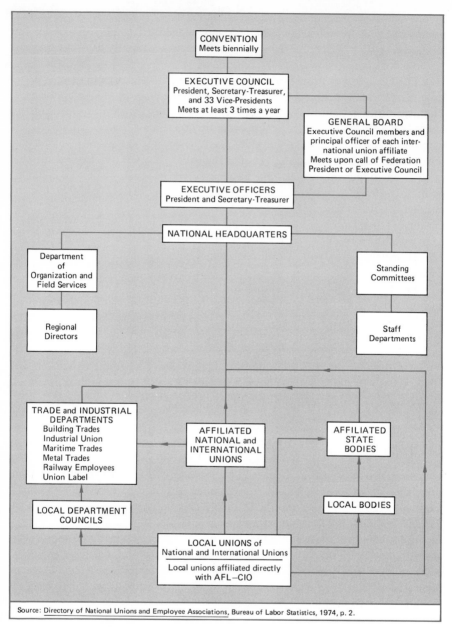

Source: Directory of National Unions and Employee Associations, Bureau of Labor Statistics, 1974, p. 2.

Figure 13–1   Structure of the AFL-CIO (1974)

union growth received new impetus because of the labor shortages and consequent increase in labor power during World War II.

Since 1965 unions have made significant gains among white-collar, professional, farm, and government employees. None of these was considered fertile

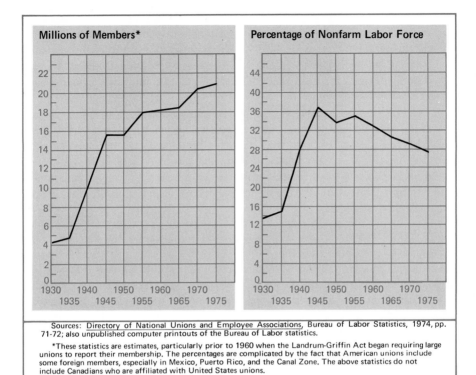

Sources: <u>Directory of National Unions and Employee Associations,</u> Bureau of Labor Statistics, 1974, pp. 71-72; also unpublished computer printouts of the Bureau of Labor statistics.

*These statistics are estimates, particularly prior to 1960 when the Landrum-Griffin Act began requiring large unions to report their membership. The percentages are complicated by the fact that American unions include some foreign members, especially in Mexico, Puerto Rico, and the Canal Zone. The above statistics do not include Canadians who are affiliated with United States unions.

Figure 13–2   Growth in Union Memberships from 1930–1975

ground for union expansion as long as large numbers of industrial workers remained outside the union and these groups were small. Since the most significant increase in the work force now lies in the service areas, consisting of white-collar, professional, and government employees, it is understandable that these areas are now selected as prime targets for unionization drives.

White-Collar and Professional Employees.   As the number of white-collar and professional employees increases, other changes occur that stimulate employee discontent. Historically white-collar workers have identified closely with management. But when hundreds of clerks or keypunch operators are assembled to perform routine tasks in a giant, impersonal organization (so-called white-collar factories), they feel much in common with the masses of blue-collar machine tenders and assembly-line workers. Under such conditions, unions tend to become attractive.

At one time school teachers did not consider joining unions, but their viewpoints are changing. The current generation of public school teachers is unwilling to tolerate low pay, arbitrary decisions by administrators and boards of education, heavy teaching loads, and abuses of students caused by permissive philosophies of child rearing. According to Albert Shanker, president of the American Federation of Teachers, that organization spends close to $30 million a year on organizing activity. A rival organization, the National Education Association, probably spends another $10 million. A unified teacher's union could be the largest and most powerful independent union in the United States. In New York State, where the two unions have merged, the membership of 218,000 includes practically every public school teacher.[2]

Although medical doctors seem most unlikely prospects for unionization, even they are moving in that direction in the large hospitals in New York City and Los Angeles. A 10,000-member Physicians National Housestaff Association voted in the fall of 1975 to bargain collectively on behalf of postgraduate interns and residents. Nurses and medical technicians have been unionized in far greater numbers than physicians.

Farm Employees. From 1970, when Cesar Chavez led the first successful drive to organize California grape growers, to 1977, when the Teamsters decided to withdraw, the United Farm Workers engaged in bitter competition with the teamsters to organize California's 226,000 farm workers. A new Agricultural Labor Relations Board has been established by the state to supervise elections and reduce the open warfare between the two unions. The unionization of farm workers, now expanding rapidly in Arizona and Florida, has been relatively successful in spite of the serious jurisdictional problems.

Government Employees. The impressive success of unionization drives among public service employees is due in no small part to President Kennedy's Executive Order 10988, in January, 1962.[3] It required recognition of and collective bargaining with certified unions of federal employees. Since 1962 unionization at all levels of government has increased rapidly in spite of legislation limiting the right of government employees to strike.

Actually no-strike legislation has proved ineffective in curbing strikes by public service employees. Strikes by San Francisco police and New York City garbage collectors have demonstrated the inability or unwillingness of public officials to deal effectively with this type of illegal behavior. When striking employees report in sick and union leaders disavow any connection with the strike, politically minded officials are reluctant to deal boldly with the situation. This reluctance to act constitutes one of the most serious problems with public service unions and one which is arousing anti-union sentiment. It is not likely that the general public will tolerate disruption of public services over an extended period of time.

Resistance to Unionization. In spite of government efforts to promote unionism, organizing efforts have encountered problems. Prior to passage of

---

[2] "A 'Teacher's War' That's Costing Millions," *U. S. News and World Report* (April, 1976), p. 90.

[3] Dale Yoder, *Personnel and Industrial Relations* (Englewood Cliffs: N. J.: Prentice-Hall, Inc., 1970), p. 427.

the Norris-La Guardia Act in 1932 unionism was contained by the use of court injunctions to stop strikes and by the requirement that employees sign the despised *yellow dog contract,* a commitment not to join a union. During this period, it was also common for employees to be fired for union activity.

After the passage of the 1932 and 1935 legislation (Norris-La Guardia and Wagner Acts), it appeared that unions would have freedom for unlimited organizing activity. This growth, in turn, was expected to provide the political power unions needed to consolidate their gains. A serious problem arose, however, when public opinion turned against unions immediately after World War II (1946). A few unions were communist dominated while others were controlled by racketeers, and voters feared that unions were becoming too strong. A number of nationwide strikes reflected the immaturity of the labor movement and showed contempt for public welfare and the national economy. This resulted in passage of the Taft-Hartley Act (Labor-Management Relations Act) in 1947. This legislation spelled out a number of unfair practices on the part of labor and permitted states to pass right-to-work laws which forbid dismissal of individuals for refusal to join unions. The Taft-Hartley Act also outlawed the *closed shop* in which only union members are eligible for employment. These and other provisions of the Act expressed some of the public's antagonism toward union power and recognized the belief that big unions as well as big business can destroy individual rights.

Concern over the power and abuses of unions was again expressed in the Landrum-Griffin Act (the Labor-Management Reporting and Disclosure Act of 1959). The Act was designed primarily to protect the rights of union members from the union itself. It includes a bill of rights for union members, requires extensive reporting by both unions and employers, and contains safeguards for democratic government within the union. Although the Act significantly improved the quality of unionism in America, its protection of individual rights also tended to restrict union power.

Regional Differences in Union Membership

The percentage of nonagricultural employees who belong to unions varies greatly from state to state. As shown in Figure 13–3 (page 284), the heaviest concentration of union employees is in the industrialized Eastern and Midwestern states and the Western seaboard states. Union membership is lowest in the South and Southwest. It is also notable that, with the exception of Nevada, states with the lowest percentage of union members are also those with right-to-work laws. Although right-to-work laws tend to weaken unions and make organizing difficult, these laws are not the major reason for the relatively low level of union activity in most of these states. As a matter of fact, it was the low level of unionization (lack of union power) that made passage of the laws possible.

Several factors contribute to the weakness of union activity in certain states. One is the paucity of large, labor-intensive industries in these states—a condition which is changing. Conservative attitudes, commitment to the Protestant work

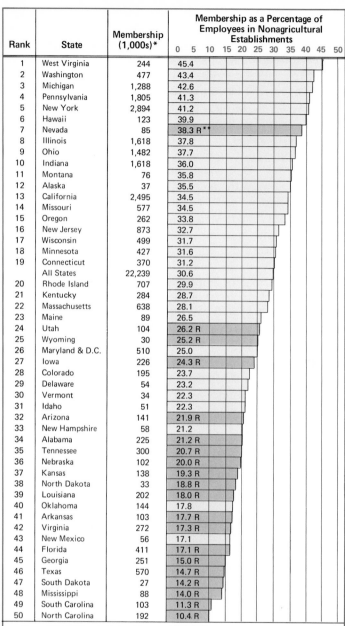

Rank	State	Membership (1,000s)*	Membership as a Percentage of Employees in Nonagricultural Establishments
1	West Virginia	244	45.4
2	Washington	477	43.4
3	Michigan	1,288	42.6
4	Pennsylvania	1,805	41.3
5	New York	2,894	41.2
6	Hawaii	123	39.9
7	Nevada	85	38.3 R**
8	Illinois	1,618	37.8
9	Ohio	1,482	37.7
10	Indiana	1,618	36.0
11	Montana	76	35.8
12	Alaska	37	35.5
13	California	2,495	34.5
14	Missouri	577	34.5
15	Oregon	262	33.8
16	New Jersey	873	32.7
17	Wisconsin	499	31.7
18	Minnesota	427	31.6
19	Connecticut	370	31.2
	All States	22,239	30.6
20	Rhode Island	707	29.9
21	Kentucky	284	28.7
22	Massachusetts	638	28.1
23	Maine	89	26.5
24	Utah	104	26.2 R
25	Wyoming	30	25.2 R
26	Maryland & D.C.	510	25.0
27	Iowa	226	24.3 R
28	Colorado	195	23.7
29	Delaware	54	23.2
30	Vermont	34	22.3
31	Idaho	51	22.3
32	Arizona	141	21.9 R
33	New Hampshire	58	21.2
34	Alabama	225	21.2 R
35	Tennessee	300	20.7 R
36	Nebraska	102	20.0 R
37	Kansas	138	19.3 R
38	North Dakota	33	18.8 R
39	Louisiana	202	18.0 R
40	Oklahoma	144	17.8
41	Arkansas	103	17.7 R
42	Virginia	272	17.3 R
43	New Mexico	56	17.1
44	Florida	411	17.1 R
45	Georgia	251	15.0 R
46	Texas	570	14.7 R
47	South Dakota	27	14.2 R
48	Mississippi	88	14.0 R
49	South Carolina	103	11.3 R
50	North Carolina	192	10.4 R

Source: U.S. Department of Labor, <u>Directory of National Unions and Employee Associations</u> (1974).
*These figures include 2,215,000 members of 35 professional and state associations plus 235,000 members of municipal associations.
**These states have right-to-work laws.

Figure 13–3   Distribution of Union and Employee Association Memberships by State

ethic, and retention of the dream that it is still possible to achieve financial independence also appear to be more prevalent in these areas. Many employees who are only one or two generations removed from the independence of farm life contrast sharply with employees in industrial centers whose industrial labor ancestry goes back to the sweatshops of the American colonies and Europe.

Personal Decisions Regarding Union Membership

We look now at the motivation of employees for joining unions. Managers have little control over the environmental factors that affect unionization on a national level. Managers do, however, influence organizational behavior and consequently need to understand employee motives with reference to union activity.

Why Employees Join Unions. Because differences exist between unions, situations, and individuals, employees join unions for many different reasons. During the early years of the 19th century, pay and working conditions were intolerable by today's standards. Adults were forced out of the job market by employers who hired children for a few cents a day to work under adverse physical and psychological conditions. A 60-hour work week was the rule, and some employees worked as long as 12 hours a day, seven days a week. The work was difficult and often dangerous. There was little job security, and supervisory styles were commonly dictatorial and arbitrary. By comparison, employees receiving the minimum wage today are well off. It is interesting to note, however, that the underlying reasons for joining unions have not changed greatly. Some of the most common of these are:

1. *Desire for security and protection.* The individual who stands alone against the organization may still feel insecure and powerless. Most employees are afraid that absolute power will be misused, and managers often behave in ways that increase the suspicion and distrust of subordinates. Collective action continues to be a means of countering organizational power.

2. *Desire for more money and better working conditions.* Employees who earn $10.00 an hour today may feel the need for money just as their grandparents who earned $1.00 a day did. A 40-hour work week is good, but a shorter work week and longer vacations are desirable. The elimination of the back-breaking labor from most jobs was admirable, but today's employees have no memory of the 19th century sweatshops or construction labor gangs. Expectations increase. Employers today are often called on to provide work that is interesting, challenging, and well paid. The point is sometimes made that more money is no longer the primary objective of unions. Indeed, an increasing amount of bargaining time is spent on other matters such as the nature of the work, supervisory practices, and guaranteed employment. It is noteworthy, however, that companies have become accustomed to granting large pay increases without a serious struggle. Should management change this policy, pay increases most certainly would gain a renewed prominence.

3. *Social pressures.* Nowhere are the informal group pressures discussed in Chapter 4 more overtly expressed than in the techniques used by unions to enlist and hold members. Since union-management problems deal with vital economic, social, and family issues, feelings become intense. Employees who refuse to join existing unions must often bear the brunt of frustration-generated hostility. When unions are successful in achieving their objectives, nonunion members are resented because they receive the benefit of union efforts without paying the price for it. When unions are unsuccessful, nonunion employees are perceived as being partially to blame because they have withheld their financial and personal support.

4. *The absence of an alternative.* Many labor contracts require a new employee to join a union within a short time after employment. Such a provision is legal in all states except those with right-to-work laws (see Figure 13–3). In organizations with a *union shop* every employee is required to join the union within a specified time or be dismissed. Although it is illegal for a company to contract with a union to hire only union members, it is not an unusual practice, especially in the building trades.

Few employees join unions for philosophical reasons. That minority believes in the economic and social benefits of unionism for society in general. But the vast majority of union members are motivated by practical concerns rather than by philosophical beliefs. Significant numbers of union members are political conservatives whose values actively support a free enterprise capitalistic economy. Most employees, union and nonunion alike, are aware that our competitive system is a principal cause of the unprecedented affluence of the United States.

Why Employees Do Not Join Unions.   The decline in union employees as a percentage of the total work force indicates that considerable numbers of employees choose not to belong to unions. Again, their reasons differ greatly.

1. Individuals in the work force who obviously lack the motivation to join unions include the self-employed and professional managers—although many such persons belong to employer and professional associations for motives similar to those of union members. Managers employed to represent the organization tend to be individualists and to prefer bargaining with the organization on the basis of personal contributions rather than collective power.

2. Employees may refuse to join because of the perceived low status of union members and a preference for identification with management or a professional group. Secretaries and engineers have traditionally fallen in this category. Many employees, even those who earn less pay than union members, want to avoid the low status society places on working with one's hands and to enjoy the high status of doing intellectual work.

3. For some employees union membership is perceived as limiting opportunities for advancement. These employees prefer performance evaluation to seniority rules. Such views are most likely to be held by ambi-

tious, self-confident individuals who have no distrust of management and who perceive themselves as having a high probability of success.

4. Some employees avoid union membership because they see in it no real benefits. On the positive side, they identify with the organization and believe that they are treated fairly. On the negative side, they want to avoid the payment of union dues and the control unions exert upon their membership. They are aware that the formation of a union could lead to costly strikes, pressures to restrict production, and other actions which could be economically destructive. Such individuals are most likely to work in organizations that already outperform many unionized companies in terms of pay, fringe benefits, and other aspects of the employment situation. In such organizations, warm, personal relationships with management are a valued aspect of the workplace which could be disrupted by unionization.

5. Employees of nonunionized companies often fear management reprisals for union involvement. The Wagner Act makes it an unfair labor practice for management to discriminate against an employee for union activity; but it is, nevertheless, a common practice in some companies. Ordinarily the action is disguised, for example, by making working conditions so unpleasant that resignation is preferable to the harassment. Nonunion employers, usually with the help of sympathetic employees, have powerful means at their disposal for influencing the behavior of employees who actively promote unionization. In the emotionally charged atmosphere surrounding a union representation election, both management and unions resort to pressure tactics which would otherwise be considered totally unacceptable.

STRATEGIES FOR UNION SECURITY

Thesis: The power and effectiveness of unions depend upon their ability legitimately to represent a united membership in bargaining with management. One of the major tasks of union leadership is to establish and maintain this legitimacy.

The right of a union to speak for part or all of an employee group must be established before meaningful collective bargaining is possible. Once the employee group and management accept the initial right of a union to serve as the bargaining agent, the union customarily bargains for agreements which will further strengthen its leadership position and protect its membership from erosion by apathy, turnover, or management action. The strategies by which the union's right and ability to represent a group of employees are maintained are called *union security agreements*. The most common of these are:

1. The exclusive bargaining agent
2. The closed shop
3. The union shop
4. The modified union shop

5. The preferential shop

6. The agency shop

7. The maintenance of membership

8. The check-off

The Exclusive Bargaining Agent

In spite of the power of unions in America and a national policy which encourages collective bargaining, virtually all companies prefer to deal with their employees as individuals. And as long as they conform to the law in their efforts to keep unions out, this *open shop* arrangement is perfectly legal.[4] An organization with an open shop makes no collective agreements and recognizes no unions even though many of its employees may be union members.

The most elementary form of union security is the organization's recognition of a union as the *exclusive bargaining agent.* This means that the company recognizes the right of a union to represent a specified group of employees in collective bargaining without regard to whether all the employees are union members. In geographical areas or in industries which are heavily unionized, this recognition may occur without government involvement. If the company insists on maintaining an open shop, however, the union will have to engage in a membership campaign and subsequently win an election, supervised by the National Labor Relations Board, in order to be recognized by the company. Figure 13–4 briefly describes the election procedure.

Representation elections may be held under a variety of circumstances, the basic criterion being that "a substantial number of employees" desire to bargain collectively with an unwilling employer. The request that a representation election be held may come from a single employee (when there is evidence that an unfair management practice has discouraged the free signing of authorization cards) or a group of employees. The election request may also be made by an existing labor union which management has refused to accept as an exclusive bargaining agent or as a bargaining agent for its own members. Ordinarily the immediate goal of union organizers is to get as many employees as possible to sign authorization cards. These are simple 3 x 5 inch cards on which employees specify their name, employer, work unit, job title, address, and phone number. The employees' signatures authorize a specified union to represent them for purposes of collective bargaining respecting pay, hours of employment, and other conditions of employment. An employer may also request an election. This would normally occur in order to demonstrate, with a strategically timed election, that most employees do not desire union representation.[5]

---

[4] Conforming to the law is a complex matter. An excellent introduction to the National Labor Relations Act, including the certification procedure, is *A Layman's Guide to Basic Law under the National Labor Relations Act,* prepared by the Office of the General Council, NLRB (1971).

[5] Arthur A. Sloane and Fred Witney, *Labor Relations* (Englewood Cliffs, N. J.: Prentice-Hall, Inc., 1977), p. 113.

YOUR GOVERNMENT CONDUCTS AN ELECTION

For You - on the job

General Information

Prior to any election conducted by the NLRB there will be posted at the place of your work a Notice of Election issued by the NLRB to inform you of:

* The date, hours, and place of the election

* The payroll period for voter eligibility

* A description of the voting unit of employees

* General rules as to conduct of elections

There is a sample ballot on the Notice of Election which, except for color, is a reproduction of the ballot you will receive when you vote.

You should read the Notice of Election so that you will be familiar with the ballot.

The Voting Place

In the voting place will be a table, a voting booth, and a ballot box. At the table there will be observers for the Union and the Employer and a representative of the NLRB, each of whom will be wearing an official badge. The observers' badges will have ''Observer'' on them. The NLRB representative will wear an "Agent" badge.

The Agent is in charge of the election. If you have questions, talk only with him.

The Voting Procedure

1 Go to the voting table, standing in line if necessary.

2 Give your name and your clock number, if you have one, to the observers. The observers will find your name on the voting list and tell the Agent your name has been found. If any questions are asked, talk only with the Agent. Do not argue with the observers.

3 After your name has been checked off, go to the Agent and he will give you a ballot.

4 Go into the vacant voting booth. Mark the ballot with one X only. Do not sign the ballot. Fold the ballot to hide the mark and leave the voting booth taking your ballot with you.

5 Put your ballot in the ballot box yourself. Do not let anyone else touch it.

6 Leave the polling place.

You will notice that only the Agent handled the blank ballots and only you handled your marked ballot. Once your marked ballot is in the ballot box it becomes mixed with all other ballots in the box and cannot be identified. No one can determine how you have voted.

Challenged Ballots

Questions sometimes arise about eligibility of certain persons. Any observer or the NLRB representative can challenge an individual's right to vote. This challenge, however, must be for good cause and not for personal reasons; for example, a name may not appear on the eligibility list because of a clerical error.

If your vote is challenged, take your ballot into the booth, mark it, fold it to keep the mark secret, and return to the voting table. The Agent will give you a challenged ballot envelope on the stub of which are written your name and clock number and the reason for the challenge. You put the ballot in the envelope. You seal the envelope, and you deposit it in the ballot box.

You will note that while your name is on the stub of the envelope it is not on the ballot. Secrecy of your vote is maintained because if challenged ballots must be counted and if later investigation reveals challenged voters are eligible to vote, the stub containing the name and clock number of the individual voter is first torn off and discarded. All challenged ballot envelopes are then mixed together. The bal- . . .

Source: Information brochure prepared by the National Labor Relations Board. Distributed in 1976.

Figure 13–4   General Information Concerning NLRB Supervised Elections

Although elections are the primary means of obtaining recognition, the NLRB may order an employer to bargain collectively on the basis of signed membership authorization cards alone.[6] This occurs when the employer engages in serious unfair labor practices, such as making selective layoffs to diminish the likelihood of a union victory. In any case, a successful union is certified by the NLRB as the exclusive bargaining agent for the unit.

The Closed Shop

Under the *closed shop,* only union members may be hired, and only members in good standing may be retained by the organization. Although the closed shop is prohibited by the Taft-Hartley Act, it is still practiced in industries where union hiring halls are the exclusive source of employees (e.g., in the maritime and construction industries). Because employees who are expelled from the union automatically lose their jobs this arrangement gives the union an inordinate amount of control over the individual employee and consequently the organization.

The Union Shop

In a union shop, nonunion individuals may be employed, but they are required to join the union after a specified probationary period, usually no longer than a few weeks. Like the closed shop, this form of agreement gives the union a high degree of control over the labor force. Over 62 percent of all labor agreements include the union shop provision. Although it is legal under federal law, it has been the prime target of state right-to-work laws. The assumption of right-to-work laws is that a person has a right to gainful employment without being forced to join a union.

The Modified Union Shop

Under the *modified union shop,* a provision in about 11 percent of the agreements, specified categories of individuals are exempted from having to join the union. Examples of employees not covered by the agreement are those who have religious objections to union membership, who are employed on a temporary or part-time basis, or who were employed prior to a certain date.

The Preferential Shop

Under the *preferential shop,* the company agrees to discriminate in favor of union members at the time of employment. This strengthens the union by reduc-

---

[6] Employers strenuously object to this because authorization cards are not notarized and may be obtained under conditions which do not allow absolute freedom of choice. As a result of numerous court decisions the NLRB has become wary of using this method.

ing the likelihood of membership attrition through the processes of separations, retirements, and death. Companies object to such an agreement because of their preference for hiring on the basis of qualifications to perform.

The Agency Shop

The *agency shop* does not require union membership, but it requires both members and nonmembers to pay union dues. The goal is to overcome the objection of certain employees to joining a union and, at the same time, to prevent nonunion members from being *free riders.* A free rider enjoys the advantages of union membership gained in collective bargaining without paying for them. About 9 percent of the agreements include an agency shop provision.

Maintenance of Membership

As a hedge against loss of union members, the maintenance of membership agreement states that employees who are union members or who join the union after a specified date must maintain their membership in good standing for the remainder of the contract period. Employees who desire to drop their membership are given a period of about two weeks to do so before the agreement takes effect. About 7 percent of all labor agreements contain this security provision.

The Check-off

One of the most serious problems encountered by early unions was the collection of dues. This problem was solved by negotiating for the *check-off,* a contract agreement by which union dues are deducted from paychecks by the employer and remitted to the union. Ordinarily this requires each individual's authorization, but this is a routine matter.

At the present time, about 86 percent of all labor agreements contain this provision, which is close to the number of contracts containing any form of union security agreement. In other words, the check-off is common practice. It often benefits management in that the organization can avoid discharging employees merely because of nonpayment of union dues. (This would be a problem, for example, under a union shop agreement.)

INDUSTRIAL DEMOCRACY AND THE RIGHT TO MANAGE

Thesis: Industrial democracy in the United States has been expressed through relatively free, two-party collective bargaining. Although managerial decisions under collective bargaining are often dictated or influenced by union power, collective bargaining is more effective than many alternative systems in protecting management's right to manage.

Although the concept of industrial democracy has been expressed in many ways, essentially it is the notion that democracy should be extended from the political to the industrial arena—that workers should participate in the governing of industry.[7] In America, it finds expression primarily in government-endorsed collective bargaining. Employees influence organizational decisions through their elected union representatives who negotiate with management on issues affecting employee welfare. Industrial democracy has also found expression in a variety of participative leadership techniques which do not involve unions.[8]

Industrial Democracy versus Industrial Warfare

The ground rules for the participation of employees in the governing of industrial organizations are expressed in a number of laws, the most prominent of which are the Wagner Act (1935) and the Taft-Hartley Act (1947). These, however, constitute only a small portion of the total body of statutory and common law governing collective bargaining and labor relations. During 1975 almost 900 labor laws were enacted at the state level alone.[9] The continuing flood of labor laws relates to all aspects of labor relations, such as wages, hours, safety, and discrimination in selection, promotion, and compensation.

Government is clearly a third party in the daily decision making and control of industrial organizations. Still, collective bargaining remains an important means by which industrial democracy is achieved. By law, the two parties are forced to discuss their differences and attempt to arrive at rational solutions. At times, government serves as a mediator to keep constructive negotiations moving. In some instances, especially in disputes over employee grievances, third-party arbitrators are used by mutual consent of labor and management to make binding decisions and thus to moderate the conflict.

In the final analysis, however, the possibility always exists that the differences between labor and management will be settled by a contest of power. The power of management lies primarily in its access to the economic resources of the organization. It can offer raises, fringe benefits, changes in working conditions, job security, and other sources of need satisfaction. Management also has a potential for using the *lockout,* for closing down operations, usually as a means of gaining an advantage in timing when a strike is expected. By using the lockout, however, management inflicts injury upon itself as well as the union.

The union's power lies in its ability to withhold strategic human resources. Although the strike is the most common means of achieving this end, the union

---

[7] For a detailed history of this concept, read Milton Derber, *The American Idea of Industrial Democracy 1865–1965* (Chicago: University of Illinois Press, 1970).

[8] Not all theorists would agree that the participative leadership techniques which have grown out of the human relations movement qualify as a form of industrial democracy. Under such systems, the voice of the employee is heard only by invitation—at the discretion of management. Under other systems, employees operate from a power base which is neither given nor controlled by managment.

[9] Deborah T. Bond, "State Labor Legislation Enacted in 1975," *Monthly Labor Review,* Vol. 99, No. 1 (January, 1976), p. 17.

may also use other tactics such as the *slowdown,* a deliberate reduction in productivity, or the *boycott,* an effort to influence union members and others to refuse to use the company's products. In a few instances, the union has bargained by promising to increase productivity, but this approach is unusual.

Although the managers of many organizations, including a number of the corporate giants, appear to have accepted the collective bargaining approach in theory as well as practice, acceptance is by no means universal. Resistance has been particularly strong from owner-managers who view the system as an infringement upon their property rights as well as their right to manage. Conscientious employers who feel that they manage fairly and have good employee relations resent what they consider to be the alienation of their employees by the union. They dislike the split loyalties of union members and the imposition of a system that interferes with an employer's ability to relate to its employees as individuals. Nevertheless, like the hundreds of federal, state, and municipal laws that regulate employee relations, union power is a reality with which managers must deal.

The Right to Manage

By the very nature of collective bargaining, management is called upon to take action that would not be taken if management had a free choice in the matter. This continually exposes the raw nerve endings around the question of management's *right to manage,* that is, management's right to make the decisions which are necessary for efficient and effective operation of the enterprise. Given the erosion of management decision-making power because of government controls (through legislation, rulings of government agencies, judicial decisions, and the endless rulings of quasi-judicial bodies such as the National Labor Relations Board), management is particularly sensitive to what it perceives to be encroachments upon its right to manage.

Legislation does not specifically limit the subject matter to be dealt with in collective bargaining. In practice, such matters as wages, hours, vacations, union security, and fringe benefits are the most common grist for the bargaining mill. But, as a union's power increases, so does its perception of its rights and legitimate interests. Who decides whether new automated machines shall be installed? Management's primary concerns are for survival, efficiency, and profits. From management's point of view the question should clearly be answered by management. The union, on the other hand, may believe that a need to protect the jobs of its members gives it a right to influence the decision. Such conflicts can hopefully be resolved through the give-and-take required for good-faith collective bargaining. Certainly this is the intent of the labor legislation which provided the guidelines for the bargaining process. Nevertheless, the element of power is ever present in collective bargaining, and at times a test of power must be made to settle the dispute. It would be naive to assume that the most powerful of the two parties is always right in a strict moral sense; but from a pragmatic viewpoint the system works, and satisfactory alternatives to it are difficult to find.

One advantage of the formal arm's length bargaining practiced in the United States is that it maintains a high degree of management autonomy in decision-making compared with the alternative systems found in several European countries. Since practices in other countries often become trends in this country, it is important that students of organizational behavior be aware of what others are doing. It also helps us to get our own practices in perspective and thus evaluate them more objectively.

In Sweden, where about 90 percent of the blue-collar workers and half the white-collar workers are union members, the influence of unions on organizational decisions is considerably stronger than in the United States. Historically Sweden's labor relations functioned under a right-to-manage concept which included the provision that management's interpretation in any rules' disagreement would prevail unless the matter was taken to the labor court by the union or employee. A 1975 law virtually eliminated management's right to manage and gave employees the right of first interpretation, with management having to appeal to the labor court.[10] As labor power in Sweden continues to grow, it is increasingly difficult for management to implement decisions of any sort without employee consultation. The effects on productivity and the survival of the private enterprise system are yet to be determined.

After a quarter century of experience with labor representatives on boards of directors, West Germany enacted a new *codetermination* law that went into effect on July 1, 1976. It provides that every company employing more than 2,000 persons will be required to establish a supervisory board, roughly equivalent to a United States board of directors, divided equally between representatives of shareholders and workers.[11] This means that workers essentially have an equal voice with management in making policy decisions and that the owner's representatives have, for practical purposes, lost the right to manage.

Although European experience has not borne out the worst prediction for codetermination, neither United States labor nor management has shown a serious interest in it. Even with all its theoretical and practical complications, collective bargaining is preferred because management still maintains the right to manage, relatively speaking, and union leaders, who really do not want the responsibilities of managing the company, are free to represent the interests of their constituents.

THE NATURE AND PURPOSE OF STRIKES

Thesis: In the short run, strikes are damaging to the national economy, the employer, the striking employees, and the general public. In a sense, collective bargaining has failed when a strike occurs. Alterna-

---

[10] Nancy Fay and Herman Gadon, "Worker Participation: Contrasts in Three Countries," *Harvard Business Review,* Vol. 54, No. 3 (May–June, 1976), p. 71–83.

[11] "When Workers Help Call the Tune in Management," *U. S. News and World Report,* Vol. 80, No. 19 (May 10, 1976), p. 83–85.

tives to the strike are becoming increasingly important because of the growing power of unions in the public sector.

Occasional strikes are necessary to make management respect the strike threat. At least management must perceive that a strike is always possible. Yet the strike itself is commonly a destructive weapon. Employees often suffer irrecoverable wage losses during a strike. Mortgage foreclosures, changes in family plans, mounting debts, and a variety of other environmental and psychological problems make strikes a serious matter. As a result, there is strong motivation for mature union leaders to bargain, compromise, and avoid a strike.

Other major costs involved in strikes are not directly related to the dispute in question. A major strike affects suppliers, subcontractors, customers, local retailers, and, at times, even the national economy. A strike by one union often prevents members of other unions from working, either because of the latter's respect for the strikers' picket line or the interrelationships in their work. These many and complex interdependencies make a strike everybody's business.

Causes of Strikes

Press releases about strikes usually oversimplify their causes. Typically, one cause is assumed: for example, a dispute over wages, working conditions, or a union security agreement. As a general rule, however, the causes are multiple, and the most publicized issue may be the least significant. Wages are often the primary focus of attention even when the more fundamental problem is a matter of pride and ego-defensiveness—say, a determination on the part of management and the union to hold to prior proclamations about a minimally acceptable settlement.

Even when a settlement is satisfactory to both employees and management, the local union is sometimes forced to strike in support of the national organization. In still other situations, the principal barrier to a settlement lies within the union. Two types of intraunion problems cause the greatest difficulty: (1) *jurisdictional disputes* (that is, disputes over the range of jobs for which a union claims the exclusive right to represent a group of employees) and (2) political problems of the union leadership.

The basic political problem is expressed in the following quotation from a labor relations director in the rubber industry:

> I had done everything I knew to back the union away from their absurd wage demands, but a strike seemed inevitable. Finally, I decided to have a beer and a private conversation with the chief union negotiator. When he was certain the talk would be confidential, he confessed that his constituency was accusing him of being too easy at the bargaining table. He had to give the image of a tough, aggressive negotiator or lose out in the next election. We decided to keep up the charade until the last possible moment and then settle on a figure we both knew was reasonable. I welcomed the opportunity to help shore up his position. His successor could have been a lot worse to deal with.

Since the strike, or threat of it, is the union's major source of power, the fact is often overlooked that management may actually provoke a strike to serve its own purposes. For example, management may take a position that is sure to result in a strike in preference to laying off employees to reduce excess inventory or when it believes that a strike will weaken union leadership. Some strikes are also precipitated by a management refusal to engage in good-faith collective bargaining. In other words some strikes are caused by management in that (1) management could easily have prevented them (2) they serve a management purpose, and/or (3) the union prefers not to strike but perceives itself to have no alternative because of management action.

Strike Effectiveness

No objective criteria exist by which a union can consistently evaluate the effectiveness of a strike—can determine whether is objectives have been achieved. By the very nature of the bargaining process the union's initial demands may be quite different from what it actually hopes to achieve, and what it originally hoped to achieve may prove to be too high or low as the bargaining progresses. In a given strike a union's objectives may be highly complex so that trade-offs between them are possible. For example, the union may be simultaneously bargaining for higher wages, better economic supplements, changes to make jobs more interesting, and the settlement of a large number of grievances in single plants or smaller work units. Evaluating the success of a strike when these union demands are achieved to varying degrees is necessarily a subjective matter. In fact, there are times when an outside observer might feel that a strike is a failure because the union's economic gains seem small compared to the cost of the strike, while union leaders and members feel quite successful because of a psychological gain (for example, an increase in the ability of union leaders and members to present a united front rather than collapse under the stresses involved in a strike). This accounts in part for the fact that both parties can feel successful after a hard fought bargaining session.

Both union and company leaders have a high capacity for rationalizing. A favorite management rationalization centers around its ability to pass along increased labor costs to the customer. Capitulation is justified because it avoids a strike, while little consideration is given to its effects on the economy, international competition, and other important, long-term factors.

The Importance of Timing. The effectiveness of a strike is often related to its timing. For example, an auto union prefers to strike at a time when it is strategically important for the manufacturer to produce an innovative model ahead of a competitor or take advantage of a surge in consumer buying. Ideally for the union, the strike is threatened when inventories of high demand items are low. If inventories are excessive the threat of a strike may have zero impact. Management may be indifferent or may even welcome the strike if the alternative is a layoff until inventories are reduced. In either case there is a work stoppage, but the strike is more likely to deplete union funds and to reflect negatively upon union leaders while only management is blamed for a layoff.

Management also may be indifferent to a strike threat when chances for negotiating a favorable contract are high. This occurs when unemployment is high, when other recently negotiated contracts have been favorable to management, or when the union appears to be weakened because of internal conflict.

Union and Management Propaganda.   Before and during a strike, both union and management propaganda is abundant. There are charges and counter-charges, trial balloons to probe the opponent's expectations and defenses, and biased announcements from both sides concerning profits and losses. Both union leaders and management are concerned with the degree of support employees are willing to give them. They are also concerned about public opinion and the likelihood of government involvement. Both parties are prone to bluff with the skill of professional gamblers.

In recent years, attention has been given to the use of propaganda films by both the union and management. A controversial, much publicized management film, *And Women Must Weep,* depicts the violence associated with a 1958 wildcat strike in Princeton, Indiana. It documents the effects of irresponsible union leadership under shop security provisions. The violence reached its peak when the four-month-old baby of a nonstriker was shot in the head while lying in her crib. This film, promoted by the National Right-to-Work Committee, has been widely used prior to certification elections. The AFL-CIO countered with an equally emotional film, *Anatomy of a Lie.* It is important to note that statistics do not support the idea that violence is a frequently used tactic by either labor or management. There are thousands of peacefully negotiated contracts every year with very few incidents of violence. When violence does occur, however, it is widely publicized, while peacefully negotiated contracts get little attention.

And Women Must Weep, the use of which was upheld by the federal courts, demonstrates the extent to which propaganda is legal as long as the information presented is factual.[12] Prior to the decision by the Fifth Circuit Court of Appeals, the NLRB had thrown out a number of elections in which the film was used. In the last ten years, court decisions have increased management's willingness to enter the propaganda arena with a growing confidence that free speech is a two-way street. The NLRB, a neutral body, has in many instances been viewed by management as pro-labor.

Arbitration as an Alternative to Strikes

One alternative to the disruptive effect of strikes is the use of third-party binding arbitration. Although approximately 95 percent of the labor-manage-

---

[12] Thomas G. Field, Jr., "Representation Elections, Films, and Free Speech," *Labor Law Journal,* Vol. 25, No. 4 (April, 1974), pp. 217–230. Also Joseph A. Pichler and H. Gordon Fitch, *"And Women Must Weep:* The NLRB as a Film Critic," *Industrial and Labor Relations Review,* Vol. 28, No. 3 (April, 1975), pp. 395–410.

ment agreements in the private sector provide for binding arbitration of griev-ances,[13] arbitration to resolve an impasse in negotiations for the basic contract has not been accepted in the private sector.

Critics of compulsory arbitration voice two major objections. First, neither labor nor management likes the idea of having an outsider make the critical decisions about their respective rights and responsibilities which normally are made at the bargaining table. The second objection centers around what former Secretary of Labor W. Willard Wirtz called the "narcotic effect," [14] Wirtz con-tended that a legal requirement that labor disputes be arbitrated would promote a narcotic effect in the sense of providing an easy, habit-forming release from the difficult task of responsible bargaining. At the present, there is little evidence either to support or deny this belief.

One approach which has recently received an increasing amount of attention is called *final offer arbitration*. Its purpose is to provide an alternative to strikes while avoiding the possible narcotic effect of traditional arbitration. In final offer arbitration, the arbitrator has only the authority to decide which of the final offers is most fair and realistic. Once the judgment is made it becomes binding on both parties. Its value over traditional arbitration lies in its purported ability to moti-vate both parties to make realistic offers rather than to adhere rigidly to absurd demands in the expectation of a down-the-middle compromise. Though perhaps less painful than the effects of a strike, final offer arbitration provides definite penalties for failure to bargain responsibly. Experience to date tentatively suggests that this approach is somewhat more effective than traditional arbitration.[15] This would especially be true where parties to the dispute are reasonably sophisticated in bargaining techniques and have the sensitivity to anticipate the standards by which the arbitrator's judgment will be made.

STUDY AND DISCUSSION QUESTIONS

1. In what ways do unions influence the policies and practices of organiza-tions which have no unions?
2. Members often have a strong identification with the union even though their standard of living is relatively high and many of the management abuses which led to the rise of unions have been eliminated. What accounts for the continuing strength of this identification?
3. What major differences existed between the AFL and the CIO? Why do you think the AFL was able to develop first?

---

[13] Sanford Cohen and Christian Eaby, "The Gardner-Denver Decision and Labor Arbitration," *Labor Law Journal,* Vol. 27, No. 1 (January, 1976), p. 18.

[14] Hoyt N. Wheeler, "Compulsory Arbitration: A Narcotic Effect?" *Industrial Relations,* Vol. 14, No. 1 (February, 1975), pp. 117–120.

[15] Peter Feuille, "Final Offer Arbitration and the Chilling Effect," *Industrial Relations,* Vol. 14, No. 3 (October, 1975), pp. 302–310.

4. In view of the pro-union legislation of 1932 and 1935, what accounts for the fact that unionism began to level off soon after the end of World War II?
5. In 1976 some union construction workers made temporary agreements to lower their wages by $1.00 to $2.00 an hour in order to avoid a continuing loss of jobs to nonunion employers. What does such action suggest about the kinds of problems unions face and possible solutions to them?
6. Recently a nonunion manufacturer, with plants in five countries, employed a national consulting firm to make a site study. The critical question was: Where should we locate our new plant in order to find personnel who will most likely fit into a nonunion organization with a participative management structure? Where would you suppose they might locate? Why?
7. Why do unions place such a high value on union security agreements?
8. What is meant by *industrial democracy?*
9. Neither labor nor management in the United States has shown an interest in a German type of labor-management collaboration. Why?
10. Describe and evelute final offer arbitration.

CRITICAL INCIDENT

A Difference of Opinion

Eric Laird immigrated to the United States at the age of 11 and began working as a printer's devil for 30 cents a day. As a result of native ability and unusually hard work, he achieved the status of master printer during his early twenties and soon founded his own printing business. At the time of this incident, he was the owner of a successful printing business in a large midwestern city in which the level of unionization was below average for the nation. Since Mr. Laird was beyond the average retirement age, his 48-year-old son, Julian, managed most of the day-to-day operation of the business. Julian's daughter, Ellen, also worked part time in the business while studying history and political science in a nearby university.

Laird's business had for many years been profitable, and he had shared generously with his employees. Their pay, fringe benefits, and working conditions were the best in the city; and management's relationship with the employees was generally good, if somewhat paternalistic. Eric Laird was sole owner of the business, the assumption being that, as an only child, Julian would inherit it upon his death.

The level of unionization of printers across the city was low. Unionization drives in the politically conservative state had been relatively unsuccessful, especially in the printing industry, where most of the firms had fewer than fifty employees and the owner-managers maintained strong personal ties with their employees. Because of an unusually concentrated drive by a national printers' union, several local printing establishments were being unionized. The Lairds reacted this way:

Eric Laird:

At this point, it appears that the NLRB will conduct an election, but as far as I'm concerned if the union wins we sell out or shut down. I started this business with my own two hands and a $20 investment in an old press. I paid a heavy price to build this company, and I don't intend to let a bunch of parasites come in here and tell me how to run it. We can't pay higher wages and still have a profitable business. With government bureaucrats already swarming all over the place, we certainly don't need any more outside interference. The payoff just isn't big enough to justify the trouble.

Julian Laird:

Dad, I don't want the union in here any more than you do, but I think we can keep it out. I've talked briefly with an attorney in Denver who specializes in legally resisting union drives. He knows as much about keeping the union out as the professional union organizers do about getting in. Don't forget that we have almost fifty years of good management going for us, too. Having an election and losing an election are not the same thing. And even if we are unionized, I don't think we should just lie down and quit. I don't want to bother with a union, but there is no way a union can take over this company.

Ellen Laird:

You both sound like right-wing 19th century bourgeois industrialists. You might take note of the fact that some of the most progressive and profitable companies in our industry are unionized. Frankly, I think a union would keep us on our toes—force us to be more efficient as well as be more considerate of our employees. Look at it this way: it is our policy to pay top wages and treat our employees fairly, so what will change? Well, one thing certainly will—our employees will be less dependent upon our generosity and may therefore have a greater sense of dignity and self-respect. They will have a little more power and we will have a little less. They won't have to come to us with hat in hand, hoping our generosity will continue.

Eric Laird:

Ellen, I've never heard such nonsense! I can't believe a member of this family would ever take such an absurd position. Doesn't private ownership mean anything? Don't we have a right to control our own. . . ?

Ellen Laird:

It is interesting that you would bring up the subject of rights. Are we the only ones with a right to have some control over our own destinies? Aren't there two sides to this issue?

Questions

1. What are the pros and cons of each position?
2. Which viewpoint is most defensible? Be prepared to take a point of view in a classroom debate, to support it with facts, and to point out the weaknesses of alternative points of view.

Chapter 14

Managerial Decision Making: Nature and Process

Of the many functions performed by managers, none contributes more directly to managerial effectiveness than decision making. Consequently, a manager's decision-making record is the principal basis for performance evaluation by superiors. Because managerial decisions reflect a manager's education, experience, and judgment, individual differences in decision-making ability are enormous.

Some managers can quickly make sound decisions in complex situations while others perform poorly under the most favorable conditions. This fact has led researchers to focus attention on the decision-making process, the techniques or methods by which decisions are made. While they have found no one *best* process for all decision makers, they have observed systematic differences in the way effective and ineffective managers decide. Managers who use this information can significantly improve their decisions.

THE NATURE OF MANAGERIAL DECISIONS

Thesis: Managerial decisions are often the product of a hodge-podge of data upon which the manager's authority, formal education, experience, reason, and emotions are brought to bear. As organizations become more sophisticated, however, managers adopt methods of decision making which are more scientific and can withstand public scrutiny.

The quality of organizational decisions bears an interesting relationship to managerial authority. Few managers avoid the experience of having a good decision vetoed by a superior whose chosen course of action is mediocre by comparison. A decision overturned by a superior is, for practical purposes, inadequate, since an act of authority prevents it from being put to the test. The practice of obscuring the quality of decisions through the nonrational use of authority is one of the most common misuses of managerial power. As managerial authority has declined, however, managers have become increasingly aware of a need to defend their decisions on the basis of reason rather than power.

Traditional Decision Making

Decision making in most organizations differs greatly from the methods prescribed by decision theorists. Most managerial decisions are on-the-spot "judgment calls" which do not lend themselves to sophisticated methods. They are highly intuitive in nature, and neither the assumptions upon which they are based, the alternatives from which a course of action is chosen, nor the criteria for decision making are clearly stated. Generally speaking, modern decision theorists stress the importance of making explicit the process by which decisions, especially major decisions, are made. This permits both the defense of a decision and the long-range improvement of a manager's decision-making capability.

Managers make many decisions by default or neglect. Reacting to problems referred to them by subordinates or superiors, they take action on the basis of habit or respond with an unthinking, mechanical application of policy. This contrasts sharply with *initiative decisions,* which are voluntarily made, after appropriate data collection and analysis, to solve or avoid specific problems. Since a manager's individual perception of a need for action is the occasion of initiative decisions, this kind of decision is avoided by mediocre, unaggressive managers.

Lindblom described an approach to decision making which maximizes personal security.[1] Its rationale holds that the safest approach to change is to proceed in the direction one has traveled in the past, while limiting the consideration of alternative action "to those policies that differ in relatively small degrees from policies presently in effect." [2] This commonly used approach is workable in a stable organization operating in a stable market. Its weaknesses surface, however, when the environment is characterized by novel situations and rapid change.

Another common approach to decision making is the "implicit favorite" model.[3] Following this model, the manager makes an implicit (not openly expressed) choice among alternatives and then continues to gather data until the implicit choice is confirmed. This often involves more rationalization than reasoning as the manager selectively perceives data that support the implicit decision and cause alternatives to appear weak by comparison.

Other people can often predict how a manager using the implicit favorite model will ultimately decide long before the decision is consciously made. This occurred, for example, when a firm's president and largest shareholder went through a prolonged, agonizing decision about promoting his son into the executive ranks. Other executives knew that the president's decision to consider his

---

[1] Charles E. Lindblom, "The Science of 'Muddling Through,'" *Public Personnel Review,* Vol. 19 (Spring, 1959), pp. 79–88.

[2] Ibid., p. 84.

[3] P. O. Soelberg, "Unprogrammed Decision Making," *Industrial Management Review,* Vol. 8 (1967), pp. 19–29.

son for the position was, in effect, his decision to promote him. Since, however, fairness and objectivity demanded a comparison with other candidates, the charade had to be played out.

A Good Decision

Managers who cannot hide behind their formal authority must devise a means of justifying their decisions. One alternative is simply to evaluate decisions in terms of their results. Another is to evaluate them in terms of the methods or processes by which they are made.

Decisions and Results.   The simplest criterion of a good decision is that it works. Given management's current interest in managing by objectives, it is reasonable to emphasize the role of results in evaluating the quality of managerial decisions. From one perspective, a single criterion seems adequate: Decisions which produce good results are good decisions; those which produce poor results are not.

The results criterion has merit. Certainly good decision makers get better results than poor decision makers, on the average. It does not, however, follow that a manager whose achievements are outstanding has necessarily been a good decision maker. Good results may be due to such opportunity factors as having effective subordinates or operating in a favorable market environment.

The results criterion offers particular problems in evaluating a specific decision. Two investors buy stock on the same day. Investor *A* plays a hunch, invests all his funds in a single speculative stock, and immediately makes a fortune. Investor *B* meticulously studies the market, calculates the risks, diversifies his purchases, and makes a reasonable profit. Which investor made the better decision? Which is the better decision maker? These questions can best be answered with another question. With whom would you prefer to trust your investment funds? It is rational to prefer the calculated risk-taker to the gambler. Under the conditions stated, a poor decision may yield good results.

The Decision Process.   Since managerial decisions are made about future events, they are made on the basis of incomplete information. Consequently, they involve risks. The possibility always exists that a good decision will have undesirable consequences. The automobile dealer who purchased a heavy stock of large automobiles just before the 1974 oil embargo could not possibly have anticipated the rush to small automobiles. Neither could automobile manufacturers predict the 1976 swing back to large automobiles. The fact that unpredictable events affect the outcomes of decisions suggests that decisions may be best evaluated in terms of the process by which they are made. From this perspective, one should not be surprised that outstanding decision makers occasionally get poor results. They qualify as outstanding decision makers because of their approach to decision making; their superior overall results are a predictable consequence of that approach. One of the major purposes of this chapter is to describe methods which are most likely to yield good results.

Rationality in Decision Making

One criterion of a good decision is its *rationality,* the extent to which a chosen course of action is designed to achieve an objective in an efficient manner. Although rationality is an ideal to be sought, in practice the decision maker must be content to settle for something less, for a *bounded* rationality. Rationality is bounded or limited by such factors as (1) time and cost considerations in data collection and analysis; (2) only partial awareness of alternative solutions; (3) inadequate knowledge of the consequences of alternative solutions; (4) poorly defined goals; (5) conflicting and continually changing goals; and (6) human limitations in the areas of memory, reasoning, and objectivity.

One of the main barriers to rational decision making in organizations arises from the fact that managers must promote their own careers while making organizational decisions. This results in continual compromises and inconsistencies. Perhaps the conflict is best exemplified when an executive whose total resources have been committed to one organization resigns to accept a high position with a competitor. To persons who are unfamiliar with the inner workings of organizations at the executive level, it could appear that such behavior is shameful and traitorous as well as irrational. How could a person whose total energies have been focused on making one company successful decide to eliminate that contribution and give a competitor the benefit of it? The answer, of course, lies in the fact that most executives are also employees. As such they have personal needs which are not always consistent with the needs of their employers. Executives compete with one another for promotions, power, and prestige; they hold tenaciously to certain ideas for ego-defensive reasons and otherwise behave irrationally when judged by organizational criteria. Thus, rationality can only be understood with reference to a point of view. Unfortunately for their employer, it is not unusual for executives to make organizational decisions of questionable rationality because they are behaving rationally in terms of enhancing their own careers.

Maximizing Behavior.   In the classical economic model, business decision makers are presumed to behave rationally in that they *maximize* profit-making behavior; that is, they supposedly make business decisions which will produce the maximum amount of profit for the firm. When applied to an individual, this theory postulates the rational weighing of alternatives with decisions ultimately made in terms of maximizing self-interest.[4]

The notion that behavior is maximized either at the level of the firm or the individual is indefensible. It assumes, for example, clarity of objectives, complete awareness of alternatives and their consequences, and unlimited reasoning capacity. In effect, all the limitations on rationality listed earlier prevent decision makers from being maximizers in a classical sense.

---

[4] E. Frank Harrison, *The Managerial Decision-Making Process* (Boston: Houghton Mifflin Company, 1975), p. 63.

Satisficing Behavior.   Under the *bounded rationality* concept, decision mak-ers may be seen as *satisficers* rather than maximizers; that is, they seek satisfactory rather than optimal solutions to problems. March and Simon distinguish the two as follows:

> An alternative is *optimal* if (1) there exists a set of criteria that permits all alternatives to be compared and (2) the alternative in ques-tion is preferred, by these criteria, to all other alternatives. An alternative is *satisfactory* if (1) there exists a set of criteria that describes minimally satisfactory alternatives and (2) the alternative in question meets or exceeds these criteria. . . .[5]

The task of searching for the optimal alternative is infinitely more difficult than finding a satisfactory alternative. Since managers always operate with limited resources, they are of necessity satisficers rather than maximizers.

The Use of Heuristics.   Bounded by limitations of time, resources, and mental capacity, real-world decision makers use imperfect models, rules of thumb, or heuristics to reduce the elements of a decision into manageable, bite-sized pieces. A *heuristic* is a technique or principle which permits limited data collection and analysis in decision making. Computers are heuristically programmed to selec-tively use information to arrive at usable, approximate solutions. Using nonquan-titative data, managers establish rules and criteria by which conclusions are reached in situations which are so complex that all the relevant variables could not possibly be considered. Recognizing that there are many other criteria which would ideally be considered, managers select a few important criteria and apply them to the most obvious alternatives.

The use of heuristics leaves the decision maker open to possible criticism. Why were the particular standards of evaluation used? Why were additional data not collected? Regardless of the methodology used, a manager's ultimate defense is: Given the available options and resources, the course of action I chose was, in my judgment, the best one. This ultimate right to decide does, of course, allow bias to enter the decision process. A manager may, for example, cite an unpredict-able economy as a reason not to expand into a new market. The overriding decision criterion, however, may be a personal desire to avoid the stress, conflict, and hard work associated with the action. Nevertheless, there is no practical alternative to a heuristic approach by a decision maker with limited rational capacity in an environment with changing and conflicting objectives.

Systems Constraints.   Effective managerial decisions are never made in a vacuum. A decision of the marketing department affects manufacturing, account-ing, personnel, purchasing, and, in a sense, every function of the organization. Because of this, a high level of participation and coordination is necessary in making organizational decisions.

---

[5] James G. March and Herbert A. Simon, *Organizations* (New York: John Wiley & Sons, Inc., 1958), pp. 140–141.

The constraints within which a decision maker must work are often political. Ideal alternatives are compromised to gain acceptance by superiors, peers, or subordinates. What appears to be an engineering and financial decision, say a change in machines or methods, turns out to be influenced more by union power than by technical or financial feasibility.

Since organizations are *open systems,* in continual interaction with the external environment, business decisions are strongly influenced by external factors. Possible consequences, such as the following, cannot be ignored:

1. The union calls for a strike or slowdown.

2. Lending institutions refuse financing.

3. New competitors enter the market.

4. The government initiates antitrust proceedings or passes unfavorable legislation.

5. An international cartel restricts supplies.

6. Public sentiment becomes negative.

7. Customers switch to a competitive product.

The complexity of organizational decision making is steadily increasing. It is not surprising, therefore, that the process by which organizational decisions are made has gradually become less individualistic and personal.

Personal Influences upon Managerial Decisions

Given the same set of facts, two decision makers often select alternative solutions that differ greatly. They perceive and evaluate the facts differently, based upon values, standards, and motives which are partially or wholly unconscious. The possibility of such biases influencing decisions can never be eliminated, but it can be reduced somewhat by making explicit each step of the decision process.

Although personal characteristics interact in complex ways to influence the decision process, it is possible to identify a number which affect decision quality. The following are among the most important of these characteristics.

1. *Intelligence.* Although superior intelligence is generally preferred, the kind of intelligence, as well as the amount, is important. For example, managers who are extremely high in abstract reasoning and low in practical judgment tend to become theoretical intellectualizers rather than practical problem solvers. Analytical ability, like practical judgment, is a significant contributor to decision quality.

2. *Cautiousness versus impulsiveness.* Managers who are unusually cautious may spend so much time gathering data that they miss important opportunities. They are risk avoiders who place a high value on safety. At the opposite extreme, impulsive decision makers become anxious when the loose ends of a complex problem are dangling. To avoid this anxiety,

they decide too quickly. As a result, they spend much time rationalizing and attempting to hide or correct their mistakes.

3. *Risk taking.* The tendency to take high risks is not perfectly correlated with the cautiousness-impulsiveness continuum although the two are related. Some managers are prone to take high risks, but only after calculating the success-failure probabilities. This tendency may result from a variety of motivations including (1) an extremely high level of aspiration, (2) a need for the thrill or excitement of taking chances, or (3) a naive optimism with reference to the probability of success.

4. *Optimism versus pessimism.* To some extent, optimism and pessimism are related to one's self-image. Decision makers who think poorly of their own abilities, who have feelings of guilt and self-doubt, are more likely than others to overestimate the probability of failure. The self-images of highly optimistic managers may be unrealistically positive because of an inability to accept self-criticism and because of a tendency to repress or rationalize away past failures. Tough-minded, mature managers attempt to calculate the actual risks rather than systematically vary in either direction. They tend to rely heavily on their own abilities and to have little use for the idea of luck.

5. *Ego defensiveness.* The decisions of managers who are constantly on the defensive suffer from lack of objectivity. Their perception and logic are distorted by a need to view themselves favorably.

6. *Dependence on others.* Managers with a strong need for the approval of others excessively weigh the reactions of others to their decisions. The course of action selected may be successful in terms of the manager's personal goal of avoiding conflict but relatively unsuccessful in achieving organizational objectives. At the opposite extreme, some managers, insensitive to the needs and reactions of others, make decisions which may be logical but are unworkable because they cannot be implemented.

7. *Level of aspiration.* Good decisions are sometimes costly to the decision maker. They require hours of hard work and may involve a high level of personal tension and interpersonal conflict. Because of this, the manager whose self-expectations are relatively low may settle for a poor solution rather than pay the price required to find a good one.

8. *Decisiveness.* Since all decisions are made in terms of certain standards, it is important that a decision maker be committed to personal values and other standards such as goals, productivity expectations, and guidelines for effective management. Having made personal decisions in these areas, the manager is able to be *decisive* on the job, that is, to make decisions without undue hesitation. Decisiveness also depends upon a manager's self-confidence and ability to face the consequences when poor decisions cannot be avoided.

9. *Creativity.* Although good decision makers are not always creative, creativity is an asset in generating alternative solutions. It is possible, however, for a manager to be too creative, to behave creatively when, for example, the situation calls for someone who can routinely implement a good decision rather than continually work at improving it.

In practice a given manager will be much stronger in some areas than in others. In certain situations, decision quality can be maintained by delegation,

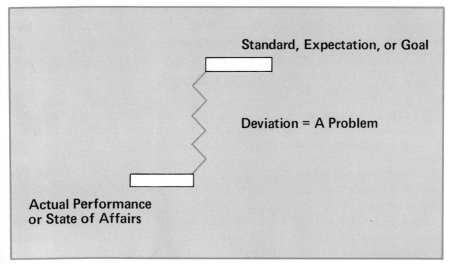

Figure 14–1   A Problem as a Deviation from a Standard

Travers' experience illustrates that problem awareness involves more than a passive registration of ongoing events. There is much a manager can do to become aware of problems before their full impact is felt.

The Problem Seeker

Effectiveness as a problem seeker begins with a manager's self-perception and problem perception. Managers who are high achievers, who have learned aggressively to seek out and solve problems, have a natural advantage over those who view problems as a source of frustration. Persons who view themselves as problem solvers are attracted to problems. Because problems provide opportunities to increase their worth to the organization, they are psychologically conditioned to notice problems that others overlook.

A simple example illustrates the importance of perception in problem solving. A toothache is a problem. From the patient's viewpoint, it is most undesirable, but the dentist sees it as an opportunity both to provide a service and to fulfill personal needs. Managers who view themselves as problem solvers should take no more delight in the occurrence of an organizational problem than a dentist takes in the pain experienced by a patient. On the other hand, solving the problem can provide managers both inner satisfaction and external rewards.

Becoming Aware of Problems

Self-perception as a problem solver can be strengthened through solving problems, although this may be a slow process. Fortunately managers can do some things to improve problem awareness, even though their initial feelings and

use of participative techniques, and other devices which permit compensati
a manager's weakness. Decisiveness is the one personal characteristic
seems to be most essential for a high level of managerial success.

PROBLEM FINDING

Thesis: A problem is a deviation from a standard or expectati
To be effective in decision making, a manager must be aware of cur
problems and must anticipate potential problems.

The formal education of the typical manager is relatively imperson
those majoring in business, it is oriented toward the content of formal ac
disciplines such as accounting, finance, organizational theory, and quar
analysis. Important as these are to managerial effectiveness, particularl
analytical aspects of problem solving, they provide a manager with little i
to be aggressive in searching for problems to be solved. In fact, the a
disciplines seldom take note of the fact that problem finding is an in
aspect of problem solving. Ignorance of this fact often produces individ
have the aptitudes and skills to solve problems but simply do not see t
look now at the nature of problems and how a person may become
effective problem finder.

Problems as Deviations from Standards

Poor managers often have problems of which they are unaware.
ple, a foreman believes that his human relations are acceptable while hi
thinks otherwise. The foreman is unaware of the problem because t
disparity between his self-expectation and his perception of his own be
disparity does exist, however, in the mind of his superior. Objectively
both have a problem, but the foreman's problem is potentially mc
because he is unaware of it.

A slightly different perspective on the nature of problems is gaine
owner of a small trucking company.

Glen Travers took great pride in the eight diesel-powere
ports he acquired to replace all but four of his aging truck fleet. *
the new trucks received heavy use, Travers felt sure it would be
another year before major repairs would become necessary.
did not know was that faulty engine parts were pouring mic
particles of metal into the oil, causing rapid wear. Within a tw
period, four of the trucks required major engine overhauls. H
ered too late that he could have learned of the problem earlier
an analytical chemist periodically check oil samples for sym
engine wear.

---

[6] Charles H. Kepner and Benjamin B. Tregoe, *The Rational Manager* (New Yorl
Inc., 1965), p. 20.

self-perceptions may not be ideal. The following behaviors are among those which are most likely to increase problem awareness.

1. Continually maintain a conscious awareness of organizational objectives relating to productivity, quality, human relations, and other important areas of achievement.

2. Establish effective controls through which deviations from standards can be conveniently and surely detected. This may require standards in areas where the organization has none, say in areas of employee turnover, level of waste, or number of grievances filed.

3. Make explicit what constitutes reasonable expectations for individual performance. For example, is there really a problem when an employee who works alone and has minimal influence on others is always grouchy and dissatisfied? If everybody must wear a happy face, the employee's behavior constitutes a human relations problem. If, however, the standard permits such behavior, and morale in general is good, the problem solver's attention can be focused elsewhere.[7]

4. Develop a sensitivity to organizational problems by identifying with the overall organization and accepting broad responsibility for its problems. Learn to view the organization from the viewpoint of the chief executive, high-level supervisors, and others for whom a problem may be defined differently.

5. Be observant. Give special attention to possible unanticipated consequences of organizational changes.

6. Respect your own feelings of apprehension about situations. Allow your hunches to develop into testable hypotheses.

7. Create problems by identifying opportunities (raising standards, goals, and expectations), thereby establishing the need for problem-solving behavior.

8. Reward problem finding among subordinates.

9. Do not confuse problem finding with negative thinking or faultfinding. This can be avoided by motivating subordinates who observe problems to propose solutions also.

10. Make your personal goals explicit and identify areas of congruence and conflict with organizational goals. This diminishes the possibility of avoiding organizational problems for strictly personal reasons.

The use of guidelines such as these is an application of behavior modeling, of behaving in ways which produce a desired outcome in anticipation of the day when such behavior will become automatic. This process may be thought of as

---

[7] Problems can often be solved by lowering expectations. If the standard is unrealistic, this practice is advisable. It is important, however, that realistic standards not be lowered as a means of finding an easy way out.

educating or nurturing the intuition.[8] Behaviors which are modeled after those of successful managers are positively reinforced by such rewards as raises, promotions, and recognition. This increases the probability that such behaviors will become an internalized, natural behavior pattern.

A DECISION MODEL

Thesis: There is no sure way to avoid decisions which are ineffective in solving organizational problems. Models are available, however, which capture the experience of management and the research of decision theorists. The use of such guides reduces the probability that poor decisions will be made.

Although terminology and explanations differ greatly, decision theorists are in general agreement that certain practices positively contribute to decision making and problem solving [9] while others diminish their effectiveness. These practices are typically embodied in decision models.

Decision models are not a panacea. When followed slavishly they may even decrease the quality of specific decisions. They are most appropriate for solving problems where sufficient time is available for research and other programmed activities. This does not mean, however, that decision models contribute nothing to the numerous, on-the-spot decisions managers make. Models often sensitize a manager to certain thought processes which should occur regardless of the urgency of the decision. Figure 14–2 presents the skeleton of a decision model which will be explained in the remainder of this chapter.

When first introduced to a decision model, practicing managers often think that it is too detailed and complex. Their attitudes typically become more favorable, however, when the model is used to solve complex, real-life problems.

The critical analysis step in decision making can become quite technical, so much so that staff specialists may be needed for support. On the whole, however, the use of models simplifies the process by which a problem is systematically sorted out and broken down into manageable units. In effect, the major decision

---

[8] See Chapter 3, "The Nature and Nurture of Intuition," in William T. Morris, *Management for Action: Psychotechnical Decision Making* (Reston, Va.: Reston Publishing Company, 1972), pp. 47–66.

[9] In this chapter, no distinction is made between the terms *decision making* and *problem solving,* although decision making is sometimes described as the choice step in a problem-solving model. These terms are used in many different ways in the literature of decision theory. See Kenneth R. MacCrimmon and Ronald N. Taylor, "Decision Making and Problem Solving," in Marvin D. Dunnette, (ed.), *Handbook of Industrial and Organizational Psychology* (Chicago: Rand McNally & Company, 1976), p. 1337.

To view decision making as simply the choice step in a broader process of problem solving conveys the misleading notion that decision making occurs at a specific, knife-edge point in time. Actually many decisions evolve over a long period of time; and those which appear to be instantaneous are interlocked with prior decisions concerning policies, goals, values, and methods. Major decisions emerge from the small decisions involved in such actions as defining the problem, establishing criteria, and gathering and evaluating data. That decision making is a continuing process is also seen in the fact that decisions made during implementation often modify the original (focal) decision.

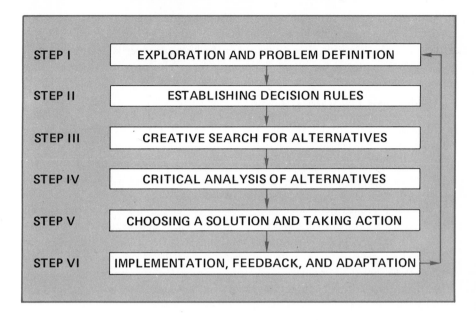

Figure 14–2 **A Decision Model**

grows out of a series of smaller, antecedent decisions. Although Step V uniquely involves choice behavior, it is noteworthy that decisions are made throughout the model.

Exploration and Problem Definition

The first step in the overall decision process is an exploration of the apparent problem and assessment of its nature and importance. The problem is then defined in terms of the standard or expectation to which it is related.

Exploration involves answering a series of questions about the apparent problem. Since a problem is defined as a deviation from a standard, one might begin by noting the applicable standard and by evaluating whether it is reasonable and worthwhile. Sometimes the apparent problem is merely a symptom of a deeper problem upon which attention should be focused. For example, an increase in the number of petty grievances may be symptomatic of employee dissatisfaction because of a seemingly unrelated management action.

It is sometimes valuable to note the time of problem observation and any changes which preceded it. This may provide a clue to its cause and its seriousness. Since several interrelated problems sometimes exist, exploration often proves to be a major technique for problem finding.

Once a problem is isolated it is defined in terms of the standards to which it relates. For example, the turnover rate among factory employees is 3 percent per month. It should be below 2 percent. Care should be taken to avoid defining the problem in terms of possible causes: The selection of factory employees has resulted in a 3 percent turnover rate when it should be below 2 percent. By implying in the definition that the cause of the high turnover is personnel selection, the way is staged for blame-fixing and for overlooking other causes.

Establishing Decision Rules

Decisions can only be described as good or bad in terms of criteria. When possible, these criteria should be made explicit before alternative solutions are developed. Such a practice reduces the likelihood that the solution choice will be based upon irrelevent criteria or that an inferior solution will be accepted because the quality of a good solution is unknown.

This step requires consideration of two interrelated areas. The first is concerned with the problem-solving process; the second is concerned with the standards by which the possible solutions will ultimately be judged. With reference to the former, decisions are made concerning who will assume responsibility for solving the problem. Similarly, management must specify the extent to which other managers will participate, the amount of time and money to be invested in research, when the decision must be made, and the probable returns from finding an outstanding solution rather than one which is minimally satisfactory.

The criteria against which alternative solutions will be evaluated may be stated in terms of organizational objectives such as maximizing short-term profits, controlling a market, or increasing cash flow. They may also be expressed in terms of constraints or parameters within which the ultimate solution must fall. The solution to a given problem, for example, must not result in loss of organizational control by the present owners, or it must not result in an expenditure of more than $100,000. Perhaps the final solution must be acceptable to the organization's employees or must not attract the attention of the Federal Trade Commission or other government agencies.

In some instances, establishing criteria involves compromises and trade-offs. In collective bargaining, for example, the decision rule might be made that a guaranteed annual wage will be granted only if the union agrees to drop its resistance to discharges of employees whose incompetence is demonstrated by management and to permit employees to be freely moved to other jobs when they have no work to do. Such criteria provide guidelines which enable decision makers to decide on a rational basis and avoid becoming confused by the pressures and preoccupations of the moment.

Creative Search for Alternatives

Managers who practice choosing from among alternatives tend to make better decisions than those who evaluate isolated solutions on an accept-reject basis. Since acceptance or rejection of the most obvious solution is easier than creatively generating alternative solutions, however, the creative step in decision making is commonly omitted.

Creativity in decision making is the process of generating new and useful solutions to problems. A creative solution, like a creative work of art, involves more than novelty or uniqueness. Anyone can produce a one-of-a-kind painting, but not everyone can produce an aesthetically appealing work of art. Anyone can offer solutions to management problems, but genuinely creative solutions require the decision maker to be disciplined, knowledgeable, and highly motivated.

Creativity and Personality.   Creativity is deliberately defined as a process rather than as a personal attribute. It is, in one sense, a personal attribute, but there is good reason for conceptualizing creativity as a behavior. Thus, an individual *behaves creatively* in a particular situation rather than *being creative* as if it were a general personality characteristic. An artist, for example, may be exceptionally creative when painting or sculpturing but abysmally uncreative when generating alternative solutions to a scientific or managerial problem.

Creativity, then, is situational. In order to be highly creative in solving a given problem, the decision maker needs depth of relevant background. By placing bits of information together in unique ways, novel and useful combinations emerge.

Managers are often so accustomed to operating within the constraints of goals, policies, rules, laws, and traditions that creative thinking appears strange and frustrating. They associate it with an uninhibited, Bohemian life style, more fitting for musicians and artists than for managers. This is an unfortunate perception since it often reduces motivation to be creative and raises questions about one's potential for it.

Actually everyone has the potential for behaving creatively. Individuals who are relatively uninhibited, open to new experiences, flexible and independent in their thinking, and committed to being creatively productive have an advantage over persons who lack these qualities. On the other hand, almost everyone with the motivation to do so can behave creatively for short periods of time. A variety of techniques has been developed to facilitate this behavior.

Techniques for Encouraging Creativity.   One of the oldest and best known techniques for encouraging creative thought is *brainstorming*.[10] Following this approach, a group of individuals applies a set of rules which encourages uninhibited free association about the problem at hand. No one is allowed to be critical, and group members are encouraged to draw upon the contributions of others in generating new ideas.

The enthusiasm, social stimulation, and permissive atmosphere of brainstorming is intended to stimulate the free flow of ideas, as indeed it does. In practice, however, the technique has its drawbacks. The ideas presented tend to direct group thinking into certain channels which inhibit the divergent thinking brainstorming purports to stimulate. Research indicates that, for the development of unique ideas and high quality ideas, the pooled efforts of individuals working

---

[10] Alex F. Osborn, *Applied Imagination: Principles and Procedures of Creative Thinking* (New York: Charles Scribner's Sons, 1941).

in isolation is better than brainstorming. There is, however, no reason why the best of the two methods cannot be achieved by following individual creativity with brainstorming.

Another technique for stimulating creativity is called *synectics.*[11] This structured group approach is designed to force participants to deviate from usual modes of thinking. Under the guidance of an experienced leader, participants engage in role-playing exercises and various forms of fantasy designed to break down traditional ways of viewing problems. In one application of the technique, people with different backgrounds are locked in a room together until they find a novel solution. Although synectics is not as simple to use as brainstorming or individual creativity, it is a workable technique.

Breaking Creativity Barriers.   The major barrier to creative thought is illustrated in Figure 14–3. Everyone has a characteristic way of viewing situations. These perceptual predispositions or "sets" are related to an individual's background, knowledge, experience, personality characteristics, attitudes, and intellectual abilities. Everyone is a victim of faulty assumptions and self-imposed constraints which restrict the freedom to form novel associations. It is common in approaching the nine dot problem, for example, to assume that the lines cannot be extended beyond the limits of the dots. As long as this unanalyzed assumption controls one's thought processes, the problem cannot be solved.

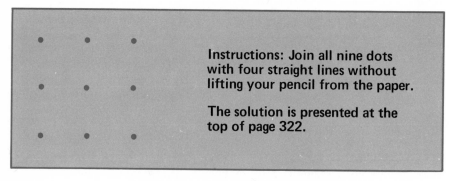

Instructions: Join all nine dots with four straight lines without lifting your pencil from the paper.

The solution is presented at the top of page 322.

Figure 14–3   The Nine Dot Problem

The primary task of thinking creatively is to break the psychological barriers to free association. In the words of James L. Adams, the task is that of "conceptual blockbusting." He defines conceptual blocks as "mental walls which block the problem solver from correctly perceiving a problem or conceiving its solution."[12] The actions listed below are helpful in breaking down these barriers and generating alternative solutions.

---

[11] W. J. Gordon, *Synectics* (New York: Harper and Row, Publishers, 1961) and G. M. Prince, "The Operational Mechanism of Synectics," *The Journal of Creative Behavior,* Vol. 2 (1968), pp. 1–13.

[12] James L. Adams, *Conceptual Blockbusting* (San Francisco: W. H. Freeman and Company, Publishers, 1974), p. 11.

1. Postpone critical analysis of solutions until the creative step in problem solving is essentially completed.

2. Avoid dogmatic, all-or-nothing thinking.

3. Do not be inhibited by how others might react to a possible solution.

4. Allow time for ideas to incubate. Pressures of time tend to inhibit free association.

5. Analyze the assumptions upon which previously developed alternatives are based and create alternatives which might work under a variety of other assumptions even if such assumptions are unrealistic.

6. Think of solutions someone else might recommend, say an engineer, accountant, politician, priest, or architect.

7. Discuss the problem with a variety of other people. Learn to see the problem from their viewpoint and to listen to their solutions.

8. Do not be too serious. Introduce humorous approaches to reduce tension and give a different perspective.

9. Discover how others have already solved the problem.

10. Imagine what an ideal solution would be like and work backward to possible means by which that end could have been achieved.

11. Work on other problems; then return to work on the focal decision problem in a different physical and psychological environment.

12. Keep a note pad accessible to jot down ideas that occur just before sleep, upon awaking from sleep, while traveling, and on other occasions which are not directly related to work.

13. Combine elements of different solutions, even when they are obviously absurd.

14. Brainstorm the problem with friends who should know little about the problem as well as with experts in the problem area.

15. Reevaluate any negative attitudes about whether a good solution can be found. Think in terms of when, not whether, the problem will be solved.

Managers who recognize the importance of generating alternative solutions and behave in the ways suggested above are, by definition, creative. They are behaving creatively at that time in the problem-solving process when such behavior is appropriate.

Critical Analysis of Alternatives

Just as the creative phase of decision making requires some analytical thinking, the critical analysis phase of necessity involves some creativity. It is generally advisable, however, to separate the two. Critical thinking inhibits creativity, and creativity may interfere with the tough-minded, analytical thinking required to determine which alternative yields the highest payoff.

Most of the literature of decision theory is concerned with critical analysis. It includes a wide assortment of models for determining which of several alternatives provides the best solution to a problem. A *model* is a simplified representation of reality and is designed to explain some part of it. Model building attempts to compensate for the limited ability of the human brain to cope with the massive data and the complex relationships involved in many decisions.

A simple decision model was suggested by Benjamin Franklin. The decision maker draws a line down the center of a page and lists all the arguments for a course of action on one side and all those against it on the other. Then the evidence is evaluated. Items of equal weight on the two sides are systematically crossed off until one side is eliminated. This model is similar to modern decision models in that a major decision is broken down into a series of small, manageable ones.

Many of the models developed by decision theorists are too technical for use by the typical operating manager.[13] They often require the expertise of a specialist in quantitative methods as well as the time to gather data and develop computer programs. In addition, many managerial decisions do not lend themselves to quantitative analysis. Both the data involved in management decisions and the evaluation criteria are often in the form of judgments and general impressions. In a recent promotion decision, for example, one criterion was that, "the new vice-president must possess attitudes and values which are compatible with those of the other members of the executive team." Such criteria and the data to which they are applied are better treated in open and rational conversation than in decision analysis models.

One approach to deciding among alternatives, which need not be highly complicated, involves the use of a payoff matrix. As shown in Figure 14–4, this is a technique for forecasting the payoff, or expected value to the organization, of each alternative under different conditions. In this illustration three *strategies* (alternative courses of action) are evaluated. The assumption is made that one of three *states of nature* (conditions which are beyond the decision maker's control) will occur. The probability of each state of nature is estimated. From the estimated profit under each condition, the expected payoff for each strategy is calculated.

The calculations shown in Figure 14–4 indicate that buying new machines will yield the highest profit. The decision maker may, however, want to apply criteria other than profitability. For example, it may be meaningful to ask whether the modest increase in potential profit is adequate to offset the personal effort required in making the transition to new machines and the 20 percent chance of a $20,000 reduction in profits (the difference between $100,000 and $80,000)

---

[13] For examples of complex quantitative decision models see V. M. Tummala, *Decision Analysis with Business Applications* (New York: Intext Educational Publishers, 1973), and Ira Horowitz, *Decision Making and the Theory of the Firm* (New York: Holt, Rinehart and Winston, 1970).

Strategies	STATES OF NATURE			Expected Payoff
	Product Demand Stays Constant	25% Increase in Demand	50% Increase in Demand	
S_1 Buy new machines	$ 80,000[1]	$130,000	$200,000	$151,500[2]
S_2 Modify old machines	90,000	135,000	170,000	141,750
S_3 Use old machines	100,000	130,000	160,000	137,500
Probability of occurrence	.20	.35	.45	1.00

[1] Estimated annual profit over a three-year period.
[2] Calculations of Expected Payoffs (EP) for each of three Strategies (S_s):

$$EP(S_1) = \$\ 80{,}000(.20) + \$130{,}000(.35) + \$200{,}000(.45) = \$151{,}500$$
$$EP(S_2) = \ \ \ 90{,}000(.20) + \ \ 135{,}000(.35) + \ \ 170{,}000(.45) = \$141{,}750$$
$$EP(S_3) = 100{,}000(.20) + \ \ 130{,}000(.35) + \ \ 160{,}000(.45) = \$137{,}500$$

Figure 14–4   Application of the Payoff Matrix

if product demand stays constant. The use of quantitative data in this matrix in no way hinders the application of numerous other criteria.

Since the data used in analyses such as this involve several judgments of varying degree of accuracy, it might appear that the expected payoff values have a false and misleading appearance of accuracy. This is an ever-present danger of such a method. On the other hand, it is infinitely more rational to make each judgment explicit than to conceal it in a muddle of half-conscious assumptions.

It is inevitable, for example, that uncontrollable variables (in our example, the changes in market conditions) will influence the outcome of decisions. Decision makers need to be aware of such variables or at least aware of the fact that such variables are unknowns in the decision process. And, whether decision makers realize it or not, they inevitably apply probabilities to the states of nature they perceive to be present. Too often the probabilities that influence major decisions are vague expressions of optimism or pessimism such as, "The chances are good that our market will improve next year," or "I see little chance of an improved market in the immediate future."

The requirement that probabilities be precisely estimated is an occasion for research, consultation, and systematic analysis. The outcome is necessarily in the form of an estimate, but, at least, it is a consciously made, informed estimate. At the worst, the decision maker becomes aware that a given decision is based on a gamble rather than on a calculated risk, and a meaningful note of caution is thus introduced into the decision process.

Many excellent publications are available to managers with an interest in learning how to use decision models.[14] Although their greatest immediate value will be found in the solution of complex organizational problems, their principles should, in the long run, find expression in all sorts of managerial decisions.

Choosing a Solution and Taking Action

The skills and personal qualities needed to analyze data critically are often possessed by staff specialists who want no part of responsibility for taking action. Analysis is primarily an intellectual process, while choosing and taking action require courage and a willingness to take personal risks. Analysis of data can always be delegated, but decisions often cannot be.

It might appear that effective analysis is synonymous with choosing a solution. In practice, however, such thinking omits two important facts. First, since decisions concern future events, alternatives are seldom so clear that they eliminate the need for personal judgment. Secondly, since the decision maker must personally assume responsibility for the decision, the ultimate criteria are both organizational and personal. They are concerned with both the achievement of organizational goals and the manager's need for self-preservation and enhancement.

Implementation, Feedback, and Adaptation

Good decisions sometimes fail to produce good results because of poor implementation and follow-up. By the same token, mediocre decisions can get excellent results if a manager shows unusual ingenuity in implementation.

In one sense, choosing a solution and taking action is an irreversible process. What is done cannot be undone—or can it? Fortunately as the implementation process unfolds and the states of nature do or do not occur as predicted, adaptation is possible. New decisions are made which alter the original one and either prevent it from being a catastrophe or, if it proves to be effective, further enhance its effectiveness.

Some decisions are *absolute* in that, once action is taken, they cannot be reversed or significantly altered. A decision to sell often falls into this category, assuming, of course, that the decision is implemented. Other decisions are *adaptive*. They can be altered because their implementation is an unfolding process rather than a single, irrevocable event. Thus, a decision to enter a new market may at first involve buying and reselling a product in a limited geographical area. Implementation may proceed gradually until the entire country is covered and the firm manufactures the products. Since the sequential nature of adaptive decisions greatly reduces risk, they are usually preferred to absolute decisions.

---

[14] The most lucid and practical introduction to decision models continues to be David W. Miller and Martin K. Starr, *The Structure of Human Decisions* (Englewood Cliffs, N.J.: Prentice-Hall, Inc., 1967). For a more recent and more general treatment of decision making, read E. Frank Harrison, op. cit., and Allen Easton, *Complex Managerial Decisions Involving Multiple Objectives* (New York: John Wiley & Sons, Inc., 1973).

Sequential decisions may be expressed graphically by means of a "decision tree." [15] By plotting the known alternatives in this fashion, a manager can simultaneously visualize both present and future decisions. By inserting probabilities and the financial implications of each alternative, the decision tree also serves the same purpose as the payoff matrix shown in Figure 14–4. Where quantitative data are not available, verbal descriptions of each alternative serve to clarify their implications.

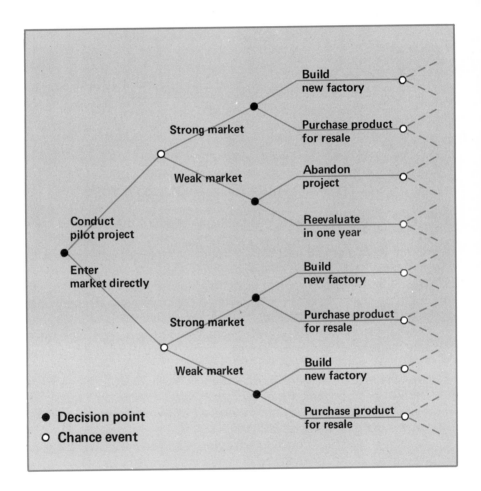

Figure 14–5   A Tree for Sequential Decisions

NOTE: The solution to the nine dot problem shown on page 316 is presented at the top of page 322. Either (A) or (B) may be used as a starting point.

---

[15] Harrison, op.cit., pp. 235–241.

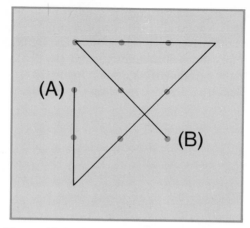

Figure 14–6   Solution to Nine Dot Problem

STUDY AND DISCUSSION QUESTIONS

1. In what sense does managerial authority obscure the quality of decisions?
2. In what ways do managers benefit from making explicit the process by which their decisions are made?
3. What is the "implicit favorite" model of decision making?
4. Two store managers of a decentralized retail chain have an opportunity to invest in an item for resale during the Christmas season. Market conditions in the two areas are comparable. Manager *A* decides not to carry the item. Manager *B* decides to carry it and, as a result, earned the highest profit in the history of the company. Their superior concluded that A made the better decision. How could this conclusion be justified?
5. Herbert Simon observed that managers seek satisfactory rather than optimal solutions. Does this hold true even when managers use the best possible decision models? Explain.
6. How is a *problem* defined in this chapter? Can you think of problems in any area of life that cannot be defined in this way?
7. One way to solve a problem is to lower the standard or expectation. When is such action appropriate? Give examples.
8. What is meant by the term *educating the intuition?*
9. What one factor is most likely to account for the great individual differences in creativity?
10. Since the purpose of critical analysis is to discover which alternative is best, why should choosing a solution and taking action be regarded as separate steps?

CRITICAL INCIDENT

A Matter of Policy

After serving for three years as assistant manager, William Lanford had recently been promoted to manager of a branch store. Goldstein Department Stores, Inc., was a privately held corporation consisting of one downtown store and four branches located in large shopping centers. Lanford's immediate superior was Lynda Wells, the president and general manager.

While serving as an assistant manager, Lanford had been concerned about the low motivation of the store employees. Soon after his promotion, he called a meeting and explained that their poor performance would no longer be tolerated. Although most of the employees recognized the problem and responded favorably, two young men who worked in the stockroom seemed to disregard his warning. Because they were members of a minority group, Lanford discussed the matter with Wells prior to giving them a second warning individually.

Lanford's consultation with Wells was not a result of indecisiveness or lack of confidence on his part. Soon after the passage of the Civil Rights Act of 1964, Wells, who had just become general manager, established the policy that prior to making any personnel decisions which might conceivably result in a discrimination charge, she should be consulted.

Three weeks after the second warning was given, Lanford observed that the behavior of the two employees in question had not improved. On one occasion, he estimated that within a four-hour period they worked no more than two hours. Accordingly, at the end of the week he informed them that their services would no longer be needed. They did not seem particularly surprised or upset about the action.

Lynda Wells learned of Lanford's action the following Wednesday as she was reviewing personnel records. Her first reaction was anger that Lanford had not consulted her before discharging the employees. She was also afraid a charge of discrimination would be made since both employees were minority group members. Although her hostility toward Lanford was intense, she thought it was better not to make an issue of it. He had, after all, followed company policy in discussing the matter with her at the time he first talked with the discharged employees.

A few days later Lanford casually mentioned his action to Wells and indicated that the termination interview was uneventful. Her icy silence and general demeanor left no question in Lanford's mind that all was not well between them. The event was not mentioned again.

Questions

1. Define the problems involved in this incident in terms of deviations from standards.
2. In what ways did organizational authority affect the decision processes?

3. In what sense did the personality characteristics of Wells and Lanford affect their decisions?
4. What "system constraints" influenced the decisions?
5. What decision criteria did Lanford apply?

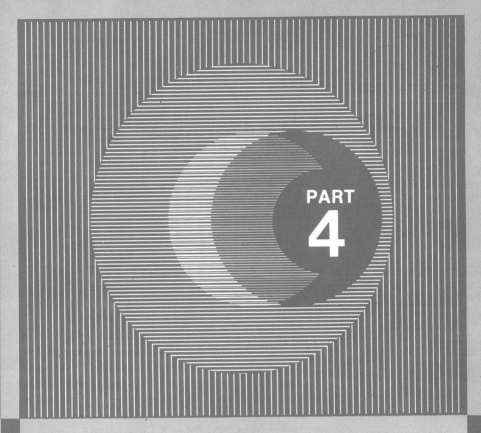

PART
4

Minimizing Human Problems in Organizations

Chapter 15

Improving Communication in Organizations

Effective communication is a prerequisite for the achievement of organizational objectives. The importance of communication problems has at times been exaggerated—there are, after all, other types of problems—but the impact of poor communication can be enormous. The potential for communication to go awry is evident in the aggregate amount of time a manager spends in communicating: giving and receiving directives, participating in conferences, instructing subordinates, hearing grievances, disciplining, counseling, selling, observing, and reading and writing a wide variety of messages. A manager is constantly involved in some form of communication.

The subject of communication is illusive because it is intertwined with so many other subjects. Effective communication is, for example, an integral part of effective leadership, decision making, motivation, the management organizational conflict, and other subjects with which the discipline of organizational behavior is concerned. Such subjects are the *content* of communication; they are concerned with communicating in order to achieve a particular objective in a particular situation. This chapter is concerned primarily with the *process* of communication: with how communication occurs in contrast to what is communicated. Implicit in this chapter is the assumption that a body of knowledge exists which can help managers communicate more effectively and thereby perform more successfully the many tasks in which communication is involved.

COMMUNICATION DEFINED

Thesis: No single definition covers the range of behaviors studied in all areas where communication occurs, and there is no definition upon which scholars in this field agree.[1] *Communication in organiza-*

[1] For an analysis of 95 definitions of communication found in published literature, see Frank E. X. Dance, "The 'Concept' of Communication," *The Journal of Communication,* Vol. 20 (June, 1970), pp. 201–210.

tions is here defined as the process by which messages are transmitted from one person to another.

The *messages* referred to in this definition may be expressed in the form of bulletins, letters, memos, job descriptions, policy statements, telephone conversations, and other forms of verbal information. They may, in addition, include a broad spectrum of nonverbal data which are transmitted through such media as voice tone, facial expressions, gestures, and clothing. The implication of stating that the messages are transmitted from one person to another is that there is no solitary communication. A manager may, for example, make an important policy statement in the text of a newsletter article that nobody reads. In such a situation communication has only been attempted. Communication occurs only when the message is received.

Some definitions imply that communication occurs only when the sender is successful in transmitting an *intended* message. One difficulty with this qualification is that people are seldom totally effective in transmitting their intended meanings to others and they often transmit messages to others when they have no intention of communicating at all (e.g., through the way they walk). In practice we must often be content with transmitting a reasonable facsimile of the intended message—a replica which is accurate enough make a point or achieve a desired objective but is short of perfection. As long as words, gestures, and other symbols are transmitted from one person to another, communication occurs, however far it may fall below an exact transmission of intended meaning. The goal of studying communication is to narrow the gap between the intended message and the message which is actually transmitted.

ESSENTIALS OF THE COMMUNICATION PROCESS

Thesis: Communication involves four elements: a sender, a message, a medium, and a receiver. Only to the extent that the sender and receiver have similar backgrounds is there a likelihood that communication will be effective, regardless of the medium employed.

Communication is complicated by the fact that each of us is experientially isolated from everyone else. We never know with certainty what is occurring in the psyche of other persons. Rather, we infer from verbal and behavioral cues what others are thinking and feeling. It is this leap of inference, this interpretation of the sensory data we experience, that makes effective communication difficult.

Encoding

Before a message can be transmitted from one person to another it must be *encoded;* that is, the intended message must be translated into a code or series of symbols (words, gestures, facial expressions, and so on) that represent the meaning the sender hopes to communicate. It should be noted, however, that only the symbols are transmitted. The meaning received depends upon the receiver's interpretation of those symbols.

Consider the case of a manager whose objective is to increase the productivity of subordinates by communicating dissatisfaction with their past performance. Encoding the message requires decisions not only about what will be said, but how, when, and where. Encoding may also involve decisions about the expression or concealment of emotion. The manager may, for example, decide not to show frustration and to communicate in a matter-of-fact, unemotional manner. He or she may ultimately decide to talk with subordinates as individuals, tailoring the message to the unique circumstances of each, informally and privately communicating with each as the appropriate occasion arises.

Encoding may occur within the span of a few milliseconds, as when one person greets another with a "Good Morning" rather than with an alternative greeting. Regardless of the time required and the degree of conscious planning, the transmission of a message originates with encoding.

The Medium

As shown in Figure 15–1, media provide the channels through which transmission occurs. The more important the message the more likely managers are to give careful thought to media selection. Since the medium used, say a face-to-face interview in preference to a memorandum, often determines the success of a communication act, the selection process deserves serious consideration. Managers commonly fail, however, to give it the attention it deserves.

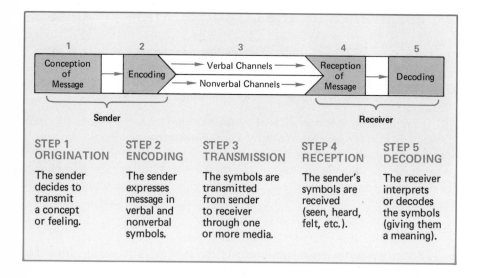

Figure 15–1   The Communication Process

Decoding

When the sender's symbols, in the form of sensory data such as light or sound waves, are received, they must always be interpreted. Words and other symbols have multiple meanings, and there is no assurance that the intended meanings of the sender-encoder are identical to those of the receiver-decoder.

The more experiences the sender and receiver have had in common the more likely it is that the sender's intended meaning will be communicated. When, for example, the sender speaks only Spanish and the receiver only English, a relatively primitive level of communication is probable. A similar experience occurs when college-educated, company-oriented managers attempt to communicate with employees whose education, attitudes, loyalties, and aspirations differ greatly from their own.

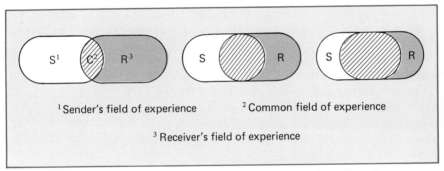

¹ Sender's field of experience   ² Common field of experience

³ Receiver's field of experience

Figure 15–2   Effectiveness of Communication as a Function of Overlapping Fields of Experience

In order for people with different experience fields to communicate, at least one must learn to speak the language of the other. In practice, this goes beyond the mastery of vocabulary. Managers who aspire to communicate with subordinates must learn how they think, feel, and characteristically respond in a variety of situations. By applying such knowledge, managers are usually able to predict with acceptable accuracy how a given message will be decoded.

Nonverbal Communication

Much of what a person communicates is transmitted nonverbally. Persons who are familiar with the sign language of the deaf or the early American Indians will recognize our ability to communicate without the use of words. What may not be so evident is the extent to which our own nonverbal language is actually used.[2] It is especially useful in expressing emotional states or reactions in contrast to complex ideas.

---

[2] For a thorough analysis of this subject, refer to Abne M. Eisenberg and Ralph R. Smith, Jr., *Nonverbal Communication* (Indianapolis: The Bobbs-Merrill Co., Inc., 1971).

Ruesch and Kees propose a threefold classification of nonverbal communication: sign language, action language, and object language.[3] A brief look at each shows that our own culture is indeed rich in nonverbal symbols of communication.

Sign Language.   Any gesture which serves as a word substitute may be classified as sign language. Examples of common signs are head movements for yes or no and an outstretched arm with the palm forward for stop. As with all nonverbal messages, sign language must be interpreted in a specific context to be meaningful. Thus, outstretched arms and clenched fists can be a joyous victory sign for the winner of the Master's golf championship and a symbol of hostility and aggression for an angry mob in front of the White House. Similarly, a wave of the hand may say either hello or goodbye.

Action Language.   All physical movements which convey a message but are not specifically used as word substitutes are classified as action language. For example, depending upon the context in which the actions occur, the way people walk, run, sit, eat, laugh, or embrace communicates something about them.

In a recent committee meeting, one member folded his arms and gradually pushed his chair away from the conference table. Everyone received the message, "If I can't have my way, I won't participate." Some actions, such as a predisposition to smile or to exhibit hand tremors and a cracking voice, communicate the presence of more lasting characteristics of the individual. The simultaneous transmission of verbal and nonverbal symbols is especially effective in giving the receiver the cues needed to decode accurately.

Object Language.   An intentional or unintentional display of material things constitutes an object language through which one's identity, aspirations, attitudes, and motivation are communicated to others. One's clothes, automobiles, and office furniture often fall into this category. Similar to some forms of action language, they are a means through which personality and self-image are projected.

PERSONAL AND ENVIRONMENTAL INFLUENCES

Thesis: Effective communication depends upon personal characteristics and skills. These qualities can be expressed to the maximum, however, only if environmental conditions are optimal.

During the heyday of the human relations movement, *it's a communication problem* became a catchall explanation and a convenient scapegoat for the many difficult-to-solve problems arising in relationships between people. Conflict between individuals, for example, was often explained away as a communication problem as though real conflict were nonexistent and labeling would somehow

---

[3] Jergen Ruesch and Weldon Kees, *Nonverbal Communication: Notes on Visual Perception of Human Relations* (Berkeley: University of California Press, 1956), p. 189.

result in a quick and easy solution. This period introduced a much needed awareness of the importance of communication in organizations; but it was a shallow, faddish emphasis which was lacking in research support and a sound basis in communication theory.

The communication fad of the 1950s has, fortunately, gone the way of all movements that lack depth and substance. Although communication theory is still relatively undeveloped, when compared with decision and leadership theory, for example, empirical research into the nature of communication in organizations has been fruitful and a steady stream of insights has resulted.[4] We look now at some of the personal and organizational qualities that determine the effectiveness of communication.

Personality Factors

Regardless of the favorability of the organizational climate, individuals differ greatly in their ability to communicate. These differences are partly the result of variations in such skills as writing, counseling, interviewing, debating, and public speaking. One's vocabulary, grammar, style of delivery, and even spelling are related to communication skills. Yet these knowledge and skill factors are often less important than certain personality characteristics such as empathy, talkativeness, assertiveness, and character.

Empathy.   People differ greatly in empathy, the awareness of the needs and motives of others. Problems caused by this insensitivity are seen in the experience of Roger Green, an engineer with a major oil company.

> Aptly described by his supervisor as having "the social sensitivity of a crowbar," Roger was repeatedly passed over for promotion into management. His technical competence, motivation, and dependability were unsurpassed, but he could not hear what others were trying to say. When Roger argued for a point of view, his position was based on facts—to a point. Unfortunately he always omitted facts about others' feelings and personal needs. One of his superiors declared that Roger, "is a mechanical genius and a social idiot who communicates better with computers than with people." Although Roger's contribution to the company was outstanding, he was always assigned jobs that involved as little human contact as possible.

Few people have as much difficulty as Roger in understanding another person's frame of reference, and those who do are not likely to change significantly. Persons with greater empathy can improve their sensitivity by consciously attempting to understand how others think and feel.

---

[4] The status of communication theory is thoroughly analyzed in the following: Lyman W. Porter and Karlene H. Roberts, "Communication in Organizations," in Marvin D. Dunnette (ed.) *Handbook of Industrial and Organizational Psychology* (Chicago: Rand McNally & Company, 1976), p. 1553; and A. Chapanis, "Prelude to 2001: Explorations in Human Communications," *American Psychologist,* Vol. 26, No. 11 (November 1971), pp. 949–961.

In some cases, *sensitivity training* seems to improve empathy. This is a group dynamics technique, related to group psychotherapy, in which participants may become more empathic through self-disclosure, increased self-awareness, and awareness of how others feel and think. Sensitivity training has been strongly criticized in recent years because its effects are unpredictable, but it is one of the few techniques with a potential for improving the communication of the person with low empathy.

Talkativeness.   It is difficult to communicate with people who refuse to talk, just as it is difficult to communicate with people who talk too much. Even in small classes, some students never say a word except in response to a direct question. Likewise, in business situations, a few quiet, withdrawn individuals attend conferences and committee meetings but speak only when forced to do so. Such persons often have more to contribute than many who talk freely, but their inability or unwillingness to voluntarily communicate suppresses their potential contribution.

Unusually quiet people are often poor communicators for another reason. Since communication is a two-way process, a good communicator motivates others to express themselves freely. But most people are inhibited in the presence of a person who talks very little. Free communication between two people has been described as a form of "mutual blackmail" in that self-disclosure develops in short, sequential steps until each understands the attitudes, beliefs, values, and needs of the other. In effect, people who refuse to disclose themselves to others fail to pay the price others demand for a full disclosure.

The importance of self-disclosure as an element in communication can hardly be overemphasized, particularly because it provides a basis for empathy. Also, the personal relationships which grow out of self-disclosure provide the channels through which informal communication among managers flows. Managers who are excluded from these channels may fail to receive the information needed to make sound decisions and take advantage of opportunities. The same holds for managers who cut themselves off from the informal, casual communication channels of subordinates.

Assertiveness.   Individuals who are excessively assertive or domineering may undermine their effectiveness as communicators. It is, nevertheless, true that assertiveness is often required for good communication. At times, a manager must be persistent and argue forcefully for a point of view in order to exert a significant influence upon the organization. The manner of presentation and the conviction with which one speaks are often more persuasive than the weight of facts and the strength of one's logic.

Character.   During Lyndon B. Johnson's last year as President of the United States and in the period prior to the resignation of President Richard Nixon, the news media overworked the term *credibility gap.* The term is, however, meaningful. It occurs when people learn through experience that what an individual says is not trustworthy. Verbal fluency matters very little if trust is low. When trust is high, on the other hand, others will accept a message and attribute honorable motives to the sender. This holds even when the actual message is poorly expressed and/or contains information others do not want to hear.

The observation that actions speak louder than words is a forceful comment about communication. Actions tend to validate or repudiate one's words. Through their decisions, managers communicate something about their character, judgment, and dependability. The cumulative effect of such decisions is to provide a broad context within which messages are interpreted and evaluated. A manager should assume that deception will always be discovered and thus should behave so that others will assume that his or her words are truthful.

The maturity with which one treats information received from others is also related to trust. For example, employees who believe that supervisors can be trusted to respect confidences are often willing to share information which they would otherwise withhold. Some managers, like the king who killed the bearer of bad news, react so unpredictably to upward communication that subordinates learn to tell them only what they want to hear.

Formal Communication Systems

Communication in small organizations is highly personal. In a small family business, for example, virtually all communication occurs in face-to-face conversations or by telephone. Even a memorandum may be considered unnecessarily impersonal and formal.

As organizations grow, the need for uniformity requires a variety of formal communication channels. Written job descriptions, policies, procedures, and rules provide a continuing flow of information throughout the organization. The standards and feedback devices of control systems automatically transmit messages up and down the hierarchy. As a part of the control system, routine reports provide management with information about current operations.

Computerized Information Systems.   Because the demands for effective decision making and for government reporting require the collection and analysis of detailed information about all aspects of the firm, large organizations could not survive without elaborate communication networks. These sophisticated information systems provide managers with both facts and various analyses needed for operational decisions.

At the present time, the most useful research in the field of organizational communication is in computerized management information systems. Nevertheless, there is no substitute for the informal communication that continually occurs. The problems which arise in the latter are less subject to scientific analysis and are more difficult to solve.

The Role of Authority.   Although little research has been conducted on the relationship between formal authority and the communication process, important interactions between the two exist. Orders which flow through the formal hierarchy determine the direction of the organization, and the manner in which they are communicated goes far in determining the organization's psychological climate. For example, authoritarian and participative leaders take quite different approaches to communicating with others while making decisions.

An individual's perceived authority is a primary determinant of how a given message will be interpreted. Formal structure and authority attest to the legitimacy of a command and suggest the likelihood of its accuracy. *Consider the source* is the first principle for decoding a message. This, of course, requires more than assessing the formal authority of the sender. An assessment of the individual's competence and motivation is also involved; yet formal authority is always an element to be considered.

Informal Communication

Informal communication includes all messages transmitted in the work setting other than those which are formally structured. These include, for example, a conversation between two supervisors about a coordination problem, between two clerks about how to post an item, or between members of an informal work group concerning personal matters or the work itself. The nature of such communication is nowhere described in the formal communication systems, but the organization could not survive without it.

One medium of informal communication is the *grapevine,* an unprogrammed communication channel which meanders through the organization carrying any and every type of information of interest to organizational members. Actually most large organizations are crisscrossed by several different grapevine channels with interconnecting links.

The individuals who comprise the links of a channel may have relatively little in common. A message originator may be an executive secretary whose sister is the best friend of the wife of a factory employee who acquires status from feeding information into an informal work group. Once a bit of information is received by a freely communicating informal group, it may fan out in several directions, say through members of a car pool in one case and employees whose work is related in another.

The development of grapevines is inevitable. Although grapevines are neither good nor bad in themselves, the messages they carry are uniquely subject to distortion. The *serial transmission effect,*[5] a problem in formal as well as informal communication, poses a particular problem for grapevine communication. This refers to the fact that as messages are transmitted from one human link to another they become progressively more garbled. Their content is misinterpreted, abbreviated, embellished, and selectively transmitted in terms of what the sender believes the receiver wants or needs to know. Since the original message may be only partially true, it is not surprising that the grapevine is sometimes referred to as a rumor mill.

---

[5] The literature on this phenomenon is summarized in W. Charles Redding, *Communication within the Organization* (New York: Industrial Communication Council, 1972), pp. 105–111.

The grapevine is an extremely fast channel of communication, but the thoroughness of its coverage is not always dependable. In a given instance, many employees may be bypassed altogether. The grapevine commonly reinforces messages which are transmitted through formal announcements, bulletins, memos, newsletters, and other formal channels. Since the truth of its messages is highly correlated with the willingness of management to communicate openly and effectively through other means, the best way to guarantee the relative accuracy of the grapevine is to provide reliable information sources against which its messages can easily be checked.

Organizational Climate

Although the concept of organizational climate is somewhat nebulous, it is valuable in understanding several aspects of organizational behavior. *Organizational climate* is the overall favorability of member attitudes and perceptions with reference to specific activities and features of an organization. Within this definition, the climate may be quite favorable for, say, good communication but relatively unfavorable for rapid change, tough-minded decision making, or some other activity.

Openness and Trust.   The human relations writers emphasized the importance of openness in communication. They advocated a participative approach to decision making and leadership which is possible only if information flows freely throughout the organization. The emphasis upon openness of communication found expression during the 1930s in programs for counseling employees on personal as well as work-related problems. As the group dynamics movement developed, emphasis shifted to problem-solving groups in which authority, status, and other barriers to communication are minimized.

A climate which is favorable to open communication is not easily achieved. Employees who have long been accustomed to authoritarian leadership fear the negative consequences of openness, having learned through experience that their interests are best served through secretiveness. Why, for example, should an employee tell the foreman about a better way to do a job when the foreman may react by raising standards or with defensiveness or hostility because he did not think of it first? Even when management rewards openness, employees often act in terms of previously learned expectations and do not easily relinquish their resistance to open communication.

A climate favorable to openness must rest upon a foundation of mutual trust,[6] but there are, unfortunately, substantial barriers to its development. Because efforts to develop open communication sometimes appear insincere, they have the effect of reducing trust levels. When, for example, supervisors who do not genuinely value the opinions of subordinates begin asking for them, their actions are met with suspicion. When information shared by employees results

---

[6] Karlene H. Roberts and Charles A. O'Reilly, III, "Failures in Upward Communications: Three Possible Culprits," *Academy of Management Journal,* Vol. 17 (June, 1974), p. 212.

in managerial action of which the employees disapprove, secretiveness and distrust are reinforced. Yet such action is, at times, unavoidable.

Managers also have reservations about open communication. Certainly managers cannot always be open without creating unnecessary anxieties and, at times, getting employees involved in complicated management problems which will interfere with employee performance. In theory, it is difficult to argue with an openness policy, but in practice a degree of closed communication is necessary.

The Open Door Policy.   Top level managers who favor open communication often establish a policy in which subordinates at all levels are invited to express their ideas and grievances directly, without going through the chain of command. Theoretically this open door policy is the essence of egalitarian leadership and freedom of communication.

In practice, few managers can use an open door policy effectively. It can be extremely time-consuming. It tends to undermine the authority of bypassed managers and to create superior-subordinate conflict. In a sense, an open door policy expresses a lack of confidence in the ability of subordinate managers to deal effectively with their subordinates. It clashes with the concept of delegation and implies that upward communication will be blocked unless bypassing occurs.

Yet an open door policy appears to be a logical corollary of an open communication philosophy. Why, after all, should it be inappropriate for any two organizational members to communicate freely with one another? An inconsistency between an open door policy and open communication appears, however, when a bypassing employee assumes that the manager's door is open for closed or confidential conversations. Managers who invite lower level employees to express their attitudes and viewpoints cannot easily relate the conversation to the employees' immediate superiors without violating a confidence. This inconsistency often undermines an open door policy over a period of time.

In practice, effective managers do not keep the door completely open. They ask the subordinate, "Have you talked this over with your immediate supervisor?" and they usually insist upon that action. Consultation with one's immediate superior is a logical first step in a genuinely open system. Another way of keeping the door only partially open is for a manager to receive those who seek an audience but to avoid the encouragement inherent in an official open door policy.

Managers must pay a price for openness. It can be highly threatening, and only mature organizations and individuals are likely to practice it over a long period of time. Yet when the disadvantages of alternatives are considered, enlightened managers opt for openness as a general goal.

BREAKING THROUGH COMMUNICATION BARRIERS

Thesis: Where the organizational climate is favorable for openness, management can improve communication by isolating and reducing the impact of specific barriers. Where the climate is unfavorable, reducing the impact of specific barriers is one means of improving it.

Individual efforts to improve communication are relatively unsuccessful if an organization is characterized by distrust and ego-defensiveness. On the other hand, trust can be developed and ego-defensiveness reduced. We look now at some means of achieving these ends and thereby improving communication.

Gatekeeping

The gatekeeper concept was developed during World War II by social psychologist Kurt Lewin.[7] Although the concept has evolved and found expression in a variety of settings, its essence remains unchanged. A *gatekeeper* is a person who decides which items of information will be retained and which will be passed on in the communication chain. *Gatekeeping* is the process through which a gatekeeper obstructs the free flow of messages.

Perhaps the most obvious gatekeeping occurs between labor and management in conflict situations. Strong social pressures erect deliberate barriers to upward communication as employees of each informal group maintain close surveillance over the activities of one another. Rule breaking, loafing, theft, and sabotage, as well as positive contributions to the organization, are painstakingly concealed from management.

First-line supervisors, caught between the demands of their superiors and subordinates, may carefully filter the information passed along to management lest they be suspected by superiors of being too close to their subordinates and by their subordinates of betraying a trust. In fact, managers at all levels become gatekeepers when open communication might jeopardize their careers or make them appear inept. If kept within reasonable bounds, these forms of gatekeeping need not be destructive. At any rate, their occurrence is inevitable.

A more subtle, and sometimes unconscious, form of gatekeeping occurs at every point in the transmission network. When information is evaluated and integrated, the resulting inferences and decisions are transmitted while at least part of the underlying information is withheld.[8] Although this filtering may not represent a deliberate distortion, it nevertheless modifies the nature of the message as it is transmitted from one person to another. The message bears the imprint of the transmitter's perceptual process, judgment, and evaluation of what the receiver needs to know. In upward transmission, information unfavorable to the sender is often suppressed while favorable information is transmitted.

Although gatekeeping cannot be eliminated, it can be reduced. Once gatekeepers are discovered, specific steps can be taken to modify their behavior. In addition to directly confronting them, the superior can discourage such behavior by verifying their reports and developing alternative channels of communication. Formal techniques such as attitude surveys may be used to uncover the facts and increase the risk involved in deliberate gatekeeping.

---

[7] Abraham Z. Bass, "Refining the 'Gatekeeper' Concept: a U.N. Radio Case Study," *Journalism Quarterly* (Spring, 1969), pp. 69–72.

[8] Thomas P. Ference, "Organizational Communication Systems and the Decision Process," *Management Science,* Vol. 17–8, No. 2 (October, 1970), p. 85.

The unconscious or semiconscious gatekeeping associated with any serial reproduction of a message is more difficult to eliminate. It is sometimes appropriate to transmit a written copy of the original message along with any necessary elaboration or special instructions. Formal management training may also be helpful. Managers who become aware of the common tendency toward unintentional distortion of communication can make improvement if they are motivated to do so.

Semantic Problems

The term *semantic* means having to do with meaning. There is a semantic difference, for example, between *bear* (to carry) and *bear* (an animal), although the spelling and sound of the words are the same. In oral communication, the meaning of each must be derived from its context.

Semantic problems are common in organizations. The terms *profit* and *efficiency* roll from the tongues of management with warmth and affection, but in the language of the rank and file they may carry a cold, impersonal message of potential wages unjustifiably withheld and speedups on the assembly line. Intellectually the two groups might easily agree upon a dictionary meaning, but in real-life communication, the words carry different emotional overtones for labor and management.

Because of the relatively common background of managers, they tend to communicate better with one another than with the rank and file. To communicate effectively with the latter they must be sensitive to the possibility of semantic problems and use words whose intended meaning will be understood. Fortunately first-line supervisors, most of whom are promoted from the ranks, typically have little difficulty at this point, and it is they who communicate most directly with employees. Higher level managers are most likely to show their insensitivity in newsletters, bulletins, statements of rules, and in other written messages.

Communication is sometimes impaired by the specialists' use of insider language. The jargon and special terminology of accountants, engineers, and scientists impede communication with other specialists and with general management. Where technical concepts are involved, this problem is difficult to overcome. If the problem is primarily one of vocabulary, an awareness of the need to translate and the motivation to do so are usually sufficient to improve communication. If specialists are regularly evaluated and rewarded on the basis of this factor, communication problems should be minimized.

Another type of insider language is *argot,* or slang. Informal work groups develop their own words for tools, parts, processes, behaviors, and people. This language serves to identify group members and to brand outsiders. The use of slang is most characteristic of adolescents, and when used extensively by adults is often accompanied by evidences of adolescent immaturity and naivete. An example of this naivete is the notion that those who know the language are somehow superior to and more sophisticated than those who do not.

Because argot is deeply imbedded in the structure of informal groups, management usually makes no attempt to do anything about it. It seldom causes a serious communication problem at the employee level where it is most common. Within management it can be more serious. New managers and outside consultants are most likely to experience a problem because of it.

Noise

In common usage, noise refers to meaningless or irrelevant sounds that sometimes disturb thought or communication. The term is difficult to define because noise at one moment becomes a highly relevant message at another. Out of the noise of a dozen conversations a person hears his or her name called, and immediately that particular conversation zooms into focus.

In the language of communication theory, *noise* may or may not refer to audible sounds. It refers to messages which are ineffectively communicated because the intended receiver sees them as meaningless. They are perceived as "that which is always being said" and, therefore, fail to get the full attention of the intended receiver. Thus, a written admonition to wear goggles while using the grinder is physically sensed but psychologically grouped with the noise of surrounding machines and other meaningless stimuli.

Redundant messages, those which are repeated for emphasis, are especially likely to be relegated to the status of noise. Perhaps the best way to prevent this is to vary the medium, on one occasion using the bulletin board, on another the public address system, and so forth. This approach has an advantage in attracting attention because people have different thresholds of awareness for different media. An individual may never be reached through the public address system but may listen carefully to what a supervisor says in personal conversation.

Status Differences

Significant differences in social status tend to inhibit upward communication. When a factory employee enters the walnut-paneled office of a well-dressed executive, bulwarked behind a massive desk, it is not surprising that some degree of intimidation occurs. This is especially true if the walls are embellished with diplomas, awards, or other evidences of a high status. After all, the symbols were carefully selected to show that the officeholder is important and powerful.

The obvious way to reduce status barriers is to remove status symbols and emphasize similarities rather than differences between the personnel at different organizational levels. One large international corporation has removed most recognized status symbols in order to achieve better communication and facilitate participative leadership. In the new plants, only the personnel manager has a private office. All the other managers work in one large room and have identical furniture.

It is noteworthy that status differences are not always a communication barrier. In fact, in downward communication, high status may be an asset. Employees, for example, generally prefer to take orders from someone they perceive to have high status rather than from their peers or from someone recently promoted from their own ranks. Since the status symbols exhibited by managers are also symbols of power, the possession of high status is an excellent means of attracting and holding attention. A casual remark by the company president may remain on the grapevine for months, while the same statement by a middle manager might never be heard.

Whether status differences are, on the whole, an asset or a liability, depends to some degree upon the dominant leadership style employed in the organization. An emphasis upon status differences is more consistent with an authoritarian than with a participative style. Status differences are, therefore, less damaging in the authoritarian structure.

System Overload

The members of an organization, like electronic devices, have a limited capacity to receive and transmit messages. Air traffic controllers in a large airport are a widely publicized example of persons whose capacity to communicate is sometimes stretched to the breaking point. Managers in large organizations also have the problem. They are often called upon to interact personally with large numbers of people and are bombarded with written correspondence, telephone calls, and a continuous stream of reports. Although skills commonly improve with practice under such circumstances, ability to communicate may deteriorate.

The capacity of computers to produce massive volumes of data often contributes more to communication problems than to their solutions. Critically important information is lost in the volume of details. Managers who receive more messages than they can judiciously interpret must isolate the messages which are most important. In addition to consuming time, this process has a disorganizing effect upon a manager's behavior. Also, the ever-present possibility that important messages will not be received produces frustration and stress.

In the case of line managers, system overload may be reduced by adding staff support and/or changing the nature of management positions in order to reduce the number of their communication contacts. Specialists in time organization and work efficiency techniques may also help managers in a variety of ways. Electronic devices for recording incoming messages or for dictating may be helpful in some instances. In most cases, however, a reduction in the flow of unnecessary information provides the most effective relief for system overload. The condensation of computerized operating reports, memoranda, and even important journal articles can be extremely helpful.

Communication specialists can provide a management team with valuable training in communication techniques. Managers can be taught, for example, when to dictate a memo and when to make a telephone call. They can learn a variety of time-saving techniques such as combining messages rather than interrupting another individual with a number of telephone calls. The mechanics of communicating may appear simplistic and unworthy of a manager's attention.[9]

---

[9] For a uniquely thorough and practical approach to improving communication skills, see George T. Vardaman and Patricia Black Vardaman, *Communication in Modern Organizations* (New York: John Wiley & Sons, Inc., 1973), p. 516.

In view of the time managers spend communicating and the cost of poor communication, however, training in this area is an unusually good investment.

Defensive Reactions

Defensiveness is among the most serious barriers to communication. Where the organizational climate is characterized by suspicion, cutthroat competition, and general insecurity, managers and employees alike are prone to filter what others say through their own fears and distrust.

An insecure employee whose supervisor says, "I suggest that in the future you set your alarm a little earlier," may incorrectly hear the supervisor say, "If you are late again for work, you will be discharged." Similarly, the foreman who is congratulated by a superior for a job well done may react with the suspicion that the boss is preparing him for an undesirable assignment or for criticism for substandard performance elsewhere.

The causes of widespread defensiveness in organizations may be correctable by instituting changes in organizational policies. Management may, for example, change from a policy of secretiveness to deliberate sharing of information. Less frequent occurrences of defensiveness that involve the same individuals are probably due to emotional immaturity. Messages directed to immature individuals must be carefully encoded to anticipate the defensive reaction and minimize distortion resulting from fear and suspicion.

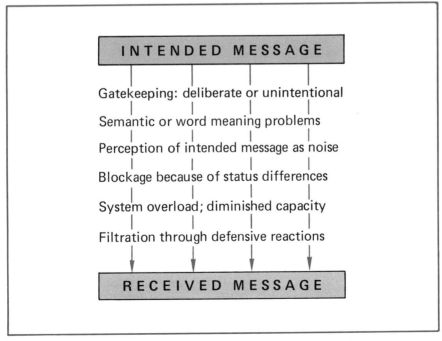

Figure 15–3   Barriers to Effective Communication

LEARNING TO LISTEN

Thesis: The assumption is commonly made that listening is an ability that requires no effort or special skill. As a result, many would-be communicators do not listen well enough to become aware of the receiver's frame of reference. No degree of logic or verbal fluency can totally overcome this obstacle.

The major objectives of active listening are the improvement of learning effectiveness and communication skills. It is obvious that good listeners, say in the classroom, learn more from lectures and discussions than do students whose listening skills are marginal. It may be less obvious that the feedback which results from listening is essential to good communication. It provides valuable insight into another person's general frame of reference and into that individual's intellectual and emotional reaction to a specific message. Effective listening, a major ingredient of empathic communication, is a skill in which people differ greatly. Fortunately, it is one which can be improved.

Active versus Passive Listening

A degree of listening occurs as the passive, involuntary registration of auditory stimuli upon consciousness. Hearing occurs because the listener is interested in what is being said or because there are no successfully competing stimuli in the form of external sounds or internal thoughts. In many situations, however, the competing stimuli are dominant, and we fail to receive relevant messages because of daydreaming or because attention is drawn to irrelevant stimuli in the environment.

Listening is most effective when one listens with a purpose. Contrast the common experience of being unable to call a person by name immediately after being introduced with the recall of the entertainer who remembers the names of a large audience after hearing each name only once. Effective listening begins with a motivation to hear, to understand, and to remember. Effective listening is not often a chance happening. It is, rather, the result of an intentional concentration effort.

Techniques of Active Listening

One difficulty in listening arises from the slowness of speech in comparison to listening. Pauses between words and phrases allow the listener time to get lost in the free association triggered by the speaker or by some irrelevant stimulus. This is most likely to occur when interest is low and/or when the speaker's content is difficult to understand.

The following activities are recommended for improving concentration, effectively using the speaker's "spare time," and consequently improving listening skills.

1. Be slow to brand any speaker as boring or uninteresting. These qualities are as often a function of the thought processes of the listener as the content and delivery of the speaker.

2. Expect to learn something when someone speaks.

3. Ask pertinent questions in order to influence the speaker toward interesting content.

4. Guard against a tendency to tune out the speaker when the content presented becomes difficult to understand. Counter with increased determination to learn and remember.

5. Make a game of self-examination after a conversation or speech to see how much of the content can be recalled.

6. Try to anticipate where the speaker is going. Establish and test hypotheses about the speaker's motives, values, and biases. Is the speaker attempting to persuade? to teach? to win friends? to entertain? to kill time?

7. Note the techniques used by the speaker. To what extent does the speaker rely upon facts, upon an emotional appeal, upon the shock effect, or upon authority?

8. Integrate what is being said with what the speaker has said before and with facts learned from other sources.

9. Evaluate the relevance of what is being said. Is it in any way practical? To what is it relevant? Should the content be classified as trivia?

10. Listen for intended meanings. Look behind the words and manner of presentation for what the speaker is attempting to communicate.

11. Be a responsive listener. Maintain eye contact with the speaker. Particularly in individual conversation use nods and facial expression to let the speaker know that contact is being made.

12. Accept the challenge to become an expert at listening and remembering.

STUDY AND DISCUSSION QUESTIONS

1. Some definitions involve the notion that communication occurs only when the intended meaning of the sender is transmitted to the receiver. In what sense is this notion inadequate?

2. Explain this statement: Only symbols, not meanings, are transferred from sender to receiver.

3. What is the difference between action language and object language?

4. Explain the relationship between empathy and ability to communicate.

5. Why do people who are unusually quiet sometimes have difficulty empathizing?

6. What is the primary relationship between character and the ability to communicate?
7. What changes are most likely to occur in the nature of the communication process as organizations grow?
8. Assuming it could be done, would it be advisable to eliminate the grapevine within an organization? Explain.
9. Be prepared to debate the pros and cons of the open door policy. In organizing each position, it may be helpful to imagine how individuals at different organizational levels might feel when the open door policy is operating.
10. Describe the nature of unintentional gatekeeping.

CRITICAL INCIDENT

The Hardhat

When Al Lemanski took an early retirement from his position as a construction executive in Newark, he vowed he would never work another day. The son of a Boston factory employee, Lemanski worked part-time as a construction laborer while in high school and college. Rising from a background of relative poverty, he amassed a sizable fortune through a variety of business investments. Within the organization, he earned a reputation for being intelligent, honest, fair, and somewhat blunt in interpersonal relations. Although his decisions were often brilliant, and no one who knew him well found occasion to question his competence, his directness was sometimes inaccurately seen as a lack of concern for the feelings of others.

After two years of inactivity, Lemanski could no longer tolerate retirement. Several months of searching finally led him to purchase a prosperous factory near Dallas. Most of the company's 200 employees, about half of whom had been with the firm since it was founded, worked on the assembly line. The former owner was a mild-mannered, affable engineer named Gus Reed. Lemanski bought the company soon after Reed suffered a severe heart attack. The employees were told only that the company had been bought by "a wealthy, retired executive from the northeast."

Between the time of Reed's heart attack and Lemanski's arrival, the company was managed by William Jackson, the factory superintendent and Reed's lifelong friend. Although Jackson had met Lemanski while negotiations for the purchase were under way, the two had no opportunity to become well acquainted. Jackson was somewhat apprehensive about his future, especially since Lemanski had no background in manufacturing.

When Lemanski arrived, he talked briefly with the office manager and then sent word for Jackson to come into his office. Since Jackson did not know what to expect, he somehow felt that he was being called on the carpet. Gus Reed would have casually talked in Jackson's office, a glass enclosure near the assembly line.

The conversation was relatively formal. Although the subject was not mentioned, Lemanski seemed to assume that Jackson would continue as plant superintendent. As was Lemanski's style, he wasted no time in speaking his mind. "As I see it, we have three problems that need attention immediately. Labor turnover is excessive, and returns for repair are running too high. Also, we need to clean up the place, especially the warehouse area."

The entire meeting was upsetting to Jackson. He had obviously lost a friend and acquired a boss. Although he felt it would be unwise to contest Lemanski's analysis, Jackson was furious by the time he left the room. Jackson would not normally have taken factory foreman Larry Bass into his confidence, but Bass was the first person he met, and he felt the need to get some things off his chest. Jackson began with:

> Who does that arrogant, fast-talking hardhat think he is? On his first day aboard, he thinks he knows more about how to run the place than I do. Well, when he discovers the hard way what the company's real problems are, he'll wish he hadn't been so high and mighty.

After a brief cooling-off period, Jackson regained his composure and wished he had not been so free in venting his feelings to Bass. The other foremen were sure to hear the story within the hour.

Questions

1. What communication problems are involved in this incident? Be specific in terms of the chapter content.
2. How could Lemanski have avoided the problem with Jackson?
3. Question 1 refers to the communication problems in this incident. Would it be just as accurate to call them human relations problems?

Chapter

16

The Management of

Conflict and Stress

An organization can achieve its objectives only if its members cooperate and coordinate their efforts toward a common end. For this to occur, everyone must subordinate a degree of individuality and personal freedom to the organization. Such behavior is not achieved, however, without a struggle. Thus, while organizations require cooperative effort, they also occasion conflict within and between the individuals of which they are comprised.

Previous chapters have dealt with many of the conflicts between individuals and between groups. In this chapter, attention is focused primarily on the individual, with particular emphasis on the practical means by which employees and managers reduce the inner tension and stress associated with work. First, however, we examine the nature of organizational conflict, since this is the context within which individual stress is experienced.

CONFLICT WITHIN ORGANIZATIONS

Thesis: Conflict is both a disruptive force within an organization and a primary source of individual stress. Yet it is not entirely destructive. The organization's goal should be to control conflict rather than to eliminate it.

Traditional organization theorists assumed that conflict within organizations is pathological, a sickness to be treated with rational principles of organization and a heady dose of formal authority. Human relations theorists agreed that conflict is pathological but believed that it could be eliminated through mutual understanding, improved communication, and a shared awareness that conflict is unnecessary. Neither of these positions is satisfying to modern theorists.

The Inevitability of Conflict

It would be comforting to believe that people are entirely rational and good, but it would not be true. As a matter of fact, all people are a blend of good and bad, rational and irrational, selfish and unselfish. It is realistic, then, to assume that unless human nature changes significantly, conflict cannot be eliminated. Experience shows, however, that it can be contained sufficiently to minimize its destructive effects.

Although organizational conflict occurs in countries with different political and economic philosophies, the United States is unique in its acceptance and institutionalization of conflict as a way of life. This is expressed in four important ways. First, every possible means is taken to protect the rights and freedom of the individual, including a strong adversary system of jurisprudence. Secondly, the combat of collective bargaining has, since the 1930s, been promoted by law. Third, the competition between organizations, long institutionalized through antitrust legislation, tends also to legitimize and promote competition between individuals. Finally, our entire system of government, from the election of officials to debate over legislation is based upon the assumption that the benefits of controlled conflict more than offset its disadvantages.

Sources of Organizational Conflict

Since managers must engage in continual combat with competitors, parties to law suits, union representatives, and a host of others encountered in operating the firm, it is understandable that a combative life-style is also expressed in manager-to-manager relations within the organization. The same competitive spirit that motivates managers to make enormous personal sacrifices for the organization also motivates a sometimes destructive struggle for power.[1] Where the pace is set at the top for cutthroat competition, managers and employees at lower levels have no difficulty justifying their own similar behavior.

Although power struggles within management are an important source of organizational conflict, they are only one of many. Prominent among other sources of conflict are the following:

1. *Line and Staff Competition.* The growth of highly specialized, creative, well-educated staff poses unique problems for line managers. Faced with a growing dependence upon staff, line managers must adjust to a reduction in organizational power and prestige. Conflict in most organizations persists between line and staff because it is virtually impossible to define precisely the responsibility and authority relationships between the two.
2. *Functional Interdependence.* Conflicts between an organization's functional units, such as sales, accounting, and manufacturing, are commonplace. The sales department is at odds with manufacturing because quality is too low or prices too high to meet the competition. Accounting is viewed as exercising excessive control over budgets, and the sales department is perceived as a culprit because of its free spending. Although departments are separated on the basis of function, they can

---

[1] For insights into the nature and effects of conflict between managers, read Alonzo McDonald, "Conflict at the Summit: a Deadly Game," *Harvard Business Review,* Vol. 50 (March, 1972), pp. 59–68.

never function as completely autonomous units. They must somehow resist the constant urge to view the organization in terms of their narrow self-interests.

3. *Labor-Management Polarization.* This is one of the most common sources of organizational conflict. Its implications have already been discussed at length.

4. *Organization-Individual Disagreements.* From one perspective, the conflict between the organization and the individual centers around the individual's failure to fulfill the organization's expectations regarding productivity or compliance with rules. From another, the conflict is often seen as resulting from excessive organizational demands. Such conflict may be overt or hidden from view, depending upon the perception each side has of the power of the other.

5. *Disagreement over Goals.* Conflict among managers is often caused by the fact that there is poor agreement over goals. One manager makes decisions as if the organization's primary goal were immediate profits, while another acts as if long-term growth were more important. Perhaps an even more common source of conflict is the clash of the personal goals of managers and employees with the goals of the organization.

6. *Overlapping or Ambiguous Responsibilities.* Organizations constantly change in response to personnel turnover, expansion or contraction, the adoption of new policies, changes in the external environment, and so forth. As a result, it is impossible to establish job responsibilities once and for all. When a change occurs, one person reaches out to assume more responsibility, while another retrenches and still another tentatively assumes responsibility for certain functions without knowing definitely who should be performing them. Thus, the stage is set for conflict.

7. *Bottlenecks in the Flow of Work.* Line supervisors in manufacturing must meet production deadlines, but they are dependent upon production schedulers, warehousing, shipping, and others for effective performance. A bottleneck at any point can prevent the line supervisors from being effective, and is, quite naturally, an occasion for interpersonal conflict.

8. *Personality Clashes.* Individual differences in such personal qualities as values, attitudes, abilities, and personality traits are often the cause of personality conflict. Two managers may learn to despise each other thoroughly for reasons totally unrelated to their work, but their performance on the job may suffer because of it. Manager *A* believes, for example, that Manager *B* blocked a promotion. As a result, information *B* needs for optimal effectiveness is withheld.

Positive Contributions of Conflict

The negative implications of conflict are obvious. Both the individuals involved and the organizations for which they work are usually hurt by it. In recent years, however, both operating managers and organization theorists have discovered positive aspects of conflict. For example, in a recent study conducted for the American Management Association, executives noted the following positive outcomes of conflict in their companies:

1. Better ideas were produced.

2. People were forced to search for new approaches.

3. Long-standing problems surfaced and were dealt with.

4. People were forced to clarify their views.

5. The tension stimulated interest and creativity.

6. People had a chance to test their capacities.[2]

These outcomes of conflict within organizations are similar to those experienced externally. For example, legislation regulating pension funds, safety on the job, pollution of the environment, or consumer protection may be frustrating and costly, but it still motivates managers to do what is needed. It is not uncommon for an economic recession or the aggressiveness of a competitor to stimulate improvement in an organization's efficiency.

Conflict within organizations, like external conflict, serves as an energizer. Like an electric shock or an injection of adrenalin, it attacks the foundations of complacency and mobilizes the resources required to meet the adversary. Although conflict within organizations is in many ways analogous to a civil war, its impact in most organizations is less destructive than the lethargy which exists where little conflict is present.

THE NATURE OF STRESS

Thesis: Stress is an exceedingly complex concept which does not lend itself to a simple definition. It can best be understood in terms of the internal and external conditions necessary for its arousal and the symptoms by which it is identified. Its identifiable symptoms are both psychological and physiological.

It is not the situation but one's perception of it that determines whether it will be stressful. Thus, Larry Jones, a recent university graduate in an entry-level management position, viewed his job as extremely taxing and wondered whether he would be able to perform adequately in it. Within two months, the job's appearance began to change. Although the work itself was at least as demanding as it first seemed to be, Larry discovered that his superiors were tolerant of his initial ineptness and realized it would take several months for him to reach the proficiency level of his predecessor. Although his job remained a challenge, he was soon able to work without the apprehension and physical tension he had felt earlier. In time he became confident that his performance was acceptable, but, because of his high level of stress-related motivation, he was able to perform at the peak of his ability during a critical time in his career.

Stress is a very imprecise term in the literature of the behavioral sciences. Joseph McGrath, a respected researcher and theorist, prefers to think in terms

---

[2] Warren H. Schmidt, "Conflict: A Powerful Process for (Good or Bad) Change," *Management Review,* Vol. 63 (December, 1974), p. 5.

of the conditions necessary for stress rather than give it a straightforward definition

> *So there is a potential for stress when an environmental situation is perceived as presenting a demand which threatens to exceed the person's capabilities and resources for meeting it, under conditions where he expects a substantial differential in the rewards and costs from meeting the demand versus not meeting it.* [Italics McGrath's] [3]

As this statement implies, stress occurs in response to an environmental demand upon an individual, but the degree of stress experienced is imperfectly correlated with that demand. It is the "stressee's" perception of the demand rather than the demand itself that determines the degree of stress experienced. That perception is greatly influenced by the individual's self-perceived abilities and overall self-confidence.

The latter part of McGrath's statement indicates that one precondition for stress is that the individual be motivated to perform in a specific situation. For example, a student who is taking an examination on which failure appears likely will experience stress only if the outcome is regarded as important. Or a manager, faced with high employee turnover, may experience stress if superiors expect turnover to be reduced but experience little stress if they view high turnover as inevitable.

McGrath gives meaning to stress in terms of the conditions necessary for its arousal. In a later section of this chapter, a further interpretation of stress is given in terms of its symptoms. Within the context of these conditions and symptoms, *stress* may be defined as a psychological and physical reaction to prolonged internal and/or environmental conditions in which an individual's adaptive capabilities are overextended. Stress is one (among many) of a person's adaptive reactions to threat.[4] One may or may not be fully conscious that threat exists. Even when such awareness is present, the source of the threat may not be known. Since some stress is necessary for life, the word normally connotes *excessive stress.*

That the perceived threat may be internal—that is, from within the person rather than in the external environment—is seen in the fact that barriers to need satisfaction are often psychological. The two major classes of such barriers are (1) *personal barriers,* in which one's own lack of ability, motivation, or education,

---

[3] Joseph E. McGrath, "Stress and Behavior in Organizations," in Marvin D. Dunnette (ed.), *Handbook of Industrial and Organizational Psychology* (Chicago: Rand McNally & Company, 1976), p. 1352.

[4] In this context, *threat* is necessarily defined in broad terms. It must encompass, for example, the situation in which an individual perceives danger where the average, healthy-minded person would feel confident and secure. It must also include many high-risk situations in which a confident, tough-minded manager accepts a long-term commitment to a near-impossible goal. Threat, viewed as the perceived possibility of self-damaging failure, is often involved in the most interesting and challenging of jobs. The stress-producing potential in the frightening and the challenging situation may be identical where the perception of high risk is involved.

for example, prevents need satisfaction and (2) *conflict barriers,* in which one's inability to decide between alternatives (say between the status quo and accepting a promotion which necessitates leaving a preferred geographical area) becomes a problem. The notion that the threat must be experienced over a prolonged (but undefined) period of time differentiates stress from short-term emotional states such as momentary fear reactions.

THE SYMPTOMS OF STRESS

Thesis: Situationally induced stress provides the psychic and physical energy needed for peak performance. When the stress-producing factor cannot be overcome and stress becomes chronic, its effects are mentally and physically destructive.

When one perceives an element in the environment to be threatening or unusually challenging, the brain sends instructions to the endocrine glands to prepare for an emergency. Hormones produced by the pituitary, adrenal cortex, and other glands trigger a series of responses which release the adaptive energies of the body. Under normal conditions the body responds with more physical strength, greater speed, prolonged endurance, deeper concentration, a sharper intellect—whatever the situation demands. But the emergency preparation is not intended to last indefinitely. If the *stressor,* the stress-producing factor, is not eliminated, the body's emergency reaction itself becomes a problem.

The General Adaptation Syndrome

Hans Selye, the world's foremost authority on stress, was the first to describe systematically the changes through which the body passes to deal with perceived threat. He describes what he called the General Adaptation Syndrome (G.A.S.), an adaptive response which occurs in three phases: *A,* an alarm reaction; *B,* the stage of resistance; and *C,* the stage of exhaustion.[5]

The alarm reaction is the preparation for emergency action, commonly referred to as preparation for *fight* or *flight* (for aggressive action to meet the threat or for the speed required for a hasty retreat). During this stage, the normal digestive functions slow down, but energy is made available through an increase in blood sugar. The heart beats faster and more strongly to improve the flow of energy resources and waste products, and the blood pressure rises to dilate the vessels and increase the flow of blood to the muscles. Rapid and deep breathing increases the oxygen needed for high energy production, and a combination of perspiration and dilation of the blood vessels near the surface of the skin offset the rising body temperature generated by the high activity level. These reactions

---

[5] The nature of the G.A.S. was first described in the 1940s. See Hans Selye, "The General Adaptation Syndrome and the Diseases of Adaptation," *Journal of Clinical Endocrinology,* Vol. 2 (1946), pp. 117–230. Selye's latest work on stress is *Stress Without Distress* (Bergenfield, New Jersey: The New American Library, Inc., 1974).

stand in sharp contrast to the state of internal equilibrium which exists under conditions of relaxation and security.

If the stressor, say a financial crisis within the firm or perceived inability to perform according to expectations of superiors, is removed, an internal state of equilibrium or homeostasis is restored. If the perceived threat continues, the body often develops an increased resistance to it. In effect, one's potential for stress is raised, but it takes a toll in use of the body's adaptational resources. In this *stage of resistance* the characteristics of the alarm reaction disappear and bodily functions return to normal.

If the stressor is removed, the body's natural resistance to stress has performed its function. Equilibrium is thereby restored. If, on the other hand, the stressor persists, the individual continues into the irreversible *stage of exhaustion* where the signs of the alarm reaction reappear, the body's adaptive energies are depleted, the lifespan is shortened. A wide range of diseases such as ulcers, heart ailments, and high blood pressure are in some instances directly traceable to stress. Many other diseases fail to respond to normal treatment because stress has greatly diminished the body's natural adaptive resources.

Detecting Signs of Unhealthy Stress

Symptoms of unhealthy stress in others may or may not be obvious. Neither do we always recognize them in ourselves. We often move in imperceptible increments from one stage to another, with our standards of normalcy shifting with changes in bodily condition. Thus, a manager whose stymied career results in perpetual stress may forget how it felt to be free from apprehension, tension,

SYMPTOM	DESCRIBES POORLY			DESCRIBES WELL		
Constant fatigue	☐	☐	☐	☐	☐	☐
Low energy level	☐	☐	☐	☐	☐	☐
Recurring headaches	☐	☐	☐	☐	☐	☐
Gastrointestinal disorders	☐	☐	☐	☐	☐	☐
Chronically bad breath	☐	☐	☐	☐	☐	☐
Sweaty hands or feet	☐	☐	☐	☐	☐	☐
Dizziness	☐	☐	☐	☐	☐	☐
High blood pressure	☐	☐	☐	☐	☐	☐
Pounding heart	☐	☐	☐	☐	☐	☐
Constant inner tension	☐	☐	☐	☐	☐	☐
Inability to sleep	☐	☐	☐	☐	☐	☐
Temper outbursts	☐	☐	☐	☐	☐	☐
Hyperventilation	☐	☐	☐	☐	☐	☐
Moodiness	☐	☐	☐	☐	☐	☐
Irritability and restlessness	☐	☐	☐	☐	☐	☐
Inability to concentrate	☐	☐	☐	☐	☐	☐
Increased aggression	☐	☐	☐	☐	☐	☐
Compulsive eating	☐	☐	☐	☐	☐	☐
Chronic worrying	☐	☐	☐	☐	☐	☐
Anxiety or apprehensiveness	☐	☐	☐	☐	☐	☐
Inability to relax	☐	☐	☐	☐	☐	☐
Growing feelings of inadequacy	☐	☐	☐	☐	☐	☐
Increase in defensiveness	☐	☐	☐	☐	☐	☐
Dependence upon tranquilizers	☐	☐	☐	☐	☐	☐
Excessive use of alcohol	☐	☐	☐	☐	☐	☐
Excessive smoking	☐	☐	☐	☐	☐	☐

Figure 16–1 Checklist of Symptoms of Stress

and a burning stomach. It is a good day when there is no pain and when life is tolerable without tranquilizers.

Another barrier to objectively diagnosing one's own stress level arises when the stage of resistance is mistaken for equilibrium. The ambitious, hard-driving manager, noting that the original symptoms of stress are gone, is tempted to assume additional stress-producing responsibilities during this stage rather than use the time wisely to reduce the stressors.

The physiological and psychological symptoms of stress occur in many combinations and degrees—enough to make self-diagnoses quite hazardous. Figure 16–1 lists some common symptoms of stress. Applying the checklist to oneself will not provide a professionally respectable analysis of one's stress level, but it should give an insight into the nature of stress.

THE CAUSES OF STRESS

Thesis: The causes of stress are found within the environment, the individual, and the interaction between the two. The stress experienced by a given individual is seldom traceable to a single source.

In exploring the causes of stress it is important that a clear distinction be made between stress and the stressor (the source of the stress). It is confusing and technically incorrect to speak of a "stressful situation," as though anyone placed in that situation would experience stress. For purposes of analysis and understanding, stressors are divided into two classes: those which lie within the individual and those which are a part of the external environment.

Internal Stimuli for Stress

The internal sources of stress are complex and difficult to isolate. Some sources are internal in that no external stimulus is needed to maintain the stress, some are internal in that they influence the perception of potential external stressors, and others are internal in that they determine an individual's threshold of resistance to potentially stress-producing stimuli. One's level of motivation is also a factor in the arousal of stress. Each of these internal influences upon stress is considered separately, although they function in continual interaction.

Inner Conflicts.   For many people, stress is a constant companion regardless of how favorable or unfavorable external conditions may be. Nonspecific fears, anxiety, and guilt feelings maintain the body in a state of readiness for emergency action on a continuing basis. The environmental events which left their impact on the individual may even be repressed from memory, but they continue to activate the endocrine glands which in turn provoke the alarm reactions.

Perceptual Influences.   Is the boss a menacing, threatening antagonist or a kind, considerate friend? Is there a constant danger of an arbitrary discharge or layoff? Does the future offer broad opportunities for personal advancement or no opportunities at all? The answers to these questions lie only partially outside oneself. And, regardless of the facts, the potential of people and situations in the environment to provoke stress depends upon perceptual processes which are uniquely individual.

Perception is influenced by a number of internal factors. Certainly people with inner conflicts which are sufficient to cause stress are more likely than self-confident people to perceive environmental conditions as threatening. Thus, perceptual distortion stimulates a circularity that is hard to break. Because the environment is presumed to be full of danger, evidences of danger are perceived everywhere. They are selectively perceived in exaggerated form.

Perception of threat is also related to all dimensions of one's self-image. To people who see themselves as problem solvers, for example, a given problem may be welcomed as a friend, while others who question their own competence may view it as dangerous.

Perception is also a function of one's attitudes. This is reflected in the attitudes of Bill Richards, a respected oil company executive, toward demotions.

The company had for many years been divided into multistate regions, each with a vice-president for exploration, production, accounting, and the other major functions. For reasons of economy, however, the company had begun to combine regions, leaving in each case a large number of competent managers faced with the choice of finding new jobs or taking a demotion. Although Richards was, in fact, one of the managers most likely to be offered a position in the merged organization, he did not so perceive himself, and he became increasingly apprehensive as the decision date drew near.

Richards' perception of his own standing within the company was inaccurate, but much of his problem stemmed from his attitude toward taking a demotion, should that be necessary. He saw a demotion as a sign of failure, incompetence, and lack of good standing with one's superiors; and he seemed totally unable to see that demotions can have different meanings, depending upon the circumstances. When he was able to see that demotion in this situation was really no different from being outpaced by a worthy competitor in a race for a promotion, his attitudes changed and his rising stress level began to subside. He got the job, but he probably would not have had his stress gotten out of control and itself contributed to further perceptual distortion.

Thresholds of Stress.   The threshold of stress is not independent of the two factors just discussed but is worth considering as a separate internal influence upon stress levels. We have already discussed the subject of stress threshold without calling it by name. People who have few internal conflicts and a minimum of perceptual distortion can withstand external conflict and pressure that weaker personalities would find intolerable. People who have *high thresholds* (that is, high entrance levels) for stress have high levels of resistance to it.

Thresholds are related both to ego strength and self-confidence and to specific personality characteristics. If, for example, a stressor is applied to two individuals, the one with the least sensitivity and concern for others is less likely to experience stress. On many occasions, the tough-minded, task-oriented manager survives a business crisis unscathed, while a more sensitive but equally mature and competent colleague develops ulcers and high blood pressure.

Resistance to stress can be due to many other factors. Purely physiological differences in the functioning of the nervous system, glands, and body organs may influence stress levels. Under identical experiences of threat and tension, people differ in their predisposition, say, to develop high blood pressure (which itself becomes a stressor and compounds the stress problem). On the psychological side, people differ in their repertoire of alternatives for coping with stressors. Personality flexibility is better than rigidity, for example. The ability to do just a little rationalizing, to blow off steam rather than to bottle up feelings, to laugh at oneself and the situation—all these and other behaviors which could be detrimental if taken too far provide resources that enable one to face pressure without stress.

Motivational Level.   People who lack a sense of direction are unlikely to be stressed by discovering that they are behind schedule. It is the ambitious, driving, goal-directed individual who is most likely to experience stress in the work environment.

Lack of career success is cause for concern only if a manager or employee's aspirations exceed present or anticipated progress. The second-string professional quarterback will experience no stress from sitting on the bench year after year unless he is deeply motivated to get into the action. Environmental events become stressors only to the person who cares what happens.

Environmental Stressors

A great many factors within an organization have the potential for provoking stress. They are not, of course, stressors in and of themselves, but for specific individuals they play such a role. Since the controlling conditions were discussed earlier, the potential stressors below are discussed only briefly.

Organizational Structure.   The extent to which the organizational structure influences stress levels depends upon the compatability of members with the organization. The rigid structure and strict rules, procedures, policies, and controls of many bureaucracies are preferred by some people while others feel grossly overcontrolled in such organizations.

Ivancevich and Donnelly studied 295 salesmen in tall, medium, and flat organizations. They found that salesmen in flat organizations experience lower amounts of "anxiety-stress" than those in medium and tall organizations. To the extent that individual autonomy is a desired quality in the workplace, this finding will probably generalize to other types of employees and other organizations.[6]

---

[6] John M. Ivancevich and James H. Donnelly, Jr., "Relation of Organizational Structure to Job Satisfaction, Anxiety-Stress, and Performance," *Administrative Science Quarterly,* Vol. 20 (June, 1975), pp. 272–280.

Leadership　Although managers have less potential today than in the past for intimidating subordinates and otherwise contributing to stress, managerial behavior is the most critical stressor for many employees. The irresistible urge of some managers to misuse power combines with the negative reaction of many people to authority to make any position of organizational leadership a potential source of threat.

Monotony.　Especially at the employee level, monotony is likely to be a stressor. Even employees who find variety and autonomy stress provoking also find monotony to be frustrating. Monotony is especially likely to be a stressor for managers and others who expect intrinsic satisfaction from their work.

A Blocked Career.　One of the most common career crises occurs when managers with high aspirations realize that their upward mobility has stopped. Another occurs when one's employment is threatened by personality clashes, company financial problems, or any other factor which appears beyond the individual's control.

Excessive Responsibility.　When organization members fail to perform according to their own expectations or the perceived expectations of their superiors, stress often results. It is interesting to note that the stress-producing effect of this condition may be independent of actual performance. Low producers with low self-expectations may experience no stress, while superior producers with demanding standards are stressed to the breaking point. Excessive responsibility may also result from an inadequate grant of formal authority.

Task Load.　In some situations, no single task demands too much, but the combination of tasks imposes an excessive work load. Time pressures are intense, and there is no let-up. For managers, especially, this situation may involve long hours of work with little time off for vacations.

Ambiguous Demands.　Although some people need more structure than others, everyone needs a general idea of performance expectations. Frustration results when employees get no feedback on performance or discover that management is using performance criteria which are arbitrary, irrelevant to organizational goals, and/or constantly changing.

Value Conflicts.　The organization sometimes requires behavior that a member cannot perform with a clear conscience. A manager may, for example, be called upon to give kickbacks or to misinform customers about a product.

Interpersonal Conflicts.　Having to work day after day with another person who is irritating, aggressive, or repulsive because of personal habits may be highly stressing.

Family Crises.　Problems relating to marriage, children, health, finances, and other aspects of personal life may cause stress which affects job performance. These problems sometimes combine with on-the-job stressors to produce a stress pattern which is extremely difficult to reverse.

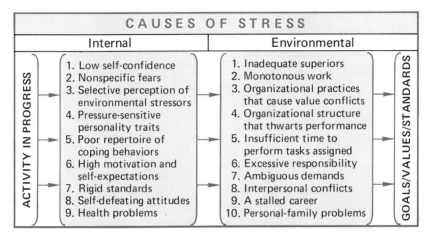

Figure 16–2   Some Interacting Causes of Stress

One of the most troublesome aspects of stressors is the fact that two or more may combine to produce an effect which is greater than the sum of the parts. This is illustrated by the case of a mature but overworked financial manager who had to be hospitalized for so-called nervous exhaustion when he discovered that his daughter was on drugs and his wife was seeing another man while he worked late at the office. Not everyone will break under a combination of intense pressures, but there is a point of frustration at which everyone will experience stress and some deterioration of performance.

THE CREATIVE MANAGEMENT OF STRESS

Thesis: Since the causes of stress lie both within individuals and their environments, there is no way management can eliminate all organizational factors which trigger undesirable stress. Management can, however, minimize stress, and individuals can control their stress-provoking reactions to the organization.

In most organizations, management assumes that reading the signs of excessive stress and adjusting intelligently are strictly personal matters. Although an increasing number of companies underwrite periodic physical examinations for their managers, any effort to monitor stress levels routinely is presumed to constitute an invasion of privacy. Accordingly, stress reduction is viewed as a personal matter, and most suggestions for the management of stress are made with this fact in mind.

Modifying the Organizational Environment

There are many opportunities for managers to modify the organization to reduce their own stress or that of subordinates. Examples of such actions are

1. Clarifying task assignments, responsibility, authority, and criteria for performance evaluation

2. Introducing consideration for people into leadership style

3. Delegating more effectively and increasing individual autonomy where the situation warrants it

4. Clarifying goals and decision criteria

5. Setting and enforcing policies for mandatory vacations and reasonable working hours

Too often managers and employees alike assume that organizational changes affecting their welfare can be initiated only by their superiors. As a result, they submissively endure excessive work loads, vague goals, inadequate decision criteria, and the like, when even the slightest initiative to propose solutions would eliminate the stressors.

Escape Techniques

Most people are creative in discovering ways to reduce stress, but their techniques are not always constructive. For example, one escape device is the reduction of level of aspiration to the point that one's productivity is unnecessarily low. Others escape through excessive daydreaming, television watching, and alcohol consumption. Even overeating is sometimes linked to unconscious attempts to reduce stress; but like so many other escape techniques, it may cause problems rather than solve them. An otherwise wholesome escape becomes destructive when its side effects cause problems (as heavy drinking usually does) or when the amount of time spent in the diversion prevents one from directly facing the stress-producing problem (e.g., watching television all evening when selected reading might help remove a stressor problem).

Among the many healthy ways of escaping work pressures and reducing stress are the development of hobbies, direct participation in sports, involvement in civic or religious activities, relaxing with family or friends, and other activities which provide a diversion from work-related problems. As long as a person can set aside time for these activities and approach them in such a way that they themselves do not cause stress, they may contribute significantly to solving the stress problem. These are escape techniques only in the sense that they provide relief from work-related stressors. Labeling them in this way is not meant to imply that they are of intrinsically less value or importance than work, although ambitious managers often behave as if they are.

The Frontal Attack

Stress is sometimes experienced because an individual is unwilling to face and solve a problem directly. While one overworked, underpaid bookkeeper, for example, nurses an ulcer and complains about lack of opportunity, another attends night school to prepare for a career in accounting. At times such a direct confrontation is the ideal way—the only way—to eliminate the source of stress.

The feeling of being boxed in may characterize the person who insists on having both the comforts of a secure position and the benefits of risk taking. But, since the stress associated with a stagnant, no-opportunity situation cannot always be managed by a psychological adaptation, bold action may be needed.

> When Calvin Janis was discharged from his four-year tour in the Navy, he took advantage of his military background to gain entry into a civil service career and for ten long, montonous years worked in a job he considered a waste of the taxpaper's money. One day he awoke to the appalling fact that he had become a clockwatcher whose one goal in life was to retire. Rather than live with the frustration, he left his lucrative civil service job, borrowed the money to go into business for himself, and launched what turned out to be a highly successful career in appliance sales. His business was not without its problems, but they were not the type that produced an unhealthy level of stress.

A frontal attack on the cause of stress sometimes requires a person to play less and work more. Hard work does not in itself cause stress, but one's reaction to failure or inadequate performance often does. It is well to keep in mind the fact that one must usually pay a price for reducing stress to acceptable levels. Students, for example, should not overlook the obvious fact that an ideal way to avoid the stress surrounding examinations is to pay the price of more studying. One might also cope by lowering aspiration levels (for example, making *C*'s rather than *B*'s). The immediate price to be paid in this case would be lower than that of a frontal attack, but in later years that price could prove to be exorbitant.

Value Clarification

Many people, including some successful managers, have never reflected on their total life situation long enough to decide what is important. As a result, they attempt to achieve career success while neglecting other aspects of their lives, such as family, religion, health, and recreation. The stress generated by the neglect in these areas is carried over to the job and effectiveness on the job is thereby undermined.

People with this problem should become introspective long enough to decide what their values really are. In many instances, the value clarification process is less a matter of developing a philosophy than of setting priorities. It may, for example, involve a decision to reject a promotion and preserve one's health or to limit time spent in a career so that more time may be spent in recreation and family activities. Value clarification may lead to the conclusion: I will not sacrifice my personal integrity by engaging in what I consider to be immoral or unethical behavior—even if it means changing jobs. To establish value priorities and to express them in the use of one's time may, for some individuals, be the only way to reduce stress to a healthy level.

The concept of value clarification has numerous applications on the job. Many of the ambiguities in managerial positions are removed when managers take the time to decide what is really important. Managers often waste time on trivia because they are not sure how to distinguish it from what really matters. Managers who decide that their most important problem is, say, improving the company's cash flow position or improving product quality, know where to concentrate their efforts and invest their resources. Such decision making decreases uncertainty and thereby decreases stress.

Value and time priorities are always closely associated, and both involve decision making. None of the techniques yet devised for helping people reduce stress has much chance of success when priority decisions need to be made. They have the effect of treating symptoms while the disease continues to spread.

Perceptual Adaptation

Some situations which provoke stress cannot be significantly changed. In the best of companies, for example, managers must weather prolonged periods of recession, the onslaught of a tough competitor, or a crisis caused by an unfortunate decision. This may result in months or years of difficult decisions, long hours of work, and intense pressures from investors, lending institutions, and others. Some managers simply walk away from these situations, but others persist and learn to cope without undue stress.

Some managers who function effectively in such situations have developed creative perceptual sets which prevent excessive stress. These are learned ways of interpreting situations and events. They may comprise frames of reference which allow people to face problems at a level which is not psychologically destructive. Two examples will show how this is accomplished. Except for their names, these are descriptions of managers with whom the author has worked in management development.

Harry Kelso's progress in management had been phenomenal, but, because his position was valued so highly and his pay was so exceptional, he became apprehensive when making what should have been routine decisions. Quite simply, he was afraid he would make a poor decision which could thwart his career or cost him his job.

His fear subsided and his ability to decide improved when he ceased to think of losing his job as the end of his brilliant career. His altered perception was something like this: My security is not based on my success in this one company but upon my competence and ability to perform. I will give this company all I have to offer. But to be sure my effectiveness here is not impaired, I will maintain my contacts within the industry and will always have somewhere else I can go—probably with a promotion. If I get fired, it will not be the end of the world. Good managers get fired every day, and I have never heard of one who failed to get another job. Making money has never been a problem for me; so all this company can really give me is a rewarding state of mind. If, in fact, the state of mind it gives is one of fear and insecurity, I don't want to work here. I will not trade my self-esteem and sense of well-being for a job, here or anywhere else.

The unhealthy stress experienced by Kelso was removable by a change in perception because the perceptual set through which he had previously viewed his situation was the cause of his difficulty. Had his stress been caused primarily by something else, say a long-standing psychological problem, the perceptual change would not have been so effective.

A slightly different type of situation, involving an inexperienced supervisor, shows how a change in perception, combined with efforts to change the situation, reduced stress.

After only eighteen months in the job, Virginia White was promoted to office manager. In this capacity, she supervised eight men and twelve women, several of whom were candidates for the same promotion. Except for a lack of supervisory experience, she was eminently qualified for the job, and her performance was excellent. She was, however, plagued by a high level of stress. Although the added responsibility was a stressor, it was less so than White's inability to accept the fact that two of her subordinates deeply resented her promotion, and, on occasion, negatively influenced the attitudes of other employees toward her. Actually her effectiveness was not in jeopardy, but she could not accept the fact that some subordinates disliked her.

White's stress began to subside when she learned to perceive being liked in a different way. Her new perceptual set was: I don't have to be liked by everyone to be effective. I am not, after all, in a popularity contest. It is enough that I do my job well and am respected. Also, I don't have to be liked by everyone in order to see myself as worthy of being liked. Especially do I not have to be liked by people whose attitudes are biased by jealousy. Actually their hostility is not directed toward me so much as toward anyone who might be in my position. Part of my job is to absorb such hostility. It is all in a day's work.

Another approach White used to reduce stress emerged from an insight she expressed this way: I have been under pressure because I've been working in a hostile, threatening environment; but I created part of that environment by getting promoted and part of it by my perception of others' reactions to that event. I have expected everyone to be hostile, and, as a result, I have seen hostility where it did not really exist.

Her solution was designed to reverse the situation: Without regard for what anyone else says or does, I am going to be the most effective, likable, considerate supervisor in the company. Although being liked is not critically important, I am going to expect that sooner or later everyone will like me and am going to act as if they already do. It would be foolish for me to feel uncomfortable in such a warm, friendly environment. As one might expect, her expectation became a self-fulfilling prophecy. Her stress subsided, and her interpersonal relations continually improved.

The technique of restructuring one's perception in order to reduce stress has merit only when it does not lead to excessive wishful thinking and escape from the real world. Nevertheless, any situation can be interpreted in many ways, and managers need the flexibility provided by a repertoire of possible interpretations. Accordingly, there is virtue in learning the ways in which effective, stress-resistant managers view their worlds.

The Medication Approach

Tranquilizers are commonly used to reduce stress. If they are taken under the guidance of a competent physician, they can be of benefit in helping to weather a crisis or maintain composure while dealing constructively with a stressor. They should not, however, be viewed as substitutes for coping with the causes of the stress. They tend to suppress the symptoms of stress and, therefore, create a false and dangerous illusion of well-being. They should not be used as a long-term solution to the stress problem.

Biofeedback

Whether the task is learning to operate a machine, to conduct an employment interview, or to maintain an inner tranquility in the presence of potential stressors, feedback on performance is essential. What situations, behaviors, and thought patterns cause a person to become tense and exhibit the bodily changes of the alarm reaction? The question is difficult to answer because the initial bodily changes are often imperceptible. By the time one finally becomes aware of the cumulative effect of many stressors, the symptoms cannot be linked to their specific causes. Immediate feedback is needed to establish this association.

Biofeedback is a process through which the bodily changes under stress are magnified and presented to an individual in such a way that the relationship between stressors and stress can be understood. Any number of bodily functions such as muscle tension, perspiration, blood pressure, and heart rate can be monitored simultaneously in a laboratory setting, and research concerning change in such bodily functions is extensive. Numerous experiments show that through feedback these functions, once considered to be involuntary or automatic, can be consciously controlled.[7]

An electronic apparatus, called an electromyograph, provides feedback on the electrical activity (tension) within the muscles and is now available at a reasonable cost. Electrodes placed on the head, for example, provide impulses which are fed back as sound beeps. As tension decreases, the beeps occur less frequently. As an individual gains insight into the thought processes and physical actions which reduce tension, the beeps occur so infrequently that the apparatus

---

[7] For an analysis of biofeedback theory and research, read Richard S. Lazarus, "A Cognitively Oriented Psychologist Looks at Biofeedback," *American Psychologist* (May, 1975), pp. 553–561, and Gary E. Schwartz, "Biofeedback as Therapy; Some Theoretical and Practical Issues," *American Psychologist* (August, 1973), pp. 666–673. (Bibliographies are included in each.)

must be reset and the process repeated until the desired level of tension reduction is achieved.

After a few hours' use of the feedback device—sometimes daily periods of fifteen to thirty minutes over a two-week span are sufficient—a person learns how to relax without using the electromyograph. Once the relaxing technique has been mastered, a busy manager can pause occasionally for short relaxation periods— three to five minutes in length—to prevent an accumulation of tension and to reinforce the need to relax.

Biofeedback is definitely useful in controlling the negative physiological effects of stress, especially when the technique is administered by a skilled professional. Its value for this purpose cannot be overemphasized. The technique does not, however, deal with the causes of stress as effectively as it might. In a sense, it treats only symptoms, but in many situations this may be sufficient.

Meditation Techniques

In recent years, writers and practitioners of transcendental meditation (TM) have popularized a variety of meditation techniques which are capable of reducing stress. Although such techniques were originally associated with Eastern religions, such as Zen Buddhism,[8] many have now lost their ideology. The meditative techniques were developed to help the deeply religious person withdraw from external stimuli into increasingly deeper levels of concentration upon deities or purifying thoughts. Today emphasis is most likely to be upon escape from external pressures and the achievement of a stressless, if not blissful, state of inner harmony.

Shapiro and Zifferblatt make the point that from the current research on biofeedback, meditation, and self-control, a new model or paradigm of the person is emerging within the scientific community.

> This paradigm conceptualizes the healthy person as an individual who can pilot his or her own existential fate in the here-and-now environment, and who can have far greater self-regulatory control over his or her own body than heretofore imagined. Concomitant with this new paradigm is an attempt to develop and improve techniques by which people can self-observe their behavior, change it (if desired), and then continually modify and monitor it according to their needs.[9]

The scientific research mentioned by these authors points to the conclusion that there is nothing inherently religious or mysterious in TM in spite of the language and thought forms within which it is usually shrouded. In fact, the essential elements of TM have been isolated and are available, less their Oriental religious trappings, for use by anyone concerned with avoiding the damaging effects of stress.

---

[8] Duane H. Shapiro, Jr., and Steven M. Zifferblatt, "Zen Meditation and Behavioral Self-Control," *American Psychologist* (July, 1976), pp. 519–532. (Extensive bibliography included.)

[9] Ibid., p. 519.

Herbert Benson, Harvard University professor of medicine, describes for the readers of the *Harvard Business Review* the essential features of TM in what he calls the "relaxation response."[10] Roughly, the technique involves the following:

1. The meditation place should be quiet. Freedom from all types of distractions is important.

2. The meditator repeats a single-syllable word, such as *one,* in a low, gentle tone. This focus upon a single point is a kind of auto-hypnotic technique for narrowing concentration and releasing oneself from external concerns. (In TM this word, called a *mantra,* would be the name of a diety or some other word with special meaning. It would be a smooth, mellifluous word with many *M*'s, *Y*'s, and vowels, and no one but the meditator should know what mantra he or she is using.)

3. The meditator assumes a passive relaxed attitude, avoiding any attempt to force a response.

4. The meditator's position should be as comfortable as possible: no tight clothes, arms and legs supported, and so forth.

5. Guidelines are provided for progressively relaxing each part of the body and for breathing in a specified manner. (The breathing exercise is apparently an adaptation from Zen meditation.)

Benson recommends practicing the relaxation response for about twenty minutes at a sitting. The research on such techniques leaves little doubt that they are effective in controlling the physiological effects of stress. They have an advantage over biofeedback in requiring no mechanical instruments and overmedication in avoiding undesirable side effects and the possible development of a dependency. TM techniques are healthy, natural, self-control methods; and, although it has not been fully demonstrated, it is possible that they have a lasting, integrative effect upon one's personality.

STUDY AND DISCUSSION QUESTIONS

1. Why is it reasonable to expect that conflict within organizations cannot be eliminated?
2. Evaluate the following statement: Although conflict within organizations is in many ways analogous to a civil war, its impact in most organizations is positive.
3. In what sense is it misleading to think of environmental factors as causes of stress?
4. What physiological changes occur in the alarm phase of the general adaptation syndrome? How is each adaptive or purposeful?

---

[10] Herbert Benson, "Your Innate Asset for Combating Stress.," *Harvard Business Review,* Vol. 52, No. 4 (July, August, 1974), pp. 49–60.

5. What are the relationships between perception and stress?
6. What personality characteristics or traits are likely to contribute to a high threshold of resistance to stress?
7. It was observed by a new chief executive of the XYZ Company that stress levels within most of the company's managers were extremely high. What hypotheses with regard to possible causes should be tested?
8. What kinds of escape from work stressors are healthful and constructive?
9. Evaluate the merits of tranquilizers for reducing stress.
10. Compare the relative merits of biofeedback and transcendental meditation in reducing stress.

CRITICAL INCIDENT

Sylvia's Stress

During her last year in college, Sylvia Carnes changed her major from business communications to management, much to the dismay of her mother who could not visualize her beautiful, feminine daughter in the manager role. Sylvia refused, however, to accept her mother's insistence that she (and all women, for that matter) would be better off to become a secretary, to avoid the pressures of a management position, and to get married at the earliest opportunity.

After graduation Sylvia began her career as a management trainee for a major United States manufacturer of soap products. For years the company had employed only the most outstanding graduates—as, indeed, Sylvia was—but this resulted in intense competition for promotion. After three years on the job, her progress was mediocre. At times she had considered marrying the man to whom she had long been engaged, if for no other reason than to enable her to quit work. Sylvia was, however, cautious about marrying. Her mother's three marriages had ended in divorce, and Sylvia was distrustful of men in general.

Sylvia's work group was highly informal. Her immediate superior, Vernon Katona, followed the lead of higher management in using an informal, participative leadership style, but Sylvia was never completely at ease around him. When he criticized her work or gave her directions, she could not help observing that he was really a male chauvinist; he reminded her of a bossy step-father whom she had thoroughly disliked.

The product development team of which Sylvia was a member worked diligently, and there never seemed to be a time when anyone felt that the pressure was off. Because there were always several projects going at once, it was difficult to attain a feeling of completion and closure. Actually no one seemed to be pushing anybody, the pay and other incentives within the company were outstanding, and everyone just seemed to perform at his or her peak with a minimum of supervision.

Sylvia found her work to be interesting and challenging, but the work pressures were almost too much for her. She sometimes went home so tired that she would sleep for ten hours without feeling completely rested. She enjoyed a few television programs, but recurring tension headaches prevented her from watching many of the programs she liked. She and her fiancé spent several hours a week together, but the relationship was never all she hoped it might be. Sylvia vacillated between thinking (1) that she should yield to her fiance's insistence that they marry, (2) that she should forget marriage altogether and become a career woman, (3) that she should combine marriage and a career, and (4) that, regardless of what she did about marriage, she should change jobs.

Questions

1. What are the probable sources of Sylvia's stress?
2. What actions would be likely to relieve the stress?
3. What further information do you need to answer the previous two questions with confidence?

Organizational Change and Management Development

All organizations—even the most stable ones—are in a continual process of change. Those which change too slowly or which change in the wrong direction decline and eventually die. Like biological organisms, organizations must constantly engage in adaptive behavior to survive and grow. They must, for example, adapt to external changes in the law, natural resources, technology, personnel demands, customer preferences, and competitors' actions.

Each internal change, made in response to environmental demands or changes in managerial personnel, tends to affect the entire system, often in unpredictable ways. An economic recession or a change in the chief executive officer may send shock waves throughout the organization and demand significant change at every level. This chapter is concerned with the process of change in organizations, especially with the role of managers in coping with change and in developing themselves to prevent their own obsolescence.

THE NATURE OF CHANGE IN ORGANIZATIONS

Thesis: One of the major challenges with which organizations are faced is the creation of an atmosphere in which rapid, meaningful change is possible. A delicate balance must be maintained between demands for continual change and the necessity for organizational stability.

In recent years the rate of change within society as a whole has accelerated rapidly. In many areas changes which have occurred during the lifetimes of our senior citizens are greater than those which occurred in all previously recorded history. Transportation, for example, has advanced from the horse and buggy to interplanetary travel and communication from the telegraph to television beamed from Mars and Venus.

367

Although technological advances are significant, they offer no greater challenge than changes in human attitudes and values. Such factors as the "knowledge explosion," decline of the Protestant work ethic, expectations of a shorter work week, rejection of traditional morality, and growing expectations of affluence strain the adaptive capacities of organizations. These changes demand sophisticated management of change.

Resistance to Change

Resistance to change often results in obsolete methods, machines, skills, and other factors which influence effectiveness. For this reason, much attention is given to understanding and reducing resistance to change. Such resistance is not inherently bad, however. Whether the resistance is from managers or employees it may serve two critical functions.

1. It forces the advocates of change to build a defensible case. Thus, ill-advised changes are sometimes avoided.

2. By limiting the degree of change, resistance provides a critical stabilizing influence. Particularly in organizations whose strategic decision makers are impulsive, conservative change-resisters may provide the balance required for survival.

The notion that resistance to change exerts a positive influence upon organizations is seldom emphasized because of the problems caused by such resistance. Why do people resist change? The following include the most common reasons:

1. *Knowledge and skill obsolescence.* In some instances an organizational change makes obsolete the knowledge and skills acquired over a lifetime of experience. Thus, a bookkeeper whose security blanket is the mastery of a complex accounting system is understandably threatened by the change to a computerized system. An employee in a petroleum refinery takes immense pride in the years of experience and responsible service through which the status of senior still operator is reached. Then a change to a totally automated process makes worthless virtually every skill of the senior operator. And, because the new units are controlled by college-educated engineers, retraining and experience can never completely restore the status enjoyed by the operator of the old distillation unit.

2. *Economic loss.* The compensation level of employees and managers whose knowledge and skills have become obsolete is often maintained during a retraining period. Such a practice obviously reduces resistance to change. In many situations, however, retraining is impossible, and a demotion or loss of employment results. The mere possibility of such a loss is enough to cause some resistance. The cynicism employees often feel about change is expressed in an anecdote about suggestion systems. In response to an excellent suggestion the boss says, "Congratulations, Snodgrass, you have just won $25 for your suggestion. It has led to the elimination of five jobs, including your own."

3. *Ego defensiveness.* For five years Elmer Post, the exective vice-president of a plastics firm, was successful in overriding the recommendation of R and D specialists to convert to a vastly superior plastics extrusion process. Why was he so adamantly against it? First, it was not his idea. When the recommendation was initially made, moreover, he went out on a limb in opposition to it. Once that action was taken, he was unable to see the facts objectively because he was afraid of losing face.

4. *Comfort with the status quo.* Change can be disrupting. A break in an established routine may force a person to think instead of daydream, to take risks rather than remain secure, and to work hard instead of loafing.

5. *Cautiousness and conservatism.* Because of personality characteristics, attitudes, and values, many people are predisposed to minimize risks and make changes slowly. Where strategic decision makers have these characteristics, an entire organization may be forced to follow their lead.

6. *Peer pressures.* Because peer cooperation is required for success in many jobs, even highly independent individuals are unable to withstand work group pressures and support organizational change. For this reason obtaining group support for change is usually more effective than soliciting the support of isolated individuals.

7. *Lack of information.* When employees and managers who are affected by a change are ignorant concerning its purpose and implications, they are unlikely to support it. In the absence of information, many people become suspicious and expect the worst to happen.

8. *Social displacement.* The social relationships which develop in the workplace are often more important to employees than commonly realized. Even where employees are fully protected against financial loss because of a change, resistance persists because it threatens to disrupt friendships through which a variety of personal needs are met.

9. *Limited perspective.* High-level managers become critical of subordinate managers when the latter protect their special interests (a specific department, for example) rather than support the whole organization. In one firm, this was expressed in the resistance of the chief financial officer to developing computer programs to provide rapid feedback on budget expenditures. Without full awareness of his own motives, he resisted the change because it would limit the power that he and other members of the accounting department exerted through personal contacts in order to control spending.

10. *Too little time to adapt.* When frequent and rapid changes are made, those affected by them may experience an unhealthy level of stress. Under such circumstances resistance is one means of slowing the process until the changes are assimilated and a degree of equanimity restored.

Traditional Approaches to Change

During the early part of this century, management's approach to change was simple and straightforward. Following classical organizational theory, changes were made by managerial decree with little concern for the response of subordinates. Because managers felt confident of their organizational power, they often misused it. This, in turn, brought aggressive challenges from labor and government. Change by decree is still practiced, but most managers have, at least, learned to be cautious in its use.

Propaganda is a traditional technique for motivating the acceptance of change. Employees who resist innovation are systematically confronted with rumors that the company will be closed or moved to a new location. They are bombarded with information supporting the change and pointing out the dire consequences of resistance. Propaganda may be supported by authoritative statements of consultants and other experts who appear to be objective. Although propaganda has been effective in some circumstances, it lacks the potential of open, two-way communication to establish trust and understanding. Propaganda may reduce resistance to change in the short run while increasing it over a long period of time.

Another power-oriented tactic used to support change is contrived personnel turnover. Employees or managers who resist change are discharged or encouraged to leave the organization. But this, too, proves to be costly. Management's growing dissatisfaction with power tactics for instituting change and the positive influences of the human relations movement have encouraged experimentation with a variety of techniques for management of change.

The greatest challenges to a change-by-decree approach occurred in response to management's practice of unilaterally raising production standards as employees improved their skills and methods. Employees believed that they should reap the benefits of their efforts, through either increased pay or shorter working hours. Management, on the other hand, was committed to increasing productive efficiency and maintaining competitive costs. In this situation, the ability of employees to restrict production, to withhold information about methods improvement, and to undermine change efforts was a formidable barrier to change by decree. Such resistance helped to convince management that changes should be managed with more finesse and greater consideration for the needs and attitudes of those whose cooperation is needed to implement change.

During the 1940s and 1950s, the new look in change management was linked to an emphasis upon participative management. Not surprisingly research studies demonstrated that employees who were given a voice in deciding upon a change were less resistant to its implementation. Some companies, applying their recently acquired knowledge of group dynamics, instituted programs through which employees participated in rule making and standard setting. Although many such efforts have been little more than crude attempts at manipulation, some have been successful. Even where participating employees do not significantly influence a given decision, they at least have an awareness that their voice has been heard. They also understand why management takes a particular course of action.

Training managers in human relations skills, especially at the supervisory level, produced a significant impact upon the management of change. Since willingness to accept change is associated with the effectiveness of superior-subordinate relations, it is understandable that management development (or manager development) should be related to the task of producing change. Manager development is itself a change process which, ideally at least, facilitates other needed changes throughout the organization.

MANAGEMENT DEVELOPMENT: PHILOSOPHY AND GOALS

Thesis: Programs of manager education, skills development, and attitude and behavior change are commonplace in modern organizations. The merits of specific programs in specific situations are justifiably called into question, but some form of continuing management development is a necessary part of organizational life.

Few operating managers or experts in organizational behavior question the importance of management development in principle, although development programs are seldom evaluated by objective methods, and many of the attempts to do so have been characterized by a misleading appearance of quantitative exactness and sophistication of experimental design. Nevertheless, experience with management development programs and both clinical and experimental evaluation of their effects have taught us much about the requirements for effectiveness.

Purposes of Management Development

The purposes of management development may be examined in terms of organizational objectives and the motivations of participants. First, the organization's primary concern is behavior change. The acquisition of knowledge (say about electronic data processing), the modification of attitudes (developing favorable attitudes toward management by objectives, for example), or the acquisition of skills (such as how to negotiate a union contract), are all intended to change behavior. Specifically, the organization is concerned with behavior change which will make a manager more effective in working with or through others to achieve organizational goals.

Although managers typically support organizational goals and value development for its own sake, they have additional, uniquely personal motives for seeking development opportunities. Development opportunities are an expected form of compensation because they increase the probability that a manager will receive raises and promotions. Development provides a hedge against managerial obsolescence and contributes to the sense of security and independence managers experience when their services are in high demand. Opportunites for growth are sometimes more influential than salary in a manager's decision to accept or continue in a position. An organization must develop its managers in order to be effective in manager recruitment and avoid excessive management turnover.

Training versus Development

During the early days of the human relations movement, the terms *supervisory training* and *management training* were commonly used. They are still used to some extent, but they are not in vogue. Training tends to convey the notion of the acquisition of skills. For example, we train employees to assemble a unit of production or to operate a machine. Perhaps because of the use of the word in connection with animal training, it is implied that the trainer, one who possesses superior knowledge and skills, is the thinking, active member of the team while the one being trained is acted upon. In contrast, the term *management development* is intended to imply that the changes which occur involve the total person.

Although line managers [1] are responsible for encouraging management development, they do not, in a strict sense, develop their subordinates. All that line managers can do is to encourage self-development and to provide opportunities for it. Thus, in the final analysis, management development is always self-development. It is not something one person can do to or for another.

Some Generalizations about Management Development

Considering the great variety of management development programs and the even greater variety of development needs, it would be presumptuous to compile a set of management development principles. We can, however, draw some generalizations which cut across the different methods and provide criteria against which their merits can be assessed.

1. *Providing feedback on performance.* Programs which provide a knowledge of results are essential for meaningful change. A major reason that managers fail to change is inadequate knowledge of the consequences of past behavior.

2. *Tailoring to the individual.* The development needs of managers differ greatly—so much so that a program (sensitivity training, for example) which is helpful to one manager may hurt another. Development programs should be matched with the carefully diagnosed needs of individual managers.

3. *Relating to the power structure.* What a manager learns will be of minimal value unless the reward structure of the organization is favorable to its implementation. Some managers, for example, learn to appreciate the virtues of participative leadership only to have all efforts to practice it undermined by their superiors. Supervisor rewards or punishments often have more to do with whether an act will be practiced than do the intrinsic merits of the act itself.

---

[1] Although staff managers, usually personnel specialists, may spend most or all their time conducting management development programs, line management must assume ultimate responsibility. Because of the importance of superior-subordinate relations, it is difficult to establish staff accountability.

4. *Selection and development.* Selection and development are closely related functions in that selection limits development potential. Development dollars may be wasted on managers who are deficient in intelligence, general education, motivation to lead, emotional maturity, and other characteristics which are related to managerial effectiveness.

There are other limits within which management development may take place. Harvard professor J. Sterling Livingston and others emphasize the importance of teaching managers to manage in ways that are consistent with their individual personalities.

One of the least rational acts of business organizations is that of hiring managers who have a high need to exercise authority, and then teaching them that authoritative methods are wrong and that they should be consultative or participative.[2]

5. *Motivational factors in development.* A manager's motivation to develop into an effective manager may exert a more critical influence upon development than the methods used. Livingston supports the notion that the *way* to manage can usually be found if there is a *will* to manage. The person who is lacking in this motivation will not invest the time, energy, and thought required to increase his or her managerial effectiveness.[3]

6. *A continuing activity.* Management development is never completed. Through on-the-job experience and formal development programs, a manager must continue to learn and change or accept the fact that obsolescence has begun.

What appears to be a need for management development may be a need for modifying the organization. The environment within which managers work may place such great demands upon them that no amount of motivation or competence will enable them to perform adequately. This may be the case, for example, where a chief executive sets the pace with poor delegation, inconsistent policies, and poorly formulated goals. For this reason, the development of managers is related to other forms of change within the organization. This theme is expanded later in this chapter under the topic of Organization Development (OD).

MANAGEMENT DEVELOPMENT METHODS

Thesis: Since the needs of managers differ greatly, there is no one *best* development method. The effectiveness of a given method also depends upon the skills and personality of the management development specialist applying it. These and other variables must be considered when deciding upon the method to be used.

---

[2] Sterling Livingston, "Myth of the Well-Educated Manager," *Harvard Business Review,* Vol. 49, No. 1 (January–February, 1971), p. 87.

[3] Ibid., p. 85.

The brief descriptions of management development methods which are presented in this section are intended to present a summary of the salient features of each method and to provide resource guidelines for persons who are interested in studying the subject in greater depth. Since virtually every manager is charged with the responsibility of providing growth opportunities for subordinates, this is a skill in which all managers should develop competence.

On-the-Job Development Programs

Management development which occurs on the job is generally preferred to off-the-job methods.[4] The former can more readily be tailored to the needs of individuals, and it takes advantage of the identification and authority relationships which exist between superior and subordinate. These and other benefits of on-the-job methods can be seen in the descriptions presented here.

Experience as a Developer of Managers.   Is experience really the best teacher? Certainly it is not always the best. There are some attributes, however, which are likely to be developed only through experience. One of these is decision-making ability. Methods of gathering and analyzing data can be learned in formal courses and simulation exercises, but there is no substitute for making real-life decisions where the data are incomplete and the risks are high. Likewise, the development of poise and self-confidence in stress-provoking situations is unlikely to occur except through experience.

Not all experiences, on the other hand, are helpful. Some destroy self-confidence, teach ineffective leadership styles, and create attitudes and habits that thwart managerial effectiveness. Because on-the-job experience can be either good or bad and because it may or may not meet the needs of a specific manager, progressive organizations structure a manager's experience to provide optimal opportunities for self-development.

Job Rotation.   A manager who has worked in one position for ten years may actually have only one year of experience ten times. Programmed job rotation occurs at the entry level where management trainees, ordinarily recent college graduates, are rotated through several short-term assignments. Some companies rotate middle managers in a similar way. A line manager, for example, may be transferred from general management of Plant A to the same position in Plant B, to staff assistant to the president, to a trouble-shooting position in manufacturing, and then to a similar position in accounting. Companies that follow this practice recognize that a manager loses some effectiveness when a new job is begun but believe that the loss is offset by the development benefits. Moving costs and disruption of family life are further disadvantages, but job rotation is excellent for creating generalists with unusual potential for top management. Job rotation also develops an appreciation of the unique problems of different posi-

---

[4] See Yoram Zeira, "Introduction of On-the-Job Management Development," *Personnel Journal,* Vol. 52, No. 12 (December, 1973), pp. 1049–1055.

tions and contributes to a cross-fertilization of ideas. It greatly reduces the likelihood that a manager will stagnate in one job and habitually resist change.

Coaching.   Many of the disadvantages of unplanned on-the-job experience can be overcome through coaching. The "coach," usually a manager's immediate superior, systematically provides feedback on performance, assists in planning for self-development, provides guidelines for goal setting, and counsels the subordinate on specific problems.

The effectiveness of coaching depends primarily upon the skills of the coach and the amount of time and effort devoted to the task. Levinson elaborates on this point:

> The coaching and appraisal process, as usually carried out in United States business, falls short of the mark because it does not support strong relationships and contacts between a boss and his subordinates.
>
> Among the most important reasons for this failure are that most line executives do not give enough time and thought to working with their juniors; the climate in business is not tolerant enough of mistakes and individual needs to learn; and rivalry between bosses and subordinates tends to be repressed instead of acknowledged.[5]

Because a wide range of development techniques may be used in coaching, managers need special training to be effective. Motivation to develop subordinates must be strong, however, before the techniques will be consistently used. This means that the organization's reward systems should make the development of subordinates profitable.

Management Counseling.   Some of the shortcomings of coaching, primarily a lack of time and expertise, are overcome by the use of outside consultants for the individualized development of managers. The specialist, often a professional industrial psychologist, performs a coaching function, as just described. DuBrin describes, in addition, a unique role the management counselor plays as an executive confidant.[6] High-level managers, in particular, sometimes lead a lonely life and need an outsider with whom they can vent their feelings of frustration and confidentially discuss problems and proposed actions.

The roles of management counselors, who may spend from a half day a month to full time counseling the managers of an organization, vary significantly. Some, with a background in clinical or counseling psychology, inadvertently gravitate toward personal problems counseling, including marital counseling, and neglect their primary goal of management development. Management counselors

---

[5] Harry Levinson, "A Psychologist Looks at Executive Development," originally published in Gene W. Dalton, Paul R. Lawrence, and Larry E. Greiner (eds.), *Organizational Change and Development* (Homewood, Ill.: Richard D. Irwin, Inc., and Dorsey Press, 1970), p. 259.

[6] Andrew J. DuBrin, *The Practice of Managerial Psychology* (Elmsford, N.Y.: Pergamon Press, Inc., 1972), p. 89.

with educational backgrounds in management or industrial psychology are more apt to avoid personal problems and concentrate on job-related problems.

One industrial psychologist, who serves as a management counselor in as many as 10 to 15 different companies simultaneously, makes use of an "Inventory of Management Behavior" to obtain descriptions of managers' behavior by subordinates, peers, superiors, and the managers themselves. Discrepancies between self-perceptions and the perceptions of others are used as a starting point for development. The manager with an unrealistic self-perception as an excellent delegator, for example, is given support in understanding delegation, in exploring the causes of his or her own failure to delegate, and in making the appropriate behavior modification.

Management counselors, like management coaches, use a variety of development techniques, including many which are described later in this chapter as OD (Organization Development) interventions. Counselors with broad business experience may also play substantial roles as advisors on matters relating to selection, development, motivational systems, disciplinary problems, supervisory practices, morale, and other areas in which they are competent.

Questions of ethics sometimes arise when clients become increasingly dependent upon the counselor's services rather than growing in self-reliance. Management counselors often accept positions in line management or management development within their client companies, posing interesting questions of ethics, especially when the consulting firm loses a client in the transaction.

The Critical Incidents Technique.   During World War II and the following decade, extensive research was conducted on a development technique in which managers are given continual feedback on "critical behaviors." Research is conducted to develop a list of positive and negative behaviors which are critical to the successful performance of a given job. On the supervisory level, for example, a negative critical behavior might be "Criticized the work of a subordinate in the presence of other employees." A positive behavior might be "Effectively involved subordinates in problem solving" or "Took the initiative to solve a long-standing problem."

After the instrument is developed, the superior systematically makes a record as critical behaviors are observed. Continual feedback then provides a basis for behavior change. Although this method is not widely used, its results have been impressive, and the principles upon which it is based are sound. It takes place on the job and makes use of the organization's power structure. It provides regular feedback. The feedback deals with behavior. It provides for positive reinforcement of desirable behaviors as well as for discouragement of the undesirable. Since the evaluation factor is built into the instrument, the manager need only observe and make a record of behavior rather than constantly make value judgments. In view of the current emphasis upon behavior modification, the Critical Incidents method should increasingly be given high marks as a development method.

This Critical Incidents technique is obviously different from the technique used at the ends of the chapters of this textbook. The latter is an abbreviated form of case study. The former is basically a feedback device concerned with very specific, critical behaviors. Although both deal with incidents which are critical to managerial effectiveness, they are distinctly different methods.

Special Projects.   Managers are in a unique position to use special projects to develop their subordinates in areas of recognized deficiency. Two diverse examples will show the nature and purpose of this technique. In the first situation, a young supervisor with a poor record of solving disciplinary problems was assigned the task of making a proposal to a supervisory development group in which he was a participant. His task was to study various methods of handling disciplinary problems, evaluate them, and make a written and oral presentation on the merits of different methods.

The second case involves a middle manager with an outstanding background in sales but a notable weakness in accounting and finance. In addition to recommending that this man take correspondence courses in the areas of accounting and finance, his superior placed him on a committee assigned to study the budgeting procedure and to recommend improvements. The assumption was that this experience would increase his awareness of and appreciation for the importance of financial controls.

Goal Setting.   Although goal setting is ordinarily associated with an organization's planning and motivational systems, it is also related to management development. Given that the organization's primary objective in developing managers is goal-oriented behavior change, it is logical to believe that goal clarification might be helpful. Critics of management development often raise questions about the relevance of the changes which occur within managers, especially in the case of attitude-change programs. Goal clarification helps a manager to know when an attitude or behavior change is relevant to improved effectiveness and when it is relevant only to the limited objectives of the development program itself. A program may be eminently successful in teaching a given skill, but unless the skill is needed for improved present or future performance, the development investment is not justified.

As indicated in Chapter 7, when managers become increasingly goal-oriented, certain changes occur in their perceptual and thought processes as well as in the results they achieve. For example, goal setting broadens a manager's perspective, focuses attention upon relevant problems, enhances leadership ability, and improves the quality of decisions. Since these and other changes associated with goal setting are sought in management development programs, it follows that an effective goals program, normally established to increase productivity, may serve as an outstanding development method.

Understudy Positions.   In many organizations, managers are given assignments as assistants or assistants-to, primarily for the developmental value of the positions. Ordinarily an *assistant* (say assistant general manager) occupies a line position while an *assistant-to* is considered to be staff. Thus, the assistant-to may be a young trainee, but an assistant is normally next in line for the superior's position or one which is comparable.

The assistant position has the advantage of allowing the understudy to assume responsibility, make decisions, and take risks. The main advantage of the assistant-to position is that the young manager has an opportunity to serve as an understudy long before he or she is capable of assuming heavy responsibility. Both provide an opportunity to study the behavior of a manager with more experience, to observe organizational life at a higher level, and to form personal identification with superiors which will potentially facilitate the acquisition of managerial skills. The effectiveness of understudy positions, however, depends greatly upon the concern of the superior for the understudy's development and the suitability of the former as a managerial model.

Off-the-Job Development Programs

If all development programs had to be of one type, either on or off the job, the former would be preferable. Fortunately the two are complementary. At times managers need to get away from the job in order to gain perspective. It is important that they exchange ideas with managers from other organizations and learn from behavioral scientists, technical specialists, and others whose viewpoints differ from their own.

Development Sites.   Off-the-job development programs ordinarily take place in one of three sites: (1) the organization's own facilities, (2) a university continuing education center, or (3) a location selected by a private management development firm. Most large organizations have a staff of professionals who do nothing but conduct development programs for first-line supervisors and middle managers. Organizations which have extensive in-house programs are also the best clients of university programs and private development firms.

Universities offer a variety of programs tailored to the needs of operating managers and ranging in length from a few hours to several months. Most of these programs avoid traditional testing and grading. Although a wide variety of methods are employed, most university programs take advantage of the broad experience of participants by providing time for information sharing.

During the past twenty-five years, a number of private organizations have been formed to offer seminars and laboratories on subjects of current interest to managers. Several of these advertise nationally through direct mail and locate their seminars in major cities across the country. Small firms, sometimes consisting of only an individual, offer courses within limited geographical areas. Some firms periodically offer seminars in which managers from different companies participate, while others tailor programs to meet the needs of selected groups within a single organization. The largest private organization in the development field is the American Management Association. In addition to providing seminars in its home office in New York City and in large cities across the United States, the AMA is a major publisher of management literature.

Conference Method.   The conference or discussion format is intended to provide maximum opportunity for participants to test their ideas, ask questions, exchange information, and challenge concepts which are presented in lectures or printed materials. The conference method holds the attention of participants over long periods of time and elicits a high degree of emotional involvement. If poorly managed, however, it can be a disaster. Unless a means is provided for injecting a core of valid and challenging information into the conference, it sometimes degenerates into an unorganized discussion session in which participants share their collective ignorance.

Although widely differing conference leadership styles may be effective, the skill of the leader is a major factor in the success of a conference. Some leaders play a *content* role; that is, they become involved in the content of the discussion: supplying information, questioning, challenging, and persuading. They also keep the discussion on track, making sure all conference members have an opportunity to participate, summarizing points of view, minimizing the unhealthy effects of arguments, and making sure the subject matter is covered. Leaders who play the *process role* limit their involvement to the latter functions (i.e., keeping the discussion on track and the like).

It takes greater skill to be successful in the content role. The possibility is always present that the content leader will dominate the conference and elicit too little participation. On the other hand, it is wasteful for a leader's expertise to be suppressed because of a commitment to the process role.

Case Study and Role Playing.   Case studies have been used extensively in management development programs in many settings. Although many variations of the method are used, the essentials are the same. Participants are presented with the details of a management problem (in human relations, finance, production, or marketing, for example) to which each arrives at a solution. The solutions are then discussed, along with the assumptions, methods of analysis, and the logic upon which they are based. In some treatments of case studies, participants may receive additional information upon request. Out of the total experience, they gain insights into their own biases, strengths and weaknesses, and typical modes of solving problems. They also learn through observing how others interpret and solve those same problems.

A major advantage of the case method is that it focuses attention upon problem situations rather than upon theory and principles. Supposedly insights gained in this way are more likely to be applied on the job than are those acquired through more abstract methods. Managers are often frustrated by the fact that no "correct" solutions are provided to case problems. Real-life problems offer the same frustration, however. The case study method is more concerned with the process through which solutions are reached than with the solutions themselves.

Role playing is often used in conjunction with case studies. In a case involving disciplinary action, for example, two managers may act out a proposed solution and then switch roles so that each can experience the feelings elicited by the proposed action. Role playing can be highly realistic or so phony as to be embarrassing to participants. The skill of the leader and the psychological climate within the development group are critical determinants of its success.

Case studies and role playing are used extensively. They are not ideal for every situation, but they are proved and valuable techniques when used properly.

Business Games. Like case studies and role playing, business games are simulated or reconstructed representations of some aspect of organizational life to which participants are asked to react. Business games describe a situation in case study form but go further to describe a set of rules and relationships concerning the relevant aspects of the problem. For example, participants may be supplied with information concerning product costs, company goals, finances, market conditions, and the actions of competitors.

The objectives of business games are to familiarize participants with the complex, interacting factors involved in a functioning organization and to develop decision-making skills. Participants play the game by making decisions concerning investments, expenditures, production, inventory, and the like. Computers provide rapid feedback on the result of each decision, and competing teams continue to make decisions for a specified period or until a trend develops. Then the results and decision processes are discussed, and the critical points are highlighted.

Some business games are quite realistic, but they are no substitute for actual decision making because the risk factors are different. Participants who are the most analytical and scholarly perform well on business games, but they may or may not have the quality of toughness required to perform in the real world. Also, some participants are able to make good decisions in a business game by deciphering the decision strategies which would be effective in real organizations. All things considered, however, business games are an excellent and extensively used development technique.

In-Basket Problems. The manner in which managers handle their in-basket items (such as routine correspondence, grievances, directives, customer complaints, reports, and requests for information or action) reveals much about their leadership and decision styles, human relations skills, personal organization, ability to communicate, and other characteristics. In-basket simulations provide development specialists with insights that are valuable in diagnosing a manager's development needs and serve as a point of reference for developmental counseling.

A professionally designed in-basket problem comes close to providing an actual job sample. Although, at this point in the method's evolution, it is more often used as a selection than a development tool, its potential for the latter is high.

Behavior Modification. The human relations movement made the point that external control through fear has serious limitations. Specifically, control through fear requires close supervision, causes resentment, and is less effective than control which results from internalized goals and favorable attitudes. Thus, the primary target of the human relations movement was attitude change.

In recent years, however, it has become obvious that favorable attitudes do not automatically lead to improved performance. High job satisfaction may result in a country club atmosphere rather than in increased productivity. These facts, together with a predisposition to think in behavioral terms, led some researchers to conclude that if behavior change is the ultimate goal of development it may as well be the immediate target. Further research disclosed that attitude change often follows behavior change—that once behavior is changed, attitude changes tend to follow in order to remove the cognitive dissonance and restore an internal equilibrium.[7]

There are many ways to approach development from a behavioral point of view, but they have in common the application of learning principles. In particular they focus on reinforcement theory. People learn to repeat those behaviors that are rewarded and to drop from use those which are not rewarded or which are punished. The following quotation from Goldstein and Sorcher is a concise statement of one behavioral approach to training and development:

> Specifically, we have defined and implemented Applied Learning as consisting of (1) modeling, (2) role playing, (3) social reinforcement, and (4) transfer training. That is, Applied Learning involves providing the trainee with numerous, vivid, detailed displays (on film, videotape, or live) of a manager-actor (the model) performing the specific behaviors and skills we wish the viewer to learn (i.e., *modeling*); giving the trainee considerable guidance in and opportunity and encouragement for behaviorally rehearsing or practicing the behaviors he has seen the model perform (i.e., *role playing*); providing him with positive feedback, approval or reward as his role playing enactments increasingly approximate the behavior of the model (i.e., *social reinforcement*); and implementing these three procedures in such a manner as to maximize the likelihood that what the trainee learns in the classroom will in fact be applied in a stable and consistent manner on the job (i.e., *transfer training*).[8]

A number of organizations, including the American Telephone and Telegraph Company, have successfully used this technique. The principles are simple but sound. They are, however, more appropriate for teaching specific skills (e.g., handling grievances and conducting post-appraisal interviews) than they are for developing complex abilities such as decision making. In terms of the way training and development were defined earlier, behavior modification is more a training than a development technique.

Behavior technology is improving, however, and is now being applied in "self-shaping" programs with middle managers. In such programs, the participants establish their own target behaviors, methods of measuring and recording behavior change, schedules of reinforcement, and means of receiving feedback on performance. In other words, they decide upon certain desired behavior changes and follow a systematic approach to achieving them.

---

[7] See Arnold P. Goldstein and Melvin Sorcher, "Changing Managerial Behavior by Applied Learning Techniques," *Training and Development Journal,* Vol. 27, No. 3 (March, 1973), pp. 36–39. (References to background literature are included.)

[8] Ibid., p. 37.

Laboratory Training. Since the late 1940s, when laboratory training (also called T-group and sensitivity training) was first used as a management development method, it has been the subject of continual controversy. Although there are many variations and applications of laboratory training, the outcomes most often sought are (1) increased self-awareness, (2) the development of sensitivity to the needs and behavior of others, (3) the clarification of personal values and goals, (4) insight into the nature of group forces upon individual growth and decision-making processes, and (5) the resolution of conflict.

The leader of a T-group always plays the process role. The group members are usually from different organizations and thus constitute a "stranger group." The sessions are often begun with a minimum of structure and without explicit goals. From a relatively innocuous beginning in which group members introduce themselves, there is a gradual deepening of relationships until members disclose their normally hidden feelings, attitudes, beliefs, and self-perceptions. Feedback provides participants with a unique opportunity to view themselves through the eyes of others to whom their inner selves have been laid bare.

One of the strongest criticisms of sensitivity training is that the outcome is unpredictable. In rare instances, the trauma of self-disclosure and feedback has even lead to a psychotic break. In other instances, managers have decided that the pressures of business life are too great and have returned to their organizations only to turn in their resignations. For some managers, no doubt, the objectives of sensitivity training have been fully realized and expressed in constructive on-the-job behavioral changes. Many of those for whom sensitivity training was a waste of time should never have become involved in it. Especially for some of the early programs, participant screening was poor or nonexistent. In addition, group leaders have sometimes shown little awareness of the objectives of management development.

Sensitivity training reached its crest of popularity in the 1960s. A 1974 mail survey conducted in 300 business firms throughout the United States led University of Cincinnati researchers William Kearney and Desmond Martin to conclude:

> At present this development tool is not an important part of the corporate development programs surveyed, nor does it emerge as being a significant part of future plans. Rather, it appears to be a tool created and refined by a few behavioral scientists to achieve ends that are difficult to measure and evaluate. Some comments from the respondents lean favorably to the T-group approach, but they reflect improvements within the organization that are hard to define. This fact could be sensitivity training's greatest liability. Although behavioral scientists may like to experiment with this tool in the research setting, the pragmatic training director has difficulty concluding that it is an effective means for developing managers.[9]

---

[9] William J. Kearney and Desmond D. Martin, "Sensitivity Training: An Established Management Development Tool?" *Academy of Management Journal,* Vol. 17, No. 4 (December, 1974), pp. 755–759.

Sensitivity training has fallen under increasingly heavy criticism during the 1970s. It is, nevertheless, a method which has been extensively used to develop managers. Had it been used only with managers who needed it and by competent professionals rather than amateurs exploiting its commercial potential, its reputation today would, no doubt, be more favorable. There is a place for sensitivity training, but it is more limited than it first appeared to be.

THE ORGANIZATION DEVELOPMENT (OD) APPROACH TO CHANGE[10]

Thesis: An organization development approach to change is committed to a Theory Y view of people, to the notion that strategies for change should involve the total organization rather than be focused upon individual managers, and to a belief that planned change should be a continual process. At this stage of its development, OD is making a significant contribution but is falling far short of its potential and professed ideals.

Organization development began in 1946 through the work of Gestalt psychologist Kurt Lewin and his associates at The Research Center for Group Dynamics (Massachusetts Institute of Technology) although the name itself did not appear in published literature until ten years later. In addition to the impetus given by Lewin and associates, organization development grew out of the laboratory training movement and the development of survey research and feedback methodology.[11]

OD: Definition and Values

Warner Burke, of the National Training Laboratory for Applied Behavioral Science, defines OD as ". . . a planned, sustained effort to change an organization's culture."[12] In this context, an organization's *culture* refers to the norms which regulate member behavior; the organization's purpose, policies, and values; its channels of communication; centers and modes of influence; and the psychological climate which determines the roles and relationships of organizational members.

In a Conference Board research report, Harold Rush expands Burke's definition to include a statement of purpose.

---

[10] Organization Development cannot be explained fully in the short space allotted to it in this chapter. For an in-depth presentation of the field, read Newton Margulies and Anthony P. Raia, *Organization Development: Values, Process, and Technology* (New York: McGraw-Hill, Inc., 1972).

[11] Wendell French and Cecil Bell, "A Brief History of Organization Development," *Journal of Contemporary Business,* Volume 1, No. 3 (Summer, 1972), pp. 1–3.

[12] W. Warner Burke, "The Demise of Organizational Development," *Journal of Contemporary Business* (Summer, 1972), p. 57.

> OD . . . is a planned, managed, systematic process to change the culture, systems, and behavior of an organization, in order to improve the organization's effectiveness in solving its problems and achieving its objectives.[13]

Although there is no universally accepted definition of organization development, Rush's definition may be deficient in omitting reference to an objective of satisfying the needs of the organization's members. Like the human relations movement, to which OD is closely related, organization development is strongly committed to the individual, to collaboration between employees and management, and specifically to employee participation through group involvement.

An OD *change agent* (OD process leader), unlike the typical management development specialist, is identified with a specific value system. Margulies and Raia state the OD values as

1. Providing opportunities for people to function as human beings rather than as resources in the productive process

2. Providing opportunities for each organization member, as well as for the organization itself, to develop to his full potential

3. Seeking to increase the effectiveness of the organization in terms of *all* of its goals

4. Attempting to create an environment in which it is possible to find exciting and challenging work

5. Providing opportunities for people in organizations to influence the way in which they relate to work, the organization, and the environment

6. Treating each human being as a person with a complex set of needs, *all* of which are important in his work and in his life.[14]

Since some organizations are not committed to all these values, OD specialists are unable to function effectively in all organizations. Management must be strongly committed to a Theory Y view of human nature and to the philosophy of management which generally characterized the human relations movement. In spite of protestations to the contrary, OD specialists often seem to be excessively concerned with employee need satisfaction and too little concerned with productivity.

OD Interventions

Because organization development is concerned with improvement of the total organizational culture, OD authors are apt to refer to virtually any means of influencing the organization as an *OD intervention*. According to French and

---

[13] Harold M. F. Rush, *Organization Development: A Reconnaissance* (New York: The Conference Board, Inc., 1973), p. i.

[14] Margulies and Raia, op. cit. p. 3.

Bell, an OD intervention refers to "the range of planned programmatic activities clients and consultants participate in during the course of an organization development program."[15] Recent literature makes reference to management by objectives and job enrichment as OD interventions. They would qualify under the above definition, but neither has historically been identified exclusively with the OD movement.

Sensitivity training is the intervention with the longest history of identification with OD. Other interventions, most of which involve sensitivity training, are briefly described below.

1. *The Grid OD Method.* The Managerial Grid, described and illustrated in Chapter 10, is used to identify the degrees of concern participating managers have for people and for production. The Grid OD method is not, however, limited to the use of this one instrument as the name would seem to imply. Other instruments used for analysis are in-baskets and organizational simulations. Analyses are also conducted of the team effectiveness of work groups, long-range planning, union-management relations, incentive systems, and other organizational variables. Over a three-to five-year period, a six-phased program, including such interventions as sensitivity training, goal setting, and team development, are used to bring about the desired changes in individuals and the organization.[16]

2. *Team Building.* The purpose of team building is to improve the effectiveness and performance of people who work together on a daily basis. Unlike traditional staff meetings, the sessions may last from two to five days and attention is focused on personal relationships within the group as well as upon group goals, work distribution, and how the group functions in order to reach its objectives (i.e., procedures, processes, and norms). The group is led by an OD change agent, and the sessions themselves are likely to involve a T-group format.[17]

3. *Confrontation Meetings.* The purpose of confrontation meetings is to resolve conflict between individuals and/or groups. In one version of this technique, the OD specialist obtains written descriptions from each group member of his or her perceptions of the members of the other group. These are exchanged for study and are followed by T-group meetings to clarify problems and find solutions.

4. *Survey and Feedback Technique.* Data concerning attitudes and perceptions of personnel toward various aspects of the organization are obtained through questionnaires, interviews, direct observation, and other means.

---

[15] Wendell L. French and Cecil H. Bell, Jr., *Organization Development: Behavioral Science Interventions for Organization Improvement* (Englewood Cliffs, N.J.: Prentice-Hall, Inc., 1973), p. 97.

[16] R. R. Blake, et al., "Breakthrough in Organization Development," *Harvard Business Review,* Vol. 42, No. 6 (November-December, 1964), pp. 133–155.

[17] For a description of the team-building purpose and process, see Richard Beckhard, "Optimizing Team-Building Efforts," *Journal of Contemporary Business,* Vol. 1, No. 3 (Summer, 1972), pp. 23–32.

The information is presented to the individuals from whom it was obtained in a variety of ways, and T-Group interventions are used to change attitudes, improve communication, and plan organizational changes.

These are just a few of the many interventions employed by OD specialists. Laboratory exercises have been produced in great numbers and generously shared by OD practitioners.[18]

Evaluation of OD

Organization development specialists make no claim that their discipline has fully matured. They are, in fact, quite introspective and aware of the many discrepancies between their ideals and their performance. The following criticisms are offered by researchers and theorists who are identified with OD.

1. Although OD claims to take a systems approach, in practice OD specialists are most often involved in localized, fragmented studies such as reducing the conflict between two work groups.[19] OD projects theoretically consist of long-term, continuing, and coordinated interventions; but to date most have been short term.

2. OD practitioners do not have sufficient knowledge of and appreciation for the role power plays in the functioning of an organization.

3. Specialists in OD should expand their knowledge and skills to include a broad base of management theory and practice and should avoid overreliance upon sensitivity training as an intervention.[20]

4. Although OD authors sometimes imply that the contrary is true, organization development is not a clearly defined discipline in terms of theory or practice.

5. The education available for OD practitioners leaves something to be desired. Most universities have been reluctant to institute professional degree programs in the area.

6. OD practitioners tend to limit themselves to a few techniques such as laboratory training, surveys, and team building. In reality, there are many other ways to change organizations. Change may be effected, for example, through modifying the work flow or organization structure.[21]

7. OD change agents usually content themselves with expressing their humanistic values in areas of job satisfaction, motivation, and productivity

---

[18] Through the efforts of two men, J. William Pfeiffer and John E. Jones, many of the more commonly used laboratory exercises have been published in booklet and ring-binder form for use by OD practitioners and others. For information, contact University Associates Press, P. O. Box 615, Iowa City, Iowa 52240.

[19] For a sensitive critique by a respected "insider," see Burke, op.cit.

[20] See Anthony P. Raia, "Organizational Development—Some Issues and Challenges," *California Management Review,* Vol. 14, No. 4 (Summer, 1974), pp. 13–20.

[21] Ibid., p. 18.

"without becoming involved in resource allocation, availability of equipment, choice of supervisors, content of jobs, allocation of rewards, and the like." [22]

Although all these criticisms are valid, the last one is probably the most significant. If carried to its logical conclusion, it supports the generalization that OD is a poorly delineated, fledgling discipline which purports to take a systems approach to organizational change but actually operates on the periphery. If and when OD specialists become sophisticated in their understanding of the role of power in organizations, greatly expand their methodologies, and begin to operate at the center rather than on the periphery of organizations, they will no longer be OD specialists. They will have become integrated into a large group of eclectic, systems-oriented behavioral science practitioners concerned with management development and organizational effectiveness.

Probably the most serious problem with OD is the narrowness it must maintain in order to continue its identification as an independent discipline. If it continues on its present course, organization development's greatest contribution will lie in the techniques it contributes to management specialists whose horizons are not limited by an identification with OD.

STUDY AND DISCUSSION QUESTIONS

1. At all levels of an organization, there are employees who resist change. What are the positive and the negative implications of this?
2. What experiences were most instrumental in convincing management that the power approach to instituting organizational change should be limited?
3. What relationships exist between the development of managers and effecting change in organizations?
4. How is management development most directly influenced by an organization's (a) power structure, (b) methods of management selection, and (c) motivational systems?
5. Evaluate the following statement as it applies to management development: Experience is the best teacher.
6. What are the similarities and differences between management coaching and counseling?
7. What are the relative merits of on-the-job and off-the-job management development programs?
8. What arguments can be made for concentrating management development efforts on behavior rather than attitudes?
9. Describe and evaluate sensitivity training.

---

[22] Robert L. Kahn, "Organizational Development: Some Problems and Proposals," *Journal of Applied Behavioral Science,* Vol. 10, No. 4 (October–December, 1974), p. 499. Robert L. Kahn is Director, Survey Research Center, Institute for Social Research, The University of Michigan.

10. Organization development is committed to a rather specific system of values. How might this orientation limit the practice of OD?

CRITICAL INCIDENT

The Big Change

In many ways, the Dameron Manufacturing Company in 1977 was amazingly like the one Charles Dameron founded in 1918. It was still family owned, had no union, and was conservatively and paternalistically managed. The company adapted to changes slowly, but it remained a profitable operation.

In 1947, the company had sent some of its first-line supervisors to a human relations training program, but management was negatively impressed with the "liberal" ideas with which they were indoctrinated. As a result, all supervisory training was conducted in-house for the next thirty years. In 1977, labor problems and conflicts between the foremen and the personnel department led management to enroll the Company's seventeen supervisors in a five-day human relations seminar. The change of policy was initiated by the president. General superintendent Kent Duran liked the new policy, however, and selected for his subordinates an outstanding program. To avoid having too many supervisors away from the factory at once, two were sent to each monthly seminar.

Robert Bass, a young supervisor who had received two years of community college education before joining the company, returned from the seminar excited about what he had learned, especially the parts about delegating decision making to the lowest feasible level, giving employees an opportunity to assume maximum responsibility, and establishing channels of open communication with employees.

After the Friday afternoon session, Bass discussed some of his ideas with Duran and his immediate superior. Both seemed genuinely pleased to learn that he had profited from the seminar.

When Bass returned to work on Monday morning, he discovered that numerous problems had to be dealt with, a report was due, and several employees needed to talk with him about various matters. It was Friday afternoon before Bass realized that he had not yet been able to make the changes about which he had become so enthusiastic. By this time, the frustrations of the week had taken the edge off his enthusiasm, and he became preoccupied with the pleasant thought of a relaxed weekend with his family. Monday morning would be a good time to begin the new approach.

Questions

1. What is the probability that the "outstanding" training program will change behavior?
2. What factors in this organization function as a deterrent to change?
3. What, if any, OD interventions would you recommend in this situation?
4. What two or three first steps would you recommend to stimulate lasting changes in supervisory behavior?

Chapter

18

Relating to

Disadvantaged Groups

Large organizations function effectively only when subdivided into relatively small units—into divisions, districts, departments, and work units, for example. Each of these groups is differentiated from the others by its function, center of power, location, product, and other attributes. Such groups are contrived and rational. They are planned to achieve specific objectives, and collectively they make up the formal organization.

Chapter 4 explained that as formal organizations grow, informal groups spontaneously emerge to meet a wide variety of individual needs. In this chapter, we look at still another basis for the grouping of employees in organizations. These groups share one feature: each is, to some degree, a victim of prejudice and discrimination within the formal organization. They are commonly referred to as *disadvantaged* groups.

Collectively members of disadvantaged groups constitute a majority of the nation's work force. Of the four groups discussed in this chapter—minorities, women, the aging, and the emotionally maladjusted—the first three have been given special legal protection against discrimination. Two groups not discussed in this chapter, the very young members of the work force and the hard core unemployed (marginal employables), are also at a disadvantage in the workplace. The most disadvantaged individuals in both of the latter groups are also members of racial or ethnic minority groups.

Although the categories discussed in this chapter overlap and interact, they are treated as separate groups for purposes of discussion. Difficulties are compounded, however, for persons who are members of more than one disadvantaged group. This is reflected in a statement attributed to singer-comedian Sammy Davis, Jr. When asked if he ever felt the effects of prejudice, he reportedly answered, "Well, I'll put it to you this way. How would you feel if you were a small, Jewish, one-eyed black man?" One way to profit from this chapter is, as far as possible, to step into the shoes of disadvantaged persons and try to feel, as well as understand, the problems they face.

389

PREJUDICE AND DISCRIMINATION

Thesis: Since discrimination involves the act of making distinctions and recognizing differences, it is a necessary aspect of managerial decision making. Thus, a manager should not avoid discrimination but should discriminate on the basis of criteria, which are relevant to the achievement of organizational objectives, which are fair, and which show a respect for human rights.

A serious indictment against management is the lack of employee confidence that its personnel decisions are impartial. The strength of unionism can be traced, in part, to the fact that managerial decisions about personnel often involve prejudice, ignorance, and seeming disregard for rationality, objectivity, and individual rights. At no point did classical theory prove to be more idealistic and naive than in its assumption that managers would make unbiased decisions about people merely because it is the rational thing to do. The insistence of some employee groups upon the seniority rule as a criterion for personnel decisions reflects a lack of confidence in management's ability or willingness to discriminate fairly.

Prejudice in Decision Making

To say that a personnel decision shows prejudice implies that the decision maker's negative attitudes toward an individual or group results in unfair discrimination. Extensive prejudice toward minority groups such as blacks, Catholics, and Jews is common in our society and has been harmful both to individual victims and to society as a whole.

Prejudice is not, of course, the exclusive property of majority groups. Some members of minority groups have developed bitter and hostile feelings because of their perceived unfair treatment at the hands of the majority. There is, for example, intense prejudice among some people toward whites, Protestants, Democrats, and other majority groups. Special attention, including legal protection, is given to minorities only because of their relative inability to protect themselves against unfair discrimination by a prejudiced and self-serving majority.

Although social and legal constraints often force prejudiced people to control their actions, these external persuaders receive internal support from the values and standards of many individual decision makers. At times, managers with strong prejudices toward particular groups or individuals will bend over backwards to behave consistently with their values and contrary to their prejudices. Therefore, prejudice does not necessarily result in unfair discrimination.

Legal constraints inhibit unfair discrimination against minority groups and others such as women and the aging, but unfair discrimination in personnel decisions cannot be controlled primarily by this means. There are so many subtle forms of unfair discrimination that the problem is never completely solved where large numbers of managers are internally motivated by prejudice. The motivation needed to contain discrimination can arise from a variety of sources such as humanistic values, a genuine concern and compassion for people, and/or economic self-interest.

Fair and Unfair Discrimination

Since discriminating is an integral part of all decision making, it is inevitable that even relatively unprejudiced managers will, at times, discriminate unfairly. Decisions are never completely objective, standards of acceptable behavior constantly change, and value judgments concerning fairness differ from person to person and within a given person over time. Society has, on several occasions, expressed its values in ways which have resulted in charges that management is unfairly discriminating. A current example of this concerns affirmative action programs for hiring and promoting members of disadvantaged groups, often at the expense of better qualified applicants and employees. In this case, society's need to make restitution for past wrongs is given higher priority than the long-accepted right of an individual to be evaluated on the basis of qualifications and past performance.

Returning veterans have also been given preferential treatment in hiring and promotions, and some companies contract with unions to discriminate in favor of union members when hiring new employees. It is common practice, particularly in unionized companies, to discriminate in favor of employees with seniority, even if it leads to promoting an irresponsible, poorly qualified employee when a conscientious, well-qualified employee is passed over. During the recession of the mid-1970s, discriminating on the basis of seniority led to mass layoffs of minority group members. This occurred because, in recent years, organizations had responded to government pressure to employ and promote an increasing number of minority employees, and the last to be hired were the first to be laid off.

The point of these illustrations is that the problems of eliminating unfair discrimination are shot through with value judgments and biased perceptions. In order to understand the content of this chapter it is important that we remain aware of the prisms through which each of us views the problems involved, that we attempt to place ourselves in the other person's shoes, and that we be cautious in judging the motives, morals, and behavior of others in this complex area.

The term *discrimination* is commonly used to imply unfair discrimination. This tends to obscure the fact that managers must constantly discriminate (differentiate or make distinctions) in their decisions about people. Many managers realize that discriminating on the basis of race, color, religion, sex, age, and national origin is inappropriate; but they are highly frustrated by their inability to discriminate consistently on the basis of qualifications and merit.

Both government pressures for quota hiring and promoting and union pressures for making seniority the main criterion in personnel decisions discourage enthusiastic management support for many of the programs others have devised for eliminating unfair discrimination. Managers are often caught between the need to eliminate discrimination and the need to maintain a competitive position in the marketplace. What appears as indifference to the needs and rights of disadvantaged groups may simply be management's quest for survival. For a business to survive, its managers must place a high value on efficiency and productivity as well as individual needs. This is not a justification for unfair discrimination, but it is a partial explanation for its occurrence.

Legal Protection Against Discrimination

The freedom marches, riots, and civil rights legislation of the 1960s marked a major turning point in the discrimination against disadvantaged groups. Although the political and social influence of blacks was the major force in calling attention to the plight of these groups, the effect was beneficial to all. Title VII of the Civil Rights Act of 1964, the "Equal Employment Opportunity" section, forbids discrimination on the basis of race, color, religion, sex, or national origin in all aspects of organizational life. The Equal Employment Opportunity Commission was created to administer and ensure compliance with the Act. Section 703A states that:

> It shall be an unlawful employment practice for an employer (1) to fail or refuse to hire or to discharge any individual or otherwise to discriminate against any individual with respect to his compensation, terms, conditions, or privileges of employment because of such individual's race, color, religion, sex, or national origin; or (2) to limit, segregate or classify his employees in any way which would deprive or tend to deprive any individual of employment opportunities or otherwise advertently affect his status as an employee because of such individual's race, color, religion, sex, or national origin.[1]

The Equal Employment Opportunity Commission (EEOC) has vigorously enforced the Civil Rights Act by making full use of its powers to negotiate with companies, unions, and employment agencies to correct specific acts of discrimination and require the development of affirmative action programs to eliminate discriminatory practices. The EEOC has, on a number of occasions, filed suit in the federal courts against private employers who did not respond to less drastic measures.

The March 1971 Supreme Court decision in the case of *Griggs* v. *Duke Power Company* strengthened the 1964 Act by requiring companies to prove that their selection procedures do not tend to discriminate.[2] This decision established the illegality of selection tests or employment standards that discriminate even though there is no intent to discriminate.

The case of the *United States* v. *Georgia Power Company* (1973) further established that any employment requirement, a high school diploma in this instance, must assess the qualifications of applicants for specific jobs rather than

---

[1] Civil Rights Act, 1964, Title VII, Section 703A.
[2] 28 L. Ed., U. S. Supreme Court Reports

for general employment by the organization.[3] These decisions have led to intensive efforts to validate selection standards, especially psychological tests. If selection criteria are not correlated with on-the-job performance and, therefore, unfairly screen out members of a protected group, they are clearly illegal.

The Civil Rights Act of 1964 was landmark legislation for the protection of disadvantaged groups; but a number of other laws, amendments, court decisions, executive orders, and policies of government agencies have also strengthened legal efforts to eliminate unfair discrimination. It is safe to say that the current problems of minorities and other disadvantaged groups are not the result of insufficient legislation.

Affirmative Action Programs

The Labor Department's Office of Federal Contract Compliance (OFCC) and the EEOC have required many organizations to evaluate opportunities for disadvantaged groups and to specify detailed plans to guarantee equal opportunities for employment and promotions. Such *affirmative action programs* include definite schedules for recruiting, hiring, and promoting members of disadvantaged groups. The programs may also include commitments to *quota* hiring and promoting based upon the populations of the different disadvantaged groups in the locality. If, for example, a company is located in an area where 30 percent of the population is Mexican-American and only 5 percent of its employees are from this group, discrimination is presumed to exist.

Although the quota requirement has merit in many cases, it is sometimes irrational and causes undue hardship on organizations. This is especially true if the personnel needed by the organization are not available locally. When an organization which is located in an area populated by unskilled workers requires large numbers of skilled and professional personnel, the problem cannot always be solved according to a timetable acceptable to the EEOC or OFCC.

Managers often feel that the administrators of the law are not sensitive to organizational needs and that they possess a zeal which interferes with good judgment and effective management. Some government administrators and members of disadvantaged groups, on the other hand, are convinced that any request by an organization for more time is necessarily an excuse to continue discrimination. Depending upon the individuals involved, governmental efforts to eliminate unfair discrimination may result either in a cooperative government-organization partnership to solve a common problem or a bitter struggle between adversaries who appear to have no common interests.

NEEDS AND PROBLEMS OF MINORITY EMPLOYEES

Thesis: The moral, social, and legal climate in America is more favorable than at any time in the past for eliminating discrimination

---

[3] 474 F. 2d 906 (1973)

against minority employees and for providing an organizational climate which will meet their needs for growth and self-esteem. There remain, however, formidable barriers to the achievement of these objectives, and both organizations and minority employees must pay a price to overcome them.

Generalizations about minorities are made difficult by the great differences among minority groups and the individuals within them. The problems of a religious minority are different from the problems of a racial minority, and both are different from the problems of minorities based on national origin. Many of these distinctions are explained below.

Changing Pattern of Discrimination

Discrimination against minority groups has persisted throughout history. Strong, pervasive prejudice against Jews and blacks, in particular, has existed for centuries and both have maintained their unique identities in contrast to other groups which have been assimilated into the general population. For many groups, such as the Irish, Polish, Slovak, and Chinese, prejudice and discrimination have centered primarily upon a recent immigrant status and concomitant characteristics of poverty, low skill levels, poor education, and culture-based characteristics that set its members apart as different and therefore inferior.

Many European immigrant groups had the further disadvantage in Protestant America of being Catholic. As their ethnic group status increased, however, and their members gained the freedom to become assimilated into the general population at will, prejudice against Catholics declined. The nation's level of general education and traditions of religious freedom have also reduced religious prejudice. The election of John Kennedy to the Presidency attests to this fact, as does Jimmy Carter's ability to carry a substantial Catholic vote in 1976. This does not mean that religious prejudice in America has ceased, but in most organizations its influence is minimal and as likely to operate in one direction as the other.

Spanish-Speaking Employees. The recent influx of unskilled Puerto Ricans into such metropolitan areas as New York City has tended to push other ethnic and racial groups up the status ladder. The social status of Mexican Americans in such states as New Mexico, Texas, Arizona, California, and Colorado is also suffering at the present time. This is, in part, due to the large numbers of illegal immigrants who continue to swell their ranks and dilute the favorable image that millions of skilled, well-educated Mexican Americans have earned for themselves. The national policy which allows employers to hire illegal immigrants from Mexico has provided a needed source of unskilled labor at relatively low rates while doing serious damage to Mexican Americans who have tried to remove the stigma of second-class citizenship.[4]

---

[4] Officially an illegal alien may be imprisoned for a period of six months, but this law is seldom enforced because of the large number of offenses. Informed estimates are that as many as ten million

Beginning in 1966, more than a half million Cubans came to the United States to escape the Fidel Castro regime. Since they represented the skilled and educated citizens of Cuba, they avoided many of the problems faced by immigrant Puerto Ricans and Mexicans. Their acceptance in the work force shows that problems associated with poor education, lack of earning potential, and consequent inability to adopt a middle-class life-style may be as much a cause of discrimination as ethnic background as such. Both prejudice and discrimination against other immigrant groups have diminished as they have gained educational and economic equality with the general population.

In 1970, persons of Spanish heritage were financially better off than blacks (see Figure 18–1), but they commonly perceive themselves to be more disadvantaged. Many Spanish-speaking Americans are strongly linked to a foreign culture, have language problems, and are Catholics. Persons of Spanish heritage often make distinctions among themselves of which outsiders are generally unaware. For example, those with white skin, reflecting a Spanish or Anglo, rather than an Indian ancestry, generally feel superior. Such within-group distinctions are present in all disadvantaged groups, further increasing the disadvantage of some.

Family Income*	Total	White	Black	Spanish Heritage
Median Income	$ 9,950	$ 9,961	$6,067	$7,534
Mean Income	10,999	11,418	7,114	8,578
Mean Income per Family Member	3,092	3,271	1,729	2,000

Source: General Social and Economic Characteristics: United States Summary, Bureau of Census, June, 1972.

*No definitive information is available on the extent to which these relationships have changed since the 1970 census. Because of inflation, the absolute figures are underestimates at the present time, and there is strong evidence that the relative position of minorities is improving.

Figure 18–1   Family Incomes of Whites, Blacks, and Persons of Spanish Heritage

American Indians.   Although Indians constitute a relatively small portion of the total work force, their numbers are growing, and their problems are increasingly gaining national attention. They are at a definite disadvantage in the workplace because of social and cultural characteristics related to reservation life which make difficult an adjustment to the fast pace and regimentation of urban-industrial life.

persons illegally enter the United States each year with about 80 percent of these crossing the Mexican border. Many, of course, remain only for a short time. The Congress has tacitly condoned this practice by refusing to pass bills that would make it illegal to employ illegal aliens. See "Border Crisis: Illegal Aliens Out of Control?" *U. S. News and World Report* (April 25, 1977), pp. 33–39.

Since 1947 the Bureau of Indian Affairs has engaged in an organized effort to relocate Indians in urban centers where employment is available. Although BIA relocation programs have not been a phenomenal success, many large cities such as Chicago, Minneapolis, Cleveland, Dallas, Denver, Los Angeles, San Francisco, Oklahoma City, and Seattle have a significant number of citizens who identify themselves as Indians and maintain close relationships with other Indians on and off reservations. Between 1950 and 1970 the Indian population of Minneapolis (Hennepin County) increased from 426 to about 10,000.[5] These growth figures are characteristic of the Indian populations of many large cities in the West and Midwest. Latest figures indicate that there are approximately 200,000 American Indians in the work force, over one-fourth of which are in some form of government work, and less than 10,000 of which are self-employed.[6]

Employment turnover among Indians who have recently left the reservation is high. They have usually left only because of economic necessity and, aside from the lack of employment opportunities, prefer reservation life. About one-third now return to the reservation, down from about three-fourths when the relocation programs began. Additional disadvantages are posed by their generally low skill levels and by work habits which are poorly suited for industrial life. Domestic problems are common among urban-dwelling Indians, and arrests associated with heavy drinking are high (for example, arrests are more than ten times as high for Navajo Indians in the Denver area as for the total population).[7] Although Indian customs and characteristics vary greatly with tribes and individuals, experts are agreed that drinking is a problem among American Indians, and it is obviously one which affects their work. The drinking appears to be associated with problems of personal, social, and economic adjustment rather than with any unique biological characteristics. For many individuals and subgroups, it is, of course, no problem at all.

Employers should be aware that American Indians identify strongly with their ethnic group long after they have adjusted to urban life and work. They seek the supportive social relationships of other Indians and often hold to many of their ancestral traditions and beliefs long after they externally appear to have been assimilated into the general population. In fact, in recent years a strong nationwide movement has emerged to develop a common bond between Indians of all tribes and to improve their well-being by encouraging ethnic pride and discouraging loss of identity through assimilation. Since problems of identity and self-esteem have long contributed to the disadvantaged condition of American Indians, the unity movement may serve to improve their general status and consequently to improve their employment situation.

---

[5] Howard M. Bahr, "An End to Invisibility," in Howard M. Bahr, Bruce A. Chadwick, and Robert C. Day (eds.), *Native Americans Today: Sociological Perspectives* (New York: Harper & Row, Publishers, 1972), p. 408.

[6] *Subject Report: American Indians.* Department of Commerce, Bureau of Census, June, 1973. These are rough estimates and do not include states with less than 25,000 Indians in the population.

[7] Theodore D. Graves: "The Personal Adjustment of Navajo Indian Migrants to Denver, Colorado," Bahr, Chadwick, and Day, op. cit., p. 443.

The many problems which have plagued American Indians, not the least of which is prejudice carried over from frontier days, should not obscure the facts that an increasing number are becoming successful vocationally and that large numbers of individuals have none of the characteristics which place the group at a disadvantage in the workplace. Because they have as a group been educationally disadvantaged, the fact is often overlooked that they are very competitive in terms of general intelligence. The latter provides a note of optimism for their educational and economic future.

Blacks in the Work Force.   In the latest United States census, 22.7 million Americans or about 12.8 percent identified themselves as blacks. Although this is by far the largest minority group, the figures themselves reflect the prejudice blacks have faced throughout history. Persons who are identifiable as having some black parentage—even a small percentage—have traditionally been classified by others and themselves as blacks. This obvious prejudice seems to imply that black genes somehow taint the racial purity of whites. At any rate, large numbers of persons who call themselves blacks are mostly white. Because there has long been a deep-seated prejudice against blacks and because their physical features are easily identified, their assimilation into the general population has been especially difficult.

As shown in Figure 18–2 the majority of blacks in the United States hold blue-collar and service jobs. They have experienced a relatively low level of

Occupational Group	Total	White	Black	Spanish-Speaking
Total: Number (thousands)	85,936	76,620	8,112	3,609
Percentage*	100.0	100.0	100.0	100.0
White-collar workers	48.6	50.6	28.9	31.5
Professional and technical	14.4	14.8	8.8	7.0
Managers and administrators, except farm	10.4	11.2	3.4	5.7
Sales workers	6.3	6.8	1.9	3.9
Clerical workers	17.5	17.8	14.8	15.3
Blue-collar workers	34.7	33.9	42.1	47.6
Craft and kindred	13.4	13.8	9.5	12.4
Operatives	16.2	15.5	23.2	26.7
Nonfarm laborers	5.1	4.6	9.4	8.5
Service workers	13.2	12.0	26.3	16.5
Farmworkers	3.5	3.6	2.8	4.5

Source: <u>Manpower Report of the President,</u> April, 1975, Superintendent of Documents, U. S. Government Printing Office.

*Percentages may not always total 100 because of rounding.

Figure 18–2   Employment of White, Black, and Spanish-Speaking Workers by Occupational Group: 1974

participation in business careers, perhaps because opportunities for success in managerial positions have been minimal. A somewhat greater number have been successful in the professions, especially as teachers and clergy. Until recently, discrimination within unions has been a serious barrier to their upward mobility within the blue-collar ranks. This and other biasing factors have forced blacks into the least desirable, least secure, and lowest paid jobs in the market. When compared with other minority groups over a long period of time, they have suffered the highest rates of unemployment and have been subjected to the greatest cultural and educational handicaps because of poverty.

The Civil Rights Act of 1964 and other legislation have greatly increased the number of job opportunities for blacks. Various branches of the government and large numbers of companies aggressively recruit blacks and provide training opportunities to ensure their promotability. In spite of these efforts and the outstanding success of many individuals, however, the problem of fully assimilating blacks into the work force is far from being solved. Here are some of the major problems and their implications.

1. Racial prejudice remains a barrier in both unions and companies. This is offset to a degree, however, by the sincere efforts of large numbers of decision makers who are committed to compensating for past discrimination.

2. Education and training problems cannot be overcome immediately, in part because there are still relatively few blacks receiving the type of formal education required to compete successfully for promotions within management. There are increasing numbers of positions open to members of minority groups, but they cannot be filled indefinitely by marginally qualified people. Although quota hiring and promoting have been forced upon organizations to compensate for past discrimination, the result may ultimately thwart minority progress. There are three reasons for this. (a) Failure to perform injures the self-image of the minority manager who is promoted without being fully qualified. (b) In order to meet quota requirements, organizations are sometimes forced to restructure positions by taking away their content and responsibility while leaving intact the title and pay. This hurts both the organization and the individual who is humiliated by occupying such a position. (c) If minority managers are kept in positions for which they are not qualified, the charade creates resentment and, in some cases, increases racial and ethnic prejudice.

3. Blacks and other minority employees are often skeptical about whether extensive educational and vocational preparation will pay off. They have learned through experience to doubt that the golden age of opportunity has finally arrived. Thus, an understandable problem of motivation slows their progress in gaining equality in education and in the workplace.[8]

---

[8] Psychological studies do not show that black and white youngsters hold different levels of aspiration or want different types of jobs, but the achievement motivation of blacks is apparently lowered by the reality-based perception that their chances of success are not as high as for whites. See Patricia Gwin, "Psychological Dimensions of Minorities' Work Force Participation," *Sloan Management Review,* Vol. 15 (September, 1974), p. 47.

4. The road to success is often so rough that it is not considered worth the effort. Members of disadvantaged groups, preoccupied with the effects of discrimination, have failed to see that the price of success can be exorbitant. Even the white, Protestant, Anglo-Saxon male with an outstanding education for business and many cultural advantages often decides that the price of becoming a successful manager is too high. The stresses and personal risks in management are sufficiently high that a person needs every advantage in order to stay motivated to succeed.

The success of blacks in management and many other professions is slow because it must follow educational preparation. There are, however, numerous reasons for optimism. Educational opportunities for blacks have improved enormously since 1964, and more high-level jobs are now available than there are persons with the skills to take advantage of them. The success of blacks in the entertainment field and in college and professional sports has helped to reduce prejudice, and, especially at the college level, school integration appears to be having the same effect. Although for specific individuals the outlook appears bleak and progress slow, the long-range employment outlook for blacks is excellent.

Orientals. The Oriental population consists mostly of Japanese, Chinese, and Filipinos, to which a number of Vietnamese and other Southeast Asians were added during the 1970s. Although prejudice still exists, Orientals as a group have been more successful than other minority groups in making a place for themselves and minimizing the minority stigma.

Oriental Americans have placed a high value on education, a fact which accounts to a significant degree for their enviable position among minorities. In fact, the average educational level of both Chinese and Japanese-American men exceeds that of white men. Although the influence of social and cultural characteristics can never be ruled out in accounting for the relatively high status of Orientals in the United States, their emphasis upon education is unquestionably a major factor. It is doubtful that any minority group can compete favorably for skilled, technical, and managerial positions when an educational barrier exists. If white males cannot overcome this handicap, it is unreasonable to expect minorities to be able to do so.

Relating to Minority Employees

A manager's effectiveness in relating to minority groups depends on many factors such as ability to empathize and the presence of genuine concern for the needs of others. These qualities are not sufficient, however, to ensure good relations with minority employees. Some degree of sophistication in understanding their special problems is helpful. The following generalizations are particularly important.

Recognizing Individual Differences. Recently a university professor of Japanese ancestory mistook a Japanese student for Chinese. When he made a remark about the Chinese student and was corrected by a colleague, the some-what embarrassed professor retorted, "Frankly, all these Orientals look alike to me!" Since the professor was himself an Oriental, his remark was humorous, but it is related here to accent the common tendency to stereotype minority groups—to expect all members of a minority group to be alike.

From a purely statistical point of view, certain predominant racial and ethnic characteristics can be identified. As minority members become assimilated into the general population, however, the likelihood that a stereotype will apply rapidly diminishes. Whether a stereotype is derogatory or not, the safest approach is to ignore it and relate to minority group members as individuals. The fact that profound differences exist within all minority groups, however, does not reduce the value of studying racial and ethnic subcultures. Managers who understand broadly held subculture norms, attitudes, and values can relate to minority group members with greater sensitivity than those who lack this awareness. They can, for example, avoid referring to the minority group by a name which is in popular use and not meant to be derogatory but is for some reason offensive to minority group members.

Allowing for Personal Defensiveness.   Experiences of early childhood and adolescence are critical in shaping attitudes, perceptions, and personal identities. James Farmer, the son of the registrar and professor of religion and philosophy at Rust College, a black Methodist school in Holly Springs, Mississippi, tells a gripping story of an unforgettable event which occurred a few blocks from Rust College. James watched through the screen door of a drugstore as a white boy enjoyed a drink at the soda fountain. The dialogue between James and his mother continued:

> "But I told you you can't get a Coke in there," she said. "Why can't I?" I asked again. Her answer was the same, "You just can't." I then inquired with complete puzzlement, "Well, why can he?" Her answer thundered in my ears. "He's white."
> We walked home in silence under the pitiless glare of the Missis-sippi sun. Once we were home she threw herself across the bed and wept. I walked out on the front porch and sat on the steps alone with my three-and-a-half-year-old thoughts.[9]

Although this specific experience would not likely happen today, many variations of it do occur, and, regardless of when such an experience took place, the memory of it is likely to remain vivid. Members of minority groups cannot be understood without an awareness of this fact.

Minority members who have suffered discrimination often harbor feelings of resentment and hostility which they express in damaging ways. Managers cannot allow unlimited expression of these feelings—most managers will not tolerate a physical attack or a verbal attack that becomes abusive. On the other hand, a mature manager can learn to absorb some hostility and to accept some

---

[9] James Farmer, "The Shock of Black Recognition," in B. Eugene Griessman, *Minorities, A Text with Readings in Intergroup Relations* (Hinsdale, Ill.: The Dryden Press, 1975), p. 239.

defensiveness without responding in kind. A smart-aleck remark or injection of sarcasm into a question need not be taken personally by a manager.

With reference to the feelings just described, a note of caution is in order. People who have been discriminated against often have feelings of hostility and resentment, but they do not necessarily have such feelings. We should be careful to avoid misinterpretations of behavior which occur because we project into minority employees the feelings we expect them to have.

Accepting Rather than Tolerating.   An Indian whose attitudes concerning punctuality have been conditioned by years of reservation life or a black whose vocabulary and diction bear the stamp of an impoverished ghetto background can be *tolerated* as "one of them" or *accepted* as a unique human being of infinite worth and potential. Some managers have an unfortunate knack for being judgmental and harshly critical of subordinates who are different from themselves. Others project a warmth—a touch of genuine human compassion—that makes subordinates want to do their best, to perform responsibly, and to communicate openly.

Managers should assume that, in the final analysis, their attitudes toward minorities will be known. It is extremely difficult for managers with deep prejudice toward minority employees to sustain good relations over an extended period of time. Where prejudice exists, attitude changes are clearly in order.

THE CHANGING ROLE OF WOMEN

Thesis: Employment opportunities for women are increasing at all levels, but equality with men in opportunities and pay will not soon be achieved. The growing number of women with the motivation and ability to compete favorably with men is handicapped by cultural stereotypes. These are, in part, based upon the behavior and attitudes of other women who prefer the traditional wife-mother-lover role or who are willing to settle for a work role that involves a minimum of conflict and responsibility.

Title VII of the Civil Rights Act prohibits discrimination on the basis of sex, and a series of court decisions and EEOC rulings have demonstrated that the Act is indeed capable of bringing some changes in the status of working women. Even past inequities have to some degree been influenced by actions of the EEOC and the Wage and Hour Division of the Department of Labor. It is impressive, for example, that the New York Telephone Company agreed, within a specified period, to give up to 57 percent of future vacancies in middle management to women, that PPG Industries paid $11,100,000 to 371 women against whom they had allegedly discriminated, and that Delta Air Lines agreed to pay 1,000 women and minorities $1,000,000 in back pay because of discrimination. AT&T paid $15,000,000 in back pay to women employees and agreed in 1973 to provide 50,000 higher paying jobs for women within a 15-month period.[10]

---

[10] William F. Glueck, *Personnel, A Diagnostic Approach* (Dallas, Texas: Business Publications, Inc., 1974), pp. 122, 353, and 557.

But such actions do not tell the whole story. Barriers to the elimination of sex discrimination are deeply embedded in the attitudes and values of men and women alike. Back pay and affirmative action programs are a positive step toward removing discrimination, but alone they are insufficient to achieve the goal.

Present Status of Working Women

Women make up an increasing proportion of the total work force. From 1950 to 1974, work force participation of women increased from 29 to 39 percent, and the latter represents over 35,000,000 women (about 45 percent of all women over 16 years of age).[11] By 1990 women should constitute about 46.5 percent of the total work force.[12]

In spite of the increasing numbers of women at work and the positive steps which have been taken to eliminate discrimination, several sex-linked problems still exist.

1. Large wage differentials between male and female employees persist.

2. Recent increases in the absolute earnings benefit only a minority of women.

3. Women remain overwhelmingly concentrated in a relatively small number of low-paying occupations.

4. Large numbers of women, especially black married women over 25 years of age, are forced to work to compensate for the low incomes of their husbands.[13]

As shown in Figure 18–3, the increase in working women is not restricted to a given marital status. There is every indication that women will continue to make up a high percentage of the work force in the foreseeable future. They will increasingly perceive their work in terms of a career and will become progressively more competitive with men for challenging, high-paying positions.

Occupational Segregation

The annual income of both women and men continues to increase, but the gap between the two is also increasing.[14] Although many factors contribute to the difference, the most influential is *occupational segregation,* the tendency for certain jobs to be occupied by men and others by women. Another contributor to the difference is the recent entry of large numbers of women into the work force, mostly in unskilled and semiskilled jobs. Pay is consistently low in those jobs which are predominantly filled by women.

---

[11] *1975 Handbook on Women Workers* (Washington D. C.: U. S. Department of Labor, Employment Standards Administration Women's Bureau), p. 8.

[12] *Manpower Report of the President* (Washington, D. C.: U. S. Government Printing Office, April, 1975), p. 57.

[13] Ibid., p. 55.

[14] *1975 Handbook on Women Workers,* op, cit., pp. 92–93.

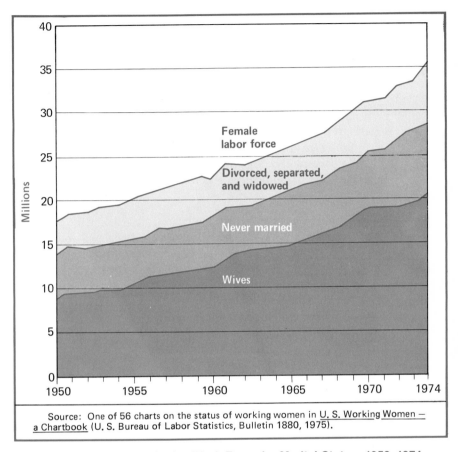

Source: One of 56 charts on the status of working women in U. S. Working Women — a Chartbook (U. S. Bureau of Labor Statistics, Bulletin 1880, 1975).

Figure 18–3   Women in the Work Force by Marital Status, 1950–1974.

Over 80 percent of all elementary school teachers, librarians, bookkeepers, and cashiers, and over 90 percent of all registered nurses, bank tellers, secretaries, telephone operators, and typists are women.[15] In contrast, women comprise only about 18 percent of all managers and a significantly lower percentage of top level executives.

In some high-level positions, the participation of women has increased since the passage of the Civil Rights Act in 1964, but these increases do not raise their total participation to high levels. For example, women accountants have increased from about 18 to 22 percent, physicians from about 8 to 12 percent, and managers from about 15 to 18 percent.[16] Such increases reflect the changing status of women but are not yet sufficient to alter significantly the income differences between men and women. Certain jobs are still considered women's work,

---

[15] Stuart H. Garfinkle, "Occupations of Women and Black Workers," *Monthly Labor Review,* Vol. 98, No. 11 (November 1975), p. 28.

[16] Ibid., p. 28.

and those jobs pay less than so-called men's work requiring comparable education, training, and responsibility.

Women in Management

Under pressure from the EEOC and other government agencies, an increasing number of women will be given opportunities to fill managerial positions. The problems involved are not, however, limited to bias in selection and promotion. A number of culture-based attitudes of both men and women are at least partially responsible for the paucity of women managers. The most important of these centers around the roles traditionally accepted as appropriate for males and females.

Role Conflicts.   Management has traditionally been viewed as man's work just as secretarial and nursing jobs have been considered the domain of women. One reason for this is that the ambitiousness, aggressiveness, and tough-mindedness normally identified with management have been considered male characteristics. The image, however arbitrary it may be, is deeply ingrained and clashes with the need of many women to maintain their femininity. This conflict prevents some very capable women from entering the management field.

A number of research studies have shown that both men and women prefer to work for men. Chapman and Luthans elaborate on this point:

> . . . research generally shows that neither males nor females themselves have a very high opinion of female leadership capabilities. Women are not generally accepted by the groups being led. The organizational situation as a whole tends to be nonsupportive of female leadership. However, it is important to note that in those situations where women have been traditionally accepted in managerial positions—such as in Air Force operations where WAFs are typically used—there appears to be no difference between the leadership styles or behaviors of men and women.[17]

One explanation for the preference of both men and women for male supervisors relates to the fact that both have usually been reared by women. The controlling influence of women continues into elementary and secondary school because of the predominance of women teachers. The male adolescent, in particular, who struggles to rid himself of maternal domination, does not willingly accept it back in the form of a woman supervisor. This is especially true for the person who harbors repressed hostility and resentment. These personality dynamics suggest that, all things considered, strong, socially dominant women will have more difficulty supervising than will men with comparable characteristics.

Motivation Problems.   Jobs in management, law, medicine, and other fields at the upper end of the employment spectrum require extensive educational

---

[17] J. Brad Chapman and Fred Luthans, "The Female Leadership Dilemma," *Public Personnel Management,* Vol. 4, No. 5 (May, 1975), p. 178.

preparation, and a high level of success on the job usually requires intense effort and persistence. For many women who have the option of staying out of the labor force and pursuing the mother-wife-lover role the price of career success offsets its benefits.

It would, however, be easy to oversimplify women's lack of motivation for entering difficult and high-paying careers. Judith Laws makes the cogent point that the failure of women to enter such career fields is partly a result of their low expectation of being successful.[18] Applying expectancy theory, she notes that, if a woman places a high value on becoming a manager but perceives the probability of success to be low, her motivation to acquire the education and endure the rigors of the competitive environment will be low. This logic is irrefutable, and as women begin to realize that their chances of success have increased, more should prepare for and succeed in the field of management.

Stereotypes about Women

Much discrimination against women at work is a result of conventional notions about women which are false or which apply to only a limited subgroup. We look now at four examples of such stereotypes and their implications.

1. *Women work only to provide short-term, supplementary income.* A sequel is that women will not remain on the job long enough to justify an investment in training for a difficult, high-paying job. Although these generalizations apply to some women, they certainly are not valid for all. About 40 percent of all women who work do so because of economic necessity. Between 1940 and 1975, families headed by women doubled in number, reaching one out of every eight families.[19] An increasing number of women regard their work as career-oriented and have no plans to quit regardless of economic necessity or family situation.

2. *Women are less concerned than men about getting ahead on the job.* Research indicates that women are as interested as men in having a job where the chances of getting ahead are good, although more women than men express no desire to be promoted from their present jobs. Since, however, a desire to be promoted is correlated with expectations of being promoted, the conclusion that women are less ambitious than men cannot be confidently drawn.[20]

3. *Women prefer jobs that are not intellectually demanding.* Research shows that more women than men perceive themselves to be in jobs which are

---

[18] Judith Long Laws, "Psychological Dimensions of Women's Work Force Participation," *Sloan Management Review,* Vol. 15 (September, 1974), p. 49.

[19] Beverly Johnson McEaddy, "Women Who Head Families: A Socioeconomic Analysis," *Monthly Labor Review,* Vol. 99, No. 6 (June, 1976), p. 3.

[20] This and other stereotypes were treated in the following research report: Joan E. Crowley, Teresa E. Levitin, and Robert P. Quinn, "Facts and Fictions about the American Working Woman," *Institute for Social Research Newsletter* (University of Michigan), Vol. 1, No. 16 (Autumn, 1972), pp. 4–5.

intellectually undemanding. When this factor is held constant, however, no differences are found between the sexes in preference for intellectually demanding work. Women have adapted to the reality of limited opportunities but not by choice.

4. *Women prefer not to take the initiative on the job.* Men do attach more importance to autonomy and are less concerned about having their responsibilities clearly defined. This, again, may be a function of the kinds of work women do, since significantly fewer women perceive themselves to have freedom on the job. The cultural roles expected of women, with its emphasis upon passivity versus assertiveness, may also be a contributing factor to this sex-linked behavior.

The research and writing on the subject are not altogether effective in debunking these and other stereotypes about women in the work force; and, in some instances, stereotypes which managers have for years used as a basis for discriminating against women are actually reinforced by statistical studies. Partisan researchers are placed in the defensive position of rationalizing their findings in terms which are favorable to women who seek an equal opportunity with men in developing their careers. The following section suggests a better way to achieve this end.

A Change in Methodology

Research on the role and status of working women should not treat women as a homogeneous group since the averaging effect will always produce misleading results. Large numbers of women still have conventional attitudes about a limited "woman's place," and it is the attitudes and behavior of this group which reinforce the attitudes of managers who consciously or unconsciously try to prevent women from gaining equality with men. It is irrelevant how most women feel or think when it comes to deciding whether a particular woman will be effective in a given position. This general point of view is supported by research conducted within the Prudential Insurance Company of America. According to researcher, Philip Manhardt:

> It was concluded that the observed sex differences could be largely accounted for by the existence of a subgroup of women who do not expect a career to be a significant factor in their lives and for whom aspects of a job related to long-range career success are essentially irrelevant since they may not expect to be working for more than a few years.[21]

The notion that research about women as a group may detract from our understanding of the potential role of career women is well expressed by researchers Reif, Newstrom, and Monezka. They conclude that

[21] Philip J. Manhardt, "Job Orientation of Male and Female College Graduates in Business," *Personnel Psychology* (Summer, 1972), p. 276.

. . . decisions made about women on the basis of their sex, without considering such individual factors as background, education, experience, personality, and potential, are likely to be wrong. It appears that many of the stereotypes of women are not representative of women who hold or aspire to responsible positions in business. Moreover, the supposed sex differences in personality, abilities, and attitudes about work for the most part have not been based upon empirical observations of women managers but have resulted from judgments about traits that have been rightly or wrongly attributed to women in general.[22]

Women who aspire to compete on an equal footing with men should not attempt to demonstrate that all women are equipped—attitudinally, educationally, motivationally, or otherwise—to perform effectively in a competitive work environment. On the other hand, women who aspire to be mothers, wives, and lovers should not feel that the role they have chosen is an inferior one. Morality and the law demand that career women be given every opportunity to succeed without sex discrimination, but this should not interfere with the freedom of other women to choose with dignity an entirely different life-style.

OPPORTUNITIES AND PROBLEMS OF AGING

Thesis: Employees with the good fortune of living long enough to grow old have many problems in common, but individuals differ greatly in the skill with which such problems are faced. Research and experience have provided satisfactory solutions to most problems of aging, but, unfortunately, many employees wait until they are too old to begin searching for them.

In contrast to many Oriental countries, the United States has always placed a premium on youth. It started with the earliest explorers and colonists who needed strength, vitality, and physical endurance to survive and conquer a new land. It continues today because of (1) the human energy demands of competitive organizations, (2) the learning demands of the knowledge explosion, and (3) the adaptability demands of rapid change in all aspects of society. It is noteworthy, however, that it is usually the older people in organizations who have the most interesting jobs and the greatest power. Aging poses some serious problems and disadvantages, but it also brings some unique satisfactions and opportunities.

Special Problems of Aging

Some of the problems of aging occur whether or not one is employed. The most common of these are:

1. Coping with an increasing number of physical infirmities

---

[22] William E. Reif, John W. Newstrom, and Robert M. Monezka, "Exploding Some Myths about Women Managers," *California Management Review,* Vol. 17 (Summer, 1975), p. 78.

2. Adapting to a decline in physical strength

3. Adjusting to becoming an "old person"

4. Facing the deaths of family members and friends

5. Having to face the implications of one's own death

6. Meeting the financial and social needs of advancing years

7. Accepting a growing dependency upon other people

Unfortunately the youth orientation of our culture encourages people to deny to themselves that they are getting old and thus to be poorly prepared for it. The millions of middle-aged people who have viewed old people as a worthless burden on society face the dilemma of either having to change their perception of old people or accepting a negative view of themselves as they grow old. The latter commonly occurs and is a major pathology of aging.

Actually the organizational problems faced by declining abilities are fewer than one might imagine. Barring organic problems, such as hardening of the arteries in the brain, employees whose work is primarily mental need not experience a noticeable decline in mental ability before age 65. Any decline that does occur usually can be offset by experience. Fortunately the physical abilities of employees who do manual work decline more slowly than those of persons who do only mental work. Because of health problems, a few manual workers must be transferred to less strenuous jobs (job reassignment), but older employees usually have the experience and seniority to claim such jobs anyway. In some cases, *job redesign* is necessary to enable a person with an age-related handicap to continue to perform (e.g., removing from a job functions that require unusually heavy lifting or rapid movements). Generally speaking, older workers perform about as well as younger ones, have a much lower rate of turnover, are more safety conscious, and, of course, have a broader base of experience upon which to draw.

Age Discrimination

Older employees who lose their jobs often have problems finding suitable employment. Many employers are reluctant to hire employees over age forty because (1) the employers question whether the necessary investment in training will pay off, (2) they are unwilling to pay the increased cost of insurance premiums, and/or (3) they want to avoid problems relating to pension plans and policies of promotion on the basis of seniority.

To protect individuals between the ages of 40 and 65, the Age Discrimination in Employment Act of 1967 makes it illegal for an employer to discriminate in compensation, terms, conditions, or privileges of employment because of age.[23]

---

[23] The Age Discrimination in Employment Act of 1967, *U. S. Code Congressional and Administrative News,* pp. 2213–2228.

The Employee Retirement Income Security Act of 1974 gives further protection to aging employees by reducing the likelihood that older employees will lose their jobs because an organization wants to avoid paying their retirement benefits. Such laws cannot eliminate the hardships faced by older employees who must begin new jobs which do not make use of their prior training and experience. The laws do, however, discourage discrimination against individuals solely because of age.

Problems of Retirement

A majority of companies require retirement at age 65. Supporters of this policy point out that it (1) avoids a number of the problems inherent in making separate decisions about each individual, (2) requires older employees to move out and give young employees an opportunity for promotions, (3) enables management to be more effective in personnel planning, and (4) is fair in that everyone is treated alike. There is, however, strong sentiment in some organizations for abolishing mandatory retirement specifically because it does treat everybody alike when in fact people are quite different. Some are capable of many years of outstanding service after age 65, while others probably should have retired earlier.

One of the advantages of compulsory retirement is that it does not imply that the retiree has become inadequate. It thus enables an employee to retire with dignity. Many companies have developed preretirement programs to help employees prepare, psychologically and financially, for retirement. Especially for individuals who have centered their lives around their work, have become dependent upon their formal status and power for self-esteem, and have few outside interests, retirement can be psychologically devastating. It may even lead to an early death. On the other hand, if begun early and taken seriously, preretirement planning will usually help one avoid such reactions.

Although a sizable number of organizations have instituted flexible retirement policies (gradual retirement by extending vacations, for example), it is unlikely that there will be a rush to plans which remove mandatory requirements. The stronger movement is in the direction of providing opportunities for voluntary early retirement. Notable among such programs are those of the federal government and the major automobile manufacturers. Both allow voluntary retirement with full pay for employees with 30 years of service. To qualify, however, government employees must be 55 years of age and employees of the automobile companies must be 56.

PERSONALITY MALADJUSTMENT IN ORGANIZATIONS

Thesis: One of the largest disadvantaged groups is made up of people with emotional problems. Their cost to organizations through employee turnover, absenteeism, substandard production, labor-management strife, and disciplinary problems is enormous. Yet most organizations make no special provision for understanding and relating to them.

Approximately 10 percent of the general population suffers from some form of emotional problem which is serious enough to interfere with performance on the job, and many of these have compounded their problem through alcoholism or drug addiction.[24] In addition to this group are an increasing number of people who are either sociopathic, in that they have an underdeveloped conscience, or who, for other reasons, have adopted an antisocial or criminal life-style. Although many of these people are institutionalized, most of them at sometime or other are part of the work force and more often than not create problems for management.

Recognizing Emotional Problems

Employees with emotional problems are beset by a chronic inability to find need satisfaction. For the past three decades, such persons have been described as mentally ill, although they are certainly not ill in the sense that persons with measles or cancer are ill; and some outstanding professionals do not agree that the medical model is a good one.[25] The emotionally maladjusted have had difficulty coping with their environmental frustrations and internal conflicts, and the symptoms they exhibit represent the inadequate means they have adopted as coping devices.[26]

Managers legitimately become involved in the personal problems of subordinates when those problems interfere with their work. Although it is not the humane or economically feasible thing to do, managers commonly treat the unacceptable behavior of an emotionally maladjusted person as if it were just another disciplinary problem. For this reason, it is important (1) that the symptoms of maladjustment be recognized, (2) that employees' emotional problems be considered in personnel decisions, and (3) that employees with serious problems be referred to someone who can give them professional help. Figure 18–4 lists some of the common symptoms of emotional maladjustment. It is especially important in detecting emotional problems that managers take notice of changes in behavior as well as the presence of combinations of the symptoms listed. It should be obvious that most of the behaviors listed in Figure 18–4 often characterize normal people. It is the nature of their onset, the degree to which they are present, the combinations in which they occur, and their negative effects in the workplace that provide a basis for viewing them as symptoms of emotional problems.

---

[24] Robert N. McMurray, "Mental Illness: Society's and Industry's Six Billion Dollar Burden," in Robert L. Noland, *Industrial Mental Health and Employee Counseling* (New York: Behavioral Publications), 1973, pp. 3–25.

[25] George W. Albee, "The Sickness Model of Mental Disorder Means a Double Standard of Care," *Michigan Mental Health Research Bulletin,* Vol. 4, No. 1 (Winter, 1970). Dr. Albee, a University of Vermont professor of psychology, is a past president of the American Psychological Association and from 1957 to 1959 was director of the Task Force on Manpower for the Joint Commission on Mental Illness and Health.

[26] Refer to the latter part of Chapter 5 for an explanation of defensive reactions, neuroses, and psychoses.

Emotional problems may be indicated by combinations of the following when such behaviors are excessive, have an acute onset, or noticeably increase over a period of time.

Irresponsibility	Absenteeism	Aggressiveness
Indifference or apathy	Tardiness	Irrationality
Forgetfulness	Low productivity	Poor judgment
Defensiveness	Errors and mistakes	Withdrawal
Procrastination	Constant complaints	Heavy drinking
Irritability	Preoccupation with	Use of narcotics
Daydreaming	health problems	Fearfulness
Memory lapses	Bizarre behavior	Perfectionism
Self-criticism	Criticism of others	Suspiciousness
Shyness	Inferiority feelings	Guilt feelings
Indecisiveness	Inability to concentrate	Chronic rule-
Inappropriate emotions	Unpredictable behavior	breaking
Self-preoccupation	Rapid personality changes	Excuse making

Figure 18–4 **Possible Symptoms of Emotional Problems**

Alcoholism and Drug Abuse

Although in recent years the use of a variety of drugs, ranging from amphetamines to heroin, has become a serious problem, the excessive use of alcohol continues to be more prevalent and more costly in terms of economic loss and destruction of lives. In 1971, the National Council on Alcoholism estimated that there were 100 million drinkers in the United States,[27] and several indicators show that the number has continued to increase. By 1974, there were about nine million alcoholics in the United States with from 100,000 to 200,000 being added each year for an estimate of about ten million by 1980. The lives of an estimated 36 million persons are adversely affected by alcohol.[28] Conservatively estimated, the annual cost of alcoholism is currently over $9 billion in lost production, over $8 billion in health and medical costs, and over $6 billion as a result of motor vehicle accidents.[29] The price which industry and others must pay for narcotic drug abuse is over and above these figures.

Although the American Medical Association and most professionals in the health sciences regard alcoholism as an illness, it must also be considered as a symptom of underlying emotional problems—as one of many inadequate means of coping with internal conflict. It provides a common avenue of escaping from

[27] National Council on Alcoholism, *Facts on Alcoholism,* 1971.

[28] Secretary of Health, Education, and Welfare, *Second Special Report to the U. S. Congress on Alcohol and Health* (Washington, D.C., May, 1974).

[29] Joseph F. Follmann, Jr., *Alcoholics and Business: Problems, Costs, Solutions* (New York: AMACOM, 1976), pp. 20–21.

present stressors and past emotional problems. Unfortunately it offers no solutions and itself increases the problem.

Managing Maladjusted Employees

Most employees who are dismissed from their jobs have the ability to perform adequately but for personality-related reasons do not do so. Even when managers are fully aware of underlying emotional problems, they cannot tolerate inadequate performance indefinitely without disrupting the work force and encouraging problem employees to continue without professional help.

Noting the seriousness of the problem, a number of companies have developed in-house programs to provide help for maladjusted employees, including alcoholics and drug addicts.[30] Such programs result both from a growing sense of social responsibility and management's awareness that the dollar loss in productivity warrants an investment in this area.[31] Whether or not one's organization provides services of this kind, managers should use their authority to persuade maladjusted employees to get professional help before treating their unacceptable performance as run-of-the-mill disciplinary problems.

Virtually every community has resources for helping people with emotional problems. Managers should become acquainted with those resources and develop skill in making referrals. Among those individuals and organizations most capable of providing help are ministers, priests, rabbis, psychologists, psychiatrists, social workers, family physicians, and organizations such as Alcoholics Anonymous, community mental health centers, and detoxification centers. Experience has demonstrated that most employees will accept a referral and profit from treatment when motivated by a desire to maintain their employment and/or good standing with their employers.

STUDY AND DISCUSSION QUESTIONS

1. In what ways are prejudice and discrimination related?
2. How does the federal government get compliance with the Civil Rights Act?
3. What evidence is there that discrimination against ethnic groups is related more to their socioeconomic status than to ethnic prejudice as such?

---

[30] For information on solutions to these problems, refer to the following sources: (1) James E. Petersen, "Insight: A Management Program of Help for Troubled People," *Proceedings of the 1972 Annual Spring Meeting, Industrial Relations Research Association,* Madison, Wis., 1972, pp. 492–495; (2) Noland, op. cit.; (3) Follman, op. cit.; (4) "New Approaches to Treating Alcoholism," *Business Week* (September 1, 1975), pp. 83–84; (5) "What Industry Is Doing About 10 Million Alcoholic Workers," *U. S. News and World Report,* Vol. 80, No. 2 (January 12, 1976), pp. 66–67.

[31] For a cost analysis, see A. E. Hertzler Knox and William E. Burke, "The Insurance Industry and Occupational Alcoholism" *Labor Law Journal,* Vol. 26, No. 8 (August, 1975), pp. 491–495.

4. What are the major problems presently faced by blacks as they attempt to gain equal standing with the majority of the work force?
5. Assuming that it is wise to avoid ethnic and racial stereotypes and relate to members of these groups as individuals, of what value to a manager is understanding subculture norms and attitudes?
6. How is it possible for the gap between the average pay of men and women to increase at a time when the status of women is obviously improving?
7. How can expectancy theory be used to explain the motivation of women to prepare educationally for management careers?
8. Statistical studies have often failed to debunk stereotypes about women which have caused unfair discrimination. What change in research methodology would improve this situation?
9. What are the pros and cons of compulsory retirement at age 65?
10. Why is it important for managers to know when disciplinary problems are a result of the offender's emotional maladjustment?

CRITICAL INCIDENT

The Hostile Irishman

Progress to master machinist was slow in the Dayton Machine Tool Company because employee turnover was low and promotions were dependent upon job openings and seniority. The line of progression was from helper to third class, to second class, to first class, and finally to master. The number of jobs at each level was relatively fixed by tradition with a large number of helpers and few masters (a total of eight). The company's reputation for fairness and excellent treatment of its employees was unusually good. Although the employees were members of a local union, there had never been any serious union-management problems.

In March of 1975, Dayton entered into an agreement with the EEOC to increase the number of minority employees hired and promoted. Because the union itself was in trouble due to years of discriminating against minorities, it reluctantly supported the agreement in spite of its implications for setting aside the seniority promotion rule.

At the time of this incident, Jim McBride had been employed by Dayton for 27 years and planned to take early retirement at age 60 which was three years away. Recognizing that his long-term opportunities were better in a technical area, McBride had taken a cut in pay from his warehousing job to begin at the bottom as a machinist's helper. After 15 years, he had become a first-class machinist with three years in grade and was next in line for master.

Juan Salinas, a 33-year-old native Puerto Rican, had been employed by Dayton for six years and had been promoted to first class at an accelerated pace in conformity with the affirmative action plan. Although he had been a first-class machinist for only 11 months and had not learned certain tasks related to die and model making, he, rather than McBride, was promoted when a master machinist retired unexpectedly.

McBride was taken by surprise when the announcement was made. At first he was merely disappointed, but he then became concerned for fear he would retire before making master machinist. That would result in less retirement pay than he had planned for. Finally he became intensely hostile, and with the support of his union steward, he took his case to management. At one point in the bargaining, he made this impassioned plea:

> Why me? Why discriminate against me? I took a cut in pay to become a machinist's helper and in fifteen years of total dedication to my work I have earned this promotion. Don't talk to me about minorities. I have never discriminated against a minority. In fact, in the Irish ghetto where I grew up, I always thought I was one. Salinas is an individual just like I am, except that he is a young man with six years of experience and I'm a not-so-young man with fifteen years experience. You're promoting an individual, not a minority group, and you're doing it at my expense. Don't old Catholic Irishmen have some rights, too?

Questions

1. What are the arguments for and against the promotion of Salinas over McBride?
2. How should the current problem be resolved? Why?
3. What additional information is needed in order to answer Question 2?

Chapter 19

Social Responsibilities of Management

Progress in the area of moral and social responsibility has not kept pace with advances in science, technology, and industrial development. Fortunately the past decade has witnessed an awakening to the need for courageous moral action in both public and private organizations. Changes required for continued social and economic progress—even the changes required for survival—will be costly for organizations as well as individuals, but they are necessary. Contrary to the predictions of many prophets of doom, there is evidence that our institutions are capable of self-renewal and internalization of values that will benefit all society.

In recent years concepts of social responsibility have dealt mostly with corporate obligations for preventing and solving major social and environmental problems such as inflation, unemployment, and pollution of the nation's waterways and atmosphere.

Social responsibility also involves the concern of employers for the safety of customers and employees, and it relates to virtually all aspects of labor-management relations since employees and their families comprise most of society. Accordingly, the subject of social responsibility touches virtually every aspect of organizational life and includes the content traditionally conceptualized as business ethics.

No attempt is made in this chapter to catalog and provide easy answers for the moral or ethical issues with which managers must grapple in the pursuit of corporate objectives. It does, however, provide an acquaintance with some of the major issues of managerial decisions involving business morality. It purports to broaden a reader's perspective by showing the complexity of the value judgments managers must make, and to increase sensitivity to moral issues in organizational life.

EVOLVING CONCEPTS OF CORPORATE RESPONSIBILITY

Thesis: Managers, scholars, politicians, judges, environmentalists, consumer advocates, and other interested groups and individuals view

corporate responsibility differently. There is, however, a growing con-
sensus that profit-making organizations must observe social values
more consistently in the future than they have in the past.

Several events and circumstances converged during the 1960s and 1970s to
focus on the need for greater responsiveness of business to the needs of society
as a whole. Prominent among these was the failure of former President Johnson's
Great Society programs to decrease crime, poverty, urban blight, and related
social problems to a significant degree. Disillusionment with the ability of government to solve society's problems turned increasing attention to private business
both as a cause of social problems and as a potential cure for society's ills.

Business as a Cause of Social Problems

A growing number of vocal consumer advocates and environmentalists have
become so vehemently antibusiness that their total perception of managerial
motives and behavior has become distorted. As self-appointed interpreters of the
business world to government and society, they shape public opinion and pose
a serious threat to the freedom of managers to control the destinies of their
organizations. The many blue-chip companies which have confessed their sins
or been exposed give credibility to the critics of business, but too often these critics
have seen only the bad side of managerial behavior.

When people are chronically frustrated and unable to deal effectively with
their problems, they commonly single out a scapegoat upon which to vent their
feelings. But good scapegoats are hard to find, and well-informed people are not
easily fooled into believing that an innocent bystander is a villain in disguise.
Business, unfortunately, has not been just an innocent bystander, and so, with
the help of consumer advocates such as Ralph Nader and other social critics,
both business and capitalism have recently fallen under heavy criticism. At least
some of the criticisms have not been justified.

It is not surprising that society's reaction to irresponsible business practices
is at times aggressive and vindictive and that the overall reputation of business
has suffered in recent years. From one point of view, it is inexcusable for industries to have dumped their untreated wastes into the nation's streams and rivers
(as, indeed, the general public has also done in disposing of its sewage). The
cement plant, oil refinery, or steel mill that unceasingly belches its pollutants into
the atmosphere and the coal company that mars the countryside and fails to
provide adequate safety protection for its employees create a negative image that
generalizes to all industry. When high-pressure pitch artists insult the public with
television advertisements that deceive rather than inform, it should be expected
that an increasingly well-educated populace would question the motives and
integrity of business leaders.

The Classical View of Corporate Responsibility

The *classical view* of corporate responsibility was accepted by both business
and society during the nineteenth and early twentieth centuries. Following Adam

Smith's belief that an "invisible hand" works to direct events for the public good,[1] management's sole responsibility was seen as maximizing profits, constrained only by the limits of the law.

In the classical view, the primary mechanisms within which the public good is preserved are inherent in the market system. The organization must produce the best possible goods and services at the lowest possible price. If low efficiency or commitment to other less selfish goals interferes with this process, the competitive marketplace rewards the efficient and punishes the inefficient, thereby protecting the public. From this viewpoint, morality lies within the workings of a competitive market rather than within an individual manager. To tamper with the system (with price controls or supports, for example) is, by definition, to compromise the best interests of society.

The most influential modern spokesman for the classical viewpoint is 1976 Nobel prize-winning economist, Milton Friedman:

> In a free enterprise, private property system, a corporate executive is an employee of the owners of the business. He has direct responsibility to his employers. That responsibility is to conduct the business in accord with their desires, which generally will be to make as much money as possible while conforming to the basic rules of society. . . . Insofar as his actions in accord with his 'social responsibility' reduce returns to stockholders, he is spending their money. Insofar as his actions raise the price to customers, he is spending the customer's money. Insofar as his actions lower the wages of some employees, he is spending their money.[2]

Generally the classical view has held to the *caveat emptor*—let the buyer beware—philosophy in the sales area. The buyer's protection results from the seller's desire to survive in a competitive market. It is the seller's self-interest rather than altruism that protects the customer.

The classical view of corporate responsibility assumes that managers have personal morals, but it relies primarily upon an impersonal force—the dynamisms of a free, competitive market—to protect society. Unfortunately, because of international cartels, oligopolies, and monopolistic labor unions, competition and pricing do not function as the classical view implies. In an environment of imperfect competition, the system provides inadequate protection for the public.

A stronger concept of individual and corporate responsibility is not, however, inconsistent with a belief in the virtues of a competitive market, to the extent that competition exists. In fact, if past generations of managers had been more moral, law abiding, and responsive to society's needs, the factors which limit free market competition would be fewer and the benefits of free market conditions would be better realized in today's economy.

---

[1] Adam Smith, *An Inquiry into the Nature and Causes of the Wealth of Nations* (1776), edited by Edwin Cannan (New York: The Modern Library, Random House, Inc., 1937), p. 423.

[2] Milton Friedman, "Does Business Have a Social Responsibility?" *Bank Administration,* April, 1971, pp. 13–14. Also see Milton Friedman, *Capitalism and Freedom* (Chicago: University of Chicago Press, 1962).

The Accountability Concept

The *accountability concept* of corporate responsibility emphasizes the belief that private businesses receive their charters—their right to operate and make a profit—from society and are therefore accountable to society for their behavior. To be specific, one result of doing business has been contamination of the nation's atmosphere and waterways. Business may be expected to bear a portion of this cost by investing in pollution abatement facilities. Business is also expected to respect society's aesthetic values by preserving the country's natural beauty and to protect employees by treating them fairly and taking reasonable measures to protect their health. In like fashion, a business has an obligation to consider the safety and other needs of its customers. None of these obligations diminishes the necessity for the firm to be efficient in producing and competitive in pricing. Its objective of increasing the wealth of its owners is unchanged and may even be made easier to achieve in the long run because of the firm's sense of responsibility.

The idea that management is accountable to anyone except the shareholders is repugnant to advocates of the classical view. Yet, even during the nineteenth century, child labor laws, the Interstate Commerce Act of 1887, and other actions of government expressed society's conviction that uncontrolled maximization of profits should not be the only goal of management. In recent years, numerous laws have been passed to express society's concept of corporate responsibility and to limit managerial freedom in areas where abuses have most often occurred. Through the passage of laws, society demonstrates that business is, in fact, society's servant and is ultimately accountable to society for its actions.

The Quality-of-Life Concept

Robert Hay and others describe a third level of corporate responsibility which goes beyond the levels just described. In it the business places emphasis upon the nation's quality of life rather than upon increasing stockholder wealth. At this level managers do not deny the importance of profits, but they believe that concern for people is more important than making money and behave accordingly. In relating to customers, *caveat emptor* is replaced with *caveat venditor* (that is, let the seller beware). Managers who operate within this philosophy go far beyond merely paying their own way in society (say by not polluting the environment or discriminating against minority groups). A firm should actively assume responsibility for curing society's ills without reference to who caused them. The quality-of-life manager, described as a humanist rather than a materialist, is characterized as follows:

> The social values of a quality-of-life manager are that a person cannot be separated into economic man or family man. His philosophy would be, 'We hire the whole man and all his problems.' He would recognize that group participation rather than rugged individualism would be a determining factor in his organization's success. His values about minority groups are different from the other managers. His view is that 'Members of minority groups need support and guidance. . . .'

His political values would dictate that government and politicians are necessary contributors to a quality of life. Rather than resist government he would state that business and government must cooperate to solve society's problems.[3]

This view of social responsibility differs from the other two in that the contributions of business to the solution of social problems are not limited to meeting obligations incurred while concentrating on the profit-making objective of the business. Contributions toward solving social problems, such as inflation, unemployment, poverty, crime, and depletion of natural resources, are not considered side ventures. They are accepted, along with making a profit, as primary organizational objectives. The quality-of-life manager "agrees that profit is essential for the firm, but that profits in and of themselves are not the end objectives of the firm." [4]

This altruistic viewpoint proposes that the lofty ideals to which many individuals aspire in their private lives should become the guiding principles for business. Its critics, on the other hand, question whether such idealism is functional in the real world where most people are not altruistic. How can the quality-of-life firm hope to compete with the firm whose managers believe that increasing shareholders' wealth is the primary goal of a business? What happens to the efficiency and productivity of a business organization once the idea is accepted "that profit is essential for the firm, but that profits in and of themselves are not the end objectives of the firm"? Should business actively attempt to achieve social objectives (which go beyond a serious concern for solving business-related social problems) when its leaders have not been educated for such work? Will such dilution of purpose lower the effectiveness of business organizations and consequently lower the entire nation's quality of life? There are no clear answers to these questions, but the remainder of this chapter offers insights which can help avoid answers which deal too lightly with the complex issues involved.

OBJECTIVES OF PROFIT-MAKING ORGANIZATIONS

Thesis: All organizations have limited objectives. The primary objective of a business is to make a profit for its investors. This does not, however, mean that profit making is the only objective of a business or that managers necessarily seek to make as much profit as they possibly can. In practice, effective managers perform a spectacular juggling act in order to meet the increasing demands of employees, government, consumers, and the general public while still earning a satisfactory return for the firm's stockholders.

While giving lip service to the idea that profit-making organizations have multiple objectives, designers of corporate financial decision models typically

[3] Robert D. Hay, Edmund R. Gray, and Jessie E. Gates (eds.), *Business and Society* (South-Western Publishing Co., 1976), p. 9.

[4] Ibid.

assume that managers attempt to maximize shareholder wealth. Some advocates of increased social responsibility, on the other hand, admit that profits and corporate growth are important but act as though profit is a dirty word, an unworthy goal of a truly moral person or organization. The daily lives of operating managers exemplify a pragmatic middle ground. One executive expressed this concept of the executive role:

> Corporate executives are really 'middlemen' in that they strive to bring a fair return to the owners. In addition, they see that employees are compensated properly and treated fairly, that customers get the product/service they paid for and the price is fair, that the product really is of use to society, and that the company's image reflects all this and a true concern for the welfare of society. This, in the long run, is in the best interest of the company.[5]

This quotation reflects the tendency of operating managers to integrate their diverse goals and to seek satisfactory rather than maximum short-term profits.

The Tainted Image of Profits

To one who favors government ownership of a nation's productive resources, profits are associated with the heartless bourgeois capitalist whose selfishness leads to a two-class society in which workers suffer in order to make the rich richer. To the employee whose already meager paycheck is eroded by inflation, corporate profits may be viewed as funds that should have been allocated for wages. To the avid sportsman-environmentalist who catches fish that cannot be eaten because of chemical wastes or to the embittered victim of a preventable industrial accident, profits may symbolize management's irresponsibility—its failure to pay its way in society.

To these individuals, profits—and perhaps even the private enterprise system—may be seen as an evil without socially redeemable qualities. It is difficult for such persons to see how managers in profit-making organizations could possibly be morally sensitive and socially responsible persons.

From the executive suite, the picture looks quite different. One executive described it this way:

> There may be a better system than capitalism, but I haven't seen any evidence of it. For all its faults, it produces a higher standard of living for everyone than alternative systems, and at the same time it allows more freedom. Profits? Certainly they're important! Labor experts say that in 1976 the United States needs 72,000 new jobs every week just to keep unemployment at its present high level. Government make-work programs can't provide them. If we don't make a profit, there won't be any investment dollars to expand the economy and create those jobs or even to keep the jobs we now have. How much

---

[5] Charles P. Edmons, III, and John H. Hand, "What Are the Real Long-Run Objectives of Business?" *Business Horizons,* Vol. 19, No. 6 (December, 1976), p. 79.

profit should we make? Well, that's another question, but you will notice that dividends and stock prices are not spectacular. A lot of the people who complain about corporate profits prefer a safe 5½ percent interest at the savings and loan to the risk and return on corporate stock.

During the rise of capitalism in America, most people had some commitment to the Protestant ethic, a system of values associated with Calvinistic theology. John Calvin saw Christianity as supporting individual responsibility, reward based on merit, and the accumulation of wealth through hard work, productivity, and frugality. This doctrine, equally applicable to the industrialist, farmer, and factory worker, involved no conflict between morality and profit making, and persons who are still committed to it see no need to abandon the profit motive in order to make business socially responsible. Leon Keyserling, former chairman of the Council of Economic Advisors, expresses this point of view:

> The system has evolved and will continue to do so. Most well-informed people in 1900 or even in 1928 would have called what we welcome today socialism rather than capitalism. But looking backward, I would say instead that we have been progressing, and still are, toward a more socially minded society rather than toward socialism, that being a system where the major instruments of production and distribution are in public hands, not guided by the profit motive as we employ it.
>
> Our system has many blemishes, and our virtue consists in recognizing them. But I am convinced that during the past four decades we have made an unparalleled record of progress—economic, social, and what might be called civil. And we have done this under our free institutions with remarkably little turmoil and upheaval by historic tests. We should aim to improve the system, not abandon it.[6]

It should be expected that persons who believe in improving rather than abandoning the system will view social responsibility differently from those who are convinced that capitalism is inherently immoral and therefore inconsistent with social responsibility.

Social Responsibility: A Central or Peripheral Value?

From society's point of view, the purpose of private business is to provide the goods and services needed by its people. Society's decision to encourage the formation of private business is an expression of a belief that the private enterprise system will more nearly meet the people's needs than will an alternative system.

Society's purpose in permitting private enterprise should not, however, be confused with the motivation of a business investor. In a capitalistic system, profit making or, more precisely, increasing investor wealth is generally regarded as the primary purpose of a business firm (though not the *only* purpose, as indicated earlier). This concept of relatively limited purpose may, as illustrated by Milton

---

6 Leon H. Keyserling, "A System Worth Improving," in Otto Eckstein, et al., "The Future of Capitalism—A Symposium," *Business and Society/Innovation,* Vol. 10 (Summer, 1974), pp. 14–15.

Friedman's position, be interpreted to mean that business should not concern itself with social responsibility goals. A less extreme position would make profit the primary goal of business and would subordinate social responsibility to it only if the two should come into conflict.

Primary and Supportive Goals.   Limited purpose is inherent in the nature of all organizations. Academic, religious, governmental, service, and social organizations, like business organizations, are formed with a primary purpose in mind. Schools are not criticized because they fail to provide the community with police and fire protection, nor is Alcoholics Anonymous condemned because it fails to teach reading and mathematics. Like these institutions, a business is formed for a limited purpose and, if it is accepted that the purpose is honorable and serves a valuable function in society, the business should be judged only on the basis of whether it fulfills that purpose in an ethical and honorable way.

Like most organizations, a business has many *supportive goals* (goals which are important in achieving the firm's primary objective and expressing the personal values of its managers and stockholders). Its primary goal, however, is to provide goods and services in order to make a reasonable profit for its stockholders. If the business cannot make a profit, it ceases to exist. A firm's supportive goals may include treating its employees with fairness and dignity, supplying its customers with superior products, providing safe working conditions, and protecting the environment.

The owners of the typical business did not form the company because they wanted to create a satisfying place for their employees to work or even because they were concerned that society needed their products or services. The company may, in fact, have been formed in a tight labor market and at a time when many effective companies were competing for a small portion of the market. The crucial question relating to corporate responsibility is not, therefore, whether profit is the firm's primary goal. It is: What happens when the primary goal cannot be reached without sacrificing one or more supportive goals?

Sacrificing Supportive Goals.   To some managers and policy-making investors, making a profit is more than the primary goal of the organization. It is the central value from which all other values derive their meaning. Profit can be the primary reason for forming the organization and the primary objective in its operation without undermining the personal values of its decision makers. Some managers, for example, are willing to fail in business rather than work employees under conditions which adversely affect their health or lie to prospective customers in order to sell a product. For these persons profits are highly desirable—they are necessary for the organization's survival—but they are not a substitute for a more comprehensive value system and are not necessary for the managers' survival as worthwhile human beings.

To managers for whom making a profit is a central value, everything is subordinated to the profit motive. Their credo is: Make a profit. Make it responsibly if you can, but make a profit! If they cannot provide safe working conditions and still make a profit, safety standards are lowered. If they cannot make a profit

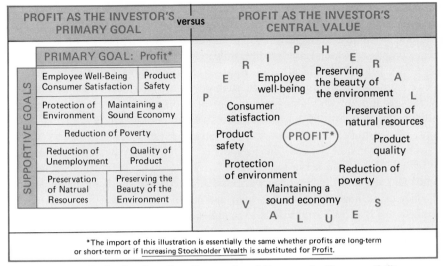

Figure 19–1 **Contrasting Concepts of Corporate Responsibility in Profit-Making Organizations**

without selling a shoddy product, quality standards are lowered. If a choice must be made between profits or fair wages, profits have first priority. These are clearly examples of social irresponsibility. Note, however, that they are not a necessary corollary of making profits the primary goal of the business. Rather, they result from placing profit making in the center of one's value system and making all other values peripheral or subordinate to it.

Some managers, like some government officials, educators, and members of the clergy, are morally bankrupt. Their values reflect a concern only for personal gain regardless of who gets hurt. Some organizations encourage unethical conduct and social irresponsibility by rewarding managers for contributions to short-term profits without reference to how the profits are made. This, too, reflects the values of individuals—the owners or policy-making executives—rather than the values of business per se. Such behavior does not have to exist in profit-making organizations and, in the long run, may detract from profits.

Not-for-Profit Business Activities. In an affluent society, especially where monopolistic or oligopolistic companies can fulfill their various obligations and still make adequate profits, some managers express their personal values by supporting social projects which are, in the short run at least, altruistic in nature. The firm may, for example, sponsor a minority business, build an unprofitable plant in a ghetto, or support a sports program in an area with a high crime rate.

Although there have been instances of monumental losses from such activities, leading to questions about management's responsibility to stockholders, these activities exemplify attempts at social responsibility beyond tokenism and minimal obligation. Notable among companies whose social action programs have led to serious problems is Boise Cascade Corporation. Its promotion of a minority enterprise in the heavy construction industry resulted in a pretax loss of about $40 million and a large drop in the price of the company's stock.[7] Other large companies which have made significant investments in social action programs are IBM, Chase Manhattan Bank, Xerox, Eli Lilly, and Coca-Cola.

Assuming stockholder support, such corporate programs may be justified by the assumption that management can be more effective than government, individuals, or nonprofit organizations in solving certain kinds of social problems—for example, alcoholism, drug addiction, and emotional problems of employees. Or it can be argued that business is failing society by engaging in such activities—that it can serve society best by paying more taxes, increasing dividends and wages if the situation warrants, and investing funds in the expansion of efficient business enterprises which are needed by society. Some critics of business feel that for corporations to retain earnings for the purpose of engaging in socially oriented activities which do not directly benefit stockholders is to increase corporate power and influence unjustifiably in areas where it lacks both expertise and a mandate from society.

CRITERIA FOR SOCIALLY RESPONSIBLE BEHAVIOR

Thesis: Managers have no uniform code of ethics or social responsibility to guide their behavior. They generally agree that socially responsible behavior is desirable but disagree about what behaviors are socially responsible.

The term *social responsibility* has been used throughout this chapter without being defined. As a matter of fact, it is best defined *operationally,* that is, in terms of the behaviors that set socially responsible managers apart from those who are irresponsible. But who is able to make such judgments? Whose criteria are objectively right? Who can decide what is right for others?

Davis and Blomstrom define *social responsibility* as the obligation of decision makers "to take actions which protect and improve the welfare of society as a whole along with their own interests." [8] Gordon Fitch defines corporate social responsibility as "the serious attempt to solve social problems caused wholly or in part by the corporation." [9] The differences between these two definitions are indicative of the even more varied views which exist among managers. Fitch's definition, the more conservative of the two, is more likely to be acceptable to a majority of managers.

In the following discussion, some of the criteria for evaluating right and wrong in the arena of business are considered. Call it business ethics, social

---

[7] Hay, Gray, and Gates, op. cit., p. 14.

[8] Keith Davis and Robert L. Blomstrom, *Business and Society: Environment and Responsibility,* (3d ed.; New York: McGraw-Hill, Inc., 1975), p. 6.

[9] H. Gordon Fitch, "Achieving Corporate Social Responsibility," *The Academy of Management Review,* Vol. 1, No. 1 (January, 1976), p. 38.

responsibility, or business morality, the question remains: Upon what basis should managers make decisions which involve value judgments?

Increasing Expectations

Not many years ago, few people took seriously the problem of environmental pollution. There were no antipollution laws and no Environmental Protection Agency. By discharging raw sewage into rivers and lakes and burning refuse at city dumps, local governments joined industry as a full partner in polluting the environment. At the same time, the public demanded large, powerful automobiles whose engines were a major source of smog and a drain on the world's already short oil reserves.

The pollution problem became intense before people became concerned enough to do something about it. Then, almost overnight, industrial polluters became villains, and an indignant society stood aghast that managers could be so selfish and immoral. This, of course, is just one of many examples of how conditions and expectations (values or standards) change.

Especially since World War II have expectations dramatically increased concerning the treatment of the physically and mentally disabled, minorities, women, the aging, and other disadvantaged groups. During the 1970s, we have seen an emphasis on safety standards and truth in lending and advertising. Far too gradually, people are beginning to develop a conscience about wasting fuel and other natural resources. When the awareness finally occurs, this may, in retrospect, prove to have been society's most serious sin against future generations, and for this a suitable scapegoat will be hard to find.

In these and other areas, society continues to formulate ever higher expectations regarding business behavior. The freedoms enjoyed by Americans permit socially destructive practices to continue unabated long after they have become serious problems. Those same freedoms, however, lead to an exposure of socially irresponsible behavior and to action to prevent its continuation. That action ordinarily takes the form of legislation. In some cases, society expects both government and business to do the impossible—to solve society's problems free of charge. In the real world, however, nothing is free. Zero-defect quality control in the auto industry means higher prices, and stricter standards on emission control must lead to small, less luxurious automobiles.

The cost of pollution controls is passed on to the customer in the form of higher prices. In some cases, the closing of pollution-emitting plants and investment in antipollution devices rather than expansion of productive capacity have increased unemployment. Enormous pay raises, at all levels of government and industry, combine with other factors to ensure continued inflation. Stringent rules regarding the mining and use of coal are desirable, but they also lead to increased fuel prices and continued dependence upon oil and natural gas. As these facts indicate, the issues of social responsibility often involve trade-offs and are seldom clear-cut matters of moral versus immoral behavior.

Legality as a Standard of Conduct

It was once popular to say that morals cannot be legislated, but this statement is not altogether true. Laws that reflect a strong sentiment within the population and involve appropriate penalties for failure to comply are often imposed upon persons who do not initially support them. Laws that receive vigorous enforcement can be singularly successful in changing behavior and subsequently modifying attitudes until they are congruent with the behavior which the laws require. Thus, a law such as the Occupational Safety and Health Act, which is deeply resented by some managers because it is regarded as unrealistic and harsh, is eventually accepted and its standards internalized.

Almost every aspect of business is controlled by laws, rulings of quasi-judicial bodies such as the National Labor Relations Board, numerous state and federal agencies, executive orders, and court rulings. Literally thousands of thou-shalt-nots, expressed both in sweeping generalizations and in minute details, specify appropriate managerial conduct with reference to employees, customers, competitors, suppliers, stockholders, the government, energy, the environment, and other business-related areas. The extent to which laws regulating business proliferate reflects (1) skepticism concerning the ability of managers to act responsibly on their own, (2) a growing conviction that the controls associated with a free market are in themselves inadequate to protect the public, (3) a high level of dependence upon government to solve social problems, and (4) a widespread preference for the security of government controls over the freedom they inevitably destroy.

Another factor in the proliferation of laws, as sociologist Etzioni points out, is strictly political:

> . . . a good part of the laws passed are not meant to be implemented, at least not systematically and effectively. Passing laws is part of the make-believe or theater of politics, in which politicians try to placate two (or more) opposing camps. They give one faction the law (saying, in effect, "You see, I took care of it") while the other faction more or less retains the freedom to pursue activities which violate the law. It's a politician's way of eating his cake and having it.[10]

Whatever the reasons for the passage of laws, it is a favorite national pastime which shows no signs of slowing down and which is having a monumental impact upon business.

The Law as an Equalizer. One positive aspect of laws relating to business behavior is that they serve as an equalizer among companies, some of which are not inclined to be socially responsible. However much the critics of business may want to cry "rationalization for irresponsibility," it is extremely difficult for one company to install costly antipollution devices while its competitors continue to pollute. And a large user of steel, for example, cannot buy expensive steel

---

[10] Amitai Etzioni, "There Oughta Be a Law—Or Should There Be?" *Business and Society Review/Innovation,* No. 8 (Winter, 1973–74), pp. 10–11.

to support a socially minded supplier while its competitors buy the same grade of steel for less.

Problems in Legislating Morality.   By equalizing the rules of the game, legislation modifies the free enterprise system by constructing a baseline of morality and responsibility. There is, of course, a point at which government controls become so extensive that the positive aspects of a free market cannot be realized, and it is the fear of many that we are rapidly approaching such a point. Another limitation in the legislation of morality is that managers may take the position that the minimum requirements specified by the law are all the morality that is needed. As one company president candidly stated:

> In many areas the law has already exceeded my conscience, and we're still getting ten new commandments a month. The situation reminds me of my childhood when mom and dad insisted that I follow their puritanical standards. I had to go along sometimes when I didn't really believe what I was doing was necessary in order to be good. They simply had too many rules and didn't give me the freedom to decide for myself what was right or wrong; so I did my own thing as soon as they turned their backs. I feel the same way about the government. Actually I'm sympathetic with the intent of most of the laws, but I despise being told that I have to do something and then having to report all my activities in minute detail. It's mom and dad forcing their religion on me all over again, only more so. The government never lets up!

Business morality can be legislated, but the legalistic approach has its drawbacks. There can never be enough laws to cover every situation. Neither can there be enough officials to police all the laws—unless most managers endorse them and conscientiously try to obey them. There is ample evidence to show that managers as a whole are motivated to behave responsibly,[11] but it remains to be seen whether the sheer number of laws will cause a significant number of managers to feel overcontrolled and to react negatively by observing the letter of the law while violating its spirit.

Professional and Organizational Codes

Most professions have codes of ethics by which the behavior of their own members is guided. These are usually taken seriously since failure to comply may result in expulsion from the organization and in professional ruin. For example, an industrial psychologist whose membership in the American Psychological Association is lost because of unethical conduct will subsequently face the withdrawal of certification and licensing which are necessary to practice in his or her state. Although such codes directly apply only to the profession's members, they indirectly affect all members of the business community with whom the professionals work.

---

[11] Davis and Blomstrom, op. cit., p. 186.

The Influence of Public Accountants. One profession having a significant impact upon the ethical behavior of managers is accounting. Certified public accountants (CPAs) not only impose their own ethical codes upon business but are also responsible, along with attorneys, for helping managers understand and obey the law.

The American Institute of Certified Public Accountants is explicit in stating its rules of conduct and insistent that those rules be followed.[12] Its rules of conduct are stated in the following areas:

1. Independence (avoidance of conflict-of-interest situations)

2. Personal integrity and objectivity

3. Professional competence with reference to work undertaken

4. Compliance with the Institute's auditing standards

5. Use of accepted accounting principles

6. Making forecasts of future transactions

7. Confidential client information

8. The payment of contingent fees

9. Encroachment upon another public accountant's practice

10. Offers of employment to a public accountant

11. Acts which discredit the profession

12. Soliciting and advertising personal services

13. Payment or acceptance of commissions

14. Engaging in incompatible occupations

15. The nature of a public accountant's practice and firm name

Standards 4 and 5, in particular, place substantial demands upon the client to maintain adequate records and to conduct its financial affairs in such a way that an audit can be performed and the firm's true condition discovered and noted in the audit report. There is a real sense in which public accountants serve as a firm's conscience in the financial area. Managers continually ask, "What will our auditors say about this?" and they often seek an opinion before deciding upon a course of action.

---

[12] "Restatement of the Code of Professional Ethics," a booklet published for its members by the American Institute of Certified Public Accounts, effective March 1, 1973.

International Business Machines. Many organizations publish their own codes of conduct and are diligent in enforcing them. Notable among these is IBM, whose *Business Conduct Guidelines* is an 84-page booklet that all managers must review each year. They must also certify that they understand it and will comply with it. Any violation is cause for dismissal from the company.

The IBM booklet provides guidelines for employee behavior relating to customers, suppliers, and competitors as well as to IBM itself. Among the specific guidelines are statements dealing with gifts and entertainment, marketing practices, tying up a source of supply, engaging in illegal activity, and a variety of statements concerning an employee's obligations to the company. One part of IBM's guidelines deals with a 1956 Consent Decree in which the firm agreed, in response to an antitrust action by the United States Government, to avoid specific practices which were allegedly monopolistic. It is especially important that IBM managers be aware of the Consent Decree because of its far-reaching implications for dealing with customers and competitors as well as with the federal government.

Organizational codes of ethics, statements of philosophy and behavior, or guidelines for conduct are not always structured in such a way that they will really influence organizational behavior. Unlike the IBM code, some are intended to be only window dressing—something to help convince government or the public that a firm's intentions and behavior are honorable.

Enlightened Self-Interest

It can be argued that organizations should promote socially responsible behavior because it is good business. It pays to be honest with customers and to provide them with a quality product just as it pays to be generous with employees and to avoid further deterioration of the environment. Farsighted managers can see that certain very costly forms of socially responsible behavior may not pay off immediately but may actually be necessary for survival a few years hence. Questionnaire responses from 144 major corporations showed enlightened self-interest to be the most important motive for social performance in the areas of urban, consumer, and environmental affairs.[13]

It is important for managers to recognize that ethical or socially responsible behavior is better for business than are the alternatives to it. Part of being a morally sensitive person is knowing why a particular action is desirable rather than doing it out of fear, obligation, or blind obedience. On the other hand, it would appear somewhat insensitive to behave morally, say by providing a safe work environment, only because of a belief that it will bring a good return on the investment. A logical corollary of the latter is that one should be morally responsible only when there is reason to believe that it will pay.

---

[13] Vernon M. Buehler and Y. K. Shetty, "Motivations for Corporate Social Action," *Academy of Management Journal,* Vol. 17, No. 1 (December, 1974), p. 769.

There is a more sophisticated version of enlightened self-interest (sometimes called intelligent selfishness). It is based on two distinctions. The first is between *self-interest* and *selfishness.* Everyone is motivated by self-interest. "I want to be a kind, generous, and compassionate person" expresses a desire to enhance oneself by acquiring some of the most noble qualities of which humans are capable. This is an expression of self-interest but not selfishness. Selfish people put their immediate interests ahead of others. Morally sensitive persons have learned that it is in their own best interest to be unselfish—to be genuinely concerned for others. Out of such a commitment and experience emerge such virtues as compassion and mercy.

The second distinction is between *intrinsic* and *extrinsic* payoffs. To say that it pays to be socially responsible can mean that being socially responsible has an intrinsic payoff (meaning that the satisfaction from performing the act is itself the payoff). Or it may have an extrinsic payoff such as higher profits and other measurable consequences. There is satisfaction in being a moral person and dealing with other people honestly, fairly, and generously. It should not be assumed that all managers who verbalize their commitment to social responsibility in terms of enlightened self-interest or intelligent selfishness are necessarily selfish, expecting an external payoff, even in the long run. Some, at least, seem to use such terms to camouflage a deeper value system—a religious belief, for example, which they have been unable to express in terms that seem appropriate in the tough, unsentimental world of business.

Social and Economic Philosophy

Managers are often pragmatists who have no particular social and economic philosophy. But there are those whose behavior is strongly influenced by a belief system other than strictly moral or religious beliefs. There are managers, for example, who believe strongly in allowing the law of supply and demand to determine wages and prices whenever possible. They believe in minimal government control, in a pay-as-you-go policy of government spending, and in other values associated with a conservative philosophy. Such managers are apt to place a high value on efficiency and to think that the benefits of free competition outweigh its shortcomings. Most managers tend to support this philosophy.

Managers of a more liberal persuasion are less likely to be concerned about deficit spending and to fear that government encroachment on the free market will destroy the system. They welcome government controls and have a deep appreciation for the buffering effect of government action upon the boom and bust swings of a free market. They minimize the positive contributions of our system of imperfect competition and are more impressed with the human suffering which results from unsuccessful businesses and other losers in the competitive market. Efficiency is valued "but not as much as people," meaning that efficiency is not viewed as highly important to the well-being of people. The rights of the individual are believed to be in constant jeopardy by the self-serving interests of big business. When the organization is pitted against an individual, the liberal's natural inclination is to identify with the underdog.

Belief systems such as these provide individuals with a philosophical predisposition to evaluate people, situations, and events in a set way. At the extremes, such predispositions distort perception and judgment to such an extent that a given situation cannot be evaluated on its merits. Extreme pro-union or anti-union philosophies also tend to distort the facts so that the observer's emotional state becomes the major criterion of good and evil in the workplace.

A Matter of Conscience

Critics of competitive, profit-oriented business focus upon its lack of warmth, compassion, and genuine concern for people. It has been argued that problems of business morality can be solved only by managers with a deep commitment to a system of humanitarian values from which these qualities emanate. Such a *moral value system*—a relatively permanent system of beliefs and attitudes concerning the worth and treatment of people—would enable a manager to follow the lead of conscience rather than be guided by pragmatic or utilitarian motives. Such a conscience begins to develop in childhood experiences, in the home and school, and is not likely to be the product of a college course in business ethics.[14]

The Personal Values of Managers.   Studies of the value systems of 356 business executives in 1972 showed that the value systems of American managers had changed very little from the time of a comparable study in 1966.[15] The managers in these studies placed highest importance on the company, customers, ability, high productivity, profit maximization, organization efficiency, and achievement, although employees, subordinates, and co-workers also ranked high among the values that influence their daily decisions. Religion, trust, honor, employee welfare, loyalty, and dignity ranked high; while social welfare, compassion, government, and liberalism were relegated to positions of secondary importance.

It appears from these studies that the value systems of American managers are more oriented toward achievement and task than toward people, as such. Managers do, nevertheless, regard people as highly important—especially those within their own companies and, more specifically, their own subordinates. Managers are, by the very nature of their jobs, committed to thinking of people at work in terms of their contributions at work, rather than in terms of their value in general. Thus, rationality in organizational decision making is a more functional value within the manager's work environment than compassion and concern for solving the ills of society.

The values held by managers probably account for their being managers rather than social workers, members of the clergy, scientists, or college professors. Their values may also account for their ability to function in an environment

---

[14] The importance of childhood experiences in the development of conscience is discussed in "It's Too Late for Ethics Courses in Business Schools," by Mary Susan Miller and A. Edward Miller, *Business and Society Review,* No. 17 (Spring, 1976), pp. 39–42.

[15] Edward J. Lusk and Bruce L. Oliver, "American Managers' Personal Value Systems—Revisited," *Academy of Management Journal,* Vol. 17, No. 3 (September, 1974), pp. 549–554.

which is highly demanding and stress provoking. Managers believe that the production of goods and services for a profit is important in and of itself. In this regard, they are like other professionals. They probably could not perform well without such a belief in what they are doing.

Pseudomorality.   There is a point of view which portrays managers as cruel and heartless because they sometimes make decisions which bring frustration and suffering to people. Managers fire employees, for example, and they close down plants on which people depend for a livelihood. Although there are some heartless and cruel managers, this perception shows an abysmal lack of insight into the attitudes and values of managers. Such decisions are usually made only after much agonizing and are often made only after great expense to the organization because of a manager's procrastination while attempting to discover a less painful course of action.

Managers who lack the courage to make unpleasant managerial decisions often convince themselves that they are motivated by compassion and goodness. Thus, we have the term *pseudomorality* (false morality). Consider this real life example:

> Too late to save the largest employer in a small city from bankruptcy, a management consultant was called in to talk with Charlene Reitz, the company's founder-president. In the course of the investigation, it was discovered that the financial vice-president, Raymon Kelly, had for years caused the company's most effective managers to resign because of his harsh, domineering personality. Kelly was a bright, powerful man. No one, including Reitz, was willing to have a head-on confrontation with him.

> Reitz had often considered replacing Kelly; but when it came to actually taking the step, she reminded herself of his years of faithful service, especially how he had worked long hours at low pay when the company was small. She also had to consider the fact that Janice Kelly, Raymon's wife and her good friend, had been supportive during times when she was ready to give up on the business.

> When all the facts were out and Reitz was able to face the truth, she frankly admitted that she had known for a long time that Kelly was destroying the company but was unable to face the unpleasantness of replacing him. In order to avoid facing the fact of her own lack of courage, she had rationalized her behavior in terms of compassion and goodness. As a result 150 employees would soon be out of work.

Examples of pseudomorality occur more often than most managers are willing to admit. Since hard decisions provoke hostility and create insecurity, it is not surprising that they are avoided and rationalized. Neither is it surprising that the depth of character often demanded of the managers who make difficult business decisions is viewed as lack of compassion. Compassion may take more forms than first meet the eye.

Everybody Is Doing It

One of the weakest foundations for a code of moral behavior is to play follow the leader—to see what others are doing and follow suit. In contrast to pace-setting managers whose behavior is constrained by deep religious convictions or a moral philosophy, some managers look primarily to common practice for a clue to right and wrong conduct

If everybody is doing it, bribing the officials of foreign governments to buy a firm's products or misrepresenting the quality of a product can be rationalized as just another cost of doing business. Concerning product quality, one manufacturer expressed this position:

> I don't like selling a product that's designed to self-destruct in eighteen months, but if I build in quality, I can't compete on price. My competitors and customers are setting the pace, and I can't change until they do.

A close look at this firm's competitors revealed that some were, in fact, charging more and building a quality product. Actually making products of varying quality levels is not in itself unethical as long as consumer safety is not involved and consumers know what they are buying. There is, however, a fundamental weakness in any ethical code based primarily on what others are doing. It is at best amoral.

MAKING ORGANIZATIONS MORE MORAL

Thesis: A high level of morality in organizations—with all its implications for the behavior of managers within and outside the firm—does not happen by chance. It is a result of planning, commitment, goal setting, and the selection of managers with depth of character.

History has shown that when organizations fail in their responsibility to society the freedom to control their own destiny erodes. Laws, passed to demand specific action, impose increasingly narrow constraints within which managers retain the freedom to make decisions. Unions, the press, special-interest groups, and the general public emerge as cohesive forces to oppose real or imagined abuses of power. If there were no other reason for business organizations to initiate internal reforms, the threat of external controls should be enough. The following recommendations are given for making organizations moral.

1. *Management Development.* Companies which elect to make high profits and at the same time achieve social responsibility must select and develop managers with character, broad education, and professional competence. Whatever their schooling, they must be liberally educated.[16] An organization must make certain that its managers are informed concerning a wide

---

[16] Kenneth R. Andrews, "Can the Best Corporations Be Made Moral?," *Harvard Business Review,* Vol. 51, No. 3 (May-June, 1973), p. 63.

range of social and economic issues in the firm's environment. Breadth of perspective should be sought and generously rewarded.

2. *Organizational Goals and Standards.* Organizations that are serious about becoming and remaining moral should define what they mean by morality. This definition can be expressed both in codes of ethics and in corporate goals. The goals may take the form of self-structured affirmative action programs relating to discrimination, the environment, employee relations, and other areas relating directly to the company. Goals may also involve whatever contribution the firm chooses to make regarding broad social issues such as crime, poverty, inflation, unemployment, and the need for more responsible government.

3. *Involvement of the Total Organization.* Rather than delegate the task to a few environmental or social responsibility specialists, managers at all levels should be made aware of their individual responsibility. They should recognize that a corporate social contribution can be developed within the context of the profit system—"not as a peripheral and purely philanthropic or moral exercise." [17] This means that the organization's goals must be made a part of the goals of each manager and find fulfillment in every aspect of organizational life.

4. *A Corporate Social Audit.* As a means of satisfying themselves and society of their own morality, companies should make periodic audits of their performance vis-á-vis their goals and objectives.[18] Contributions may be measured, for example, in terms of dollars spent to abate pollution, to improve safety on the job, and to support community projects. They may also be measured in terms of time spent by managers and employees in community affairs.

5. *Rewarding Desired Behavior.* The organization's motivational systems must be structured to reward socially responsible behavior as well as contributions to profit.

6. *Professionalization of Management.* For many years, writers in the field of management have indicated a need for the professionalization of management in the sense that medicine, law, and accounting are professions. This can be accomplished only if a substantial number of business organizations give their support to the development of competence criteria and a code of ethics against which to evaluate the qualifications and conduct of managers. Businesses will also need to initiate a professional organization to assume responsibility for the certification of managers. Such an organization will have an impact only as companies favor certified managers in selection and promotion and as its ethics committee becomes known for excluding incompetent or unethical managers from membership. This

[17] Robert C. Gunness, "Social Responsibility: The Art of the Possible," in Robert L. Heilbroner and Paul London (eds.), *Corporate Social Policy* (Reading, Mass.: Addison-Wesley Publishing Company, 1975), p. 26. Robert Gunness is vice-chairman of the board of Standard Oil Company (Indiana).

[18] Raymond A. Bauer and Dan H. Fenn, Jr., "What Is a Corporate Social Audit?" *Harvard Business Review,* Vol. 51, No. 1 (January-February, 1973), pp. 37–48.

professionalization task is enormous, but it can be accomplished with the support of America's major corporations and schools of business.

STUDY AND DISCUSSION QUESTIONS

1. How does a competitive free enterprise system purport to protect society? Evaluate this position.
2. What are the major differences between the accountability and quality-of-life concepts of corporate social responsibility? Do you agree with one or the other of these? Why?
3. Contrast the purpose of business from the points of view of society and the investor. Does this distinction imply that the investor places no value on society's purpose?
4. What is the significance of the distinction which is made between profit as the investor's primary goal versus profit as the investor's central value?
5. Professional (hired) managers who invest corporate funds in nonprofit projects (for example, an antipoverty project in a ghetto of a distant city) are often hailed as expressing the highest form of social responsibility. What moral or ethical conflicts might such activities involve?
6. The way Davis and Blomstrom define *social responsibility* appears on the surface to be much like Fitch's definition. Why is the latter more likely to be acceptable to management?
7. Evaluate the statement: Morals cannot be legislated.
8. How do professional codes of ethics influence the behavior of managers?
9. Explain and evaluate the following statement in the light of the contents of this chapter: In my role as a manager, my motivation for involvement in solving social problems is intelligent selfishness.
10. As purchasing agent for her firm, Jane Strauss had for ten years bought from the Stanton Company because of price, product quality, and good service. On December 24, 1978, Mr. Stanton sent her a $100 gift certificate with a card on which was written, "Thank you for ten years of warm friendship and good business relations." What criteria should Strauss use in deciding whether to accept the gift?

CRITICAL INCIDENT

Closing Time

Diversified, Inc., acquired the Delta Corporation after months of study, debate, and negotiation. The data presented by Diversified's financial vice-president, Marie Vela, finally convinced the board of directors that the operations could become acceptably profitable in spite of the fact that two of Delta's plants had shown a loss for sometime.

The major job of increasing Delta's profitability became the responsibility of production vice-president Robert Webb. He was successful in increasing the efficiency of Delta's ten plants almost immediately, and it appeared that in the second year the company would make about $1 million profit. The Mercedes plant, named after its founder, was the only one that continued to lose money into the second year of operation. The Executive Committee met to decide what action should be taken.

Webb established to the satisfaction of the Executive Committee that the major problem was the age of the machines. While competitors had gradually replaced several models of manually operated metal-stamping machines with semiautomated models, the Mercedes plant had become obsolete. The new machines were expensive, and Delta had for several years had financial problems that forbade their making the needed investments.

It soon became apparent that the Committee was polarized along two lines represented by Webb, who wanted to keep Mercedes, and Vela, who thought it should be closed. Vela showed that Diversified would be better off to close the plant and take a tax write-off than to sell it for the unimpressive price it would bring. Webb had learned to appreciate the integrity and competence of the Mercedes managers and was concerned about the unemployment problem that closing the plant would bring.

Vela got a decisive no from Webb when she asked whether he would recommend buying the plant if Diversified did not already own it. Webb's response was similar when she asked whether he believed Diversified could make as much money building up Mercedes as it could investing its funds in expansion of its more profitable plants.

Webb argued that Mercedes could become profitable within three years and that a decision to keep the plant would avoid a great deal of human suffering. He expressed part of his viewpoint in these terms:

> We know we can make more money elsewhere, but this is a chance to do some good. So we lose $50,000 during the next three years. What's $50,000 out of a million dollars?

Vela, not inclined to buy Webb's logic, responded with:

> I supported acquisition before the board of directors when we acquired this company. Our directors thought we were engaging in a business venture, not a welfare project. We don't help anybody—certainly not our stockholders—when we artificially keep a company alive that deserves to die. If you want to be humanitarian, think of the people we will be able to rehire in South Chicago if we expand our operation there with the money you want to lose at Mercedes.

Questions

1. What are the issues?
2. What additional information is needed to make a sound decision?
3. What action should be taken?

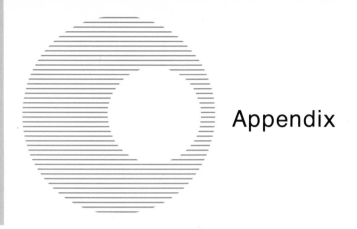

Appendix

PART 1—CRITICAL INCIDENT

Conflict at the Summit

George Cummins, founder of what is now Cummins Building Products, Inc., began the Tennessee-based company in 1900 as a small, underfinanced sawmill. As a result of outstanding management decisions, the company expanded rapidly into a variety of fields related to the construction industry. With the exception of a severe slump during the depression of the 1930s, the company has been unusually profitable and in order to finance rapid expansion became a publicly held corporation in 1950.

By the late 1970s, Cummins Building Products had sales outlets throughout the United States. Among the company's major holdings were extensive forests in the Deep South, Washington, and Oregon. In conjunction with these, the company had several large sawmills, plants for making plyboard and lumber by-products, and two plants for making doors, windows, and cabinets. Wholesale outlets for the company's lumber and manufactured products were strategically located throughout the United States.

The Management Team

At the time of this incident, the company was headed by its president, Ronald Cummins, the founder's grandson. His competence and powerful personality enabled him to maintain control over the company, with support from a closely knit management group, in spite of the fact that the Cummins family had been able to retain only about 20 percent of the stock through the series of public stock issues.

Although Cummins left no doubt about who had the right to the last word, he worked closely with the company's Executive Committee which consisted of the individuals described below.

Joe Reyna—Executive Vice-President. At age 63, Reyna was almost the same age as Cummins and had worked closely with him since the two graduated from engineering school. Because of his age, Reyna had little chance of becoming president and was considered by many to be almost an appendage or alter ego of his boss. He often disagreed with Cummins, however, and freely voiced his convictions.

Curtis Moser—Financial Vice-President. Moser had been employed by the corporation for twenty years. Previously he was a partner in a major auditing firm. His competence was well established.

Paula Lemke—Personnel Vice-president. Lemke worked for a management consulting firm prior to joining Cummins as a plant personnel director. She was oriented toward a sophisticated level of quantitative research which had originally brought her to the attention of Ronald Cummins and which continued to win his admiration.

Henry Finch—Vice-President for Advertising and Public Relations. Finch did his job well, basked in the status of being a member of the Executive Committee, and was especially careful never to cross Cummins.

Richard Kruse—Marketing Vice-President. Kruse was a master salesman and sales manager who, in the opinion of many, was tough-minded, money-motivated, and interested only in the sales end of the business.

William Clay—Production Vice-President. At age 45, Clay was by ten years the youngest member of the Executive Committee and by far the most recently employed. He had joined the company five years prior to this incident after a brilliant career with a competitor that was and is well known for its progressive management practices.

Managerial Policy and Practices

If profits were the only measure of a company's success, Cummins Building Products, Inc., would have few peers, but in spite of its overall success the company had its problems. Ronald Cummins' management philosophy was strongly influenced by his father and grandfather whose success, personal courage, and entrepreneural spirit he greatly admired. Perhaps because of this, the company retained some of the qualities of the original sawmill operation. George Cummins, who was considered an honest and fair man, believed in getting a full day's work for a fair day's pay and was unsympathetic to the modern emphasis upon fringe benefits and what he viewed as "a preoccupation with making employees happy" which had begun during the last few years of his life. Ronald Cummins, like his predecessors, believed that for best results an organization should have a large number of supervisors and relatively small work groups.

Like the first sawmills owned by George Cummins, the mills and factories of Cummins Building Products employed more than their share of poor, uneducated, often undisciplined employees who would work for low wages under unfavorable environmental conditions. Turnover among plant employees had always been high and was accepted by Ronald Cummins as inevitable—perhaps even desirable since he believed that it discouraged union organizers from gaining a foothold in the company.

Most of the company's first-line supervisors had been promoted from within and tended to follow the supervisory practices of their immediate superiors. Cummins believed that to teach the supervisors modern ideas about leadership would disrupt practices which had proved workable over many years. "Our supervisors," he reasoned, "know the kind of people they're supervising and use methods that they understand. If we try to change them, it will just create chaos, and before long our employees will be telling us how to run our business."

Not everyone agreed with the management philosophy often expressed by Cummins, but because of his awesome power and influence they went along with him. Part of his influence came from the fact that his business decisions—especially his investment decisions—were often brilliant. In the final analysis, he provided a type of leadership that led to profit and company growth, but his methods were sometimes frustrating to his subordinates. They suspected that he intentionally kept them in the dark about his goals and plans for the organization as a means of enhancing his own power and control. The corporation's current goals and policies always seemed to be posited in his brain rather than in the company's planning and policy manuals.

Cummins did a good job keeping in touch with the organization at all levels, considering its size and dispersion over the United States. He insisted that all employees and managers feel free to talk with him, and he often made commitments or issued directives without going through official channels. Reyna confronted him about this practice more than once, but he insisted that to confine himself to the so-called chain of command would undermine his own effectiveness and make him subservient to his own subordinates. The effect of his actions was to reverse decisions made by other managers.

The William Clay Situation

William Clay spent more time away from the home office than the other members of the Executive Committee. Many contacts with plant managers which he could handle by mail or telephone he preferred to make in person. He felt a need to keep in close touch with the problems and challenges his subordinates faced rather than manage from a distance. He thought of himself as providing subordinate managers with guidance rather than giving them direct orders. He also believed that personal contacts were an important part of his push to upgrade the quality of management, and occasionally he personally conducted one-day management training programs.

A morale survey showed that the company had some really serious personnel problems. With Lemke's help, Clay discovered that employee identification with the company was poor and that employee turnover was excessively high for the industry. In one plant, Clay found that supplying employees with uniforms was a positive factor in improving morale and that, in the short run at least, it reduced turnover. However, when Cummins discovered what Clay had done, he was critical of the action. He believed uniforms were an unnecessary expense and a bad precedent. Cummins did not question Clay's authority to make the decision but believed that it was a poor one. His reaction was such that Clay did not feel free to expand the practice to other plants, and although he knew that getting rid of the uniforms in the one plant would be inadvisable, he knew they were an irritant to Cummins.

The other members of the executive team, Reyna in particular, believed that many of the actions Clay was taking in the production division were needed. They were aware, however, that Cummins and Clay tended to view situations differently and to make different assumptions about people and problems. They were unwilling to take sides against Cummins. Anyway, they understood Cummins' approach to managing the company, knew his record of success, and were less certain about Clay's approach since he was a relative newcomer.

Moser, Lemke, Finch, Kruse, and their families were often together socially. Especially during these times, they discussed Clay's situation and were critical of him because of his poor judgment in trying to buck the system. They also spent hours discussing specific business problems and sharing ideas and attitudes about various aspects of the organization. These informal relationships were valuable for the purpose of coordinating and planning. Because of his closeness to Cummins, Reyna was often absent from such sessions.

The Meetings

Official Executive Committee meetings were always announced so that everyone could plan to attend, but unofficial meetings of all or most of the members were called on the spur of the moment. Since Clay was out of the city more than the others, he very often missed these meetings. Although Cummins did not feel justified in directly criticizing Clay for not attending, he was sometimes irritated by his absence and expressed his feelings to the others.

On one occasion, Cummins' suppressed feelings about Clay burst into the open:

> I'm not sure Clay is going to work out. His judgments about people are poor, and he spends so much time in the field that he's never here when we need him. He has no business out their conducting attitude surveys and supervisory training programs when there's serious work to be done. Sometimes I get the feeling that he's more concerned about our employees than he is about the company. I think it's time for a showdown.

Reyna was the only one with a good word for Clay, but he recognized that Cummins was in no mood to be reasoned with. Reyna's statement was brief:

I will say this for him, Ron: he tries hard, and he's done a good job of holding costs down while increasing production. I wonder how he was so successful with Hardwick before we got him.

Lemke, who had conducted the company's one attitude survey at Clay's request, decided this would be a bad time to speak up. No one experienced the positive feelings toward Clay needed to motivate a strong stand for him. Even Reyna, who admired him greatly, was a little envious. Clay was doing some things that Reyna wished he had done while he was in that position.

Questions

1. What perceptions of human nature seem to be expressed by the managers of the Cummins Company? What does the behavior of the managers themselves say about human nature?

2. What does this situation demonstrate about the factors which contribute to managerial success? Give specific examples.

3. In what ways did informal group behavior affect Clay's success as a manager?

PART 2—CRITICAL INCIDENT

A Project Gone Awry

Control Systems, Inc., is a relatively new subsidiary of an international manufacturer of sophisticated electronic components and hardware. Although the parent corporation originally viewed itself as a mass producer of semiconductors, its range of products gradually expanded to include several pocket-size calculators and other products for use by the ultimate consumer. Control Systems was the company's first venture into a new field—the production of electronic sensors and control devices. The initial line of products was designed to detect the presence of smoke and other gases and to respond in a variety of ways, including the production of a continuous graphic record.

Site Selection

Although the town selected for the first Control Systems plant had a population of only 40,000 it was located in a densely populated agricultural area in which labor was abundant. During the past several years an increasing number of small, inefficient farms had been consolidated, and the use of heavy machinery greatly reduced the number of people needed in agriculture. Nevertheless, the farm communities remained relatively stable, and the managers responsible for the site selection were convinced that the location was ideal.

The site was viewed with favor primarily for two reasons. First, and most obvious, was the availability of a large number of potential employees, considering that they could be drawn from a radius of up to fifty miles. Second, and perhaps more important, were the characteristics of the area residents. They were viewed as being more committed to the Protestant work ethic than the average city dweller—more likely to work hard, appreciate a good employment opportunity, and identify with their employer. When compared with employees in some localities, who over several generations had developed a labor class identity, the residents of this area were perceived to have retained more of the enterprising spirit that built America, a sense of independence that comes from working the land, and a sense of responsibility that would be needed if the management philosophy of Control Systems was to be implemented.

The Management

Only four people from the home office were permanently assigned to the Control Systems operation although the parent corporation made specialists available on a temporary basis as needed to solve specific problems or to establish the production and control systems needed to form a viable company. A brief description of each of the key managers is given below.

Lynn Jordan, General Manager.   Lynn Jordan, age 45, had been employed by the parent corporation for 23 years and had assumed a wide range of responsibilities. She joined the company in a staff capacity after completing a bachelor's degree in industrial engineering and an MBA. For several years her work primarily involved time and motion studies. She was later promoted to a production planning position and finally to assistant production manager of a large semiconductor plant. At one point in her career, she directly supervised ten first-line production supervisors and through them about 300 factory employees. Her performance in each position was considered outstanding.

Max Stringer, Quality Control Manager.   Stringer, a 26-year-old quality control specialist, had been with the company for four years. Although his college major was in management, he had nearly three years in the basic sciences as a premed student before deciding upon a business career. He thoroughly understood the technical nature of his work and prided himself on an ability to get along with everybody. As a matter of fact, everybody liked Stringer and seemed to regard him as a personal friend.

Jerry Burch, Manager of Shipping and Receiving.   Burch, at age 55, was the oldest of the group and the least educated. He was only a high school graduate, but he was highly intelligent, responsible, and experienced. Actually he did more than his title implied. This included making small purchases not easily handled by the parent corporation and managing the warehouse.

Burl Voth, Director of Personnel. Voth, age 40, was a professional personnel director with previous plant start-up experience in the parent corporation. In this particular operation, his duties included timekeeping and payroll functions in addition to those typically performed by the personnel director in a large organization. His job was simplified somewhat by the fact that many record-keeping and other functions, including the preparation of payroll checks, were handled by the parent corporation. This was facilitated by the use of a computer terminal connected directly with the home office.

Start-up Operation

The four key managers, with support from various specialists, temporarily assigned, spent several months planning, preparing facilities, installing equipment, and establishing themselves within the community before locally hiring six first-line supervisors. Although none of the supervisors had experience within the industry, all had manufacturing experience and were regarded as highly trainable. In preparation for their new jobs, they were given two months of intensive training and indoctrination in similar plants owned by the company. At the end of this period Control Systems began to hire and train local employees for assembly work.

Within three months, six work units of 20 employees each were in operation. At this time, Control Systems had a total of 145 employees and managers, and plans were underway for gradual expansion up to about 1,000 employees, depending upon product demand. Because Control Systems was recognized as a stable organization and paid more than the going wage, it was able to hire the most stable, responsible, and talented personnel in the area. Although unemployment was relatively high, most of the people hired were drawn from other companies in the area. Extreme care was taken to avoid any form of discrimination against minority groups, and roughly half of the employees were drawn from each sex.

Approach to Management

Both Jordan and Stringer were of the opinion that the start-up operation should not be rushed and that from the beginning product quality should be emphasized. Experienced operator trainers were temporarily brought in to get the new employees off to a good start.

During the training period all aspects of the operation looked good. Relations between employees and management were outstanding. Although it was understood that assembly workers would ultimately be paid on a unit basis, the hourly training rate was considered high for the area; so the employees seemed unconcerned about not receiving bonus pay for quantity of production. Morale was high, work quality was superior, and employee identification with the organization was strong. It became a mark of status within the community to be employed by Control Systems, and the backlog of qualified applicants increased daily.

Relations between managers and employees were personal and informal. This was consistent with the leadership philosophy of Jordan and her immediate superior in the home office, David Goodrich, and with their belief that the type of personnel they had employed would respond favorably to maximum autonomy and minimum supervision.

The Surfacing of Problems

Once the operators learned the basic assembly operations, time studies were meticulously performed and piece rates established. Since most of the employees had not had previous factory experience, the performance of the trainers, as well as the regular operators, was timed and the data were incorporated into the final production standards. When compared with studies performed in other factories of the parent company, the standards were about average in difficulty. Since trust within the organization was high, no one paid much attention to the time and motion studies. The production employees knew what was taking place and looked forward to the results.

The first sign of trouble occurred when the production standards were posted. Although the trainers demonstrated that the standards could be achieved and explained how speed increases with practice, most of the employees remained skeptical. They began to suspect that the trainers had unusual abilities, and they were not altogether satisfied by the reminder that prior to their employment each Control Systems employee had demonstrated superior manual dexterity on a validated test. There was some sentiment among the employees that even if they could produce at a pace which would earn them additional income—possibly increasing their base pay by as much as 100 percent—the fatigue involved would be unbearable.

Over a period of weeks, production began to increase, but very slowly. Few employees were earning above their base rate, and in some cases, where the ability of employees to produce was limited by the pace of others, the entire work group was slowed down by the actions of a few. Some employees whose work was not limited by the pace set by others did not appear motivated to produce as many subassemblies as they could.

Production was not the only problem in the Control Systems plant. Tardiness and absenteeism gradually began to increase after the price-rate system of pay was installed. Two of the first-line supervisors wanted to take a tough stand against the offenders but believed that company policy forbade it. It was their impression that strong disciplinary action would disturb employee morale and generally disrupt the outstanding interpersonal relations within the plant. That result, they were convinced, would reflect negatively upon their own effectiveness. They could not help but call to mind what they knew to be true about the high quality of employees in the plant and the company's emphasis upon individual autonomy and responsibility. Consequently, the disciplinary action for tardiness or an unexcused absence was usually a mild reprimand.

A Recommended Solution

When it became obvious that the problems were not being solved, Jordan met with Goodrich, Stringer, and Voth to discuss possible solutions. One conclusion reached was that they would have been better off to have stressed productivity rather than quality until the desired level of productivity was reached, even if it meant having to make extensive repairs before the units could be sold. But nothing could be done now about that mistake.

Growing out of the meeting was the recommendation to higher management that a system be established to provide employees with an end-of-year bonus based on a profit-sharing formula. This, the managers reasoned, would call attention to the need for maximum productivity and increase the general level of motivation within the plant. This was expected to mobilize group pressures to achieve the objectives sought by management. With most employees reaching the production standard, a profit should be forthcoming within 12 to 18 months.

Questions

1. In view of the motivation theories and models discussed in Part 2, what are the probable causes of the motivation problems experienced by Control Systems, Inc.?

2. What do you think led to the conclusion that productivity rather than quality should have been stressed first?

3. Assuming that the recommended profit-sharing plan is implemented, what effect would you expect it to have on employee motivation?

4. How would you cope with the disciplinary problems?

5. What questionable assumption appears to have been made about the motivation of employees who are strongly committed to the Protestant work ethic?

6. What actions would you take to improve overall motivation of the production employees?

PART 3—CRITICAL INCIDENT

The Applicant

The NASCO plane touched down just before sundown with its lone passenger, Lee Mercer, The pilot drove him directly to the Bay City Country Club where he met Board Chairman, Vince Seely, and a management consultant, Dr. Eileen Calvert, who had worked for NASCO (North American Shoe Company) for many years in management selection and development. Mercer was a handsome man in his early fifties. With his rugged features, athletic build, and impeccable social skills, his impact was phenomenal. After several months of searching for a company president, Seely and Calvert were hopeful that Mercer might be the ideal applicant.

NASCO is the publicly held parent organization of five companies which manufacture shoes of varying quality under about fifteen brand names. Although NASCO effectively controls its subsidiaries, its management prefers to allow them maximum autonomy while providing a superior quality of consultation from the home office. This system had proved to be highly satisfactory since NASCO had for fifteen years operated profitably under the progressive leadership of its president, Howard Putnam. However, the office of president was vacated unexpectedly when Putnam accepted a high-level political appointment in the federal government.

Mercer was executive vice-president of a competing firm which was twice as large as any of the NASCO companies but much smaller than the parent organization. Mercer was not particularly dissatisfied with his present job but had very discreetly inquired about the NASCO presidency when it appeared that the company was having difficulty filling the position. Although Mercer was quite interested in the position, he preferred to think of the meeting with Seely and Calvert as an exploratory visit rather than a formal employment interview. To a degree they took the same position although they would have preferred to study a brief of Mercer's qualifications before the meeting.

The evening began with drinks, dinner, and light conversation. The three mostly discussed mutual friends, trends in the industry, and current events. Mercer came across as a person with a deep sense of personal integrity, a responsible family man, and a person who loved his work. After graduating with highest honors as an industrial engineer, he had held several engineering and managerial positons in four companies before occupying his current position.

After dinner, the three withdrew to a small conference room which provided greater privacy. Becoming impatient with what she perceived to be the somewhat frivolous or surface content of their conversation, Calvert decided to restructure the situation.

Calvert:
Lee, do you mind if I ask you some questions of a more formal nature? Perhaps we could save some time by taking a direct and businesslike approach to getting to know one another better.

Mercer:
I don't mind at all. Fire away.

Calvert:
First of all, why don't you just tell us about yourself—who you really are. Describe yourself as we might describe you a year from now if you became the president of NASCO.

Mercer:

Well, I'll try. That's a tough one. If at times I sound as though I'm boasting, don't forget that you asked the question. *(Pause)* To begin with, I'm a fair-minded person. I expect a lot from other people, but I believe in paying them well for their efforts. I think of myself as being intelligent—more intelligent than the typical manager. I'm well organized. I've been called tough-minded and hardheaded, and I suppose I've been called a few names that are not repeatable. *(Pause)* Where do you want me to go from here?

Calvert:

We have been working on an interesting project at NASCO recently. We're trying to improve our selection of first-line supervisors. Could you give us some suggestons?

Mercer:

Probably none you would regard as new and different. We have that problem, too. We have tried assessment centers and professional appraisal services, but nothing has proved to be better than a good interview by someone with common sense judgment. Basically we try to pick a person who is friendly and outgoing—somebody who gets along with others, is an outstanding worker, and tough enough not to be intimidated by hostile subordinates.

Seely:

What have you done in the area of supervisory training?

Mercer:

Most of our training is done on the job. Experience is still the best teacher. I don't mean, of course, that there is no place for supervisory training, but the seminars conducted in the companies I've been with - don't really seem to have done much to change behavior on the job.

Calvert:

I'm sure that at one time or other you have had an opportunity to advise supervisors or managers about improving their leadership performance. What do you tell them?

Mercer:

That would probably require more time to answer than you want me to take. Well, let's see. . . . I think I would tell them to first be sure where they stand with their boss. A manager needs to know that his superiors will back him. He needs to know that he has the authority to get the job done, to take whatever action must be taken to get the production out the back door at a profit. I would also tell them to be sure the policies, procedures, and rules they expect their subordinates to follow are clearly communicated. You can't expect subordinates to perform if they don't know what you want them to do.

Seely:

From what you said during dinner, your experience negotiating with unions has been extensive. Why do you think employees join unions?

Mercer:

I'm sure there are many reasons. For example, we have a union shop; our employees can either join the union or lose their jobs. I suspect, however, that, where employees have a choice, the drive for security is the main factor. Union members don't have to worry as much about being fired. They can do less work and make more money than non-union employees. I suppose it's just human nature for workers to want to live on easy street if they have the clout to pull it off.

Calvert:

If you could structure an organization for optimal decision making on the part of management what would you do?

Mercer:

I'm not sure I know what you mean, but I strongly believe that poor decision making is most often associated with two things. First, the decision maker may lack the authority to make the decisions which are necessary to get a job done. Decision-making authority must accompany assigned responsibility. Second, a committee can't make a decision. Someone has said that a camel is a horse put together by a committee, and I tend to agree. In the final analysis, if you have responsibility for getting a job done, you must have the courage to make decisions and live with the consequences. If your organizational superior makes a decision, you must accept it—you don't have to like it, but you do have to abide by it. If you make a decision, you have a right to expect your subordinates to carry it out whether they like it or not. That's the nature of organization.

Hours later Seely drove Mercer back to the airport and promised to call him within the next week. On the way back to the city, Seely thought about Mercer's answers and looked forward to a conference about him with Calvert the following day.

Questions

1. What can be inferred about Mercer's leadership style from the portion of the interview reported in this incident?

2. From the data presented what success-related characteristics would you assume that Mercer possesses?

3. Evaluate Mercer's views about supervisors.

4. What do Mercer's views on why employees join unions indicate about him?

5. Describe Mercer's approach to making decisions.

PART 4—CRITICAL INCIDENT
The Metropolitan Herald

To an outside observer, the *Metropolitan Herald* sometimes appeared to be a hodgepodge of business activities. To its president, Leonard Thomason, a multimillionaire entrepreneur, it was at first a favorite pastime, but it had become more than a full time job. Originally a weekly newspaper in a metropolitan area dominated by two large dailies, the *Herald* received new life when Thomason acquired it, merged it with a weekly want ad magazine with wide circulation, and converted the combination into a daily newspaper.

At the time of the merger, Thomason also acquired a company which specialized in the contract printing of magazines and paperback books. Although the acquisition was made primarily to obtain the company's buildings and a large press for use by the *Herald,* the contract printing was continued under the *Herald* management. The two operations were relatively compatible, and both were highly profitable.

Over the twenty years since the Herald was established, Thomason relinquished direct control of his other business interests and devoted his time exclusively to the newspaper. He was an excellent businessman—so much so that his subordinates were awed by him. People outside the business who knew him well regarded Thomason as a warm, friendly individual; but his immense wealth, superior ability, and ownership of the business created a marked status difference between him and his employees and managers.

The *Herald* was a fast-moving, exciting place to work; and, although salaries were not as high as some, they were acceptable. Turnover among managers was virtually nonexistent. Prior to the merger, Cheryl Payne, a highly intelligent individual with three years of business school, had worked with the want ad magazine for five years in responsible bookkeeping and accounting positions. For ten years she had been office manager for the *Herald* and during this period occupied the top financial position in the organization. Her technical skills in accounting were adequate for her job but were not outstanding. She was, however, highly skilled in planning, organizing, and supervising; and she knew more about the inner workings of all aspects of the company than anyone else with the possible exception of Thomason. Because of her position, she knew everyone's salary, a situation which proved to be a source of frustration for her because her own salary had not kept pace with those of the other top managers in the company.

Payne's dissatisfaction became acute when Dennis Redden was promoted into a new position, that of financial vice-president, at a salary of $38,000. This was exactly $10,000 more than she was earning. Redden, a Harvard MBA, had worked in the management services division of Arthur Andersen for four years before Payne hired him as a systems analyst and general problem solver in the area of systems, accounting, and finance. After working in this capacity for three years, he held two staff positions in advertising and marketing before Thomason made him assistant to Mark Manske, the production vice-president. After ten years with the *Herald,* Redden held the position that Payne thought she should have been promoted to, and Payne reported to him.

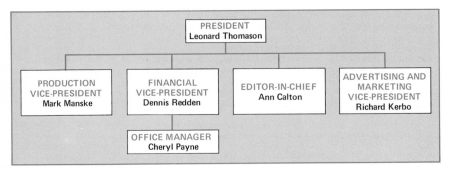

The Metropolitan Herald Organization Chart

At first Payne was so disturbed that she thought it unwise to talk with Thomason about her dissatisfaction. Within a few days, however, she regained her composure and decided to confront him. The heart of the conference included this dialogue:

Payne:
I have never been led to believe that my performance was anything but satisfactory. On a number of occasions you have said . . .

Thomason:
Let me assure you that I have never been dissatisfied with your work. You have brought outstanding people into your department and managed it admirably. There's nobody in the company who does the job you do of managing people. I have said it before and will say it again: Your contribution to the company has been invaluable, and I hope I have shown my appreciation through the years.

Payne:
I don't want to seem ungrateful, but if I have done so well, why do I now report to a man I brought into the company and helped train? I just don't get the picture.

Thomason:
Redden's promotion was not meant to reflect negatively on your performance. As you have told me many times, Redden is one of the best problem solvers in the organization and is an outstanding manager in every way. He has one of the most analytical minds in accounting and finance that I have ever observed in action, and we very much need his skills right now. In view of the progress he has made in recent years I honestly didn't believe he would stay with us if I placed him back under your supervision.

Payne:

I suppose you're right, but you can understand how I must feel about the move. I will admit that it's been a crushing blow.

Having expressed the fact of her frustration, Payne felt somewhat better. She had not really expected Thomason to back away from his decision, and she was glad to know that he still held her in high esteem. But, in spite of this, she still believed strongly that she should have had the promotion.

After her talk with Thomason, Payne had dinner with Ann Calton, the Editor-in-Chief, and spent several hours discussing the events of the day. Calton had a masters degree in English and had taught several years in a community college before becoming an editor. Her salary was $35,000 a year.

Calton:

Well, did you get around to asking him about your salary?

Payne:

No, and I'm not sure why. I had intended to, but somehow it just didn't seem appropriate. Maybe I didn't want to hear what he would say, or maybe I didn't believe he would give me a straight answer. At any rate, I'm not likely to ever bring up the matter now.

Calton:

Why do you think your salary hasn't kept pace?

Payne:

I'm not sure. Perhaps it's because of my unimpressive formal education or because I started out as a bookkeeper and the image stuck. But I think salary should be based on performance, not education. What I learned in school is such a small part of what I know now that I consider my formal education almost irrelevant. Actually my salary is not bad in an absolute sense, but everything is relative. I hired an accountant last month with no experience at a starting salary of $13,000, and next year starting salaries will probably jump another $1,000. I can't help but wonder where I would be today if I were a man.

Calton:

Do you mean you think being a woman has something to do with your salary and failure to get the promotion?

Payne:

At this point I'm not sure. I wouldn't rule it out altogether.

Soon after Thomason's conference with Payne, he met with a management consultant, Frank Parsons, with whom he had earlier discussed the creation of the new position.

Parsons:

Have you received any feedback yet on Payne's reaction to the promotion?

Thomason:

Yes, I have, and it wasn't good. I guess I really expected her to be upset but hoped she wouldn't find it necessary to unload on me. You would think that anybody in his right mind could see that Redden is being groomed to take my place. At 65 I can't be expected to stay around too many years, and Redden is the only person with the education, breadth of experience, and potential sophistication in dealing with policy matters to take my place. I haven't even told Redden directly what I have in mind for him. Certainly I'm not going to make the announcement first to someone else.

Parsons:

Is there any chance that Payne might be able to handle the Financial V-P position if and when Redden moves up?

Thomason:

I'm not sure yet. I will be watching her performance, and Redden may be given a voice in the matter. She's such an excellent delegator that she could probably handle it. With Redden as president, I'm not sure that we would need a super financial analyst in that slot.

In the days that followed, Payne lost much of her enthusiasm for the company and performed her work in a satisfactory but emotionally detached manner. Unaware that Redden might soon be promoted to company president, she felt confident that her career had peaked out and at an unacceptably low level. She thought about resigning, but she had been with the company too long for that and knew that there was no possibility of finding a comparable position elsewhere. She decided to do what was required of her and no more, to find her main satisfaction in off-the-job activities, and to take an early retirement.

Questions

1. Analyze the nature of the communication which occurred in this incident. In what ways was it related to the conflict between Thomason and Payne?

2. How might management development have prevented this problem?

3. What, if any, elements of business morality are involved in this incident?

4. Understanding the situation as you do, place yourself in Parsons' position. What action would you advise Thomason to take?

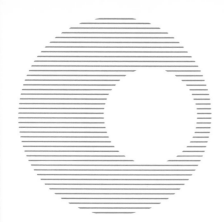

Name Index

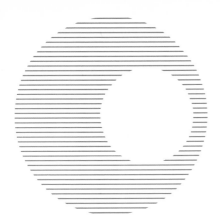

Subject Index

T

U